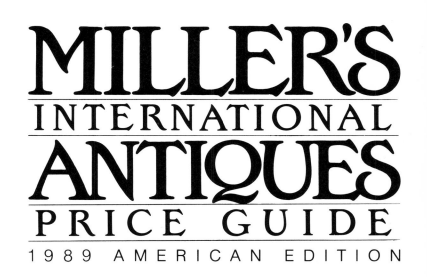

MILLER'S
INTERNATIONAL
ANTIQUES
PRICE GUIDE
1989 AMERICAN EDITION

1

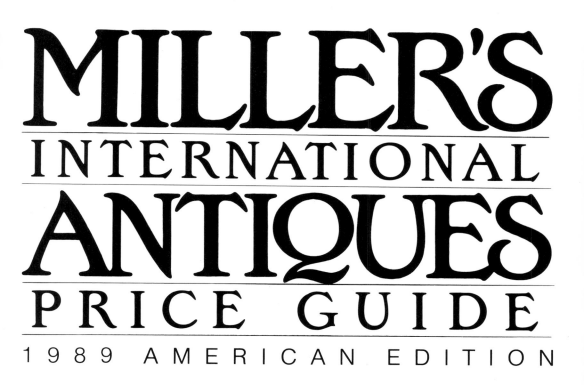

MILLER'S
INTERNATIONAL
ANTIQUES
PRICE GUIDE

1989 AMERICAN EDITION

COMPILED AND EDITED BY
JUDITH AND MARTIN MILLER

VIKING

HOW TO USE THE BOOK

Miller's uniquely practical *International Antiques Price Guide* has been compiled to make detailed information immediately available to the consumer.

The book is organized by category of antique: e.g. Pottery, Porcelain, Furniture, etc. (see Contents List on page 6); within each major category there are sub-categories of items in alphabetical order: e.g. basket, bowl, candlestick, etc., and these in turn are ordered by date. There are around 9,000 photographs of antiques and collectibles, each with a detailed description and price range. There is also a fully cross-referenced index at the back of the book.

In addition to individual entries there are special features throughout the book, giving pointers for the collector – likely condition, definitions of specialist terms, history, etc – together with general articles, chapter introductions, glossaries, bibliographies where further reading is important, tables of marks etc. As all the pictures and captions are new every year the selection of items included quickly builds into an enormously impressive and uniquely useful reference set.

PRICES

All the price ranges are based on actual prices of items bought and sold during the year prior to going to press. Thus the guide is fully up-to-date.

Prices are *not* estimates: because the value of an antique is what a willing buyer will pay to a willing seller, we have given not just one price per item but a range of prices to take into account regional differences and freak results.

This is the best way to give an idea of what an antique will *cost*, but should you wish to *sell* remember that the price you receive could be 25-30% less – antique dealers have to live too!!

Condition
All items were in good merchantable condition when last sold unless damage is noted.

ACKNOWLEDGEMENTS

Judith and Martin Miller wish to thank a large number of International auctioneers, dealers and museums who have helped in the production of this edition. The auctioneers can be found in our specialist directory towards the back of this edition.

Copyright © Millers Publications 1988

Viking Penguin Inc.,
40 West 23rd Street, New York,
New York 10010, U.S.A.
Penguin Books Canada Ltd.,
2801 John Street, Markham,
Ontario, Canada L3R 1B4

Designed and created by
Millers Publications
Sissinghurst Court
Sissinghurst
Cranbrook
Kent, England
in association with
A.G.W. International Ltd.,
Chicago, Illinois.

All rights reserved.
First published in 1988 by Viking Penguin Inc.
Published simultaneously in Canada
ISBN: 0-670-82489-5
ISSN: 0893-8857

Typeset in England by Ardek Photosetters,
St. Leonards-on-Sea, England.
Color originated by
Spectrum Reproductions, Colchester.
Printed and bound in England by
William Clowes Ltd, Beccles

Editor's Introduction

by

Judith Miller

Martin and I started *Miller's Antiques Price Guide* in 1979. We produced a book which we believed was greatly needed by virtually everyone who had some interest in antiques, whether professional or as a collector.

We firmly believed that what was needed was a guide to the antiques market which was photographically illustrated, with detailed, concise descriptions and price ranges. The last ten years have convinced me that this is what the buying public want. Initially, of course, we produced the kind of book that Martin and I wanted – and since we now sell well in excess of 100,000 copies of the British edition, it would seem we were not alone. The book in its various editions is now used all over the world as a major reference work to antiques and since we use in the region of 10,000 new photographs every year, the first ten issues of the British Guide provide an unrivalled source to 100,000 different antiques.

Four years ago we decided, in conjunction with Viking Penguin, to produce a U.S. edition of the Guide. We were convinced that the U.S. market needed the clear, high quality photographs, detailed descriptions, and the price ranges which give a "ball-park" figure for the thousands of items featured in *Miller's International Antiques Price Guide*. These price ranges are researched from sold items and give readers an essential tool for buying and selling antiques and collectibles. We are constantly trying to improve our product and give the U.S. consumer information relevant to the antiques market in the States.

One interesting development I have noticed over the years is that the antiques market is becoming more international. Of course, each country has a special interest in items made by native craftsmen and it is the general trend that such pieces will sell better at a major saleroom in their country of origin. However, to balance this, when general prices achieved at auction in New York, London, Geneva and Hong Kong are compared, they show a striking similarity.

We try to include as many color photographs as is possible, and again this year we have nearly 1,000 items illustrated in color, all of which have been on the market in the year prior to compilation. All the pieces included, either in color or black and white, are antiques which have been available through dealers or auction houses; they are not museum pieces. The result is a strongly visual and encyclopedic reference guide to recognizing and buying antiques, to detecting trends and to planning one's future collecting. On my monthly trips to the U.S. I am in constant touch with dealers, antiques centers and auction houses to check and verify prices.

Finally our thanks are due to all those experts whose invaluable help and guidance has contributed so much toward this new edition.

CONTENTS

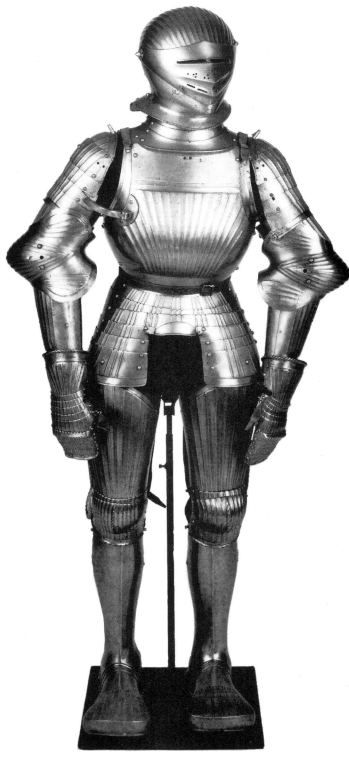

A composite "Maximilian" armour, comprising closed helmet with bellows visor and lifting peg, chin-piece, collar with spring peg hinges, which attach spaulders, both with assembly marks, one stamped with Nuremburg mark, sabatons with right toe fibreglass replacement, all elements fluted and enhanced with incised lines except greaves, main borders turned, early 16thC, approx. 66in (167.5cm).
$32,000-50,000

6

POTTERY

The market for pottery has continued along very much the same lines as last year. Occasional sales of well-known collections stimulate prices and these new levels remain stable or fall slightly over the next few years. The dearth of top class wares continues and selectivity amongst collectors ensures that only the best decorated amongst commoner wares arouse any real interest. If in good condition such pieces rise slightly above prevailing price levels.

Anything unusual has sold well. In particular, unusual examples of moulded white saltglaze have exceeded expectations. Coloured saltglaze in good condition remains popular but the market for run-of-the-mill pieces is less buoyant. The

number of collectors of pottery appears to be growing. Even quite badly damaged pieces will find a ready market if they have decorative appeal or are unusual in some way.

This desire for pieces with decorative appeal extends into the market for 19th century pottery. It is hard to understand the chemistry by which a trend develops so widely in such a relatively short space of time. Within a year it appears that large numbers of collectors, in a variety of fields, have decided to display their pieces within room settings rather than in cabinets, and the resultant enthusiasm for ornamental pieces has been obvious.

Selective buying is evident but

the market for large decorative pieces such as Mason's Ironstone vases or majolica garden seats is exceptionally buoyant. In this area of the market decorative appeal even outweighs considerations of attribution so that a pair of Minton's garden seats, whilst selling well at $16,000, were outshone in every way by a charming pair of unattributed seats modelled in the form of Egyptian slave girls which made $28,500.
General price levels for Wemyss ware continue to increase. A pair of piglets fetched $15,000 last year whilst prices in the region of $6,000-$10,000 became the norm for adult pigs or rarities. Royal collecting interest has also stimulated demand.

Baskets

A Leeds creamware basket, handpainted with fuchsias in puce, blue and green, c1775, 3 by 9in (7.5 by 23cm).
$400-550

Bowls

A Bristol delft blue and white bowl, on a domed circular foot, slight rim chips, crack to base and slight restoration to foot, c1730, 10½in (26.5cm) diam.
$3,000-4,500

An English delft blue and white straining bowl, glaze chipped, mid-18thC, 8½in (21.5cm) diam.
$1,000-1,400

A Rogers blue and white chestnut basket stand, Camel pattern, pierced, slight damage, impressed mark, c1815, 7 by 9in (18 by 23cm).
$60-100

A Liverpool delft blue and white water bottle, small glaze imperfection, slight restoration, c1760, 9in (23cm).
$300-500

Bottles

A Liverpool delft blue and white bottle, decorated with woman and child and a figure in a pavilion in a garden, c1760, 9in (23cm).
$1,300-2,000

A Wedgwood silver gilt mounted three-colour jasper scent bottle, the pale blue ground with 2 green medallions in white relief, mid-19thC, 3in (8cm).
$700-900

A creamware bowl, c1770, 4 by 8½in (10 by 21.5cm).
$800-1,200

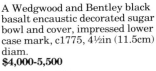

A Wedgwood and Bentley black basalt encaustic decorated sugar bowl and cover, impressed lower case mark, c1775, 4½in (11.5cm) diam.
$4,000-5,500

A Lambeth delft bowl, painted in blue, manganese, yellow and green with buildings in a continuous landscape, minor glaze chips, c1760, 10in (26cm) diam.
$700-900

A Prattware coloured pottery bowl, possibly Liverpool, c1790, 11in (28cm) diam.
$1,500-2,600

An Adams blue and white jasper sugar bowl and cover, applied in white relief, the cover with swan finial, impressed mark, c1800, 6in (15cm) wide.
$1,200-1,750

A creamware bowl and cover, in mint condition, c1800, 8in (20.5cm).
$800-1,200

CREAMWARE

★ a low fired earthenware glazed in a cream or butter colour with a porcelain effect
★ first produced in 1740
★ perfected by Josiah Wedgwood in the 1760s
★ named Queen's Ware by Wedgwood in honour of Queen Charlotte

A Sunderland lustre bowl, transfer printed with portrait of Sir Robert Peel, speech and mariners compass, splash lustre, c1840, 10in (25cm) diam.
$450-700

A Mason's patent Ironstone china dish, painted with Interior of the Hall of Kenilworth Castle, Warwickshire, impressed mark, c1820, 10½in (26.5cm) wide.
$800-1,200

A George Jones majolica strawberry dish, for cream and sugar, with a thrush between 2 nests, relief decoration of strawberry blossom, leaves and fruit, 1878, 11in (28cm) wide.
$1,000-1,400

A Staffordshire majolica dish in the shape of a begonia leaf, c1885, 9½in (24cm).
$60-100

A Copeland parian bust of The Veiled Bride, marked, c1850, 14½in (37cm).
$2,000-3,000

Busts

A George Jones majolica nut dish, with a squirrel holding a hazel nut, the dish decorated with hazel leaves and ferns in relief on a pink ground, 1886, 10in (25cm) wide.
$700-900

An Enoch Wood bust of Wesley, c1800, 4½in (11cm).
$400-550

An Enoch Wood bust of the
Madonna, c1810, 16in (40.5cm).
$2,000-3,000

A Staffordshire bust of Maria Foot
Obadiah Sherratt type, wearing
a yellow-edged pink dress, on a
marbled blue socle and moulded
four-footed base, some restoration to
base and socle, c1816, 11½in (29cm).
$3,000-4,500

A Wedgwood black basalt library
bust of Sir Francis Bacon, impressed
marks to bust and socle, the socle
with deleted 'made in England'
marks, late 19th/20thC, 16in
(40.5cm).
$900-1,300

A parian bust of Henry Wilson, after
H F Libby, inscribed on the reverse
'H.F. Libby, Sculpt. Boston.
Copyrighted', 'The Death of Slavery
is the Life of the Nation', H Wilson,
late 19thC, 13in (33cm).
$800-1,200

*Henry Wilson (1812-75), the
American politician, was an ardent
anti-slavery advocate. He joined the
American (Know Nothing) party in
1854 but soon withdrew because of
its intolerance and failure to take a
positive stand on the slavery issue.
He was US Senator for
Massachusetts (1855-73), one of the
founders of the Republican party
and Vice President of the United
States (1873-75).*

A parian bust of The Duke of
Wellington, after the sculpture by
Comte D'Orsay, wearing the collar
and badge of the Order of the Golden
Fleece, some damage, impressed
marks and dated 1852, on an
ebonised wood stand, 13in (33cm)
overall.
$200-350

A Staffordshire pottery bust of
The Duke of Wellington, forming a
jug, decorated in colours and gilt,
7in (18cm).
$200-350

A Staffordshire pottery bust of The
Duke of Wellington, forming a
tobacco jar and cover, decorated in
colours, chip to hat, 7½in (19cm).
$150-250

Commemorative

A Staffordshire bust of the virgin,
wearing a yellow robe and a head
scarf in crimson lined with blue, on a
marbled socle and square base, 15in
(38cm).
$150-250

A Staffordshire silver lustre
commemorative jug, Molineux and
Cribb, c1815, 5½in (14cm).
$700-900

A commemorative jug of Princess
Charlotte and Leopold, creamware
with green enamel and purple
lustre decoration, c1816, 6½in
(16.5cm).
$400-550

A blue transfer printed plate inscribed 'Her Majesty Queen Caroline of England', c1821, 6½in (16.5cm) diam.
$400-550

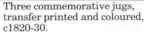

Three commemorative jugs, transfer printed and coloured, c1820-30.

l. Queen Charlotte, 5in (12.5cm).
$450-700

c. William IV and Adelaide, 6in (15cm).
$700-900

r. King George IV, 4in (10cm).
$700-900

A commemorative plate, George IV visit to Edinburgh 1822, enamelled, lustred and titled, 8½in (21.5cm) diam.
$800-1,200

A commemorative pottery jug of Viscount Clive of India obtaining his majority, November 5th, 1839.
$150-250

A Staffordshire children's plate to commemorate the union of Queen Victoria and Prince Albert, with painted enamel decoration to the rim, c1840, 5in (12.5cm) diam.
$400-550

A mug with underglaze black transfer of the 14th Earl of Derby, decorated with enamelled blue circles, c1852, 3in (7.5cm).
$250-350

A Staffordshire mug printed in blue with a half-length portrait of Queen Victoria, 1837, 3½in (9cm).
$1,300-2,000

A porcelain underglaze transfer mug, with portrait and captions in black, February 4th, 1874, 3in (7.5cm).
$200-350

A footed porcelain mug with black transfer print, underglaze, c1852, 3½in (9cm).
$300-500

A porcelain mug with underglaze black transfer of the Wesleyan Methodist Chapel at Spilsby, Lincolnshire, c1890, 3½in (9cm).
$100-200

A mug with portrait of Robert Burns and Mrs Burns on the reverse, by C W McNay, Bo'Ness, Scotland, c1896, 3in (7.5cm).
$100-200

A Staffordshire commemorative mug, Wesley on one side, temple on other side and inside, c1891, 3in (7.5cm).
$100-200

An earthenware mug with large portrait of Queen Victoria in a surround of national flowers, for the 1887 Jubilee, titled 'Queen of England – Empress of India', 3½in (9cm).
$200-350

A brown saltglaze stoneware jug by Doulton to commemorate the wedding of George, Duke of York, and Princess May of Teck, 1893, 4in (10cm).
$300-500

A Copeland stoneware teapot, in buff with olive green glaze, decorated in white, the reverse with portrait of Queen Victoria with indented wording Diamond Jubilee 1897, 7½in (19cm).
$200-350

A Copeland three-handled loving cup, commemorating the end of the Boer War, brown outline with detailed hand colouring in enamels and gilding, titled on base 'Subscribers copy', 1900.
$900-1,300

A pottery mug with portrait of General Sir Redvers Buller, brown underglaze transfer with overglaze enamel clobbering, Boer War, c1900, 3½in (9cm).
$100-200

A Doulton glaze stoneware mug, commemorating the Trafalgar Centenary, portrait of Nelson and a rope twist border enclosing a depiction of the battle, 1905, 3in (7.5cm).
$250-350

A Doulton saltglaze stoneware jug, commemorating the centenary of Trafalgar, with relief portrait of Nelson and his famous signal, 'England expects every man will do his duty', 1905, 8½in (21.5cm).
$450-700

A mug commemorating the marriage of King George V and Queen Mary on July 6, 1893.
$75-150

A pottery mug commemorating the coming of age of Lewis Frederick Davis, Esq, Ferndale, 1912, 3in (7.5cm).
$75-150

A Staffordshire Toby jug, modelled as Thomas Woodrow Wilson, President of The United States, designed by Francis Carruthers Gould, in a limited edition of 500, c1917.
$800-1,200

A porcelain mug with portrait of the Rt Hon David Lloyd George, in 2 shades of brown, c1918, 3in (7.5cm).
$200-350

A Staffordshire Toby jug, modelled as Admiral Beatty, designed by Francis Carruthers Gould, in a limited edition of 350, c1918, 11in (28cm).
$700-900

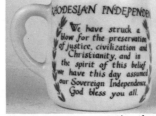

A pottery mug commemorating the Unilateral Declaration of Independence of Rhodesia, November 11th, 1965, with portrait of Ian Smith on the reverse.
$60-100

A commemorative jug of Admiral Sir David Beatty, at the German surrender, November 21st, 1918, 6in (15cm).
$200-350

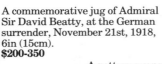

A pottery mug with portrait of George Washington, First President of The United States of America, celebrating the Bicentenary of Independence, 1976, 3½in (9cm).
$60-100

Cottages

A pottery 'organ' pastille burner, late 18thC, 6in (15cm).
$450-700

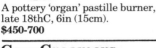

A Staffordshire model of Stanfield Hall, c1850, 7in (18cm).
$300-500

A Prattware money box in the form of Gothic cottage, sponged in blue, ochre, yellow and black, c1800, 5½in (14cm).
$1,000-1,400

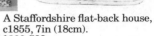

A Staffordshire flat-back house, c1855, 7in (18cm).
$300-500

A cow creamer, probably North Country, sponged in purple and black, c1800, 5in (12.5cm).
$1,500-2,600

Cow Creamers

A Whieldon cow creamer, with unusual markings, c1770, 5in (12.5cm).
$3,000-4,500

A Yorkshire cow group, coloured in blue, ochre, black and yellow, c1800, 5½in (14cm).
$1,200-1,750

A creamware cup and saucer, with green decoration, c1775, saucer 5in (12.5cm) diam.
$700-900

A Wedgwood and Bentley black basalt encaustic decorated cup and saucer, the borders painted in iron red and white, impressed lower case mark to saucer, c1775.
$1,500-2,600

Cups

A Staffordshire moulded white saltglaze coffee cup with ribbed loop handle, and a saucer, minor chip to saucer and hairline crack, c1775.
$1,200-1,750

A pair of Staffordshire stirrup cups, c1820, 5in (12.5cm).
$3,000-4,500

A Nottingham stoneware loving cup, inscribed 'Made at Nottm. Novr. the 4th 1779 – Sarah Howels of Headwalton, Nottnsh', restored, 9½in (24cm).
$2,000-3,000

A Wedgwood green and white jasper teabowl and saucer, the dipped pale lime green ground moulded in white relief, impressed marks and 3, the saucer in lower case, c1790.
$1,300-2,000

Ewers

A pair of Wedgwood black basalt water and wine ewers, after designs by Flaxman, on spreading feet and square bases, impressed marks, late 19thC, 17½in (44cm).
$2,000-3,000

A Staffordshire pearlware fox mask stirrup cup, streaked in iron red and highlighted in black, one ear with slight chip, c1790, 5½in (13.5cm) long.
$2,000-3,000

A dog's head stirrup cup, marked Turner, c1800, 6½in (16cm) long.
$2,500-3,500

Figures – Animals

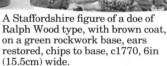

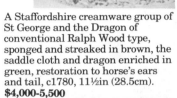

A pair of Wedgwood pale lilac jasper ewers, applied in white relief on the dipped ground, impressed marks and S, c1880, 8in (20cm).
$2,500-3,500

A Staffordshire figure of a doe of Ralph Wood type, with brown coat, on a green rockwork base, ears restored, chips to base, c1770, 6in (15.5cm) wide.
$1,500-2,600

A Staffordshire creamware group of St George and the Dragon of conventional Ralph Wood type, sponged and streaked in brown, the saddle cloth and dragon enriched in green, restoration to horse's ears and tail, c1780, 11½in (28.5cm).
$4,000-5,500

A Ralph Wood model of a lion, with deeply incised mane covered in a translucent olive green glaze, streaked in yellow on the shoulder, on a brown washed base, moulded with green foliage, part of tail lacking, slight chips to base, c1775, 12½in (31cm) wide.
$4,000-5,500

A Ralph Wood whistle in the form of a lion, c1780, 3in (7.5cm).
$1,000-1,400

A Ralph Wood bull baiting group, c1780, 6in (15cm).
$4,000-5,500

It is rare to have black spots, usually manganese.

A Mosbach figure of a dog, naturalistically painted in colours, tail missing, c1785, 4in (9.5cm).
$1,000-1,400

A rare 'birds in tree' group, possibly from the Wood factory, underglazed decorated in green and yellow, c1785, 7½in (19cm).
$1,500-2,600

A Prattware cockerel, c1790, 4in (10cm).
$1,500-2,600

A Yorkshire figure of a ram, with brown curling horns and spots on a blue, brown and green base, horns restored, minor chips to base, c1790, 6½in (16cm).
$1,500-2,600

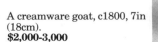

A Prattware deer with bocage, c1790, 4in (10cm).
$1,000-1,400

A creamware goat, c1800, 7in (18cm).
$2,000-3,000

A pearlware 'birds in branches' group, in ochre, yellow and blue, probably Staffordshire, chips to tree and base, c1790, 7½in (19.5cm).
$1,300-2,000

A Staffordshire dog, with splashed brown markings and on yellow and blue cushion base, c1790, 3½in (8.5cm).
$250-350

A pair of pottery figures of dogs, by John Bell, Waynesboro, Pennsylvania, each modelled as a recumbent greyhound with black collar, on yellow base, impressed mark, c1850, 9½in (24cm) long.
$5,000-6,000

A Staffordshire pearlware figure of a recumbent stag, sponged in brown with green leaved tree, leaves and ears restored, antlers lacking, c1800, 8in (20.5cm).
$700-900

A Staffordshire pearlware figure of a cow, with brown patches, on a green and brown base applied with moss and coloured flowers, some restoration to horns and tail, c1800, 13in (32.5cm) wide.
$1,200-1,750

A Staffordshire pearlware figure of an eagle with brown plumage, pink sponged base, one wing with slight chip, minor flaking to enamel, c1810, 7½in (19.5cm).
$450-700

A Staffordshire creamware figure of a lion, with red coat and grey mane and paws, with yellow ball, on a shaped green base edged in red and pink, tail restored, c1810, 6½in (16cm).
$1,300-2,000

A Tittensor figure of a stallion with brown coat and yellow saddle, on an incised green base, tree damaged, ears chipped, impressed mark at back, c1815, 6½in (17cm).
$3,000-4,500

A Staffordshire pearlware figure of a cockerel, with multi-coloured plumage, tail restored, c1820, 10in (25cm).
$1,300-2,000

A pair of early Walton type dogs, c1820, 5½in (14cm).
$2,000-3,000

A Walton type figure of a deer, with white spotted iron red hide with black muzzle and hooves, on moulded base with blue scrolls and enriched in green, ears restored, tree chipped, antlers lacking(?), c1820.
$450-700

A pair of Staffordshire creamware leopards, with pale yellow coats and brown markings, one with a lump of meat, on green bases, ears chipped, one with some flaking to green enamel, c1820, 8½in (21cm) wide.
$10,000-13,500

In the Ceramics section if there is only one measurement it usually refers to the height of the piece

A slipware figure of a lion, his forepaw resting on a ball, with cream slip marbling beneath a treacle glaze, tail restored, early 18thC, 10in (25cm) long.
$600-900

An Obadiah Sherratt figure of a
pointer with black markings, tail
restored, c1825, 6in (15cm).
$450-700

A pair of stoneware lions, c1830, 4in
(10cm).
$100-200

A Staffordshire miniature cow with
bocage, marked salt, c1830, 2in
(5cm) wide.
$450-700

A Staffordshire figure of a dog with
black markings, entitled Rover,
damage to bocage, c1840, 4½in
(11cm).
$1,300-2,000

A rare Staffordshire cat, in black
and white on blue base, c1840, 6in
(15cm).
$800-1,200

A Staffordshire equestrian group of
Obadiah Sherratt type, modelled as
a gallant in opaque blue jacket and
brown breeches, astride a sponged
grey horse with a yellow saddle
cloth and bridle, some restoration,
c1830, 8½in (22cm).
$3,000-4,500

A large Staffordshire greyhound,
c1845, 11in (28cm) long.
$900-1,300

*This model was produced over a long
period. Examples vary enormously
in quality and therefore price.
The illustrated example is of good
quality.*

A pair of Staffordshire mares and
foals, late 18thC, 11in (28cm).
$800-1,200

A Staffordshire pair of brightly
coloured birds, c1850, 13in (33cm).
$1,500-2,600

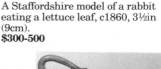

A Staffordshire model of a rabbit
eating a lettuce leaf, c1860, 3½in
(9cm).
$300-500

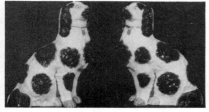

A pair of Staffordshire zebras,
c1855, 6in (15cm).
$800-1,200

A pair of Staffordshire spaniels,
with separate moulded forepaws,
with gilt collars and black
markings, both restored, c1860,
15½in (39cm).
$600-900

An early Staffordshire tiger,
probably Portobello, Death of
Lieutenant Monroe, c1875, 6½in
(16.5cm).
$900-1,300

A Staffordshire spaniel, c1860, 13in
(33cm) wide.
$1,500-2,600

A Wedgwood black basalt jackdaw,
with black glass eyes, modelled by
E W Light, impressed mark, tail
restored, c1915, 7in (17.5cm) wide.
$75-150

A Wedgwood black basalt cat, with
later yellow glass eyes, modelled by
E W Light, impressed mark and C,
c1915, 4in (10cm) wide.
$300-500

A Wedgwood black basalt bulldog,
with yellow glass eyes and wearing
a copper collar, modelled by
E W Light, impressed mark and C,
c1915, 5in (12.5cm) long.
$300-500

A Wedgwood black basalt egret,
with yellow glass eyes, perched on
pierced rockwork, modelled by
E W Light, impressed mark at back,
c1916, 8in (20cm).
$100-200

*Ernest William Light was a
celebrated modeller and sculptor in
the Potteries who was later to become
headmaster of Hanley School of Art.
Wedgwood commissioned him to
model this series of bird and animal
figures between 1913 and 1919.*

A rare Staffordshire dismal hound,
4in (10cm).
$700-900

A Staffordshire figure of a spaniel,
with possibly the Princess Royal,
6½in (16.5cm).
$400-550

A pair of Staffordshire dogs with
pheasants, 9in (23cm).
$800-1,200

A figure of a *lion passant*,
Staffordshire or perhaps Yorkshire,
one paw resting on a ball, the body
yellow with black spots and brown
mane, 6in (15cm).
$6,000-8,000

A Yorkshire ram group with
attendant, typical dotted decoration
in ochre, blue and black, 5in
(12.5cm).
$1,500-2,600

A pair of painted chalkware doves,
American, each perched on a stump
base with leaf and cherry
decoration, one tail restored and
some restoration to paint, late
19thC, 11½in (29cm).
$600-800

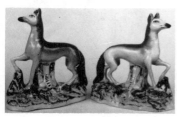

A rare pair of Staffordshire foxes,
6½in (16cm).
$800-1,200

A Wedgwood white pottery model of
a bison by John Skeaping, printed
and impressed marks, 9in (23cm).
$300-500

Figures – People

A Ralph Wood group, St George and the Dragon, cream with brown trim, c1780, 11in (28cm).
$1,500-2,600

A Ralph Wood figure of a gospeller, c1780, 9in (23cm).
$1,500-2,600

A figure of a sailor in blue uniform and yellow striped waistcoat, on a marbled base, possibly Yorkshire, chip to hat, flag and base, c1780, 9½in (24.5cm).
$2,250-3,500

A Ralph Wood figure of a harvester in brown hat, grey waistcoat and green breeches, left hand and handle of scythe restored, impressed mark Ra. Wood Burslem, c1775, 8in (20cm).
$3,000-4,500

A Neale & Co figure of Apollo, impressed under base, c1785, 6in (15cm).
$800-1,200

A Ralph Wood type figure, Venus coming out of the sea, c1790, 9in (23cm).
$700-900

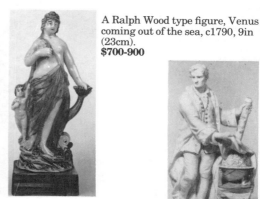

A Yorkshire figure of Liverpool Volunteer, in ochre and green, c1785, 5in (12.5cm).
$1,500-2,600

A Ralph Wood figure of Sir Isaac Newton, in pale flowered clothes, on a marbled base, top of telescope lacking, impressed mark Ra. Wood Burslem 137, c1790, 12in (30.5cm).
$2,250-3,500

A Wood and Caldwell figure, c1800, 8½in (21.5cm).
$1,300-2,000

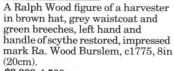

A rare pair of R Wood II rustic groups, c1795, 11in (28cm).
$3,000-4,500

A pair of Staffordshire cradles, l. enamel, r. 'Pratt' decorated, c1800, 4½ and 5in (11 and 12.5cm).
$300-500

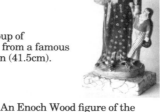

An Enoch Wood group of quarrelling Cupids, from a famous bronze, c1800, 16½in (41.5cm).
$2,250-3,500

An Enoch Wood figure of the 'Sailor's wife', c1815, 9½in (24cm).
$1,500-2,600

ENOCH WOOD OF BURSLEM

* ★ during the late 18thC and early 19thC one of the most productive factories
* ★ Enoch Wood commenced his apprenticeship in the early 1770s
* ★ went into business with his cousin Ralph Wood in 1784
* ★ a new firm Wood and Caldwell was established in 1790 changing to Enoch Wood & Sons in 1818
* ★ good figure models produced using overglaze colours
* ★ in-glaze colours used on earlier figures by Ralph Wood and Whieldon
* ★ blue-printed ware also produced, being exported to the USA in large quantities

A pair of figures of
The Lovers and
The Sailor and his
Lass, with unusual
blue bocage, c1815,
8½in (21.5cm).
$3,000-4,500

A pair of Staffordshire musicians,
after the Derby models, probably
E Wood, with enamel finish, c1810,
6in (15cm).
$700-900

A Staffordshire figure of a
gentleman, in black top hat and
tails, blue waistcoat and striped red
trousers, base chipped and repaired,
slight chipping to enamels, c1810,
9in (22.5cm).
$600-900

A Staffordshire group of Dandies,
c1815, 7in (18cm).
$1,000-1,400

A pair of Walton figures, Flight and
Return from Egypt, enamel colours,
marked, c1815, 6in (15cm).
$2,500-3,500

A Staffordshire pottery group of The
Dandies, in multi-coloured enamels,
c1815, 8½in (21.5cm).
$1,000-1,400

A Staffordshire tithe pig group, with
a very rare figure of a clergyman,
c1815, 10in (25cm).
$1,500-2,600

A Staffordshire figure of Diana with
dog, painted in enamel colours,
c1815, 11in (28cm).
$700-900

A pair of enamel decorated figures of
St Peter and St Paul, c1820, 10in
(25cm).
$1,500-2,600

A Staffordshire figure, Tenderness,
c1820, 6½in (16cm).
$1,000-1,400

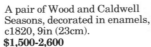

A Staffordshire group, Flight to
Egypt, marked Walton, c1820, 7½in
(19cm).
$1,500-2,600

Three Staffordshire groups, marked
Walton, c1820.
l. Reaper, 7½in (19cm).
$1,000-1,400

c. Songsters, 9in (23cm).
$1,300-2,000

r. Ewe and lamb, 6in (15cm).
$600-900

A pair of Wood and Caldwell
Seasons, decorated in enamels,
c1820, 9in (23cm).
$1,500-2,600

An early Staffordshire group of Dandies, in mint condition, c1820, 8in (20cm).
$1,200-1,750

A pair of John Dale Staffordshire figures of rural musicians, decorated in enamels, c1820, 4½in (11cm).
$1,500-2,600

An Obadiah Sherratt group of Grecian and Daughter, some restoration, c1820, 10in (25cm).
$2,000-3,000

An Obadiah Sherratt figure entitled 'The Reading Maid', c1820, 11½in (29cm).
$900-1,300

A Staffordshire figure of a shepherd, c1860, 12in (30cm).
$400-550

A Staffordshire figure of a sheep shearer, c1855, 6in (15cm).
$200-350

A pair of Obadiah Sherratt figures, Elijah and the Widow, c1825, 11in (28cm).
$1,300-2,000

A pair of Staffordshire cupids, by Ralph Wood, 7in (18cm).
$1,500-2,600

A set of 3 early Staffordshire pottery figures, 2 country men and one bare footed woman, all on bases with single iron red line to border, 6½in (16cm).
$400-550

A rare early Staffordshire figure of a girl in a chair, 3in (7.5cm).
$750-1,000

Staffordshire Figures

STAFFORDSHIRE FIGURES c1835-95

- ★ can be made from either pottery or porcelain type body
- ★ 'Staffordshire Portrait Figures' by P D Gordon Pugh is the standard reference book and some collectors only buy examples appearing therein
- ★ unusual animals and theatrical figures very collectable
- ★ damage, wear, flaking all affect value as well as restoration
- ★ beware of fakes!

A Staffordshire pottery group of portrait figures, Victoria and child, and Albert, c1848, 7½in (19cm), (A,16,37) and (A,15,36).
$450-700

A pair of Staffordshire figures, Tam O'Shanter and Souter Johnny, c1840, 5in (12.5cm).
$300-500

Two Staffordshire groups, Before and After Marriage, c1840.
$450-700

A Staffordshire model of Shakespeare's house, c1850, 7½in (17cm), (H,7,22).
$300-500

A Staffordshire figure of 'Omer Pacha', c1850, 10½in (27cm), (C,64,166).
$700-900

A Staffordshire quill holder, c1845.
$300-500

A Staffordshire bird, c1845, 5½in (14cm).
$200-350

A rare Staffordshire figure of James Blomfield Rush, in dark blue jacket, green waistcoat and pink trousers, named in gilt script on the oval base, minor restoration to the nose, c1850, 10in (25cm), (G,23,48).
$2,000-3,000

A Staffordshire figure of Admiral Napier, c1850, 9in (23cm), (C,42,101).
$400-550

A rare Staffordshire figure of Marietta Alboni as Cinderella, in long blue dress, c1850, 9in (23cm), (E,20,43).
$1,000-1,400

A Staffordshire hunting group spill vase, c1850.
$300-500

A rare and unusual Staffordshire figure of the actor Menier in the part of Thelsitor from the play, *Porga*, with white turban, green sleeved jacket and stockings, named in French on the underside of the base and also inscribed with a part from one of the main songs, one finger restored, c1850, 10½in (26cm), (E,).
$700-900

A pair of dogs, c1850, 10in (25cm).
$700-900

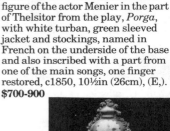

A pair of red and white dogs, c1850, 12in (30cm).
$450-700

A Staffordshire castle, c1850.
$75-150

A Staffordshire sailor figure, T P Cooke as Ben Backstay, c1850, 8½in (21cm).
$100-200

Make the Most of Miller's

CONDITION is absolutely vital when assessing the value of an antique. Damaged pieces on the whole appreciate much less than perfect examples. However a rare, desirable piece may command a high price even when damaged

A figure of a pirate, or maybe Will Watch, c1850.
$150-250

A Staffordshire pastille burner, c1850, 8in (20cm).
$300-500

A Staffordshire group of Princess Alice with Prince Louis of Hesse, c1860, 14in (35cm), (A,70,218).
$300-500

A pair of Staffordshire figures of the Duke and Duchess of Cambridge, c1860, 14in (35cm), (C,59,157,158).
$1,000-1,400

A Staffordshire figure of a gentleman wearing a tam o'shanter, dark blue jacket and pink half cape, perhaps Prince Alfred, c1860, 12½in (31cm).
$200-350

A pair of Staffordshire Moody and Sankey figures, American, c1870, (D,5,9a,10a).
$600-900

A Staffordshire model of a hunter seated beside a dead tiger draped across the back of an elephant, c1870, 9in (23cm).
$450-700

A pair of Staffordshire figures of the Prince and Princess of Wales, c1870, 12in (30cm), (A,65,200,201).
$900-1,300

A Staffordshire flatback group, 'The Murder of Smith and Collier', 19thC, 13in (32cm), (G,27,54).
$400-550

Two Staffordshire figures of Edward VII and Queen Alexandra, c1900, 13in (32cm), (A,85,242,3).
$300-500

A Staffordshire figure of the King of Sardinia, glaze chip to base, 17in (42.5cm), (C,38,90).
$600-900

A Staffordshire figure of Jumbo the elephant, painted in splashed brown glaze and named in raised capitals on the brown and green base, c1870, 11in (28cm).
$600-900

A model entitled 'The Wounded Soldier', 13in (32cm), (C,71,194).
$700-900

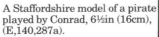

A Staffordshire model of a pirate played by Conrad, 6½in (16cm), (E,140,287a).
$150-250

A Staffordshire model of Palmers House, 8in (20cm), (G,18B,43).
$900-1,300

A pair of Staffordshire figures of Queen Victoria and Prince Albert, 8in (20cm), (A,27,71).
$400-550

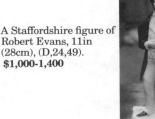

A Staffordshire figure of Robert Evans, 11in (28cm), (D,24,49).
$1,000-1,400

A Staffordshire figure of St Winifred, 11in (28cm).
$300-500

Two Staffordshire apes, 3in (8cm).
$200-350

A Staffordshire model of Potash Farm and Stanfield Hall, 8in (20cm), (G,20,44,46).
$1,000-1,400

A colourful pair of Staffordshire pottery figures depicting the American evangelists Dwight Lyman Moody and Ira David Sankey, one damaged and one re-stuck, 14in (35.5cm), (D,5,9a,10a).
$300-500

A Staffordshire pottery portrait figure of Wellington, decorated in colours and gilt, hairline cracks, 13½in (34cm), (B,2,17).
$300-500

A Staffordshire pottery figure of a bearded sailor, 13½in (33.5cm).
$600-900

A Staffordshire pottery group depicting the eccentric young women known as Alphington Ponies, identically dressed with yellow hats, orange check coats and green dresses, 4½in (11.5cm), (I,18,41).
$400-550

Flatware

A London delft blue and white Royalist portrait plate, painted with half-length portraits of William III and Queen Mary flanked by the initials WMR wearing coronation robes, within a turquoise line rim, slight glaze cracks and flaking to rim, c1690, 9in (22cm).
$3,000-4,500

A London delftware moulded dish, c1710, 10in (25cm).
$1,500-2,600

A Lambeth delftware blue and white dish, painted with Chinese stylised landscape, late 17thC, 14in (35cm).
$800-1,200

An English delftware farmyard plate, sponged in yellow, blue, red and manganese, restored, c1725.
$1,200-1,750

An English delftware plate with a colourful design, c1730, 9in (23cm).
$1,200-1,750

An English delftware manganese Wincanton plate, some chips, c1745, 9in (23cm).
$900-1,300

A pair of London delft polychrome plates, c1750.
$450-700

A very rare London delftware plate depicting 2 birds cock-fighting, c1760, 8½in (21cm).
$6,000-8,000

A saltglaze dish with enamel decoration, c1765, 6½in (16cm) wide.
$6,000-8,000

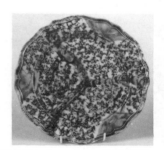

A Whieldon type plate, c1765, 10in (25cm).
$800-1,200

A Whieldon type plate, with leaf decoration, c1765, 9in (23cm).
$1,500-2,600

A Lambeth delft ballooning plate, with a green balloon in flight between blue trees, 2 pieces re-stuck to rim at 5-o'clock, rim chips, c1785, 9in (23cm).
$400-550

An enamelled creamware plate, c1770, 10in (25cm).
$600-900

MAKE THE MOST OF MILLER'S

Every care has been taken to ensure the accuracy of descriptions and estimated valuations. Where an attribution is made within inverted commas (e.g. 'Chippendale') or is followed by the word 'style' (e.g. early Georgian style) it is intended to convey that, in the opinion of the publishers, the piece concerned is a later – though probably still antique – reproduction of the style so designated. Unless otherwise stated, any description which refers to 'a set', or 'a pair' includes a valuation for the entire set or the pair, even though the illustration may show only a single item

A Rogers meat draining dish, printed with a view of the Boston State House, impressed mark, c1820, 18in (46cm) wide.
$1,000-1,400

A Staffordshire blue and white plate, c1820, 10in (25cm).
$100-200

A Rogers meat dish, printed with Britannia seated before the Horn of Plenty, minor glaze chip to rim, impressed mark, c1820, 21in (53cm) wide.
$300-500

An Enoch Wood & Sons meat dish, with a rare print of hunting polar bears, crazed and stained, impressed mark, c1825, 16½in (42cm) wide.
$700-900

A rare Staffordshire meat dish, printed with the Durham Ox with his owner John Day, c1825, 22in (55cm) wide.
$1,300-2,000

A Mason's meat dish, printed with the Classical Landscape pattern, reverse with some crazing, c1830, 16in (40cm) wide.
$300-500

A Brameld Rockingham plate, c1830, 7in (18cm).
$400-550

A Brameld Rockingham plate, damaged, c1830, 7½in (19cm).
$100-200

An English lustre saucer with the Print of Charity, c1840, 8in (20cm).
$75-150

A pair of Middlesbrough pottery plates, c1840, 6in (15cm).
$200-350

A South Wales pottery dish, with damask border in shades of brown, W Chambers, c1839-54, 20in (50cm) wide.
$200-350

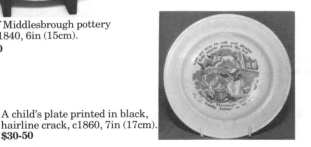

A child's plate printed in black, hairline crack, c1860, 7in (17cm).
$30-50

A set of 20 Wedgwood plates with blue pattern taken from a painting by Claude, c1860.
$700-900

A pair of pottery nursery plates, each printed in purple, one with the bust of King William IV, the other with Queen Adelaide, 7in (18cm).
$1,000-1,400

An English majolica dish, modelled with flowering strawberry vines, with separate cream jug, sugar bowl and spoon, 14½in (36cm) wide.
$800-1,200

A pottery nursery plate, the centre printed with portrait of the Princess Royal, 6in (15cm).
$200-350

A pair of pottery nursery plates, the centres printed in black with portraits and inscribed 'The Lily of England, Princess Royal' and 'The Swedish Nightingale, Jenny Lind', within moulded borders, 7in (17cm).
$200-350

A Staffordshire solid agateware saucer, 5in (13cm).
$1,300-2,000

A large Spode charger, decorated in blue and gilt, pattern number 3702, 20in (50cm).
$450-700

A Liverpool delft dish, painted in polychrome in Chinese taste, 13½in (34.5cm).
$400-550

A Castelli tazza, painted in the Grue workshop with the fall of Samson, extensively repaired, replacement foot, c1690, 11½in (29cm).
$1,200-1,750

A Dutch Delft polychrome dish, painted in iron red, blue, green and yellow, rim chips, c1740, 14in (35cm).
$400-550

A Dutch Delft dish, painted in iron red, blue and green, chipped, early 18thC, 14in (35cm).
$450-700

A Dutch Delft canted meat dish, brightly decorated in manganese, yellow and green, on a bright green ground, damaged, mid-18thC, 17½in (44cm).
$1,500-2,600

A pair of Luneville dishes, painted in polychrome, with puce rims, slight glaze chips to rims, c1770, 13in (33cm).
$6,000-8,000

A pair of Marseilles, Veuve Perrin, plates painted 'en camaieu vert', minute rim chips, manganese and brown VP monogram marks, c1765, 10in (25cm).
$800-1,200

A Low Countries blue and white majolica dish, painted with a portrait bust of a woman, the border with 3 blue lines, rim glaze chips, 17thC, 12½in (31cm).
$1,300-2,000

A Rouen plate painted in a 'famille verte' palette, rim chips, c1740, 10in (25cm).
$2,250-3,500

A slipware plate decorated in brown and green, on a yellow/cream ground, incised 1723, 11½in (29cm).
$450-700

Two Sienna polychrome plates, with scenes of the deer hunt and the wolf hunt, one plate broken and riveted, c1740, 9½in (23.5cm).
$1,500-2,600

Jars

A London delft blue and white drug jar, rim chips and cracks at back, c1690, 7in (18cm).
$800-1,200

A London delft blue and white wet drug jar of 'man smoking pipe' type, named for Oxymel:Scill, cracked rim, handle, spout and foot chipped, c1680, 8in (20.5cm).
$4,000-5,500

A London delft drug jar, c1760, 3½in (8.5cm).
$1,000-1,400

A Wedgwood black basalt Capri-decorated pot pourri jar and cover, painted in colours and gilt, impressed and moustache marks, c1830, 13½in (35cm).
$1,300-2,000

A Dutch Delft drug jar and metal cover, hairline crack to neck, 11in (27cm).
$400-550

A Berrettino baluster blue and white wet drug jar, the contents named in Gothic script on a ribbon scroll above an oval pharmacy mark of 2 clasped hands, repaired, spout chip, Marchigian, c1580, 9½in (24cm).
$1,000-1,400

A Dutch Delft drug jar and metal cover, 10½in (26cm).
$450-700

A Deruta bottle for A Graminis, painted in blue, yellow, orange and copper-green, old repair to neck and body, c1530, 16in (40cm).
$10,000-13,500

A pair of Sicilian wet drug jars, with contents inscribed on yellow and green labels, the scroll handles with mask terminals and the pharmacy mark S beneath, one with repair to rim, chips, 17thC, 10in (25cm).
$2,000-3,000

Jugs

Three Sicilian waisted albarelli, painted in yellow, green and blue with scroll cartouches between blue bands, blue rims, small chips, 17thC, 9in (23cm).
$1,500-2,600

A Staffordshire saltglaze milk jug and cover, with aubergine crabstock handle and finial, on 3 mask and paw feet, cracks to rim, minor rim restoration, c1755, 6in (15.5cm).
$4,000-5,500

A Jackfield type pottery sparrow beak jug, c1760, 5in (12.5cm).
$200-350

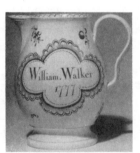

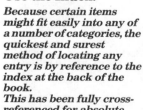

A creamware jug, painted in iron red and black and the inscription 'God Speed y Plough', and the inscription 'John & Mary Beckitt' beneath the handle, minute rim chips, c1770, 8in (20.5cm).
$1,500-2,600

A Leeds creamware dated baluster jug, with ear-shaped handle, painted in iron red with the inscription 'William Walker, 1777', minute rim chips and cracks, 8in (20cm).
$2,250-3,500

An English delft blue and white puzzle jug, the handle attached to the hollow rim with 3 short spouts above the cylindrical neck pierced with hearts and ovals, perhaps Liverpool, c1760, 7½in (19cm).
$3,000-4,500

Use the Index!

Because certain items might fit easily into any of a number of categories, the quickest and surest method of locating any entry is by reference to the index at the back of the book.
This has been fully cross-referenced for absolute simplicity

A pottery jug with polychrome decoration, possibly Liverpool, c1775, 2½in (6cm).
$200-350

A pearlware jug, moulded with a female mask to the spout, inscribed 'A & T, 1779', chips to rim and body, 7in (18cm).
$400-550

A pearlware blue and white jug, inscribed 'Success to Trade', c1780, 7in (18cm).
$300-500

A Prattware jug, Farewell and Return, c1790, 5½in (14cm).
$450-700

A Staffordshire pearlware Fair Hebe jug, moulded as a youth and companion in bright blue and ochre clothes, impressed mark R.MA (?), c1800, 5in (12.5cm).
$1,200-1,750

A Wedgwood green and white jasper cream jug, the dipped ground moulded in white relief with classical figures in medallions, impressed mark, c1800, 2½in (7cm).
$700-900

A Prattware jug with serpent pattern handle, the body decorated with the Duke of York and the reverse with a figure holding 3 leopards, and initialled I.P., late 18thC, 7½in (19cm).
$400-550

A Wedgwood creamware jug, transfer printed in black with an allegory of the Peninsular Wars, chips to bottom rim, impressed mark, c1800.
$1,300-2,000

A Staffordshire lead glazed redware bear jug and cover, the loop handle applied with a monkey, removable head wearing a muzzle, his coat covered in frit chippings, some minor chipping, early 19thC, 11in (27.5cm).
$1,200-1,750

STAFFORDSHIRE JUGS

★ made by many Staffordshire potteries
★ commenced manufacture c1825
★ very collectable, marked examples particularly, while value affected by damage and moulding quality
★ usually in 3 sizes and can be buff, pale blue, pale green, grey or white

---

An Elsmore & Foster ale jug, the white ground decorated with typical transfers depicting The Great Cashmore Clown, 19thC, 14in (35.5cm).
$1,300-2,000

A Prattware military review jug, with underglazed colours and traces of original gilding, c1800, 6in (15cm).
$800-1,200

A pearlware bear jug and cover, the black bear with mulberry muzzle and collar clutching Boney in his paws, perhaps Scottish, some damage, c1810, 11½in (28.5cm).
$800-1,200

A silver lustre jug with a rural scene, c1820, 6½in (16cm).
$300-500

A pair of Mason's Ironstone jugs printed and coloured in iron red, blue, green and gilt, with serpent handles, c1820, 8in (20.5cm).
$300-400

A Prattware jug with rose, thistle and shamrock design, c1829, 6½in (16cm).
$900-1,300

A jug depicting The Oddfellows, multi-coloured transfer printed with arms and motto on reverse, lustre rim, c1835, 5½in (14cm).
$450-700

A puzzle jug, with coloured enamels and lustre decoration, c1835, 8in (20cm).
$700-900

A brown and saltglaze jug, with greyhound handle and moulded with stag and boar hunting scenes, made expressly for I D Bagster, c1830, 7in (18cm).
$250-350

On later 19thC wares, the greyhound does not look over the rim of the jug.

A Tyne lustre jug with coloured transfer prints, c1835, 7in (18cm).
$450-700

A pearlware puzzle jug, the centre containing a white figure of a girl in Turkish dress, with ochre serpent handle with 3 spouts beneath a pierced blue neck, the body and foot boldly painted in Pratt colours with trailing flowers, some rim restorations, c1820, 11in (29cm).
$600-900

A Minton majolica jug, moulded as a pineapple, c1869, 8½in (21cm).
$400-550

An unusual Staffordshire jug, in the form of a seated monkey in yellow tricorn hat and orange jacket playing a cello, c1860, 12in (30.5cm).
$250-350

A majolica jug by Holdcroft, with fishes in low relief on a cobalt blue ground and bamboo handle, c1870, 8in (20cm).
$300-400

A Staffordshire majolica jug with ramshead mask and textured surface in lilac and green, c1870, 9in (23cm).
$100-150

A Carltonware pottery jug, with blue background with brown and yellow decoration, 14in (35.5cm).
$100-150

A delft puzzle jug, perhaps Liverpool, painted in blue with a verse, 7in (18cm).
$1,500-2,600

A Staffordshire majolica owl jug with pink interior, c1875, 9½in (24cm).
$300-500

A Mason's Patent Ironstone fluted jug, with ribbed handle, cracked and repaired, printed factory marks, 12in (30.5cm).
$600-900

A set of 10 Mason's Patent Ironstone graduated jugs, decorated in Chinese style in iron red and blue, with green and red lizard handles, 2 handles repaired, 3 not marked, 3 to 9½in (7.5 to 24cm).
$1,500-2,500

A white saltglaze cream jug, modelled in relief with pecten shells and formal flower sprays, on 3 shell and paw feet, 3in (7cm).
$800-1,200

A Mason's Patent Ironstone jug, decorated in the Chinese taste in bright colours, with dragon handle and lifting mask below the spout, printed mark in blue Mason's Patent Ironstone china and crown, 12½in (32cm).
$800-1,200

A Staffordshire jug, printed in puce with a fluted pink lustre ground, the neck with flowers in relief in colours, 5½in (13.5cm).
$200-350

A Staffordshire jug, modelled in relief in pink and copper lustre and green with a hunting scene, *The Kill*, marked B in copper lustre, 5in (14.5cm).
$200-350

WEDGWOOD BLUE PRINTED POTTERY

★ Wedgwood started by buying in printed wares from other factories, e.g. Minton
★ in 1805 Wedgwood produced its first blue and white printed pottery, using the Blue Bamboo pattern
★ from c1810 floral patterns introduced, with Chinese landscapes following on
★ impressed marks, normally Wedgwood plus numbers, letters or symbols appear on products

A Wedgwood creamware jug, with botanical design, 4½in (11cm).
$400-550

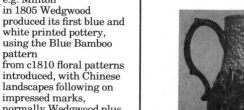

A Westerwald stoneware baluster jug, moulded all-over with relief rosettes on a blue ground, later metal cover, 12½in (32cm).
$800-1,200

A Wedgwood milk jug of cauliflower design, 8in (20.5cm).
$1,000-1,400

A Savona blue and white fountain with loop over handle, mask head terminal, tapering spout and mask spout below, handle repaired, chips to feet and spout, blue crowned shield mark, c1700, 23in (59cm).
$8,000-11,000

Toby Jugs

A Staffordshire Toby jug of Ralph Wood type, in dark brown hat, pale brown coat, white waistcoat, pale yellow breeches and dark brown shoes, c1775, 10in (25cm).
$10,000-13,500

A rare and particularly well modelled example.

A Toby jug of Ralph Wood type, in mottled brown hat, pale green jacket, brown breeches and shoes, hand and base cracked, glaze chipping, c1770, 9½in (24cm).
$1,000-1,400

A Toby jug of Ralph Wood type, in brown hat, sponged brown jacket, yellow breeches and brown shoes, chips to jug, paint flaking, c1770, 9½in (24cm).
$2,000-3,000

A miniature Ralph Wood Toby jug, on unglazed base, c1780, 6½in (16.5cm).
$1,500-2,500

A Staffordshire creamware Toby jug of Ralph Wood type, with translucent glazes, in dark brown hat, brown jacket, green waistcoat and yellow breeches, some restoration to hat, c1780, 10in (25cm).
$1,000-1,400

A Staffordshire Toby jug of conventional type, with blue sponged edging, yellow waistcoat and blue shoes, chip to rim of hat, c1780, 10in (25cm).
$1,300-2,000

A Staffordshire Toby jug, with translucent glazed manganese hat, hair, breeches and shoes, in a mottled brown coat, chips and flaking to hat and jug, c1780, 10½in (26cm).
$1,000-1,400

A Staffordshire 'Thin Man' Toby jug of Ralph Wood type, his tricorn hat and coat splashed in grey and with blue waistcoat, seated on a green framed chair, c1780, 9½in (23.5cm).
$10,000-13,500

An early Staffordshire Toby jug, c1790, 9½in (24cm).
$1,500-2,500

A miniature Prattware Toby jug, damaged, c1790, 4in (10cm).
$300-500

A Staffordshire Toby jug of conventional type, in mottled brown hat, sponged brown jacket, brown breeches and shoes, on a green base, hat rim restored, c1790, 10in (25cm).
$1,200-1,750

A Prattware Toby jug, c1790, 9in (23cm).
$700-900

A Toby jug, possibly Yorkshire, Hearty Good Fellow, decorated in Pratt palette, c1790.
$2,500-3,500

An Enoch Wood Toby jug, Dr Johnston, decorated in black and red enamels, c1790, 6½in (16cm).
$1,300-2,000

A pearlware Toby jug, possibly Yorkshire, painted in Pratt colours, in blue hat, ochre jacket, flowered waistcoat, green breeches and blue shoes, c1800, 9½in (23.5cm).
$1,000-1,400

A Staffordshire creamware Toby jug, in mottled brown coat, yellow waistcoat and splashed aubergine breeches holding a brown jug, restoration to hat, handle, jug and pipe, c1800, 10½in (25.5cm).
$800-1,200

An early Staffordshire sailor Toby jug, in enamel colours, c1800, 12in (30.5cm).
$1,500-2,600

A Staffordshire planter Toby jug, in brown hat, ochre and yellow jacket and blue breeches, hat, hair and foot restored, c1800, 12½in (31cm).
$2,500-3,500

A snuff-taker Toby jug, with detachable tricorn hat, barrel and crossed pipes on base, c1845, 14in (35.5cm).
$700-900

A Staffordshire Toby jug, in brown and ochre hat and sponged all-over with brown and green, pipe stem broken, glaze chipping, c1800, 10in (25cm).
$1,500-2,600

A Prattware 'Martha Gunn' Toby jug, decorated in typical palette, 9in (23cm).
$4,000-5,500

Mugs

A sailor Toby jug, with jug and beaker in his right hand, with blue decorated jacket and striped trousers, inscribed 'Dollers', 12in (30.5cm).
$2,000-3,000

A Bristol delft blue and white cylindrical mug, painted with an all over chequer pattern, minute glaze flaking to rim, c1730, 5in (12cm).
$1,500-2,600

A Liverpool tin-glazed stoneware cylindrical mug, painted in manganese with a tree with yellow-centred flowers and with grasses, crack at front, c1760, 2½in (6.5cm).
$3,000-4,500

A Yorkshire Toby jug, with impressed crown mark, 9½in (24cm).
$1,500-2,600

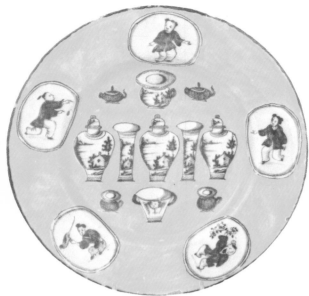

A Bristol delftware charger, painted with a chinoiserie figure, with tin-glazed back, c1715, 13in (33cm). **$7,000-10,000**

An English delft plate, the ground reserved on the rim with 5 roundels, each with Chinese figures, and centrally decorated with delft vases, 9in (23cm). **$12,000-20,000**

This is probably a retailer's sample plate, and similar Dutch examples are recorded.

l. A Staffordshire slipware press moulded dish, by 'I.C', some areas with glaze lacking, c1680, 14in (35cm). **$12,000-20,000**

r. A Staffordshire slipware press moulded dish, by John Simpson, damage and repairs, c1680, 13½in (34cm). **$10,000-17,500**

A saltglaze stoneware coffee pot decorated with enamels, possibly Staffordshire, c1755, 8in (20.5cm). **$16,000-25,000**

A documentary Wrotham slipware tyg, by Nicholas Hubble, damage, 1656, 6½in (16.5cm). **$20,000-30,000**

A Staffordshire creamware 'pebble dash' teapot and cover of Whieldon type, minor restoration, c1760, 5in (13cm). **$24,000-35,000**

l. A blue and white delft dish, chips, mid-18thC. c. & r. Polychromed delft dishes, 13in (33cm). **$800-1,500**

34

A Whieldon cornucopia wall pocket, depicting flora, translucent glazes, c1760, 11in (28cm). **$2,000-3,000**

A pair of decorative grazing cows, on typical Obadiah Sherratt rainbow bases, c1820, 7in (18cm). **$2,000-3,000**

A Staffordshire Whieldon school tea caddy and mask wall pocket, c1765, mask 10in (25.5cm) long, l. **$7,000-10,000** r. **$5,000-7,500**

A Staffordshire saltglaze bear jug and cover, all covered in chippings, minor repairs and cracks, c1740, 9½in (24cm). **$14,000-22,500**

A rare Obadiah Sherratt rural musical group including 12 sheep and a dog, enamel decorated, 9in (23cm) wide. **$5,600-8,750**

A Staffordshire saltglaze stoneware bear baiting jug and cover, slight damage, restored, 10in (25.5cm). **$11,000-18,750**

A Toby jug with long face, in translucent coloured glazes, c1770, 10½in (26cm). **$4,000-6,250**

A Bristol delft polychrome dish, probably Limekiln Lane, minute rim chips, c1740. **$6,000-10,000**

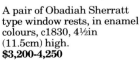

A pair of Obadiah Sherratt type window rests, in enamel colours, c1830, 4½in (11.5cm) high. **$3,200-4,250**

A massive Wedgwood black basalt encaustic decorated volute krater, minute chip to one handle, impressed and comma marks, c1800, 24in (61cm). **$24,000-35,000**

An Urbino Istoriato dish, with the death of Achilles, painted by Nicola Pellipario, broken in many pieces and re-stuck, c1535, 10in (25.5cm). **$19,000-28,750**

A Wedgwood black and white Jasper copy of The Portland vase by John Northwood, impressed and incised marks, c1878, 10in (25.5cm). **$32,000-45,000**

An assembled Creil creamware part dinner service, comprising 92 pieces, each decorated with a black transfer reserve, mid-19thC. **$8,000-12,500**

A Deruta dish, with a portrait medallion of a young woman in renaissance dress and cap, small chips to rim, c1500, 13in (33.5cm). **$24,000-35,000**

An Italian Istoriato plate, painted with the Judgement of Paris, inscribed on the reverse, probably Urbino, c1544, 10½in (27cm). **$24,000-35,000**

A Minton majolica stick stand, after a model by J. Henk, damage, marked, c1885. **$5,000-7,500**

An Urbino Istoriato plate, painted with the Temptation of Adam, damage, c1560, 9in (23cm). **$8,000-15,000**

A pair of Venetian vasi a palli, late 16thC, 13in (33cm). **$28,000-40,000**

A Deruta lustre dish, with Hercules lifting the giant Antaeus, cracked, c1520, 16in (40.5cm). **$60,000-85,000**

l. A German faience tankard, painted by a
Nuremburg Hausmaler, with pewter cover, damage,
the faience c1740, 10in (25.5cm). **$24,000-35,000**
c. A Crailsheinm faience tankard, cracked, c1750,
almost contemporary pewter cover. **$2,200-3,250**
r. A German faience tankard, cracked, c1740,
probably Erfurt. **$2,400-3,500**

A Böttger teapot and cover, painted in
'Schwarzlot', enriched in gilding by Ignaz
Preissler, in the Ming style, the handle with
'Laub-und-Bandelwerk', the shoulders and cover
moulded with Chinese archaistic motifs, c1720,
6in (15cm). **$80,000-112,500**

A Berlin two-handled campana vase in the neo-
classical taste, blue sceptre and dash mark and
impressed 4 to inside of foot, c1805, 17½in (45cm).
$20,000-35,000

A Böttger stoneware tankard and cover,
with contemporary 18thC silver acorn thumbpiece,
incised 'mock-seal' mark to the base of the
handle, chips to footrim, c1715, 8½in (21.5cm).
$42,000-57,500

Two Sicilian vases, small chips to
feet and rims, probably Sciacca,
c1650, 9½in (24cm). **$6,000-10,000**

A Habaner ware beer jug, inscribed
and dated 1680, chips to foot,
neck reinforced with a metal band, old
metal mount to handle, 12in (30cm).
$9,000-16,250

A Champion's Bristol plate, with flat rim, 'X' mark in blue and '22' mark in red, 7in (18cm) diam. **$700-1,000**

A Champion's Bristol sauceboat, with shaped iron red enamelled rim and leaf capped scroll handle, the body enamelled, blue enamelled cross mark and numeral '11', 6½in (16.5cm). **$900-1,375**

An unrecorded Capodimonte, Carlo III, group of 3 figures, modelled by Guiseppe Gricci, probably representing a doctor and youthful assistant attending to a patient, the doctor's left arm missing, chipped, c1750, 6in (15cm). **$40,000-62,500**

A Champion's Bristol ovoid tea jar, with gilt line and dentil neck borders and foot, unmarked, 5½in (14cm). **$600-875**

A Bristol rustic figure, allegorical of Winter, from a group of The Seasons, depicted as a boy skater, impressed mark 'To', 11in (28cm). **$2,000-3,000**

A Champion's Bristol tankard, with groove moulded plain loop handle and enamelled rim, decorated with floral sprays, blue enamelled cross mark and numeral '17' to base, 3in (7.5cm). **$900-1,375**

A Champion's Bristol oval dessert dish, the sides moulded with 4 broad 'pleats', blue enamelled cross mark and numeral '1', 11½in (28cm) wide. **$1,600-2,500**

A Champion's Bristol shallow dish, with gilt dentil rim, enamelled with floral festoons pendant from a gilt line, and centred with scattered sprigs, enamelled blue cross and numeral '5' mark, 8in (20cm). **$1,000-1,500**

A Champion's Bristol double lipped cream jug, with entwined loop handle, unmarked, 4in (10cm). **$1,600-2,250**

A Champion's Bristol coffee pot and domed cover, underglaze blue crossed swords and cross mark, 7½in (18cm). **$800-1,250**

A Champion's Bristol baluster shaped jug, blue enamelled cross mark and numeral '1', 8in (20.5cm). **$900-1,250**

A Champion's Bristol dessert dish, in the Double Ribband pattern, blue enamelled cross and gilded numeral '6' mark, 7in (18cm) square. **$800-1,250**

A Champion's Bristol butter boat, Cookworthy mould, with relief moulded flowers, fruit and leaves, unmarked, 4in (10cm) long. **$700-1,125**

A Champion's Bristol écuelle, stand and cover, with gilded and moulded husk decoration, and gilt dentil rims, gilded cross mark and numeral '3', the stand 6½in (16.5cm) diam. **$600-875**

A pair of Champion's Bristol plates, decorated in the Double Ribband pattern, one with blue enamelled cross mark, 9in (23cm). **$800-1,250**

A Champion's Bristol dessert dish, with fluted raised ogee sides and petal shaped gilt dentil rim, enamelled blue cross mark and numeral '5', 11in (28cm) wide. **$1,400-2,000**

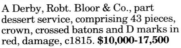

A Derby, Robt. Bloor & Co., part dessert service, comprising 43 pieces, crown, crossed batons and D marks in red, damage, c1815. **$10,000-17,500**

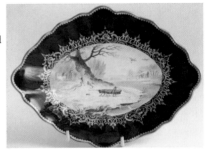

Two Frankenthal groups by J. F. Luck, firing cracks, chips and restoration, crowned CT marks, c1765, 6½in (17cm).
top: **$12,000-17,500**
bottom: **$16,000-22,500**

A Höchst group by J. P. Melchior, underglaze blue wheel mark, c1770, 9in (23cm). **$10,000-15,000**

A Derby dish, painted in the manner of Jefferyes Hamet O'Neale, firing crack, Derby mark in puce, c1785, 9½in (24cm). **$4,000-6,250**

A Chantilly bordalou, decorated in Kakiemon enamels, with twig handle, 18thC. **$9,000-12,500**

A Caughley kidney-shaped dish, painted in underglaze blue. **$440-625**

A pair of Derby campana vases, painted with figures among ruins in wooded landscapes, 'On The River Dove, Derbyshire', and 'A View of Scotland', iron red crown, crossed batons and D marks, c1815, 13in (33cm). **$14,000-22,500**

A pair of Fürstenberg white portrait busts, by J. C. Rombrich, probably of Herr Schrader von Schliestedt and his wife, parts of his cuirass and her lace coiffe missing, chip to her nose, c1758, 6in (15cm). **$13,000-18,750**

A Meissen group of Mezzetin and Columbine, modelled by J. J. Kändler, her head re-stuck, chips to tree, blue crossed swords mark on base, c1740, 7in (18cm). **$8,000-15,000**

A Meissen coffee cup and saucer, from the Swan Service, modelled by J. G. Ehder for Count Bruhl, bearing the arms of Heinrich, Graf von Bruhl and his wife Anna von Kolowrat-Krakowska, handle restored, blue crossed swords mark to both pieces, c1741. **$22,000-32,500**

A pair of Louis XVI ormolu mounted Meissen figures, modelled by J. F. Eberlein, restorations, the porcelain c1750, 16½in (42cm). **$11,000-16,250**

A Böttger porcelain Hausmalerei teabowl and saucer, painted by the Breslau Hausmaler Ignaz Preissler in Eisenrot and Schwarzlot, c1720. **$26,000-37,500**

A Meissen figure of a girl pancake seller, blue crossed swords mark to rear of base, c1750, 7½in (19.5cm). **$5,000-7,500**

A Ludwigsburg group of dancers, modelled by Franz Anton Bustelli, dressed for the Masque, minor chips, blue crowned crossed C mark and incised UM3 to base, c1760, 6½in (16cm). **$26,000-37,500**

A Meissen ormolu mounted ornament, from the Cris de Paris series, modelled by J. J. Kändler and P. Reinicke, c1756, 7½in (19cm) wide. **$12,000-17,500**

A Meissen silver mounted tankard, painted by J. E. Stadler, c1728, with contemporary Augsburg silver cover, by Hans Jacob Wild II, with the thaler of 1695, 7in (18cm). **$34,000-50,000**

Meissen figures of The Courtesan, by J. J. Kändler and P. J. Reinicke, and The Marquis, from the Cris de Paris, repairs, blue crossed swords marks, c1755, 5½in (14cm). l. **$4,000-6,250** r. **$5,000-7,500**

A Meissen Marcolini tête-à-tête, chips to 2 covers, crossed swords and star mark to all pieces, various impressed numerals and gilder's mark S, c1795. **$12,000-17,500**

A Meissen deckelpokal and cover, repairs, blue crossed swords marks and gilder's 2. to both pieces, c1730, 8in (20cm). **$8,000-12,500**

A Meissen tankard, painted by Johann Gregor Höroldt, c1728, 4in (10.5cm). **$36,000-50,000**

Meissen teapots and covers, l. painted by P. E. Schindler, r. perhaps by Mehlhorn, chips and repairs, blue KPM marks and gilder's marks, c1724, 6in (15cm). l. **$16,000-22,500** r. **$10,000-15,000**

A Meissen group of lovers, modelled by Eberlein, repairs, blue crossed swords mark, c1745, 5½in (14.5cm). **$3,000-5,000**

An ormolu and Sèvres porcelain encrier with 2 troughs, sander and inkwell, 11in (28cm) wide. **$6,000-10,000**

A pair of hard paste porcelain pot pourri vases in the St. Cloud style, with silvered mounts, with pseudo incised mark for St. Cloud, Trou, 10½in (26.5cm). **$8,000-12,500**

A Vienna tray, painted by Joseph Nigg, signed on the marble ledge, inscribed on the reverse, c1834, 16½in (41.5cm). **$28,000-40,000**

A pair of Sèvres pattern Napoleonic vases and covers, painted by J. Pascault, both covers restored, imitation M Imple de Sèvres marks, late 19thC, 60in (152.5cm). **$50,000-75,000**

A Vienna, Du Paquier, baroque moulded sauceboat, painted in the Imari style with flowers, c1740, 9½in (24.5cm) wide. **$11,000-15,000**

A garniture of 5 Spode vases, each painted with an Oriental design in enamel colours and gold, pattern No. 967, early 19thC, central vase 6½in (16.5cm). **$9,000-12,500**

A pair of Directoire ormolu and Vincennes ewers, the porcelain with blue interlaced L mark and twin dots, c1753, 8½in (21.5cm). **$5,000-7,500**

Vienna, Du Paquier, beakers, teabowl and saucers. l. **$24,000-35,000** c. **$4,000-7,500** r. **$6,000-10,000**

A First Period Worcester teacup and saucer, painted on a blue scale ground, with exotic birds, insects and flowers. **$800-1,250**

A pair of Worcester, Flight & Barr, armorial ice pails and covers, painted with a baronet's arms within a Garter Motto, liners missing, some rubbing, script mark, c1802, 11in (28cm). **$11,000-16,250**

A Worcester plate from the Duke of Gloucester Service, the underside with fruit sprays, gold crescent mark, c1775, 9in (22.5cm). **$30,000-42,500**

A pair of Flight, Barr & Barr ice pails and covers, each with slight chip below rim, early 19thC, 9in (22.5cm). **$6,000-8,750**

A Worcester blue scale vase and cover, painted with exotic birds and scattered butterflies, blue square seal mark, c1770, 13in (33cm) high. **$12,000-17,500**

A pair of First Period Worcester leaf dishes, moulded with overlapping vine leaves, painted with butterflies and insects, hair crack, 18thC, 8in (20cm). **$1,900-2,625**

A Meissen clock case and stand, repairs, some damage, blue crossed swords mark and Pressnummer 25 to stand, c1745, 20in (50cm) high. **$11,000-16,250**

A pair of Worcester blue scale ground chestnut baskets, pierced covers and stands, damage, blue seal mark, c1770, stands 11in (28cm). **$15,000-21,250**

A Royal Worcester porcelain plaque, with painting of a sow and piglets around a water pump and tree in a farmyard, signed H. Davis, fully marked and with date code for 1924, 9 by 6in (23 by 15cm), in gilt frame. **$14,000-22,500**

A Barr, Flight & Barr porcelain tureen and stand, the cover with applied 'pearls' and gilded with classical border, the tureen with painted panel attributed to Thomas Baxter, each piece impressed BFB below crown, the cover and stand with script mark, c1810, 7½in (19cm) wide overall. **$10,000-15,000**

A Würzburg coffee pot and domed cover, painted with 2 large landscapes, neck, spout and cover restored, impressed CGW mark, c1775, 9½in (24cm) high. **$30,000-42,500**

A painted grey pottery jar and cover, of bronze form, with animal head masks to each side, crack, minor damage to one handle, Han Dynasty, 26½in (67cm) high. **$14,000-20,000**

l. A painted grey pottery figure of a soldier, left hand pierced for sword attachments, restorations, Han Dynasty, 20in (50cm). **$60,000-100,000**

r. A white painted buff pottery figure of a matron, with light earth encrustation, surface wear, some restoration, Tang Dynasty, 20in (50cm) high. **$22,000-32,500**

A pair of buff pottery figures of Bactrian camels, with raised heads and jaws agape, the necks and humps well modelled with tufted hair, the backs with simple oval saddle cloths, some traces of red pigment remaining, some restoration, Tang Dynasty, 30in (76cm) high. **$70,000-100,000**

A Sancai buff pottery figure of a horse, the well-modelled body and head under a straw glaze, the saddle cloth under a deep green glaze splashing on the haunches, some restoration, Tang Dynasty, 18½in (46.5cm) high, tall wood stand. **$44,000-62,500**

A Jun Yao tripod censer, with short neck and everted rim, the crackled lavender glaze liberally splashed with purple to the exterior and rim above the pale stoneware short feet, Song Dynasty, 3in (7.5cm) diam.
$36,000-50,000

A Yuan blue and white broad baluster jar, guan, painted with an arching peony scroll, the neck with a band of formalised breaking waves, the shallow broad foot unglazed, minor chip to inside rim, c1350, 9in (23cm) high.
$130,000+

A Dingyao bowl, carved and incised on the exterior with 2 lotus heads and scrolling foliage, under an ivory white glaze, pooling in tears above the deeply cut foot, the rim left in the biscuit, Northern Song Dynasty, 6½in (16.5cm) diam. **$14,000-22,500**

A Ming blue and white saucer dish, painted at the centre of the interior with 3 cloud scrolls, the exterior with 2 five-clawed dragons in pursuit of a flaming pearl, foot flakes from the biscuit, surface scratches on the interior, encircled Zhengde six character mark and of the period, 8½in (22cm) diam, fitted box.
$14,000-20,000

A Yuan blue and white broad jar, guan, painted in soft cobalt with 4 fish swimming amongst water plants, comprising 3 carp and a pike perch, above a band of classic scrolls and lappets of circlets on the lower part, the shallowly-cut broad foot unglazed, horizontal crack to shoulder, minute rim chips, c1350, 13in (33cm) diam.
$340,000+

A Yaozhou celadon bowl, the centre freely carved with lotus blossom and downturned leaf with combed veins on a ground of foliate scrolls, the flaring unglazed foot fired brown, all under a transparent olive green glaze, Northern Song Dynasty, 7½in (18.5cm) diam, fitted box. **$18,000-27,500**

A Ming blue and white dish, the reverse with 2 birds in flight, minor fritting, Wanli, 18½in (46.5cm). **$10,000-15,000**

A Ming blue and white box and cover, painted with dragons chasing flaming pearls, minor cracks, cover restored, Wanli six-character mark and of the period, 12in (30.5cm) wide. **$12,000-20,000**

A Ming blue and white jar, encircled Jiajing 6-character mark and of the period, 5in (12cm). **$20,000-30,000**

A late Ming dish, painted in the centre with 2 herons, the sides with fish, frogs and crustacea, Tianqi/Chongzheng, 8in (20cm), fitted box. **$14,000-20,000**

A late Ming blue and white saucer dish, encircled Wanli six-character mark and of the period, 7in (18cm), fitted box. **$12,000-20,000**

l. A fine, rare blue and white Magnolia vase, Kangxi, 18in (46cm) high. **$28,000-40,000**

r. A fine, rare Ming blue and white armorial pilgrim flask, with emblems of Leon and Castille for Spain, c1590, 12in (30cm) high. **$160,000+**

A Transitional blue and white brush pot, painted with military scene, incised rim, c1640, 8in (20cm) high. **$6,000-10,000**

47

An Imperial 'famille verte' coral red ground bowl, with everted rim and plain white interior, painted with exotic flowers, underglaze blue Kangxi 'yuzhi' mark within a double square and of the period, 4½in (11cm) diam. **$38,000-52,500**

A Ming tilemaker's pottery figure of a seated Warrior Immortal, edges restored, 16th/17thC, 25in (63cm) high, wood stand. **$14,000-20,000**

A 'famille verte' Month cup, rim chip, Kangxi six-character mark and of the period, 2½in diam. **$6,000-8,750**

l. A blue and white vase, painted with a hunting scene, observed by dignitaries, Kangxi, 19in (48cm) high. **$11,000-16,250**

r. A pair of 'famille verte' vases, painted with flowers and butterflies, minute glaze line to neck interior, Kangxi, 17in (43cm) high. **$40,000-62,500**

A pair of Transitional Wucai sleeve vases, vividly painted with dragons, one cracked, small rim chips, mid-17thC, 17in (43cm) high. **$12,000-20,000**

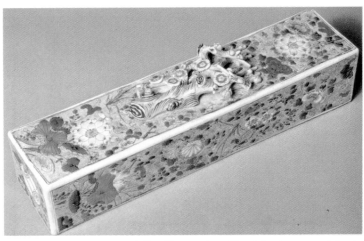

A 'famille verte' rouleau vase, slight enamel flaking, Kangxi, 17in (43.5cm) high. **$7,000-11,250**

A 'famille verte' scroll weight, the top with high relief prunus spray, the sides painted with flowers on a seeded green ground, edges rubbed, Kangxi, 14in (36cm). **$11,000-16,250**

A pair of Doucai wine cups, delicately painted, one with glaze imperfection to interior, encircled Kangxi six-character marks and of the period, 2½in (6cm) diam, wood stand. **$50,000-67,500**

A pair of 'famille rose' Laughing Twins, Hehe Erxian, neck crack, minor chips and fritting, Yongzheng, 12in (31cm) high. **$14,000-22,500**

A Dehua blanc-de-chine group of 4 Europeans, minor damage to extremities, Kangxi, 6½in (16cm) wide. **$8,000-12,500**

An underglaze copper red and white bowl, encircled Kangxi six-character mark and of the period, 6in (15cm) diam. **$22,000-32,500**

A sang-de-boeuf pear-shaped vase, encircled Yongzheng six-character mark and of the period, 11in (28.5cm) high. **$16,000-25,000**

A 'famille verte' flat-backed wall cistern, cover and oval basin, boldly painted with fish and crabs, restored, Kangxi, 18in (45cm) high. **$8,000-15,000**

A massive blue and white tapering cylindrical vase, painted with panels of figures, neck crack, some fritting, Kangxi, 37in (94cm) high. **$9,000-13,750**

A small yellow, green and aubergine glazed saucer dish, incised and painted with dragons contesting a flaming pearl, encircled Kangxi six-character mark and of the period, 4½in (11cm) diam. **$8,000-12,500**

A 'rose-verte' dish, painted in strong colours with figures in a walled garden, below scroll landscape panels on a green ground with peony and magnolia sprays, rim restored, Yongzheng, 21½in (55cm) diam. **$20,000-30,000**

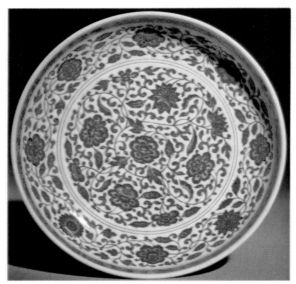

A blue and white yellow-ground saucer dish, painted at the centre with flowers on leafy stems, the exterior similarly painted, glazing flaw, Yongzheng six-character mark and of the period, 8½in (21cm). **$42,000-57,500**

A 'famille rose' hunting punchbowl, painted with hunting scene on the interior, the exterior with unusual scene of a royal tiger hunt, some cracks, late Qianlong, 16in (41cm) diam. **$18,000-25,000**

A garniture of 5 blue and white vases and 3 covers, each decorated with a peach-shaped panel of a pavilion, one cover odd, some restoration, early 18thC, vases 17½in (44cm) high, beakers 15in (38cm) high. **$8,000-15,000**

A blue and white jar, each lobe painted with gourds, Yongzheng six-character mark and of the period, 3½in (9cm) high. **$10,000-15,000**

An export armorial neo-classical punchbowl, painted after a European engraving in the manner of Bartolozzi, the interior with coat of arms, some damage and rubbing, c1790, 22in (55cm) diam. **$16,000-25,000**

A Louis XVI ormolu-mounted Chinese 'famille rose' pot pourri vase, the porcelain Yongzheng, 5½in (14cm) high. **$8,000-12,500**

A Chinese Imari armorial shaving bowl, painted in underglaze blue, iron red and gilt at the centre, two rim chips restored, c1720, 11in (28cm). **$6,000-8,750**

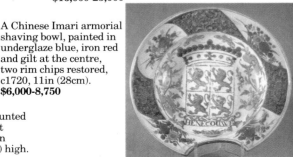

A pair of green dragon jars and covers, painted with dragons, in pursuit of flaming pearls, below bands of Buddhist emblems within ruyi heads and scrolls, rim chip, Qianlong six-character seal marks and of the period, 8in (20cm). **$12,000-20,000**

A Doucai saucer dish, with 8 Buddhist emblems, Qianlong seal mark and of the period, 20½in (52cm) diam. **$22,000-32,500**

A pair of 'famille rose' neo-classical urns and covers, in the style of Marieberg faience, one restored, one cover chipped, gilding rubbed, Qianlong, c1770, 16in (40cm) high. **$11,000-16,250**

A pair of 'famille rose' Mandarin palette vases and covers, with iron red seated lion finials, repaired, Qianlong, 20in (49cm). **$16,000-22,500**

A pair of 'famille rose' turquoise ground vases and covers, painted on both sides with figures, minor restorations, Qianlong, 18in (45cm) high. **$16,000-25,000**

A 'famille rose' 'Pronk' plate, painted with The Doctor's Visit, slight wear, 9in (23cm). **$8,000-12,500**

A 'famille rose' Doctor's Visit plate, Cornelis Pronk style, c1735, 9in (23cm). **$19,000-26,250**

A pair of export armorial basins, enamelled in colours, minute rim chips, one border with large haircrack, c1745, 15in (38cm). **$12,000-17,500**

An unrecorded documentary export shipping bowl, inscribed Elizabeth Cook 1747 and William Hillyard 1747, enamel restored, c1747, 10in (25cm). **$16,000-25,000**

A set of 8 'famille rose' figures of Daoist Immortals, holding their appropriate attributes, one head re-stuck, extremities chipped, c1800, all about 8½in (21.5cm) high. **$9,000-13,750**

A pair of celadon ground and gilt candlesticks, rim chipped, Qianlong seal mark and of the period, 11in. **$7,000-10,000**

A pair of 'famille rose' armorial dishes, centres with European style landscapes, possibly Fort St. George, India, damage, c1745. **$9,000-13,750**

A pair of blue and white garden seats, with 2 sides centrally pierced with interlocking cash on a band of scrolling lotus, c1800, 19in (48cm) high. **$8,000-12,500**

A pair of export models of hawks, the wings and tails carefully detailed with sepia simulated feather markings, some restoration, Qianlong, 11in (28cm). **$38,000-52,500**

A set of 4 'famille rose' erotic panels, each elaborately painted with a pair of lovers in a pavilion, a terrace, a garden and a chamber, mid-Qing Dynasty, 8 by 5in (20 by 12.5cm), wood frames. **$12,000-17,500**

A 'famille rose' turquoise ground vase, painted with iron red bats in flight, repairs, Qianlong seal mark, 27in (68cm). **$24,000-35,000**

A pair of export glazed models of cockerels, painted with iron red bodies, head extremities restored, 18th/early 19thC, 11in (27.5cm) high. **$8,000-12,500**

A pair of 'famille rose' 'tobacco leaf' tureens and covers, with flowerhead handles and pomegranate finials, painted with overlapping coloured leaves scattered with flowersprays and peony, one spare cover, one tureen with handles missing, chipped, Qianlong, 12in (31cm) wide. **$11,000-16,250**

Twenty-four blue and white plates, painted with peony below flowering pomegranate branch, within a band of trellis pattern, c1750, 9in (23cm) diam. **$8,000-12,500**

A pair of 'famille rose' millefleurs vases, reserved with large oval landscape panels, each with figures in boats and on a promontory in a wooded river landscape, on brightly enamelled gilt and floral ground, 19thC, 28in (71cm) high. **$10,000-15,000**

Twelve blue and white chocolate cups and saucers, painted with chrysanthemum, bamboo and daisy issuing around a jagged outcrop of rockwork, with elaborate loop handle of European inspiration, c1750, the cups 2½in (7cm), the saucers 5in (13cm) diam. **$6,000-10,000**

Provenance: Nanking Cargo sale, 1986.

The Lord Mayor of London punchbowl, a 'famille rose' bowl for the English market, enamelled with views taken from prints of 18thC City of London, cracks stabilised, one area overpainted, c1805, 16in (40cm) diam. **$56,000-80,000**

A blue and white vase and cover, with seated lady Immortal finial, boldly painted with lotus in leafy meanders, finial restored, 19thC, 40in (101cm) high. **$8,000-12,500**

A pair of 'famille rose' celadon ground bottle vases and domed covers, with peach finials, the bodies decorated in bright enamels, trailed white slip and gilding with flying bats, wispy cloud scrolls, floral roundels and Buddhist emblems, beneath spearheads at the rims, one cover and rim restored, early 19thC, 35½in (90cm) high. **$14,000-20,000**

A pair of 'famille rose' yellow ground fish bowls, moulded and brightly painted in relief on the mustard yellow ground with vases of flowers, stands of scholars' utensils, archaistic vessels and scattered flowers, the interiors with swimming carp amongst water weeds, 19thC, 20in (51cm) diam. **$18,000-27,500**

A pair of 'famille verte' figures of seated Buddhistic lions on detachable bases, with green bodies and bushy tails, one with a pierced ball beneath its forepaw, the other with a cub, the bases pierced with kidney-shaped apertures, restorations, 19thC, 20in (50cm) high. **$8,000-12,500**

53

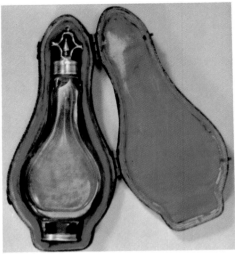

A red scent bottle, with white enamel decoration, gilt metal mount with finger ring and chain, c1880, 3in (8cm) long. **$140-225**

A red cut 'opera glass' scent with embossed silver gilt mounts and picture frame inside, c1880, 5½in (13.5cm). **$400-625**

A French clear glass scent bottle of pear shape, with silver gilt mounts, engraved 'E & B', c1780, 3½in (9.5cm), in a fitted black shagreen case. **$900-1,250**

A glass beaker, with gilt flower sprays and insects, attributed to Michael Edkins, c1780, 4½in (11.5cm). **$2,200-3,250**

A clear scent with pink on white overlay, cut with printies, c1850, 3in (8cm). **$150-212**

A red double ended scent with chased silver gilt mounts, c1880, 3in (8cm). **$400-625**

A blue satin scent, with embossed silver mount, c1880, 5in (12.5cm). **$360-550**

A French scent bottle with black bead cover, with fleur-de-lys and 'Vive le Roi' in white beads, silver mount, c1780, 2in (5cm). **$400-625**

A blue scent bottle with facet cut body, gilt floral decoration, c1800, 5in (13cm). **$700-1,000**

Three clear glass scent bottles, c1815:—
l. Oval with diamond cutting, silver mount, 4in (10cm).
c. Rectangular with prism and diamond cutting, silver mount, 5in (13cm).
r. Round with diamond cutting, gold mount, 3in (8cm) diam. **$140-225 each**

A pair of blue cruet bottles of urn shape, with gilt inscriptions 'Soy' and 'Anchovy' in gilt roundels, c1800, 4½in (11.5cm) high. **$520-750**

A Nailsea olive green bottle of tapered form, with white looped decoration, c1810, 9½in (23.5cm). **$400-600**

A set of 3 green spirit bottles, with canted corners and cut shoulders, pouring lips and cut ball stoppers, with gilt inscriptions, c1800, 6in (15cm). **$1,600-2,250**

A pale green crown glass flagon, of Nailsea type, c1840, 10in (25cm). **$440-650**

Two blue overlay scent bottles:
l. Diamond cut with embossed silver gilt mount, c1860, 3½in (8.5cm). **$300-425**

r. Fan cut with plain silver mount, c1860, 4in (10cm). **$300-425**

A set of 3 spirit bottles, embossed silver mounts with hallmark Birmingham 1839, in a silver plated stand, bottles 13in. **$900-1,375**

A pair of spirit bottles, hallmark Birmingham 1839, 13in. **$680-950**

A fine Nailsea bottle of olive green tint, with white splashes, c1800, 10½in (27.5cm) high. **$800-1,125**

A pair of green wrythen moulded spirit bottles, of slightly different tints, with cork and metal stoppers, c1840, 12in (29cm). **$740-1,050**

A rare green shouldered decanter, with scale cut base and double band of looped stars and printies, facet cut neck and cut spire stopper, c1770, 10in (25cm). **$1,700-2,375**

A green mallet shaped decanter, with 3 plain neck rings, bevelled lozenge stopper, c1790, 7½in (19cm). **$400-625**

A Nailsea crown glass cream pan, of light green tint, with folded rim, c1810, 4½in (11cm) high, 8½in (22cm) diam. **$160-300**

A set of 4 Venetian paintings on glass, after Pietro Longhi, depicting The Lady's Awakening, The Meeting of the Procurator and his Wife, The Declamation and The Dancing Lesson, mid-18thC, 20 by 16½in (51 by 42cm), in giltwood frames. **$38,000-52,500**

A pair of ormolu and blue cut glass vases, with twin handles, foliate socles and square bases, one cracked, Swedish or Russian, late 18thC, 9½in (24cm) high. **$7,000-10,000**

A pair of giltmetal and Bohemian glass candlesticks, the shaped storm shades painted with lions and trailing foliage, the square bases on winged lion feet, mid-19thC, 15in (38cm) high. **$10,000-15,000**

A North Country blue sugar basin and cream jug, the basin with hollow stem, folded foot, c1800, jug 3½in (9.5cm) high, basin 4in (10cm) high. **$500-700**

A pair of English blue leaf dishes, with gilt decoration, one repaired, c1860, 4in (10cm) and 4½in (11cm) diam. **$140-225**

A North Country amethyst cream jug, with faint wrythen decoration and folded rim, c1780, 4in (9.5cm) high. **$300-425**

A transfer printed pottery mug, with unusual salmon pink ground, c1845, 4in (10cm).
$100-200

A creamware mug, c1765, 4in (10cm).
$1,300-2,000

An early Staffordshire coloured print creamware mug with frog in it, c1815, 6in (15cm).
$900-1,300

A creamware mug inscribed in black 'Rodney for ever', flanked by 4 coloured flower sprays, slight crack to rim and above handle, c1785, 5in (12.5cm).
$800-1,200

A John Aynsley black glazed cylindrical mug, inscribed with a verse proclaiming the virtue of good ale and the danger of credit, reserved within a cream painted cartouche, minor chip to rim, signed J. Aynsley, Lane End, late 18thC, 4½in (11cm).
$900-1,300

A Staffordshire majolica mug with relief decoration of a kingfisher above water lilies, c1882, 4½in (11cm).
$100-200

A Mettlach pewter-mounted beer mug, decorated after C Wurth, incised and painted in colours with an inscription on a ribbon cartouche on a pale blue ground, the cover with pewter mount and moulded mask thumbpiece, incised signature, impressed marks and numbers, c1910, 17in (42.5cm).
$1,200-1,750

Plaques

A Sunderland lustre mug, printed on one side with the head and shoulders of 'Frederick King of Prussia' and on the other with a view of the iron bridge, slight chip under foot rim, early 19thC, 6in (15cm).
$400-550

A large Prattware plaque of Bacchus and Venus in typical Pratt palette, c1800, 6in (15cm).
$1,000-1,400

A Wedgwood black basalt plaque moulded in high relief and under-cut with Death of a Roman Warrior, cracked across and restored, impressed mark 4 times, c1800, 11 by 19½in (27 by 48.5cm).
$3,000-4,500

A Sunderland lustre plaque, with Adam Clarke, the Wesleyan minister, impressed Dixon & Co, c1815, 8 by 9in (20 by 22.5cm).
$150-250

A Wedgwood & Bentley jasper medallion, the dipped slate blue ground moulded in high grey/blue relief with Andromache, impressed lower case mark, E. & F. and W, 3in (8cm).
$1,300-2,000

A Sunderland lustre plaque, with ships in full sail, c1825, 8½ by 9½in (21 by 24cm).
$150-250

A Sunderland lustre plaque, 'May Peace & Plenty', impressed Dixon & Co.
$150-250

A pearlware plaque of Queen Caroline moulded in high relief, wearing a blue dress with pink lustre collar within a pink lustre and iron red moulded frame pierced for hanging, slight corner chip, c1820, 5½ by 4½in (14 by 12cm).
$1,200-1,750

An orange lustre plaque, with Adam Clarke, c1870, 7½ by 8½in (19 by 21cm).
$75-150

A Staffordshire green lustre plaque with Field Marshall Lord Roberts, c1900, 7½ by 8½in (19 by 21cm).
$75-150

Pots

A Wedgwood and Bentley creamware large flower pot and stand, with bands of brown and black sponging, some glaze degradation and crack to stand, the stand with impressed upper case mark, c1775, the stand 10½in (27cm) diam.
$1,300-2,000

A Minton majolica cache pot, the sides decorated with panels of landscape and seascape by Rischgitz, 1878, 10in (25.5cm).
$1,200-1,750

A Wedgwood four-colour jasper dip flower pot, applied in white, impressed mark, and date code for 1882, 7in (17cm).
$1,300-2,000

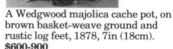

A Wedgwood three-colour jasper jardinière, the dipped pale lilac ground with green flower heads beneath an anthemion border, the rim with green leaves, some minor chipping, impressed mark and z, 3½in (9cm), and a green ground stand similar, impressed mark, 6in (15.5cm) diam, c1790.
$1,300-2,000

A Wedgwood majolica cache pot, on brown basket-weave ground and rustic log feet, 1878, 7in (18cm).
$600-900

A Castle Hedingham, Essex, pottery two-handle pot, c1890, 8½in (21cm).
$150-250

Make the most of Miller's

Miller's is completely different each year. Each edition contains completely NEW photographs. This is not an updated publication. We never repeat the same photograph

Two Wedgwood caneware flower bowls and pierced liners, the rims applied with a band of black trailing vine, on circular spreading feet, minor damage to one liner and foot, impressed marks and A, c1815, 8in and 7½in (20.5 and 18.5cm).
$700-900

A pair of Wedgwood three-colour jasper flower pots, in pale lavender and green with lion mask supports, impressed marks, c1880, 5in (13cm).
$1,200-1,750

Redware

A glazed redware figure of a dog, probably John Bell, Pennsylvania, modelled as a recumbent greyhound, with flint enamel glaze, c1850, 10in (25.5cm) long.
$1,800-2,200

A Moravian slip decorated redware bowl, probably Salem, Forsyth County, North Carolina, Jacob Christ type, decorated in brown with a central stylised flowerhead within concentric rings and wavy line border, on a mustard yellow ground, some damage, 19thC, 13½in (34cm) diam.
$250-300

A slip decorated redware dish and bowl, American, with wavy line decoration, some damage, 19thC, dish 10½in (27cm) diam.
$400-500

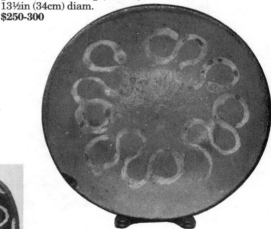

Two slip decorated redware plates, American, one decorated with wavy lines, the other with 4 stylised snakes, damage, 19thC, 11 and 12in (28 and 30.5cm) diam.
$400-500

A slip decorated redware dish, probably New England, decorated in yellow slip, 19thC, 11½in (29cm) wide.
$750-850

Two slip decorated redware dishes, American, one with central star, the other with central stylised flower, some damage, 19thC, 9 and 11in (23 and 28cm) diam.
$400-500

A manganese decorated redware jar, by John W. Bell, Waynesboro, Pa., the unglazed exterior decorated around the shoulder with a band and manganese flowers, the interior with manganese glaze, rim chips, impressed mark, c1885, 12½in (32cm).
$550-650

Services

A creamware part tea service, painted with stylised iron red flower sprays beneath a band of entwined turquoise foliage and beaded rims, comprising: a teapot and cover, 5in (13cm) high, sugar bowl and cover, 4½in (11cm) high, a milk jug, 5½in (14cm) high, a cylindrical tea caddy, 3½in (8.5cm) high, and a slop bowl, 6in (15cm) diam, some damage, c1785.
$1,200-1,750

A Clews stone china part dinner service decorated in an Imari palette, comprising: a two-handled soup tureen, cover and stand, 3 vegetable dishes and covers, a square salad bowl, 2 oval two-handled sauce tureens, covers, stands and ladles, 2 sauceboats, an oblong carving dish, an oval pierced liner, 11 various serving dishes, 4 deep dishes, 2 small shell dishes, an oval hors-d'oeuvre dish with central carrying handle containing 3 shaped dishes, and 71 assorted plates, some damage, impressed Clews Stone China Warranted, enclosing a crown mark, c1830.
$10,500-15,000

A pearlware botanical part dessert service, painted with named specimens within silver lustre borders, comprising: 2 oval sauce tureens, covers and stands, 3 octagonal dishes, 2 lozenge shaped dishes, 2 square dishes, 3 shell dishes, and 19 plates, each plant named in red script on the reverse, perhaps Swansea, some damage, c1805.
$13,000-17,500

A Ridgway dessert service, decorated in iron red and green on a light green ground with brown edges, comprising: an oval footed centre dish, 3 leaf shape dishes and 11 plates.
$1,200-1,750

A Staffordshire part moulded smearglaze service, comprising: 12 plates, 9in (23cm) and 6 dessert dishes, 11in (28cm) long, c1840.
$2,000-3,000

A Mason's Ironstone china part dinner service, comprising 24 pieces, with richly coloured chinoiserie decoration, late 19thC.
$1,500-2,500

An ironstone china part dinner and dessert service, printed in colours, comprising 12 soup plates in 2 sizes, 14 meat plates in 2 sizes, 4 dessert dishes and 6 dessert plates, printed Royal Arms and Ironstone China mark.
$700-900

A Mason's Ironstone polychrome dinner service of Mughal pattern, comprising: tureen, cover and stand, 4 lidded entrée dishes, 2 lidded sauce tureens, 2 rectangular dishes, 3 stands, 11in (28cm), 5 stands, 9in (23cm), 73 assorted plates, 14 soup bowls, 3 large roast dishes, 6 large game dishes and a square bowl, standard printed crown mark.
$16,500-23,000

A Staffordshire pearlware dessert dish, printed in blue with classical figures in panels on a floral ground, 3 oval dessert dishes, and a pair of pierced oval baskets and stands of the same pattern, perhaps by Rogers.
$1,200-1,750

Stoneware

A saltglaze stoneware 1½ gallon jar, by Cowden & Wilcox, Harrisburg, Pa., painted in blue slip with a man-in-the-moon, hairline cracks, impressed mark, c1880, 9in (23cm).
$1,600-1,800

A saltglaze stoneware 2 gallon jug, by George A. Satterlee and Michael Morey, the New York Stoneware Co., Fort Edward, New York, painted in blue slip depicting a cock and bull, minor firing defects to decoration, with impressed mark and 2, c1870, 14½in (37cm).
$1,800-2,000

A saltglaze stoneware 3 gallon jar, by Cowden & Wilcox, Harrisburg, Pa., painted in blue slip with cherry decoration, hairline cracks, rim chips, impressed mark and number 3 and blue highlights, c1880, 12in (30.5cm).
$450-500

A saltglaze stoneware 2 gallon batter jug, by Cowden & Wilcox, Harrisburg Pa, painted in blue slip floral decoration, minor rim chips, impressed mark with number 2 and highlights, with tin covers, c1880, 11in (28cm).
$2,000-2,500

A saltglaze stoneware 2 gallon jar, by George A. Satterlee and Michael Morey, New York Stoneware Company, Fort Edward, NY, painted in blue slip with a bird, with impressed mark and 2, cracked and chipped, c1865, 11½in (29cm), and a 2 gallon crock, by Philip Riedinger and Adam Caire, Poughkeepsie, NY, with 2 applied handles and painted in blue slip with a bird, chipped, impressed mark and 2, c1865, 9½in (24cm).
$400-500

Two saltglaze stoneware jugs, North Carolina, each with applied handle and threaded neck, one incised with 2 fish, the other with a salamander with cobalt slip highlights, 19thC, 8½ and 10½in (22 and 27cm).
$800-900

Tankards

A Staffordshire saltglaze stoneware tankard, with impressed 'AR' stamp, early 18thC, 5in (12.5cm).
$1,500-2,500

An agateware tankard, with grooved loop handle and spreading foot with striated brown and cream clays, slight chip to handle, c1745, 3in (8cm).
$1,500-2,500

A Bayreuth, Pfeiffer, tankard, with contemporary hinged pewter cover and foot rim painted in colours, the crowned JGH monogram dated 1771, minor chip to handle and rim, puce O.B.P. marks of Pfeiffer and Oswald, 14in (35cm).
$3,000-4,500

A German faience cylindrical tankard painted in colours, with pewter mount and cover with ball thumb-piece, the cover engraved No. 10 and initials J.C.K., body cracks, dated 1759, 8½in (21.5cm).
$1,000-1,400

A Westerwald oviform tankard, painted in blue and manganese on grey body, crowned AR within roundel, reeded neck and foot, chips to neck, early 18thC, 9½in (24cm).
$600-900

A London delftware tankard with glass base, late 18thC, 5in (12.5cm).
$3,000-4,500

Tea Caddies

A creamware tea caddy of Wedgwood/Whieldon type, enriched in green and yellow on a moulded cell pattern ground, some minor restoration, c1760, 5½in (14cm) wide.
$3,000-4,500

A Wedgwood Whieldon type tea caddy, c1765, 5½in (14cm).
$900-1,300

An English delftware blue and white tea caddy, 4½in (11cm).
$1,500-2,500

Tea & Coffee Pots

A black glazed pottery teapot, 18thC.
$200-350

A saltglaze teapot, decorated in polychrome, c1745, 4½in (11cm).
$1,500-2,500

A Staffordshire glazed redware moulded teapot and cover, glaze chip to rim above spout, c1745, 4in (10.5cm).
$5,000-7,500

A Staffordshire saltglaze teapot and cover, painted and gilt with trailing flowering branches and roses, spout restored, crack to base, c1750, 4½in (12cm) high.
$1,500-2,500

A Whieldon type teapot and cover, moulded with flowering plants covered in a brown, manganese, yellow and blue glaze, repair to tip of spout and chip to cover, c1750, 7½in (18cm) wide.
$450-700

A redware teapot, possibly Wedgwood, c1750, 7in (18cm).
$800-1,200

A Whieldon type teapot and cover, with green spout and scroll handle, the spout mounted with a silver tip, the cover with chain attachment, cover chipped, the spout slightly damaged beneath the mount, 4½in (11cm), with a similar dish, repaired and rim restorations, c1760, 6½in (16cm).
$1,500-2,500

A creamware coffee pot, with applied sprigging, c1765, 7½in (19cm).
$1,500-2,500

A creamware teapot, c1765, 6in (15cm).
$1,300-2,000

A Staffordshire saltglaze pecten shell moulded teapot and a cover, the spout moulded with a skeletal man, minute rim chips, c1755, 5in (13cm).
$2,000-3,000

A Whieldon teapot in blue, white and yellow, c1770, 3in (7.5cm).
$1,000-1,400

A Staffordshire saltglaze teapot and cover, painted with panels of pink flowers on a dark green ground with black geometric designs, c1760, 6in (15cm) wide.
$1,300-2,000

A Staffordshire saltglaze teapot, c1765, 4½in (11cm).
$2,250-3,500

A Wedgwood creamware teapot and cover, with foliage moulded spout and handle painted in the atelier of David Rhodes, in purple and grey, minute chips to spout and staining to body, c1770, 5½in (13.5cm).
$5,000-7,500

Price

Prices vary from auction to auction – from dealer to dealer. The price paid in a dealer's shop will depend on:

1) what he paid for the item
2) what he thinks he can get for it
3) the extent of his knowledge
4) awareness of market trends

It is a mistake to think that you will automatically pay more in a specialist dealer's shop. He is more likely to know the 'right' price for a piece. A general dealer may undercharge but he could also overcharge

A Whieldon teapot, in typical mottled brown glaze, c1770, 5in (12.5cm).
$1,200-1,750

A Wedgwood creamware coffee pot and cover, transfer printed in iron red, minor chips to spout and inside cover, c1770, 10in (25cm).
$1,500-2,600

A creamware teapot, William Greatbach, c1770, 6in (15cm).
$2,250-3,500

A Wedgwood pale lilac and white jasper teapot and cover, the dipped ground moulded in white relief, chips to spout, impressed mark, c1790, 4in (10.5cm).
$1,200-1,750

A Staffordshire majolica teapot, c1878, 7½in (19cm).
$300-500

A creamware coffee pot, dated 1778, 9½in (24cm).
$1,500-2,600

A Wedgwood creamware teapot and cover, transfer printed in black on both sides, chip to cover and spout, impressed lower case mark, c1780, 5½in (13.5cm).
$1,300-2,000

A Wedgwood green and white jasper teapot and cover, slight rim chip, some staining, c1800, 3½in (9.5cm).
$700-900

A Wedgwood blue and white jasper teapot and cover, in white relief with Domestic Employment, slight rim chip to cover, impressed mark and o, c1790, 4in (10.5cm).
$1,000-1,400

A Wedgwood pottery teapot, with widow figure on lid, burnt orange background, restored, 7in (18cm).
$200-350

Tiles

A delft tile picture of 6 tiles, painted in colours, 18thC, 16 by 11in (40 by 27.5cm).
$700-900

A delft tile picture of 6 tiles, painted in manganese with touches of yellow, the ground in green, yellow and manganese, 18thC, 16 by 10½in (40 by 26.5cm).
$800-1,200

A Holdcroft majolica teapot, modelled as a bird on its nest, on a separate stand of rustic logs, c1867, 7in (18cm).
$400-550

A London delftware blue and white tile, c1730, 5in (12.5cm) square. **$75-150**

A Liverpool delftware religious tile, c1750, 5in (12.5cm) square. **$75-150**

A delft tile picture consisting of 15 tiles, finely painted in colours, c1720, 26 by 16in (66 by 40cm). **$4,000-5,500**

A set of 2 tiles by Craven Dunnill of Brossley, Shropshire, c1895, 6in (15cm) square. **$30-50**

A Liverpool blue and white tile, c1760, 5in (12.5cm) square. **$60-100**

A Liverpool blue and white tile, c1760, 5in (12.5cm) square. **$60-100**

A Liverpool blue and white tile, c1760, 5in (12.5cm) square. **$30-50**

A Liverpool Sadler black printed tile depicting a dentist at work, c1765, 5in (12.5cm) square. **$200-350**

A Lambeth blue and white tile, c1780, 5in (12.5cm) square. **$75-150**

A very rare Prattware coloured tile, c1790, 5½in (13.5cm) square. **$600-900**

A very rare Prattware coloured tile, c1790, 5in (12.5cm) square. **$600-900**

Two Dutch Delft manganese tile pictures, depicting a cat and a dog, both with cracks and restoration, late 18thC, 15 by 10in (38 by 25cm), in black painted wood frames. **$700-900**

A Victorian tile, 'Summer', depicting stag hunting, c1870, 6in (15cm) square. **$60-100**

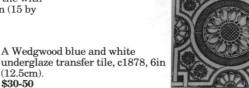

A Maws relief moulded tile with children, c1860, 6 by 6in (15 by 15cm). **$60-100**

A Wedgwood blue and white underglaze transfer tile, c1878, 6in (12.5cm). **$30-50**

A Minton blue and white tile designed by William Wise, 1879, 6in (15cm) square.
$60-100

A Minton tile, designed by William Wise, printed blue on white, 1879, 6in (15cm) square.
$60-100

A Minton tile, with underglaze printed design of poppy seed heads in ochre colours on pale grey ground, c1885, 6in (15cm) square.
$60-100

A solid clay tile, with painted design in 'Persian' style in shades of brilliant blue and green, with black and brown, impressed mark: William de Morgan, Merton Abbey, c1885, 6in (15cm).
$150-250

A Victorian pressed-dust tile, with relief design of flowers in yellow on green ground, c1890, 6in (15cm) square.
$20-40

A set of 5 English delft tiles, probably Liverpool, each painted in manganese enamel with Christ on the cross, some glaze chipping, 4 reduced in width, 5in (12.5cm).
$400-550

Tureens

A Wedgwood creamware sauce tureen, cover and pierced stand, painted in the manner of James Bakewell in purple monochrome, finial restored, c1770, the stand 10½in (26.5cm) wide.
$1,500-2,500

A pair of matching tiles depicting the martyrdom of Stephen, slight glaze chipping, one reduced in width.
$60-100

A Continental stove tile with blue decoration, 17thC, 7 by 8in (18 by 20cm).
$400-550

A pair of ironstone serving dishes with blue transfer printed decoration, with lions head finials, 19thC, 16in (40cm) wide.
$200-350

A Wedgwood majolica game dish with liner, marked, c1860, 6in (15cm).
$1,000-1,400

A Derbyshire creamware tureen on stand, c1770, 7½in (18.5cm).
$2,000-3,000

A Wedgwood majolica sardine box, moulded as a roped crate floating on waves surrounded by rocks and seaweed, 1873, 8½in (21.5cm) wide.
$450-700

An English creamware vegetable dish and cover, painted in brown on both sides of the cover and base with an entwined monogram above the inscription 'Worlingworth Hall 1800' on a ribbon within brown line rims, c1800, 13in (33cm) wide.
$700-900

A George Jones majolica sardine box, with basket-weave base in blue and green, 1865, 7 by 8in (17.5 by 20cm).
$450-700

A Wedgwood earthenware tureen by Eric Ravilious, with vignettes of train, motor car and snow scene, part of Travel series, 1936, 9½in (23.5cm) diam.
$200-350

A type of ware becoming increasingly interesting to collectors.

A Wedgwood pie dish of fine grained vitrified stoneware, c1790.
$450-700

These dishes were made from 1790 as substitutes for the pastry cases. Great pies of standing crust filled with meat or game appeared in every well-to-do household until banished by the Flour Tax levied during the Napoleonic Wars.

A Staffordshire majolica sardine box, with high relief fish handle and plant decoration, on brown ground, c1875, 7in (18cm) wide.
$300-500

A Brameld Rockingham miniature pie dish, with green trim, 3½in (8.5cm) wide.
$400-550

Vases

A Stilton cheese dish and cover in the style of Wedgwood, c1900, 12in (30cm).
$200-350

A Wedgwood and Bentley solid agate vase, on black basalt base, some restoration to handles and top rim, impressed lower case mark, c1775, 10in (25cm).
$4,000-5,500

A Staffordshire spill vase of Ralph Wood type, modelled as a youth in black hat, green jacket, flowered waistcoat and yellow breeches, some minor chipping, c1780, 9in (23cm).
$800-1,200

A George Jones majolica game dish, cover and liner, the exterior moulded and painted against a light blue ground, liner and cover cracked, impressed marks, c1880, 13½in (34cm) long.
$1,500-2,500

A Staffordshire triple spill vase of Ralph Wood type, crook and sheep's ears restored, c1780, 11in (27cm).
$1,000-1,400

A Staffordshire creamware spill vase of Ralph Wood type, modelled as a gallant in translucent green glazed jacket and yellow breeches, on a green and brown rockwork base, slight chip to vase, c1780, 8in (20cm).
$800-1,200

A pair of Wedgwood blue and white jasper altar vases, the solid blue jasper grounds moulded in white relief, one vase with handle damaged and rim chip, the other with one handle lacking, impressed mark, c1785, 5½in (13.5cm).
$1,300-2,000

A Wedgwood blue jasper dip replica of the Portland vase, decorated in white, 19thC, 10½in (26cm).
$1,300-2,000

A Wedgwood black basalt encaustic-decorated vase, painted in grey and sepia, between bands of anthemion and iron red key pattern, repair to handles, rim and foot, impressed mark, c1800, 12in (30cm).
$1,200-1,750

A Wedgwood black basalt encaustic-decorated pot pourri vase, lid and pierced cover, painted in red and highlighted in white, minute chip to rim and lid, impressed and moustache and comma marks, c1820, 13½in (34cm) wide.
$2,000-3,000

An Obadiah Sherratt spill vase group with a boy and a girl in Turkish costume, the vase painted in splashed black, green and purple glazes, crack to vase, c1820, 7in (18cm).
$4,000-5,500

A Staffordshire spill vase in the form of a bull baiting group, c1820, 10½in (26cm).
$2,000-3,000

A pair of Staffordshire spill vases, c1845, 5in (12.5cm).
$450-700

A Staffordshire spill vase musician group, the spirally moulded striped pink and white flared vase with salmon pink interior, on a shaped green mound base, some restoration to vase, base and extremities, c1830, 9in (22.5cm).
$3,000-4,500

An unusual Staffordshire spill vase modelled as a ram with applied fur, standing before a tree outlined in pink and green, minor damage to horns, c1845, 4½in (11cm).
$200-350

A Wedgwood three-colour jasper vase, the dipped blue ground with a lilac medallion of a sacrifice subject, the neck with 7 lilac portrait medallions and raised prunus blossom in white relief, slight chips to relief, impressed mark, c1880, 6in (15cm).
$900-1,300

A pair of Staffordshire spill vases in the form of hounds with hares, c1860, 7in (17.5cm).
$600-900

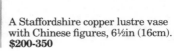

A Staffordshire copper lustre vase with Chinese figures, 6½in (16cm).
$200-350

Wemyss Ware

A Wemyss tray with roses, 10in (25cm) wide.
$200-350

A Wemyss Ware basket, painted with dog roses and turquoise borders and handle, c1920, 16in (40.5cm) wide.
$400-550

A pair of black and white Wemyss cats, Bovey Tracey, painted by Joseph Nekola, c1930, 12½in (31.5cm).
$3,000-4,500

A Wemyss pig, modelled in a squatting position, its coat with large black splashes, pink ears and snout, impressed mark, 6½in (16.5cm) long.
$1,000-1,500

A Wemyss Plichta cat, 1930-47, 6in (15cm).
$100-200

A Wemyss mug, painted with a black cockerel and 5 hens on grass below a red line rim, rim chips to foot rim, impressed Wemyss, 6in (15cm).
$450-700

A rare Wemyss tabby cat.
$9,000-12,500

A Wemyss spirally moulded bowl, painted with pink cabbage roses, painted mark, 8½in (21.5cm) diam.
$300-500

A Wemyss dog bowl, painted with apples, 6½in (16.5cm) diam.
$200-350

A Wemyss vase, painted on a multi-coloured ground with thorny foliage, signed Crail, Wemyss, 213, 8in (20cm).
$300-500

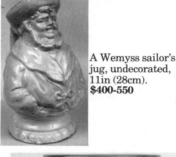

A Wemyss sailor's jug, undecorated, 11in (28cm).
$400-550

A Wemyss teapot with plum design, 4½in (11.5cm).
$700-900

A Wemyss plaque, inscribed on the reverse 'Wemyss, T. Goode & Co., London', and impressed Wemyss, 7½in (19cm) diam.
$200-350

A Wemyss three-handled tyg, restoration, 9½in (24cm) diam.
$900-1,300

A Wemyss plaque, inscribed Wemyss on the reverse and having Thomas Goode's retailing mark, 7½in (19cm) diam.
$200-350

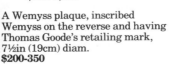

A Wemyss plate decorated with cockerels, c1880, 8½in (21.5cm) diam.
$200-350

MINTON MAJOLICA

Throughout ceramic history, but particularly in the 18th and 19th centuries, there have been numerous examples of rediscoveries or reintroductions of types of body or techniques of decoration.

Minton majolica is an example of the reintroduction of an earlier type of ware following a period of intense experimentation to replicate and improve upon it. In 1848 Joseph Leon Francois Arnoux was appointed Art Director at Minton. His primary task was to introduce new products and to promote them in such a way that the reputation of the factory was enhanced and new markets created.

Arnoux sought to exploit the fashion for classical design and the growing interest in bright colour evident in paintings and architecture of the period. He turned for inspiration to the work of Bernard Palissy, whose naturalistic, brightly coloured maiolica wares had been popular in the 16th century.

Arnoux recreated Palissy's brightly coloured glazes but avoided the easily damaged delft-type body used by Palissy, employing instead a high-fired durable body akin to stoneware.

The body was given a coating of opaque white glaze which provided a surface for overpainting in brightly coloured opaque glazes. Later, transparent coloured glazes were also used over relief moulding. The new ware was specially promoted at the 1851 Great Exhibition in London where it was well received. These early wares included wine coolers, jardinières, flower pots and stands, all decorated in the majolica style.

Minton cleverly exploited the market over the next 40 years by introducing models in response to the dictates of fashion. Rival firms, notably Wedgwood and George Jones, were quick to copy the new product; like Minton their work, which is also of high quality, is usually impressed with factory marks. Some lesser factories also cashed in on Minton's innovation. Some of the work of these lesser factories is less impressive as the body is not always as highly fired as it should be.

Interest from the USA in the late 1970s and early 80s stimulated the price of majolica. For a time everything, whether marked or unmarked, perfect or damaged, found a ready market. By the mid 1980s damage or the lack of a factory mark severely limited interest and this trend still continues. Most saleable are wares with a strong decorative impact, regardless of factory. Of marked pieces Minton remains the market leader with some favour shown towards George Jones, Wedgwood and marked pieces from lesser factories.

Minton Majolica

A Minton majolica dish painted by Leon Arnoux after a design by Alfred Stevens, with Ceres in blue on an ochre ground within a wide border of manganese and white on a blue ground, the reverse with stylised radiating foliage, signed L.A....x, and Minton 1859, 17in (43.5cm).
$9,000-12,500

A Minton majolica oyster plate, in pink with relief decoration of shells and seaweed, 1878, 9in (23cm).
$100-200

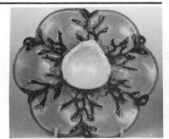

A Minton majolica oyster plate, with turquoise blue ground and relief decoration of seaweed, 1880, 8in (20cm).
$100-200

A pair of Minton majolica table-centre dishes, 1877, 15in (38cm).
$1,300-2,000

A Minton majolica pierced tazza supported by 3 sparsely clad cherubs, impressed marks, dated cypher 1864, 10in (25cm).
$700-900

A Minton majolica centrepiece in the form of 3 cherubs supporting a basket, painted in typical enamel colours, impressed marks, c1870, 11½in (28.5cm).
$1,000-1,500

A Minton majolica game tureen and cover, moulded with pheasants on one side, the reverse with a hare, enriched in coloured glazes, the cover with recumbent hound finial, the interior covered entirely in a turquoise glaze, impressed marks, date code for 1867, 14in (36cm) long.
$2,000-3,000

A Minton majolica bowl covered in a bright blue glaze, impressed mark and date code for 1872, 12in (30cm).
$450-700

A Victorian Minton majolica comport, with dish supported by putto on naturalistic green and brown circular base, 14½in (36cm).
$300-500

A Minton majolica bowl, the base modelled as 3 doves, with a border of white flowerheads and green foliage joined by pink ribbon, with turquoise glazed interior, 2 chips to foot, hair crack to bowl, impressed marks, numerals and date code for 1874, 12½in (31.5cm).
$1,500-2,500

A Minton majolica vase, painted in typical enamel colours, one head re-stuck, impressed marks and date code for 1873, 16½in (41cm).
$1,000-1,500

A Minton majolica jug, modelled as a young girl with a fan and a purple cloak, impressed marks, 11in (28cm).
$700-900

A Minton majolica jug moulded and painted with mediaeval figures dancing, impressed mark and date code for 1871, 9½in (24cm).
$400-550

A Minton majolica salt modelled as a dog begging, on a pink cushion with orange tassels, impressed mark, 15in (38cm).
$800-1,200

A Minton majolica garden seat in the Oriental taste, the bright yellow ground moulded in low relief and decorated in a green glaze, impressed mark and date code for 1873, 20in (50cm).
$1,000-1,500

A pair of Minton majolica tiles, decorated on a turquoise ground, impressed mark, year cypher, 8in (20cm).
$400-550

A Minton majolica figure, 8in (20cm).
$1,000-1,500

A Minton majolica model of a cockatoo, its plumage coloured in cream heightened in green and with yellow crest, impressed marks, 12½in (31cm).
$400-550

Miscellaneous

A London delft flower brick, c1730, 3½in (8.5cm).
$1,000-1,500

A Mason's Patent Ironstone foot bath, of fluted form and with twin mask handles, numerous cracks, printed marks, 20in (50cm) wide.
$800-1,200

A pair of Bristol delft blue and white flower bricks, one with slight cracks to rim, both with rim chips, c1740, 6in (15cm) wide.
$1,500-2,500

A Wedgwood blue and white foot bath, printed inside and out, large impressed mark, early 19thC, 20in (49cm) wide.
$2,250-3,500

A pair of delft blue and white flower bricks, 18thC.
$1,000-1,500

A Staffordshire pottery pipe in the form of John Bull with small lion, decorated in enamel colours, c1815, 4in (10cm).
$1,500-2,500

A foot bath printed with the Elephant pattern, probably Rogers, c1825, 18½in (46cm) wide.
$1,500-2,500

A Victorian Spode foot bath with polychrome decoration, in browns and blues.
$1,300-2,000

A pearlware pipe modelled as a man, impressed with the name 'Jolly Pickman', in ochre collared and cuffed blue coat and ochre breeches, seated on a green basket and smoking a sponged blue and yellow pipe, perhaps Yorkshire, restoration to pipe and his hands, c1800, 6in (14.5cm).
$1,500-2,500

A creamware pipe modelled as a lady, wearing blue and ochre sponged clothes, the pipe stem going through her body and the bowl modelled as a face, perhaps Yorkshire, pipe bowl restored, c1800, 7in (17cm).
$1,500-2,500

A pearlware pipe modelled as a man in a dark green hat, blue jacket, ochre waistcoat and striped trousers, the pipe bowl moulded with happy and sad faces, perhaps Yorkshire, minor stem restoration, c1800, 6in (15.5cm).
$1,500-2,500

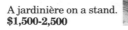

A jardinière on a stand.
$1,500-2,500

A Jerome Massier Vallauris jardinière and stand, the lilac ground washed in cream and painted with iris in shades of green, yellow and white, impressed marks, 53in (134cm).
$2,000-3,000

18th Century Porcelain

Influenced largely by the American market, wares with a strong decorative appeal are in great demand. Enthusiasm is running particularly high for 'botanical' wares, especially from the Chelsea and Bow factories. Other wares which would enhance the overall decoration of a room in 18th century style are equally popular.

Condition is of paramount importance in this area of the market. Wares in perfect condition command a premium but 'invisibly' repaired pieces also find a ready market through reputable dealers. As a result such dealers are often willing to buy damaged wares which can then be repaired. A customer should, of course, only buy from a dealer who can be trusted to make the degree of restoration clear.

19th Century Porcelain

The demand for quality continues unabated. Over the last year there has been a noticeable growth of interest in 19th century porcelain on behalf of buyers from the USA. Perfect condition, fine hand-painted decoration, size and shape are key factors affecting value.

Bearing these factors in mind, good quality ornamental vases of sufficient size to make a bold statement within a decorative scheme sell well, as do decorative services and centre pieces.

This interest in the decorative quality of 19th century wares does seem to have its negative side. In the American market decorative bone china saucers are in great demand as ash trays or for serving nuts. The cups which would normally accompany them are discarded, even left behind in the shop as not worth the trouble of carrying and certainly not suitable for nuts!

Baskets

A Belleek opalescent basket, with triple strands applied with a ribbon and inscribed Belleek, Co. Fermanagh, one handle re-stuck, 12in (30cm) wide.
$3,000-4,500

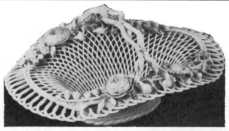

A First Period Belleek basket, impressed Belleek, Co. Fermanagh on a ribbon mark, 10½in (27cm) wide.
$600-900

A Coalbrookdale basket and pierced cover, the handle with mayflowers tied with a pink ribbon bow, 6½in (16cm).
$200-350

A Meissen basket, with green rope twist handles with coloured flower terminals, the exterior with blue flowerheads at the intersections, slight chips to terminals, blue crossed swords marks, c1880, 16½in (42cm) wide.
$1,300-2,000

A Rockingham primrose leaf moulded pot pourri basket, stand and cover, enriched in gilding, the cover with flower and foliage finial, cover repaired, the stand with puce griffin mark, c1835, 5½in (14cm).
$800-1,200

A pair of Spode Imari pattern pot pourri baskets and pierced covers, with gilt handles, painted beneath a white bead and gilt line rim, some slight rubbing to gilding, red marks and pattern No. 967, c1820, 5½in (14cm) wide.
$4,000-5,500

A Worcester quatrefoil basket, pierced cover and stand, one handle lacking to stand, some chipping to flowers, the cover incised 58, the base of the basket 13, c1760, the basket 8in (20cm) wide.
$2,000-3,000

A pair of Spode baskets, pattern No. 2600, marked, 8in (20cm) wide.
$300-400

A Chamberlain's Worcester apple green ground basket, painted with a view of Derwent Water, script mark, c1820, 8½in (21.5cm) wide.
$700-900

A Chamberlain's Worcester blue ground basket with gilt carrying handle, painted with a view of Malvern, the underside with grey marbling, on 4 gilt paw feet, 2 feet chipped, script mark in iron red, c1830, 8in (20.5cm).
$800-1,200

A Chamberlain's Worcester miniature foliage moulded basket, the exterior enriched in puce, green and gilding, minor restoration to handle and slight crack to base, script mark in puce, c1840, 5in (12.5cm) wide.
$800-1,200

A Berlin ornithological basket, with blue sceptre mark and 3 incised lines and a 4, c1790, 11½in (29cm) wide.
$4,000-5,500

Bottles

A Worcester blue and white bottle and a basin, transfer printed with The Pine Cone and Foliage pattern, blue W marks, c1775, the bottle 8½in (22cm).
$1,500-2,500

A Derby miniature bowl and jug set, c1820, jug 1in (3cm).
$450-700

Bowls

A Chelsea sunflower bowl and cover, enriched in yellow, with a green leaf finial, slight rim chips, cover repaired, finial restored, the cover with red anchor mark, c1756, 5in (13cm) wide.
$1,300-2,000

A Chelsea dish, c1760, 10½in (26.5cm) wide.
$450-700

A Liverpool Herculaneum sugar bowl and cover, with fixed gilt ring handles, with a wide band of pink roses between gilt line rims, pattern No. 368 in gold, c1810, 5½in (14cm) wide.
$900-1,300

A lustre bat printed teabowl, c1810, 2½in (7cm) diam.
$45-75

A Miles Mason sugar bowl and cover, with fixed gilt ring handle and moulded spire finial, painted in the 'famille verte' palette, with The Dragon in Compartments pattern between gilt lines, c1810-15, 6½in (16cm) wide.
$1,000-1,500

l. A First Period Worcester blue printed teabowl, Prunus Root pattern, slight damage, c1765, 2½in (6cm) diam.
$100-200

A Pinxton pale yellow ground sugar bowl and cover, with fixed gilt ring handles and finial, minor rubbing to gilding, script P No. 241 inside cover, c1795, 6in (15.5cm) wide.
$1,000-1,500

r. A First Period Worcester polychrome enamelled teabowl, c1750, 3in (7.5cm) diam.
$300-500

A Wedgwood Fairyland Lustre bowl, inscribed on base with printed urn mark and numbers Z4968, 11in (28cm) diam.
$2,000-3,000

A Ridgway bowl, Nutcracker and Siskin, 6½in (16.5cm) diam.
$450-700

A Worcester blue and white bowl, mid-18thC, 9in (23cm).
$400-550

A Worcester blue scale bowl of Lady Mary Wortley Montagu pattern, painted in the atelier of James Giles, enriched with gilt, some rubbing, blue square seal mark, c1770, 6½in (16.5cm) diam.
$1,200-1,750

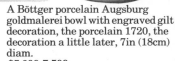

A Worcester powder blue ground bowl, painted within gilt circular and fan shaped medallions, 6in (15cm) diam, and an unglazed waster of a similar bowl from the factory site, c1770.
$600-900

A Royal Worcester bowl, painted by Jas Stinton, signed, with shaded gilt borders, printed mark for 1916, 9in (23cm).
$1,000-1,500

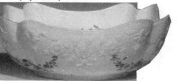

A Böttger porcelain Augsburg goldmalerei bowl with engraved gilt decoration, the porcelain 1720, the decoration a little later, 7in (18cm) diam.
$5,000-7,500

A Meissen purple ground sugar bowl and cover, with gilt and iron red bud finial, reserved on a purple ground, blue crossed swords mark and Pressnummer 80, painter's mark 5, to each piece, c1740, 4½in (11.5cm) diam.
$8,000-11,000

A Böttger porcelain bowl, the exterior with a band of Böttger lustre foliage edged in gilt, 2 minute rim chips, c1725, 7in (17.5cm) diam.
$14,000-19,000

A Höchst bowl, painted with scattered flower sprays, with gilt rim, puce wheel mark and impressed IS, c1760, 8½in (21cm) square.
$1,000-1,500

A Meissen slop bowl, painted by Mehlhorn, with Böttger lustre gilt and iron red foliage surround, repaired, c1722, 7in (18cm) diam.
$5,000-7,500

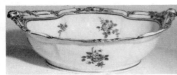

A Sèvres basin, painted in colours with gilt and blue lines, star crack in base, blue interlaced L marks enclosing date letter F for 1758, 12½in (31.5cm) wide.
$1,300-2,000

Boxes

A Meissen sugar box with gilt rim, cover missing, blue crossed swords mark, incised dreher's mark of 3 dots, gilder's number 30, c1730, 5in (13cm) wide.
$700-900

TYPES OF PORCELAIN

The distinction between hard and soft paste porcelain is:
★ **hard paste (or true porcelain)** – fired at a higher temperature than soft paste; feels cold to the touch; chip is flint or glass like; hard, glittery glaze
★ **soft paste (or artificial)** – file will cut easily into soft paste (not a test to be recommended!); chip is granular; warmer feeling to the touch; less stable in the kiln, figures in particular were difficult to fire; soft glaze – liable to crazing; the early soft paste was prone to discolouration

A Meissen chinoiserie bowl, the exterior painted in colours, the interior with an 'en camaieu rose' chinoiserie panel within gilt panelled and foliage rim, blue crossed swords mark, Pressnummer 8 and traces of gilder's mark 38, c1740, 6½in (17cm) diam.
$10,500-15,000

A Sèvres punch bowl, painted in colours between 'bleu celeste' and gilt bands, blue interlaced L marks enclosing the date letters for 1785, the painter's mark of Micaud, and the gilder's mark of Vincent, 13in (33cm) diam.
$10,000-13,500

A Vienna Du Paquier bowl, the interior decorated, and with iron red rim, c1735, 7in (17.5cm) diam.
$5,000-7,500

A Meissen silver mounted snuff box and cover, on green base, the interior and the cover with scattered 'deutsche Blumen', the silver mount chased with foliage, c1750, 2½in (6cm) wide.
$7,000-10,000

A Spode box and cover, reserved on a blue ground gilt with scale pattern, pattern No. 1166, c1820, 3in (7cm) diam.
$1,500-2,500

A bowl by Samson of Paris, decorated within gilt scroll borders on a gold diaper ground, the inside with flowers and butterflies, 11½in (29cm) diam.
$450-700

A Vienna Du Paquier quatrefoil bowl, painted in Schwarzlot with continuous 'Laub-und-Bandelwerk', enriched with gilt, and 4 Schwarzlot lappets, gilt rims, c1735, 7in (18cm) diam.
$2,000-3,000

A Mennecy silver mounted oval snuff box, modelled as a hen and chick, c1760, 2in (5cm) wide.
$5,000-7,500

A Meissen snuff box and cover, the cover painted in the manner of Wagner with Plenty attended by cupids, with gilt metal mounts, minor chip to interior of cover, mid-18thC, 3in (7.5cm) wide.
$2,000-3,000

Caddies

A Staffordshire porcelain box, modelled as a sleeping infant, c1840.
$450-700

A Chelsea copper gilt mounted bonbonniere, with diamond chip eyes, the interior painted with scattered flowers, the enamel cover similarly painted, cracks to cover, c1755, 3in (8cm).
$1,500-2,500

A pair of inscribed Lowestoft tea caddies for Bohea tea and Green tea, Bohea with minute rim chip to circular aperture, painter's number 5, c1765, 5in (12cm).
$6,000-9,000

A Meissen tea caddy and cover with pine cone finial, cover repaired, blue crossed swords mark, c1750, 6in (14.5cm).
$2,000-3,000

A Meissen lime green tea caddy, blue crossed swords mark, c1740, 4in (10cm).
$3,000-4,500

Candelabra

A set of 4 John Bevington two-branch candelabra, in the form of figures emblematic of the Seasons, in turquoise, puce and gilt, some damage, crossed swords and monogram mark in blue, 13½in (34cm).
$900-1,300

A pair of Bow candlestick figures of a stag and doe, with mottled brown coats, brightly coloured foliate nozzles, the bases enriched in turquoise and blue, restoration to trees, antlers and doe's ears, crack to one nozzle, some minor chipping and restoration to extremities, c1765, 9½in (23.5cm).
$5,000-7,500

A pair of Bow candlestick figures of The New Dancers, enriched in underglaze blue and gold, she restored through waist, both with restoration to trees and nozzles, c1765, 11½in (29cm).
$2,250-3,500

A pair of Bow candle groups of Cupid with dog and bird, one restored, 9in (22.5cm).
$1,500-2,500

Use the Index!

Because certain items might fit easily into any of a number of categories, the quickest and surest method of locating any entry is by reference to the index at the back of the book.
This has been fully cross-referenced for absolute simplicity

A pair of Coalport ormolu-mounted simulated bronze candlesticks, on pink lustre spreading bases and with gilt rims, rubbed, c1810, 11in (27cm).
$1,500-2,500

A pair of Chelsea fable candlesticks, modelled as The Dog and The Ass, the beast of burden carrying dead game in its panniers, and The Dog in the Manger barking at an ox, enriched in gilding, chips and restorations, repairs to nozzles, gold anchor marks at back, c1765, 13in (33cm).
$5,000-7,500

Centrepieces

A Derby blue and white centrepiece, surmounted by a kingfisher, minor damage, patch marks, c1768, 6½in (16.5cm).
$1,300-2,000

A Doccia white glazed centrepiece modelled as a bridge, fitted with 4 vases on pedestals with silver gilt flowering plants, the bridge 13in (33cm) wide, c1750, fitted with gilt wood supports simulating rippling water.
$1,200-1,750

A German porcelain floral encrusted tablecentre.
$450-700

A pair of Meissen candelabra, c1845, 12in (30.5cm).
$3,000-4,500

A pair of Bloor Derby vases of flowers, on a dark blue ground, on pierced white and gilt stands and 4 gilt paw feet, circular Bloor Derby mark and crowned Gothic D in red, 6½in (16.5cm).
$800-1,200

A pair of Meissen armorial candlesticks, modelled after silver originals, painted in colours with scattered 'Holzschnitt Blumen' enclosing the armorial device of Smith of Essex between gilt lines, one nozzle broken off and repaired, blue crossed swords marks and Pressnummer 46 to both pieces, c1745, 8½in (22.5cm).
$2,500-3,500

A Crown Derby bough pot, encrusted with flowers in a white and gilt panel on a rich blue ground, with pink rose handles, the cover composed of a mass of flowers, including irises, pansies and carnations, printed mark in red, crowned Gothic D, 7in (17cm).
$2,250-3,500

A colourful Meissen centrepiece, decorated with flowers and on either side with Chinese figures under a parasol, the interior painted with gold scrolling foliate designs, restored, inscribed B.195, 20in (53cm) wide.
$2,000-3,000

Clock Cases

A late Meissen clock case, modelled as a putto reading from an open book, cockerel's tail feathers re-stuck, 11in (28cm).
$4,000-5,500

A Sèvres pattern gilt bronze mounted centrepiece, painted on a blue ground, late 19thC, 11in (27.5cm).
$800-1,200

A large Meissen centrepiece group, painted in bright enamel colours, very slight damage, late 19thC, 14in (36cm).
$2,500-3,500

Cups

A Bow coffee cup, decorated with continuous chinoiserie scene of fishermen, c1770.
$400-550

A miniature Bow trio, c1758.
$1,300-2,000

A Caughley polychrome teabowl and saucer, with Target pattern, c1780.
$200-350

A rare Coalport John Rose faceted coffee can, c1800, 2½in (6cm).
$30-50

A Coalport egg cup, c1820, 2in (5cm).
$75-150

A Chelsea teabowl, with classical ruin decoration, raised anchor period, c1750, 3½in (9cm) diam.
$2,250-3,500

A Coalport trio, c1825.
$200-350

A Chelsea beaker painted with The Red Dragon pattern, the interior with scattered flowerheads, chip to foot rim, 2½in (7cm), and an octagonal saucer en suite, raised anchor mark, c1750.
$3,000-4,500

A Chelsea Derby cup and saucer, c1765, saucer 5in (12.5cm) diam.
$400-550

A Chelsea Derby cup and saucer, c1770, saucer 5in (12.5cm) diam.
$400-550

An English stirrup cup, probably Derby, with Tally Ho on the collar, c1835, 3in (7.5cm).
$900-1,300

A Derby teacup and saucer, painted in monochrome, pattern No. 33, c1810.
$100-200

A Christian's Liverpool polychrome teabowl and saucer, c1770.
$300-500

A Minton cup and saucer with Sèvres mark, pattern No. 90, 2in (5cm).
$200-350

A New Hall teabowl, cup and saucer, 'en grisaille', pattern No. 171, c1790, cup 2½in (6cm).
$100-200

A Pennington's Liverpool coffee cup, c1775, 2½in (6cm).
$150-250

A Pinxton teacup and saucer, with pink and gilt swags with iron red tendrils and gilt line rims, cup cracked, the saucer with impressed J, c1795.
$800-1,200

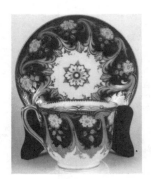

A Ridgway cup and saucer, pattern No. 5/3647, c1850.
$100-200

A Spode coffee can, c1820, 2½in (6cm).
$75-150

A Staffordshire stirrup cup, c1835, 5in (12.5cm).
$1,300-2,000

A Worcester Flight & Barr teabowl and saucer, scratch B mark, c1790, saucer 5½in (13cm) diam.
$100-200

NEWHALL

★ Newhall was the second Staffordshire pottery to successfully make porcelain, Longton Hall being the first (although Neale may have been making porcelain)

★ the usual date for the commencement of the factory is 1782, however then it was known as Hollins, Warburton & Company

★ they used the Cookworthy method of making a class of porcelain known as hybrid hard-paste

★ porcelain is a greyish colour to transmitted light and is seldom crazed

★ Duvivier, who had worked at Derby and Worcester, also painted at New Hall from 1782-90 — because of the rarity of attributable pieces one wonders if some of his work at New Hall has been wrongly attributed to another factory

★ very few pre-1790 wares had a pattern number

★ around 1812 a new bone-china body was introduced and the factory was by this time known as New Hall

★ after 1820 the bone-china wares seemed to lose some quality and the factory closed in 1835

★ New Hall, above all other 18thC English factories, has seen what can only be called an explosion in price in recent years. This has probably been caused by the disparaging attitude of many porcelain dealers to the more ordinary Newhall wares in the past and hence their underpricing

A Wedgwood Fairyland Lustre melba cup, decorated with a version of the Leapfrogging Elves design under a sky studded with stars, pattern No. Z4968, 4in (10cm) diam.
$450-700

A Staffordshire teacup and saucer, by Charles Bourne, in colours and flaming orbs in iron red, mark in red C.B. and pattern No. 320.
$100-200

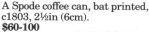

A Spode coffee can, bat printed,
c1803, 2½in (6cm).
$60-100

A Chamberlain's Worcester egg cup
in yellow and gilt, pattern No. 151,
c1800.
$450-700

A Copeland Spode London teacup
and saucer, pattern No. 2693, c1855.
$150-250

A Worcester Flight & Barr beaker,
the wide top border painted in sepia,
the lower part yellow with narrow
gilt borders, inscribed in brown
Flight & Barr, Worc. Manufacturers
to their Majesties, a crown above,
4in (9.5cm).
$5,000-7,500

A Flight, Barr & Barr teacup and
saucer, impressed mark, c1820.
$100-200

A Worcester three-piece by Giles,
with rare twisted handles, saucer
5in (12.5cm) diam.
$800-1,200

A Worcester three-piece set
comprising:
l. A thunderbolt teabowl and saucer,
c1770, saucer 5in (12cm) diam.

r. A saucer dish decorated with iron
red sunbursts, c1775, 7in (18cm)
diam.
$800-1,200

l. A First Period Worcester coffee
cup, hand painted in puce, green
and gold, c1775, 2½in (6cm).
$100-200

r. A Pennington's Liverpool coffee
cup, hand painted in pink and
green, c1775.
$100-200

WORCESTER PORCELAIN DATES	
1751-1783	First Period
1751-1774	Dr Wall Period
1776-1793	Davis/Flight or Middle Period
1783-1793	Flight Period
1793-1807	Flight and Barr Period
1807-1813	Barr, Flight and Barr
1813-1840	Flight, Barr and Barr
1840-1852	Chamberlain and Company
1852-1862	Kerr and Binns (W H Kerr & Company)
1862	Royal Worcester Porcelain Company

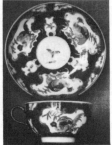

A Worcester blue and white coffee
cup and saucer, c1780.
$200-350

A First Period Worcester cup and
saucer, decorated with exotic birds
in reserves on a scale blue ground.
$900-1,300

A Worcester cup and saucer, in the
Kakiemon palette, with the Brocade
pattern, saucer 4in (10cm) diam.
$800-1,200

A Worcester teabowl and saucer,
printed in blue within a blue line
border, disguised numeral 7 mark,
c1780.
$100-200

A hand painted cup and saucer, with dark blue borders and polychrome flowers, c1830.
$60-100

A Böttger beaker and saucer, moulded with bands of stiff leaves and gilt with symmetrical foliage with solid gilt interior, c1720.
$2,500-3,500

A Meissen teabowl and saucer, the interior of both pieces with gilt 'Laub-und-Bandelwerk' borders, the interior of the teabowl with Schwarzlot indianische Blumen, blue crossed swords marks and the gilder's mark v., c1730.
$3,000-4,500

A Meissen teabowl and saucer, with a spray of 'purpurmalerei' flowers to the well of the teabowl, c1735.
$1,500-2,500

A Berlin teacup and saucer, painted with pink floral garlands within shaped pink borders gilt with foliage, blue sceptre marks, c1780.
$3,000-4,500

A pair of Höchst cups and saucers, painted in the neo-classical taste 'en grisaille' within gilt surrounds, one saucer with chip and small crack, blue wheel marks and incised PI and IE marks, c1785.
$1,200-1,750

A pair of Meissen celadon fond cups and saucers, reserved on gilt and turquoise grounds, the handles with iron red dots, blue crossed swords marks, c1738.
$10,500-15,000

A Berlin cup and saucer, the cup dated 1813 in foliage, the saucer with a map of Leipzig and inscribed 'Volkerschlacht bei Leipzig am 18 u 19 Oct', blue sceptre marks.
$3,000-4,500

A Doccia teacup, coffee cup and saucer, moulded with mythological figures and monuments in landscapes, gilt rims, c1750.
$2,000-3,000

A Meissen beaker and saucer, painted with harbour landscapes, blue crossed swords marks and gilder's marks 8 to each piece, c1730.
$16,000-22,500

A Meissen dead leaf ground teabowl and saucer, painted with sprays of 'indianische Blumen' in the Kakiemon palette, blue crossed swords marks and impressed dreher's marks, c1738.
$4,000-5,500

A pair of Meissen Hausmalerei teacups and saucers, painted by F F Meyer von Pressnitz, the cups with brightly coloured birds and flowers, the interiors gilt with 'Laub-und-Bandelwerk', blue crossed swords marks, c1740.
$6,000-9,000

A Meissen teacup and saucer, painted with scenes, gilt rims, crossed swords mark to both pieces, and Pressnummern 64 and 66, c1750.
$700-900

A Meissen teacup and saucer, painted in colours with gilt rims, blue underglaze crossed swords marks and Pressnummern 64 and 66, c1750.
$700-900

KAKIEMON
★ the Kakiemon family worked at the Japanese Arita factory towards the end of 17thC
★ their patterns are executed in a distinctive palette in iron red, pale yellow, turquoise and green
★ the Meissen factory copied from the Japanese originals and became fashionable in Europe

A Meissen chinoiserie teabowl and saucer, painted with Chinese figures, blue crossed swords marks, gilder's marks 38 to each piece, c1740.
$3,000-4,500

A Meissen green ground quatrefoil teacup and saucer, with 'ombrierte' gilt cartouches, saucer broken and re-stuck, crossed swords marks to base, c1740.
$1,300-2,000

A Meissen chinoiserie cup and saucer with gilt scrolled handle, the reverse of the saucer with scattered 'indianische Blumen', blue crossed swords marks, the cup with Pressnummer 24, gilder's numbers 38 to each piece, c1740.
$3,000-4,500

A Meissen armorial teacup and saucer, painted with a monogram flanked by military trophies and surmounted by the Imperial crown and with gilt trellis and lambrequin borders, blue crossed swords marks and Pressnummer 24 to each piece, c1740.
$4,000-5,500

A Meissen teacup and saucer, with shaped rim and entwined handle, decorated on a blue ground, mark in blue, 19thC.
$800-1,200

A Nyon teabowl and saucer, painted in colours with gilt dentil borders, blue fish marks, c1785.
$1,300-2,000

A Nyon cup and saucer, painted in colours, minor chip to foot of cup, blue fish marks, c1785.
$2,250-3,500

A Nyon trembleuse cup, cover and saucer, with gilt pine cone finial, painted with panels of roses divided by puce, green and gilt lines within borders of iron red chain pattern, blue fish marks, c1790.
$2,250-3,500

A Paris cup and saucer, with floral painting in shades of brown and gilt, c1820, cup 3in (7.5cm).
$450-700

A Sèvres green ground cup and deep saucer, painted with garlands of pink roses in white reserves on a green ground heightened with gilding, interlaced L marks and date letter V for 1774, and painter's mark B.g.
$600-900

A Sèvres green ground cup and saucer, with gilt dentil rims, interlaced L marks, date letters D for 1756 and R for 1770, decorators' marks L B and E.
$1,000-1,500

A Sèvres cup and saucer, painted between shaped pale blue 'oeil-de-perdrix' and gilt seeded bands with gilt dentil rims, blue interlaced L marks enclosing the date letter Q for 1759, and with painter's mark of Thévenet père, incised marks.
$2,000-3,000

A Sèvres 'bleu nouveau' coffee cup and saucer, the panels reserved on 'bleu nouveau' ground with gilt, blue interlaced L marks enclosing the date letter N 1766 and painter's mark of Morin, incised marks.
$2,000-3,000

A Paris, Jacob Petit, cup, cover and trembleuse stand, the sides encrusted with coloured bouquets, the cover with pink rose finial, chips to flowers, blue JP marks, c1840, the stand 6½in (16.5cm) diam.
$700-900

A Sèvres reeded cup and fluted saucer, painted in colours with a composite band of blue and yellow, alternating with green and yellow shells between brown and gilt bands with a blue line and gilt dash border and dentil rim, small chip to rim of cup, the saucer with interlaced L marks, date letter for 1768, and painter's mark of Thévenet père.
$800-1,200

A Vienna Du Paquier beaker, rim chips, perhaps decorated outside the factory, c1730.
$400-550

A Sèvres premier Empire coffee cup and saucer, painted with a broad band of gilt and silver chinoiseries on a black ground, various incised marks and red stencilled 'M.Imp. le de Sevres' marks to both pieces, c1808.
$2,250-3,500

A Vienna chocolate cup and square galleried tray, painted in green and black, within green and gilt beaded borders, blue beehive marks, the tray with crowned mark, the cup impressed 3, c1770, the tray 6½in (17cm) square.
$5,000-7,500

Ewers

A Vincennes teabowl and saucer, with gilt rims, minor rim chips, the teabowl with blue interlaced L marks enclosing a dot, c1752.
$1,500-2,500

A Coalport ewer, hand painted, unsigned, c1910, 7in (18cm).
$400-550

A pair of Sèvres style ormolu mounted decorative faux ewers, with turquoise ground base, on acanthus moulded foot set on rounded plinth, 13in (33cm).
$1,500-2,500

A pair of Sèvres pattern gilt bronze mounted ewers, on blue grounds, with gilt bronze necks, on studded spreading circular feet, late 19thC, 9½in (24.5cm).
$900-1,300

A Royal Worcester ewer with foliate moulded handle, pedestal foot and moulded shoulder, in muted enamels and gold, inscribed under the base January 4th 1980, 10½in (27cm).
$600-900

Figures – Animals

A Samuel Alcock dog, impressed numeral 311, c1835.
$450-700

A Bow white model of birds in branches, some restoration, c1755, 7in (18cm).
$450-700

A Bow figure of a dismal hound, with light brown markings, base with applied flowers, 3in (8cm).
$4,000-5,500

A Bow group of a hen and cockerel, with brown, puce and purple feather markings, restoration to hen's neck and through the base, c1760, 4½in (11cm).
$8,000-11,000

A Bow hare, with brown fur markings, the base enriched in green and applied with a flower, restored through top of front legs and re-stuck to base, ears restored, c1760, 5½in (14.5cm).
$5,000-7,500

A Bow figure of a begging pug bitch, wearing a pink collar tied with a rosette, base applied with 2 coloured flowers, minute chip above left eye, c1758, 3½in (8.5cm).
$4,000-5,500

A Bow bird group, well coloured, some restoration, c1760, 6½in (16.5cm).
$2,250-3,500

A Chelsea sheep, with brown markings, mound enriched in green, ears restored, red anchor mark, c1755, 3in (8cm) wide.
$1,300-2,000

A Derby dry edge figure of a boar, perhaps painted in the workshop of William Duesbury, tusks and one ear restored, Andrew Planché's period, c1753, 4½in (11.5cm).
$6,000-9,000

An English group of 3 pug dogs at play, chip to base, one tail and 2 legs repaired, c1850, 7in (18cm) wide.
$200-350

A Derby dry edge figure of a goat, perhaps painted in the workshop of William Duesbury, restoration to horns, cracked through base and re-stuck to base, Andrew Planché's period, c1753, 6in (15cm).
$3,000-4,500

A Derby figure of a leopard, with puce marked pale yellow coat, on a base applied with coloured flowers, tip of tail lacking, right forepaw and ear repaired, Wm Duesbury & Co, c1765, 3½in (9cm) wide.
$1,500-2,500

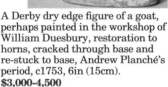

A pair of Derby spaniels, white with gilding, marked, c1815, 4in (10cm).
$1,000-1,500

A Derby porcelain pug, c1800, 2½in (6cm).
$450-700

A pair of Bloor Derby models of peacocks, painted in gilt and blue enamel, chips to flowers, head feathers and beak of one, red painted marks and No. 8, 6½in (16.5cm).
$2,000-3,000

A Derby King Street cat group, c1870, 4in (10cm) wide.
$400-550

An English group of a recumbent cat with kittens playing at the side, painted in black and yellow and on pink rectangular and gilt lined base, perhaps Derby, minor restoration, c1825, 4½in (11.5cm).
$1,500-2,500

A Longton Hall white figure of a turkey of so-called 'Snowman' type, the stump perhaps originally surmounted by a nozzle, some minor chipping, c1750, 7½in (18.5cm).
$3,000-4,500

A Staffordshire porcelain dalmatian, c1840, 3in (7.5cm).
$450-700

A Staffordshire porcelain swan, c1840, 3½in (9cm).
$400-550

A Staffordshire porcelain Lloyd Shelton type eagle, unmarked, c1840, 7½in (19cm).
$600-900

A Royal Worcester equestrian group, modelled by Doris Linder, 'Prince's Grace & Foal', No. 288 of a limited edition, 9½in (24cm), complete with a fitted wood stand and certificate.
$1,000-1,500

A pair of Staffordshire porcelain figures of dogs, with black and tan markings on a white ground, with gilt borders, 3½in (9.5cm).
$450-700

A Royal Worcester model of the racehorse Nijinsky, by Doris Linder, No. 193 of a limited edition, 11in (28cm), complete with fitted wood stand and certificate.
$1,000-1,500

A Höchst white figure of a dog, chips to ears, crack through hind legs, blue wheel mark to base, c1765, 4½in (12cm).
$450-700

A Meissen figure of a peacock, restoration to neck, minor frits to base, blue crossed swords mark, c1728, 7in (18cm).
$6,000-9,000

A Meissen miniature figure of a bear, with brown fur markings on mound base with foliage, ears restored, blue crossed swords mark at back, c1745, 3in (8cm).
$4,000-5,500

A Meissen white figure of a carthorse, modelled by P Reinicke, minor repairs, blue crossed swords mark at side, c1750, 8in (20cm) long.
$1,000-1,500

A pair of Meissen canaries, in mint condition, c1850, 4½in (11cm).
$1,000-1,500

A Meissen figure of a swan, modelled by J J Kändler, on waterweed mound base, blue crossed swords mark at back, c1750, 4½in (11.5cm).
$10,000-13,500

A Meissen finely modelled figure of a Bolognese terrier dog, in tones of white and brown, late 19thC, 9in (23cm).
$2,000-3,000

A Meissen bonbonniere base, moulded in the form of a lion's head and painted in naturalistic colours, the interior painted gold, cover missing.
$300-500

A pair of porcelain Bolognese hounds in the Meissen style, seated on breccia marble plinths with gilt bun feet, 6½in (16.5cm) wide.
$5,000-7,500

A late Meissen group of a cockerel, hens and chicks, cockerel with damaged comb, chips to tail feathers, blue crossed swords, incised and impressed numerals, 8in (20.5cm).
$2,000-3,000

Figures – People

A pair of Minton porcelain poodles, c1845, 5in (12cm) wide.
$900-1,300

A Belleek parian figure entitled 'The Prisoner of Love', after the model by Giovanni Fontana, named on the base, tassel at corner of drapery on base lacking, incised Giovanni Fontana Sc. at the back of the base, black printed Belleek, Co. Fermanagh, Ireland marks, second period, 25½in (65cm).
$10,000-13,500

A Bow white figure of a sphinx said to represent the actress Peg Woffington, some minute chipping to headdress and tassels at back, c1750, 5in (12cm).
$3,000-4,500

A Bow white figure of Urania, by the Muses modeller, left hand and dividers lacking, chip to veil, c1752, 6½in (16cm).
$1,500-2,500

A Bow white figure of a toper, some minute chipping, one jug with handle lacking, c1755, 5in (13cm).
$1,500-2,500

A Bow white figure of Smell from a set of the Senses, slight chip to hem and tree, c1752, 5in (13cm).
$1,500-2,500

A Bow white figure of Air, in flowing dress, c1758, 8½in (21cm).
$1,300-2,000

A Bow figure of a gallant, in pink lined blue frock coat, flowered waistcoat, pale yellow breeches and black shoes, with a black tricorn hat, left hand a replacement, flaking to enamel on coat, F mark in black, c1756, 6½in (16cm).
$1,500-2,500

A Bow figure of a lady in Turkish dress, after the Meissen model by J F Eberlein, in pale brown headdress, pale yellow flowered dress and pink skirt, crack to wrist, chips to tree and dress, one finger lacking, c1758, 6½in (17cm).
$2,000-3,000

A Bow figure of a fish vendor, after the Meissen model in pink lined pale blue bodice and pink and flowered skirt, holding a white apron, on a green base, slight chips to fingers, tub, one fish lacking and chips to base, c1758, 6½in (16cm).
$2,250-3,500

An unmatched pair of Bow porcelain figures, of a shepherd and a shepherdess, c1760, 11½in (29cm).
$4,000-5,500

A pair of Bow porcelain figures of the Seasons, Autumn and Winter, in mint condition, c1760, 7in (18cm).
$2,000-3,000

A Bow figure of Pedrolino, with gilt edged pale yellow jacket, flowered culottes and black shoes and hat, some restoration to arms and jacket, c1765, 6in (15cm).
$1,300-2,000

A pair of Bow figures of a seated monk and nun, he in lime-green-lined blue cloak, plum coloured hood and scapular and pale pink tunic edged in gold, reading a red bound breviary, she in plum coloured pink lined veil and scapular and lime-green-lined blue habit, holding a gilt rosary, anchor and dagger marks in iron red, c1765, 5in (14cm).
$3,000-4,500

A Bow figure of a lady in red hat, pink jacket, striped and flowered dress and yellow underskirt, flowers chipped, fingers restored, c1765, 6in (15cm).
$1,300-2,000

A Bow sweetmeat figure, modelled as a new dancer in blue and pink hat, green bodice, iron red lined flowered apron and striped and patterned yellow dress, restoration to hat, hands, right arm and tree, c1765, 6½in (16cm).
$450-700

A pair of Derby figures of Juno and Jupiter, in pink and yellow flowered clothes, lightly enriched in gilding, Juno with restoration to peacock and left hand, both with minor chipping, Wm Duesbury & Co, c1765, 10½in (25.5cm).
$3,000-4,500

A Derby figure of General Conway, draped in a puce cloak, on a scroll moulded base enriched in gilding, slight damage to shield and cannon, Wm Duesbury & Co, c1770, 12½in (32cm).
$1,200-1,750

A Derby figure of a gallant, in pale yellow hat, flowered jacket and turquoise breeches, the base enriched in puce, green and yellow, slight chips to hat, left hand restored, minor chipping, Wm Duesbury & Co, c1760, 5in (13cm).
$1,300-2,000

A pair of Derby figures of a sailor and his lass, wearing pale striped and flowered clothes, he with restoration to arms, she to hat and right arm, trees chipped, Wm Duesbury & Co, c1765, 9½in (24cm).
$2,250-3,500

Two Derby figures of John Wilkes and General Conway, Wilkes in gilt edged white clothes and pink cloak, Conway in white cuirass, turquoise jacket and pink cloak, some minor restorations, Conway with restorations to base and back, Wm Duesbury & Co, c1765.
$2,250-3,500

A Derby figure of a singer, in turquoise lined pink cloak, iron red flowered jacket and yellow breeches, on a green rockwork base applied with flowers, some minute chipping, Wm Duesbury & Co, c1775, 8½in (21cm).
$800-1,200

A pair of Derby porcelain figures of a Welsh tailor and his wife, c1800, 10in (25.5cm).
$3,000-4,500

Large pairs are much rarer than small pairs which tend to be about 6in (15cm) high.

A Derby figure of a singer, in iron red lined black cape, pale yellow flowered jacket and pale yellow breeches, head re-stuck, some chipping, Wm Duesbury & Co, c1775, 8in (20.5cm).
$800-1,200

A pair of small Derby porcelain figures of a Welsh tailor and his wife, c1800, 6in (15cm).
$1,000-1,500

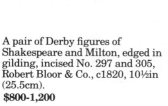

A pair of Derby figures of Shakespeare and Milton, edged in gilding, incised No. 297 and 305, Robert Bloor & Co., c1820, 10½in (25.5cm).
$800-1,200

Make the most of Miller's

When a large specialist well-publicised collection comes on the market, it tends to increase prices. Immediately after this, prices can fall slightly due to the main buyers having large stocks and the market being 'flooded'. This is usually temporary and does not affect very high quality items

A pair of Derby figures of Autumn and Winter after the original model by Pierre Stephan, 9 and 8½in (23 and 21.5cm).
$1,000-1,500

A Derby white figure of Harlequin after the Meissen model, hat and foot chipped, sword lacking, Robert Bloor & Co, c1815, 5½in (14cm).
$1,200-1,750

A pair of Plymouth bocage figures of a gardener and his companion, some damage, late 18thC, 10½in (25.5cm).
$1,000-1,500

A Rockingham white biscuit bust of William IV, c1830, 6½in (17cm).
$800-1,200

A Staffordshire porcelain figure of a girl with a doll, c1835, 6in (15cm).
$600-900

A Staffordshire porcelain figure of Dr Syntax, Landing at Calais, c1835, 5in (12.5cm).
$400-550

A Rockingham biscuit figure of a paysanne du Mongfall en Tirol, hat, fingers and handle of basket restored, incised No. 15 and impressed marks, c1830, 7½in (19cm).
$1,200-1,750

A large Royal Worcester parian model 'The Bather Surprised', after an original model by Sir Thomas Brock, draped in pale green, some damage, impressed marks, late 19thC, 26in (66cm).
$1,300-2,000

A Royal Worcester figure of a water carrier, coloured in tones of cream and with gilt highlights, bowl and urn restored, impressed marks, 16½in (42cm).
$300-500

A pair of Royal Worcester figures of children carrying baskets, after models by James Hadley, impressed and printed marks for 1883, 8½in (22cm).
$1,300-2,000

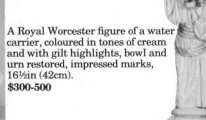

A Royal Worcester model, Stroller and Marion Coakes, modelled by Doris Lindner, No. 376 of a limited edition of 750, with certificate.
$300-400

A Robinson and Leadbetter parian bust of Sir Isaac Pitman, modelled by T Brock, plinth chipped on reverse, impressed factory marks, impressed sculptor's name and dated 1887, 2½in (6cm).
$250-350

A pair of Berlin figures, painted in
bright enamel colours, some
damage, sceptre mark, 7in (18cm).
$800-1,200

A Berlin figure of the Farnese
Hercules, blue sceptre mark, 18thC,
6½in (16cm).
$100-200

A pair of Berlin figures from a set of
the Months, one inscribed 'Marts',
with a sign for Aries attached to the
tree stump base, the other inscribed
'Februari', with the sign of Pisces,
minor chips, blue sceptre marks,
c1785, 4½in (11cm).
$1,000-1,500

A Berlin Wegely figure of
Cupid, in disguise as a
lawyer, restoration to
hands and cape, blue mark
at back, various impressed
marks, c1755,
4½in (11cm).
$2,000-3,000

A pair of Berlin figures, decorated
predominantly in blue, K.P.M.
mark, late 19thC, 14½in (37.5cm).
$1,300-2,000

A French figure of a seated
Chinaman, in Kakiemon colours,
cover of globe missing, painted
Chantille mark, 19thC, 10½in
(26cm).
$600-900

A Capodimonte Carlo III figure of a
man, modelled by Guiseppe Gricci,
extensive repair to his head and
right arm, c1750, 9½in (24cm).
$4,000-5,500

*Apparently unrecorded in the
literature of Capodimonte.*

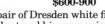
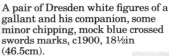

A pair of Dresden white figures of a
gallant and his companion, some
minor chipping, mock blue crossed
swords marks, c1900, 18½in
(46.5cm).
$2,250-3,500

A pair of Royal Dux figures of water
carriers, each wearing blue, 15½in
(40cm).
$800-1,200

A Royal Dux group, 28½in (72cm).
$700-900

A Frankenthal figure of a peasant
woman, restored, blue lion rampant
mark, c1758, 5½in (13.5cm).
$1,200-1,750

A Fürstenberg figure of a boy
allegorical of Winter, wearing a
brown ermine-lined cap and a lilac
ermine-lined coat, some gilding, left
hand and foot repaired, incised
script B L and impressed 3 to base,
c1780, 4½in (11.5cm).
$1,000-1,500

A pair of Russian porcelain figures
of young girls, both damaged, blue G
marks for the Gardner's Factory,
8in (20cm).
$600-900

A Heubach porcelain figure of lady of mystic origin.
$700-900

A pair of Höchst figures of musicians, he in a pale orange jacket, pink trousers, a black hat with white feathers, she in a yellow dress, white pinafore, pink hat and bodice, restoration to his hand, the end of her mandolin, blue wheel marks to bases, c1765, 6½in (16.5cm).
$8,000-11,000

A Höchst bust of a helmeted warrior, painted in colours, enriched with gilding, red wheel mark to base and painter's mark C, c1755, 4½in (11cm).
$700-900

A Höchst figure of Harlequin, wearing a multi-coloured suit and a conical hat, his head restored, chip to hat, one of the goat's horns missing, the bagpipe broken, red enamel wheel and painter's c and incised $\frac{I}{K}$ marks to base, c1755, 6½in (16cm).
$8,000-11,000

A Höchst figure of a Chinaman, modelled by der Meister des Türkischen Kaisers, his coat with yellow border with scattered flowers over a green robe, chips to sleeves and tips of shoes, piece of base re-stuck, c1755, 4in (9.5cm).
$1,200-1,750

A Höchst figure of a dancing girl, modelled by Johann Peter Melchior, wearing a blue and iron red laced bodice, with gilt edged white skirt and yellow underskirt, thumb and forefinger of right hand missing, blue crowned wheel mark, c1775, 5½in (13.5cm).
$1,000-1,500

A pair of Kloster Veilsdorf figures of a sultan and sultana, after the Meissen model, his right hand, sword hilt and right boot restored, restoration to her hat, the sultan with incised G on the base, c1775, 7½in (19cm).
$6,000-9,000

A Höchst figure of a lady, modelled by Johann Peter Melchior, her left hand missing and chips to base, blue crowned wheel mark, c1770, 7in (18cm).
$1,500-2,500

A Ludwigsburg figure of an apple seller, by Pierre François Lejeune, blue crowned interlaced C mark, and painter's mark L, c1770, 5in (12.5cm).
$2,250-3,500

A Limbach figure of a lady emblematic of Winter, with puce topcoat and puce flowered white skirt with orange hem, c1775, 6in (15cm).
$4,000-5,500

A Ludwigsburg figure of a lady with a muff, modelled by Pierre François Lejeune, in puce, orange, white and blue, chip to cape, blue crowned double C mark, and incised IC3 to base, c1760, 5in (12.5cm).
$1,500-2,500

A pair of Meissen figures of children, on high domed silver bases repoussé with swags and stiff leaves, minor chips, the porcelain c1750, the silver mounts Fribourg and probably bearing the maker's mark of Gotthard Leberecht Krumbholz, 1749-93, 6in (15cm).
$2,000-3,000

A Meissen figure of a sleeping child, the gown with floral ornament and 4 bands of blue and gilt and wrapped in a chequered cloth tied with a ribbon bow and fastened at the end with a gilt pin, crossed swords mark in underglaze blue, incised marks and impressed number 122, 16½in (42cm).
$3,000-4,500

The original was modelled by Kändler in 1741. These figures were given as New Year gifts in Saxony and were modelled after the figure of the Holy Child in the church of Santa Maria in Aracoeli in Rome.

A Meissen figure of Columbine, modelled by J J Kändler, in puce, yellow, white and gilt 'indianische Blumen', yellow shoes, repair to hat and left hand, chips to leaves, blue crossed swords mark to rear of base, c1750, 5½in (13.5cm).
$1,500-2,500

A Meissen equestrian group of a sportsman, in black, yellow and brown, restorations, blue crossed swords mark on base, c1750, 11in (27.5cm).
$2,000-3,000

A Meissen figure of a youth, holding a rooster and a long walking stick, in white, blue, yellow, pale puce and green, repair to hat, cane and right foot, traces of blue crossed swords mark to the rococo scroll moulded base, c1755, 6in (15cm).
$800-1,200

A Meissen figure of a tailor, from the series of Craftsmen, modelled by J J Kändler, in black, red and white, head restuck, hat and collar repaired, blue crossed swords mark at back of base, c1753, 9½in (23.5cm).
$4,000-5,500

A Meissen figure of a coquille seller, modelled by P. Reinicke and J. J. Kändler, repair to his hat, right arm and basket, blue crossed swords mark and Pressnummer 21 to base, c1755, 6in (15cm).
$3,000-4,500

A Meissen figure of Cupid as a soldier, repairs to one wing, sword, and catagan, blue crossed swords mark at back, c1755, 3½in (9.5cm).
$600-900

A pair of Meissen figures of a shepherd and a shepherdess, in pale puce, yellow and green, with 'indianische Blumen', some restoration, faint blue crossed swords marks on bases, c1755, 5½in (14.5cm).
$3,000-4,500

A Meissen figure of a cellist, in white jacket with 'indianische Blumen', blue breeches, yellow shoes, extensive restoration, c1755, 4½in (11.5cm).
$1,300-2,000

A pair of French porcelain figures of a gallant and his lady, dancing in bright 18thC costume, slight damage, late 19thC, 13in (33cm).
$700-900

A pair of Continental coloured bisque figures of an 18thC courtier and his companion, wearing elaborate costumes.
$800-1,200

A Vienna figure of a man, painted in black, puce, yellow, green and blue, restoration to his hat, right hand and monkey's paw, blue beehive mark, impressed 3H and painter's mark 20, c1770, 7½in (19cm).
$1,000-1,500

Flatware

A Bow blue and white dish with twig handle, the centre painted within a blue rim, slight glaze damage, mid-18thC, 9in (22cm).
$450-700

A parianware group of 2 American Civil War soldiers, 20in (51cm).
$1,000-1,500

A French biscuit group emblematic of Plenty, minor repairs, 18thC, 13½in (34cm).
$1,000-1,500

Two Bow blue and white pickle dishes, 3 and 4½in (7.5 and 11.5cm).
$700-900

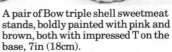

A pair of Bow triple shell sweetmeat stands, boldly painted with pink and brown, both with impressed T on the base, 7in (18cm).
$3,000-4,500

A Caughley blue and white asparagus server, c1780.
$100-200

A miniature Caughley plate, hand painted with the Island pattern in underglaze blue, c1775, 4.4cm.
$300-500

> ### Make the most of Miller's
>
> *Unless otherwise stated, any description which refers to 'a set' or 'a pair' includes a valuation for the entire set or the pair, even though the illustration may show only a single item*

A Caughley kidney-shaped dish, c1780, 11in (28cm) wide.
$200-350

A Caughley fluted bread and butter plate, transfer printed with the Temple pattern, c1780, 7½in (19cm).
$200-350

An early Coalport armorial plate, c1805, 9in (23cm).
$200-350

A pair of Coalport dessert dishes, painted in the manner of Thomas Baxter, with gold painted foot rim, marked 899 in gold, c1810, 11in (28cm) wide.
$2,250-3,500

A pair of Coalport dessert dishes, hand painted in polychrome, c1820, 10½in (26.5cm) high.
$400-550

A Coalport plate, c1820, 9in (23cm).
$150-250

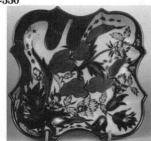

A Coalport finger and thumb pattern dish, c1825, 7in (18cm).
$1,000-1,500

A pair of Coalport shell-moulded plates, with hand painted yacht design on mother-of-pearl and gilded ground, c1880, 9½in (24cm).
$300-500

A Coalport dessert plate from the service presented by Queen Victoria to the Emperor of Russia in 1845, with gold gadrooned shaped edge, rich dark cobalt border, 6 panels edged in gold with pale lemon ground bearing Imperial Russian orders, the white centre panel painted with Russian-Polish crowned two-headed eagle, marked on reverse with Royal Coat of Arms, surrounded by A.B. & R.P. Daniell Manufacturers to Her Majesty and The Royal Family, 120 New Bond St. and 18 Wigmore St., London, 10in (25.5cm).
$4,000-5,500

A Coalport plate with scale blue ground, a copy of Dr Wall Worcester version, c1885, 9in (23cm).
$200-350

A Coalport dinner plate, painted by Percy Simpson, with a named view of the River Severn near Shrewsbury, c1909, 10½in (26.5cm).
$300-500

Two matching Coalport lobed dishes, with a rare combination of fruit and flowers, painting attributed to Thomas Brentnall, impressed 2 mark.
$1,300-2,000

A Copeland and Garrett meat draining dish, printed with figures leading out dogs, printed mark, named on the reverse, c1835, 19in (48cm) wide.
$900-1,300

A Davenport blue and white plate, printed with a profile bust portrait of George III as an emperor, c1820, 7in (18cm).
$400-550

A pair of Coalport two-handled dishes, with named scenes of Ben Lomond and Hawthorden, on a royal blue ground, c1910, 11½in (29cm) wide.
$1,000-1,500

A Copeland and Garrett meat dish, printed with Shooting a Leopard, c1835, 20½in (52cm) wide. **$1,000-1,500**

A Derby armorial plate with a leopard, red mark, c1805, 9in (23cm). **$400-550**

A Derby plate with salmon ground, red mark, c1810, 10in (25cm). **$400-550**

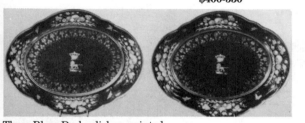

Three Bloor Derby dishes, painted and gilt with the Shrewsbury crest, 16th Earl, on dark green grounds, printed mark, c1825, 8½in (21.5cm) wide. **$900-1,300**

A Doccia blue and white charger painted with an oriental pattern, c1755, 12½in (31.5cm). **$400-550**

A Doccia blue and white platter with Stampino floral decoration, c1745, 12in (31.5cm) wide. **$900-1,300**

A pair of Doccia shell-shaped dishes, painted in an Imari palette, c1755, 12in (30.5cm). **$1,300-2,000**

A Doccia shell-shaped dish decorated with flowers, painted in colours, c1760, 10in (25.5cm) wide. **$450-700**

An initialled Doccia dinner plate, decorated in blue and gold, c1780, 9½in (24cm). **$200-350**

A pair of Doccia dishes with floral decoration, painted in colours, c1770, 9in (23cm). **$300-500**

A Liverpool, William Ball, saucer printed in blue with The Apple Picking pattern, c1760, 5in (12cm). **$100-200**

A Doccia plate decorated with fruit and flowers, enclosed by blue 'feuille-de-choux' borders in the Sèvres style below a gold band, c1780, 9½in (24cm). **$75-150**

A Limoges plate, by Haviland & Co, signed A. Nicol, c1910, 9½in (24cm).
$200-350

A Longton Hall leaf dish, painted in the manner of the Trembly Rose painter, c1755, 11in (27.5cm).
$1,500-2,500

A Longton Hall strawberry leaf-moulded plate, painted within a naturally moulded and coloured border of trailing strawberries and leaves with purple tendrils, slight rim chips, c1755, 9in (23cm).
$4,000-5,500

A Longton Hall dish with twig handle, painted in bright enamel colours, the rim painted with a dark red line, small chip to rim, mid-18thC, 8½in (21.5cm).
$1,500-2,500

A Longton Hall leaf dish with green rope twist handle, painted in the manner of the Trembly Rose painter, within a lobed chocolate line rim, slight rim chips, c1755, 9in (23cm) wide.
$800-1,200

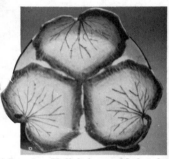

A Longton Hall dish, moulded and naturally coloured with 3 cucumber leaves with puce veins and edged in green and yellow, cracks to rim, c1755, 6in (15cm).
$1,300-2,000

A Meissen saucer, painted with merchants on a quayside with sailing vessels, blue crossed swords mark and gilder's mark 8, c1730.
$4,000-5,500

A Meissen armorial plate from the Sulkowski Service, modelled by J J Kändler, blue crossed swords mark and impressed Dreher's mark, c1737, 9in (23cm).
$5,500-7,750

A Meissen blue and white barbed plate with brown rim, painted with 8 panels of chinoiserie figures and garden scenes, the reverse with continuous flowering foliage to the rim, blue crossed swords mark at the foot of the tree, and Pressnummer 20, c1740.
$4,000-5,500

A Meissen chinoiserie saucer, painted with iron red and gilt, the reverse with 3 sprays of 'indianische Blumen', blue crossed swords mark and gilder's mark 58, Pressnummer 2, c1740.
$1,300-2,000

A Berlin plate with raised gilt chinoiserie figures, with iron red border and gilt lines, rim chip repair, blue sceptre mark and Pressnummer 15, c1805, 9½in (24.5cm).
$3,000-4,500

A Minton plate, hand painted and signed, A. Boullemier, c1870, 9in (23cm).
$450-700

A pair of Mintons yellow ground cabinet plates, painted within gilt dentil rims, impressed marks and pattern No. G1276, 1874 and 1881, 9½in (24cm).
$1,000-1,500

A Mintons plate, the centre painted 'en camaieu rose' within a gilt key-pattern band, on the turquoise ground, impressed and printed marks and date code for 1874, 9½in (24cm).
$900-1,300

A pair of Minton plates, painted in colours, artist's initials A.H.W. within printed gilt diaper borders, impressed factory marks and printed New York retailer's mark, 9in (23cm).
$400-550

A pair of Mintons dessert plates, painted in white enamel on turquoise enamel ground, one signed Leroy, impressed Mintons and clay mark for 1877, stamped A.B. Daniell & Son, 46 Wigmore St., London, 9½in (24cm).
$2,500-3,500

MINTON

★ factory site bought in 1793 by Thomas Minton at Stoke on Trent
★ Minton had worked at Caughley and Spode
★ factory first produced earthenware, started to make porcelain c1798
★ factory mainly famous for its bone china
★ early patterns tend to be very similar to Newhall, Pinxton and Spode
★ early wares not marked but did often have a pattern number, sometimes with N. or No. in front
★ Minton palette is closest to Pinxton
★ much pre 1850 Minton is wrongly ascribed to other factories, particularly Rockingham, Coalport and Pinxton
★ the early figures are prone to damage – watch for restoration
★ very few heavily flower encrusted wares have escaped without damage
★ some beautiful ground colours with excellent gilding. Minton had particular success with a turquoise ground
★ as with most other factories, signed pieces are most desirable
★ artists of note include: G Hancock, J Bancroft, T Kirkby, T Allen, R Pilsbury, Jesse Smith and A Boullemier
★ note marks: MINTON became MINTONS from c1873

Did you know

MILLER'S Antiques Price Guide builds up year by year to form the most comprehensive photo-reference system available

A set of 6 Minton dessert plates, produced for Thomas Goode & Co, decorated by Anton Boullemier after an original design by William Coleman, each on a pale green ground within gold rims, one with crazed glaze, impressed and printed marks, 9½in (24cm).
$1,500-2,500

A Minton dessert service, printed in puce 'camaieu', within a gilt spearhead border, comprising 12 plates, 3 damaged, and 4 low stands, 3 damaged, impressed marks for 1865.
$700-900

A Mintons plate, painted with a spray of pink roses and forget-me-nots, impressed mark Mintons and year mark for 1878, and printed mark from William Mortlock, 18 Regent St. London Mintons China, 9in (23cm).
$300-500

A Mintons plate, with a gilt key pattern rim, impressed mark Mintons and year mark for 1879, printed mark Mintons Bailey Banks & Biddle Philadelphia, 9½in (24.5cm).
$200-350

A Minton dessert plate with pierced gilded border, slight restoration to rim, signed L. Solon, c1880, 9in (23cm).
$600-900

A pair of Mintons plates, painted with Sunrise on the Danube and Cottage near Kie, impressed Mintons and year mark for 1880, 8½in (22.5cm).
$300-500

A set of 4 Nymphenburg plates, impressed mark, late 18thC, 9½in (24.5cm).
$1,500-2,500

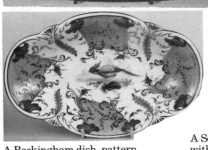

A Pinxton saucer dish, slight rubbing, c1795, 7½in (19.5cm).
$300-500

A J M W Ridgway dessert plate, with relief moulded pattern No. 1017, c1825, 9in (23cm).
$200-350

A Rockingham dish, pattern No. 700, 11½in (29cm) wide.
$700-1,000

A Sèvres 'rose pompadour' tray, with pierced scroll border, reserved on a pink ground, enriched with gilding, minor damage to rim, blue interlaced L marks enclosing date letter E For 1759, and painter's mark of Noël and incised square, 5½in (14.5cm).
$8,000-11,000

A Sèvres 'bleu celeste' tray, with pierced scroll border, painted on a turquoise ground, enriched with gilding, one border flowerhead restored, traces of blue interlaced L mark, incised A, c1757, 5½in (14.5cm).
$1,500-2,500

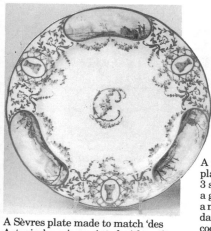

A Swansea lobed plate, c1805, 9in (23cm).
$200-350

A matched set of 10 Sèvres dessert plates, the rim painted with 3 sprays within a gold cartouche on a green ground, 9½in (24.5cm), and a matching bowl, 8in (20.5cm), some damage, printed marks and date code for 1770.
$1,500-2,500

A Sèvres plate made to match 'des Asturies' service, painted with a gilt and floral monogram of CL for Charles IV of Spain and his consort Louise of Parma, blue interlaced L marks enclosing the date letter for 1759, and later painter's mark of Vieillard, 9½in (24cm).
$2,000-3,000

A Sèvres style dish, set on a gilt metal stand with foliate handles, reserved on a gold decorated deep blue band, late 19thC, 17in (43cm).
$800-1,200

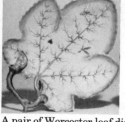

A pair of Worcester leaf dishes with green stalk handles, raised puce veins and edged in green, one with 2 slight rim chips, c1760.
$5,000-7,500

A pair of Strasbourg hexafoil plates, painted in colours, rim chips, mid-18thC, 9½in (24cm).
$2,000-3,000

A Swansea crested dish with gilt twig handles, with motto 'Y DDUW BOR DIOLCH', c1819, 11in (28cm) wide.
$2,000-3,000

A pair of Swansea botanical plates, painted by William Weston Young, with Myosotis rupicola and Menziesia caerulea named on the reverses, perhaps some retouching to the enamels, c1820, 8½in (21.5cm).
$1,200-1,750

A Worcester blue and white pickle leaf, moulded underside and painted with flowers, rim chip, workman's mark, c1760.
$300-500

A Worcester blue and white butter boat, with moulded feet and painted floral spray, crescent mark, c1760.
$400-550

A First Period Worcester blue and white butter shell, painted with The Two Peony Rock Bird pattern in underglazed blue, painter's mark in underglaze blue, c1760, 5in (12.5cm).
$900-1,300

A set of 7 Worcester plates, in mint condition, open crescent mark, c1775, 8in (20.5cm).
$3,000-4,500

A First Period Worcester dish, in black, turquoise, gilt and deep blue, open crescent in underglaze blue, 10½in (26.5cm).
$1,300-2,000

A Worcester fluted dish, painted in the Kakiemon palette, within a border for flower sprays divided by bands of iron red scrolls and gilt diaper pattern, c1770, 10½in (27cm).
$2,000-3,000

A set of 32 Worcester, Flight, Barr & Barr, plates and soup plates, c1815, 10in (25.5cm).
$10,500-15,000

A Chamberlain's Worcester dish, with gilt dentil rim, script mark, c1800, 10½in (26cm).
$3,000-4,500

A pair of Worcester Imari pattern leaf dishes, painted with The Kempthorne pattern, one with minute rim chip, the other repaired, blue square seal marks, c1770, 10½in (26.5cm).
$1,200-1,750

A Grainger's Worcester comport, c1820, 5½in (14cm).
$300-500

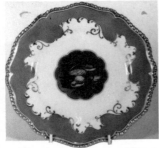

A Worcester, Flight, Barr & Barr, dessert plate with gilded edge, apple green border and central panel painted on a white ground, painting attributed to Smith, impressed FBB mark under crown, printed circular factory mark with Royal coat of arms and fleur-de-lys, c1815, 8in (20cm).
$1,300-2,000

A pair of Chamberlain's Worcester dessert plates, brightly painted within a band of gold leaves, reserves on a green ground, impressed marks, mid-19thC, 9in (23cm).
$450-700

A Grainger's Worcester fine painted plate, printed and impressed marks, c1875, 9½in (24cm).
$300-500

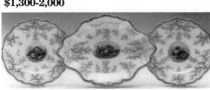

c. A Worcester, Flight, Barr & Barr, dessert dish, brightly painted within a gold gadroon rim, impressed marks, c1825, 12½in (31cm) wide.
$1,500-2,500

l. and r. A matching pair of dessert plates, printed on the reverse Royal Porcelain Works, Flight, Barr & Barr, Worcester & Coventry Street, London.
$2,000-3,000

A Royal Worcester dish, boldly painted within a gold rim on an apricot and ivory ground, shape No. 1275, printed mark and date code for 1906, 9in (23cm).
$450-700

A Dr Syntax plate by Charles Ford, 'Doctor Syntax makes free of the cellar', signed, c1871, 9in (23cm).
$200-350

A Dr Syntax plate by Charles Ford, 'Doctor Syntax and the Dairymaid', c1871.
$200-350

An important Fairyland Lustre plate, with coloured scene of imps walking over bridge in blue/grey floral border, 10½in (26.5cm).
$900-1,300

A pair of English porcelain deep dishes, each painted with a coat of arms and the motto 'Praemium. Virtutus. Honor', probably made for the Cheere family, the deep blue border painted with a scrolling foliate design, early 19thC, 9½in (24.5cm).
$600-900

An English porcelain sample plate, the centre gilt with St George and the Dragon, the border with the emblems and arms of England, Scotland, Ireland and Wales, perhaps Minton, c1860, 9½in (23.5cm).
$300-500

A pair of Berlin ornithological deep plates, painted with bright colours, within green 'feuille de chou' and shaped gilt chain pattern borders with pink flowerheads, blue sceptre marks, c1790, 9½in (24cm).
$5,000-7,500

A set of 7 Nymphenburg plates, late 18thC, 9½in (24cm).
$2,000-3,000

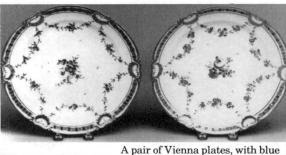

A pair of Vienna plates, with blue beehive marks, Pressnummer 34, puce painter's marks, c1775, 10in (25cm).
$150-250

Flasks

A rare Davenport blue and white moon flask with ring handles, with a profile bust portrait of George III, c1820, 6in (15cm).
$600-900

A Meissen pear shaped flask, decorated in Holland in the Oriental manner in green and red, the porcelain c1730, the decoration slightly later, 8½in (21cm).
$2,500-3,500

A First Period Worcester pickle dish, painted in underglaze blue with vines and flowers, with blue serrated edge, workman's mark a fylfot, 3½in (8.5cm).
$200-350

Ice Pails

A pair of Derby ice pails, covers and liners, painted in blue and gilt, with twisted scroll finials, one cover restored, puce crown cross batons and D mark, 10in (25.5cm).
$1,300-2,000

A pair of Coalport ice pails, covers and liners, the bodies painted in sepia and gilt on white grounds, some damage, replacement wooden pine cone finials, 13in (33cm).
$3,000-4,500

A Flight, Barr & Barr ice pail, cover and liner with pine cone finial and loop handles with ram mask terminals, on a ground of whorls and leaves in iron red, blue, green and gilt, on a low spreading foot to the square base, impressed marks, c1810, 14½in (36.5cm).
$10,500-15,000

Inkwells

A Samson desk set, applied with coloured porcelain flowers, cherub with small repair, 8in (20.5cm).
$600-900

A Royal Worcester pen and inkstand, printed mark and date code for 1899, 10½in (26cm) wide.
$450-700

A rare moulded Chamberlain's Worcester inkwell, c1820, 1½in (4cm).
$400-550

A Worcester, Flight & Barr, inkstand, centrally painted on a blue ground, finely gilded, 2 covers restored, incised B mark, c1800, 7in (18cm) wide.
$3,000-4,500

A Chamberlain's Worcester inkstand, in yellow on a matt blue base, heavily enriched in gilding, putto restored, script mark in gold, c1820, 5½in (14cm).
$900-1,300

A very rare Stevenson & Hancock Derby jewelled inkwell, painted mark, c1880, 4in (10cm).
$1,000-1,500

A rare Grainger's Worcester inkstand with named view of Chepstow, c1820, 5in (12.5cm).
$1,500-2,500

Jardinières

A pair of Meissen jardinières, with 'Alt-ozier' borders, painted in colours with 'deutsche Blumen', one restored, blue crossed swords marks, c1745, 12in (31cm).
$1,500-2,500

A Royal Worcester 'Hadley style' jardinière, with gilded rim and foot, signed W. E. Jarman, pattern No. 276, green mark, 1907, 8in (20.5cm) diam.
$2,250-3,500

Jars

A Royal Worcester pot pourri jar, painted by Reginald Harry Austin, printed mark and date code for 1911, 7½in (18.5cm).
$1,000-1,500

A Mintons jardinière with brilliant turquoise enamel and gilded decoration, painting attributed to Antonin Boullemier, slight crack to rim, marked on base with gold crown and globe, also impressed Mintons and clay mark for 1875, 14in (35.5cm) wide.
$3,000-4,500

A Royal Worcester jardinière with pierced rim, boldly painted by Albert Shuck, shape No. H295, printed mark and date code for 1919, 9in (22.5cm).
$900-1,300

A garniture of 5 Chelsea Derby covered jars, applied overall with green and gold flowerheads and branches with red berries, some damage, late 18thC.
$2,000-3,000

A pair of Sèvres Louis XVI style gilt-bronze mounted cobalt ground and gilt jars and covers, 21in (53cm).
$2,000-3,000

A pair of German pot pourri jars and covers, each brightly painted, slight damage, 15½in (39cm).
$3,000-4,500

A pair of French porcelain jars and covers, potted and painted in the Chinese manner, in bright enamel colours and gold, slight damage, 14½in (37cm).
$800-1,200

A Wedgwood Fairyland Lustre black ground jar and cover, outline printed in gold and coloured, the ground gilt with a spider's web, printed Portland Vase mark and pattern No. Z4968i, c1925, 3½in (8.5cm).
$3,000-4,500

A pair of ormolu-mounted octagonal baluster jars, gilt and painted in iron red and underglaze blue in the Imari style, fitted for electricity, some damage, 13in (32cm).
$2,250-3,500

Jugs

A Caughley milk jug, transfer printed with the Fishermen pattern in underglaze blue, c1785.
$450-700

A Böttger gold Chinese milk jug and later domed cover, gilt in the Seuter workshop, reserved on a solid gold ground, chip to spout, the porcelain c1725, 7in (18cm).
$1,500-2,500

A Sèvres jar, cover and stand, painted within a decorated blue and gold rim, minor damage to one handle of the stand, painted mark with date code for 1780, stand 7in (17cm) wide.
$1,000-1,500

A Minton jug with loop handle, pattern No. 248, c1805, 6½in (16.5cm) wide.
$400-550

A Miles Mason jug, bat-printed in grey between gilt line rims, minute chip to lip, c1810, 8½in (21cm).
$450-700

A Meissen inverted baluster jug, modelled after a silver original, small chip to rim, blue crossed swords mark, c1755, 7½in (19cm).
$1,000-1,500

A Meissen jug with hinged cover and contemporary silver-gilt mount, slight restoration to spout and cover, blue crossed swords mark, the mount with the décharge of Julien Berthe, fermier-général 1750-56, the porcelain c1740, 7½in (18.5cm).
$6,000-9,000

A Rockingham jug, unmarked, 4½in (11cm).
$1,000-1,500

A Plymouth blue and white jug, minute chips to foot, blue 24 mark, c1770, 6½in (16.5cm).
$2,250-3,500

LIVERPOOL

- ★ porcelain from all Liverpool factories is eagerly collected
- ★ **Richard Chaffers & Co** 1754-65 – produced first a bone ash and later a soapstone porcelain, mainly blue and white, good painting, with some polychrome wares of high quality
- ★ **Samuel Gilbody** c1754-61 – rarest of Liverpool porcelains, soft glaze colours which tend to sink into glaze, very difficult to correctly attribute wares
- ★ **William Ball** 1755-69 – blue and white slightly more common from this factory, decoration very Bow-like, glaze can be confused with Longton Hall, but frequently has a greenish-blue appearance
- ★ **William Reid & Co** 1756-61 – mainly quite crude blue and white, often sanded, chinoiserie based decoration, sometimes resembling contemporary style on Liverpool delftware
- ★ **Philip Christian & Co** 1765-76 – greyish tone to underglaze blue, some fine painting, flatware is rare, but bowls were something of a speciality
- ★ **Seth Pennington** 1770-99 – many copies of Christian's wares, standard not as high as earlier factories, mainly blue and white
- ★ **Wolfe & Co** 1795-1800 – polychrome wares with chinoiserie decoration, blue and white extremely rare

A Sèvres cream jug with branch handle, painted with flowers, on 3 branch feet, with gilt dentil rim, blue interlaced L marks enclosing the date letter O for 1767 and painter's mark, 3½in (8.5cm).
$800-1,200

A Worcester blue and white feather moulded cream jug, with workman's mark, c1760.
$600-900

A Chamberlain's Worcester blue ground jug, the neck with the monogram GR in gold within a gilt oak leaf cartouche, minor restoration to lip and foot, script mark, c1815, 7in (18cm).
$1,200-1,750

Mugs

A Bow blue and white cylindrical mug, c1758, 2in (5.5cm).
$1,200-1,750

A pair of Chantilly Kakiemon mugs, with manganese branch handles and leafy terminals, iron red hunting horn marks, c1740, 2½in (6.5cm).
$10,500-15,000

A miniature Copeland Spode mug, c1900, 2in (5cm).
$75-150

A Lowestoft blue and white mug, the interior rim with blue loop pattern, painter's numeral 5, c1765, 4in (9.5cm).
$9,000-12,500

A Sèvres coffee can, with rare chinoiserie painting, crowned red mark, c1778, 2in (5cm).
$600-900

A Chelsea tea plant beaker, enriched in colours beneath a chocolate line rim, rim chips, c1745, 3in (7.5cm).
$3,000-4,500

A Coalport mug, c1810, 3in (7.5cm).
$400-550

A miniature Royal Crown Derby mug, c1902, 1½in (3.5cm).
$100-200

A Chelsea white tea plant beaker, slight rim chip and repair, c1745, 3in (7.5cm).
$2,250-3,500

A Coalport two-handled mug, dated 1877, 4in (10cm).
$200-350

l. A Derby Imari style coffee can, c1800, 2½in (6in).
$100-200
r. Spode monochrome coffee can, c1800, 2½in (6cm).
$100-200

A miniature Royal Crown Derby mug, c1909, 1½in (3.5cm).
$100-200

A Staffordshire porcelain lilac and gilt moulded mug, 19thC, 3in (7.5cm).
$45-75

A Rockingham mug, the loop handle with gilt hoof terminal, painted between gilt line rims, some minor staining, puce griffin mark and Cl 2 in red, c1835, 4in (10cm).
$1,300-2,000

Plaques

A pair of Rockingham documentary plaques, painted by W W Bailey, with Sunset, view on the Welsh coast and The Clyde, from Erskine Ferry, some very minor flaking to enamels, signed and inscribed in red on the reverses, c1835, 4½ by 5½in (11 by 14cm).
$4,000-5,500

An English porcelain plaque, inscribed on reverse, 'painted by W. Corden', and dated February 4th, 1823, 6 by 5in (15 by 12.5cm).
$700-900

A Flight, Barr & Barr plaque, painted by Samuel Astles, impressed mark FBB, crowned and incised number 22, 10½ by 8½in (26.5 by 21cm), in gilt frame.
$13,000-17,500

An early Victorian portrait miniature of Major General T S Nicolls.
$300-500

A Flight, Barr & Barr plaque, painted by Samuel Astles, with classical statuary in the background, 21½ by 16½in (55 by 42.5cm) frame.
$42,500-55,000

The plaque was exhibited at the Royal Academy in 1827.
After the mezzotint by Richard Earlom, from the original painting by Jan Van Huysum in the Houghton Collection, sold by Lord Orford, son of Sir Robert Walpole, to the Empress Catherine of Russia.

A Berlin hand painted plaque, c1870, 8 by 6in (20.5 by 15cm).
$700-900

An Austrian plaque, reserved on an intricate gold decorated iron red ground, the border on a deep blue ground, inscribed on the reverse, 'Die Toilette der Esther', 12½in (31.5cm).
$1,300-2,000

A Berlin plaque, painted after Murillo, impressed sceptre and KPM marks, c1875, 11 by 8½in (28 by 22.5cm), carved gilt-wood frame.
$4,000-5,500

A Berlin plaque, painted by S A D Fordyce after Van Dyck, with the three eldest children of Charles I, signed and dated 1882, impressed sceptre and KPM marks, gilt metal frame, 9 by 11in (22.5 by 28cm).
$3,000-4,500

A Berlin named plaque of Princess Louise, hand painted, signed Knoniller, impressed mark, KPM and sceptre, c1880.
$3,000-4,500

A Berlin plaque, painted after A Kauffmann with a vestal virgin, in a white dress, impressed KPM, sceptre, F and 5 marks, late 19thC, 10½in (27cm).
$3,000-4,500

A Berlin plaque, painted after Raphael with the Madonna di San Sisto, impressed KPM marks, late 19thC, 12½ by 10in (32 by 25.5cm).
$2,000-3,000

A pair of Berlin plaques, impressed KPM marks, sceptre and H/G marks, late 19thC, carved giltwood frames, 9½ by 5½in (23.5cm by 14.5cm).
$3,000-4,500

A Berlin plaque, painted with a young servant girl in a pink dress and white apron, impressed marks, late 19thC, 9½ by 6½in (24 by 16cm), with a gilded carved wood frame.
$3,000-4,500

A Berlin plaque, impressed KPM mark, 13in (33cm).
$4,000-5,500

A German plaque painted by Louis Renders after David Neal, with Mary Queen of Scots' first encounter with Rizzio, inscribed on the reverse 'premiere rencontre de Marie Stuart avec Rizzio d'apres le tableau de David Neal/8 juin, 1887', small patch of flaked paint, signed, 11½ by 8½in (29 by 21.5cm), gilt metal frame.
$1,300-2,000

A Berlin plaque, painted by Carl Muller, impressed marks, 10 by 8in (25.5 by 20.5cm).
$3,000-4,500

A German plaque, painted with a nude young woman, after a painting by Ingres entitled The Spring, late 19thC, 8 by 4in (20 by 10cm).
$1,500-2,500

A German plaque, 5½in (14cm), with wood frame.
$2,000-3,000

A German plaque, painted with a portrait of a young girl in a white robe, 7½in (19cm), wood frame.
$1,200-1,750

A Vienna plaque, painted with Cleopatra and Anthony, in red, gold, pink and blue, the back with shield mark in underglaze blue and inscribed Kleopatra, 13½in (34cm), in wood and velvet frame.
$900-1,300

Pots

A Coalport yellow ground bough pot and pierced cover, perhaps painted in the studio of Thomas Baxter, slight chipping to cover, c1805, 11½in (28.5cm) wide.
$2,500-3,500

A pair of 'Vienna' gold ground plaques, painted by C Heer and E Lat, with a scene from Othello and with Sir Francis Drake standing before Queen Elizabeth I, signed, traces of titles on the reverses, imitation blue shield marks, late 19thC, 19½in (49cm) diam.
$6,000-9,000

A Coalport chocolate pot, painted in reds, blues and greens, heavily gilded, c1800, 6in (15cm).
$200-350

A Coalport bough pot, the chocolate brown ground incised and stencilled and heightened in brown, c1810, 12½in (31cm) wide.
$450-700

A pair of Derby iron red ground D-shaped bough pots and one pierced cover, with gilt rams' mask handles, crown, crossed batons and D marks in iron red, Duesbury & Kean, c1800, 10in (25cm) wide.
$5,000-7,500

A pair of Liverpool Herculaneum flower pots and 2 stands, with gilt mask handles, c1815, 6½in (17cm) wide.
$2,000-3,000

A Royal Crown Derby rouge pot, with Old Derby Witches pattern, c1921, 2in (5cm) diam.
$150-250

A Spode bough pot, with gilt 'feuille-de-choux' cartouche, and bronzed winged cherubs, slight cracks to edges and one foot, c1820, 12in (30.5cm) wide.
$600-900

A Miles Mason bough pot and cover, bat-printed with Cupid and Psyche, within elaborate gilt cartouches divided by moulded blue and gilt pillars with Ionic capitals between gilt line rims, the cover with blue and gilt gadroons, minute chips to rim, cover chipped and cracked, finial lacking, c1810, 11in (28cm).
$1,500-2,500

A Meissen cream pot and cover, painted in colours with 'Watteaumalerei' scenes of figures from the Commedia dell'Arte, blue crossed swords mark to base, c1745, 4½in (11cm).
$2,250-3,500

A Meissen pomade pot and cover, painted in colours with 'Holzschnittblumen' in the manner of Gottfried Klinger, gilt rims, handle restored, faint crossed swords mark to base, c1745, 6in (15cm).
$3,000-4,500

A Chamberlain's Worcester salmon pink ground bough pot and pierced cover, painted with Venus Attired by the Graces, slight restoration to finial, script mark in gold, the base inscribed, c1800, 7½in (18.5cm).
$4,000-5,500

A Worcester, Flight & Barr, salmon pink ground jam pot, cover and fixed stand, painted in colours within gilt cartouches, the rim of the stand gilt with key pattern, finial restuck, incised B mark, c1800, 4½in (12cm).
$2,000-3,000

Sauceboats

A Bow blue and white sauceboat, on 3 mask and paw feet, with a drab glaze, slight lip chips and some firing cracks to rim and handle, c1750, 9in (22cm) wide.
$1,300-2,000

A Caughley sauceboat, with the Fisherman pattern, c1780, 3in (7.5cm).
$300-500

A pair of Buen Retiro cache pots with shell and satyr's mask handles, minor chips and restorations to both handles, blue fleur-de-lys marks and incised interlaced C on both pieces, c1770, 10in (25.5cm) wide.
$6,000-9,000

A Liverpool blue and white moulded sauceboat, attributed to William Ball's factory, c1758, 5½in (14.5cm) wide.
$5,000-7,500

A pair of Derby sauceboats in mint condition, c1765, 5in (12cm).
$1,500-2,500

A Longton Hall cos lettuce leaf-moulded sauceboat, the stalk handle with fruit terminal, with blue rim, c1758, 6½in (16.5cm) wide.
$1,000-1,500

Two Meissen sauceboats, painted with 'deutsche Blumen' beneath 'ozier' bands, blue crossed swords mark, c1750, 9in (23.5cm) wide.
$400-550

A large Worcester blue and white sauceboat, painter's mark, c1754, 9½in (24cm) wide.
$1,500-2,500

A Worcester blue and white silver shaped sauceboat, c1755, 7½in (19cm) wide.
$1,500-2,500

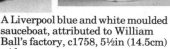

A small Worcester sauceboat, hand painted with the rare Little Fisherman pattern, 2 small chips to rim, c1765.
$600-900

A Worcester blue and white double-lipped two-handled sauceboat, minute extending firing crack to one flute, painter's mark, c1756, 7in (17.5cm) wide.
$1,500-2,500

A pair of Worcester blue and white sauceboats, with scroll handles, one with minute chip to foot and rim, blue crescent marks, c1770, 7½in (18.5cm) wide.
$800-1,200

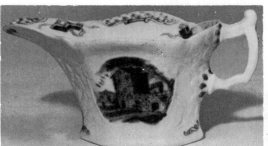

An English porcelain blue and white creamboat, perhaps Reid's Factory, Liverpool, c1755, or Newcastle-under-Lyme, c1750, 5½in (14cm) wide.
$4,000-5,500

Scent Bottles

Services

A Rockingham scent bottle and stopper, encrusted with coloured flowers between gilt line rims, slight chipping to flowers, crack to one side, puce griffin mark and C1 2 in red, c1835, 3in (8cm) square.
$900-1,300

A Coalport Imari pattern part dessert service, painted in iron red and underglaze blue, enriched in gilding, comprising: 2 sauce tureens, covers and stands, a centre dish, 11 dishes and 30 plates, some damage, c1810.
$4,000-5,500

An English part tea service, probably by John Rose & Co, Coalport, in enamel colours and gold, comprising 27 pieces, pattern No. 299, early 19thC.
$600-900

A Coalport part dessert service, consisting of 7 pieces, painted by W Waterson and H Hughes, impressed date 1908, plate 9in (22.5cm).
$2,000-3,000

A Coalport blue ground part dessert service, comprising: an ice pail, cover and liner, 2 sauce tureens, covers and stands, a centre dish on 4 feet, 10 dishes, 18 plates, some damage, c1810.
$10,000-13,500

A Copeland 51-piece part dinner service, painted with a Japan pattern in iron red, green, blue and gilt, comprising: 37 plates, 8 dishes, 3 tureens and covers on stands, c1875.
$4,000-5,500

A tea and coffee service by H & R Daniel, comprising: teapot stand, bowl, 2 cake plates, 19 cups and 11 saucers, pattern No. 4367, c1827.
$3,000-4,500

An H & R Daniel blue ground part tea service, painted in yellow and gilt, comprising: a teapot, a sugar bowl and cover, a milk jug, a slop basin, 8 teacups and saucers, pattern No. 3859, some damage, c1825.
$1,000-1,500

A Derby coral red ground part tea and coffee service, comprising: a teapot and cover, a sugar bowl, a milk jug, a slop basin, 2 saucer dishes, 22 cups, 11 saucers, crown, crossed batons and D marks and pattern No. 745 in iron red, Duesbury & Kean, c1805.
$5,000-7,500

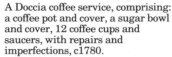

A Doccia coffee service, comprising: a coffee pot and cover, a sugar bowl and cover, 12 coffee cups and saucers, with repairs and imperfections, c1780.
$2,250-3,500

Price

Prices vary from auction to auction – from dealer to dealer. The price paid in a dealer's shop will depend on:
1) what he paid for the item
2) what he thinks he can get for it
3) the extent of his knowledge
4) awareness of market trends
It is a mistake to think that you will automatically pay more in a specialist dealer's shop. He is more likely to know the 'right' price for a piece. A general dealer may undercharge but he could also overcharge

A Gotha coffee pot and cover, milk jug and cover, sugar basin and cover, and a coffee cup and saucer, the cup and saucer marked in underglaze blue R.g. for Rotberg, the proprietor, 1783-1805.
$900-1,300

A Nymphenburg part tea and coffee service, painted in a pastel palette of green and red, comprising: a slop bowl, a sugar bowl and cover, 16 cups, 19 saucers, some damage, impressed Bavarian shield marks, c1760.
$8,000-11,000

A Nymphenburg part tea and coffee service, painted in green and black with iron red borders, comprising: a coffee pot and cover, a teapot and cover, a sugar box and cover, 8 cups and saucers, some damage, impressed Bavarian shield marks, c1765.
$3,000-4,500

A Meissen travelling tea service, comprising: a teapot and cover, an ogival teapot stand, a tea caddy and cover, a slop bowl and 12 cups and saucers, some repairs, blue crossed swords and dot marks and various Pressnummern, c1770, in contemporary green silk lined tooled leather case with brass lock and drop handles.
$15,000-21,000

A Paris, Restoration, purple ground tea service, the teapot and hot water pot with animal mouth spouts, comprising: a teapot and cover, a hot water pot and cover, a sugar bowl and cover, a bowl and 12 cups and saucers, c1820.
$6,000-9,000

A Sèvres mocha set, comprising: 5 small cups with scroll handles, a stand with moulded 'feuille-de-choux' painted with bands of flowers 'en camaïeu rose' and with gilt rims, small chip to rim of stand, blue interlaced L marks enclosing the date letter G for 1759 and painter's mark of Catrice, the stand incised M.ai CU.
$1,000-1,500

A Sèvres part dessert service, painted in blue and manganese, comprising: 4 shaped plateaux bouret, 4 saucer dishes, 11 plates, some damage, interlaced L marks enclosing various date letters, 1783-90, various painter's marks.
$3,000-4,500

A Sèvres gilt and white part tea and coffee service, comprising: 2 sugar bowls and covers, a pair of oviform jugs, a bowl, 16 cups and 14 saucers, some damage, printed fleur-de-lys marks, interlaced L's and various date codes for 1824-26.
$2,000-3,000

A Sèvres pattern armorial royal blue ground coffee service, comprising: a coffee pot and cover, a hot milk jug and cover, a two-handled sugar bowl and cover, 8 coffee cans and saucers, some damage, imitation Sèvres marks in iron red, c1900.
$1,500-2,500

Tea & Coffee Pots

A Bristol teapot and cover with moulded spout and grooved loop handle, blue X11 mark, Richard Champion's factory, c1775, 5½in (13.5cm).
$1,300-2,000

A Bristol teapot and cover, brightly decorated in coloured enamels, knop chipped, 6in (15cm).
$800-1,200

A miniature Caughley teapot and cover, hand painted, slight chip inside cover, c1775, 3½in (8.5cm).
$1,000-1,500

A Caughley barrel shaped teapot, with the Temple pattern, c1780, 6in (15cm).
$300-500

A Derby teapot, c1750, 6in (15cm).
$900-1,300

A Derby teapot and cover, edged in gilding, body cracked, Wm Duesbury & Co, c1770, 5½in (14cm).
$1,200-1,750

A Doccia coffee pot and cover, with purple landscape decoration, the rims gilt, one engaging tooth inside cover missing, c1780, 6in (15cm).
$450-700

A Mettlach pewter mounted 'castle' stein, the reverse with an inscription on a panel beneath the handle and suspending a red seal, impressed marks and numbers, date code for 1898, 16in (40cm).
$2,250-3,500

A Caughley polychrome teapot, c1780, 5½in (13.5cm).
$600-900

A Chelsea fable teapot, painted in the manner of Jefferyes Hammet O'Neale with the fable of The Fox and The Goat in the Well, the reverse with 2 pieces restuck, c1752, 4in (10.5cm), the cover a late 18thC enamelled tin replacement painted with flower sprays.
$3,000-4,500

A Doccia coffee pot and cover, painted in dark pink, green and gilt, c1785, 6in (15cm).
$300-500

A Longton Hall cabbage leaf moulded teapot and cover, crack to base and one side, part of handle terminal missing, c1755, 4½in (11cm).
$25,000-34,000

A Lowestoft teapot with Curtis-type decoration, c1782.
$800-1,200

A Rockingham baluster teapot and cover, painted beneath a gilt dentil rim, 7in (17.5cm), a baluster milk jug, 6in (15.5cm), a two-handled sugar bowl and cover, 5½in (14cm), c1830.
$2,000-3,000

A Plymouth yellow ground coffee pot and cover, painted in purple, crack to rim and top of handle, chips to spout and cover, c1770, 10in (25cm).
$800-1,200

A miniature Spode teapot and cover, with gilt mons on a blue ground gilt with scale pattern, chip ground to foot rim, red mark and pattern No. 1166, c1820, 2in (5cm).
$900-1,300

A Worcester teapot and cover with flower finial, decorated in 'famille rose' colours, 18thC, 6in (15cm).
$250-350

A Royal Worcester white porcelain teapot and cover, probably decorated by George Owen, the handle, spout and cover applied with pale blue beads, impressed mark, c1890, 5in (12cm).
$6,000-9,000

A Berlin coffee pot and cover, painted in red with scenes after Watteau, blue sceptre mark and Pressnummer 3, c1785, 9in (23cm).
$4,500-7,000

A Böttger porcelain Goldchinesen Hausmalerei inverted baluster coffee pot, the handle, spout, knop and rims gilt all over, c1725, with contemporary silver-gilt footrim, 8½in (21cm).
$3,000-4,000

A Böttger porcelain Hausmalerei coffee pot and domed cover, by Johann Philipp Dannhöfer, enriched with gilding, spout, rim and foot chipped, finial lacking, the porcelain c1725, the decoration slightly later, 7½in (19.5cm).
$7,000-10,000

A Böttger white porcelain teapot and cover, minor chips to rim, c1720, 6½in (16.5cm) wide.
$15,000-21,000

A Meissen gold Chinese teapot and cover, shaped panels on solid gold ground, chips to spout and rims, c1725, 5½in (13.5cm) wide.
$1,200-1,750

A Meissen yellow ground coffee pot, painted 'en camaïeu rose', reserved on a yellow ground, minor chip to the underside of cover, blue crossed swords mark and incised cross, c1740, 7½in (18.5cm).
$4,000-5,500

A Meissen gold Chinese teapot and cover, gilt at Augsburg by Bartolomaüs Seuter, with silver-gilt chain attachment, minor chips to foot rim, one chip to rim, interior of cover chipped, c1725, 6½in (16.5cm) wide.
$13,000-17,500

A Meissen cylindrical chocolate pot and cover, with turned wood gilt metal mounted handle, chip to cover, c1745, 5in (13.5cm).
$900-1,300

A Meissen spirally moulded baluster coffee pot and cover and a hot milk jug, repair to lip of jug, blue crossed swords marks, c1750, coffee pot 9½in (24cm).
$600-900

A Meissen Goldmalerei teapot and cover, painted in puce, gilt at Augsburg in the Seuter workshop, minute chips to spout and finial, c1730, 7in (18cm) wide.
$4,000-5,500

A Meissen teapot and cover, painted in the manner of C J Albert, chips to spout and handle terminal, finial restored, blue crossed swords mark, c1755, 6in (15.5cm) wide.
$1,200-1,750

A Meissen baluster coffee pot and domed cover, picked out in colours and gilt and painted in sepia, hairline crack, rim chip repair, blue crossed swords mark, mid-18thC, 9in (23cm).
$600-900

A Meissen Marcolini chocolate pot, with gilt fittings, c1763, 7in (17.5cm).
$1,500-2,500

A Weesp lilac ground teapot and cover, painted with Italian Comedy figures, the handle and spout with blue foliage scrolls, minor chip to rim of cover, c1760, 6in (15.5cm) wide.
$14,000-19,000

Tureens & Butter Tubs

A blue and white Goldfinch pattern sauce tureen, cover and stand, c1820, 6½in (16cm).
$300-500

A Meissen quatrefoil tureen, cover and stand painted in colours with 'Watteaumalerei' vignettes, gilt rims to all pieces, repair to knop, blue crossed swords marks and Pressnummern to base, c1750, the stand 11½in (28.5cm) wide.
$10,500-15,000

A Meissen Marcolini tureen and cover, naturalistically painted in yellow, red, green and grey, repairs, blue crossed swords marks and various incised marks to base, c1770, 11in (28cm) wide.
$1,300-2,000

Vases

A Belleek white porcelain vase, light damage, first version printed mark in brick red, 8in (20.5cm).
$300-500

A pair of Meissen tureens and covers, moulded with 'Neuebrandenstein', painted in colours, piece restuck to one cover, chips to handles, blue crossed swords marks, c1750, 11in (28cm) wide.
$4,000-5,500

A Meissen soup tureen, cover and stand, with cut lemon finial, painted with bouquets of 'deutsche Blumen', blue crossed swords marks, Pressnummern, c1750, the stand 17in (43cm) wide.
$3,000-4,500

A Meissen two-handled tureen stand, moulded with pierced scrolls, edged in puce and gilt, blue crossed swords and dot mark, c1770, 17in (44cm) wide.
$1,500-2,500

A Belleek spill vase, with black marks, c1895, 12½in (31.5cm).
$2,000-3,000

A Meissen tureen and cover, with cut lemon finial, painted with bouquets of 'deutsche Blumen', base repaired, blue crossed swords mark, c1750, 13½in (34cm) wide.
$300-500

A Meissen tureen and cover, with cut lemon finial, painted with bouquets of 'deutsche Blumen' within 'ozier' bands, minor chips to handles, blue crossed swords mark, c1750, 12in (30.5cm) wide.
$1,000-1,500

A Sèvres two-handled ecuelle, cover and stand, painted in colours on a blue and gilt 'oeil-de-perdrix' ground, chip to handle of stand, blue interlaced L marks, date letter for 1775, and blue decorator's mark for Thévenet, 10in (25.5cm) wide.
$2,000-3,000

A pair of Bow vases and covers, painted in the 'famille rose' palette, one body cracked and restored, c1750, 7½in (19.5cm).
$4,000-5,500

A Chelsea blue ground vase, painted in blue and gilt, some minor rubbing, gold anchor mark, c1760, 13in (33cm).
$2,250-3,500

A matched pair of Derby beaker shape vases, painted on a dark blue ground with gilt, on 3 paw feet, 5in (12.5cm).
$1,000-1,500

A Liverpool Herculaneum buff ground vase, slight rubbing, printed mark in puce, c1815, 4in (9.5cm).
$1,200-1,750

A Minton pale turquoise ground 'munster pot pourri' vase and cover, some damage, the cover with blue crossed swords mark, c1830, 10½in (26cm).
$800-1,200

A pair of Minton pink ground campana vases, painted on shaded pink and yellow grounds, c1820, 6½in (17cm).
$3,000-4,500

A pair of Minton pâté-sur-pâté vases by A Birks, c1890.
$1,000-1,500

A pair of Minton vases, c1880.
$900-1,300

A Ridgway & Sons vase, on a bronzed foot, one handle damaged, impressed Ridgway & Sons and inscribed Brunswick, No. 326 in red, c1810, 7in (18cm).
$450-700

A Wedgwood Fairyland Lustre vase, decorated on a pale blue and mauve ground, 9in (23cm).
$800-1,200

A Pinxton yellow ground vase and 2 covers, painted 'en grisaille' in the manner of William Billingsley and highlighted in yellow, one cover repaired, c1797, one cover later, 10½in (27cm).
$3,000-4,500

A pair of Spode vases, the base marked Spode 2575, c1815, 5in (12.5cm).
$3,000-4,500

A Rockingham blue ground vase and cover, painted in blue and edged in gilding, the cover with gilt seated monkey finial, c1828, 19in (48cm).
$2,000-3,000

A Rockingham vase, c1830, 8in (20cm).
$1,500-2,500

RIDGWAY

- ★ one of the most important factories manufacturing English bone china
- ★ most of the early Ridgway porcelain from 1808-30 is unmarked; some, however, do have pattern numbers which are fractional, as did Coalport, with which it is often confused
- ★ the quality of the early porcelain is excellent, brilliant white and with no crazing in the glaze
- ★ there were many skilled flower painters employed at the Cauldon Place works including George Hancock, Thomas Brentnall, Joseph Bancroft
- ★ the development of the Ridgway factory is as follows:
  John Ridgway & Company, 1830-55
  Bates, Brown-Westhead & Moore, 1859-61
  Brown-Westhead, Moore & Company, 1862-1905
  Cauldon Ltd, 1906-20
  Cauldon Potteries Ltd, 1920-62

A Rockingham garniture, some damage, all with puce griffin marks, c1835, 6½in (17cm) and 8½in (21cm).
$5,000-7,500

A Rockingham vase, with painted sea shell motif, slight repair, puce mark, 4½in (11cm).
$900-1,300

A pair of Royal Worcester Persian style vases, decorated in gold on an ivory ground, printed mark and date code for 1890, 12½in (32cm).
$1,000-1,500

A Spode 'New French Jar' shaped vase, the base marked Spode 711, c1820, 9in (23cm).
$4,000-5,500

A Ridgway & Sons Imari pattern vase and cover, some rubbing, impressed Ridgway & Sons and 4, c1810, 8½in (21cm).
$450-700

A Worcester blue ground vase, painted by Jefferyes Hamet O'Neale, cracked through and restored beneath the cartouches, blue square seal mark, c1770, 13½in (34cm).
$5,000-7,500

A Chamberlain's Worcester salmon pink ground vase, cover and finial stopper, with gilt ram's mask handles, minute rim chip to inside, script mark in gold and incised 27, c1800, 14in (35.5cm).
$4,000-5,500

A Worcester, George Owen, vase and cover, repair to finial, gilt mark, date code for 1894, 5in (12.5cm).
$2,250-3,500

A Royal Worcester vase in Art Nouveau style, shape No. 2472, c1891, 9½in (24cm).
$300-500

◄ A Royal Worcester pilgrim flask vase in Persian style, impressed and printed marks and date code for 1876, 13½in (34cm).
$1,500-2,500

A Royal Worcester vase, applied and moulded in high relief, printed mark and date code for 1883, 11½in (29cm).
$800-1,200

A Minton vase, interior stained, gilt worn, one handle with cracked terminal, the interior with monogram J.W, 7in (18cm).
$600-900

A Worcester, Flight, Barr & Barr, simulated shagreen ground vase, painted with flowers, inscribed 'Thy long lost Edwin from Goldsmith' on the base, restoration to one handle and part of rim, script mark, c1825, 8in (20cm).
$1,000-1,500

A pair of English vases and covers, perhaps Royal Worcester, one with restorations to handles, finial restuck and hair cracks, the other with hair cracks to base, c1870, 15in (37.5cm).
$800-1,200

A Royal Worcester garniture, with hand painted mask handles, initialled, shape No. 1716, c1895, 8 to 10in (20 to 25.5cm).
$2,000-3,000

WORCESTER PATTERNS

★ early period wares mainly confined to chinoiserie decoration

★ in the late First Period polychrome wares

★ most valuable standard type of decoration is birds, particularly if painted by James Giles

★ this is followed by English flowers

★ then Continental flowers

★ and finally the rather stylised Oriental flowers

★ it cannot be stressed strongly enough with Worcester that any rim rubbing or wear will greatly reduce the value, often by as much as half

---

A Grainger's Worcester vase, printed mark and date code for 1899, 13½in (34.5cm).
$800-1,200

A Royal Worcester moon flask, boldly painted with flowers on an ivory ground, printed mark, late 19thC, 15in (38cm).
$1,500-2,500

A pair of Grainger's Worcester Persian style vases, painted in muted enamel colours and gold on an ivory ground, printed mark and date code for 1897, 12½in (31cm).
$900-1,300

A Royal Worcester vase and cover, with griffin handles, boldly painted on an apricot and cream ground, cover damaged and slight chip, printed mark and date code for 1898, 15in (38.5cm).
$600-900

A Hadley's Worcester 'faience' vase, painted in sepia, slight glaze damage, c1898, 9in (22.5cm).
$400-550

A Royal Worcester vase with dragon handles, the body painted by John Stinton, signed, printed mark, shape No. G953, date code for 1905, 7in (18cm).
$1,300-2,000

A Royal Worcester two-handled vase, signed by Harry Davis, shape No. G995, c1912, 6in (15cm).
$1,300-2,000

A pair of Royal Worcester vases, painted on peach grounds, date code for 1914, 10½in (26cm).
$800-1,200

A Royal Worcester Crownware lustre vase, with galleon, shape No. CW281, c1926, 9½in (24cm).
$300-400

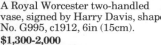

A Royal Worcester porcelain vase, signed Sedgley, 12in (30.5cm).
$1,000-1,500

A vase and cover, painted by Barker, c1930, 9in (23cm).
$1,300-2,000

A Royal Worcester vase, painted by Harry Stinton, shape No. G42, printed mark and date code for 1931, 6in (14.5cm).
$1,000-1,500

A Flight, Barr & Barr vase, the blue ground heightened in gilt, handles missing, impressed and painted factory marks with London retailers mark, 7in (18cm).
$1,300-2,000

An English porcelain vase, perhaps Spode, painted in pink, with gilt panels on an apple green ground and with white beaded borders, c1815, 6in (15cm).
$450-700

A pair of English porcelain vases, with gilt dentil rims, one neck with hairlines, 5½in (14cm).
$300-500

A Dresden vase, gilt worn, blue A.R. marks, 7in (18cm).
$400-550

A pair of Berlin pot pourri vases and covers, sceptre marks, c1880, 13in (34cm).
$3,000-4,500

A Böttger white vase and cover, modelled by Johann Jacob Irminger, minor chips to roses, c1715, 6in (15cm).
$14,000-19,000

A pair of Dresden spill vase groups, 15in (38cm).
$3,000-4,500

A pair of Berlin vases and covers, sceptre mark in underglaze blue, 19thC, 19in (48cm).
$3,000-4,500

A pair of Meissen pot pourri vases and pierced covers, some chips and repairs to foliage, one with traces of blue crossed swords mark, c1745, 7½in (28.5cm).
$5,000-7,500

A pair of Paris royal blue ground vases, painted after Teniers, on richly gilt square bases, c1820, 14½in (37cm).
$5,000-7,500

A pair of Paris vases, modelled as figures of a boy and a girl, painted in colours and enriched in gilding, minor chips to flowers, blue JP marks, c1850, 8½in (22cm).
$700-900

A Meissen vase, the 'Frauenkopf' handles with iron red and puce headdress, painted by F F Meyer von Pressnitz, chip to underside of base, the porcelain c1725, 5in (13cm).
$3,000-4,500

A pair of Meissen Marcolini presentation vases and covers, each painted with floral monograms for JP and MCP, one cover damaged and crack to one handle, blue crossed swords and star marks, c1810, 11in (28cm).
$1,200-1,750

A Paris neo-Renaissance pot pourri vase and cover, finial repaired, blue JP marks, c1840, 8½in (21.5cm).
$300-500

A Viennese vase and cover.
$300-500

A Frankfurt blue and white baluster vase, painted in the Ming manner, hair cracks, rim chips, c1690, 15½in (40cm).
$3,000-4,500

A massive Paris blue ground 'Medici' vase, richly painted, body and one handle with restorations, chips to underside of rim, c1820, 21½in (54.5cm).
$4,000-5,500

A pair of Paris pink ground vases, blue JP marks, c1840, 7in (18cm).
$1,300-2,000

A Sèvres pattern gilt metal mounted turquoise ground vase, damage to one handle, c1865, 27½in (70cm).
$4,000-5,500

A Paris Sèvres vase, with turquoise ground, interlaced L's mark, 19thC, 12in (30.5cm).
$1,200-1,750

A massive Sèvres pattern green ground Napoleonic vase and cover, decorated by Desprez, richly gilt and silvered with crowned initial 'N', on a square ormolu base, cover restored, imitation M. Imple de Sèvres marks, late 19thC, 54in (138cm).
$10,500-15,000

A pair of Sèvres pattern green ground vases and covers, with white and gilt caryatid handles, the covers gilt with white and gilt knob finials, one vase with chip to rim, one cover riveted, both finials restuck, imitation interlaced L marks, late 19thC, 16½in (42cm).
$3,000-4,500

Miscellaneous

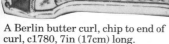

A Berlin butter curl, chip to end of curl, c1780, 7in (17cm) long.
$1,300-2,000

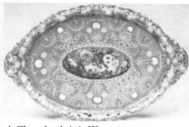

A Chamberlain's Worcester tray, painted in white and gold on a matt blue ground, script mark in red Chamberlain's Worcester, 155 New Bond Street, London, 17in (43cm).
$3,000-4,500

A Doccia triple salt with centre figure, shell restored, c1750, 7in (18cm).
$300-500

A Rockingham miniature tray, minute chipping to flowers, puce griffin mark and C1 2 in red, c1835, 4in (9.5cm) wide.
$800-1,200

A Ridgway teapot stand, painted with a sandpiper, c1815, 6½ by 8in (16 by 20cm).
$450-700

A Coalport mantel ornament, painted in sepia and gilt, slight rim chips and cracks, c1810, 11½in (29cm) wide.
$2,250-3,500

A Schrezheim cane handle, modelled as the head and shoulders of a young woman with her hair 'en chignon' with a pink ribbon, small chips to one shoulder, impressed box twig at front, c1765, 3in (8cm).
$10,000-13,500

A Caughley patty pan, decorated with the Fisherman pattern in underglaze blue, S mark, c1780, 4in (10cm) diam.
$450-700

A Doccia porcelain handled knife, fork and spoon set, with silver and metal blades, c1770.
$200-350

A Flight, Barr & Barr porcelain pin tray, signed Flight, Barr & Barr, Worcester, and Coventry Street, London.
$100-200

A Staffordshire porcelain tulip, c1840, 6in (15cm).
$800-1,200

A pair of Sèvres pattern gilt bronze mounted lamps, fitted for electricity, c1875, 26in (65cm) high overall.
$5,000-7,500

A Mennecy white pot pourri and cover, some damage to the flowers, incised D.V. mark to base of basket, c1760, 4in (10cm) wide.
$800-1,200

A German porcelain coffee strainer, with boxwood handle, 9in (23cm) long.
$400-550

A Sitzendorf chariot and cherub, wing missing, c1865, 10in (25cm).
$150-250

A pair of Berlin porcelain hand painted eggs, ormolu mounted on alabaster stands, silk lined, c1840, 6½in (16cm).
$1,300-2,000

A Copeland Spode bidet printed with the Tower pattern, printed mark, c1850, 19in (47cm) wide.
$450-700

A Vienna, Du Paquier, bourdalou, painted in 'Schwarzlot', extensively repaired, c1730, 9in (22cm) long.
$1,000-1,500

A European lithophane of an eagle, probably German, c1880, 5½in (14cm) square.
$150-250

ORIENTAL POTTERY & PORCELAIN

Bottles

A pair of black ground bottle vases, one with hairline crack to neck, Qing Dynasty, 17½in (45cm).
$4,000-5,500

A pair of 'famille verte' pear-shaped bottles, rims restored, Kangxi, 7in (17.5cm).
$900-1,300

A late Ming blue and white 'kraak porselein' bottle, frit chip and firing crack to rim, Wanli, 11in (28cm).
$1,300-2,000

A pair of blue and white bottles, Yongzheng mark in underglaze blue within a double circle, and of the period, 4in (10cm).
$2,000-3,000

A celadon glazed bottle, Qianlong seal mark in underglaze blue and of the period, 11in (28cm).
$2,000-3,000

A 'famille rose' bottle, with underglaze blue garlic neck, painted with figures at leisure, Qianlong, 10in (25cm), lamp mount.
$800-1,200

A large 'famille rose' bottle, painted in blue enamel on a yellow ground, blue enamelled Qianlong mark, 21½in (55cm), wood stand.
$3,000-4,500

A blue and white pilgrim bottle, painted in violet blue tones, rim crack, 17thC, 10½in (26.5cm).
$7,000-10,000

A flambé bottle vase, covered in a mottled lavender flecked burgundy glaze thinning at the rim, glaze ground at footrim, 18thC, 16in (40.5cm).
$800-1,200

A pair of Arita apothecary bottles with silver mounted rim, painted in underglaze blue with song birds perched on trailing flowering and fruiting branches, late 17thC, 7in (18cm).
$2,250-3,500

A pair of 'Empress Dowager' 'famille jaune' bottle vases, with a yellow ground, turquoise interior, the underside with inscription of praise: Eternal Prosperity and Enduring Spring, c1900, 12½in (31.5cm).
$1,500-2,500

A pair of Chinese Imari bottles and covers, covers restored, early 18thC, 10in (25.5cm).
$3,000-4,500

A pair of iron red painted powder blue ground bottle vases, enriched with gilt, the base with concentric circles in underglaze blue, 19thC, 16½in (42cm).
$1,500-2,500

Bowls

A green and straw glazed water pot, the interior splashed in a straw glaze, the mouth and exterior covered with a finely crackled leaf green glaze stopping irregularly short of the foot, Tang Dynasty, 5in (13cm) wide.
$5,000-7,500

A Dingyao bowl, freely carved, the ivory glaze pooling slightly irregularly in 'tears' on and around the vertical foot and covering the base, minor rim polish, Song Dynasty, 7½in (18.5cm) diam.
$8,000-11,000

A Yingqing bowl, with a fine transparent glaze of delicate blue tones pooling heavily around the foot, minute chip, Song Dynasty, 8in (20.5cm) diam, fitted box.
$8,000-11,000

A Junyao bowl, with a pale lavender glaze with a purple splash to the interior thinning to a celadon at the rim, Song/Yuan Dynasty, 7½in (19.5cm).
$3,000-4,500

Two Longquan celadon bowls, covered in a pale olive green glaze oxidised in places, cracks, Yuan Dynasty, 5in (12cm) diam.
$1,000-1,500

A celadon tripod bulb bowl, with a crackled pale olive glaze, 14th/15thC, 12½in (32cm) diam.
$2,000-3,000

An Annamese blue and white stem dish, 15thC, 12in (30.5cm) diam.
$3,000-4,500

A large Ming celadon dish, incised under a pale olive green glaze with traces of gilt to rim, 14th/15thC, 15½in (40cm) diam.
$2,000-3,000

A large Ming blue and white saucer dish, Jiajing six-character mark in a line below the rim exterior and of the period, 19½in (49cm) diam.
$10,000-13,500

A rare pair of blue and white 'kraak porselein' bowls, one repaired, chips, Wanli, 14in (35.5cm) diam.
$4,000-5,500

A Ming red dragon saucer dish, with a five-clawed dragon in underglaze blue, slightly warped, red enamels retouched, encircled Jiajing six-character mark and of the period, 7½in (18.5cm) diam, fitted box.
$3,000-4,500

A late Ming blue and white saucer dish, hair crack, encircled Wanli six-character mark and of the period, 6½in (17cm).
$2,250-3,500

A Ming dated brown glazed saucer dish, with a thick white slip reserved on a brown glazed ground, Wanli dated mark to base and of the period, 8in (20.5cm) diam.
$3,000-4,500

A Chinese bowl with flared rim, the celadon glazed exterior incised with dense flowering peony, 9in (23cm) diam.
$700-900

A Kangxi blue and white bulb bowl, c1700, 5½in (14cm).
$3,000-4,500

A Chinese blue and white bowl and cover, with metal handles and finial, Kangxi, 8in (20cm).
$1,000-1,500

A large Ming blue and white bowl, fritted, cracked, encircled mark 'fu gui jia qi' (fine vessel for the rich and honourable), late 16thC, 15in (38.5cm) diam, fitted box.
$3,000-4,500

A 'famille verte' bowl and cover, handles missing, restored, Kangxi, 5½in (13.5cm) diam, wood stand.
$1,500-2,500

A large 'famille verte' dish, painted on a dense green cracked ice pattern ground scattered with iron red and blue daisy heads, 3 small rim chips, Kangxi, 20in (51cm) diam.
$10,500-15,000

A Chinese 'famille verte' fish bowl, painted in Kangxi style on a seeded ground, 17in (43cm) diam.
$1,000-1,500

A pair of 'famille verte' dishes, enamelled within an iron red diapered border, one with minor rim restoration, Kangxi, 7in (18cm) square.
$800-1,200

A Japanese Imari bowl, painted in typical palette, late 17thC, 14in (36cm) diam.
$5,000-7,500

An aubergine and green glazed bowl with white interior, the exterior painted on a dark green ground, cracked, encircled Kangxi six-character mark and of the period, 4in (10cm) diam.
$1,200-1,750

A pair of 'famille verte' biscuit bowls with white interiors, both cracked, encircled Kangxi six-character marks and of the period, 5½in (15cm) diam.
$4,000-5,500

A blue and white phoenix bowl, Kangxi six-character mark and of the period, 8in (20.5cm) diam, wood stand.
$4,000-5,500

A gilt metal mounted Chinese Imari bowl, the porcelain 18thC, the mounts and cover later, 9½in (24cm) wide.
$2,000-3,000

A pair of 'verte' Imari bowls, early 18thC, 6½in (16.5cm) diam.
$2,000-3,000

An aubergine ground Brinjal bowl incised and painted in green, yellow and cream enamels, square seal mark, Kangxi, 4½in (11cm) diam.
$3,000-4,500

A blue and white bowl, the interior partially unglazed, 18th/19thC, 17½in (44.5cm) diam.
$1,300-2,000

A blue and white bowl, painted in the Ming style, Qianlong, 8½in (21.5cm) wide.
$1,500-2,500

A blue and white bowl, Qianlong, c1770, 10½in (26cm) diam.
$700-900

A Doucai bowl, painted in enamels with the eight Daoist Immortals, small rim chip, encircled four-character mark, 18thC, 7½in (18.5cm) diam.
$3,000-4,500

A Chinese 'famille rose' bowl, restored, Qianlong, c1770, 10in (25.5cm).
$450-700

A Chinese blue and white basket and stand, c1800, 9in (23cm) diam.
$1,200-1,750

A massive Canton 'famille rose' punch bowl, enamelled in the interior, restored, c1830, 20½in (52.5cm) diam.
$6,000-9,000

An export mythological subject bowl, the exterior painted with a panel scene depicting 'The Judgement of Paris', within gilt and iron red borders, Qianlong, 10½in (25.5cm) diam.
$2,000-3,000

A Canton 'famille rose' basin, enamelled in the Mandarin palette, heightened in gilt, 19thC, 18½in (47cm) diam.
$2,000-3,000

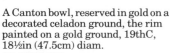

A Canton bowl, reserved in gold on a decorated celadon ground, the rim painted on a gold ground, 19thC, 18½in (47.5cm) diam.
$4,000-5,500

JAPANESE ART PERIODS

★ *Prehistory and Protohistory*
c7000 BC Jomon culture; first recorded pottery with simple design
c300 BC Yayoi culture; bronzes and more sophisticated pottery
1st to 4thC AD Haniwa culture; bronzes and distinctive red pottery
AD 220; first influence from Korea

★ *Asuka Period* – 552-645
★ *Hahuko Period* – 672-85
★ *Nara Period* – 710-94
★ *Heian Period* – 794-1185
★ *Kamakura Period* – 1185-1333
★ *Muromachi (Ahikaga) Period* – 1338-1573
★ *Momoyama Period* – 1573-1615
1598: immigrant Korean potters begin kilns at Kyushu, producing the first glazed pottery
★ *Edo (Tokugawa) Period* – 1615-1867
1616: first porcelain made by Ninsei (1596-1666)
1661-73: great age of porcelain; Arita, Nabeshima, Kutani and Kakiemon
1716-36: popularity of lacquering and netsuke as art forms
★ *Meiji Period* – 1868-1912
Strong influence of Western cultures developing and growing. Japanese art appears to decline in many respects. Much trading with the West

A pair of 'famille rose' chargers, decorated with flowers and butterflies, 19thC, 14in (35.5cm) diam.
$700-900

A Japanese Satsuma bowl, by Yabu Meizan, signed, chipped, c1880, 9½in (24cm) diam.
$14,000-19,000

A 'famille jeune' fish tank, early 20thC.
$1,000-1,500

A pair of lime green glazed bowls, one cracked, Guangxu six-character marks and of the period, 6in (15cm).
$2,000-3,000

A large 'famille verte' fish bowl, enamelled in bright colours, the interior enamelled with iron red fish swimming amongst seaweed, late Qing Dynasty, 22in (56cm) diam.
$3,000-4,500

Censers

A Ming blue and white tripod censer, cracked, Wanli/Tianqi, 7in (18cm) diam.
$1,500-2,500

A Chinese blue and white censer, Kangxi, 9½in (24cm).
$900-1,300

A blue and white censer, Kangxi, c1690, 6½in (16cm).
$5,000-7,500

Cups

A Longquan celadon stem cup, covered in an even olive green glaze stopping above the oxidised exposed footring, Yuan Dynasty, 3in (8cm) diam.
$900-1,300

A Dehua blanc-de-chine censer, with a glaze of pale ivory tones, rim chip polished, seal mark to base, 17thC, 5½in (13.5cm) diam.
$900-1,300

A Dehua blanc-de-chine two-handled censer and cover, with a fine glaze of ivory tone, minute chip to lug handle, 17thC, 7½in (19cm), wood stand.
$10,000-13,500

An Imperial yellow wine cup with white interior, encircled Kangxi six-character mark and of the period, 3in (7cm) diam.
$7,000-10,000

A 'famille rose' mug, painted with an elaborate coat of arms above an inscription in black, 'Moses, Adams, boat builder Gravesend', restored, c1750, 5½in (14cm).
$900-1,300

A 'famille verte' erotic cup, painted with a couple engaged in amorous pursuits on a floor rug, rim cracks, Kangxi, 4in (10cm).
$1,300-2,000

A 'famille rose' European subject teabowl, depicting Water from the 4 Elements after a design by Albani, early Qianlong.
$1,300-2,000

A Chinese export ware mug, decorated in colours, with underglaze blue borders, 6in (15cm).
$4,000-5,500

Ewers

A Chinese blue and white kendi, Wanli, 7½in (18.5cm).
$1,500-2,500

A Ming blue and white ewer, minor fritting, early 17thC, 7½in (19.5cm) diam.
$5,000-7,500

A 'famille noire' wine ewer, minor damage, Kangxi, 6½in (17cm) wide.
$700-900

A pair of 'famille verte' lobed globular ewers, one spout restored, pierced, Kangxi, 9in (22cm).
$8,000-11,000

A rare Dehua blanc-de-chine Montgolfier balloon shaped ewer, supported on a pierced wave base, Qing Dynasty, 9½in (23.5cm).
$2,250-3,500

A rare 'famille verte' ewer, modelled as a standing Buddhistic lion, decorated in iron red and green with a yellow character 'wang' (virtuous king) below an aubergine horn, chipped, spout damaged, Kangxi, 8in (21.5cm).
$3,000-4,500

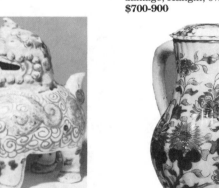

A pair of Chinese Imari ewers and covers, painted with lotus and chrysanthemum clusters, one restored, early 18thC, 7½in (19cm).
$4,000-5,500

Figures – Animals

A pair of red painted grey pottery horse heads, traces of white and ochre painted harnesses, some rubbing, one repaired, Han Dynasty, 5½in (14cm).
$1,300-2,000

A Sancai glazed buff pottery model of a caparisoned horse, glazed in ochre, pale straw and green, broken and restored, Tang Dynasty, 18½in (47cm), wood stand.
$20,000-28,000

A pair of painted red pottery earth spirits, some restoration, Tang Dynasty, 17½ and 18½in (44 and 47cm).
$6,000-9,000

A flambé glazed model of a parrot, in tones of pale lavender, purple and deep burgundy, 18th/19thC, 12in (30.5cm).
$1,200-1,750

A green glazed red pottery figure of a dog, restored, Han Dynasty, 11in (28.5cm) wide.
$2,000-3,000

A painted red pottery equestrian group, painted in white, black and red, right arm restored, Tang Dynasty, 14½in (36.5cm).
$7,000-10,000

A painted red pottery camel, traces of red, black, white and orange pigment, legs restored, Tang Dynasty, 18in (46cm).
$3,000-4,500

Make the Most of Miller's

CONDITION is absolutely vital when assessing the value of an antique. Damaged pieces on the whole appreciate much less than perfect examples. However a rare, desirable piece may command a high price even when damaged

A pair of painted grey pottery owls, painted with orange and white plumage and features, the heads pierced, Han Dynasty, 7in (18cm).
$1,300-2,000

A straw glazed Bactrian camel, traces of red pigment, the glaze degraded, some restoration, Sui/Tang Dynasty, 13in (33cm), wood stand.
$2,250-3,500

A buff pottery equestrian group, old repair and damage, early Tang Dynasty, 12in (30.5cm).
$4,000-5,500

A pair of Chinese pottery tilemaker's figures, Ming/Qing Dynasty, 14in (35.5cm).
$1,500-2,500

A pair of Fujian blanc-de-chine models of European figures seated on elephants, with rockwork bases, some restoration, firing crack, Kangxi, 12in (30cm).
$6,000-9,000

131

A pair of white glazed cockerels, with deep scarlet combs and eyes heightened in cobalt blue, one comb with restoration, 19thC, 16in (40cm).
$6,000-9,000

A large export model of a white glazed goat, the horns, beard, eyes and short tail painted in a cobalt blue firing to an olive green, the base with impressed seal mark, late Qing Dynasty, 15in (38cm).
$5,000-7,500

A rare Sichuan red pottery figure of a dog, splashed with dots of pale buff glaze, damage to tail, Sichuan nine-character mark in relief within a recess roundel, late Qing Dynasty, 16in (40cm) wide.
$8,000-11,000

A pair of 'famille rose' models of phoenix, on pierced iron red rockwork painted with peony, the birds with multi-coloured feathers, impressed marks, 10in (25.5cm).
$700-900

A pair of export figures of cranes, naturalistically moulded and coloured, one beak end chipped and short body crack, some damage, 19thC, 14in (35.5cm).
$5,000-7,500

Figures – People

Two grey pottery figures of dancers, the grotesque heads with traces of pigments, Han Dynasty, 5½in (14.5cm).
$7,000-10,000

A red pottery grotesque figure of a fat man, some restoration, Six Dynasties/Tang Dynasty, 14in (36cm).
$2,000-3,000

A Qingbai figure of Avalokitesvara, covered in a thick greyish-white glaze, where exposed, burnt orange in the firing, some restoration, Yuan Dynasty, 14in (35.5cm).
$5,000-7,500

A large Chinese pottery green, turquoise and ochre glazed figure of a seated Buddha, with detachable head, Ming Dynasty, 22½in (57cm).
$3,000-4,500

A pair of Cizhou painted figures of ladies, with a pale ivory slip and painted in dark brown, red and olive brown, Song Dynasty, 5in (12.5cm), fitted wood stands, fitted cloth box.
$900-1,300

A late Ming blue and white figure of Guanyin, damaged, Wanli, 16in (41cm).
$1,500-2,500

A Ming tilemaker's figure of Guandi, with detachable head, dressed in an elaborate armour, with turquoise and amber glazes, the hands unglazed, chips, 16th/17thC, 19½in (50cm).
$2,000-3,000

A Dehua blanc-de-chine figure of Guanyin, holding a scroll in her left hand, impressed seal mark, virtue extends even to fishermen, Qing Dynasty, 6½in (17cm).
$2,250-3,500

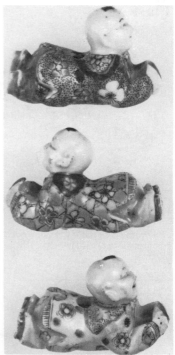

Three 'famille verte' miniature figures of boys, each pierced at the back with a small aperture, in green, iron red, and yellow, seeded green ground and cracked ice pattern, chips, one with hands restored, Kangxi, 2in (5cm) wide.
$3,000-4,500

A tilemaker's equestrian figure, formed as a heavily armoured warrior, under green and yellow glazes, some restoration, Ming/Qing Dynasty, 15½in (39cm).
$1,500-2,500

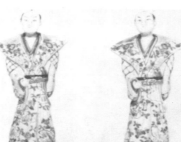

A pair of Arita figures, painted in iron red, green enamel, gilt and black, glaze cracks, 2 feet damaged, late 17thC, 9in (23cm).
$4,000-5,500

A blanc-de-chine figure of Guanyin, under an ivory glaze, some chips, 17th/18thC, 9½in (24cm).
$1,300-2,000

A Dehua blanc-de-chine figure of Damo, standing with his arms crossed, small chips, early 18thC, 15in (38cm).
$7,000-10,000

A Satsuma figure of Kannon, signed at back, Seto Seizan with Shimazu mon, late 19thC, 15in (38cm).
$2,000-3,000

A pair of large soapstone figures, touched with red pigment and engraved with floral borders, damaged, 18thC, 11½in (29cm), wood stands.
$800-1,200

A pair of pottery tilemaker's figures, coiffed and dressed elaborately in ceremonial robes, glazed in turquoise, blue and brown, 13in (33cm).
$700-900

A large Japanese figure of Hotei, late 19thC, 19½in (49cm).
$1,000-1,500

Make the Most of Miller's

Every care has been taken to ensure the accuracy of descriptions and estimated valuations. Price ranges in this book reflect what one should expect to pay for a similar example. When selling one can obviously expect a figure below. This will fluctuate according to a dealer's stock, saleability at a particular time, etc. It is always advisable to approach a reputable specialist dealer or an auction house which has specialist sales

Flasks

A pair of triple neck moon flasks, enamelled in 'famille rose' with Shou Lao and Liu Hai, with his attendant three-legged toad, the rims edged in gilt, iron red seal marks for Qianlong, but 19thC, 4½in (12cm).
$600-900

A pair of large 'famille verte' moon flasks, with diaper grounds enriched with orange, green, and aubergine enamels, the shoulders with elaborate dragon handles, one neck restored, late Qing Dynasty, 18in (47cm).
$4,000-5,500

A Satsuma moon flask, enamelled in colours and gilt, the reverse reserved on a mottled glaze ground, signed underneath Dai Nihon Taizan tsukuru, late 19thC, 7½in (19cm).
$1,500-2,500

Flatware

An early Ming celadon dish carved with a quatrefoil panel, under a semi-translucent olive glaze, border crack, late 14th/15thC, 13in (32.5cm).
$1,300-2,000

A late Ming blue and white saucer dish with lobed floral rim, painted with a pair of deer by a river beneath pine, each moulded lobe with a floral spray, the exterior with emblems, minor fritting, Wanli, 8½in (22cm) diam.
$2,000-3,000

The moulded lobe developed into the so-called 'meisanda' style of decoration, featuring roundels instead of panels, which first appeared shortly after c1600 and was common among pieces of export blue and white porcelain recovered from the wreck of the 'Witte Leeuw', sunk in 1613.

A Ming blue and white dish, painted in pale blue and white, chipped, late 16thC, 16½in (42cm) diam.
$2,000-3,000

A late Ming blue and white saucer dish, painted with scrolling pencilled lotus washed in a greyish-blue, Wanli six-character mark and of the period, 6in (15cm) diam, fitted box.
$3,000-4,500

Two late Ming blue and white saucer dishes, fritted, Wanli, 8in (20cm) diam.
$1,500-2,500

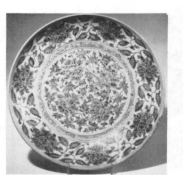

A large Ming blue and white dish, centrally painted with 4 peony heads, minutely fritted, c1500, 20in (51cm) diam.
$3,000-4,500

A Ming blue and white 'kraak porselein' dish, minor fritting, Wanli, 19½in (50.5cm) diam, fitted box.
$5,000-7,500

A late Ming blue and white 'kraak porselein' dish, small rim chips, Wanli, 14in (36cm) diam.
$3,000-4,500

A blue and white foliate saucer dish, painted in inky blue tones, slight glaze nibbles to rim, Chenghua six-character mark, Kangxi, 6½in (16.5cm) diam.
$1,200-1,750

A large blue and white dish, minutely fritted, leaf mark, Kangxi, 20in (51cm) diam.
$16,500-23,000

A pair of 'famille verte' plates, reserved on floral green ground at the border, the plain white exteriors lightly incised with leafy sprays, one chipped and with original glaze imperfections, Kangxi, 9½in (25cm) diam.
$3,000-4,000

A 'famille verte' plate, painted within an elaborate green floral ground, Kangxi, 9in (23cm).
$5,000-7,500

A Ming white glazed saucer dish, decorated in 'anhua' with a central peony, on a cruciform floral spray, chipped, encircled Jiajing six-character mark and of the period, 9in (22.5cm) diam.
$1,200-1,750

A pair of 'famille verte' dishes, boldly painted in strong enamels, one cracked, chipped, Kangxi, 14in (35.5cm) diam.
$6,000-8,000

A 'famille verte' dish, painted, with a green seeded floral border and gadrooned rim, Kangxi, 13in (33cm) diam.
$2,250-3,500

A 'famille rose' green ground tea tray, the central reserve panel calligraphically inscribed in iron red and with a date corresponding to AD 1797, painted on a pale green ground, iron red Jiaqing six-character seal mark and of the period, 6½in (16cm) wide.
$2,250-3,500

A blue and white saucer dish, six-character mark 'Qiulin Langbai ziwan' (curio belonging to Qiulin Langbai), early Kangxi, 7in (17cm) diam.
$1,500-2,500

A 'famille verte' saucer dish, reserved on an iron red cell pattern ground at the well and underglaze blue leaves at the rim, the reverse with simple flower sprays, cracked and chipped, encircled lotus mark, Kangxi, 10½in (27cm) diam.
$2,000-3,000

A yellow glazed saucer dish, incised under the mustard yellow glaze with a pair of confronted phoenix, rim crack, encircled Kangxi six-character mark and of the period, 6in (15.5cm) diam.
$1,500-2,500

An 'egg and spinach' glazed plate, with a mottled glaze of yellow, green and aubergine, the footrim reserved in the biscuit, the base white glazed, crack, some rubbing, Kangxi, 8in (20cm) diam.
$1,000-1,500

A Chinese 'famille verte' plate, decorated in typical palette with a garden scene, the rim with flower and foliage border, Kangxi, c1725, 9in (23cm).
$900-1,300

Six 'famille verte' plates, painted with an equestrian dignitary and a foot attendant, rim chips, restorations, Kangxi, 9in (22.5cm).
$4,000-5,500

Six 'famille verte' plates, painted with 5 lotus heads in iron red, yellow, black, blue and aubergine, below floral cell pattern borders, rim chips, one rim restored, Kangxi, 8½in (21cm).
$2,000-3,000

A pair of blue and white saucer dishes, boldly painted on a scale pattern ground, Kangxi, 15in (38cm) diam.
$1,500-2,500

A 'famille verte' saucer dish painted in vivid colours, border restorations, encircled Kangxi six-character mark and of the period, 9½in (24.8cm).
$4,000-5,500

A pair of blue and white saucer dishes, centrally painted below trellis ground floral panels at the compass points, one cracked, small rim chips, Kangxi, 14in (35cm) diam.
$1,500-2,500

A pair of blue and white saucer dishes, painted in the Ming style, one small rim chip, encircled Yongzheng six-character marks and of the period, 7½in (19.5cm) diam, fitted box.
$2,250-3,500

A set of 6 'famille rose' soup plates, decorated with pink and green diaper, the exterior with iron red prunus sprigs, Yongzheng, 9in (23cm).
$5,000-7,500

A blue and white dish, solidly potted and painted in the early Ming style, Yongzheng, 13in (33cm) diam.
$2,250-3,500

A 'famille rose' cockerel dish, Yongzheng, 14½in (37cm) diam.
$3,000-4,500

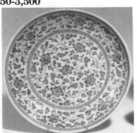

A pair of 'famille rose' saucer dishes, painted in iron red, shaded yellow, pink, white and green, one with 3 cracks, Yongzheng, 7½in (20cm) diam.
$2,500-3,500

A large 'famille rose' dish, painted after a design by Francesco Albani, within a gilt floral border, restored, Yongzheng, 16in (40cm).
$4,000-5,500

A large 'famille rose' deep saucer dish, painted with butterflies, insects and flowers, the rim gilt, encircled Yongzheng six-character mark and of the period, 21½in (54cm) diam.
$18,000-25,000

A blue and white and underglaze copper red deep dish, Qianlong seal mark and of the period, 14in (37.5cm) diam.
$4,000-5,500

A large Chinese blue and white deep dish, rim chip, Qianlong, 19in (48cm) diam.
$900-1,300

A Chinese meat dish, boldly painted in the Tobacco Leaf palette, the rim painted with a gold scrolling design on a brown band, Qianlong, 15in (38cm).
$2,500-3,500

A 'famille rose' Canton enamel yellow ground saucer dish, decorated with blue 'shou' roundels, surface wear, blue enamel Qianlong seal mark and of the period, 9in (22.5cm) diam.
$900-1,300

A 'famille rose' wavy rimmed plate, outlined in gilt against reserves of iron whorls, Qianlong, 12½in (31.5cm).
$3,000-4,000

A large blue and white saucer dish, painted in the early Ming style, the deeply cut foot unglazed, Qianlong, 15½in (39cm) diam.
$4,000-5,500

A pair of 'famille rose' meat dishes painted and gilt within a spearhead border, both cracked, Qianlong, 12½in (32cm).
$2,000-3,000

A rare Cantonese enamel 'famille rose' quatrefoil dish, painted with 3 European figures in a wooded landscape, Qianlong, 11½in (29cm) wide.
$4,000-5,500

A pair of 'famille rose' 'Judgement of Paris' plates, painted in bright enamels with the 3 goddesses Juno, Minerva and Venus, one with rim chips restored, the other minute rim chips, Qianlong, 9in (22cm).
$2,000-3,000

A large 'famille rose' dish, painted in pink, blue, green and brown, small rim chip, Qianlong, 20in (49.5cm) diam.
$3,000-4,500

A pair of 'famille rose' armorial plates, painted with a small central coat of arms and flower festoons at the border, one with minor chips, Qianlong, 9in (23cm).
$4,000-5,500

A pair of Doucai saucer dishes, painted in underglaze blue and enamelled in green, red, orange and yellow, one rim minutely chipped, Qianlong seal marks and of the period, 9½in (24cm) diam.
$5,000-7,500

A Chinese dish, the centre painted in 'famille rose' enamels, Qianlong, 16½in (41.5cm) wide.
$2,000-3,000

A pair of 'famille rose' pseudo Tobacco Leaf plates, painted with flowerheads, chrysanthemum and leaves, Qianlong, 9in (23cm).
$3,000-4,000

A pair of blue and white meat dishes, Qianlong, c1760, 14in (35.5cm) wide.
$2,000-3,000

A blue and white shaped dish, Qianlong, c1780, 10in (25cm) diam.
$750-1,000

A large blue and white saucer dish, minor rim chips, four-character mark 'yu tang jia qi' within a double circle, 17thC, 14in (35.5cm) diam.
$3,000-4,500

The mark reads 'fine vessel for jade hall'.

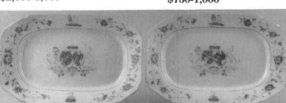

A pair of 'famille rose' dishes, decorated with the arms of the Duke of Grafton, one chipped, Qianlong, 10in (25.5cm).
$2,000-3,000

Two blue and white European design plates in the Japanese style copying a Dutch Delft original, in the manner of Frederik van Frytom, the pattern traditionally known as Deshima Island, one chipped, the other fritted, one with imitation Japanese spur marks, late 17th/early 18thC, 7½in (19cm).
$1,300-2,000

A blue and white European subject plate, painted after the Dutch draftsman Cornelius Pronk with the design 'la dame au parasol', c1737, 8½in (22cm).
$9,000-12,500

Six dessert plates with pierced borders, painted in green and white on iron red bands, 5 with cracks, 2 chipped, late Qianlong/Jiaqing, 7½in (19cm).
$1,000-1,500

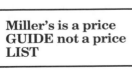

Miller's is a price GUIDE not a price LIST

A pair of small Wucai dishes, painted in underglaze blue, green, iron red and mustard yellow enamels, minutely fritted, 17thC, 5½in (13.5cm) diam.
$2,000-3,000

Garden Seats

A late Ming blue and white garden seat with lion mask handles, some restoration, Wanli, 15in (38cm).
$4,000-5,500

A Komai dish, richly decorated in takazogan and Komai numezogan, signed in a rectangular seal 'Kyoto ju Komai sei', 19in (48cm) diam.
$20,000-28,000

A Satsuma pottery plaque, decorated with shaped panels of figures dancing and feasting, 19thC, 14in (35.5cm) diam.
$1,500-2,500

A pair of Guangdong stoneware barrel shaped garden seats, the mask handles and pierced sides covered in blue, green and cream glazes, 19thC, 20in (50cm).
$2,000-3,000

A Canton 'famille rose' garden seat, painted with panels of figures and birds and pierced with double cash, between bands of moulded bosses on a ground of dense floral meander, late Qing Dynasty, 18½in (47cm).
$3,000-4,500

A Chinese blue glazed pierced garden seat, moulded in white relief, 19thC, 20in (50cm).
$1,200-1,750

A pair of 'famille rose' and 'famille verte' barrel shaped garden seats, decorated on a closely patterned gilt ground, 19thC, 18½in (47cm).
$7,000-10,000

A Canton 'famille rose' garden seat, decorated on a dense gilt floral ground, late Qing Dynasty, 18½in (47cm).
$3,000-4,000

Jardinières

A Longquan celadon jardinière, the sides moulded with flowerheads, all covered in a rich green glaze thinning around the edges, cracked, Yuan/Ming Dynasty, 9½in (24cm) diam, wood stand, fitted box.
$1,300-2,000

A pair of Chinese 'famille rose' jardinières and stands, brightly decorated with alternate panels of inscriptions and Immortals, Daoguang seal marks and of the period, 9½in (24cm).
$2,000-3,000

A massive blue and white jardinière, applied with 2 brown and gilt lion mask handles, rim chipped, 18thC, 25½in (64cm) diam, wood stand.
$7,500-10,500

A Satsuma jardinière, Meiji period.
$750-1,000

A Chinese blue and white porcelain jardinière, decorated with panels of landscape vignettes alternating with peonies, lotus and chrysanthemum, 18thC, 9in (23cm).
$3,000-4,500

A Canton jardinière and stand, with reserves on a gold decorated blue ground, the inside of the stand decorated with butterflies, fruit and flowers, stand repaired, jardinière 16in (41cm) diam.
$1,500-2,500

A pair of 'famille rose' jardinières, painted and enamelled in reserves with birds and flowering blossoms on floral grounds and pierced bases, one damaged, 10½in (26cm) diam.
$5,000-7,500

Jars

A green glazed jar, some restoration, Han Dynasty, 7½in (19.8cm) diam.
$2,000-3,000

A glazed pottery baluster jar, in brown and blue chevrons, on an olive and straw streaky ground over a white slip, both slip and glaze stopping irregularly above the crisp recessed foot, some restoration, Tang Dynasty, 8in (20.5cm).
$6,000-9,000

A Longquan celadon funerary jar and cover, with a widely crackled bluish green glaze, crack, finial damage, Southern Song Dynasty, 7in (18cm), stand, fitted box.
$4,000-5,500

A spotted Jizhou jar, covered with a black glaze and grey spots, rising to a wide neck and an everted lip, the base glazed, chips, Southern Song Dynasty, 7½in (18.5cm).
$2,250-3,500

A Transitional blue and white oviform jar, painted in inky blue tones with a continuous scene from Sanguo Yanyi (Romance of the Three Kingdoms), with 'anhua' bands, c1640, 12in (30cm).
$3,000-4,500

A Ming blue and white jar and cover, c1650.
$1,300-2,000

A Ming white glazed jar, with an even milky white glaze, some wear, Jiajing six-character mark in a double square and of the period, 5in (12.5cm), fitted box.
$4,000-5,500

A large Ming blue and white baluster jar, 'guan', painted in brilliant violet tones, the rim bound in metal, cracks, Jiajing six-character mark and of the period, 13in (33cm).
$6,000-9,000

A Ming blue and white oviform jar, painted in bright tones, with dot lappets at the foot and cloud and pendant dot lappets at the shoulder, the tapering neck with stylised wave motifs, restored, Jiajing six-character mark and of the period, 9in (23cm).
$4,000-5,500

A Ming white glazed squat jar, lightly incised under the glaze with 2 phoenix, encircled Jiajing six-character mark and of the period, 4in (10.5cm).
$3,000-4,500

A Ming Wucai jar, painted with 8 boys at play, some surface fritting, base star crack and short neck crack, encircled Wanli six-character mark and of the period, 5in (12.5cm).
$15,000-21,000

A rare 'famille rose' armorial jar, painted in black, gilt and iron red, feather scroll at the lowest point, foot restored, c1720, 8in (20.5cm).
$6,000-9,000

A pair of blue and white square jars, with white metal mounted necks, edges fritted and chipped, body crack, Kangxi, 10½in (26.5cm).
$1,300-2,000

A pair of blue and white jars, painted in a bright blue, Kangxi, 8½in (22cm), wood covers and stands.
$5,000-7,500

A pair of blue and white square tea jars and covers, painted within borders of trellis pattern divided by 'ruyi' lappets at the corners, chipped, one cover damaged, Kangxi, 11½in (29.5cm).
$10,000-13,500

A pair of 'famille verte' jars, painted in reserve with 2 vertical panels of 'bajixiang', drilled bases, one chipped, one cracked, Kangxi, 12½in (31cm), wood covers and stands.
$7,000-10,000

A Chinese blue and white baluster jar, painted with Buddhistic lions playing with brocade balls below a border of emblems, Kangxi, 12½in (31.5cm).
$2,000-3,000

Two blue and white baluster jars, freely painted, one neck with minor damage, Kangxi, 13in (33cm).
$2,000-3,000

A Transitional Wucai baluster jar and domed cover with knop finial, cover rim chip and finial restored, mid-17thC, 16in (40.5cm).
$5,000-7,500

An ormolu mounted 'famille rose' jar and cover, on a pink ground, the porcelain c1800, 22in (55cm).
$3,000-4,500

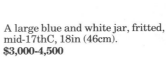

A large blue and white jar, fritted, mid-17thC, 18in (46cm).
$3,000-4,500

Tea & Coffee Pots & Services

An export part tea service, painted in extensive 'grisaille', iron red and gilt, comprising: teapot and cover, cream jug and cover, spoon tray, 6 teabowls and saucers, old damage, Yongzheng/early Qianlong, and a teapot, possibly decorated in Holland, and 2 saucers, cracked, Qianlong.
$2,000-3,000

An export teapot and cover, painted to each side 'en grisaille' and gilt, the cover with a peach finial within iron red husk and simple green enamel bands, chips to spout and cover, some enamel flaking, Qianlong, 9½in (23.5cm) wide.
$1,000-1,500

A Chinese export teapot and cover, Qianlong, 5in (12.5cm).
$400-550

Tureens

A 'famille rose' and blue and white tureen and domed cover, cover chipped, Qianlong, 11½in (28.5cm) wide.
$9,000-12,500

A pair of 'famille rose' jars and covers, painted with phoenix, magpies, cranes and other birds, among trees and chrysanthemum issuing from rockwork, one damaged, 17in (43cm).
$1,000-1,500

A pair of Imari jars, painted on an inky blue ground, one cover damaged, early 18thC, 10½in (26cm).
$1,300-2,000

A Chinese export miniature part tea service, painted in bright enamel colours, comprising: a teapot and cover, 2 teabowls, 2 cups and 8 saucers, slight glaze chipping, Qianlong.
$1,300-2,000

A 'famille rose' teapot and cover, the cover with small knop finial enamelled in yellow, Qianlong, 4½in (12cm).
$450-700

A 'famille rose' teapot and cover, restoration to lower spout and body, c1760, 6in (15cm).
$4,000-5,500 ▶

A Satsuma wine pot and cover, late 19thC, 4½in (12cm) wide.
$800-1,200

IMARI PATTERNS
- ★ Imari named after port of shipment
- ★ decoration of Japanese porcelain often based on brocade patterns
- ★ made at Arita, Hizen Province, from early 18thC to early 19thC
- ★ Imari patterns copied and adapted by Derby, Worcester, Spode, Minton, Mason and others
- ★ patterns also made in China

A miniature partridge tureen and cover, moulded and painted in black and iron red with realistic feather markings, small chips, tail restored, Qianlong, 3in (8cm) wide.
$2,250-3,500

A Chinese white glazed tureen and cover, the base with rabbit's head handles, the cover with pierced crown finial, Qianlong, 12in (30cm).
$4,500-7,000

A blue and white soup tureen and cover, c1760, Qianlong, 10½in (26cm).
$4,000-5,500

A pair of blue and white bombé tureens and covers, one painted in slightly darker tones than the other, one cover restored, late 18thC, 14½in (37cm) wide.
$4,000-5,500

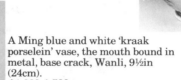

A blue and white tureen and cover, frits to the handles, 18thC, 10½in (26cm) wide.
$2,000-3,000

Vases

A 'famille rose' tureen and cover, with iron red bud finial and pairs of lion mask handles suspending metal loops, late Qing Dynasty, 14½in (36.5cm) diam.
$4,500-7,000

A Nanking vegetable dish with boars head handles, the cover with fruit finial, Chien Lung, 14in (35.5cm) wide.
$2,000-3,000

A Ming blue and white 'kraak porselein' vase, the mouth bound in metal, base crack, Wanli, 9½in (24cm).
$1,000-1,500

A Chinese blue and white double gourd vase, Wanli, 10½in (26cm).
$1,000-1,500

A Transitional blue and white bottle vase with garlic neck, c1640, 14in (35cm), wood stand, fitted box.
$5,500-7,750

A pair of late Ming blue and white vases, meiping, minor fritting, Wanli/Tianqi, 10½in (27cm), wood stands, fitted boxes.
$5,000-7,500

A late Ming blue and white vase with 4 mask handles to the shoulder, cracks to neck, Wanli, 10in (25.5cm).
$600-900

A metallic brown glazed vase, the glaze stopping above the deeply cut recessed brown washed pale stoneware foot, 18thC, 3½in (9cm).
$3,000-4,500

143

A Japanese Arita vase, decorated in blue, some damage, 17thC, 19in (48cm).
$2,000-3,000

A blue and white vase, painted in grey-blue, rim probably polished, Kangxi, 10in (25cm), wood stand, fitted box.
$1,500-2,500

A blue and white celadon ground vase, meiping, lightly moulded and painted with 3 Immortals including 'Shoulao', minor glaze crack near luting line, Kangxi, 15½in (39cm).
$2,500-3,500

A 'famille rose' relief moulded square baluster vase, painted in colours, some damage, Yongzheng/Qianlong, 20in (51cm), lamp fitting.
$3,000-4,500

A Dehua blanc-de-chine sleeve vase, incised and applied with relief lion masks, under a pale creamy ivory glaze, the broad foot unglazed, Kangxi, 9½in (24.5cm).
$3,000-4,500

A Dehua blanc-de-chine gu-shaped beaker vase, 17th/18thC, 15½in (39.5cm), the interior with a lamp fitting.
$10,000-13,500

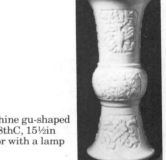

A pair of Imari vases and covers, painted with panels of flowering plants, the covers with 'shi-shi' knops, early 18thC, 10in (25cm).
$1,000-1,500

A large sang-de-boef hu-shaped vase, under a rich glaze firing white at the angles, c1800, 17in (43cm).
$2,000-3,000

A Doucai vase, meiping, delicately pencilled in underglaze blue and enamelled in pale green, yellow, aubergine and coral red, repaired, 18thC, 14in (35.5cm).
$1,200-1,750

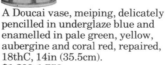

A tall bottle vase, by S Ichino, covered in a pale bluish white glaze with iron brown flecks, impressed Ichino character and St. Ives seals, Yingqing, 12½in (31.5cm).
$200-350

A Satsuma trumpet vase, enamelled in gossu blue, green and iron red and gilt, small rim flake, 19thC, 9in (23cm).
$700-900

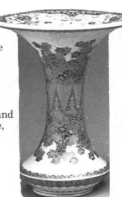

A large Canton 'famille rose' vase, with trumpet neck, cracked, early 19thC, 28in (71.5cm).
$2,250-3,500

A baluster vase, in iron red painted on powder blue ground, 19thC, 17in (43cm).
$1,200-1,750

A pair of 'famille verte' yellow ground vases, painted on a mustard yellow ground, 19thC, 14in (35cm), wood stands.
$4,000-5,500

A cloisonné vase, decorated with birds and flowers on a blue ground, damaged, 19thC, 21in (53cm).
$3,000-4,500

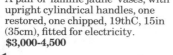

A pair of 'famille jaune' vases, with upright cylindrical handles, one restored, one chipped, 19thC, 15in (35cm), fitted for electricity.
$3,000-4,500

A pair of Canton 'famille rose' vases, applied on the sides of the neck and shoulder with 6 relief dragons, 19thC, 22½in (57.5cm).
$6,000-8,000

A Satsuma vase of faceted form, painted with alternate panels containing vases of flowers or blossom between a lappet foot and shoulder, 19thC, 9½in (24.5cm).
$6,000-8,000

A pair of 'famille rose' pink ground baluster vases and domed covers, with crouching lion cub finials and blue enamel lion mask fixed ring handles, late Qing Dynasty, 19in (48.5cm).
$5,000-7,500

A robin's-egg glazed double gourd vase, standing on a slightly recessed base, the gilt rim with 3 circular apertures, Daoguang, 3½in (8cm).
$700-900

A 'famille rose' vase painted in blue, puce, yellow and gilt, star crack to base, iron red Jiaqing seal mark, 15in (38cm).
$3,000-4,500

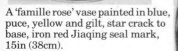

A pair of 'famille verte' vases, one vase with hairline at rim, 19thC, 18in (45cm).
$1,200-1,750

A blue and white vase, painted with a dignitary and attendants receiving 3 officials upon a walled terrace, 19thC, 17½in (44cm).
$1,000-1,500

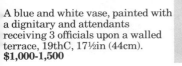

A pair of Japanese porcelain polychrome vases, late 19thC, 11in (28cm).
$600-900

A pair of Imari vases, painted all over, gilded and enamelled in typical palette with birds of paradise, prunus and dragons, 18in (45.5cm).
$3,000-4,500

◀ An Imari vase and cover, with Dog of Fo finial, 22in (56cm).
$900-1,300

A pair of Canton vases, brightly painted with panels, late 19thC, 15in (38cm).
$1,300-2,000

A blue Imari vase decorated with storks, 48in (122cm).
$1,500-2,500

A near matching pair of Japanese vases, 22in (57cm).
$1,200-1,750

A pair of Japanese slender cloisonné vases, decorated with hanging pendants of 'ho-o' below bands of stylised flowers and emblems, 9½in (24cm).
$750-1,000

A Chinese blue and white cinquefoil tulip vase, 9½in (24cm).
$1,200-1,750

A pair of Japanese cloisonné vases, finely enamelled with birds and orchids, 14½in (37cm).
$1,500-2,500

A pair of Canton vases, reserved on a gold ground painted with flowers, foliage and moths, some damage, 23in (60cm), wood stands.
$7,000-10,000

A Chinese blue and white vase, brightly decorated with ducks and a kingfisher, and flowering plants, Transitional, 10in (25cm).
$3,000-4,500

A pair of 'famille rose' vases, 18in (45.5cm).
$5,000-7,500

A pair of 'famille rose' vases, with grounds of pink, turquoise, blue, yellow and brown, 22½in (57cm).
$3,000-4,500

Miscellaneous

A blue and white and underglaze copper red box and cover, painted in a strong blue on a moulded panel, four-character hallmark to base, Qing Dynasty, 3½in (8cm) wide.
$5,500-7,750

The hallmark reads 'Xingtang Qingwan'.

A Canton 'famille rose' enamel plaque, inscribed with the letters 'PASDIA'(?), restored, early Qianlong, 7in (18cm).
$3,000-4,500

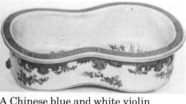

A Chinese blue and white violin shaped bidet, Qianlong, 22in (56cm) long.
$3,000-4,500

A pair of Chinese blue and white candlesticks, painted with Buddhist emblems and mythological birds flying amongst clouds, some damage, 10in (25cm).
$600-900

A 'famille verte' biscuit porcelain grotto, in aubergine, yellow and green and daubed in the 'egg and spinach' style around the perimeter of the exterior, slight damage and restoration, Kangxi, 7in (18cm).
$2,500-3,500

A pair of blue and white silver-shaped candlesticks, one stem restored, Qianlong, 7½in (19cm).
$4,000-5,500

A 'famille rose' Meissen style stand, painted in shades of brown and iron red imitating bark, turquoise, green, yellow and pink, minor damage, c1775, 12in (30cm), mounted in pierced gilt-metal as a table lamp.
$1,500-2,500

A 'famille verte' joss stick holder, Kangxi, c1720.
$450-700

An ormolu mounted Chinese 'famille rose' brush pot, painted in colours including puce, yellow, black and shades of blue, the porcelain Yongzheng, the mounts stamped E. F. Caldwell Co., Inc., New York, 7½in (19cm) diam.
$7,000-10,000

A 'famille rose' stupa reliquary, painted with lotus and Buddhistic lion masks on a deep blue ground, the base painted in iron red and gilt, the top mounted with an enamelled copper lotus supporting a lapis lazuli sphere, slightly chipped, mid Qing Dynasty, 12in (30cm).
$1,200-1,750

A blue and white model of a well bucket, painted with wrythen panels of various diapering, blue four-character mark, 18½in (47cm).
$1,000-1,500

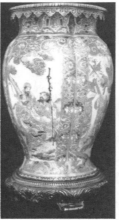

A pair of Chinese blue and white tea caddies and domed covers, 6in (15cm).
$1,200-1,750

A Satsuma pottery gilt bronze mounted oil lamp base, finely enamelled and gilded, lacking oil lamp receiver, 12in (30.5cm).
$900-1,300

A Cizhou white glazed oval pillow, the curving top incised to an ochre slip with a young boy holding a lotus spray, all under a finely crackled glaze over a white slip pooling at the edges, Song Dynasty, 8in (20cm) wide.
$2,500-3,500

A blue and white fan shaped water dropper, Yi Dynasty, 2½in (6cm) wide.
$750-1,000

A Cizhou pillow, modelled as a recumbent tiger, with bold deep brown stripes on a salmon brown ground, the head rest with an ivory white ground, minor chips, Jin Dynasty, 15in (38cm) wide.
$2,500-3,500

A white glazed water dropper, in the form of a young boy on the back of a seated buffalo, irregularly splashed with iron spots, Yuan Dynasty, 3½in (8.5cm) long, fitted box.
$2,000-3,000

A pair of coral glazed water pots, in the form of conjoined tomatoes, Qing Dynasty, 4in (10cm) wide, wood stands.
$1,000-1,500

A rare Ming blue and white tablet, with arched top painted with a border of foliate scrolls, a pair of phoenix contesting a flaming pearl above a horizontal calligraphic band and 11 smaller vertical bands, firing crack, some glaze degradation to lower part, inscribed Jiajing 34th Year corresponding to AD 1555 and of the period, 13½in (34cm).
$6,000-8,000

A 'famille rose' candle holder, painted in pink, blue and green, with a long tailed bird, painted in green, salmon and blue enamel perched to one side, minor damage to extremities, Qianlong, 5½in (13.5cm) wide.
$4,000-5,500

A dark olive glazed double gourd rosewater sprinkler, under an even shiny glaze thinning to a pale celadon at the rim of the neck and pooling between the gourds and at the base, traces of gilding remaining, minute rim glaze crack, 17th/18thC, 11in (28cm).
$2,000-3,000

A blue and white brush pot, painted in a rich blue with 2 rectangular panels, Kangxi, 5½in (13.5cm).
$2,000-3,000

A blue and white centrepiece, modelled after a Meissen original, fritting, cracked, restoration, Qianlong, 15in (38cm).
$2,000-3,000

Chinese dynasties and marks

Earlier Dynasties

Shang Yin, c.1532-1027 B.C.
Western Zhou (Chou) 1027-770 B.C.
Spring and Autumn Annals 770-480 B.C.
Warring States 484-221 B.C.
Qin (Ch'in) 221-206 B.C.
Western Han 206 BC-24 AD
Eastern Han 25-220
Three Kingdoms 221-265
Six Dynasties 265-589
Wei 386-557

Sui 589-617
Tang (T'ang) 618-906
Five Dynasties 907-960
Liao 907-1125
Sung 960-1280
Chin 1115-1260
Yüan 1280-1368

Ming Dynasty

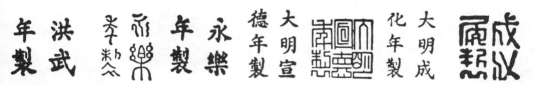

Hongwu (Hung Wu)
1368-1398

Yongle (Yung Lo)
1403-1424

Xuande (Hsüan Té)
1426-1435

Chenghua (Ch'éng Hua)
1465-1487

Hongzhi
(Hung Chih)
1488-1505)

Zhengde
(Chéng Té)
1506-1521

Jiajing
(Chia Ching)
1522-1566

Longqing
(Lung Ching)
1567-1572

Wanli (Wan Li)
1573-1620

Tianqi
(Tien Chi)
1621-1627

Chongzhen
(Ch'ung Chêng)
1628-1644

Qing (Ch'ing) Dynasty

Shunzhi
(Shun Chih)
1644-1661

Kangxi (K'ang Hsi)
1662-1722

Yongzheng (Yung Chêng)
1723-1735

Qianlong (Ch'ien Lung)
1736-1795'

Jiaqing (Chia Ch'ing)
1796-1820

Daoguang (Tao Kuang)
1821-1850

Xianfeng (Hsien Féng)
1851-1861

Tongzhi (T'ung Chih)
1862-1874

Guangxu (Kuang Hsu)
1875-1908

Xuantong
(Hsuan T'ung)
1909-1911

Hongxian
(Hung Hsien)
1916

149

Bottles

A condiment bottle, with plain lozenge stopper, c1780.
$150-250

An English blue engraved port decanter, c1800, 9in (23cm).
$1,500-2,500

An amethyst onion shaped bottle decanter, c1830, 11in (28cm).
$400-550

An amethyst apothecary jar, c1840, 15in (38cm).
$600-900

Three blue apothecary bottles, c1860, 9in (23cm).
$60-100

A pair of bottle green pharmacy jars, c1840, 12in (30.5cm).
$300-500

Bowls

A Jacobite glass bowl, engraved with the words 'God Bless Prince Charles', 9in (23cm).
$1,000-1,500

A bowl with applied blue rim, c1800, 6in (15cm) diam.
$100-200

A sweetmeat bowl with facet knopped stem and egg-and-dart border, c1800, 6½in (16cm).
$450-700

A cut glass turnover fruit bowl, damage, 18thC, 9in (23cm).
$900-1,300

A pair of 'Lynn' finger bowls and one stand, c1775, the bowls 4½in (12cm) diam.
$450-700

A well cut bowl with turnover rim, c1820, 13in (33cm) diam.
$1,500-2,500

An Irish ovoid cut dish with prism cutting and serrated rim, fan cut handles, c1800, 9in (22.5cm) wide.
$300-400

Four rinsers, double lipped with honeycomb moulding, c1830, 5in (12.5cm).
$45-75

A pair of cut fruit bowls with strawberry and cross cut diamonds, and fan cut rims, c1830, 6½in (17cm).
$700-900

A set of 3 salts and stands, with panels of strawberry diamonds and prism cutting, c1830, 3in (7.5cm).
$300-500

A fine cut covered bowl on pedestal base, c1840, 14in (35cm).
$800-1,200

A set of 6 star-cut finger bowls, c1860, 2½in (6.5cm).
$300-400

A set of 9 trailed glass bowls and under-dishes, c1880.
$600-900

A Cork Glass Co engraved finger bowl, impressed mark to base, early 19thC, 5in (13cm) diam.
$1,300-2,000

Candelabra

A diamond facet cut taperstick, with bladed collar and base knop, c1770, 6½in (16.5cm).
$800-1,200

An Irish candlestick with hollow stem, on lemon squeezer base, c1800, 6½in (17cm).
$400-550

A pair of cut candlesticks with prism and flute cut sockets, diamond and ladder cut stems and step cut feet, c1810, 9in (22.5cm).
$1,200-1,750

An opaque twist taper stick, c1765, 7½in (18.5cm).
$5,000-7,500

A pair of Regency bronze candle lustres in the shape of cranes, 9in (23cm).
$700-900

A pair of glass candlesticks, with faceted stem and hexagonal knop, the nozzle with petal cut rim, early 19thC, 10in (25.5cm).
$1,000-1,500

A pair of Regency cut glass and ormolu candelabra, the nozzles on oblong trip tray, supported on twin scrolling gilt arms with grotesque eagle heads.
$5,000-7,500

A pair of Regency ormolu and cut glass three-light candelabra, the faceted shafts flanked by scrolling foliate branches, adapted and restored, 17½in (44.5cm).
$4,000-5,500

Decanters

l. & r. A pair of blue decanters with lunar cut stoppers, c1800, 9½in (24cm).
$1,300-2,000
c. A smaller decanter with bevelled lozenge stopper, c1800, 8½in (21.5cm).
$450-700

A pale green decanter with steeple shaped stopper, c1840, 14in (35.5cm).
$300-500

A pair of honeycomb moulded decanters, c1830, 11½in (29cm).
$400-550

A swag cut decanter, c1820, 9½in (24cm).
$200-350

A pair of English chrysoprase decanters, with original stoppers, c1840, 12in (30.5cm).
$800-1,200

A decanter with 'A.M' monogram within a laurel leaf circle, c1780, 9½in (24cm).
$600-900

Two ovoid shaped decanters:
l. Flute cut with lozenge stopper, c1810, 8½in (21.5cm).
$300-500
r. Plain with target stopper, engraved 'M', c1800, 9in (22cm).
$300-500

Two decanters with cut mushroom stoppers, c1810, 8½in (22cm).
$300-500

A pair of Georgian decanters, c1820.
$900-1,300

A pair of papier mâché coasters, c1820.
$600-900

l. & r. A pair of Irish decanters with spiral neck rings and lozenge stoppers, c1790, 9½in (23.5cm).
$1,500-2,500
c. An unusual Irish barrel shaped decanter with alternate panels of cut diamonds and sunbursts, c1810, 8in (20cm).
$800-1,200

A papier mâché coaster with gilt decoration, c1810, 5in (12.8cm) diam.
$150-250

A set of 3 Georgian green decanters, 8½in (22cm).
$1,000-1,500

A pair of decanters with 3 cut neck rings and target stoppers, c1815, 8½in (21.5cm).
$1,200-1,750

A set of 3 Georgian decanters in blue, with stand, c1800, 9½in (24cm).
$1,200-1,750

Drinking Glasses

An early ale glass, the wrythen bowl set on a propellor stem and folded conical foot, c1700.
$1,500-2,500

A wrythen moulded ale glass, the body on a short collared stem, c1690, 6in (15.3cm).
$700-900

Three dwarf wrythen moulded ale glasses, on folded conical feet, c1745, 4½ to 5in (11.5 to 13cm).
$400-550

Two champagne flutes, c1800, 7½in (19cm).
$60-100

A wrythen ale glass, engraved with a thistle, c1740.
$100-200

An ale glass, the stem with shoulder and basal knops enclosing an elongated tear, on a folded conical foot, c1730, 6in (15cm).
$800-1,200

A set of 6 dwarf ale glasses, moulded and engraved with hops and barley, c1810.
$600-900

A set of 8 facet cut ale glasses, engraved with hops, 7½in (19cm).
$600-900

A champagne glass on a Silesian stem and folded domed foot, c1750, 5½in (14.5cm).
$900-1,300

An ale glass with funnel bowl, on a stem with collar, 2 knops and multiple spiral air-twist, c1750, 7½in (19cm).
$600-900

An ale glass, the engraved bowl on a stem with multiple spiral air-twist and 2 knops, plain conical foot, c1750, 7½in (18cm).
$900-1,300

An unusual wine glass with honeycomb moulded bowl, on a plain stem with elongated tear and conical foot, c1745.
$900-1,300

A wine glass, the bowl on a stem with mercury air-twist, on plain conical foot, c1750, 6½in (17cm).
$450-700

A baluster wine glass, with tear in base on a drop-knop above a true baluster stem and domed and folded foot, c1700.
$1,200-1,750

A mercury-twist wine glass, the drawn bowl on a double spiral air-twist stem and conical foot, c1750.
$600-900

A Jacobite air-twist wine glass of drawn trumpet shape, engraved and inscribed with the motto 'Fiat', the stem filled with spiral threads above a conical foot, c1750, 6½in (17cm).
$1,500-2,500

A dark blue/green tint wine glass, the bucket shaped bowl lightly ribbed and drawn from a plain stem, on a plain foot, 18th/early 19thC, 6in (15cm).
$400-550

A wine glass with waisted bucket bowl, on plain conical foot, c1745, 6½in (16cm).
$450-700

A composite stem wine glass, with bell bowl on a stem with multiple spiral air-twist, above a beaded air-knop, and plain section with base knop, c1750, 6½in (16.5cm).
$800-1,200

A wine glass, the stem with multiple spiral air-twist and vermicular collar, c1750, 6½in (16.5cm).
$800-1,200

A wine glass with bell bowl, on a shoulder knopped multiple spiral air-twist stem, and folded conical foot, c1750, 7in (18cm).
$300-500

A dram glass, with engraved bowl, on a double series opaque twist stem and thickened plain foot, c1760.
$450-700

A Newcastle engraved composite stemmed goblet, with 2 knops above a hexagonally moulded pedestal section and basal knop, on a folded conical foot, mid-18thC, 6½in (16.5cm).
$600-900

A set of 6 deep green drinking glasses, on swelling knopped stems, 5in (12cm).
$400-550

An engraved wine glass, on plain conical foot, c1750, 6½in (16cm).
$1,500-2,500

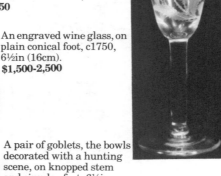

A pair of goblets, the bowls decorated with a hunting scene, on knopped stem and circular foot, 6½in (17cm).
$250-350

A façon-de-Venise engraved goblet, on a tapering hollow stem and plain foot, Liège or France, c1800, 5in (13cm).
$400-550

An engraved ratafia glass, with double series opaque twist stem, plain conical foot, c1760, 7in (17.5cm).
$900-1,300

A large suite of table glass, engraved below a decorated gold band, comprising: 12 goblets with conical bowls, 8½in (22cm), and 67 matching glasses.
$3,000-4,500

A light green export wine glass, the stem with an inverted baluster knop and ball knops, c1760, 5½in (13.5cm).
$400-550

A cut bowl goblet, c1820, 4½in (11.5cm).
$100-200

l. and r. Three barrel shaped rummers with looped laurel leaf decoration, and cushion knop stems, c1820, 4½in (11.5cm).
$300-400
r. A similar rummer with double ogee bowl, c1820, 5in (12cm).
$100-200

l. A balustroid wine glass, with engraved ogee bowl and ball knop, 5in (14cm).
$400-550

c. A balustroid wine glass, with hatched rose decoration, and ball knop, 6in (15cm).
$400-550

r. A balustroid wine glass with hatched loop decoration and swelling knop, 5½in (14.5cm).
$400-550

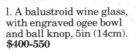

A Netherlandish flute with wrythen moulded funnel bowl, the stem with spiral pincered ornament above a wrythen moulded conical foot, 18thC, 6½in (16cm).
$600-900

A baluster goblet, the funnel bowl on an inverted baluster stem and folded conical foot, c1700.
$1,500-2,500

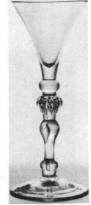

A light baluster wine glass with a trumpet shaped bowl, inverted baluster section enclosing a tear and basal knop, on a conical foot, c1750, 7½in (18.5cm).
$1,000-1,500

A wine glass, with trumpet bowl, on a stem with air-tear and ball knop, c1740, 5½in (13.5cm).
$1,200-1,750

A heavy baluster wine glass, on a stem with inverted baluster and base ball knops, c1700, 5½in (14cm).
$1,500-2,500

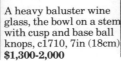

A heavy baluster wine glass, the bowl on a stem with cusp and base ball knops, c1710, 7in (18cm).
$1,300-2,000

A Newcastle glass, Dutch engraved with leaf and fruit design, c1745, 8½in (21.5cm).
$1,200-1,750

A Lynn tumbler, c1800, 2½in (6cm).
$150-250

A tumbler engraved with Sunderland bridge and a ship beneath, inscribed 'Sunderland Bridge', with hops and barley decoration, c1810, 4in (10cm).
$450-700

A Mary Gregory glass tumbler, c1880, 3½in (8.5cm).
$75-150

A large Masonic goblet, engraved with Masonic emblems, initials and dated 1840, for the Scottish, Scoon & Perth No. 3. Lodge, 6½in (17cm).
$600-900

A Dutch goblet, engraved with a bird above a basket of flowers, set on a baluster stem and folded conical foot, 8½in (21.5cm).
$450-700

A Bavarian goblet, engraved on one side with a woman and a wolf in a landscape, reserved within an inscribed band, on a foliate engraved conical foot, 7in (18cm).
$700-900

A pair of Bohemian amber goblets, with numerous Rhineland scenes, 9in (23cm).
$2,000-3,000

A rummer, engraved with a barons coronet and the initials 'RDR', the reverse side with initials 'CR', capstan stem and plain foot, c1830, 5½in (13.5cm).
$400-550

A Masonic rummer, engraved with 3 panels of Masonic symbols and monogram 'IHG', on a domed lemon squeezer foot, c1800, 5in (12.5cm).
$600-900

An Absolon rummer with emerald green tint, the ovoid bowl decorated in gilt, heightened in black, inscribed above 'Success to......' the reverse inscribed 'A Trifle from Yarmouth', gilding rubbed, c1800, 5in (12cm).
$1,000-1,500

A set of 7 rummers, engraved with egg and tulip decoration, on domed lemon squeezer feet, c1800, 5½in (13cm).
$2,000-3,000

l. A rummer, the ovoid bowl engraved with band of laurel leaves and bows, c1810, 4½in (11.5cm).
$100-200

c. A rummer, engraved 'I.M.Lang', with capstan stem, c1800, 5½in (14cm).
$250-350

r. An ovoid bowl rummer, c1810, 4½in (11.5cm).
$150-250

A well cut Georgian rummer, c1825, 5in (13cm).
$75-150

A large bucket shaped Orange Lodge rummer, flute cut with Masonic symbols, on short knopped stem, c1825, 9in (22.5cm).
$400-550

A sweetmeat with honeycomb moulded bowl, on a stem with coarse incised twist, plain conical foot, c1750, 5½in (14cm).
$1,000-1,500

A Masonic rummer, engraved with various Masonic symbols and 'PSP' and 'CSK', the reverse with 'Joined Nov 25th, 1840, Lodge No. 5', Perth Lodge, with star cut foot, 6½in (17cm).
$1,000-1,500

A Masonic rummer, engraved with symbols, dated 1848, 5½in (14cm).
$300-400

A sweetmeat, with double ogee bowl, on a stem with double series opaque twist, on domed and folded foot, c1760, 5½in (14.5cm).
$1,000-1,500

A baluster toastmaster's glass, set on an inverted baluster stem enclosing a tear above a folded conical foot, c1710, 4½in (12cm).
$700-900

A German Royal Armorial goblet and a cover, engraved with the motto and arms of England as borne by King George I, goblet slightly criselled, the glass perhaps Thuringia, the engraving Potsdam, c1725, 12½in (32cm).
$3,000-4,500

A German engraved colour-twist double bowl goblet, the 2 opposing bowls joined by a wrythen moulded section enclosing entwined dark blue and white thread, late 18thC, 9in (22.5cm).
$700-900

Flasks

A sweetmeat, with rib moulded bowl, pedestal stem with star studded shoulders, c1750, 6in (15.5cm).
$800-1,200

A cranberry flask in a boot shape, c1870, 10½in (26cm) long.
$300-500

A flask of flattened oviform, with short neck and everted rim, minor chipping to trailing, c1695, 5½in (13.5cm).
$1,000-1,500

Jelly Glasses

A two-handled jelly glass, with gadrooned bowl and domed foot, c1760, 4in (10cm).
$200-350

A jelly glass, with applied double loop handles, some damage to bowl, c1720.
$400-550

A set of 5 bonnet glasses, with egg and tulip engraved decoration, c1800, 3½in (10cm).
$300-500

Three jelly glasses with hexagonal bowls, mid-18thC.
$250-350

A cut cream jug, with diamond and prismatic cutting and star cut base, c1820.
$450-700

A jelly glass with thumb facets, and applied handle, c1880, 3½in (9cm).
$30-50

A bonnet glass with scalloped foot, 3in (7.5cm).
$100-200

A water jug, cut with vertical and horizontal prism, c1830, 8in (20.5cm).
$400-550

Jugs

A Georgian jug, blow moulded with wide tape handle, c1800, 7in (18cm).
$300-500

A water jug with flute, prism and diamond cutting, and cut strap handle, c1810, 7in (17.5cm).
$300-500

A water jug, with diamond and prism cutting, and scalloped rim, c1825, 6½in (16cm).
$400-550

A cream jug with prismatic, diamond and facet cutting, c1820.
$400-550

A pair of wine jugs, with flute cut necks and bodies, c1860, 7in (18cm).
$250-350

A jug, c1840, 8½in (21.5cm).
$300-500

A ruby trailed glass ewer, with
applied snake trim.
$300-500

A Victorian jug and lid, engraved
with floral decoration, c1870, 5½in
(14cm).
$100-200

Paperweights

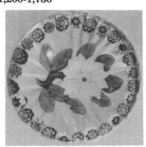

A Baccarat dated scattered
millefiori weight, with a cane
inscribed 'B1848', 3in (7cm) diam.
$1,200-1,750

A Baccarat garlanded white double
clematis weight, on a star cut base,
2½in (6.5cm) diam.
$1,200-1,750

A Stourbridge lemonade set,
consisting of jug and 2 goblets,
engraved with convolvulus
decoration, c1880, jug 13in (33cm).
$400-550

An Apsley Pellatt sulphide and
heavy cut glass jug, with cameo
portrait of George IV wearing the
collar of the Order of the Garter,
very small chips to foot, 8in (20cm).
$10,000-13,500

A Baccarat garlanded spray weight,
on a star cut base, 2½in (6.5cm)
diam.
$2,500-3,500

A Clichy blue double overlay
concentric millefiori mushroom
weight, in shades of green, purple,
bright blue, green and white, on a
strawberry cut base, 3in (8cm) diam.
$2,500-3,500

A rare Clichy faceted red ground
sulphide weight, set with a sulphide
profile portrait of the young Queen
Victoria, cut with a window, the
sides with 5 printies alternating
with flutes, 3in (7.5cm) diam.
$2,000-3,000

A Baccarat garlanded primrose
weight, the flower set within a
garland of alternate white and
claret canes, on a star cut base, 2½in
(6.5cm) diam.
$1,200-1,750

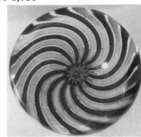

A Clichy blue and white swirl
weight, the alternate royal blue and
white staves radiating from a
central pink, white and green cane,
3in (8cm) diam.
$1,500-2,500

A Clichy turquoise ground patterned millefiori weight, with a bright opaque turquoise ground, 3in (8cm) diam.
$1,200-1,750

A St Louis crown weight, the red and green twisted ribbon radiating from a salmon pink, green and white central cane, 2½in (6.5cm) diam.
$2,000-3,000

A St Louis faceted blue double clematis weight, the flower set on a cushion of spiral white latticinio thread, cut with 6 printies, 3in (8cm) diam.
$1,000-1,500

Scent Bottles

A pair of blue tapering scent bottles and stoppers, gilt in the atelier of James Giles, in a contemporary Birmingham gilt metal filigree case with hinged cover, one stopper repaired, c1760, the case 2in (5cm) high.
$2,000-3,000

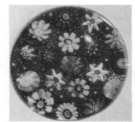

A Clichy moss ground concentric millefiori weight, with a ground of moss canes, 2½in (5.5cm) diam.
$3,000-4,000

A St Louis faceted upright bouquet weight, the sides with all-over honeycomb facets, 3in (7.5cm) diam.
$2,000-3,000

A St Louis pink double clematis weight, the ten striped pink petals about a yellow centre, with a green leaf showing behind, 3in (7.5cm) diam.
$600-900

A Paul Stankard daisy spray weight, with a translucent ruby ground, etched 'Paul J. Stankard, B977 1983', 3in (7.5cm) diam.
$1,500-2,500

A Clichy patterned concentric millefiori weight, 2½in (6.5cm) diam.
$700-900

A St Louis pansy weight, on a star cut base, 2½in (6cm) diam.
$1,200-1,750

A St Louis faceted garlanded blue flower and bud weight, cut with a window and 5 printies, 3in (7.5cm) diam.
$1,000-1,500

A large English green glass dump triple flower in pot paperweight/door stop, c1870, 5in (13cm) high.
$100-150

A paperweight with a single pansy with yellow and purple leaves, having a star cut base, 2½in (6cm) diam.
$600-900

A facet cut green scent bottle, stopper and gold screw cover, gilt in the atelier of James Giles, c1765, 2½in (6cm) high.
$2,000-3,000

An opaque white scent bottle, of tear drop form with facet cut sides, gilt in the atelier of James Giles, the sides and neck enriched in gilding, minute chip to rim, later metal stopper, in a contemporary shagreen case, c1770, 3in (8cm) high.
$1,000-1,500

An opaque scent bottle, one side inscribed 'I E Cay', Newcastle-upon-Tyne, c1785, 3½in (8.5cm) high.
$300-500

A dated opaque scent bottle, one side inscribed 'A B 1780' within blue and green foliage scrolls, with blue 'feuille-de-choux' rim, Newcastle-upon-Tyne, 3in (7.5cm) high.
$800-1,200

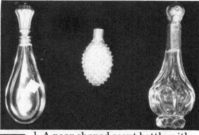

l. A pear shaped scent bottle with embossed silver gilt mount, c1830, 4½in (11.5cm).
$300-500
c. A diamond cut scent bottle with silver cap, c1840, 2in (5.5cm).
$100-200
r. A fluted moulded scent bottle, with chased hinged silver mount, c1830, 5in (12cm).
$150-250

l. A clear glass scent bottle with an embossed gilt metal mount with bloodstone end, c1830, 4in (10.5cm).
$300-500
c. A moulded scent bottle with embossed gilt brass mount, c1850.
$250-350
r. A double ended facet cut scent bottle with plain silver gilt mounts, c1860, 5½in (13cm).
$200-350

A pair of English dressing table bottles, c1840, 9in (23cm).
$300-500

A cameo citrine ground silver mounted scent bottle, overlaid in opaque white, the silver mount to the neck with hinged ball cover, the silver with maker's mark JNM, London, 1884, 5½in (14.5cm) long.
$600-900

A commemorative cut glass perfume bottle, engraved 'Jubilee 1887', and a family crest on the reverse.
$400-550

A cameo silver gilt mounted scent bottle and screw cover, the turquoise body overlaid in pale blue, with silver gilt mount and screw ball cover, maker's mark of Sampson Mordan, London, 1884, 6in (15cm) long.
$400-550

A group of cut crystal boudoir items, comprising: a pair of Russian cut cologne bottles, a cruet, a cologne bottle with enamel stopper and printed oval of Marie Antoinette, and 5 other scent bottles, one with broken stopper.
$450-700

Tankards

A Milch glass cylindrical tankard, with applied looped handle, the body painted in colours, small hairline crack in the body, 5in (12.5cm) high.
$400-550

Vases

A selection of coloured Victorian bulb vases.
$60-100

Note: shape, age and colour are important factors.

A pair of Victorian vaseline glass bulb vases, 4in (10cm) high.
$150-250

A garniture of 3 green and white layered glass vases, with cut lozenge shaped decoration, painted in gilt, mid-19thC, 10½ to 12in (26 to 30.5cm).
$1,500-2,500

A French enamelled opaque glass vase, c1860, 7in (18cm).
$200-350

A vase, engraved with celery, c1870, 10in (25.5cm).
$100-200

A Peking glass vase in jasper green, overlaid with yellow, c1880, 9½in (24cm).
$450-700

A pair of Shropshire glass vases after the antique, in black with enamelled colours, possibly Paris taking Helen to Troy, 10in (25.5cm).
$400-550

A ruby glass oil lamp, c1820, 31in (79cm).
$900-1,300

Miscellaneous

A diamond cut glass table lamp and shade, 17in (43cm).
$450-700

A hollow stem lacemaker's lamp, c1830, 7½in (19cm).
$400-550

A cameo glass biscuit barrel, with plated mount and cover, the citrus coloured body decorated in pink and white, 6in (15.5cm) high.
$2,000-3,000

A French blue opaline oil lamp, c1880, 21in (53cm) high, converted to electricity.
$450-700

TYPES OF GLASS

★ **Cased Glass:** Glass of one colour covered with one or more layers of different coloured glass. Decoration is engraved through the upper layer. First made in Bohemia in the early 19thC

★ **Cut-glass:** Fashionable during the late 18thC. Decorated with facets in the form of geometric patterns

★ **Engraved Glass:** Type of decoration done with the aid of a diamond point

★ **Etched Glass:** Hydrofluoric acid was used to decorate glass during 19thC

★ **Frosted Glass:** Glass with a matt, opaque outer surface

★ **Fruit Glass:** First made in Venice during the 18thC. Revived in the 19thC at Stourbridge. Usually arranged in a basket with glass leaves

★ **Lacy Glass:** Pressed glass with a stippled background. Manufactured in America by the Boston and Sandwich Glass Co

★ **Lime Glass:** Substitute for lead glass discovered in 1864 by William Leighton

★ **Lutz Glass:** Thin, transparent glass striped with coloured twists. Sometimes called 'candy stripe' glass. Introduced by Nicholas Lutz, a French glassworker

★ **'Mary Gregory' Glass:** Glass printed with figures of children c1870

★ **Vaseline Glass:** Decorative glass often known as yellow opaline. Best qualities are greenish-yellow. Produced end of 19thC

A square base salt, with lemon squeezer foot, 3½in (8.5cm) high.
$60-100

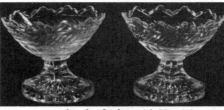

A pair of salts, with Vandyke cut rims, c1810, 3in (7.5cm).
$300-400

A square base salt with lemon squeezer foot, c1790, 3½in (8.5cm).
$60-100

A selection of pairs of Victorian cranberry coloured salts.
$100-200

An amethyst cornucopia, with fold-over rim, 6½in (16.5cm) high.
$300-500

A pale green opaline glass hat, with applied white rim and gilt headband, 2in (5cm).
$150-250

A pair of French turquoise opaline tazze with gilt decoration, c1830, 3in (7.5cm) high.
$600-900

A pair of potichomania glass ornaments, decorated with various birds and butterflies on a blue and green background, 15½in (39cm) high.
$1,200-1,750

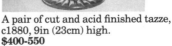

A pair of cut and acid finished tazze, c1880, 9in (23cm) high.
$400-550

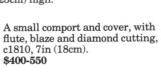

A small comport and cover, with flute, blaze and diamond cutting, c1810, 7in (18cm).
$400-550

OAK & COUNTRY FURNITURE

MONARCH CHRONOLOGY		
Dates	**Monarchs**	**Period**
1558-1603	Elizabeth I	Elizabethan
1603-1625	James I	Jacobean
1625-1649	Charles I	Carolean
1649-1660	Commonwealth	Cromwellian
1660-1685	Charles II	Restoration
1685-1689	James II	Restoration
1689-1694	William & Mary	William & Mary
1694-1702	William III	William III
1702-1714	Anne	Queen Anne
1714-1727	George I	Early Georgian
1727-1760	George II	Georgian
1760-1812	George III	Late Georgian
1812-1820	George III	Regency
1820-1830	George IV	Late Regency
1830-1837	William IV	William IV
1837-1860	Victoria	Early Victorian
1860-1901	Victoria	Late Victorian
1901-1910	Edward VII	Edwardian

An oak bed with panelled headboard, on square legs with rollers, late 16thC, 52in (132cm) wide.

$5,000-7,500

Provenance:
Possibly made for the new grammar school at Thame, Oxon, opened in 1570 and associated with John Hamden. Edmund Waller the poet may have been responsible for the initials E.W. and date 1617. The carving 'Kipling' on the frame refers to one of John Kipling's sons, who was headmaster 1729-68. The school closed in 1877.

Beds

An oak tester bedstead, the headboard with arched panels carved with scrolling foliage and guilloches centred by the monogram GD.AD, partly 17thC, with box spring and mattress, 59in (150cm) wide.

$3,000-4,500

An early Victorian oak day bed in the Gothic style, the seat covered in close nailed green leather, on square Gothic panelled legs with pierced angles, 77in (196cm) wide.
$5,500-7,750

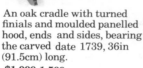

An oak cradle with turned finials and moulded panelled hood, ends and sides, bearing the carved date 1739, 36in (91.5cm) long.
$1,000-1,500

A Continental oak single bed, 18thC.
$800-1,200

A French provincial walnut 'banc de lit clos' with hinged top, fielded panels to the front and a shaped apron centred by a shell, mid-18thC, 71in (180cm) long.
$1,200-1,750

BEDS

Beds have invariably been altered. The most common change being in length – we are simply much taller now. This is regarded as acceptable generally if the bed is to be used. Size can account for considerable differences in price – a good Charles II four poster of, say, 4ft 7in wide by 6ft long might well be less desirable than a less good bed measuring 5ft 6in wide and 7ft long. Most bed buyers *do* want to use their 'fantasy' furniture while retaining 20thC comfort

Bookcases

An oak book press of the Pepys model, with carved cornice and bun feet, 57in (145cm).
$9,000-12,500

The celebrated 12 bookcases commissioned by Samuel Pepys, Secretary to the Navy, in the late 1660s from 'Sympson the joyner' were bequeathed to Magdalene College, Cambridge. Pepys is credited with the invention of the free-standing case book-press. A similar press was commissioned by Charles Sergison of Cuckfield Park, Sussex.

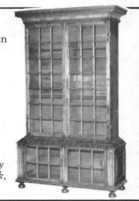

A Regency pollard oak bookcase, with channelled beaded angles and claw feet, 40½in (103cm).
$5,000-7,500

A carved oak breakfront bookcase, 62in (157cm).
$1,500-2,500

A late Victorian oak bookcase, with heavily carved decoration, the upper doors with coloured leaded light glazing, 89in (226cm) high.
$800-1,200

Bureaux

An oak bureau, 18thC.
$1,300-2,000

An oak bureau, with graduated fitted interior with well, brass swan neck handles and bracket feet, some damage, 18thC, 30in (76m).
$3,000-4,500

A William and Mary oak bureau, with a fitted interior, on later bracket feet, bearing a rare contemporary trade label of John Gatehouse, 38½in (98cm).
$4,000-5,500

An oak kneehole desk, on reduced shaped bracket feet, early 18thC, 29½in (75cm).
$3,000-4,000

A George II walnut veneered bureau, inlaid with chevron lines, enclosing a stepped interior with a cupboard, pigeonholes, drawers and a well, 35½in (90cm).
$5,000-7,500

A mid-Georgian walnut bureau, inlaid with boxwood lines, the sloping flap enclosing a fitted interior, on later bracket feet, 34½in (86cm).
$9,000-12,500

A George III oak bureau cabinet, with moulded cornice above a pair of fielded panelled doors over a fall enclosing a fitted interior, on bracket feet, 38½in (98cm).
$4,000-5,500

A Dutch oak and floral marquetry bombé fronted bureau, with an enclosed fitted interior, and 2 pen drawers in the frieze, late 18th/early 19thC, 38½in (97cm).
$6,000-9,000

A pair of Directoire fruitwood corner cabinets, with mottled black marble tops and 2 panelled doors, enclosing shelves, flanked by pilasters on plinth bases, 30½in (76cm).

$4,000-5,500

An American Dutch style bombé fronted walnut and oak glazed display cabinet, with brass handles, 72in (182.5cm).

$3,000-4,500

An oak bureau cabinet, the sloping fall front enclosing a fitted interior, on bracket feet, 45in (114cm).

$6,000-9,000

Chairs

A pair of Carolean decorated oak armchairs, the cane panel seats on scroll supports.

$1,200-1,750

A pair of Charles II oak side chairs, on scrolled legs joined by pierced front stretchers carved with foliage and baluster H-shaped stretchers.

$3,000-4,500

A Charles II ebonised oak side chair, with padded seat, on baluster turned legs, joined by an H-stretcher on turned feet.

$750-1,000

A single oak chair with bobbin turned uprights, solid seat, turned front stretchers and 5 flat stretchers, feet renewed, late 17thC.

$300-400

A Victorian oak child's chair, the seat on inverted cup turned legs joined by a matching stretcher and fitted with a foot rest.

$1,000-1,500

A set of 8 Charles II style oak dining chairs, including 2 armchairs, with leather panelled backs above matching seats on bobbin turned legs joined by barleytwist stretchers.

$1,200-1,750

A William and Mary American walnut elbow chair, the back with a dip crest for a periwig, the front turned block legs with a bulbous apron stretcher, front Spanish feet, plain H-stretchers, with a squab cushion, cane seat distressed.

$1,300-2,000

A matched set of 9 late Georgian elm dining chairs, including 2 armchairs.

$5,000-7,500

A William and Mary maple armchair, Boston or New York, feet slightly reduced, c1715, 50in (127cm) high.
$7,500-8,000

A brown painted ladderback side chair, Delaware River Valley, paint restored, mid-18thC, 43½in (110cm) high.
$500-600

A brown painted ladderback side chair, Delaware River Valley, mid-18thC, 43½in (110cm) high.
$1,500-2,000

A Chippendale cherrywood side chair, New England, with painted rush seat, c1740.
$700-800

Two Queen Anne black painted side chairs, New England, restoration to paint, late 18th/early 19thC, 41in (104cm).
$300-400

A green painted sack back Windsor armchair, by Joseph Henzey, Philadelphia, Pa, formerly a potty chair, cut-down, paint restored, late 18thC, 36in (91.5cm) high.
$350-450

A black painted comb back Windsor side chair, by E. Tracy, Lisbon Ct., later painted, late 18th/early 19thC, 36in (91.5cm) high.
$500-600

A pair of fan back Windsor side chairs, Connecticut River Valley, late 18thC, 37in (94cm) high.
$5,500-6,500

A child's black painted cage back Windsor chair, stamped S. Hamlin, New England, later painted, early 19thC, 29in (74cm) high.
$350-450

A Windsor fan back writing armchair, New England, red painted over old green, c1810, 44in(111.5cm).
$15,000-20,000

A sack back Windsor armchair, American, 19thC, 36in (91.5cm).
$300-350

A black painted sack back Windsor chair, American, later painted, 19thC, 36in (91.5cm) high.
$1,500-2,000

A child's slat back high chair, New England, early 19thC, 36½in (92cm) high.
$800-1,000

A black painted slat back rocking armchair, New England, one arm restored, rockers replaced, c1790, 40in (102cm) high.
$750-850

A mahogany platform rocking chair, by George Hunzinger, New York, patented 1882, 41½in (105cm) high.
$1,000-1,200

A set of 9 'Korenaarstoelen', comprising one armchair and 8 dining chairs, 18th/19thC.
$4,000-5,500

A matched set of 14 spindle back chairs, including 2 armchairs, on turned legs with pad and ball feet, late 18th/early 19thC.
$6,000-9,000

An oak wing armchair with solid wings, rope seat and velvet lined squab cushion, on square legs and conforming stretchers, early 19thC.
$2,000-3,000

An ash and elm comb back Windsor armchair on turned supports and H-stretcher, early 19thC.
$450-600

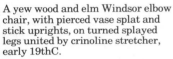

A yew wood and elm Windsor elbow chair, with pierced vase splat and stick uprights, on turned splayed legs united by crinoline stretcher, early 19thC.
$2,000-3,000

A yew wood and elm Windsor armchair, with a spindle filled hoop back, early 19thC.
$2,000-3,000

A set of 8 yew wood and elm Windsor armchairs, probably North Midlands, some replacements, early 19thC.
$20,000-28,000

A set of 6 Wigan ash and elm ladderback chairs, c1780.
$2,000-3,000

A George III oak corner chair, with cabriole front leg and pad foot.
$1,200-1,750

A George III yew wood and elm Windsor armchair in the Gothic taste, the splayed seat on cabriole legs and pad feet joined by shaped stretchers.
$5,000-7,500

A pair of Jacobean oak elbow chairs, profusely carved with mythical beasts, 19thC.
$1,200-1,750

A yew wood and elm Windsor armchair, with pierced fret carved vase splat and stick uprights, on turned splayed legs united by a crinoline stretcher, late 18thC.
$3,000-4,500

A pair of elm children's chairs, 19thC.
$300-400

An elm spindle back chair, 19thC.
$200-350

An elm Windsor wheel back elbow chair.
$400-550

A set of 4 carved oak chairs, 19thC.
$1,500-2,500

A set of 8 Victorian elm chairs, including 2 armchairs, on club legs joined with cross stretchers, and a set of 4 similar side chairs.
$7,000-10,000

A pair of oak bobbin turned elbow chairs, with vertical splats and finials, the solid seats on similar turned underframe.
$750-1,000

Six ash and elm Windsor armchairs, with spindle filled hoop backs, horseshoe arms, solid seats and on turned legs joined by stretchers.
$3,000-4,000

An oak framed chair, with carved narrow back and shaped arms.
$800-1,200

A pair of oak framed Ecclesiastical chairs.
$1,000-1,500

A pair of French provincial fruitwood fauteuils, upholstered in brown repp, on partly fluted turned tapering legs headed by rosettes.
$4,500-7,000

Two ash and elm Windsor chairs.
$450-600

An oak and chestnut settle, 18thC, 58in (147cm).
$2,000-3,000

A set of 6 oak chairs of Louis XV style, with cartouche shaped cane filled backs and seats, with moulded frames on foliate cabriole legs.
$5,000-7,500

Chests

A yew wood chest with a moulded edge, late 17thC, on later bun feet, 35in (90cm).
$7,000-10,000

An Anglo-Dutch elm, walnut and oak chest in 2 sections, with oak panel sides, on bun feet, late 17th/early 18thC, 51in (131cm).
$6,000-9,000

An oak chest, one drawer initialled A.F in brass studs, ovolo carcase mouldings and on stile feet, late 17thC, 38in (96.5cm).
$2,250-3,500

An oak chest with panelled top enclosing a fitted interior, on moulded feet, early 18thC, 55in (141cm).
$3,000-4,500

A South German walnut and oak crossbanded chest, with moulded overhanging top and carrying handles to the sides, on moulded base, 18thC, with later feet, 43in (110cm).
$4,000-5,500

An oak chest of drawers, 18thC, 33½in (85cm).
$1,500-2,500

A walnut chest, with moulded top above 2 short and 4 long graduated and banded drawers, on bracket feet, 18thC, 42in (106.5cm).
$1,500-2,500

A French provincial carved walnut serpentine commode, with moulded edge and arched fielded panel sides, shaped apron with neo-classical paterae and garland ornaments, on scroll feet, 18thC, 56in (142cm).
$5,000-7,500

A Dutch oak chest, inlaid with marquetry, on later bracket feet, 18thC, 34in (86cm).
$5,000-7,500

A burr elm chest of drawers, with original handles, and fielded panels to sides, c1760, 36in (91.5cm).
$4,000-5,500

An oak mule chest, with hinged moulded top above an ogee arched fielded panel front, on a stand with 3 short drawers and a shaped apron, 18thC, 56in (142cm).
$1,500-2,500

A mid-Georgian Lancashire oak and mahogany banded chest, with hinged planked lid above a simulated drawer front and 3 drawers, with an undulating apron and ogee bracket feet, 56in (142cm).
$1,200-1,750

A French provincial oak commode, with panelled sides and shaped feet, mid-18thC, 47in (119cm).
$5,000-7,500

A George III crossbanded oak mule chest, with brass drop handles, on bracket feet, 49in (124.5cm).
$1,300-2,000

A Dutch oak kettle base commode, late 18thC, 34in (86cm).
$1,300-2,000

A George III miniature chest of drawers with original brass handles, 13in (33cm).
$700-900

A French provincial walnut buffet, with black fossil marble slab top, short fluted square tapered legs, restorations, early 19thC, 83in (210cm).
$4,000-5,500

A French provincial oak chest of drawers, with original cast handles, early 19thC.
$2,000-3,000

A French provincial oak commode, on cabriole feet headed by foliate clasps, 51½in (130cm).
$7,000-10,000

An oak chest, on block feet, 38½in (98cm).
$4,500-7,000

A massive German oak, maple, rosewood and ebonised coffer, with inverted front, the hinged lid inset with 2 bird's eye maple panels enclosing a small hinged cupboard and 2 later trays, the architectural front and sides inlaid with foliate scrolls flanked and divided by pilasters, the sides with carrying handles, on bun feet, the frieze inlaid ANNO 1648, with grey steel hinges and lock, 78in (198cm).
$6,000-9,000

Cupboards

A carved oak coffer with panelled top.
$750-1,000

A James I oak joined press cupboard.
$7,500-10,500

A William and Mary oak cupboard, with original cornice dated 1694 and initialled I.H.A.
$9,000-12,500

A Jacobean oak cupboard with arcaded frieze, 49in (124.5cm).
$5,000-7,500

An English oak cupboard base, c1710.
$9,000-12,500

A George III oak hanging corner cupboard.
$600-900

A small George I oak panelled tridarn, good colour and patination, c1725, 53in (135cm).
$13,000-17,500

A Georgian oak cupboard, with moulded cornice and a pair of cupboard doors above 3 false drawers, flanked by turned pilasters, with 2 short and 3 long drawers, on bracket feet, 55in (139.5cm).
$4,000-5,500

An oak corner cupboard with a drawer, 18thC, 30in (76cm).
$600-900

A George III oak press, the base fitted with 2 long drawers and 4 false drawers, on block supports, 72in (182.5cm).
$2,000-3,000

An oak tallboy, made for Amy Thomas on her 21st birthday in 1778.
$7,000-10,000

A Louis XVI provincial carved oak armoire, c1770, 67in (170cm).
$6,000-9,000

An oak wall cupboard, 18thC, 19½in (49cm).
$800-1,200

An oak corner cupboard, 18thC, 31½in (80cm).
$700-900

An elm bacon cupboard, with brass drop handle and iron 'H' shaped hinges, over a plain box seat with 2 rising panels, shaped arms and plain panelled base, 18thC, 49in (125cm).
$7,000-10,000

A French provincial oak armoire, 18thC.
$6,000-8,000

A William and Mary walnut schrank, Pennsylvania, probably Lancaster County, restorations, 18thC, 74in (188cm).
$8,000-10,000

An oak clothes press, on stile feet, 19thC, 53in (134.5cm).
$3,000-4,500

A Flemish rosewood and oak kas with ebony mouldings, fitted with a long drawer, on brown glazed earthenware bun feet, 18thC, 80in (204cm).
$6,000-8,000

A Federal cherrywood corner cupboard, probably Ohio or Kentucky, c1820, 43in (109cm).
$6,500-7,500

A Federal pine corner cupboard, American, early 19thC, 41in (104cm).
$2,500-3,000

A Chippendale pine step-back cupboard, Pennsylvania, in 2 sections, minor repairs, 18thC, 73in (185cm).
$15,000-20,000

A Chippendale poplar hanging cupboard, Pennsylvania, base moulding restored, mid/late 18thC, 27in (68.5cm).
$1,200-1,500

An oak clothes press with 2 false drawers, 2 short drawers and on bracket feet, 49in (124.5cm).
$2,000-3,000

A poplar hanging cupboard, Ephrata, Pennsylvania, c1750, 18½in (47cm).
$1,000-1,200

Dressers

A mid-Georgian oak dresser, inlaid with mahogany bands, adaptations, 75½in (192cm).
$5,500-7,750

A George III Shropshire inlaid oak dresser, some restoration, 72in (182.5cm).
$4,000-5,500

A George III oak cabriole legged dresser and rack, with cupboards crossbanded with mahogany, c1820.
$9,000-12,500

A George III oak dresser, with mahogany crossbanding and brass swan neck handles, on shaped bracket supports, 71in (180cm).
$6,000-8,000

A late Georgian oak dresser, the later plate rack with waved cornice, the front fitted with 3 drawers above a shaped apron, on square tapering legs, 72½in (183cm).
$2,500-3,500

A George III oak dresser, the shelf superstructure with a moulded cornice above a scroll fret frieze and flanked by panelled pilasters, 69in (175cm).
$6,000-9,000

A late Georgian oak dresser, with iron hooks, 55in (120cm).
$4,000-5,500

An oak dresser, with bracket feet, 18thC and later, 57½in (145cm).
$6,000-9,000

A late Georgian oak dresser, the front fitted with 7 short drawers, each with a bone diamond escutcheon, with 2 arched panel doors, on bracket feet, 67in (170cm).
$8,000-11,000

An oak dresser, with plate rack beneath a dentil moulded cornice and pierced frieze and fitted with 2 arched panel doors, the base with 3 frieze drawers, banded in mahogany and chequered lines, on cabriole legs and pad feet, part 18thC, 78in (198cm).
$4,000-5,500

An oak dresser, the rack with an ogee moulded cornice above shelves, the base with a moulded edge above 5 short frieze drawers and fan brackets, on turned columns joined by a pot board, the base 18thC with a later rack, 69in (175cm).
$2,000-3,000

An oak dresser base, 18thC, 72in (182.5cm).
$6,000-9,000

An early Georgian oak dresser, on ogee bracket feet, 73in (185cm).
$6,000-9,000

An oak dresser base with 9 drawers, a pair of panelled doors to central cupboard, on ogee feet, 18thC.
$7,000-10,000

An oak three drawer dresser base, crossbanded in walnut, with backboard, shaped apron and cabriole legs at the front, oak lined, brass knobs and escutcheons, early 18thC, 70in (177.5cm).
$7,000-10,000

An oak dresser, with moulded cornice and 3 shelves, with 3 frieze drawers, on turned supports, joined by a pot rack, 54in (137cm).
$5,000-7,500

An oak dresser base, late 17thC, 77in (195.5cm).
$6,000-9,000

An oak low dresser, with brass drop handles and moulded edges, turned front supports, late 17thC, 68in (172.5cm).
$5,000-7,500

An oak low dresser, with moulded top and 3 frieze drawers, on baluster legs, 18thC, legs partly replaced, 72in (183cm).
$4,000-5,500

A George III oak dresser base, fitted with 3 frieze drawers above an undulating frieze, on square tapering legs, adaptations, 75in (190cm).
$4,000-5,500

A George II oak long dresser, with pierced undulating apron, on cabriole legs with hoof feet, 73in (185cm).
$6,000-8,000

An oak lowboy, 18thC, with later handles, 33in (84cm).
$1,000-1,500

A mid-Georgian oak low dresser, with moulded top, 3 drawers above the waved frieze, on cabriole legs and pad feet, 80in (203cm).
$10,000-13,500

An oak low dresser, on baluster turned legs and block feet joined by a stretcher, 71in (180cm).
$4,500-7,000

A Glasgow style stained oak dresser, fitted with 4 drawers with metal bale handles, 72in (182.5cm).
$14,000-19,000

Tables

A gateleg table, with oval twin-flap top and moulded channelled trestle ends, basically 17thC, 46in (116.5cm).
$3,000-4,500

An oak and grained elm gateleg table, with oval twin-flap top and one frieze drawer, on baluster legs, minor restorations, mid-17thC, 68in (172cm).
$8,000-11,000

An oak side table, c1670, 33in (84cm).
$5,000-7,500

An oak refectory table with plank top, on ring turned legs and moulded stretchers, basically 17thC, 97½in (246cm).
$18,000-25,000

A Tuscan walnut refectory table, with solid top, on H-shaped baluster supports and plinth bases with foliate mouldings, the top 17thC, 105in (267cm).
$8,000-11,000

An oak gateleg table, with turned baluster legs, c1680, 34in (86cm).
$1,500-2,500

A William and Mary oak gateleg table, fitted with 2 later drawers.
$2,250-3,500

An oak gateleg table, with single drawer with brass knob, baluster turned legs and moulded stretchers, late 17thC, 45½in (115cm).
$3,000-4,500

An oak twin-flap gateleg table, with a drawer at each end, late 17thC, with later brass knob handles, 54in (137cm).
$6,000-9,000

An oak side table, the top with moulded edge and frieze drawers, on turned legs united by stretchers, late 17th/early 18thC, 30½in (78cm).
$2,250-3,500

An oak gateleg dining table, the planked folding oval top above a frieze drawer on baluster underframe, late 17thC and later, 51½in (130cm).
$2,000-3,000

A French oak table, fitted with 2 inlaid drawers, late 17thC, 70in (178cm).
$3,000-4,000

A burr yew wood side table, the top with a moulded edge and frieze drawer, on baluster turned legs united by stretchers, late 17th/early 18thC, 30in (76cm).
$6,000-8,000

A Regency oak and holly side table by George Bullock, with banded top and drawer, on turned tapering legs, 28in (71cm).
$13,000-17,500
Provenance:
Great Tew Park, probably one of the 4 chamber tables, invoiced in 1817 at a cost of $6 each.

An early Georgian oak side table, on cabriole legs and trifid feet, 31in (79cm).
$2,250-3,500

An early Georgian oak side table, with 5 drawers around a kneehole with pierced scrolling fretwork, on square tapering club legs and pad feet, 34in (86cm).
$5,000-7,500

An oak cricket table, 18thC, 28in (71cm) diam.
$800-1,200

An oak cricket table with shelf, 18thC, 20in (52cm).
$700-900

A fruitwood refectory table with triple plank top, arched frieze and ring turned tapering legs, early 19thC, 88½in (224cm).
$8,000-11,000

An oak tripod table, 18thC, 18in (46cm).
$600-900

An early Victorian oak occasional table in the style of A W N Pugin, with parquetry top, on a spirally turned and foliate carved pedestal with arched brackets pierced with trefoils, on a quadripartite splayed base, 20in (51cm).
$2,000-3,000

A Victorian Gothic Revival oak extending dining table, on a central column and 4 leaf headed columnar supports, 57in (144.5cm), with 2 extra leaves.
$3,000-4,000

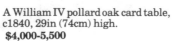

A mid-Victorian oak dining table, on ring turned baluster legs, with 6 large leaves and one small leaf, stamped Gillow and Company, Lancaster, 216in (548cm) extended.
$3,000-4,000

A William IV pollard oak card table, c1840, 29in (74cm) high.
$4,000-5,500

A pair of William IV pollard oak tea tables, with hinged D-shaped crossbanded tops, with foliate scroll and paw feet, one surface with veneer missing, 35in (90cm).
$13,000-17,500

Beds

A Federal carved cherrywood four-poster tester bed, New England, c1810, 64in (162.5cm) high.
$7,000-10,000

A Regency mahogany and brass campaign bed, with double arched tester and turned tapering posts with brass urn finials, with inscribed brass plaque 'Butler's Patent, Catherine St', 26in (66cm) wide.
$9,000-12,500

A Regency parcel gilt and fruitwood four-poster bed, with solid headboard, possibly later, box-spring and mattress, on tapering feet, with valance, 43½in (110cm) wide.
$8,000-11,000

A Federal grain painted bedstead, probably New Hampshire, c1820, 49in (124.5cm).
$5,500-6,500

A Regency ivory and green-painted beechwood day bed, upholstered in crimson damask on fluted sabre legs, 87in (221cm) wide.
$5,000-7,500

A George III mahogany day bed with scrolled padded ends, seat and squab, on square legs joined by moulded stretchers, 92in (234cm) wide.
$9,000-12,500

A Regency mahogany day bed, on ribbed splayed legs and brass feet, upholstered in green repp with a squab, with pen inscription 'Ferguson Christie', 74½in (189cm) wide.
$13,000-17,500

A George III mahogany four-poster bed, with fluted ring turned baluster shaped foot and head posts, later tester, 62in (157cm) wide.
$4,000-5,500

> In the Furniture section if there is only one measurement it usually refers to the width of the piece

Make the most of Miller's

Unless otherwise stated, any description which refers to 'a set' or 'a pair' includes a valuation for the entire set or the pair, even though the illustration may show only a single item

A four-poster bed in Chippendale style, with mahogany cluster columns, giltwood carved frieze, c1780.
$3,000-4,000

A George III painted cradle, with ogee arched hood and cane filled sides suspended from spreading uprights on splayed legs, later decorated with berried foliage, 41in (102cm) long.
$2,000-3,000

A Victorian mahogany half tester bed, with shaped footboard centred with an oval panel.
$2,000-3,000

A mahogany four-poster bedstead, on block feet, with box-spring and mattress, labelled Heal & Son, Makers of Bedsteads and Bedding, London, W., 74in (188cm).
$8,000-11,000

A pair of walnut day beds, each upholstered in yellow damask, on pierced S-scroll supports applied with roundels, early 19thC, 84in (213cm).
$3,000-4,000

A Louis XVI green painted 'lit d'alcove', with padded sides, the seat rail carved with 'guilloche', upholstered in apricot velvet, restorations, 74in (188cm) wide.
$4,000-5,500

A pine deception bedstead, Pennsylvania, in the form of a slant front desk with 4 sham graduated cockbeaded drawers, the back enclosing a hinged bedstead, late 18th/early 19thC, 48in (122cm) high.
$1,000-1,500

A small mahogany four-poster bed with arched canopy, turned supports and solid headboard, with box-spring and mattress and hangings, 43in (109cm) wide.
$6,000-8,000

An unusual parcel gilt and polychrome hanging cradle of navette form, the prow carved with a putto, the stern with the Virgin and Child, on scroll feet with bronze handles, Spanish or Venetian, early 18thC, 49½in (125cm) wide.
$5,500-7,750

A mahogany bowfront half-tester bed, 19thC.
$3,000-4,000

Bonheur du Jour

A Regency mahogany bonheur du jour, with three-quarter gallery and 6 small drawers with one frieze drawer and ring turned tapering legs, 19in (48cm).
$4,000-5,500

A Regency rosewood bonheur du jour with shelves and cupboards, with enclosed cedar-lined drawers, the frieze drawer with leather-lined easel, above a pair of cupboard doors on square tapering legs, 34½in (87cm).
$8,000-11,000

A decorated satinwood bonheur du jour, 19thC.
$4,500-7,000

Breakfront Bookcases

A George III mahogany bookcase chest, with 2 long and 2 short drawers, and 3 shallow frieze drawers on ogee bracket feet, 50in (127cm).
$1,500-2,500

A Regency mahogany breakfront library bookcase, on a plinth base, 105in (267cm).
$24,000-32,500

A mid-Georgian style elm and mahogany breakfront library bookcase, the arcaded dentilled moulded cornice above 4 glazed astragal doors and 4 panel cupboard doors applied with radial and shell mouldings, divided by reeded quadrant pilasters, on ogee bracket feet, 93in (236cm).
$4,000-5,500

A Regency mahogany bookcase, with figured panelled doors flanked by outset spirally reeded columns continuing to ring turned legs, the upper section possibly of different origin, 48in (121cm).
$2,000-3,000

A Regency rosewood bookcase, brass inlaid and panel gilt with ebonised reeded edge, fitted with guilloche moulded gilt gesso shelves flanked by stiles with caryatid masks and cut brass inlay, on a plinth base.
$4,000-5,500

A George III mahogany breakfront bookcase, the base with a pair of doors enclosing slides, flanked by 10 drawers, 100in (254cm).
$10,000-13,500

A George III mahogany breakfront bookcase, on a plinth base, 78in (198cm).
$8,000-11,000

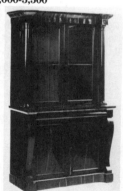

An early Victorian calamander bookcase, on a plinth base, 46in (117cm).
$4,000-5,500

A mahogany breakfront bookcase, with fitted secretaire flanked by cupboards, 19thC.
$8,000-11,000

A George III mahogany and band inlaid breakfront library bookcase, fitted with adjustable shelves enclosed by 2 pairs of barred glass doors, the base with folio trays enclosed by a pair of oval panelled doors flanked by 10 drawers with brass handles, 73in (185cm).
$10,000-13,500

Bureau Bookcases

A George III mahogany bureau bookcase, the upper part with architectural dentil cornice, with fitted interior, the lower part with 4 long drawers, original brass handles, on bracket feet, 39in (99cm).
$9,000-12,500

A Georgian mahogany bureau bookcase, with fitted interior, 6 drawers and bracket feet.
$6,000-8,000

A George I walnut bureau bookcase, the sunburst mirrored doors enclosing adjustable shelves, the fall front enclosing oak lined fitted interior, with brass drop handles and escutcheons, on bracket feet.
$9,000-12,500

A George III mahogany tambour cylinder bureau bookcase, the fall enclosing a satinwood veneered fitted interior and slide with a leather lined ratcheted adjustable slope, above 3 long drawers, on swept bracket feet, 41in (104cm).
$16,000-22,500

A George III mahogany bureau bookcase with a swan neck pediment, the sloping front with fitted interior, on ogee bracket feet 48in (122cm).
$9,000-12,500

A George III inlaid mahogany bureau with a bookcase top, the fall front opening to reveal a well fitted interior, 42in (106.5cm).
$6,000-8,000

A late Georgian mahogany bureau bookcase with broken scroll pediment, astragal glazed doors, on splay bracket feet, 44in (111.5cm).
$4,000-5,500

A George III elm bureau bookcase, the upper section with moulded cornice above a pair of lozenge astragal glazed doors, the fall enclosing a fitted interior, 39in (99cm).
$7,000-10,000

A mahogany bureau bookcase with fitted interior, dentil moulded cornice under a broken architectural pediment, some restoration, late 18thC, 84in (213cm) high.
$6,000-8,000

A mahogany bureau bookcase, with a fitted interior enclosed by writing flap, 19thC, 38in (96cm).
$5,500-7,750

Dwarf Bookcases

A burr walnut breakfront side
cabinet bookcase, 19thC, 73in
(185cm).
$3,000-4,000

A rosewood dwarf cabinet, the top
inlaid with brass paterae, above a
pair of glazed and trellis filled
recessed panelled doors, flanked by
columns with chased ormolu
capitals, on bun feet, 36in (91.5cm).
$6,000-8,000

A pair of William IV rosewood dwarf
bookcases, with gilt scrolling foliate
uprights, the lower ones headed by
lion's masks, on moulded base and
foliate bun feet, 37in (94cm).
$10,000-13,500

BOOKCASES

★ check that the glazing
bars match the rest of the
bookcase in quality,
timber and age.
Breakfront wardrobes of
the mid to late 19thC can
be turned into bookcases
by removing the solid
panels to the doors and
glazing the frames

★ during the late 19thC
many old glazed door
cabinets were removed
from their bureau or
cupboard bases to have
feet added and the tops
fitted in to make
'Georgian' display or
bookcases. This was not an
18thC form; the correct
version was much taller
and often had drawers to
the frieze base. The low
'dwarf' bookcases without
doors became popular
during the late 18thC

★ the earliest form of
adjustable shelf on the
better quality bookcases
was achieved by cutting
rabbets into the sides of
the cabinet into which the
shelves could slide. Next
came a toothed ladder at
each side, the removable
rungs forming the shelf
rests. Finally, by the end
of the 18thC, came
movable pegs fitting into
holes. Regency examples
were often made of gilt
metal or brass

★ check when a bookcase
sits on a bureau or
cupboard base that it is
slightly smaller than the
base, and it is preferable
that the retaining
moulding is fixed to the
base not the top; also, it is
unlikely that the top
surface to such a base
would have been veneered
originally

★ a bureau made to take a
bookcase on top will have
a steeper angle to the fall
front to create a greater
depth to accommodate the
case or cabinet

Library Bookcases

A Georgian carved mahogany
breakfront library bookcase, with a
swan neck pediment, and pierced
trellis dentil cornice, 99in (250cm).
$40,000-52,000

A George III mahogany bookcase,
with geometrically glazed cupboard
doors, the base with oval panelled
doors, 52in (132cm).
$16,000-22,500

A George III mahogany bookcase
with moulded cornice, astragal
glazed doors, a shaped apron below
and on splayed bracket feet, 62in
(157cm).
$4,500-7,000

A Victorian
mahogany bookcase,
the top section with
a bolection moulded
cornice, on plinth
base, 75½in (192cm).
$4,000-5,500

A George III mahogany secretaire
library bookcase, with moulded
dentilled swan neck breakfront
pediment above 2 glazed cupboard
doors, the lower part with secretaire
drawer and fitted interior, on
moulded base, 67in (170cm).
$26,000-35,000

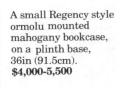

A small Regency style ormolu mounted mahogany bookcase, on a plinth base, 36in (91.5cm).
$4,000-5,500

A Regency mahogany bookcase, with 2 panelled doors to the lower section, on bun feet, 37½in (95cm).
$7,000-10,000

A late Georgian mahogany bookcase, inlaid with chequered boxwood lines, spandrels and roundels, the top with a broken pediment, on splayed bracket feet, 76in (193cm).
$6,000-8,000

A pair of Regency mahogany bookcases with ebony stringing and later scrolled broken pediment, adapted, 52in (132cm).
$25,000-34,000

A Regency rosewood library bookcase, with gilt metal grillwork applied with rosettes with green silk behind, enclosing a shelf, on moulded plinth, 43in (109cm).
$5,000-7,500

A George IV mahogany breakfront library bookcase, on plinth base, 113in (287cm).
$9,000-12,500

A carved mahogany bookcase, with interlaced blind fret decoration, on a plinth base, 19thC, 57in (146cm).
$6,000-8,000

A William IV mahogany open bookcase, with 5 shelves and a raised border, with ring turned supports and turned legs, 42in (106.5cm).
$4,000-5,500

A late Regency mahogany pedestal bookcase, the top with a banded frieze above open adjustable shelves and 2 long base drawers, between gilt metal sphinx headed turned pilasters, on plinth base, adaptations, 30in (76cm).
$1,000-1,500

A Victorian mahogany bookcase, the top section with a bolection moulded cornice enclosed by 4 glazed latticed astragal doors, on plinth base, 66½in (168cm).
$3,000-4,000

A Victorian burr walnut breakfront open bookcase, 48in (122cm).
$2,500-3,500

A Victorian mahogany bookcase, the moulded cornice above a pair of arched plain glazed doors, the base with a pair of arched panelled doors, on plinth base, 57in (145cm).
$3,000-4,500

A George III style mahogany breakfront library bookcase, c1900, 74in (188cm).
$7,500-10,500

A mid-Victorian walnut bookcase, with moulded cornice above 3 glazed cupboard doors and 3 arched panelled doors, on plinth base, 89in (226cm).
$10,500-15,000

A pair of ebonised and green painted bookcases, with fall flaps decorated with ribbon tied scrolling foliage, on square tapering legs, 30in (76cm).
$10,500-15,000

An Edwardian satinwood banded mahogany revolving bookcase, 19½in (50cm).
$2,500-3,500

A bookcase, the sides painted with diamonds within wave borders, the 2 cupboard doors painted with animals leaving the Ark, beneath the inscription 'The rain is over and gone', 56in (142cm) high.
$1,300-2,000

A mahogany bookcase, with plinth base, 83in (211cm).
$5,000-7,500

A Biedermeier satinbirch bookcase, the upper part with a moulded cornice and enclosed by a pair of ebonised arched astragal glazed doors, with a pair of panel doors below, on bracket feet, 51½in (131cm).
$1,200-1,750

A pair of George III mahogany bookcases, with moulded dentilled cornices and geometrically glazed doors enclosing shelves, on moulded plinths, 52in (132cm).
$16,500-23,000

Secretaire Bookcases

A George III mahogany secretaire bookcase, applied with radial mouldings, 47½in (120cm).
$4,000-5,500

A mahogany bookcase, with moulded arcaded cornice above 3 glazed cupboard doors and 3 panelled cupboard doors, lacking plinth base, 54½in (164cm).
$4,500-7,000

A Federal carved and inlaid cherrywood secretaire bookcase, in 2 sections, Connecticut, c1800, 42in (106.5cm).
$20,000-25,000

A Federal inlaid mahogany secretaire bookcase, in 2 parts, probably New York, minor restoration to inlay, c1800, 58in (147cm).
$7,500-8,500

A Federal inlaid mahogany and bird's-eye maple writing desk and bookcase, in 2 sections, North Eastern Massachusetts, c1800, 41½in (104cm).
$12,000-15,000

A classical mahogany veneered desk and bookcase, in 2 sections, mid-Atlantic States, restorations, mid-19thC, 51in (129.5cm).
$1,200-1,500

A William IV carved mahogany lady's bookcase, in the manner of Richard Brown, the upper part enclosed by a pair of brass grille and glazed panel doors, 28½in (72cm).
$16,500-23,000

A William IV mahogany secretaire bookcase, 49in (125cm).
$3,000-4,500

A mahogany secretaire bookcase, the 2 doors with satinwood strung astragal glazing enclosing adjustable shelves, the secretaire drawer with pigeonholes and small drawers faced in maple, early 19thC, 51in (130cm).
$4,000-5,500

A mahogany secretaire bookcase, with 2 simulated drawers enclosing a writing slide and lidded compartments, the 2 panelled doors applied with C-scrolls, foliage and flowers, on acanthus carved bracket feet, 40½in (103cm).
$2,500-3,500

An inlaid mahogany secretaire bookcase with key pattern cornice, on bracket feet, 19thC, 40in (101cm).
$5,000-7,500

A George III mahogany secretaire cabinet, with moulded dentilled cornice above a pair of geometrically glazed cupboard doors, the baize lined secretaire drawer enclosing a fitted interior, on bracket feet, 48in (122cm).
$6,000-8,000

A George III mahogany secretaire bookcase, the base with a baize lined secretaire drawer above 3 graduated long drawers, on bracket feet, replacements, the top and base possibly associated, 43½in (110.5cm).
$6,000-8,000

A George III mahogany breakfront secretaire bookcase, now adapted into 3 separate bookcases, with fall front writing drawers and fitted interiors, the centre bookcase 51in (129cm) wide, the pair of bookcases each 32½in (82.5cm).
$13,000-17,500

A Regency mahogany secretaire bookcase, 41in (104cm).
$3,000-4,500

A Regency mahogany secretaire bookcase, c1820, 48in (122cm).
$3,000-4,500

A late Regency mahogany secretaire bookcase, inlaid with satinwood, shells and boxwood lines in rosewood banded borders, 38½in (98cm).
$6,000-8,000

A Regency mahogany secretaire bookcase, inlaid with ebony and applied with ormolu mounts, the lower section with a satinwood fitted interior above 2 panelled doors between pilasters headed by anthemions, on lion's paw feet, 50in (127cm).
$4,500-7,000

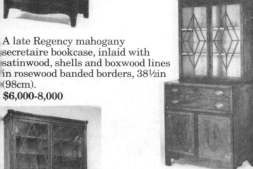

A Regency mahogany secretaire bookcase, the secretaire drawer enclosing a fitted interior with a leather inset writing surface, on lobed ball feet, 45in (114cm).
$4,500-7,000

A Regency mahogany secretaire bookcase, the fall front secretaire drawer revealing lidded document wells and baize covered writing part, 54in (137cm).
$13,000-17,500

A Regency mahogany and satinwood banded secretaire bookcase, the lower section with a secretaire drawer enclosing pigeonholes above 3 oval panelled cupboard doors, on outswept bracket feet, 69in (175cm).
$8,000-11,000

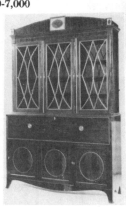

A Georgian mahogany satinwood banded and boxwood strung secretaire bookcase, with tooled leather-lined fall enclosing a fitted interior, on bracket feet, 45½in (115cm).
$6,000-8,000

187

Buckets

A Georgian mahogany plate bucket, banded in brass, c1760.
$3,000-4,500

A Regency mahogany brass bound plate bucket, with carrying handle and tapering sides, 16½in (42cm) high.
$2,500-3,500

A Regency mahogany brass bound bucket, with tin liner and tapering body with a carrying handle, 12in (30.5cm).
$2,500-3,500

Bureaux

A walnut bureau, the crossbanded and herringbone banded fall enclosing a fitted interior, early 18thC with restoration, 36in (91.5cm).
$3,000-4,500

A walnut and herringbone banded bureau, the fall with fitted interior, on bun feet, early 18thC, 40in (101.5cm).
$8,000-11,000

A walnut, crossbanded and featherstrung bureau, the sloping fall enclosing a fitted interior with pigeonholes, the lower part with 2 short and 2 long drawers, on bracket feet, restored, early 18thC, 34½in (87cm).
$5,500-7,750

A George I walnut, crossbanded and featherbanded bureau, the fall enclosing a graduated interior with secret compartments, on bracket feet, 36in (91cm).
$5,000-7,500

A Dutch walnut and floral marquetry bombé printed bureau, the sloping fall enclosing a fitted interior, with a rocaille palmette spray in the apron, terminating in claw-and-ball feet, 18thC, 48in (123cm).
$13,000-17,500

A Dutch walnut and floral marquetry bombé bureau, with stepped fittings and well enclosed by a decorated fall, on carved paw feet, 18thC, 40in (101.5cm).
$10,500-15,000

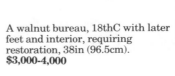

A George I walnut veneered bureau, inlaid with featherbanding, on bracket feet, re-polished, 31in (79cm).
$24,000-32,500

A walnut bureau, 18thC with later feet and interior, requiring restoration, 38in (96.5cm).
$3,000-4,000

A Georgian figured mahogany bureau, the fall front revealing a central cupboard with fitted interior, 40in (101.5cm).
$1,300-2,000

A George I walnut bureau, inlaid with featherbanding, the sloping front enclosing a fitted interior, on later base and bracket feet, 39½in (100cm).
$7,000-10,000

A George I walnut bureau, inlaid with chequered lines, the sloping front enclosing a fitted interior, on later bracket feet, 41½in (105cm).
$26,000-35,000

A mahogany bureau, with fitted interior, brass swan neck handles, and bracket feet, 30in (76cm).
$3,000-4,500

A Georgian mahogany bureau, with fitted interior, on bracket feet.
$3,000-4,500

An early Georgian burr yew and burr walnut bureau, the crossbanded sloping front enclosing a fitted interior, on later bracket feet, possibly formerly with a well, 39in (99cm).
$7,000-10,000

A Georgian mahogany bureau, the fall front revealing a mahogany veneered interior, the drawers boxwood strung and inlaid with shell patera, 48in (122cm).
$2,000-3,000

A Georgian mahogany bureau.
$1,500-2,500

A Georgian mahogany writing bureau with fitted interior, on bracket feet.
$1,000-1,500

A George II burr yew-wood bureau, the sloping fall enclosing an oak fitted interior with secret compartments, on bracket feet, 34½in (88cm).
$1,200-1,750

BUREAUX

Points to look for:
- ★ originality and condition
- ★ good colour and patination
- ★ good proportions
- ★ quality of construction
- ★ original handles and escutcheons
- ★ original feet
- ★ small size (3ft is about average)
- ★ stepped interior and a central cupboard
- ★ fitted 'well' with a slide
- ★ oak drawer linings
- ★ secret compartments

A late George III mahogany bureau, the sloping front enclosing a fitted interior, on ogee supports, 44in (111.5cm).
$2,250-3,500

A Chippendale birch slant front desk, New England, feet restored, top re-set, c1770, 44½in (112cm).
$2,500-3,000

A Chippendale walnut slant front desk, Pennsylvania, c1770, 42in (106.5cm).
$6,500-7,500

A Chippendale mahogany slant front desk, Massachusetts, feet lacking, c1780, 40in (101.5cm).
$16,000-18,000

A Chippendale mahogany reverse serpentine slant front desk, Massachusetts, writing surface and lid restored, drawers pieced, c1770, 42½in (107cm).
$4,000-5,000

A George III mahogany cylinder tambour front bureau, the fall enclosing a satinwood veneered interior, with lozenge inlay and tambour shuttered enclosed compartments, with a green leather hinged slope, 40in (101cm).
$5,000-7,500

A George III mahogany bureau, the sloping flap enclosing a fitted interior above 4 long drawers, on partly replaced bracket feet, 36in (91.5cm).
$4,000-5,500

A Dutch walnut and floral marquetry bombé cylinder bureau, the inlaid fall enclosing a baize lined slide and fitted interior, on splayed bracket feet with gilt metal sabots, late 18th/early 19thC.
$8,000-11,000

NOTES ON DUTCH MARQUETRY BUREAUX

★ beware badly split flaps and slides
★ marquetry on walnut fetches more than marquetry on mahogany, which in turn fetches more than marquetry on oak
★ cylinder bureaux as a general rule fetch less than fall front bureaux
★ always look out for marquetry which includes bone and/or mother-of-pearl
★ marquetry including birds and insects is slightly rarer than the usual floral marquetry

A Dutch mahogany bureau à cylindre, inlaid with marquetry in boxwood line borders, on fluted block and bracket feet, early 19thC 45in (114cm).
$7,000-10,000

A Dutch mahogany bombé bureau, the fall flap enclosing a fitted interior, on large claw-and-ball feet, 19thC, 52in (132cm).
$5,500-7,750

A Dutch walnut and foliate marquetry bombé bureau, with fitted interior, 19thC, 50in (127cm).
$13,000-17,500

A French tulipwood bureau, banded in rosewood, with chased gilt metal mounts, on cabriole legs, late 19thC, 25in (63cm).
$2,500-3,500

An early Victorian rosewood escritoire, 43½in (110cm).
$1,500-2,500

A Victorian figured walnut and gilt metal mounted bureau de dame, inlaid with boxwood lines and arabesques, the top with a mirrored superstructure, 32in (81cm).
$3,000-4,500

An Edwardian inlaid lady's cylinder writing bureau, with fitted interior 2 drawers, and brass gallery to back.
$1,300-2,000

A French mahogany bureau de dame, applied with metal mounts, with three-quarter galleried marble top above 3 frieze drawers, between fluted uprights above a cylinder painted in the manner of Vernis Martin, enclosing a fitted interior, late 19thC, 31in (79cm).
$3,000-4,500

Bureau Cabinets

A late Victorian walnut cylinder bureau, with pierced gallery and frieze drawer, the cylinder enclosing fitted interior and pull-out writing slide, 30in (76cm).
$900-1,300

A walnut crossbanded and featherstrung bureau cabinet, on bracket feet, reveneered, early 18thC, 42½in (107cm).
$13,000-17,500

A walnut secretaire cabinet, early 18thC.
$26,000-35,000

A George III mahogany bureau cabinet, on bracket feet, 38½in (98cm).
$5,000-7,500

A Dutch marquetry escritoire, the fall front enclosing an arcaded shelf, drawers and central cupboard, on turned feet, early 19thC, 40in (101cm).
$4,000-5,500

A Dutch mahogany and gilt metal mounted secretaire à abattant, with 2 glazed panel doors above a fall front, enclosing an elm and ebony inlaid interior, early 19thC.
$3,000-4,500

A Dutch mahogany secretaire à abattant, inlaid with brass geometric lines, the top with a frieze drawer above a fall writing panel, enclosing a fitted interior, early 19thC, 40½in (102cm).
$4,000-5,500

A Dutch mahogany crossbanded and inlaid escritoire, with a frieze drawer and fall with ebony lines of broken outline and chequer stringing, on square tapered legs, the interior converted, early 19thC.
$5,000-7,500

A French boulle cabinet, the lower doors decorated in red tortoiseshell and cut brass, the sides with conforming boulle panels, gilt brass bun feet, 38in (96.5cm).
$18,000-25,000

A late Empire mahogany secretaire à abattant with brass mounted outlines, with marble top above a fall writing panel with enclosed fitted interior, on tapering feet, 37½in (95cm).
$5,000-7,500

An Empire ormolu mounted secretaire à abattant, with mottled black marble top, the leather lined fall flap enclosing a fitted interior, on shaped feet, 39in (99cm).
$5,000-7,500

A Scandinavian mahogany bureau cabinet, decorated with flutings and roundels, with geometric boxwood lines, on block feet, early 19thC, 45in (114cm).
$5,000-7,500

A Louis XV tulipwood and kingwood secretaire à abattant, with later red marble top above a fall flap inlaid 'à quatre faces' enclosing a fitted interior, stamped L Boudin twice, JME 4 times, and J. Tuart once, 36in (91.5cm).
$5,000-7,500

A German mahogany secretaire à abattant, the arched panelled fall enclosing a fitted interior, on a plinth base, late 19thC, 42in (106cm).
$6,000-9,000

An Italian walnut and marquetry secretaire cabinet, the fall flap inlaid with scrolling foliage, enclosing 15 various-sized drawers, on later bracket feet, 41in (104cm).
$6,000-9,000

Cabinets on Stands

A Flemish gilt metal mounted tortoiseshell and ebony cabinet-on-stand, with panelled cupboard doors enclosing later rosewood specimen drawers, the stand with a slide and panelled frieze on moulded legs headed by female caryatids, 55½in (140cm).
$14,000-19,000

A Flemish ivory inlaid, ebony and tortoiseshell cabinet-on-stand, the central cupboard doors enclosing a mirrored interior, the cabinet 17thC, 40in (101.5cm).
$6,000-9,000

A Flemish rosewood, ebony and tortoiseshell cabinet-on-stand, 17thC, with later turned baluster supports and bun feet, joined by a rectangular undertier, 34in (86cm).
$5,000-7,500

A Flemish walnut, tortoiseshell and ebonised cabinet-on-stand, inlaid with ivory and ebony strapwork, the later stand with spirally turned legs and H-shaped stretcher, 30in (76cm).
$3,000-4,500

A Flemish padouk, tortoiseshell, ebony and amboyna cabinet-on-stand, the stand with foliate cabriole legs and pad feet, 19thC, 33in (84cm).
$4,000-5,500

A Flemish tortoiseshell and ebonised cabinet-on-stand, the drawers with oval tortoiseshell panels applied with gilt metal foliate cast borders, the whole veneered in red stained tortoiseshell with ebonised borders, 52in (132cm).
$20,000-28,000

A North Italian kingwood and fruitwood dressing cabinet-on-stand, with moulded cornice and inlaid with light lines, with central ratchet mirror glass, Lombardy or Piedmont, late 18thC, 43in (109cm).
$7,000-10,000

A German carved walnut and burr veneered serpentine cabinet-on-stand, the stand with a pierced undulating apron, on cabriole legs, united by an undertier and scroll feet, 19thC, 38in (98cm).
$3,000-4,500

A walnut escritoire, with quarter-veneered and herringbone banded fall, enclosing a mirrored interior, 45in (114cm).
$2,000-3,000

A South German marquetry table cabinet-on-stand, the panel doors decorated with japanned chinoiserie, the base on square tapered legs united by an undertier, early 18thC, the stand later.
$6,000-9,000

A Spanish marquetry cabinet-on-stand, the pierced moulded cornice with gilt metal fretwork, the reverse painted with a bull and a ram with inscriptions, 19thC, 49in (124cm).
$9,000-12,500

Collectors' Cabinets

A 17thC style Antwerp ebonised parquetry coin cabinet, mid-19thC, 25in (63cm).
$14,000-19,000

A William IV mahogany table cabinet, with concealed frieze drawer, on carved bun feet, 19in (48cm).
$700-900

A South German walnut, ash and marquetry table cabinet, inlaid with chequered boxwood lines, fitted with a fall front, the sides fitted with carrying handles, late 18thC, 20in (51cm).
$2,500-3,500

An Italian ebonised and gilt metal mounted cabinet, with ripple mouldings and inlaid with lines, the drawers mounted with verre églomisé panels, the central compartment with 4 enclosed drawers, carrying handles, 17thC, 58in (148cm).
$7,000-10,000

A William and Mary trinket cabinet, with star inlaid panels, fitted with drawers and enclosed by a single door, 9½in (24cm).
$1,500-2,500

A pair of mahogany chart cabinets with walnut crossbanding, each with 36 slides, c1935, 28½in (72cm).
$5,000-7,500

Made for the Greenwich Maritime Museum.

Display Cabinets

A William and Mary style burr walnut display cabinet-on-stand, on inverted cup turned legs joined by a waved stretcher, on ball turned feet, 63in (160cm).
$1,500-2,500

An early 18thC style walnut china cabinet, the stand with 3 featherbanded drawers above a shaped apron, on shell headed hipped cabriole legs and acanthus scroll feet.
$2,250-3,500

An 18thC style mahogany display cabinet, with acanthus carved waist moulding, 2 moulded doors and on acanthus carved cabriole legs with claw-and-ball feet, 52in (132cm).
$3,000-4,500

A Regency rosewood dwarf breakfront display cabinet, inlaid with boxwood lines.
$24,000-32,500

A George III mahogany corner display cabinet, outlined with boxwood stringing, the panelled doors veneered with ovals and on bracket feet, 45in (114cm).
$7,000-10,000

A rosewood display cabinet, inlaid in various woods and ivory in the Mannerist style, on square tapering legs, late 19thC, 72½in (186cm).
$6,000-9,000

A pair of mahogany and brass mounted display cabinets, with pierced gallery above 2 glazed panel doors between reeded three-quarter column uprights, on toupie feet, late 19thC, 55½in (140cm).
$9,000-12,500

A George III mahogany display cabinet with later pierced arched pediment, the base with a geometrically glazed sloping front and silk lined interior, 40in (101.5cm).
$6,000-8,000

A pair of William IV rosewood display cabinets, applied with bead and reel split mouldings, on later turned feet, 25½in (64.5cm).
$16,000-22,500

A Victorian walnut and marquetry pier cabinet, the inlaid frieze over a shaped plain glazed door flanked by gilt metal mounted and marquetry inlaid pilasters, on a plinth base, 30½in (77.5cm).
$1,000-1,500

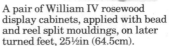

An Edwardian inlaid mahogany display cabinet.
$3,000-4,500

An Edwardian mahogany and satinwood crossbanded display cabinet, on square tapering legs with a platform undertier, 49in (125.5cm).
$3,000-4,500

An Edwardian satinwood display cabir .t, outlined with ebony stringing, the lower section with inlaid panelled doors, on square tapered legs and spade feet, 49in (124.5cm).
$2,500-3,500

An Edwardian Sheraton design mahogany display cabinet, decorated with satinwood stringing and chequered crossbanding, on square tapering supports and spade feet, 45in (114cm).
$2,000-3,000

An Edwardian satinwood display cabinet with chinoiserie decoration.
$6,000-9,000

An Edwardian mahogany hanging corner display cabinet, with swan neck pediment and moulded cornice, 26in (66cm).
$800-1,200

An open display cabinet, on chamfered legs, joined by stretchers, 53in (134.5cm).
$3,000-4,500

A mahogany china display cabinet, with fabric back interior, on claw-and-ball feet, 59in (149.5cm).
$2,000-3,000

A Sheraton revival china cabinet, decorated with satinwood crossbanding and central inlaid portrait panel.
$5,000-7,500

A burr yew display cabinet, inlaid with boxwood lines and applied with gilt metal mounts, on turned tapering feet, 38in (96.5cm).
$3,000-4,500

A Dutch walnut and floral marquetry display cabinet, heightened in harewood, on bun feet, 19thC, 34½in (88cm).
$7,000-10,000

A Dutch marquetry display cabinet, with glazed cupboard doors with bead-and-reel border, the base with 3 drawers and chamfered waved angles, on claw-and-ball feet, 66in (167.5cm).
$13,000-17,500

A Dutch walnut and floral marquetry china cabinet, on ebonised bun feet, 19thC, 50in (126cm).
$10,500-15,000

A French vitrine display cabinet, with serpentine front and figure panels after Watteau.
$2,000-3,000

A Dutch marquetry display cabinet, on a plinth base inlaid with foliage, 35in (89cm).
$2,500-3,500

An Italian hardwood display cabinet, inlaid with ivory in the Moorish style, on block supports, bearing the wax seal of Dogani di Milano, 19thC, 42in (106.5cm).
$5,500-7,750

Side Cabinets

A Louis XV style kingwood display cabinet, applied with gilt brass mouldings, on cabriole legs, bearing Fontainbleu railway labels and an inventory number, 37½in (95cm).
$4,000-5,500

A Regency mahogany secretaire chiffonier, inlaid with geometric ebonised lines, the top with a shelved ledge back on turned supports, the frieze drawer with fitted interior, 34in (86cm).
$3,000-4,500

A late Regency mahogany chiffonier, inlaid with brass in beaded banded borders, the mirror lined back with S-scroll supports, above 4 mirror panelled cupboard doors, divided by voluted pilasters, 81in (205.5cm).
$6,000-8,000

A Regency faded rosewood chiffonier, the upper part with mirrored back and giltmetal galleries to shelf, the gilded panelled doors with pleated silk, enclosing shelves, 39in (99cm).
$4,500-7,000

A kingwood, rosewood crossbanded, ormolu mounted and inlaid breakfront side cabinet, with a marble top, the panel door with a floral spray and fruit, with parquetry panels to either side, marble top broken, 19thC, 45in (115cm).
$4,000-5,500

A parcel gilt and rosewood side cabinet with later Verde Antico marble slab, adapted, early 19thC, 42½in (108cm).
$4,000-5,500

A boulle dwarf corner cabinet, brass inlaid into red tortoiseshell, with shaped marble top, 19thC, 30in (76cm).
$1,500-2,500

A late Federal mahogany veneer cabinet, probably New York, c1820, 33½in (85cm).
$1,200-1,500

A Victorian figured walnut side cabinet, inlaid with boxwood lines and applied with painted porcelain plaques in ebonised and giltmetal mounted borders, 57in (144.5cm).
$4,000-5,500

An early Victorian inlaid burr walnut side cabinet, 48in (122cm).
$1,500-2,500

A late Regency rosewood chiffonier, the shelved back on scroll metal supports with a pierced three-quarter gallery, above 2 frieze drawers and 2 silk pleated panel doors, 38½in (98cm).
$3,000-4,500

A pair of walnut cabinets, with marble tops and Sèvres plaques in the centre, Waring and Gillow, c1870, 25in (63.5cm).
$9,000-12,500

An early Victorian mahogany chiffonier, with 2 short frieze drawers and brass lattice work doors, 60in (152cm) high.
$2,500-3,500

A Dutch inlaid mahogany side cabinet, with crossbanded top, 46in (116.5cm).
$3,000-4,000

Canterburies

An Italian stained walnut and inlaid secretaire side cabinet, geometrically decorated 'a la certosina', the top fitted with short drawers and stationery compartments beneath a moulded pediment, the frieze fitted with a secretaire drawer, 19thC, 53in (134.5cm).
$4,500-7,000

A Dutch satinwood side cabinet, crossbanded and inlaid with barber-pole stringing, later painted with flowers and foliage, the frieze drawer above a tambour shutter and deep drawer, 24in (61cm).
$2,250-3,500

A Regency mahogany canterbury with central handle, on ring turned supports, the frieze with a drawer on turned legs, 21in (53cm).
$4,000-5,500

A George IV mahogany canterbury, on turned column with platform base.
$1,200-1,750

A late Regency rosewood canterbury, the frieze fitted with a drawer, on splayed legs, 24in (61cm).
$3,000-4,500

A Regency mahogany music canterbury, with one drawer, on slender turned supports, with brass feet and casters.
$2,500-3,500

A William IV rosewood canterbury, on turned moulded legs with casters, 22in (56cm).
$2,250-3,500

A Federal mahogany canterbury, probably New York, mid-19thC, 17½in (44.5cm) high.
$1,300-1,500

A mahogany canterbury, on turned supports and casters, 19thC, 21in (53cm).
$1,200-1,750

A mahogany canterbury, with ring turned uprights and slatted sides on turned tapering legs and brass feet, 18in (46cm).
$2,000-3,000

A Victorian walnut writing canterbury, the frieze drawer with an adjustable reading rest, the 4 divisions pierced and carved with scrolls, a concave fronted drawer below on bell shaped feet, 27in (68.5cm).
$3,000-4,500

An early Victorian rosewood canterbury, on turned tapering legs with brass casters, 20½in (52cm).
$2,000-3,000

A rosewood canterbury, with X-shaped divisions centred by roundels with one frieze drawer and ring turned legs, 20in (51in).
$3,000-4,500

Chairs – Open Armchairs

A Charles II walnut open armchair, the moulded arms on baluster legs, joined by conforming stretchers, minor restoration.
$3,000-4,500

A walnut framed armchair, upholstered in crimson velvet, late 17thC.
$1,000-1,500

A Charles II walnut farthingale chair, with spirally turned and square legs with stretchers, later blocks, minor restoration.
$1,300-2,000

A William and Mary walnut open armchair, the waved stretcher centred by a later urn, later blocks, minor restoration.
$2,000-3,000

A George II mahogany library armchair, re-railed.
$8,000-11,000

A Georgian mahogany open armchair of Gainsborough type, with square legs united by stretchers, parts replaced.
$2,000-3,000

A George II mahogany elbow chair with pierced vase splat, slip-in seat, on cabriole legs with trifid pad feet.
$2,250-3,500

An early George III mahogany armchair.
$2,000-3,000

An early George III mahogany open armchair, on square chamfered legs joined by stretchers.
$2,500-3,500

A Georgian mahogany elbow chair, in the French style.
$4,500-7,000

A pair of George III carved mahogany elbow chairs, re-railed.
$2,500-3,500

A George III cream painted and parcel gilt open armchair, with fluted seat rail and fluted tapering legs, later blocks.
$3,000-4,000

A pair of George III mahogany open armchairs, each with a bowed bar toprail above a railed back, with upholstered seats, on ring turned tapering legs, with 5 similar George III mahogany dining chairs.
$4,500-7,000

A George III carved mahogany frame elbow chair in the French Hepplewhite taste, on cabriole legs with fan mouldings.
$2,500-3,500

A George III carved mahogany elbow chair in the Chippendale taste, on square chamfered legs united by H-stretchers.
$1,300-2,000

A pair of George III mahogany open armchairs, with woolwork upholstered drop-in seats, and on tapering square legs joined by stretchers.
$2,000-3,000

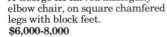

A George III carved mahogany elbow chair, on square chamfered legs with block feet.
$6,000-8,000

A George III mahogany library armchair, the arched padded back and seat with gros point floral needlework upholstery, later blocks, partly re-railed.
$3,000-4,000

Miller's is a price Guide not a price List

The price ranges given reflect the average price a purchaser should pay for similar items. Condition, rarity of design or pattern, size, colour, pedigree, restoration and many other factors must be taken into account when assessing values.

A Chippendale walnut armchair, Maryland or Pennsylvania, rear skirt restored, stamped 1B, c1770, 34in (86cm) high.
$450-550

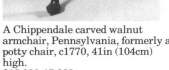

A Chippendale carved walnut armchair, Pennsylvania, formerly a potty chair, c1770, 41in (104cm) high.
$13,000-15,000

A Federal inlaid mahogany lolling chair, Massachusetts, c1800, 46in (116.5cm) high.
$13,000-15,000

A George III mahogany library chair, upholstered in blue floral needlework, the square channelled legs joined by pierced fret stretchers, reduced, later blocks and restorations.
$4,000-5,500

A Federal mahogany lolling chair, Massachusetts, legs slightly reduced, c1800, 25in (63cm).
$3,500-4,500

A George III mahogany Gainsborough chair, repairs to back legs.
$2,000-3,000

A George III giltwood open armchair attributed to Thomas Chippendale, on turned tapering legs headed by stiff leaves with ribbed feet.
$4,000-5,500

A pair of Federal style mahogany armchairs, 23in (58cm).
$1,500-2,000

A George III Chippendale design mahogany framed Gainsborough chair, with serpentine seat and back upholstered in foliate patterned crimson satinised brocade.
$2,000-3,000

A Regency mahogany library bergère, with cane filled back, arms and seat with buttoned olive green leather cushions.
$2,500-3,500

A pair of mahogany open armchairs of George III design, each with a serpentine padded back, arm-rests and serpentine seat covered in light cream damask.
$7,000-10,000

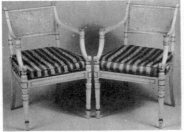

Four Regency white and gilt painted elbow chairs, with turned bamboo effect frames, cane seats and backs, with loose cushions in striped damask.
$14,000-19,000

A pair of Regency blue painted and parcel gilt armchairs, stamped T. Gray, redecorated.
$24,000-32,500

A parcel gilt and white painted open armchair of Regency design.
$9,000-12,500

A pair of Regency rosewood and brass mounted elbow chairs.
$10,000-13,500

A Regency ebonised and parcel gilt open armchair, the split caned seat on ring turned tapering legs with green damask covered squab, redecorated.
$3,000-4,000

A pair of Regency mahogany open armchairs, inlaid with ebonised lines, with blue brocade covered drop-in seats, later front rails.
$5,000-7,500

A Regency mahogany library bergère, on reeded uprights and tapering legs, terminating in brass cappings and casters.
$2,000-3,000

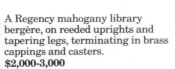

A late Regency mahogany bergère, buttoned and upholstered in green leather.
$3,000-4,500

A George IV mahogany library armchair, with buttoned chamois covered squab.
$4,000-5,500

A Victorian walnut three-piece drawing room suite, comprising a chaise longue, a gentleman's armchair and a lady's chair.
$2,500-3,500

A George IV mahogany library armchair, the yoke shaped back with cane filled centre carved with flowers, the cane filled seat with leather squab cushion.
$3,000-4,500

A marquetry inlaid open armchair with stuffover seat, 19thC.
$800-1,200

A mahogany bergère chair, upholstered in leather, c1860.
$2,000-3,000

A William IV mahogany framed library armchair, with leatherette cushions, the cane back damaged.
$750-1,000

A mid-Victorian ebonised oak open armchair, with a label of J. Kendell & Co., No. 53536, and the workman's name Hill.
$1,000-1,500

An early Victorian simulated rosewood open armchair.
$450-600

A Victorian carved walnut button back gentleman's armchair.
$1,200-1,750

An early Victorian walnut open armchair.
$800-1,200

A Victorian mahogany tub chair, upholstered in red leather.
$800-1,200

A Louis XVI giltwood fauteuil with padded oval back and circular seat covered in green damask, fluted turned tapering legs, later blocks.
$3,000-4,500

A pair of Louis XV style parcel gilt and cream painted fauteuils, upholstered in blue and white striped silk, the moulded frame with shell cresting and centre to the seat rail.
$2,000-3,000

A set of 6 Louis XV style beech fauteuils.
$8,000-11,000

A Louis XVI stained beechwood fauteuil.
$1,500-2,500

A Louis XVI giltwood bergère, with stuffover serpentine seat, on fluted tapered legs.
$2,000-3,000

A set of 4 Louis XVI style giltwood fauteuils, upholstered in tapestry, mid-19thC.
$3,000-4,500

A pair of Louis XVI style giltwood fauteuils, upholstered in machined floral tapestry, the moulded frames carved with berried foliage.
$3,000-4,500

A set of 4 Louis XVI walnut fauteuils, late 18thC.
$9,000-12,500

A French walnut fauteuil, early 18thC.
$2,000-3,000

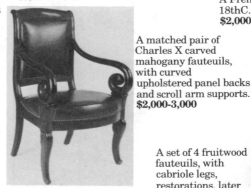

A matched pair of Charles X carved mahogany fauteuils, with curved upholstered panel backs and scroll arm supports.
$2,000-3,000

A French carved beechwood fauteuil, upholstered in petit point needlework, 18thC.
$1,200-1,750

A set of 4 fruitwood fauteuils, with cabriole legs, restorations, later blocks, mid-18thC.
$7,000-10,000

Upholstered Armchairs

A pair of George II style walnut wing armchairs, upholstered in gros point with leaves and flowerheads.
$5,000-7,500

A George III mahogany bergère, with brass feet and casters.
$4,000-5,500

A George III white and green painted bergère, upholstered in pale green cloth, the decoration later.
$1,200-1,750

A George III mahogany wing armchair, upholstered in yellow damask.
$2,000-3,000

A George III mahogany wing armchair, on square chamfered legs joined by later stretchers.
$3,000-4,500

A George III mahogany wing armchair, the shaped back, arms and squab cushion upholstered in pale blue repp, on fluted square legs joined by an H-shaped stretcher.
$5,000-7,500

An early Georgian beechwood wing armchair, with high arched back, outscrolled arms and squab covered in pale green velvet, with later stretchers.
$6,000-8,000

A George IV rosewood bergère armchair, with loose cushion.
$3,000-4,500

A Georgian mahogany wing armchair, on square supports united by plain stretchers.
$1,000-1,500

A George IV rosewood library armchair, with ratcheted buttoned padded back.
$2,500-3,500

A Regency mahogany library chair with cane filled back, arms and seat with squab cushions, and another library chair.
$2,000-3,000

A Queen Anne walnut easy chair, Rhode Island, dated 1735/6, 47½in (120cm) high.
$50,000-55,000

A Queen Anne carved mahogany wing chair, Rhode Island, one foot pieced, c1750, 46in (116.5cm) high.
$18,000-22,000

A Federal easy chair, Massachusetts, c1810, 46in (116.5cm) high.
$8,000-10,000

A Chippendale walnut easy chair, mid-Atlantic States, c1770, 45in (114cm) high.
$4,500-5,000

A Regency mahogany bergère.
$800-1,200

A Regency mahogany bergère.
$3,000-4,500

A pair of George IV mahogany bergères.
$2,500-3,500

A pair of Regency mahogany tub shape chairs, upholstered in green, with sabre legs, one repaired.
$2,000-3,000

A Regency mahogany library armchair, with cane filled back and seat with red leather squab cushions.
$4,000-5,500

A Victorian mahogany armchair, the spoon back with a C-scroll carved frame headed by a flower and acanthus carved crest.
$1,500-2,500

A pair of Regency mahogany wing armchairs, upholstered in hide.
$9,000-12,500

A late Regency mahogany framed bergère.
$1,200-1,750

A late Regency mahogany bergère library armchair.
$2,500-3,500

A pair of Regency design mahogany bergères with caned backs, sides and seats with upholstered squab cushions.
$2,500-3,500

A wing easy chair with reclining action, late 19thC.
$1,200-1,750

A Victorian rosewood scroll back nursing chair.
$450-600

A pair of Victorian walnut armchairs.
$3,000-4,000

A library chair, with buttoned leather upholstery, on reeded legs.
$900-1,300

A suite of upholstered furniture comprising a two-seat sofa, 2 small armchairs with shaped backs and 4 matching chairs, 19thC.
$900-1,300

A Victorian spoon back nursing chair, the walnut frame with a flowerhead carved surmount above a deep buttoned back and seat, upholstered in pale blue silk damask.
$1,300-2,000

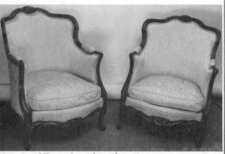

A pair of French walnut bergère chairs, re-upholstered in silk moire, mid-19thC.
$3,000-4,500

A pair of French wing armchairs, with carved gilded frames, 19thC.
$3,000-4,500

Dining Chairs

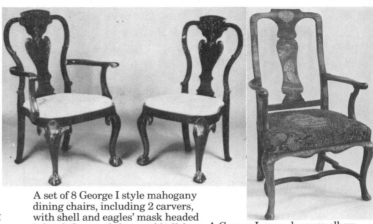

A pair of George I walnut dining chairs.
$3,000-4,500

A set of 8 George I style mahogany dining chairs, including 2 carvers, with shell and eagles' mask headed cabriole legs and claw-and-ball feet.
$7,000-10,000

A George I green lacquer elbow chair, with woolwork tapestry seat.
$1,500-2,500

A set of 8 George III mahogany dining chairs, including a pair of open armchairs, re-railed and one armchair with a later beechwood leg.
$10,000-13,500

A pair of George III cream painted dining chairs, each with a shield shaped back with ribbon tied plume splat.
$2,250-3,500

A set of 4 George III dining chairs, including two armchairs.
$2,250-3,500

A set of 6 George III mahogany dining chairs, including one open armchair, on square tapering legs with later blocks, the armchair partly re-railed, one chair with later legs.
$3,000-4,500

A set of 8 George III mahogany chairs.
$7,000-10,000

A set of 8 George III mahogany dining chairs, including 2 carvers, the carving later, renovations.
$4,000-5,500

A set of 6 George III mahogany, satinwood inlaid and painted dining chairs, including one armchair, the caned seats on satinwood inlaid square tapered legs.
$7,000-10,000

A set of 6 George III mahogany
dining chairs, including
2 armchairs, the seats on fluted
square tapered legs with spade feet.
$4,000-5,500

A set of 4 George III mahogany
dining chairs.
$2,000-3,000

A set of 8 George III carved
mahogany dining chairs, including
a pair of elbow chairs with urn
shaped arm supports.
$13,000-17,500

A set of 6 George III Hepplewhite
design mahogany dining chairs.
$4,000-5,500

A set of 8 George III carved
mahogany dining chairs, including
one elbow chair, the backs with
turned bar top rails and paterae
decorated interlaced oval splats.
$6,000-8,000

A set of 8 George III mahogany
dining chairs, including a pair of
elbow chairs, the backs with brass
and ebony strung curved bar top
rails.
$7,500-10,500

A set of 6 George III mahogany
dining chairs.
$4,000-5,500

A set of 10 George III mahogany
dining chairs, repaired.
$22,000-30,000

A set of 6 George III mahogany
dining chairs, stuffed needlework
seats.
$4,000-5,500

A set of 6 George III carved
mahogany dining chairs, in the
manner of Gillows.
$6,000-8,000

A set of 4 George III
mahogany dining
chairs, inlaid with
rosewood, on square
tapering legs.
$4,000-5,500

A set of 7 George IV mahogany
dining chairs, including
2 armchairs.
$1,500-2,500

A set of Georgian mahogany
Hepplewhite style dining chairs.
$2,500-3,500

A pair of Georgian mahogany
Hepplewhite style carver chairs.
$1,000-1,500

A set of 6 mid-Georgian mahogany
dining chairs, the drop-in seats on
cabriole legs with pad feet, later
blocks.
$9,000-12,500

A set of 6 mid-Georgian walnut
dining chairs, the drop-in seats
covered in striped silk.
$6,000-8,000

A set of 5 late Georgian
mahogany dining chairs, on
reeded legs and with carved
decoration to backs.
$1,000-1,500

A set of 6 mid-Georgian walnut
dining chairs, including one open
armchair.
$7,000-10,000

A set of 8 Georgian mahogany
dining chairs, including 2 carvers,
with reeded backs within wrythen
and bobbin turned cross rails.
$4,500-7,000

A set of 7 late Georgian mahogany
dining chairs, including 2 carvers,
with turned and carved supports
and wide top rail.
$2,000-3,000

A set of 8 late Georgian mahogany
dining chairs, including 2 carvers,
on reeded legs with drop-in seats.
$4,500-7,000

A set of 6 mid-Georgian style mahogany dining chairs, including 2 carvers.
$3,000-4,500

A pair of Regency beechwood dining chairs, the moulded stiles with geometric brass tablets, stamped GEE.
$1,000-1,500

A set of 10 Georgian style shield back dining chairs, including 2 elbow chairs, the shields decorated in Chinese manner with pagodas and central oval flowerheads, stamped Maple & Co.
$5,000-7,500

A set of 6 Regency mahogany dining chairs, including 2 elbow chairs, with scrolled reeded bar backs, drop-in seats, on sabre supports.
$5,000-7,500

A set of 6 Regency brass inlaid simulated rosewood dining chairs, the cane filled seats with needlework squabs.
$2,500-3,500

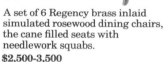

A set of 6 Regency mahogany dining chairs.
$2,500-3,500

Six Regency carved mahogany dining chairs.
$6,000-9,000

A set of 8 Regency mahogany dining chairs, with brass inlaid cresting rails, some replaced by wood.
$6,000-9,000

A set of 8 Regency mahogany dining chairs, including 2 armchairs, the panelled top rails above moulded horizontal splats.
$5,000-7,500

A set of 6 Regency mahogany dining chairs, including an armchair.
$3,000-4,500

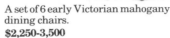

A set of 6 early Victorian mahogany dining chairs.
$1,500-2,600

A set of 6 early Victorian mahogany dining chairs.
$2,250-3,500

A set of 3 William IV simulated rosewood dining chairs, the tops of the seat rails pierced with slits for squabs, one reduced, and a similar pair.
$2,000-3,000

A set of 4 Victorian mahogany dining chairs.
$600-900

A set of 5 rosewood dining chairs, with turned vertical splats and supports, early 19thC.
$1,300-2,000

A set of 6 Victorian dining chairs with shaped backs, serpentine fronts and cabriole legs.
$3,000-4,500

A set of 6 Victorian mahogany dining chairs, with stuffover serpentine shaped seats.
$1,500-2,500

A set of 8 Victorian mahogany dining chairs.
$5,000-7,500

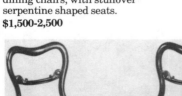

A set of 6 Victorian rosewood balloon back dining chairs.
$3,000-4,500

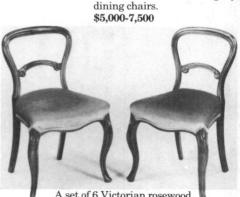

A set of 6 Victorian rosewood balloon back dining chairs.
$2,000-3,000

A set of 6 Victorian walnut dining
chairs, the scrolling balloon and
pierced foliate splat backs above
upholstered serpentine seats on
cabriole legs with knob feet.
$2,000-3,000

A set of 6 Victorian walnut framed
dining chairs, with carved
decoration to back, on cabriole legs.
$2,500-3,500

A set of 10 late Victorian mahogany
dining chairs of Queen Anne
influence, including 2 carvers, the
central splats inlaid with satinwood
and ebony stringing.
$4,000-5,500

A set of 8 Victorian cabriole leg
dining chairs, with carved
decoration.
$3,000-4,500

A set of 6 Victorian rosewood dining
chairs.
$2,500-3,500

An Edwardian mahogany dining
room suite, comprising 12 chairs,
including 2 carvers, a mahogany
draw leaf dining table, 96in
(243.5cm), a mahogany and brass
sideboard of stepped form, 85in
(216cm), and a mahogany three-tier
buffet, 48in (122cm).
$10,000-13,500

A set of 10 Edwardian
mahogany and
satinwood crossbanded
dining chairs, inlaid
with boxwood and
ebony lines.
$5,000-7,500

A pair of Dutch
mahogany and floral
marquetry chairs,
early 19thC.
$1,000-1,500

A pair of Continental walnut and
gilt embellished dining chairs in the
Queen Anne taste, Spanish or
Italian, 18thC.
$1,500-2,500

A harlequin set of 3 Indian silvered and brass repoussé covered dining chairs in Regency taste, the curved bar top rails with ram's head terminals, one with all over meandering floral repoussé decoration.
$2,000-3,000

A Dutch floral marquetry inlaid carver chair, 19thC.
$800-1,200

A set of 4 Dutch walnut and floral marquetry dining chairs in the Queen Anne taste, the balloon shaped backs inlaid with vases of flowers and birds, with slip-in serpentine floral gros point needlework seats, 19thC.
$3,000-4,500

Hall Chairs

A pair of George III mahogany hall chairs, each with pierced wheel back with tapering splats, and shaped plank seat.
$3,000-4,500

A George III mahogany hall chair, the pierced oval back centred by a foliate rosette and edged with fluting, later blocks, stamped W.S.
$2,250-3,500

A pair of late George III mahogany hall chairs, with shield panel backs and shaped seats with oval moulding.
$700-900

A set of 4 Regency mahogany hall chairs, with pierced wheel shaped splats, the central oval panel with a gilt monogram 'P'.
$9,000-12,500

A William IV mahogany hall chair, with a ferret/weasel crest.
$200-350

A Regency mahogany hall chair, with scroll and shell carved shaped back, requiring restoration.
$600-900

A pair of Regency carved mahogany hall chairs, with solid seats and sabre legs.
$450-700

Lord Kitchener's campaign chair, the headrest embroidered with a crown above a wreath with (S) H.K.K, 1896, with letter of authentication.
$600-900

A pair of Continental walnut and beech hall chairs, decorated with simulated marquetry vignettes etched with figures and animals in landscape settings, late 19thC.
$300-500

Side Chairs

A harlequin pair of walnut side chairs, 17thC and later.
$1,000-1,500

A pair of George III white painted side chairs, with close nailed padded oval backs and bowed seats covered in pale blue silk.
$1,500-2,500

A pair of George II walnut side chairs.
$6,000-9,000

A pair of George III mahogany side chairs, upholstered in blue and gold striped velvet.
$4,000-5,500

A pair of Chippendale chairs with carved back splats.
$1,500-2,500

A set of 4 Regency blue painted and parcel gilt side chairs, with cane filled backs and seats with squabs.
$3,000-4,500

A Regency painted chair, with trellis back and decorated with flowers and acorns, on a dark ground.
$100-200

When it comes to Antique Exporting . . .
WE HAVE ALL THE ANSWERS

There are many pitfalls in the antique world awaiting the novice and experienced buyer alike. The largest doubt in the mind of the potential container buyer must be, 'How will they know what to send me and will the quality be right?' British Antique Exporters Ltd have the answers to these and other questions.

Q = QUESTION

A = ANSWER

Q How many items will I get for my money?

A A typical 20-foot container will have 75 pieces of furniture and approximately 50 pieces of china-ware packed in it. We can regulate the price of the container with the quantity of small items; the higher the value of the shipment, the higher the number of small pieces. Of course the type and style of furniture, for example period Georgian, Victorian or Edwardian, also regulates the price.

Q What type of merchandise will you send me?

A We have researched all our markets very thoroughly and know the right merchandise to send to any particular country or region in that country. We also take into consideration the type of outlet eg auction, wholesale or retail. We consider the strong preferences for different woods in different areas. We personally visit all our markets several times a year to keep pace with the trends.

Q Will we get the bargains?

A In the mind of any prospective buyer is the thought that he or she will find the true bargains hidden away in the small forgotten corners of some dusty Antique Shop. It is our Company policy to pass on the benefit of any bargain buying to our client.

Q With your overheads, etc, how can you send these things to me at a competitive price?

A Our very great purchasing power enables us to buy goods at substantially less than the individual person; this means that we are able to buy, collect and pack the item for substantially less than the shop price.

Q Will everything be in good condition and will it arrive undamaged?

A We are very proud of the superb condition of all the merchadise leaving our factory. We employ the finest craftsmen to restore each piece into first class saleable condition before departure. We also pack to the highest standards thus ensuring that all items arrive safely.

Q What guarantee do I have that you will do a good job for me?

A The ultimate guarantee. We are so confident of our ability to provide the right goods at the right price that we offer a full refund, if for any reason you are not satisfied with the shipment.

Q This all sounds very satisfactory, how do we do business?

A Unlike most Companies, we do not require pre-payment for our containers. When you place your order with us, we require a deposit of £1500 and the balance is payable when the container arrives at its destination.

BRITISH ANTIQUE EXPORTERS LTD
School Close, Queen Elizabeth Avenue
Burgess Hill, West Sussex RH15 9RX, England
Telephone BURGESS HILL (044 46) 45577
Telex 87688   Fax 2014

Member of L.A.P.A.D.A. Guild of Master Craftsmen

Bruno Liljefors: A Fox in the Snow, (detail), oil on canvas, 28 x 35½ in.

is picture by Liljefors was recently sent for sale through one of our Regional Offices after the owner had been advised that it might sell to his best advantage in London.

The painting was sent for sale at Christie's and sold for £26,400.

ou wish to buy or sell at our auctions your local representative will be pleased to advise you. Each one s wide experience of antiques and works of art and can call upon the expertise of our specialist staff when required. Valuations for insurance purposes and for probate can also be arranged.

For further information please telephone your nearest Christie's representative.

ristie's South Kensington,
85 Old Brompton Road,
London SW7 3LD
Tel: (01) 581 7611

Christie's Scotland,
164-166 Bath Street,
Glasgow G2 4TG
Tel: (041) 332 8134/7

CHRISTIE'S

8 King Street, St. James's, London SW1Y 6QT. Telephone: (01) 839 9060

A Charles I oak and fruitwood livery cupboard, the base with an arched door flanked by carved foliate panels, mid-17thC, 38½in (98cm). **$12,000-17,500**

A Spanish walnut vargueno, the fitted interior with drawers and cupboards, 45in (114cm). **$8,000-12,500**

A George I oak press cupboard, dated 1723, probably Welsh, 55in (140cm). **$8,000-12,500**

A Charles II oak low dresser, with moulded rectangular top and 4 geometrically panelled drawers, on baluster turned legs with block feet, 88½in (225cm). **$19,000-25,000**

A spice cupboard with secret drawer in lid, original inside drawers, Romayne head carved decoration on door, c1700, 15½in (39cm). **$3,200-4,500**

An oak court cupboard, with convex frieze drawers, 17thC and later, 44½in (113cm) wide. **$8,000-12,500**

A rare Gothic oak cupboard, in original condition, late 15thC. **$60,000-125,000**

Above. A Spanish walnut and red painted cabinet, late 16thC, 48in (122cm) wide. **$42,000-57,500**
Left. An oak table, mid-18thC, 27in (68cm) wide. **$100-1,375**

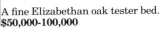

A joined oak and poplar chest with drawer, probably Central Coastal Connecticut, c1700, 48½in (122cm) wide **$200,000-300,000**

A fine Elizabethan oak tester bed. **$50,000-100,000**

A George III oak and fruitwood dresser, the plate rack with moulded canopy and pendant finials, 64½in (164cm) wide, c1775. **$28,000-40,000**

Huntington Antiques Ltd.

Early Period Furniture, Works of Art and Tapestries
Fine Country Furniture, Metalware, Treen and Textiles
The Old Forge, Church Street, Stow-on-the-Wold.
Gloucestershire. Tel: 0451 30842
Direct dialling from the U.S.A: 01144-451 30842

We offer a substantial stock of fine early oak,
walnut and country furniture. Always a
selection of refectory, gateleg and other tables;
dressers and court cupboards; wainscots and
sets of chairs; and usually some rare examples
of Gothic and Renaissance furniture. We
would always welcome the opportunity to
purchase such items.
Open Mon–Sat 9-6 and by appointment.

Most important Inlaid Oak Court Cupboard.
Leeds, South Yorkshire. Charles II Period.
8'W × 59"H × 21"D.

A harlequin set of 14 oak dining chairs, including 2 armchairs. **$8,000-12,500**

An original pine lambing chair, with ash arms, c1780, 25in (63cm) wide. **$3,600-5,000**

An original ash and elm three-legged spindle back chair, mid-18thC, 24in (61cm) wide. **$2,000-3,000**

A rare Cromwellian maple and oak chair, Massachusetts, c1665, 34in (86cm) high, 18in (46cm) wide. **$10,000-17,500**

A Charles II walnut armchair, with later scrolling X-stretcher. **$8,000-12,500**

A pair of George I walnut chairs, inlaid with the coat of arms of the Suckling family, the needlework seats with the same arms, motto and date 1732, arms possibly later. **$44,000-62,500**

A James I oak armchair, the toprail with inscription and initials IT, the carved back dated 1609, with later solid seat, Welsh. **$12,000-17,500**

A Chippendale maple corner chair, on Marlborough legs, Rhode Island or Massachusetts, c1770, 32½in (82.5cm) high. **$4,000-7,500**

A pair of Yorkshire yew wood Windsor armchairs, with arched spindle filled backs, bearing label. **$8,000-12,500**

220

Graham Price Antiques Limited

Wholesalers, Importers, Exporters and Restorers

A27 Antiques Complex, Units 2, 4, 5 Chaucer Trading Estate
Dittons Road (A27 Coastal Trunk Road)
Polegate, East Sussex BN26 6JD
Tel: (03212) 7167 and 7681 or 5301, out of hours (0435) 882553
Fax No. (03212) 3904

part of our modern, spacious, heated showrooms

We offer a large and varied selection of quality merchandise including: antique pine;
English and French country furniture; decorative items; formal furniture and accessories;
victoriana; porcelain; antique prints and kitchen ware displayed in 30,000 square feet
of showrooms, warehouses and restoration workshops on the Sussex Coast
in the small town of Polegate. We are close to the intersection of the A27 (coastal) and
A22 (Eastbourne/London) trunk roads giving a driving time from Gatwick of 1 hour
and just 5 minutes from Polegate mainline railway station which is 1 hour's journey
from London Victoria.

Container packing to all destinations; frequent truck deliveries throughout U.K. and Europe;
courier services; full restoration facilities. Friendly efficient service in all departments.

Open Mon-Fri 9am-6pm   Sat 10am-4pm   Other times by appointment

One of the most comprehensive calls
in Europe.

Clients met from Gatwick or Heathrow
or railway terminals.

Free colour brochure on request.

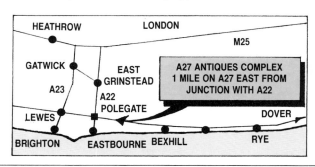

An original Queen Anne painted pine dresser, 60in (150cm) wide. **$12,000-17,500**

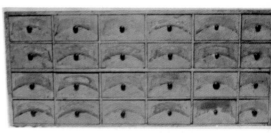

A Continental painted pine cupboard, mid-18thC, 29in (73cm) wide. **$1,600-2,250**

An original French painted pine food cupboard, mid-18thC, 30½in (76cm) wide. **$1,900-2,500**

An East Anglian painted pine chest, in original condition, 18thC, 25in (63cm) wide. **$1,200-1,750**

A painted pine flight of drawers, c1830, 44½in (112cm). **$800-1,125**

A pine spoon rack, c1850, 12in (30cm) wide. **$400-625**

A French painted pine hanging cupboard, containing a collection of children's plates, 18thC, 31in (78cm) wide. **$1,200-1,750**

A pine papered decorative box, c1740, 16in (40cm) wide. **$600-875**

A George III mahogany breakfront bookcase, the base with a fitted secretaire drawer, flanked by 8 graduated drawers and 2 panelled doors, 132½in (335cm) wide. **$360,000+**

An early George III mahogany breakfront bookcase, the base with 3 frieze drawers above 4 panelled doors with applied roundels, 85½in (217cm) wide. **$160,000-250,000**

A fine Continental neo-classical patinated bronze and ormolu mounted mahogany bed, German or Austrian, early 19thC, 71in (180cm) wide. **$100,000-150,000**

A George III mahogany double breakfront library bookcase, adapted, 220in (559cm) wide. **$26,000-37,500**

A mahogany four-poster bed, the blind fret carved canopy with giltwood foliate clasps and coronet at the end, 54½in (139cm) wide. **$6,000-12,500**

An Empire ormolu-mounted mahogany bed, now with large casters, boxspring and mattress, 59½in (151cm) wide. **$44,000-60,000**

Left. A mahogany four-poster bed, with painted arched canopy, part early 19thC, 58in (147cm) wide. **$8,000-12,500**

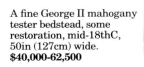

A pair of George II mahogany bookcases, minor variations, 69in (175cm) wide. **$80,000-125,000**

A fine George II mahogany tester bedstead, some restoration, mid-18thC, 50in (127cm) wide. **$40,000-62,500**

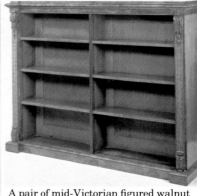

A pair of mid-Victorian figured walnut open bookcases, by Morant, Boyd & Morant, 66in (167.5cm). **$8,000-15,000**

A Regency mahogany bookcase in Gothic style, with central recessed section, slightly distressed, possibly adapted, 132in (336cm). **$28,000-40,000**

A late George III mahogany library cabinet, with moulded broken dentilled pediment and cornice, above glazed doors with chinoiserie blind fret carved strapwork, c1800, 109in (276.5cm). **$22,000-32,500**

A pair of satinwood bonheur du jour, banded with amaranth, 26½in (67cm). **$10,000-15,000**

A pair of Regency brass inlaid mahogany dwarf bookcases, the panelled sides with lion mask and ring handles, on tapering feet, 33½in (85cm). **$60,000-87,500**

A pair of Regency rosewood open bookcases, with galleried tops, the bases with Siena marble tops, the tops with later simulated rosewood oak shelves, 32in (81cm). **$20,000-30,000**

A Regency rosewood revolving bookstand, with pierced brass gallery, 57in (144.5cm) high. **$50,000-75,000**

A Louis XV style amboyna and partridge-wood bonheur du jour, applied with gilt brass foliate mouldings and inlaid with arabesques, the base with a frieze drawer with adjustable writing rest, on cabriole legs, 33in (84cm). **$8,000-12,500**

A pair of Regency satinwood dwarf bookcases, with adjustable shelves and recessed turned tapering pilasters, on tapering feet, 36in (91.5cm). **$30,000-42,500**

A George IV mahogany bookcase, with 3 Gothic glazed doors, flanked and divided by foliate volutes, 66in (167.5cm). **$20,000-30,000**

Lakeside Antiques

Old Cement Works
South Heighton
Newhaven, East Sussex
England
Tel: (0273) 513326
Fax: (0273) 515528

*Large manufacturer of bookcases
for American and Continental market.*

20,000 sq. ft. of factory and showroom.

20 minutes from Brighton.

A George I walnut bureau, with cross-banded top, the sloping lid enclosing a fitted interior, on later bracket feet, 24in (61cm).
$22,000-32,500

A George III yew wood bureau, with pierced brass carrying handles, on bracket feet, 37in (94cm).
$12,000-17,500

A Chippendale mahogany desk, the thumb moulded sloping front enclosing a blocked and fitted interior with 3 fan carved drawers, Salem, Massachusetts, c1755, 43½in (110cm). **$22,000-32,500**

A mid-Georgian walnut bureau, inlaid with boxwood and ebonised stringing, on bracket feet, 2 replaced, 38½in (97cm). **$14,000-20,000**

A George I walnut bureau, the feather-banded sloping lid enclosing a fitted interior, on later bracket feet, minor restorations, 39in (99cm).
$14,000-22,500

A Chippendale cherrywood desk, minor repairs, Pennsylvania, probably Lancaster County, c1770, 41½in (105cm).
$44,000-60,000

An early Georgian walnut bureau, banded with elm, on bracket feet, 36½in (92cm). **$12,000-20,000**

A William and Mary stained burr elm kneehole bureau, in the manner of Coxed and Woster, crossbanded with walnut and inlaid with pewter lines, on later bun feet, 39½in (100cm).
$24,000-35,000

A George III flame mahogany veneered bureau, the sloping front enclosing a fitted interior with a Gothic blind fret decorated door, on ogee bracket feet, 39in (99cm).
$6,000-10,000

An oyster veneered laburnum bureau, the sloping lid enclosing a fitted interior with a well and central door, on bun feet, 32in (81cm).
$10,000-15,000

A Chippendale carved figured maple desk, the interior drawers and prospect door in red cedar, repair to prospect door, Rhode Island, c1770, 38in (96cm).
$12,000-17,500

A laburnum bureau, the crossbanded sloping front enclosing fitted oak interior, all inlaid with a chevron pattern, on bracket feet, 38in (96.5cm).
$8,000-12,500

226

A Queen Anne green japanned bureau cabinet, finely gilt with chinoiserie figures, birds and landscapes, 40in (102cm). **$90,000-125,000**

A late George II mahogany bureau cabinet, the shaped mirrored doors with foliate carved gilt slips, the fall enclosing a fitted interior, 39in (99cm). **$8,000-12,500**

A George I burr walnut bureau cabinet, with enclosed fitted interior and leather lined featherbanded sloping front, on reduced bracket feet, 42in (106.5cm). **$64,000-90,000**

A Queen Anne walnut and featherstrung secretaire cabinet on chest, 41½in (105cm). **$22,000-37,500**

A Queen Anne figured walnut secretaire, the fall flap enclosing fitted interior, on later bun feet, 43in (109cm). **$34,000-50,000**

A George II parcel gilt mahogany and olive wood bureau bookcase, in the manner of William Kent, 40½in (102cm). **$150,000-237,500**

A Queen Anne black and gold lacquer bureau cabinet, the mirrored doors enclosing a later partly fitted interior, partly re-decorated, 42in (106.5cm). **$80,000-125,000**

A George I cream lacquer secretaire cabinet, decorated with painted figures in domestic pursuits, gardens and flowers, 44in (111.5cm). **$600,000+**

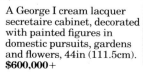

An Empire mahogany secretaire à abattant, with mottled black marble top, 38in (96.5cm). **$38,000-55,000**

A pair of Regency mahogany library cabinets, with alterations, early 19thC, 44in (112cm). **$10,000-17,500**

A Dutch walnut and floral marquetry bureau cabinet in 3 parts, c1800, 55in (139cm). **$24,000-35,000**

A George III mahogany library cabinet, with moulded swan neck pediment pierced with spreading flutes, the lower part with crossbanded doors, late 18thC, 39in (99cm). **$8,000-12,500**

A George III mahogany secretaire cabinet, 43in (109cm). **$24,000-35,000**

A George III mahogany secretaire cabinet, inlaid with boxwood lines, 44½in (112cm). **$11,000-16,250**

A giltmetal mounted bureau à cylindre in the Empire style, with enclosed drawers and leather lined writing surface, 51in (130cm). **$8,000-12,500**

A Federal mahogany bookcase/writing desk, in 2 sections, minor repairs and veneer losses, Massachusetts, c1805, 41in (104cm). **$6,000-10,000**

A Danish Empire mahogany and fruitwood bureau cabinet, on ebonised claw feet, 51in (129.5cm). **$10,000-15,000**

A Charles II style shagreen cabinet on silvered stand, the cabinet and doors edged with ivory, and with strap-work hinges and lockplate, fitted interior with 2 glass bottomed drawers, 26in (66cm). **$12,000-20,000**

An early Georgian red lacquer cabinet-on-stand, 40½in (103cm). **$12,000-20,000**

A William and Mary oyster veneered walnut marquetry cabinet-on-stand, the spirally turned legs joined by a later shaped flat stretcher, and later ebonised bun feet, 51in (130cm). **$26,000-40,000**

A Florentine parcel gilt and walnut bureau cabinet, by Luigi Frullini, 52in (132cm). **$22,000-32,500**

An English oak and ormolu mounted neo-Gothic cabinet-on-stand, c1840, 27½in (70cm). **$5,000-7,500**

An early Victorian display cabinet, 64in (162.5cm). **$8,000-12,500**

A South German ebonised, walnut and marquetry cabinet-on-stand, late 17thC, 60in (152cm). **$20,000-30,000**

A Biedermeier fruitwood secretaire à abattant, the fall front enclosing an architectural fitted interior, c1800, 44in (112cm). **$8,000-15,000**

A Charles II black and gold lacquer cabinet-on-stand, the later silvered stand with gadrooned border, 41in (104cm). **$22,000-32,500**

A George III mahogany cabinet-on-stand, the panelled doors with re-entrant corners, enclosing drawers, the stand with chamfered square legs headed by pierced brackets, 32in (81cm). **$8,000-12,500**

A Louis XVI style ormolu mounted mahogany and parquetry vitrine, late 19thC. **$16,000-30,000**

A Regency parcel gilt and rosewood side cabinet, the white marble top with concave sides and ribbed edge, above a pair of cupboard doors cross-banded with calamander and filled with brass trellis backed with pleated silk, 38½in (97cm). **$26,000-40,000**

A Regency ormolu mounted rosewood and ebonised side cabinet, 29in (74cm). **$44,000-60,000**

A Portuguese Colonial, ebony and hardwood cabinet, Goanese, 18thC, 32½in (82cm). **$38,000-57,500**

A Regency rosewood and parcel gilt side cabinet in the Southill manner, with breakfront D-shaped front, regilded, 59½in (150cm). **$60,000-80,000**

A pair of Italian rococo inlaid walnut corner cupboards, mid-18thC, 26½in (67cm). **$24,000-37,500**

An Italian ebony and pietra dura cabinet-on-stand, the sides with cartouches centred by the Medici coat-of-arms, the later stand with cabriole legs, 47in (119cm). **$38,000-55,000**

A pair of Regency ormolu mounted dwarf cabinets, with grey marble tops, later glazed panel door, 41½in (105cm). **$14,000-22,500**

A pair of Régence ormolu mounted kingwood and parquetry encoignures, with 'arc en arbalette' tops, possibly German, 29in (74cm). **$50,000-75,000**

A mid-Victorian figured walnut folio stand and cupboard, locks stamped J. Bramah, 124 Piccadilly, 43in (109cm). **$30,000-45,000**

A pair of Regency brass and ebony inlaid side cabinets, with later tops, 29½in (75cm). **$20,000-30,000**

A pair of George III mahogany library armchairs, covered in close nailed velvet, with sloping arm supports, on square legs joined by stretchers, one re-railed. **$14,000-20,000**

An early George III walnut wing armchair, the bowed seat with a squab cushion, with claw-and-ball feet. **$18,000-27,500**

An early George III mahogany library armchair, some repairs. **$40,000-62,500**

A pair of mahogany and parcel gilt library armchairs, the channelled arm supports and seat rails carved with ribbon tied rosettes, on cabriole legs headed by scrolling foliage, with pad feet and foliate toes. **$50,000-75,000**

A Regency mahogany bergère, the sides filled with split cane, the reeded frame with scroll arm supports. **$7,000-11,250**

A pair of George II mahogany library armchairs, the drop-in seats covered with restored contemporary gros and petit point needlework, c1760. **$200,000-312,500**

A George II mahogany library armchair, with cartouche shaped padded back and seat covered in cut velvet, extensively re-railed. **$19,500-28,750**

A set of 8 George III giltwood open armchairs, with moulded frames on fluted seat rails and tapering fluted legs headed by oval beaded paterae. **$60,000-87,500**

A Regency ebonised bergère, with deep curved toprail and upholstered back and seat covered in leather, the ribbed scrolled arms on sabre legs headed by anthemions. **$19,000-28,750**

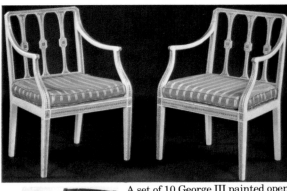

Left. A Regency ebonised open armchair, decorated with gilt, later feet.
$5,000-8,750
Right. A Regency mahogany Windsor chair.
$6,000-10,000

A set of 10 George III painted open armchairs, restorations.
$24,000-35,000

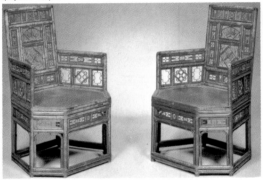

A pair of Regency bamboo bergères, in the Brighton Pavilion taste, early 19thC.
$6,000-10,000

A set of 6 George III black japanned open armchairs, later caned, re-decorated.
$8,000-12,500

A pair of George IV parcel gilt and cream painted bergères, in the style of Morel & Hughes, previously blue painted. **$36,000-52,500**

A George IV simulated rosewood bergère, stamped T. Bradley twice.
$12,000-20,000

A George III chair.
$4,000-7,500

A pair of Régence walnut fauteuils.
$7,000-11,250

A set of 5 Regency painted and parcel gilt open armchairs, the caned seats with silk squab cushions, and another en suite, of later date.
$30,000-45,000

Left. A George IV simulated rosewood bergère.
$4,000-6,250
Right. A pair of Regency painted bergères, with bowed toprails centred by panels of frolicking putti and trellis splats. **$19,000-28,750**

A set of 8 early Victorian rosewood open armchairs in George II style, profusely carved with shells and foliage, with eagle's claw-and-ball feet. **$22,000-32,500**

A pair of Russian mahogany, parcel gilt and ebonised open fauteuils, early 19thC, redecorated, 26in (67cm). **$22,000-32,500**

A Chippendale mahogany corner chair, Newport, Rhode Island, c1760. **$28,000-40,000**

A set of 4 early George II mahogany side chairs, upholstered in part-18thC gros point, c1735. **$12,000-17,500**

An Empire mahogany fauteuil, one back foot spliced. **$8,000-12,500**

Two similar George IV rosewood and parcel gilt bergères, attributed to Morel and Seddon, one with cresting deficient, the other with later finials and lacking leg mouldings. **$18,000-27,500**

A pair of Empire mahogany fauteuils, with slightly bowed panelled toprails carved with fruiting foliage, upholstered in damask, the foliate scrolling arms on dolphin supports, on ribbed cabriole legs headed by foliage and rosettes. **$36,000-50,000**

A pair of early Victorian rosewood open armchairs, carved with flowerhead crestings and centres to the seat rails. **$16,000-25,000**

A set of 11 George II walnut dining chairs, probably by Giles Grendey, restorations to front feet, c1740, and a side chair and an armchair of a later date. **$60,000-87,500**

An early Victorian oak open armchair, attributed to A. W. N. Pugin, upholstered in contemporary foliate cut velvet. **$12,000-20,000**

A giltwood suite of seat furniture of Louis XV style, comprising a canapé and a set of 4 fauteuils, labelled E.G. Gaze Meubles Anciens Dorures Rue Charles V, No. 8 Paris, late 19thC, the canapé 86in (219cm). **$19,000-28,750**

A set of 9 Regency mahogany dining chairs including a pair of armchairs, and one of a later date.
$22,000-32,500

A set of 8 Regency rosewood and parcel gilt dining chairs, including 2 armchairs. **$42,000-57,500**

A set of 12 George III carved mahogany dining chairs in the Hepplewhite taste.
$32,000-45,000

A set of 12 Regency simulated rosewood and parcel gilt dining chairs, variously stamped. **$38,000-57,500**

A harlequin set of 11 mahogany dining chairs of Chippendale design, stamped Hindley & Wilkinson.
$20,000-30,000

A set of 12 early George III style mahogany dining chairs, the chamfered legs carved with Gothic panels and headed by C-scroll brackets.
$20,000-45,000

A set of 4 George III mahogany dining chairs, including an open armchair, later blocks.
$12,000-17,500

A set of 12 Regency mahogany dining chairs in the style of Gillows, including 2 armchairs. **$40,000-57,500**

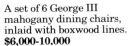

A set of 6 George III mahogany dining chairs, inlaid with boxwood lines.
$6,000-10,000

A set of 10 Regency painted and parcel gilt dining chairs, variously stamped.
$34,000-47,500

A set of 8 mahogany dining chairs, including a pair of armchairs.
$9,000-13,750

A set of 3 Russian neo-classical ormolu mounted Karelian birch side chairs, the crest panels mounted with ormolu martial trophies, c1820. **$7,000-11,250**

A set of 12 Portuguese walnut dining chairs, including a pair of open armchairs, mid-18thC. **$18,000-27,500**

A set of 21 George IV mahogany dining chairs, in the manner of Gillows, 7 stamped F.F. **$66,000-95,000**

Left. A pair of George II painted hall chairs. **$12,000-17,500**   Right. A pair of Queen Anne walnut side chairs, c1750. **$20,000-30,000**

A set of 8 George IV simulated rosewood dining chairs. **$11,000-16,250**

Above. A William & Mary scarlet and gold lacquer side chair, partly redecorated, c1700. **$3,000-5,000**
Left. A set of 10 Louis XVI painted dining chairs, upholstered in red leather. **$36,000-50,000**

A set of 8 mid-Georgian mahogany hall chairs, the solid backs with the crest of a cockatrice. **$15,000-21,250**

A set of 6 Louis Phillippe carved giltwood and gesso salon chairs, in the manner of Fournier, with pierced tassel crestings and inter-laced rope twist splats and frames. **$12,000-17,500**

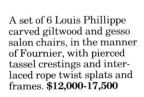

A Queen Anne walnut bachelor's chest, the crossbanded folding top inlaid with pollard oak, bordered with herringbone lines, 31½in (80cm). **$80,000-112,500**

An early Georgian walnut kneehole coffer, the hinged leather lined top enclosing a fitted interior, 35in (89cm). **$6,000-10,000**

A Queen Anne walnut chest, with crossbanded top above a slide, on later bracket feet, 27in (68.5cm). **$16,000-37,500**

A George III mahogany serpentine chest of drawers, fitted with a brushing slide, easel and compartments, c1760, 41½in (105cm). **$6,000-10,000**

A Dutch lacquered and japanned bombé chest, with brass handles and escutcheons, 22in (56cm). **$8,000-12,500**

A George I walnut bachelor's chest, the crossbanded top lined with velvet, enclosing a fitted interior, on later turned feet, 33in (84cm). **$18,000-27,500**

A Chippendale mahogany chest of drawers, on straight bracket feet, with patch to one side, Massachusetts, c1765, 36in (92cm). **$56,000-75,000**

A George III mahogany chest, crossbanded with rosewood, fitted with a brushing slide, 37in (94cm). **$12,000-20,000**

A figured walnut chest, with featherbanded top, basically early 18thC, with later bun feet, 30in (76cm). **$13,000-18,750**

A William & Mary fruitwood chest, the top with geometric walnut crossbanding 31½in (80cm). **$22,000-35,000**

A George III mahogany bombé chest, with baize lined slide, easel and enclosed compartments, 49in (124.5cm). **$16,000-25,000**

A Chippendale carved maple chest, attributed to the Dunlap family, New Hampshire, c1780. **$22,000-32,500**

A Queen Anne walnut bachelor's chest, the top crossbanded and the drawers inlaid with featherbanding, on later bracket feet and back, 32in (81cm). **$26,000-37,500**

A Régence bronze mounted kingwood commode, the bowfronted top inlaid with strapwork, the drawers with Bacchic mask lockplates and foliate handles, 51in (129.5cm). **$34,000-50,000**

A George I figured walnut chest-on-stand, crossbanded with elm, 42in (106.5cm). **$17,000-23,750**

A George I walnut tallboy, 42in (106cm). **$15,000-21,250**

A George III satinwood commode, banded with mahogany, the top edged with boxwood, the doors with rosewood banded oval centres, 54in (137cm). **$34,000-47,500**

A George III ormolu mounted mahogany and marquetry commode, crossbanded with satinwood and rosewood, 55in (140cm). **$50,000-70,000**

A George III mahogany and marquetry commode, with rosewood banded top, the legs restored, 48½in (123cm). **$24,000-35,000**

A George III painted commode, 48in (122cm). **$32,000-45,000**

A George I burr walnut tallboy, the drawers inlaid with chevron pattern lines, 39½in (100cm). **$6,000-10,000**

A Queen Anne walnut cabinet-on-chest, fitted interior, on later bracket feet, 44in (109cm). **$24,000-35,000**

A Chippendale carved walnut chest-on-chest, restorations, Philadelphia, c1775, 45in (114cm). **$40,000-62,500**

An Empire ormolu mounted bois citronnier and purpleheart commode, possibly Russian, 51in (127cm). **$60,000-87,500**

A pair of North Italian lacquer bombé commodes, some redecoration, minor variations, mid-18thC, 59in (150cm). **$70,000-100,000**

A Louis XV lacquer bombé commode with marble top, 53in (134cm). **$84,000-110,000**

A Régence ormolu mounted kingwood commode, later mouldings, 51½in (130cm). **$14,000-22,500**

A Régence ormolu mounted kingwood bombé commode, stamped Mondon, 52in (132cm). **$32,000-45,000**

A Louis XV kingwood and parquetry commode, by P. F. Quéniard, 32in (81.5cm). **$12,000-20,000**

Pierre-François Quéniard, maître in 1767.

A Transitional tulipwood and purpleheart commode, the marble top with three-quarter gallery, the drawers inlaid with harewood lines, back replaced, 52½in (133cm). **$14,000-22,500**

A Louis XV kingwood crossbanded and ormolu mounted bombé commode, by Pierre Roussel, with quarter veneered cartouche shaped panels with stringing, 53in (135cm). **$18,000-30,000**

A Louis XV ormolu mounted tulipwood and kingwood bombé commode, stamped D. Genty JME, partly remounted, 45in (114cm). **$16,000-25,000**

A pair of Italian walnut, rosewood and marquetry commodes, with crossbanded tops, with fitted secretaire drawer, 40in (101.5cm). **$42,000-57,500**

A pair of ormolu mounted première and contra partie boulle side cabinets, with foliate friezes and panelled doors, mid-19thC, 54½in (138cm). **$22,000-32,500**

An early George III mahogany clothes press, 49in (124cm). **$10,000-15,000**

A German Renaissance oak, marquetry cupboard, restorations, probably Cologne, late 16thC, 47in (119cm). **$8,000-15,000**

An Italian rosewood, crossbanded and inlaid commode, the top with a central panel depicting Pan, the drawers veneered à traverse with Hippodamia struggling with Eurytus, restored, part 18thC, 50in. **$8,000-15,000**

A Regency satinwood clothes press, with enclosed slides, 50½in (127cm). **$20,000-30,000**

A Dutch brass mounted mahogany armoire, late 18thC, 74in (188cm). **$20,000-30,000**

An Italian rococo Lacca Povera armoire, decorated with hand coloured engravings, mid-18thC, 49in (124cm). **$10,000-15,000**

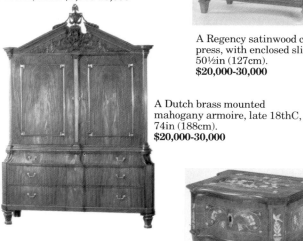

A pair of North Italian, Milanese, walnut and ivory bedside commodes, 2 feet replaced, late 18thC, 24in (61cm). **$22,000-32,500**

A South German baroque walnut armoire, probably Bayern, early 18thC, 85in (216cm). **$18,000-27,500**

An early George III mahogany partners' desk, with leather lined top, each kneehole with recessed panelled cupboard, 57in (145cm). **$15,000-21,250**

A William III walnut and featherstrung kneehole bureau, the fall enclosing a graduated fitted interior, on later bun feet. **$18,000-27,500**

A George III mahogany architect's desk, with enclosed pigeonholes and drawers, late 18thC, 55½in (140cm). **$4,000-7,500**

A George II mahogany library pedestal desk, the kneehole surrounded by 13 drawers with 2 open shelves, the back also with 13 drawers, 60in (152cm). **$32,000-45,000**

A George III faded mahogany architect's desk, the crossbanded easel top with removable bookrest, the figured frieze drawer with writing slide, central easel and compartments, 48in (122cm). **$9,000-13,750**

A George III mahogany architect's desk 6 drawers enclosed by panelled doors, 43½in (109cm). **$8,000-12,500**

An Italian walnut kneehole desk, the moulded quartered top above a slide, the frieze with 3 drawers, 18thC 42½in (107cm). **$14,000-20,000**

A George I walnut kneehole bureau, the quartered and crossbanded top above a frieze drawer, 30in (76cm). **$12,000-17,500**

A George III kneehole gentleman's dressing chest, fitted with a baize lined slide and an adjustable mirror flanked by various compartments, on later ogee bracket feet, 41½in (105cm). **$4,000-7,500**

A George I walnut kneehole desk, crossbanded and featherstrung, fitted with a long frieze drawer, arched apron and 6 short drawers, with central recessed cupboard, 30in (76cm). **$8,000-12,500**

A George I walnut kneehole desk, with cross-banded top and a moulded arched kneehole flanked by pilasters and 9 drawers, 50in (127cm). **$54,000-75,000**

An early Victorian oak and burr walnut partners' desk of Gothic style, the moulded top inset with leather, and 6 pedestal drawers to either side, 84in (213cm). **$10,000-15,000**

A Regency mahogany Carlton House desk, three-quarter brass gallery and brass letter slot, the back inlaid with oval panels, 61½in (156cm). **$264,000-350,000**

A William IV walnut pedestal desk, with leather lined top and 2 frieze drawers with waved panelled front, 63½in (161cm). **$16,000-25,000**

An early George III lacquer kneehole desk, the top decorated in raised gilt, 48in (122cm). **$12,000-20,000**

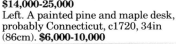

Above. A Regency satinwood Carlton House desk, 41½in (105cm). **$14,000-25,000**
Left. A painted pine and maple desk, probably Connecticut, c1720, 34in (86cm). **$6,000-10,000**

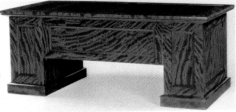

A mahogany library desk, the leather lined top with 4 easel flaps, late 19thC, 79in (200cm). **$7,000-11,250**

A George III satinwood Carlton House desk, crossbanded with rosewood, 42in (107cm). **$56,000-75,000**

A William IV mahogany pedestal desk, with frieze drawers, 52in (132cm). **$12,000-20,000**

A Queen Anne giltwood overmantel, arched bevelled triple plates, in faceted bevelled surround 35 by 62½in (89 by 158cm). **$60,000-87,500**

A William and Mary walnut and paper mirror, with bevelled plate and moulded slip, the divided glazed frame with panels of gilded and coloured rolled paper, the top one with a miniature of Christ and the Paschal Lamb, 31½ by 28½in (80 by 72cm). **$22,000-32,500**

A George II giltwood mirror, mid-18thC, 53 by 25in (135 by 64cm). **$5,000-8,750**

A George II giltwood mirror, with later bevelled plate, the frame previously with candle branches, 51 by 31in (130 by 79cm). **$15,000-21,250**

A pair of early George II giltwood girandoles, with later candle arms, 44 by 24in (112 by 61cm). **$28,000-40,000**

A George I giltwood mirror, early 18thC, 61 by 37in (155 by 94cm). **$12,000-20,000**

A George II giltwood pier glass, attributed to John Boson, 93 by 62in (236 by 157cm). **$84,000-112,500**

A George I style giltwood mirror, with divided bevelled plate and 2 brass candle branches, 28in wide. **$8,000-15,000**

A George I giltwood mirror, the bevelled plate bordered with egg-and-dart ornament, the pierced foliate cresting centred by channelled strap-work, 38 by 25½in (97 by 63.5cm). **$28,000-40,000**

A George III giltwood overmantel, with centre plate in ogee mirror-borders overlaid with scrolling foliage, restorations and re-gilded, 57½ by 82in (145 by 208cm). **$16,000-22,500**

A George III silvered overmantel by Thomas Chippendale, restoration, 69½ by 91in (176 by 231cm). **$54,000-75,000**

A George III giltwood overmantel, 88 by 71in (224 by 180cm). **$58,000-80,000**

A George III giltwood mirror, mid-18thC, 52in (132cm) high. **$6,000-12,500**

A George III giltwood mirror, with later plate, 60 by 31in (152 by 78.5cm). **$20,000-30,000**

Left. A pair of George III giltwood mirrors, partially re-gilded, late 18thC, 79in (200cm) high. **$200,000-312,500**
Right. A Queen Anne walnut mirror, 45½in (114cm) high. **$8,000-12,500**

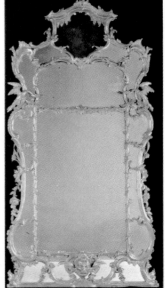

Left. A pair of Queen Anne gilt gesso girandoles, with 2 later scrolled brass candle branches and nozzles, 37in (94cm) high. **$66,000-87,500**
Right. A pair of early George III giltwood mirrors, 90in (229cm) high. **$76,000-100,000**

A pair of George III giltwood mirrors, with later
plates, the surrounds
carved with rushes and
flowerheads, 43½ by 26½in
(110 by 66cm).
$34,000-50,000

A Louis XVI giltwood trumeau, the
frieze centred by a cartouche of putti
painted en grisaille in the manner of
P. Sauvage, with a strapwork and trailing foliage surround, possibly Italian,
late 18thC, 58 by 38½in (147 by 96.5cm).
$17,000-23,750

A giltwood overmantel, with triple
divided plate, inset with a painting
of a harbour scene in the manner
of van Diest, the frame carved with C-
scrolls and rockwork foliage, 59 by
63in (150 by 160cm).
$44,000-62,500

Left. A German gilt lead framed mirror, early
18thC, 51 by 29½in (129.5 by 75cm).
$28,000-40,000
Right. A Chippendale period carved giltwood
mirror, 23in (60cm) wide.
$10,000-15,000

Left. A pair of Regency convex mirrors, early
19thC, 34 by 20in (86 by 51cm).
$6,000-10,000
Right. A George III giltwood mirror, with later
plate, 64 by 34½in (162.5 by 87.5cm).
$14,000-22,500

Left. A Louis XV giltwood mirror, with arched
crest above a divided plate within mirrored
borders, carved throughout with flowering
branches, C-scrolls and wave pattern, mid-18thC,
80in (203cm). **$7,000-11,250**
Right. A pair of George III giltwood mirrors,
48 by 30in (122 by 76cm). **$64,000-87,500**

Left. A Chippendale period carved giltwood
mirror, with contemporary plate, 43½ by 21in
(110 by 53cm). **$13,000-18,750**
Right. A Regency convex giltwood mirror, the
crest with a painted and parcel gilt seahorse
standing on rockwork suspending chains from its
mouth, 44in (112cm) high. **$10,000-15,000**

A Dutch chinoiserie painted and gilt leather 6 leaf screen, mid-18thC, 95½in (242cm) high. **$9,000-13,750**

Two Persian sunken panelled gilt and lacquered doors, minor damage, 19thC, 75in (190cm) high. **$3,000-6,250**

A Louis XVI giltwood and painted fire-screen, stamped G. Jacob, late 18thC, 42½in (107cm) high. **$14,000-22,500**

A walnut and parcel gilt mirror, possibly Danish, mid-18thC, with later plate, 59in (150cm) high. **$10,000-15,000**

An Empire ormolu mounted firescreen, the central column with 2 silk embroidered leaves, with moulded base, 46in (116.5cm) high. **$50,000-75,000**

An early George III walnut polescreen, with needlework scene, 51in (129.5cm) high. **$5,000-7,500**

A lacquer toilet mirror, the sloping lid enclosing a fitted interior, 18in (46cm). **$4,000-6,250**

A brass mounted, mahogany and parcel gilt cheval mirror, probably German, late 18thC, with later plate, 77½in (196cm) high. **$6,000-10,000**

An 8 panel coromandel carved and incised screen, Qianlong, each panel 97 by 17in (246 by 43cm). **$14,000-22,500**

A Chinese 8 leaf coromandel lacquer screen, early 19thC, each leaf 111 by 19in (282 by 48cm). **$11,000-16,250**

A Dutch 8 leaf painted and gilded leather screen, 18thC, each leaf 96½ by 22in (244 by 56cm). **$34,000-47,500**

A Chinese 8 leaf lacquer and hardstone screen, with rosewood borders and glass panels, 19thC, 91in (231cm) high. **$22,000-32,500**

A Regency 3 leaf painted screen, decorated with panels of chinoiserie landscapes, each panel 63½ by 24½in (161 by 62cm). **$17,000-23,750**

A rare Chinese export 7 leaf armorial lacquer screen, c1802, each panel 84 by 20in (213 by 51cm). **$70,000-100,000**

A French 6 leaf painted canvas screen, the painted canvas panels mid-18thC, 77in (195.5cm) high. **$9,000-13,750**

A 6 leaf lacquer screen, 97in (246cm) high. **$34,000-50,000**

A George II mahogany sofa with padded back, arms, and seat upholstered in linen, with spliced claw-and-ball feet, frame possibly altered, 62in (157cm). **$20,000-30,000**

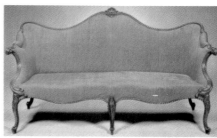

A George III mahogany settee, upholstered in 18thC moiré, 71in (180cm). **$50,000-75,000**

A Regency oak and parcel gilt sofa, attributed to George Bullock, the seat rail inlaid in cut brass with silk covered wooden bobbin fringe, 61½in (156cm). **$132,000-175,000**

A William and Mary style walnut sofa, with fragments of 17thC tapestry, 82in (208cm). **$12,000-20,000**

A George III carved mahogany twin chairback settee in the Gothic and Chinese Chippendale taste. **$17,000-23,750**

A George II giltwood sofa, re-decorated, the frame adapted, 67in (170cm). **$5,000-8,750**

An early George III giltwood sofa, in the manner of John Linnell, 89in (226cm). **$15,000-21,250**

A pair of George III giltwood settees, upholstered in silk, partly re-gilded, late 18thC, 65½in (166cm). **$20,000-30,000**

A George I walnut double chairback settee, upholstered in floral needlework, stamped IH twice, 62½in (158cm). **$24,000-35,000**

247

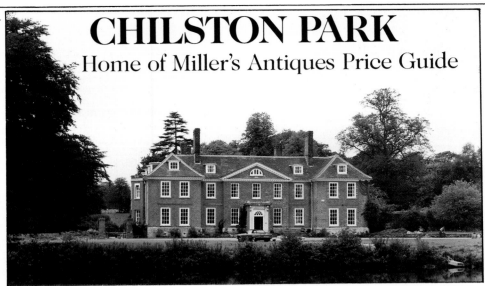

The Private Dining Room...

English cooking and fresh food are the main principles of Chilston's excellent Dining Room. Breakfast, for instance, might include porridge, kidneys, bacon, scrambled and coddled eggs, kippers, kedgeree and muffins. A baron of beef, roast saddle of lamb, game, hams...and a variety of proper puddings feature on the menu.

The Reception Hall...

Atmosphere, warmth and light flickering from chandeliers welcome you to Chilston. Gleaming wood, bright with the patina of age, sets off a gathering of family portraits...dogs doze in front of a blazing log fire...and your hosts wait to receive you.

The Drawing Room...

With an emphasis placed upon comfort, the Drawing Room provides a quiet retreat. Somewhere to rest after a journey or a day's entertainment...to take tea in the afternoon or foregather with friends for a drink before dinner...and to relax completely at the end of the day.

The Bedrooms...

There are 25 bedrooms at Chilston, all of which have private bathrooms en suite. All are luxuriously appointed and delightfully furnished and guests are quite likely to find themselves in a four-poster bed. A special degree of personal comfort is provided by traditional hot-water bottles, complete with hand-knitted woollen covers.

A Russian parcel gilt and green painted sofa, with heavily carved back, arms and frieze, partly re-railed, mid-18thC, 74in (188cm). **$8,000-12,500**

A Louis XV walnut canapé, stamped I. Avisse, 82½in (209cm). **$7,000-11,250**

Jean Avisse, maître in 1745.

A pair of early Victorian rosewood sofas, the moulded shaped backs and bowed seats with buttoned upholstery, 96in (244cm). **$20,000-37,500**

A Charles X mahogany canapé, bearing pencilled inscription Joseph Pillon, 66in (167.5cm). **$4,000-7,500**

A Dutch painted hall bench, the arched back centred by a large shell framed by pierced trellis and flowerhead decoration, early 18thC, 72in (182.5cm). **$10,000-15,000**

A Regency rosewood sofa, with padded back, arms and seat covered in floral patterned wool damask, replaced front rail, 81in (206cm). **$12,000-20,000**

A Federal mahogany, flame birch and bird's eye maple veneered sofa, North Shore, Massachusetts, c1805, 78in (198cm). **$52,000-75,000**

A classical mahogany sofa, re-upholstered in woven horsehair with brass nails, attributed to Duncan Phyfe, New York, c1815, 94in (236cm). **$20,000-37,500**

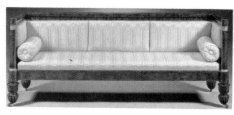

A classical mahogany sofa, with veneered front rail, New York, c1820, 80in (203cm). **$22,000-37,500**

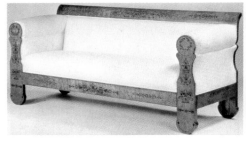

An Empire bird's eye maple sofa, the toprail inlaid with rosewood foliate arabesques, upholstered in calico, 76in (193cm). **$4,000-7,500**

A George III mahogany stool,
19in (48cm).
$4,000-6,250

An Empire giltwood tabouret,
stamped L. Ternisien A Paris,
25½in (64cm).
$14,000-22,500

A Regency oak footstool, attributed to George
Bullock, with ormolu borders and rosettes,
13½in (34cm) square. **$28,000-40,000**

A pair of Regency oak and ebonised
stools, attributed to George
Bullock, 24½in (62cm).
$42,000-60,000

A pair of giltwood stools of Régence design,
covered in 18thC tapestry woven with DVF
monogram, 32½in (82cm). **$18,000-27,500**

A pair of Charles X fruitwood
tabourets, upholstered in silk,
early 19thC, 21in (53cm).
$8,000-15,000

A George IV parcel gilt and
cream painted oak stool,
probably designed by A. W. N.
Pugin and made by Morel &
Seddon, for Windsor Castle,
redecorated, c1828, 17in
(43cm) square.
$30,000-50,000

A set of 6 Federal mahogany side chairs and table, repairs, New York, c1825. **$26,000-37,500**

A William and Mary walnut card table, with crossbanded folding suede lined top, 33½in (85cm). **$17,000-23,750**

A George III mahogany reading table, with easel supported top, later brackets. **$6,000-10,000**

A Regency rosewood breakfast table, the tip-up top with plain frieze, 54in (137cm) diam. **$8,000-12,500**

A George I mahogany games table, with hinged triple flap top, 36in (91.5cm). **$22,000-37,500**

A George I burr walnut card table, the crossbanded baize lined top with candle stands and counter wells, with frieze drawer, 2 feet spliced, 35in (89cm). **$30,000-50,000**

A pair of George IV rosewood breakfast tables, with tip-up tops and hexagonal shafts with quatrefoil panels centred by giltmetal rosettes, on carved paw feet, 47½in (120cm). **$18,000-27,500**

A George III satinwood games table, with baize lined top crossbanded in rosewood, 23½in (60cm). **$8,000-12,500**

A Federal mahogany breakfast table, repairs, New England, c1810, 46in (116.5cm). **$4,000-7,500**

A George III mahogany architect's table, with easel top, the frieze with a drawer with divided interior and baize lined slide, scalloped edge and pierced angle brackets, 40in (100cm). **$10,000-15,000**

A George III mahogany breakfast table, the tilt top crossbanded with satinwood and rosewood, late 18th/early 19thC, 54in (137cm) diam. **$14,000-25,000**

A pair of Regency Anglo-Indian rosewood card tables, the tops opening to reveal baize lined surfaces, early 19thC, 36in (91.5cm). **$20,000-30,000**

A George III mahogany library table, with leather lined top, 4 frieze drawers and 4 false drawers, on ring turned shaft with moulded splayed legs and brass paw feet, 47in (119cm). **$18,000-27,500**

A George IV rosewood games table, the folding top enclosing an inlaid chessboard, with bone chess pieces, stamped BS&P Patent, 23in (58cm). **$4,000-7,500**

A pair of George IV rosewood card tables, each with canted folding top with gadrooned edge, with ormolu shell feet, 36in (91.5cm). **$24,000-35,000**

Left. A Regency rosewood games table, the crossbanded sliding top enclosing a leather backgammon board, 28in (71cm). **$9,000-13,750**
Right. A Chinese export lacquer games table, mid-19thC, 60in (152cm), open. **$6,000-10,000**

A Louis XVI ormolu mounted mahogany trictrac table, with inset leather top reversing to a baize lined surface, the table with ebonised and inlaid backgammon board, restorations, 45½in (115cm). **$5,000-8,750**

A Sheraton period mahogany crossbanded and strung drum table, 23½in (60cm). **$10,000-17,500**

A George IV mahogany and marquetry games table, the top inset with an ebony and ivory chessboard inlaid with flowerheads, c1825, 34½in (88cm). **$18,000-30,000**

A Regency rosewood card table, with burr yew crossbanded baize lined top, early 19thC, 36in (91.5cm). **$7,000-12,500**

A George III mahogany centre table, adapted, 28in (71cm). **$5,000-8,750**

A Regency rosewood games table, attributed to Gillows, for bagatelle and troumadame, with a cue, rake and 9 balls, 60in (152cm). **$72,000-100,000**

A Regency ormolu mounted rosewood centre table, 42in (106.5cm). **$18,000-27,500**

A Regency rosewood and parcel gilt centre table, with moulded tip-up top, 53½in (135cm) diam. **$36,000-50,000**

An early Victorian amboyna and marquetry centre table, in the style of E. H. Baldock, with inlaid top and crossbanded frieze, 54in (137cm). **$12,000-20,000**

A tortoiseshell, walnut and parcel gilt centre table, the crossbanded top bordered with ivory 33in (84cm). **$15,000-21,250**

A Regency mahogany library table, with leather lined top and cedar lined drawers, 48½in (122cm). **$18,000-25,000**

An ormolu mounted boulle centre table, with inset breccia marble top and coved frieze inlaid with strapwork, inscribed, early 19thC, 27in (69cm). **$10,000-15,000**

A mahogany centre table, with moulded verde antico marble top with centred chessboard, c1830, 37in (94cm) diam. **$42,000-57,500**

A William IV parcel gilt, oak veneered and crossbanded centre table, 51in (129.5cm). **$18,000-25,000**

A pair of George IV mahogany centre tables, with later tops, 67in (170cm). **$34,000-50,000**

A pink and grey veined marble table, with brass bound specimen marble top, on baluster support and plinth base, mid-19thC, 34in (86cm) diam. **$12,000-20,000**

A Dutch oak centre table, in the manner of H. Vredeman de Vries, 17thC, the apron and top possibly later, 56in (142cm). **$7,000-11,250**

Above. An ormolu mounted mahogany centre table, stamped Jacob D. R. Meslee, 37in (94cm). **$8,000-15,000** Right. A mahogany veneer drum table, Baltimore, c1815, 20in (51cm). **$12,000-20,000**

An Irish mahogany centre table, with heavily carved frieze, on faceted cabriole legs and hairy paw feet, 73in (185cm). **$8,000-12,500**

A walnut centre table, with moulded verde antico marble top, the concave frieze with moulded edge, on cabriole legs with pad feet, 51in (130cm). **$8,000-12,500**

An Empire mahogany and parcel gilt gueridon with marble top, on bearded centaur monopodia supports and tripartite base, 34in (86cm). **$11,000-16,250**

An Empire ormolu and porphyry gueridon, early 19thC, 36in (91.5cm). **$50,000-75,000**

An early Victorian ebonised and parcel gilt centre table, with Italian scagliola painted top and ebonised rosewood moulding, 36in (91.5cm). **$16,000-25,000**

An Empire mahogany gueridon, with specimen marble top, 30in (76cm). **$22,000-32,500**

An ormolu mounted kingwood bureau plat in Louis XV style, mid-19thC, 55in (140cm). **$16,000-25,000**

A figured mahogany veneer drum table, New York, c1810, 24in (61cm). **$12,000-20,000**

255

A late George III mahogany pedestal dining table, early 19thC, 130in (331cm). **$18,000-30,000**

A Louis XV giltwood console table, mid-18thC, 52½in (133cm). **$10,000-20,000**

An Italian neo-classical painted and parcel gilt console table, c1780, 52½in (133cm). **$10,000-17,500**

A James I oak dining table, 165in (419cm). **$36,000-55,000**

A George III mahogany dining table, with 2 extra end sections, 106in (269cm). **$34,000-50,000**

A George III mahogany pedestal dining table, with 2 additional leaves, restorations, late 18thC, 152½in (387cm). **$16,000-25,000**

A Swiss walnut refectory extending table, with initials IBR MCATM 1782, 84in (213cm). **$20,000-30,000**

A pair of George II giltwood console tables, partly re-gilded, mid-18thC, 51in (129.5cm). **$12,000-20,000**

A Regency mahogany dining table, in the manner of Gillows, 235in (597cm) including 7 extra leaves. **$34,000-50,000**

A giltwood centre table, restored, early 18thC, 42in (107cm). **$14,000-25,000**

A George II pine console table, with marble top and Greek key pattern frieze, 48½in (123cm). **$60,000-87,500**

A Louis XV style coiffeuse, c1900, 59in (150cm). **$8,000-15,000**

A George III satinwood, tulipwood crossbanded and marquetry dressing table in the French taste, 27in (69cm). **$7,000-11,250**

A George III satinwood and marquetry Pembroke table, in the manner of John Cobb, 35in (89cm) wide, open. **$20,000-30,000**

An early George III mahogany dressing table, crossbanded and inlaid, 24in (61cm). **$22,000-32,500**

A Queen Anne walnut dressing table, Pennsylvania, c1750, 34in (86cm). **$44,000-62,500**

A Charles X ormolu mounted amboyna dressing table, 32in (81cm). **$14,000-25,000**

A Queen Anne cherrywood dressing table, Connecticut River Valley, c1750, 32in (81cm). **$92,000-125,000**

A Federal inlaid mahogany Pembroke table, old break to one leg, New York, c1800, 39in (99cm) wide, open. **$8,000-15,000**

A Transitional kingwood and tulipwood table, with hinged writing flap enclosing a fitted interior, 29in (74cm). **$22,000-32,500**

A Queen Anne walnut dressing table, Pennsylvania, c1745, 36in (91.5cm). **$20,000-30,000**

A Louis XV kingwood and tulipwood parquetry dressing table, 35in (89cm). **$10,000-17,500**

A George III satinwood and rosewood banded bonheur du jour, in Sheraton style, 30in (76cm). **$10,000-15,000**

257

A George IV oak writing table, early 19thC, 29in (74cm).
$12,000-20,000

A pair of mahogany pier tables, with marble tops, early 19thC, 19in (48cm).
$20,000-30,000

A Regency mahogany writing table, with later X-stretcher, 48in (122cm).
$52,000-75,000

A Regency mahogany and ormolu mounted library table, in the manner of McLean, the crossbanded top with Gothic arched brass gallery, 48in (122cm).
$24,000-37,500

A painted and gilded pier table, with marble top, early 19thC, 41in (104cm).
$48,000-65,000

A George III satinwood and marquetry pier table, 50in (127cm).
$15,000-21,250

A George III mahogany writing table, with leather lined top, additions, 47in (119cm). **$56,000-75,000**

An Empire mahogany dressing table, the shelf with inset marble, 20in (51cm).
$5,000-8,750

A George III mahogany writing table, with leather lined top and 3 frieze drawers, 43½in (110cm).
$10,000-20,000

A Regency mahogany writing table, formerly with leather lined top, with 3 drawers each side, 58in (147cm).
$84,000-112,500

A George III mahogany table, the top inlaid with a boxwood outline, one leg spliced, 60in (152cm).
$20,000-30,000

A George II mahogany side table, with marble top, 39½in (100cm). **$34,000-50,000**

A George II giltwood side table, late 18thC, now with marble top and the back carved identical to the front, 66in (168cm). **$11,000-16,250**

A pair of George II satinwood and marquetry side tables, late 18thC, 50in (127cm). **$54,000-75,000**

A George I walnut side table, the quartered top cross-banded with burr walnut, 31in (79cm). **$18,000-27,500**

A George I gilt gesso side table, with verde antico marble top, 36in (91.5cm). **$10,000-24,500**

A George III sycamore, marquetry and gilt gesso side table, with satinwood inlaid top, 48in (122cm). **$14,000-22,500**

An Empire ormolu mounted mahogany and bronze table à écrire, with gilt tooled leather lined top, 43in (109cm). **$32,000-50,000**

Below. A Continental rococo walnut writing table, restorations, mid-18thC, 50in (127cm). **$10,000-15,000**

A pair of George III mahogany side tables, 64in (162.5cm). **$44,000-62,500**

A pair of George III painted side tables, some re-decoration, 44in (112cm). **$42,000-57,500**

An Empire mahogany pier table, 43in (109cm). **$15,000-21,250**

259

A pair of Regency mahogany serving tables, with scrolling three-quarter galleries and D-shaped tops, 89in (226cm) wide. **$12,000-20,000**

A George III mahogany serving table, with bowed breakfront top, tapering legs carved with acanthus, 82in (208cm) wide. **$36,000-50,000**

A pair of Regency mahogany side tables comprising a card table and a tea table, 36in (91cm). **$14,000-22,500**

A rosewood side table, with specimen marble top, three-quarter brass gallery, mirror-glazed back, 45½in (116cm) wide. **$10,000-17,500**

A George III mahogany and satinwood banded sofa table, with boxwood and ebony lines. **$14,000-22,500**

A Regency rosewood and carved giltwood serving table, the marble top with a gadrooned frieze, 93in (236cm) wide. **$12,000-20,000**

A Régence walnut side table, with moulded serpentine top, 58½in (148cm) wide. **$40,000-55,000**

A satinwood and marquetry demi-lune sideboard, 19thC, 58½in (148cm). **$12,000-20,000**

A George III mahogany serving table, with blind fret frieze, 71½in (182cm). **$8,000-15,000**

A George III mahogany serving table, late 18thC, 73½in (187cm) wide. **$28,000-40,000**

A Regency mahogany wine table, in the manner of Gillows, damaged, 54in (137cm). **$10,000-17,500**

A Regency rosewood sofa table, with rounded crossbanded twin-flap top and 2 frieze drawers, 56½in (144cm) wide, open. **$8,000-15,000**

An early Victorian giltwood and composition side table, with serpentine moulded marble top, 81in (205cm) wide. **$8,000-15,000**

A Regency rosewood sofa table, the twin-flap top crossbanded with yew-wood and zebrawood, 60in (152cm) wide, open. **$16,000-25,000**

A Regency brass-inlaid rosewood sofa table, the twin-flap top crossbanded with mahogany and inlaid with ebonised stringing with brass roundels, 60in (152cm). **$80,000-112,500**

A Regency faded rosewood sofa table, with crossbanded twin-flap top above 2 frieze drawers and 2 false drawers, 60in (152cm) wide, open. **$16,000-25,000**

A Charles X rosewood sofa table, the top crossbanded and inlaid with trailing foliage and fleur-de-lys above 2 frieze drawers, 60in (152cm) wide, open. **$8,000-15,000**

A George III mahogany tea table, the folding top edged with ebonised and boxwood stringing, 35in (89cm) wide. **$6,000-12,500**

A Regency figured mahogany sofa table, the twin-flap top crossbanded with calamander wood, the frieze with 2 drawers and 2 false drawers, 60in (152cm) wide. **$6,000-12,500**

A George III satinwood and inlaid sofa table, the 2 frieze drawers with stringing, 62in (157cm). **$28,000-40,000**

261

A pair of George IV figured maple tripod tables, the top inlaid with dark lines and the edge moulded with gadrooning, repaired, 18in (45cm) diam.
$8,000-17,500

A William IV japanned tray top tea table, 26in (67cm) wide. **$6,000-12,500**

A late Federal bird's-eye maple work table, Mass., 16in. **$8,000-15,000**

A Queen Anne walnut tray top tea table with candleslides, repaired, Massachusetts, c1750, 21in (53cm) wide. **$24,000-37,500**

A kingwood and marquetry work table, the shaped top inlaid with a townscape, 14½in (37cm) wide. **$4,000-7,500**

A mahogany tripod table, 21½in (54.5cm) diam. **$10,000-15,000**

A George III mahogany tripod table, the tripartite triangular stem with moulded incurved side, ending on hoof feet, 29in (73cm) wide. **$4,000-7,500**

A pair of Regency brass-inlaid rosewood tables, 18in (45cm). **$26,000-37,500**

A Regency mahogany work table, 23in (58cm) wide. **$20,000-37,500**

A pair of George III painted and gilt penwork tea tables, 36in (92cm) wide. **$130,000-187,500**

A George III mahogany and tulipwood tea table, with D-shaped folding top, divided by boxwood lines, 40in (101cm). **$16,000-25,000**

A Queen Anne figured maple tilt-top tea table, Connecticut, c1735, 33in (84cm) wide. **$24,000-37,500**

262

A Chippendale carved cherrywood tilt top tea table, repaired, inscribed E.B.W.Parsons, Hartford, Conn., c1765, 36in (92cm) diam. **$24,000-37,500**

A George II mahogany basin stand, with frieze drawer and domed covered box, 29in (73.5cm) high. **$6,000-10,000**

A Regency mahogany wine cooler of sarcophagus shape, with lead lined interior, 32in (82cm) wide. **$16,000-25,000**

A George II faded mahogany library writing table, c1730, 48in (122cm) wide. **$12,000-22,500**

A Regency brass and rosewood étagère, the top tray with pierced border, 16½in (42cm) wide. **$16,000-25,000**

An early Victorian low table, with out-curving foliate border and gadrooned frieze, on legs carved with foliage and bellflower clasps, 29½in (75cm) wide. **$8,000-15,000**

A Continental neo-classical simulated porphyry and parcel gilt jardinière, possibly Italian, 19thC, 48in (121cm) wide. **$12,000-20,000**

A pair of George III satinwood cheveret tables, with boxwood line inlay, 19½in (50cm). **$14,000-22,500**

A nest of 4 Chinese scarlet and gold lacquer quartetto tables, decorated with dragons, flower and bamboo sprays and butterflies, 19thC, largest 22in (56cm) wide. **$8,000-15,000**

A Directoire mahogany cellaret, the hinged top with canted corners enclosing a fitted interior, 23in (59cm) wide. **$3,000-5,000**

An early Victorian slate snap top table, painted and gilded with flowers and birds, on turned wood vase shaped stem, 36in (91cm) wide. **$8,000-12,500**

An Irish George III mahogany wine waiter, with divided and undulating galleried top, 26in (66cm) wide. **$16,000-25,000**

A set of 5 ebony and rosewood wall brackets, the shelf inlaid with Gothic-pattern bands, with giltwood finials, 22in (56cm) wide. **$3,000-5,000**

A pair of early George III giltwood torchères in the Thomas Johnson style, 50in (127cm) high. **$24,000-37,500**

A pair of George III painted torchères, re-decorated, 55in (140cm). **$10,000-15,000**

A pair of early Louis XVI ormolu chenets, with silvered rockwork on partly ribbed bun feet, 12in (30cm) high. **$8,000-15,000**

A pair of Continental rococo limewood blackamoors, possibly German, early 18thC, 57½in (146cm). **$20,000-37,500**

A Regency mahogany torchère, fitted for electricity, 54in (137cm) high. **$18,000-25,000**

A pair of ormolu torchères, c1830, now on ebonised circular plinths, 68in (173cm) high, plinths 4½in (11cm) high. **$14,000-22,500**

Right. A Regency Cork teapoy, with 2 metal canisters, 43in (108cm) high. **$20,000-30,000**
Left. A pair of George III giltwood torchères, with later inset tops, 49in (124cm) high. **$50,000-75,000**

A pair of ormolu chenets, after Claude-Jean Pitoin, the concave fronted base with lion masks, on ball feet, 16½in (42cm) wide. **$10,000-15,000**

A pair of Louis XV giltwood corner wall brackets, with specimen marble tops, possibly German, 21in (54cm) wide. **$10,000-15,000**

A pair of giltwood torchères, on square simulated porphyry stepped bases, 48½in (123cm) high. **$6,000-10,000**

A pair of George III giltwood and composition wall brackets, 16½in (42cm) high. **$12,000-17,500**

BRITISH ANTIQUE EXPORTERS LTD

WHOLESALERS, EXPORTERS, PACKERS, SHIPPERS

RH15 9RX, ENGLAND

HEAD OFFICE: QUEEN ELIZABETH AVENUE, BURGESS HILL, WEST SUSSEX

FAX 2014

TELEX 87688 ANTIQE G

TELEPHONE BURGESS HILL (044 46) 45577

To: Auctioneers, Wholesalers and Retailers of antique furniture, porcelain and decorative items.

Dear Sirs

We offer the most comprehensive service available in the UK.

As wholesalers we sell 20ft and 40ft container-loads of antique furniture, porcelain and decorative items of the Georgian, Victorian, Edwardian and 1930's periods. Our buyers are strategically placed throughout the UK in order to take full advantage of regional pricing.

You can purchase a container from us for as little as £5,000. This would be filled with mostly 1880's to 1930's furniture. You could expect to pay approximately £7,000 to £10,000 for a shipment of Victorian and Edwardian furniture and porcelain. £10,000 to £25,000 would buy a Georgian, Queen Anne and Chippendale style container.

Containers can be tailored to your exact requirements - for example, you may deal only in office furniture and therefore only buy desks, file cabinets and related office items.

Our terms are £1,500 deposit, the balance at time of arrival of the container. If the merchandise should not be to your liking for any reason whatsoever, we offer you your money back in full, less one-way freight.

We have now opened a large showroom where you can purchase individual items.

If you wish to visit the UK yourself and purchase individually from your own sources, we will collect, pack and ship your merchandise with speed and efficiency. Our rates are competitive and our packing is the finest available anywhere in the world. Our courier-finder service is second to none and we have experienced couriers who are equipped with a car and the knowledge of where to find the best buys.

If your business is buying English antiques, we are your contact. We assure you of our best attention at all times.

Yours faithfully
BRITISH ANTIQUE EXPORTERS LTD

Norman Lefton
Chairman & Managing Director

A. FIELD, MSC FBOA DCLP FSMC FAAO.

THE RT. HON. THE VISCOUNT EXMOUTH,

REGISTERED No. 893406 ENGLAND

THE CHASE MANHATTAN BANK, N.A., 410 PARK AVENUE, NEW YORK

P. V. LEFTON,

DIRECTORS: N. LEFTON (Chairman & Managing),

REGISTERED OFFICE: 12/13 SHIP STREET, BRIGHTON

BANKERS: NATIONAL WESTMINSTER BANK LTD 155 NORTH STREET, BRIGHTON, SUSSEX

THERE ARE A GREAT MANY

but few, if any, who are as quality conscious as Norman Lefton, Chairman and Managing Director of British Antique Exporters Ltd of Burgess Hill, Nr Brighton, Sussex.

Twenty-five years' experience of shipping goods to all parts of the globe have confirmed his original belief that the way to build clients' confidence in his services is to supply them only with goods which are in first class saleable condition. To this end, he employs a cottage industry staff of over 50, from highly skilled, antique restorers, polishers and packers.

Through their knowledgeable hands passes each piece of furniture before it leaves the BAE warehouses, ensuring that the overseas buyer will only receive the best and most saleable merchandise for their particular market. This attention to detail is obvious on a visit to the Burgess Hill showrooms where potential customers can view what must be the most varied assortment of Georgian, Victorian, Edwardian and 1930's furniture in the UK. One cannot fail to be impressed by, not only the varied range of merchandise but also the fact that each piece is in showroom condition awaiting shipment.

As one would expect, packing is considered somewhat of an art at BAE and the manager in charge of the works ensures that each piece will reach its final destination in the condition a customer would wish. BAE set a very high standard and, as a further means on improving each container load their customer/container liaison dept. invites each customer to return detailed information on the saleability of each piece in the container, thereby ensuring successful future shipments.

This feedback of information is the all important factor which guarantees the profitability of future containers. 'By this method' Mr Lefton explains, 'we have established that an average £7,500 container will the moment it is unpacked at its final destination realise in the region of £11,000 to £14,000 for our clients selling the goods on a quick wholsesale turnover basis'.

When visiting the warehouse various container loads can be seen in the course of completion. The intending buyer can then judge for himself which type of container load would best be suited to his market. In an average 20-foot container BAE put approxiamtely 75 to 150 carefully selected pieces to suit the particular destination. There are always at least 10 outstanding or unusual items in each shipment, but every piece included looks as though it has something special about it.

BAE have opened a spacious new showroom based at its 15,000 square feet headquarters in Burgess Hill. The showrooms together with the restoration and packing departments are open to overseas buyers and all potential customers.

Based at Burgess Hill 7 miles from Brighton and on a direct link with London 39 miles (only 40 minutes journey) the Company is ideally situated to ship containers to all parts of the world. The showrooms, restoration and packing departments are open to overseas buyers and no visit to purchase antiques for re-sale in other countries is complete without a visit to their Burgess Hill premises where a welcome is always found.

BRITISH ANTIQUE EXPORTERS LTD
School Close, Queen Elizabeth Avenue, Burgess Hill, West Sussex RH15 9RX, England
Telephone BURGESS HILL (044 46) 45577
Telex 87688   Fax 2014

ANTIQUE SHIPPERS IN BRITAIN

Member of L.A.P.A.D.A. Guild of Master Craftsmen

A Queen Anne side chair, New England, with later grain painting, c1740, 42in (106.5cm) high.
$2,000-3,000

A Queen Anne carved walnut side chair, Pennsylvania, c1770, 38½in (97cm) high.
$3,500-4,500

A William and Mary maple side chair, Massachusetts, restorations, c1730, 44in (111.5cm) high.
$2,000-3,000

A Chippendale carved walnut side chair, Philadelphia, minor break to splat shoe, c1770, 38½in (97cm) high.
$9,000-12,000

A Chippendale carved walnut side chair, Philadelphia, old break to one stile, c1770, 40in (101.5cm) high.
$15,000-20,000

A Queen Anne maple slipper chair, Massachusetts, repairs to crest junctures and splat, formerly fitted as a rocker, c1750, 37in (94cm) high.
$1,500-2,500

A Queen Anne walnut side chair, Massachusetts, old repairs to front left foot and rear left foot, c1750, 39in (99cm) high.
$3,500-4,500

A Federal carved mahogany shield back side chair, New York, one front leg pieced, c1800, 39in (99cm) high.
$1,500-2,000

A Federal carved mahogany shield back side chair, New York, c1800, 37in (97cm) high.
$2,000-3,000

A classical mahogany side chair, New York, loss to foot, c1815, 33in (84cm) high.
$45,000-55,000

A pair of Federal mahogany side chairs, Philadelphia or New York, minor repairs to backs, c1810, 38in (96.5cm) high.
$6,000-8,000

A Federal inlaid mahogany side chair, Boston, Massachusetts, c1810, 36in (91.5cm) high.
$3,000-4,000

An inlaid and ebonised walnut side chair, New York, c1890, 34½in (87cm) high.
$600-800

A set of 9 painted fancy chairs, New York, c1825, 34in (86cm) high.
$3,500-4,500

A laminated rosewood side chair, attributed to J. and J. W. Meeks, Philadelphia, the laminated rosewood carved and pierced in a rococo design, 42in (106.5cm) high.
$2,500-3,000

Chests

A Chippendale mahogany
serpentine chest of drawers,
Massachusetts, c1775, 37in (94cm).
$25,000-30,000

A Chippendale walnut tall chest of
drawers, Franklin County,
Pennsylvania, one foot restored,
piece to other foot, c1780, 45in
(114cm).
$10,000-12,000

A Chippendale walnut chest of
drawers, Philadelphia, thin blocks
added to bottom of feet, c1770,
37½in (95cm).
$10,000-12,000

A Chippendale mahogany chest of
drawers, Pennsylvania, patches to
drawer fronts and case, c1770, 39in
(99cm).
$6,000-8,000

A Chippendale mahogany
serpentine chest of drawers,
mid-Atlantic Colonies, 3 facings on
one foot and one facing on another
foot replaced, c1780, 42in (106.5cm).
$4,500-5,500

A Chippendale cherrywood
serpentine front chest of drawers,
Connecticut, some repairs to feet
and brackets, c1790, 39in (99cm).
$9,000-10,000

A Federal cherrywood bowfront
chest of drawers, Connecticut,
c1800, 42½in (107cm).
$5,000-6,000

A Chippendale carved mahogany
chest of drawers, Massachusetts,
c1790, 35in (89cm).
$18,000-22,000

A Federal inlaid mahogany
bowfront chest of drawers,
Massachusetts, with French feet,
c1800, 39in (99cm).
$8,000-10,000

A Federal mahogany bowfront chest
of drawers, New England, with
French feet, c1800, 40½in (102cm).
$6,500-7,500

A Federal inlaid mahogany
serpentine chest of drawers,
Southern, c1800, 42in (106.5cm).
$5,000-6,000

A Federal mahogany bowfront chest
of drawers, New England, with
French feet, c1800, 41½in (105cm).
$2,500-3,500

A Federal cherrywood chest of
drawers, Hartford area,
Connecticut, with modified French
feet, c1810, 42in (106.5cm).
$2,500-3,500

A Federal cherrywood bowfront
chest of drawers, Connecticut, with
French feet, feet pieced, c1800, 37in
(94cm).
$3,000-4,000

A Federal mahogany and bird's-eye maple chest of drawers, North Eastern Massachusetts, c1810, 42in (106.5cm).
$4,500-5,500

A Federal cherrywood bowfront chest of drawers, probably Kentucky, minor damage, c1810, 41in (104cm).
$4,500-5,500

A Federal inlaid cherrywood miniature chest of drawers, probably Connecticut, on French feet, c1820, 22in (56cm).
$5,000-6,000

A late Federal mahogany bowfront chest of drawers, New England, c1810, 37in (94cm).
$1,500-2,000

A Federal mahogany bowfront chest of drawers, New England, c1810, 38½in (97cm).
$5,000-7,000

A Federal inlaid walnut chest of drawers, Kentucky, c1815, 41in (104cm).
$2,000-2,500

A Federal inlaid mahogany bowfront chest of drawers, Massachusetts, on French feet, various small veneer chips, c1800, 38½in (97cm).
$2,000-3,000

A Federal inlaid cherrywood bowfront chest of drawers, probably Connecticut, on French feet, retains original brasses, c1810, 40½in (102cm).
$3,500-4,500

Small Chests

A Queen Anne burr walnut chest, the quarter veneered and crossbanded top with feather inlay and cushion edge, 37½in (94.5cm).
$1,000-1,500

An oyster walnut and crossbanded chest of drawers, late 17th/early 18thC, 39in (99cm).
$14,000-19,000

A William and Mary style miniature chest of drawers, the top crossbanded in satinwood, with brass drop handles and lock escutcheons surrounded by a half round moulding, 15½in (40cm).
$2,000-3,000

A George I walnut chest, with crossbanded and quartered chamfered top, 35in (89cm).
$4,500-7,000

A George I oyster veneer walnut chest with moulded top, later crossbanded and inlaid with geometric stringing, 37½in (95cm).
$8,000-11,000

A George I walnut chest, with quartered crossbanded moulded top, adapted, 38in (96.5cm).
$4,000-5,500

A George I walnut tall chest, with crossbanded top, alterations, 29in (74cm).
$4,000-5,500

A George II mahogany chest, with brushing slide, above 4 graduated drawers, 28½in (72.5cm).
$8,000-11,000

A George II mahogany chest with brushing slide, 36½in (92.5cm).
$2,000-3,000

A George III mahogany serpentine chest, the top drawer partly fitted, 38in (96cm).
$4,500-7,000

A George III mahogany dressing chest, the top drawer fitted with lidded compartments and bottles, 38½in (97cm).
$2,000-3,000

A George III mahogany chest in the style of Gillows, with 3 graduated drawers banded with satinwood, flanked by reeded pilasters, 40in (102cm).
$4,500-7,000

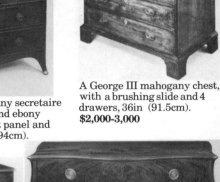

A George III mahogany chest, with a brushing slide and 4 drawers, 36in (91.5cm).
$2,000-3,000

A George III mahogany chest of drawers with satinwood banded top, inlaid edge, 4 crossbanded graduated drawers, the second drawer with sliding inset leather writing surface, 41in (104cm).
$4,000-5,500

A George III mahogany secretaire chest, the boxwood and ebony strung fall with inset panel and fitted interior, 37in (94cm).
$4,000-5,500

A George III faded mahogany chest of drawers, with eared moulded burr yew banded top, 4 graduated drawers between engaged pilaster angles inlaid with stop fluting, 38in (97cm).
$6,000-8,000

A George III mahogany chest of drawers, with serpentine top above 4 well figured drawers, between canted angles, 49in (124.5cm).
$5,000-7,500

A George III mahogany chest, with moulded serpentine top, 44½in (112cm).
$4,000-5,500

A George III mahogany chest with moulded top, 38in (96.5cm).
$3,000-4,500

A George III satinwood, rosewood crossbanded and ebony strung secretaire chest, the baize lined fall enclosing a fitted interior, 46in (116cm).
$5,000-7,500

A mid-Georgian walnut miniature chest, with crossbanded top above 5 drawers, the base with one long drawer, 13½in (34cm).
$3,000-4,500

A Georgian mahogany serpentine fronted chest, the 4 graduated drawers with brass swan neck handles, 45in (114cm).
$5,000-7,500

An early Georgian burr yew chest with moulded cornice, on later bracket feet, 43in (109cm).
$10,000-13,500

A small Georgian mahogany chest of 4 drawers.
$2,500-3,500

A Regency satinwood chest, inlaid with ebonised lines and escutcheons, 36in (91.5cm).
$3,000-4,500

A Regency cream painted chest, the drawers decorated with Oriental figures fishing, framed by simulated bamboo mouldings, 39in (99cm).
$7,500-10,500

A Regency mahogany chest, with 5 drawers between square reeded pilasters, inlaid with ebony and mounted with giltmetal paterae and anthemions, later feet, 45in (114cm).
$1,200-1,750

A Regency mahogany satinwood crossbanded and boxwood lined chest, 47½in (120cm).
$1,000-1,500

A Regency mahogany chest of 4 drawers, with shaped apron and reeded turned feet, 41in (104cm).
$600-900

A Regency mahogany chest, with dressing slide and 3 graduated drawers, 36½in (92cm).
$1,500-2,500

A Victorian mahogany chest of 5 drawers, with bun feet.
$700-900

A walnut veneered crossbanded chest of 5 drawers, on bracket feet, 19thC.
$1,500-2,500

A brass bound military chest, comprising a chest of 5 drawers with countersunk handles, flanked by 2 cupboards, 19thC, 82in (208cm).
$2,250-3,500

A Dutch walnut, marquetry and boxwood strung chest, the bombé front with 4 long drawers flanked by projecting hinged angles enclosing 4 short drawers, late 18th/early 19thC, 40in (101cm).
$6,000-8,000

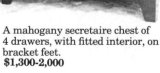

A mahogany secretaire chest of 4 drawers, with fitted interior, on bracket feet.
$1,300-2,000

A late Victorian teak military chest in 2 sections, fitted with a secretaire drawer with easel supported maple writing slope and lidded interior, on turned feet, labelled Army & Navy, C.S.L. Makers, 44in (112cm).
$2,250-3,500

Chests-on-Chests

An early George III carved mahogany tallboy, the upper part with a moulded dentil cornice and blind fret decorated frieze, 45in (114cm).
$7,500-10,500

A George III mahogany tallboy, with rosewood banded cornice, 43in (109cm).
$5,500-7,750

A George III mahogany tallboy, with dentilled cornice and fluted frieze interspersed with roundels, 47in (119cm).
$5,500-7,750

A George III mahogany chest-on-chest, on shaped bracket feet, 42½in (108cm).
$2,500-3,500

A George III mahogany tallboy, with a dentilled cavetto cornice and a blind fret frieze, 45in (114cm).
$5,500-7,750

A George III mahogany tallboy, with key pattern cornice and fretwork frieze, 49in (125cm).
$5,500-7,750

A George III mahogany tallboy, with 2 short and 6 long graduated drawers, 46in (116.5cm).
$2,000-3,000

A George III style mahogany tallboy, inlaid with satinwood and boxwood lines, 19thC, 44in (111.5cm).
$1,300-2,000

A George III mahogany secretaire tallboy, the base with a leather-lined fitted secretaire drawer with pigeonholes and short drawers, surrounding a prospect door, 44in (111.5cm).
$3,000-4,500

A George III mahogany secretaire tallboy, with central writing drawer, 47½in (120cm).
$5,500-7,750

STONE HALL
antiques

We have one of the largest and most varied stocks of good quality English and Continental Furniture in England. (20,000 sq. ft. furniture).

Always a large selection of Georgian, Victorian, Edwardian and Shipping Goods for the trade buyer.

We specialise in Linen Presses, Inlaid Sideboards, Chest on Chest, Desks, Writing Tables, Chest of Drawers, Chairs, Bookcases etc.

Plus small and decorative items.

*All items in mint condition.
Restored in our own workshop.*

1 hour drive from London
10 minutes from Stanstead Airport

Open 9 a.m. – 5.30 p.m. Monday to Friday. Weekends by appointment

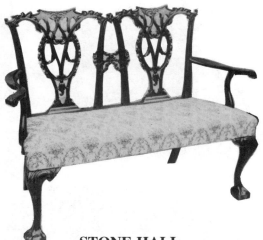

**STONE HALL
DOWNHALL ROAD
MATCHING GREEN
NR. HARLOW
ESSEX**

**Telephone: Peter, Chris or Trevor
011 44 279 731440**

Chests-on-Stands

A George II leather mule chest, the top decorated with the initials MDG and dated 1734, the associated George III pine stand with one long drawer and cabriole feet, 47½in (120cm).
$2,000-3,000

A William and Mary design walnut veneered chest-on-stand, with reeded chamfered sides.
$1,500-2,500

A William and Mary walnut chest-on-stand, on trumpet turned legs, 38½in (97cm).
$7,000-10,000

A George I crossbanded walnut chest-on-stand, on later cabriole supports, 39in (99cm).
$5,000-7,500

A George I. fruitwood chest, on later stand, with cabriole legs and pad feet, 40in (101.5cm).
$2,000-3,000

An early George III mahogany chest-on-stand, the two frieze drawers applied with blind fret, the stand carved with foliage on a punched trellis ground, 31in (78cm).
$10,500-15,000

A walnut chest-on-stand, 18thC.
$6,000-9,000

A walnut tallboy, with 3 small and 3 long drawers, on an arched stand with 3 frieze drawers, part early 18thC, 41in (104cm).
$3,000-4,500

A George I walnut chest-on-stand

A black japanned chest-on-stand, decorated with gilt chinoiserie figures, birds and houses, the stand with one long drawer, early 18thC, the stand later, 42in (106.5cm).
$3,000-4,500

A burr walnut and inlaid chest of 2 short and 3 long drawers, the separate stand with shaped apron and later turned feet, early 18thC, 37in (94cm).
$2,000-3,000

A Queen Anne walnut high chest of drawers, New England, in 2 sections, drawer edges pieced, some restoration, c1750, 37in (94cm).
$10,000-12,000

A Chippendale carved cherrywood chest-on-chest, Connecticut, in 2 sections, 3 drawers lipped, minor patches, c1780, 38½in (97cm).
$13,000-15,000

A Queen Anne carved walnut high chest of drawers, Massachusetts, in 2 sections, restorations to legs, c1750, 41½in (105cm).
$12,000-15,000

Wellington Chests

A Chippendale tiger maple high chest of drawers, New Hampshire, in 2 parts, c1770, 36½in (92cm).
$15,000-20,000

A Victorian walnut Wellington chest, with 7 graduated drawers, the top drawer with fragment of maker's label, 22½in (57cm).
$3,000-4,500

A Victorian walnut secretaire Wellington chest of 5 drawers, and a double fronted fitted drawer, 23in (58cm).
$3,000-4,500

A walnut and marquetry hall chest with marble top, mid-19thC, 20in (51cm).
$2,250-3,500

A French rosewood, tulipwood and maple semainier, crossbanded and veneered with a cube parquetry design, the rounded corners applied with ormolu floral mounts, c1860, 21½in (54cm).
$3,000-4,500

A small walnut Wellington chest of 7 drawers.
$800-1,200

Coffers

A painted blanket chest, Pennsylvania, with inscription AD 1760 JH, NIE, with a blue shaped surround, feet cut down, 51½in (130cm).
$400-500

A painted pine blanket chest of drawers, New England, with later red paint, 18thC, 39in (99cm).
$4,500-5,500

A painted pine blanket chest, Pennsylvania, possibly Hanover area, York County, painted with eagles and foliate decoration, with initials ELBKS, 1808 and 1790, 52in (132cm).
$10,000-12,000

This chest is unusual in bearing 2 dates, possibly representing birth and marriage of the owner.

A Mediterranean ivory inlaid olivewood coffer, the front decorated with geometric compass stars and urns of flowers, late 18thC, 67in (170cm).
$4,000-5,500

A Spanish rosewood and ivory inlaid table cabinet, the fall enclosing 11 drawers, on later bun feet, some replacements, 17thC, 15½in (40cm).
$4,000-5,500

A painted blanket chest, New England, cut down, now on casters, some restoration to paint, mid-19thC, 45½in (115cm).
$9,000-12,000

Commodes

A George III mahogany night table/bedside steps, with one cupboard and two drawers, one converting to a commode drawer, 19in (48cm).
$1,500-2,500

A George III mahogany bowfront commode, the bowed top above a slide, 42in (106.5cm).
$2,000-3,000

A George III mahogany commode with crossbanded top, the sides applied with flowerheads, scrolls and foliage, re-polished, 45in (114cm).
$4,500-7,000

A satinwood and marquetry commode, the top with tulipwood and kingwood crossbanding, the frieze with central drawer, 54in (138cm).
$7,500-10,500

A Louis XVI ormolu mounted amaranth and tulipwood commode, the drawers inlaid with quarter veneered tulipwood panels within chequered lines, 36½in (92cm).
$4,500-7,000

A Dutch kingwood and tulipwood commode, the top inlaid with 2 quartered panels with geometric borders, mid-18thC, 53in (134.5cm).
$6,000-8,000

A Dutch mahogany crossbanded giltmetal moulded bombé commode, with quarter veneered top, 18thC, 54in (137cm).
$4,000-5,500

A Louis XV ormolu mounted kingwood and amaranth commode, with brown and grey marble top, the 3 drawers with ormolu handles, escutcheons, chutes and sabots, some mounts with the C couronné poinçon, 40in (101cm).
$10,500-15,000

The C couronné poinçon was a tax mark used between March 1745 and February 1749, on any alloy containing copper.

A Louis XV ormolu mounted tulipwood commode with breccia marble top, stamped Mondon Jme, restorations, 38½in (97cm).
$14,000-19,000

François Mondon, maître c1728.

A Louis XVI ormolu mounted mahogany commode, with white marble top above a fielded panelled frieze drawer, 50½in (128cm).
$4,500-7,000

A Louis XVI style mahogany commode, outlined with plain brass mouldings, the later top with a pierced brass gallery, 49in (124.5cm).
$9,000-12,500

A French rosewood commode, inlaid in marquetry, with bronze gilt handles and mounts, rouge marble top, early 19thC, 27in (68.5cm).
$1,200-1,750

A Louis XV style rosewood and foliate marquetry bombé commode, inlaid with satinwood and applied with ormolu mounts, 53½in (134cm).
$3,000-4,500

A Louis XV/Louis XVI Transitional commode, parquetry veneered in kingwood, tulipwood, ebony and other woods, marble repaired, and small pieces of veneer missing, 33in (84cm).
$5,000-7,500

281

A Louis XVI style ormolu mounted mahogany and marquetry commode, after Beneman, with 3 frieze drawers and 3 cupboard doors, on toupie feet, 61in (155cm).
$6,000-8,000

A Continental crossbanded bombé commode, with gilt metal mounts.
$3,000-4,500

A South German walnut and crossbanded commode, late 18th/early 19thC, 42in (107cm).
$5,000-7,500

A South German walnut and banded commode, 18thC, 47in (119cm).
$5,000-7,500

An Italian walnut crossbanded commode, 18thC, 43in (110cm).
$3,000-4,500

A Charles X mahogany commode, with moulded concave top, above 3 drawers, flanked by fluted pilasters, 36in (91.5cm).
$3,000-4,500

A South German rococo parcel gilt and white painted commode, possibly Munich, with simulated marble top, above 2 drawers with rocaille lockplates and applied with gilt flowerheads, wave pattern, C-scrolls and handles, mid-18thC, 39½in (100cm).
$20,000-28,000

A South German bombé serpentine commode, 18thC.
$18,500-26,000

A North Italian walnut and marquetry commode, late 18thC, 48½in (123cm).
$13,000-17,500

A French chinoiserie commode in black lacquer and gilt with marble top, mid-19thC.
$4,000-5,500

A late Federal marble top mahogany commode, Mid-Atlantic States, c1820, 24in (61cm).
$4,000-5,000

A fruitwood commode, with later marble slab, probably German, late 18thC, 32½in (81cm).
$2,250-3,500

A pair of Italian walnut bedside commodes, with galleried tops, crossbanded with fruitwood and inlaid with boxwood lines, late 18th/early 19thC, 16in (41cm).
$6,000-8,000

A North Italian rosewood bombé commode, with damaged marble top, 18thC, 59in (149.5cm).
$14,000-19,000

A North Italian walnut secretaire commode, inlaid with ivory, mother-of-pearl and marquetry panels, with a writing drawer above 3 long drawers, late 18thC, 66in (167.5cm).
$20,000-28,000

A North Italian walnut and parquetry commode, with frieze drawer, 50½in (128cm).

A pair of Italian cream painted and decorated bombé commodes, with breccia marble tops with moulded edges, 41½in (105cm).
$6,000-9,000

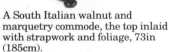

A South Italian walnut and marquetry commode, the top inlaid with strapwork and foliage, 73in (185cm).
$7,000-10,000

A North Italian rosewood and marquetry commode, with canted top centred by a floral medallion above a frieze drawer and 2 drawers inlaid 'sans traverse', 39½in (100cm).
$13,000-17,500

A North Italian walnut and marquetry bedside commode, the top with a centred flower within a tulipwood banded foliate border, 22in (56cm).
$6,000-9,000

Cupboards – Armoires

A Dutch neo-classical mahogany armoire, inlaid with kingwood and marquetry, the top section with 2 moulded panel doors enclosing shelves, late 18thC, 71in (180cm).
$7,000-10,000

A Dutch carved mahogany armoire, the upper part with a spindle gallery and moulded dentil cornice, fitted with shelves and drawers enclosed by a pair of paterae decorated panel doors, early 19thC, 66in (167cm).
$4,000-5,500

A decorative Italian green painted and parcel gilt armoire, 18thC, 73½in (184cm).
$8,000-11,000

Cupboards – Corner

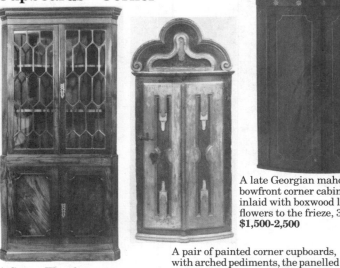

A late Georgian mahogany bowfront corner cabinet, the doors inlaid with boxwood lines and flowers to the frieze, 30in (76cm).
$1,500-2,500

A George III mahogany corner cupboard, the interior with serpentine front shelves, enclosed by glazed doors, the base with a slide above a pair of panel doors, 38in (96.5cm).
$7,000-10,000

A pair of painted corner cupboards, with arched pediments, the panelled doors enclosing shelves, possibly Scandinavian, late 18th/early 19thC, 26in (66cm).
$4,000-5,500

A George III mahogany veneered corner cupboard, the velvet lined interior with 3 shaped shelves, enclosed by glazed doors, 54in (137cm).
$5,000-7,500

A Georgian painted corner cupboard, 36½in (92cm) high.
$800-1,200

A George III mahogany bowfront corner cupboard, the doors inlaid with urns and enclosing shelves, with one drawer under, brass H-hinges, 27½in (70cm).
$2,000-3,000

A mahogany corner cupboard.
$3,000-4,000

CORNER CUPBOARDS

★ these cupboards were made right through the 18thC in various woods including walnut and mahogany, as well as oak

★ examples in oak are usually 'country' versions of the more sophisticated pieces made in walnut or mahogany

★ corner cupboards with glazed doors, that are suitable for the display of porcelain or other objects, are the most sought after type. They are, however, far more difficult to find and are consequently more expensive

★ bow fronted examples are usually considered the most desirable, especially if they are fitted inside with two or three small drawers and the shelves are shaped

★ these cupboards are usually constructed in two parts; 'marriages' do exist and whilst these may be acceptable, it should be reflected in a lower price. Check that the backboards of the two parts match and that the quality of timber and style of construction correspond

A Georgian mahogany bowfront corner cupboard, 39in (99cm) high.
$2,000-3,000

A Continental kingwood and marquetry bowfront corner cupboard, fitted with a frieze drawer, recessed panel stiles with brass sunburst boss ornament, basically French, 18thC, parts later, 30½in (78cm).
$1,500-2,500

Cupboards – Linen Presses

A George III mahogany linen press, the doors with fielded panels enclosing sliding trays, 52½in (133cm).
$2,500-3,500

A George III mahogany secretaire press, the baize lined fitted secretaire drawer above 4 graduated drawers, the panels in the doors possibly later, 46in (116.5cm).
$4,000-5,500

An early George III mahogany clothes press, the base with 2 short and one long drawer, on reduced bracket feet, 54½in (138cm).
$6,000-9,000

A George III mahogany linen press, the swan neck pediment centred by a turned finial and a satinwood banded tablet, the rosewood banded oval panelled doors over 4 long drawers, 51½in (130cm).
$3,000-4,000

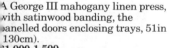

A George III mahogany linen press, with satinwood banding, the panelled doors enclosing trays, 51in (130cm).
$1,000-1,500

A George III mahogany clothes press, the base with 2 short and one long drawer, on ogee bracket feet, 53in (134.5cm).
$4,000-5,500

A Regency mahogany linen press, with urn shaped decorated cornice, the interior fitted with 4 trays enclosed by panelled doors, 48in (122cm).
$4,000-5,500

A Regency mahogany clothes press with eared cornice, above panelled doors with acorn angles, the base with 2 short and 2 long drawers on paw feet, stamped 'Wilkinson, Ludgate Hill', 56in (142cm).
$8,000-11,000

A mahogany linen press, with moulded cornice, 2 cupboards and 4 drawers, on splay feet, 19thC.
$1,500-2,500

An early Victorian mahogany clothes press, inlaid with satinwood bands, spandrels and patera banded and inlaid geometric line borders.
$2,500-3,500

Cupboards – Wardrobes

A Sheraton inlaid mahogany bowfront wardrobe, with 2 short and 2 long drawers, on shaped feet.
$6,000-8,000

A George IV mahogany wardrobe, the panelled doors enclosing cedar shelves, the sides with panelled doors, on bun feet, 55in (139.5cm).
$3,000-4,000

A George III mahogany breakfront wardrobe, the dentilled moulded cornice above 4 fielded radial panel doors, 101in (256.5cm).
$3,000-4,500

An early Victorian mahogany breakfront wardrobe, the bolection moulded cornice above 4 inset panelled doors, on plinth base, 92in (233.5cm).
$1,500-2,500

A mahogany wardrobe, with satinwood banded and boxwood line borders and dentil moulded cornice, basically early 19thC, 47½in (119cm).
$1,000-1,500

A Dutch mahogany and floral marquetry wardrobe, decorated with boxwood and chequer lines, with a moulded cornice and cushion frieze, on moulded turned feet, early 19thC, 71in (181cm).
$7,000-10,000

A Dutch mahogany and marquetry wardrobe, decorated with scrolling floral stems, vases of flowers and birds, with chequer strung cornice and moulded cavetto frieze, 19thC, 60½in (154cm).
$4,000-5,500

Davenports

A late Regency rosewood davenport, with a leather inset fall, with a fitted interior, on a column of 4 graduated drawers to one side, 20½in (51cm).
$3,000-4,000

A William IV mahogany davenport, with sliding top and brushing slide.
$4,500-7,000

A Dutch mahogany wardrobe, with 2 panelled doors enclosing shelves and drawers, late 18thC.
$3,000-4,500

Desks

A George III mahogany cylinder desk, with tambour shutter enclosing a fitted interior, 37½in (95cm).
$6,000-9,000

A George III mahogany kneehole desk, the frieze drawer over an arched kneehole fitted with a cupboard door, 43in (109cm).
$1,500-2,500

A George III mahogany partners' kneehole writing desk, the crossbanded top inset with a tooled leather panel, with 5 drawers to either side, on square tapered legs, with brass carrying handles to the sides, 58in (148cm).
$18,000-25,000

A George III mahogany desk, with crossbanded top, 34½in (87cm).
$5,000-7,500

A George III mahogany kneehole desk, with a moulded edge and inset with a panel of green leather.
$3,000-4,500

A mid-Georgian walnut kneehole desk, the crossbanded top with re-entrant front corners, the recessed arched kneehole with a cupboard, restored, 34in (86cm).
$4,000-5,500

A late George III mahogany pedestal writing table, attributed to Gillows of Lancaster, with scarlet inset leather top above arched fitted frieze drawer forming sham side drawers, above 6 small drawers surrounding the kneehole, 49in (125cm).
$3,000-4,500

A George III satinwood and mahogany banded writing desk, with domed tambour shutter front enclosing a fitted interior, 36in (91.5cm).
$7,000-10,000

A George II red walnut kneehole desk, with folding leather lined top enclosing a flap with divided interior, 37in (94cm).
$6,000-9,000

A George III mahogany tambour cylinder desk, with satinwood fitted interior with pigeonholes, drawers and slide, with a baize lined ratcheted adjustable slope, 39in (99cm).
$6,000-9,000

A George III mahogany kneehole desk, the crossbanded top inset with a panel of red tooled leather, 48in (122cm).
$6,000-9,000

An early George III style walnut partners' desk, with bellflower and C-scroll headed cabriole legs, on claw-and-ball feet, 67½in (171cm).
$7,000-10,000

A mahogany desk, with long frieze drawer and 6 small drawers flanking a kneehole cupboard panel door, basically 18thC, 35in (89cm).
$1,000-1,500

A mid-Georgian style partners' mahogany kneehole pedestal desk, the inset leather lined top above 6 drawers and a simulated panel cupboard door, 66in (167.5cm).
$3,000-4,500

A Georgian style pedestal partners' desk, c1840, 92in (233.5cm).
$10,000-13,500

A Georgian mahogany kneehole desk, with central recessed cupboard and secret frieze drawer, surrounded by 7 further drawers, 38in (96.5cm).
$3,000-4,500

A Regency mahogany pedestal desk with leather lined top, the frieze with one central drawer and 2 side drawers, the kneehole flanked by a pair of panelled cupboard doors, 61in (155cm).
$4,000-5,500

An English rosewood pedestal writing table, with gilt tooled green inset leather crossbanded top, above 9 drawers surrounding the kneehole, the opposing 3 frieze drawers above cupboard doors, mid-19thC, 59in (149.5cm).
$10,000-13,500

A Regency mahogany roll top desk with ebony stringing, the cylinder enclosing a fitted interior with leather lined slide, 37in (94cm).
$3,000-4,500

A Regency mahogany partners' desk, one side with 9 drawers, the other with 3 drawers and 2 panelled cupboards, 54in (137cm).
$4,000-5,500

A padouk and featherbanded kneehole desk, with a fitted interior, above a single frieze drawer, and a recess panelled cupboard door, 19thC, 37½in (95cm).
$1,500-2,500

A Regency mahogany partners' desk with 9 drawers around a kneehole each side, 67in (170cm).
$6,000-9,000

An early Victorian mahogany partners' desk, 60in (152cm).
$10,000-13,500

A William IV mahogany pedestal desk, fitted with 3 frieze drawers and 6 pedestal drawers, 48in (122cm).
$13,000-17,500

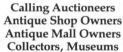

A mahogany desk, with 3 frieze drawers opposed by 3 dummy drawers, on pedestals each with 3 short drawers, 19thC, 43in (109cm).
$4,000-5,500

An early Victorian burr yew kneehole desk, with 2 panelled doors, the left enclosing slides, the right enclosing 4 drawers, 48in (122cm).
$5,000-7,500

A Victorian mahogany pedestal desk, in partners' style, the front frieze with 3 drawers, the pedestals each with 3 drawers, the reverse with false drawers, 60in (152cm).
$5,000-7,500

A Victorian walnut desk, 37in (94cm) high.
$8,000-11,000

A Victorian mahogany rolltop kneehole pedestal desk, with fitted interior and sliding leather lined writing plateau, 60in (152cm).
$1,500-2,500

A Victorian figured walnut kneehole writing desk with 5 drawers, the top with 8 green tooled leather faced drawers, the centre drawer impressed with maker's name, Grunden, Brighton, 54in (137cm).
$5,000-7,500

A Federal inlaid mahogany tambour desk, probably New Hampshire, in 2 sections, c1800, 37½in (95cm).
$5,000-6,000

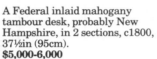

A Victorian mahogany pedestal desk, 58½in (148cm).
$2,000-3,000

A Federal cherrywood tambour ladies writing desk, Kentucky, in 2 sections, small patches to prospect door, c1810, 38in (96.5cm).
$10,000-12,000

A Chippendale walnut desk, Pennsylvania, c1770, 35in (89cm).
$7,000-9,000

A Victorian mahogany writing desk, inlaid and crossbanded in satinwood, 48in (122cm).
$4,000-5,500

A mid-Victorian burr walnut and mahogany kneehole desk, the kneehole flanked by 2 drawers and 2 fielded cupboard doors, 51in (129.5cm).
$20,000-28,000

A Victorian mahogany kneehole
desk, with leather incised top.
$1,000-1,500

A Victorian partners' pedestal desk,
81in (205cm).
$40,000-52,000

A Victorian mahogany writing
desk, 53in (134cm).
$2,500-3,500

A Victorian walnut writing desk
inlaid with ebony and kingwood,
with ormolu mounts.
$5,000-7,500

A small Victorian mahogany twin
pedestal writing desk, with
9 drawers.
$1,500-2,500

A Victorian mahogany desk, c1870,
60in (152cm).
$3,000-4,000

A Victorian carved mahogany
writing desk of Carlton House type,
the top inset with panels of tooled
green leather centred by an
adjustable ratcheted slope, stamped
W. Priest, 1 & 2 Tudor St,
Blackfriars, 75½in (192cm).
$10,000-13,500

A late Victorian mahogany
kneehole writing desk, inlaid
with harewood foliate
marquetry, satinwood bands
and boxwood lines,
41½in (105cm).
$4,000-5,500

A Sheraton Revival rosewood and
marquetry desk, stamped Maple &
Co. Ltd., late 19thC.
$1,500-2,500

An Edwardian mahogany ladies
writing desk, decorated with
satinwood inlay and rosewood
banding, 48in (122cm).
$2,000-3,000

An Edwardian inlaid rosewood
desk, with 2 mirror panels, two-door
cupboard and 4 small drawers,
hinged reading flap and 8 drawers
to pedestals.
$1,500-2,500

An Edwardian Wootton style
mahogany desk, with fielded panel
front and sides opening to an
interior fitted with short drawers
and stationery compartments, with
upholstered tread, 28in (71cm).
$4,000-5,500

A Wootton Desk Company American Bankers' desk, with fitted interior.
$4,000-5,500

A burr walnut and cockbeaded pedestal partners' desk, with bowfront pedestals and shaped top, c1920, 60in (152cm).
$5,000-7,500

A Chippendale style mahogany pedestal desk, the leather lined top with a gadrooned edge above a blind fret carved frieze, 54in (137cm).
$3,000-4,500

A mahogany Carlton House desk, with crossbanding and yellow stringing, 20thC, 41in (104cm).
$1,500-2,500

A mahogany partners' desk, each side 9 drawers inlaid with fruitwood letters, 70in (177.5cm).
$10,500-15,000

A mahogany library desk, the top inset with embossed leather, the sides with 8 drawers, on gadrooned ogee bracket feet, 61½in (156cm).
$20,000-28,000

A mahogany partners' desk, one side with 9 drawers, the other side with 3 drawers and cupboards, with carrying handles, 61½in (155cm).
$5,000-7,500

A Dutch satinwood marquetry rolltop desk, the superstructure with 2 drawers above a solid cylinder and an oak fitted interior, early 19thC, 42in (106cm).
$6,000-8,000

A Chippendale design mahogany pedestal desk, with scale carved border and blind fret decoration to drawer fronts, 48in (122cm).
$5,000-7,500

DESKS

★ desk correctly describes a piece of furniture on which to read or write and which has the top sloping at an angle. In this form it has medieval origins, but the term now embraces various types, such as bureaux, secretaires and the flat top 'kneehole'

★ the davenport desk is highly sought after. Found after the 1790s, the earliest have the upper desk part sliding forward or swivelling to accommodate the knees of the sitter

★ later Regency and Victorian models have column supports to the desk. Look out for the rising nest of drawers that works on weights and pulleys, when a secret button is depressed. After the 1840s, the 'piano front' became fashionable and is still most in demand. While it matters not if the price is right and the description fair, remember that single sided kneehole desks have been made out of Victorian washstands

★ kneehole desks have also been made out of 18thC chests of drawers. Because of cost these are rare and can be detected by incompatible drawer sides

★ an original leather top in good condition is desirable, but a fine new one is better than a bad old one

★ a bureau made to take a bookcase on top will have a steeper angle to the fall front to accommodate the case or cabinet

A kneehole desk, 47½in (120cm).
$2,000-3,000

Dumb Waiters

A brass mounted mahogany writing desk, with a tambour rolltop enclosing 3 short drawers, 26½in (67cm).
$3,000-4,500

A George III mahogany two-tier dumb waiter, each tier with drop leaves, brass terminals.
$3,000-4,500

An early George III mahogany dumb waiter, the graduated trays revolving on turned waisted spiral cut stems, 24in (61cm) diam.
$3,000-4,500

A George III style mahogany dumb waiter, the tiers with chip carved borders, 46in (116.5cm) high.
$1,300-2,000

A late Georgian mahogany two-tier dumb waiter, 41½in (105cm) high.
$1,200-1,750

A mid-Georgian mahogany dumb waiter, 43½in (110cm) high.
$4,000-5,500

An early Victorian mahogany three-tier dumb waiter, 32in (81cm).
$600-900

DUMB WAITERS

★ there is some controversy about when dumb waiters made an appearance
★ they were certainly produced in the 1720s but are rare until the 1750s
★ defined by Sheraton (Cabinet Dictionary 1803) as 'a useful piece of furniture, to serve in some respects the place of a waiter, whence it is so named'
★ 18thC dumb waiters *generally* consist of three tiers
★ made usually from mahogany
★ in Chippendale period supports often carved with foliage, acanthus leaves, broken scrolls, etc
★ Robert Adam's neo-classical style radically changed the design
★ the pillars now tended to become plainly cylindrical with turned collars at top and bottom
★ the late 18thC and early 19thC saw the introduction of pierced galleries often made of brass
★ during the Regency period some dumb waiters made from rosewood
★ marriages are around so beware
  – differing turning on 3 trays
  – two-tier examples (they can be right but are often 'naughty')

Mirrors and Frames

A Queen Anne style walnut mirror, restored, 24in (61cm) high.
$800-1,200

A George I walnut toilet mirror, the base with 3 short drawers and a concave long drawer, 17in (43cm).
$3,000-4,500

A George I giltwood and gesso wall mirror, fitted with a later plate with bevelled edge, 45in (114cm) high.
$9,000-12,500

A pair of giltwood mirrors, 18thC, 38 by 20in (96.5 by 51cm).
$10,500-15,000

A cream painted and gilded mirror, redecorated, late 18thC, 55 by 27in (139.5 by 68.5cm).
$4,000-5,500

A George I style walnut and parcel gilt mirror, carved on the back with an armorial crest and the initials A.H. London, 40 by 21½in (101.5 by 54cm).
$1,500-2,500

A George II giltwood mirror, 40 by 27in (101.5 by 68.5cm).
$4,000-5,500

An early George III mahogany and parcel gilt fret carved wall mirror, inset with a contemporary bevelled plate, 51 by 26½in (130 by 67cm).
$10,500-15,000

A George III giltwood mirror, the frieze with an églomisé panel, later plate, 44½ by 24in (111.5 by 61cm).
$3,000-4,000

A Regency carved giltwood
girandole, 35½ by 19in (90 by 48cm).
$3,000-4,500

A Regency giltwood convex mirror,
35 by 25in (89 by 63.5cm).
$2,000-3,000

A Regency ebonised, gilt and gesso
convex mirror, 51½ by 23½in (131
by 59cm).
$4,000-5,500

Regency giltwood girandole, the
later flat mirror plate within a leaf
moulded and sphere applied frame.
5,000-7,500

A Regency giltwood convex mirror,
43 by 26in (109 by 66cm).
$2,000-3,000

A Regency giltwood convex mirror,
40 by 24in (101.5 by 61cm).
$6,000-8,000

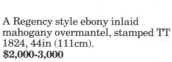

A Regency giltwood overmantel,
29½ by 53in (75 by 135cm).
$2,500-3,500

A Regency giltwood mirror, the
frieze with verre églomisé panel,
38½ by 22½in (97 by 57cm).
$1,500-2,500

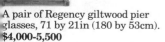

A pair of Regency giltwood pier
glasses, 71 by 21in (180 by 53cm).
$4,000-5,500

A Regency style ebony inlaid
mahogany overmantel, stamped TT
1824, 44in (111cm).
$2,000-3,000

A Chippendale mahogany and gilt mirror, New York, the scrolled cornice centering a spread winged eagle, c1770, 22in (57cm).
$6,000-8,000

A Queen Anne walnut veneer looking glass, labelled by John Elliot, Philadelphia, glass replaced, 2 tips of scrolls pieced and side veneer strip, 22in (56cm).
$4,000-5,000

An Empire carved giltwood girandole mirror, American, some flaking, c1830, 45in (114cm) high.
$22,000-25,000

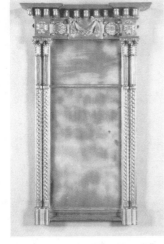

A Federal carved giltwood mirror, by Isaac L. Platt, New York, bearing label, c1825, 26in (66cm).
$3,000-4,000

A Federal gilt and églomisé pier mirror, American, early 19thC, 30in (76cm).
$2,000-2,500

A late Federal gilt and églomisé mirror, American, c1815, 30in (76cm).
$1,500-2,000

A Federal gilt and églomisé mirror, c1820, 21½in (54.5cm).
$2,500-3,500

A giltwood and gesso convex mirror early 19thC, 52 by 32in (131 by 81cm).
$4,500-7,000

A giltwood mirror with bevelled plate, possibly Irish, 53 by 43 (134 by 109cm).
$2,500-3,500

A giltwood mirror of Régence style, 50 by 44in (127 by 112cm).
$4,000-5,500

An easel mirror with bevelled plate, makers J.D. W.D., Chester 1898, 19 by 12½in (48 by 31cm).
$1,200-1,750

An Empire giltmetal frame, the back inscribed 'The Honble Mrs Duff', 12 by 8in (30.5 by 20.5cm).
$2,500-3,500

A Flemish red tortoiseshell and ebonised picture frame, distressed, late 17thC, 48 by 41in (122 by 104cm).
$18,000-25,000

A giltwood mirror, possibly German, late 18thC, 49 by 29in (124.5 by 74cm).
$9,000-12,500

A Venetian giltwood picture frame, painted with a sleeping boy, the frame late 17thC, 29 by 16in (73 by 41cm).
$3,000-4,500

An Italian neo-classical giltwood mirror, Liguria or Emilia, with divided plate, re-gilt, restorations, c1775, 69in (175cm) high.
$4,000-5,500

A German parcel gilt and ebonised mirror, late 18thC, 65 by 29in (165 by 73cm).
$3,000-4,500

An Italian silvered wood mirror, with scrolled feet, mid-19thC, 73 by 40in (185 by 101.5cm).
$5,000-7,500

An Italian giltwood wall mirror, 19thC, 43 by 27in (109 by 68.5cm).
$1,500-2,500

A fruitwood and ebonised pier glass, with bevelled plate, possibly Russian, early 19thC, 48 by 24in (122 by 61cm).
$4,500-7,000

A pair of parcel gilt and white painted mirrors, probably Scandinavian, 41 by 28in (104 by 71cm).
$5,000-7,500

A Spanish giltwood mirror of 17thC design, 39½ by 27in (100 by 68cm).
$1,500-2,500

Screens

A four-leaf screen covered in Brussels verdure tapestry, the tapestry 17thC, each leaf 84½ by 25½in (214 by 63.5cm).
$14,000-19,000

A Georgian mahogany polescreen, with turned column, 58½in (148cm) high.
$600-900

A George II style firescreen, on scrolling foliate tripod base, 64in (162.5cm) high.
$800-1,200

A pair of William IV rosewood polescreens, 41in (104cm) high.
$2,000-3,000

A Regency mahogany firescreen, with sliding panels and gilt capitals, on arched tapering feet, 25in (63.5cm).
$600-900

A mid-Georgian mahogany polescreen, on arched foliate tripod base and pointed pad feet, 54½in (137cm) high.
$1,200-1,750

A Regency carved giltwood three-fold freestanding firescreen, incorporating 10 mirrored glass panels, 42in (106.5cm).
$1,200-1,750

George III mahogany firescreen,
ith arched glazed sliding panel in a
oxwood lined frame with
atinwood band, distressed, 19in
8cm).
600-900

An early George III carved
mahogany polescreen, with petit
point needlework banner, 60in
(152cm) high.
$4,000-5,500

A Victorian crewel work four-fold
screen, 54in (137cm) extended.
$100-150

A Chippendale mahogany pole
screen, probably Massachusetts,
pole and foot restored, c1770, 45in
(114cm) high.
$600-1,000

A late Victorian ebonised, parcel
gilt and scrapwork three-leaf
screen, the back with green
patterned paper, distressed, each
leaf 70 by 24in (177.5 by 61cm).
$4,000-5,500

A Victorian giltwood and gesso
firescreen, 38in (96.5cm).
$900-1,300

n Edwardian mahogany screen,
th silk embroidered panels,
910, 66in (167.5cm) high.
00-500

A parcel gilt and gesso polescreen on
tripod base, with silk embroidered
panel, 53in (134.5cm) high.
$800-1,200

A giltwood three-fold screen of
rococo form, with shaped glazed
panels and embroidered silk panels,
19thC, 76in (193cm) high.
$3,000-4,500

Settees

A George III white painted and parcel gilt sofa, with rounded arched back, sides, seat and squab covered in green repp, on turned tapering fluted legs, 98½in (250cm).
$2,000-3,000

A George III style humpback sofa, covered in yellow moiré, on chamfered legs, carved with blind fretwork and pierced angles, 47½in (119cm).
$4,000-5,500

A George III parcel gilt and cream painted sofa, on cabriole legs headed by foliage, later blocks, redecorated, 84in (213cm).
$4,000-5,500

A Regency parcel gilt and ebonised sofa, with moulded frame and ring turned legs, reinforced seat rail, 72in (182.5cm).
$2,000-3,000

A Regency mahogany hall settee, the drop-in seat covered in green striped silk, on square tapering legs and spade feet, 77½in (196cm).
$4,000-5,500

A George III cream painted and parcel gilt sofa, with spirally turned spreading arm supports and conforming tapering legs, the seat rails strengthened, 77in (195.5cm).
$2,000-3,000

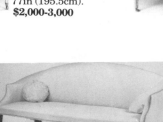

A George III mahogany window seat, covered in blue and cream striped material, on moulded cabriole legs, 45½in (114cm).
$8,000-11,000

A George III white painted and parcel gilt sofa with moulded ribb frame and fluted seat rail, on squar tapering legs headed by paterae, 75½in (190.5cm).
$4,500-7,000

A George III mahogany sofa, re-railed, 49in (124.5cm).
$4,000-5,500

A George III mahogany sofa, upholstered in yellow repp, on square tapering legs, 3 back legs spliced, one replaced, 74in (188cm).
$2,000-3,000

A Regency simulated rosewood and parcel gilt quadruple chairback settee, the white calico covered seat flanked by scrolled arms on turned tapering legs, 71in (180cm).
$2,000-3,000

A Georgian style carved mahogany settee, with stuffover arched back with outswept scroll arm supports terminating in eagles' heads, on cabriole legs with C-scroll and foliate shell decorated knees, terminating in paw feet.
$4,000-5,500

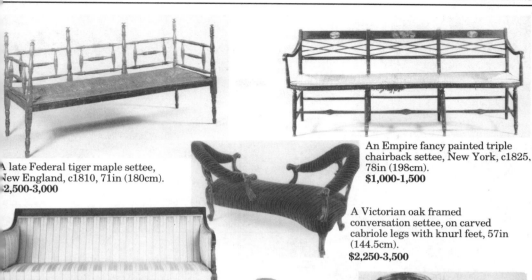

A late Federal tiger maple settee, New England, c1810, 71in (180cm).
$2,500-3,000

An Empire fancy painted triple chairback settee, New York, c1825, 78in (198cm).
$1,000-1,500

A Victorian oak framed conversation settee, on carved cabriole legs with knurl feet, 57in (144.5cm).
$2,250-3,500

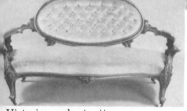

A late Federal carved mahogany sofa, New York, c1820, 72in (182.5cm).
$10,000-12,000

A Victorian walnut conversation sofa, the seats and backs upholstered in figured damask, on scrolling feet, 50in (127cm).
$1,000-1,500

A Victorian walnut chaise longue, upholstered in green velvet, on cabriole legs with knob feet, 66in (167.5cm).
$2,250-3,500

Victorian walnut settee, upholstered in green in a moulded ame decorated with stylised liage, the arms terminating in crolls on cabriole legs, scroll feet nd casters, 70in (177.5cm).
2,000-3,000

A Victorian carved walnut framed chaise longue, with buttoned back.
$2,500-3,500

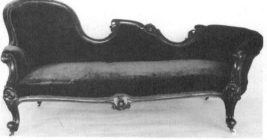

Victorian walnut sofa, with twin poon back, 66in (167.5cm).
2,000-3,000

An Anglo-Indian carved rosewood four piece suite, comprising a pair of pierced framed sofas, 69in (175cm), and 2 side chairs, late 19thC.
$4,000-5,500

walnut chaise longue, pholstered in yellow velvet, on abriole legs with knob feet, late 9thC, 70in (177.5cm).
2,500-3,500

A mid-Victorian carved rosewood settee, 78in (198cm).
$2,000-3,000

A seven-piece Edwardian mahogany parlour suite, with boxwood stringing and rosewood panels, comprising a settee, 2 carver chairs and 4 other chairs.
$4,500-7,000

A mid-Victorian walnut sofa, upholstered in buttoned slate blue velvet, on cabriole legs, 80in (203cm).
$2,500-3,500

An Edwardian inlaid mahogany parlour suite, comprising a two-seater settee with foliate inlaid splat, padded back and rounded arms, on cabriole legs, 2 armchairs and 4 side chairs.
$2,000-3,000

A mid-Victorian walnut sofa, upholstered in bottle green velvet within a moulded frame with scrolling arm terminals, on cabriole legs, carved with foliage and strapwork, on scrolled toes, 79½in (202cm).
$2,000-3,000

A pair of mid-Victorian amboyna ottoman window seats, by Morant, Boyd & Morant, each with a calico covered hinged seat and red velvet covered sides, on a plinth base and casters, 49in (124cm).
$2,000-3,000

Invoiced on 20 December 1858. $20.

A Louis XV walnut duchesse brisee, with rounded sloping back and flowerhead crestings, the moulded seat rail carved with flowerheads, on moulded cabriole legs, 73½in (186cm).
$2,250-3,500

A Louis XV parcel gilt and grey painted canapé, with moulded frame carved with foliage, on cabriole legs joined by an X-shaped stretcher, restored, 77in (195.5cm).
$4,000-5,500

A Biedermeier walnut sofa, cover in striped silk with 2 bolsters on scrolling legs, 62½in (158cm).
$6,000-8,000

A Louis XVI style giltwood sofa, on brass caps and casters, 19thC, 75in (190.5cm).
$2,000-3,000

A Louis XV style beech framed settee, upholstered in camel corded velvet, 81in (205.5cm).
$5,000-7,500

A Louis XVI grey painted lit-en-bateau, one leg later, the rails partly reinforced, 78½in (198cm).
$6,000-8,000

A Louis XVI style cream painted and parcel gilt suite, variously upholstered, comprising: a pair of chaises, a pair of fauteuils and a canapé with machined tapestry, the canapé 56in (142cm).
$4,000-5,500

An Empire style mahogany canapé en cabriolette, upholstered in gold velvet with rams heads terminals, on turned tapering legs with sabots and paterae headings, 62in (157cm).
$2,250-3,500

An Italian Louis XV style salon suite, including a chair back settee and 4 occasional chairs with cane panel backs and floral and foliate crestings, late 18th/early 19thC, later green painted and gilt.
$4,000-5,500

A German Empire mahogany and boxwood strung sofa, with an upholstered panel arched back and padded scroll arm supports, a stuffover seat and panel frieze with a classical scene, on outswept feet.
$1,500-2,600

Shelves

A set of Regency mahogany and brass mounted twin hanging shelves, with beaded edges, on turned baluster uprights, 29½in (74cm).
$1,500-2,600

A pair of late Regency mahogany standing bookshelves, supported by ball, spiral turned and fluted tapering legs with paw feet, 48in (122cm).
$8,000-11,000

A pair of Regency parcel gilt and mahogany open corner étagères, with white marble tops and pierced three-quarter galleries, mirror glazed backs, flanked by lappeted moulding, on bobbin turned tapering legs, 23in (58cm).
$3,000-4,500

A set of Regency mahogany hanging shelves, with turned finials and feet, 28½in (72cm).
$1,300-2,000

Sideboards

A Georgian bowfront sideboard, with string and sunburst inlay in fruitwood.
$5,000-7,500

A Georgian mahogany bowfront sideboard, decorated with an American eagle and 'E. Pluribus Unum', on 6 tapered supports with spade feet, 74in (188cm).
$4,000-5,500

A Georgian mahogany serpentine sideboard, decorated with pollarded bandings, with brass curtain rail, 72in (182.5cm).
$4,000-5,500

A George III mahogany serpentine front sideboard, with satinwood banding, replacement brass plate ring handles, the square tapering legs on socket feet, 53in (134.5cm).
$7,000-10,000

A George III mahogany and rosewood banded sideboard, with brass gallery, on boxwood strung square tapered legs with spade feet, 84in (213cm).
$4,000-5,500

A George III mahogany sideboard, with triple bowed top, on tapering legs and spade feet, 90in (228.5cm).
$6,000-8,000

A George III mahogany and satinwood crossbanded bowfront sideboard, fitted with drawers, cellaret and cupboard, 55½in (140cm).
$8,000-11,000

A Regency mahogany pedestal sideboard, with pierced gilt metal gallery, the breakfront top with 3 frieze drawers inlaid with ebony scrolls and foliate designs, with ebony inlaid panelled doors, 100in (254cm).
$5,000-7,500

A Federal inlaid mahogany sideboard, New York, some veneer loss, back edge now cut for plate rest, c1800, 74in (188cm).
$15,000-18,000

A Victorian rosewood and inlaid sideboard, with mirrored superstructure and doors, 54in (137cm).
$2,000-3,000

A Sheraton period kneehole sideboard, with brass swan neck handles, on 6 inlaid tapered supports with spade feet, 57in (144.5cm).
$8,000-11,000

A Regency mahogany breakfront sideboard, in the manner of Thomas Hope, c1810, 96in (243.5cm).
$26,000-35,000

A Federal inlaid mahogany sideboard, New York, various inlay chips, small missing sections, c1800, 75in (190.5cm).
$12,000-15,000

A Federal inlaid mahogany sideboard, New York, various small veneer and inlay chips and patches, c1800, 71½in (181cm).
$10,000-12,000

A mahogany Sheraton Revival marquetry breakfront sideboard with satinwood crossbanding, needing some restoration, 19thC, 84in (213cm).
$5,000-7,500

A late Victorian rosewood veneered sideboard, with ivory and boxwood marquetry inlay, 66in (167.5cm).
$4,000-5,500

A mahogany bowfront sideboard, with 2 drawers and cupboards.
$2,000-3,000

A Victorian ebonised sideboard, inlaid with marquetry arabesques, in various woods and in bone, on graduated plinth base, 80in (203cm)
$4,500-7,000

A mahogany breakfront sideboard, with central drawer, flanked by cellaret and napery.
$2,000-3,000

Stands

A Regency mahogany pedestal, with stepped top and tapering panelled sides with canted angles, on a plinth base, 50in (127cm) high.
$2,500-3,500

An early George III style mahogany urn stand, 11in (28cm).
$2,000-3,000

An early George III mahogany reading stand, with adjustable elevating ratcheted slope with candleslide, on knopped column and tripod legs, terminating in pad feet, 25in (63cm).
$2,000-3,000

A George III mahogany reading stand, on fluted column and splayed tripod legs, terminating in blocks, brass cappings and casters.
$4,000-5,500

A George IV rosewood folio stand, with later base.
$2,000-3,000

A Regency style gilt jardinière, with marble top, 45in (114cm).
$750-1,000

A Victorian mahogany folio stand, with adjustable ratcheted and slatted slopes and book rests, 27½in (70cm).
$5,000-7,500

A Queen Anne carved mahogany tilt-top candlestand, probably Delaware, minor patch to one knee, c1750, 19in (48cm) diam.
$5,000-6,000

A Queen Anne carved walnut tilt-top candlestand, Pennsylvania, repair to one leg, c1750, 21½in (55cm) diam.
$8,000-10,000

A Federal mahogany candlestand, Massachusetts, top possibly not original, c1790, 27in (68.5cm) high.
$750-850

A Federal cherrywood candlestand, New England, c1790, 26½in (67cm) high.
$1,500-2,000

A Chippendale mahogany dish-top stand, Eastern Long Island, minor patch to pedestal base, c1800, 20in (51cm) diam.
$2,000-2,500

A Federal birch tilt-top candlestand, New England, now painted with old red and black paint, c1800, 27in (68cm) high.
$2,000-2,500

A Chippendale walnut dish-top birdcage stand, Philadelphia, c1785, 22in (56cm) diam.
$10,000-12,000

A Federal cherrywood stand, probably Kentucky, c1800, 27in (68.5cm) high.
$12,000-15,000

A Federal cherrywood candlestand, New England, 2 feet repaired, top re-set, c1800, 26in (66cm) high.
$900-1,200

A Federal mahogany tilt-top candlestand, attributed to Joseph Short, Newburyport, Massachusetts, c1800, 26in (66cm) high.
$5,000-6,000

A Federal mahogany candlestand, New England, late 18thC, 17in (43cm) diam.
$800-1,000

A Federal mahogany candlestand, Massachusetts, minor repair to pedestal, c1800, 28½in (72cm) high.
$1,200-1,500

A Federal inlaid cherrywood stand, probably Kentucky or Ohio, c1810, 24in (61cm).
$3,000-4,000

A rosewood stand, the top inlaid with composite marble, 18in (46cm) diam.
$3,000-4,500

A heart-shaped étagère, c1920, 30in (76cm) high.
$600-900

A pair of giltwood plant stands in the French style, 40in (101.5cm) high.
$4,000-5,500

Steps

A set of Regency mahogany leather lined library steps, with panelled sides, on ring turned tapering legs with casters, 38in (96.5cm).
$4,000-5,500

A set of Regency mahogany leather lined library steps, early 19thC.
$3,000-4,500

Stools

A pair of giltwood window seats, with different upholstery, flanked by ring turned foliate rails, c1800, later blocks, redecorated, 26½in (67cm).
$4,000-5,500

A William and Mary walnut stool, upholstered in close nailed gros point needlework, on later turned feet, 25in (63.5cm).
$4,000-5,500

A Regency carved mahogany X-frame stool with cane seat, on reeded supports united by a turned stretcher, terminating on bun feet.
$4,000-5,500

A pair of walnut long stools, with close nailed upholstered top, on 8 baluster supports joined by a moulded stretcher, basically early 18thC, 78½in (199cm).
$2,250-3,500

A pair of George I walnut stools with slip-in seats.
$16,000-22,500

A Regency rosewood X-frame stool, with padded blue velvet seat, the seat rail strengthened, 21½in (54.5cm).
$1,300-2,000

A Regency mahogany piano stool, with adjustable leather lined seat, on ribbed tapering legs joined by a concave sided stretcher, 14in (35.5cm) diam.
$1,200-1,750

A George II mahogany stool, covered in yellow velvet, 24in (61cm).
$4,000-5,500

A pair of rosewood foot stools, 19thC.
$800-1,200

A Regency style low fender stool, covered in leopard skin on giltmetal scrolling hoof feet, 42½in (106.5cm).
$1,500-2,500

An early Victorian parcel gilt and cream painted stool, the seat with needlework vine leaves, on cabriole legs headed by flowerheads, with scrolled feet, stamped 4 times Saunders & Woolley, 20½in (52cm).
$800-1,200

A carved mahogany stool, mid-19thC, 24in (61cm) high.
$1,300-2,000

A Victorian walnut stool, upholstered in cut velvet, above a projecting scroll moulded rail, on cabriole legs, scroll feet and casters, 62½in (158cm).
$1,000-1,500

A walnut music stool, c1860, 24in (61cm) high.
$1,000-1,500

A Victorian rosewood stool, with loose needlework seat, 18in (46cm) square.
$450-700

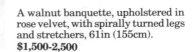

A walnut banquette, upholstered in rose velvet, with spirally turned legs and stretchers, 61in (155cm).
$1,500-2,500

Tables – Architects

An early George III mahogany architect's table, the top ratcheted and fitted with a sprung ledge above a sliding drawer, fitted with a lined writing surface, 35in (89cm).
$6,000-9,000

A mahogany architect's table, with double hinged ratcheted top, above a frieze drawer with brass swan neck handles and pierced brass escutcheons, on square chamfered legs with C-scroll brackets, 34½in (87cm).
$4,000-5,500

Tables – Breakfast

A George III mahogany breakfast table, with twin flap rounded top, frieze drawer, on baluster shaft and ribbed splayed legs, with brass paw feet, 43in (109cm).
$2,000-3,000

A George III mahogany breakfast table, with crossbanded top, on ring turned spreading shaft and shaped moulded tapering quadripartite base, with gilt metal claw feet, re-supported, 52in (132cm).
$4,000-5,500

A Regency mahogany breakfast table, with tip-up top and baluster shaft, moulded splayed quadripartite base and brass claw feet, 53in (134.5cm).
$5,000-7,500

A Regency mahogany breakfast table with tilt-top, on turned baluster shaft and downswept quadripartite base, with foliate brass caps and casters, 60in (152cm).
$4,000-5,500

A Regency mahogany breakfast table, the snap top crossbanded in rosewood, on a turned column and quadruped base, terminating in brass cappings and casters, 52in (133cm).
$3,000-4,500

◄

A Regency mahogany breakfast table, the tip-up top crossbanded in rosewood with brass inlay, 65in (165cm).
$6,000-9,000

A Regency rosewood pedestal breakfast table, inlaid with satinwood bands and boxwood lines, with brass paw terminals, 52½in (133cm).
$10,000-13,500

A Regency rosewood and gilt metal mounted breakfast table, the snap top with a cut brass crossbanded border, on gilt paw feet and casters, 50in (127cm) diam.
$17,000-23,000

A Regency mahogany breakfast table, the tip-up top with ribbed border on a ring turned pedestal and quadripartite ribbed splayed legs with brass feet, 48in (122cm).
$2,250-3,500

A Regency mahogany breakfast table, with tip-up top, on a square pedestal inlaid with ebonised lines and 4 splayed legs with paw feet, restorations, 53½in (135cm).
$3,000-4,500

An early Victorian rosewood breakfast table, 57in (144.5cm).
$3,000-4,500

A mahogany breakfast table, with crossbanded top and ring turned columnar shaft, with quadripartite base and brass feet, 58in (147cm) diam.
$2,000-3,000

Tables – Card

A William and Mary scarlet japanned and gilt chinoiserie decorated half round card table, on later supports, 30in (76cm).
$1,000-1,500

A George I red walnut card table, with enclosed guinea wells and candlestands, 33in (84cm).
$4,000-5,500

A George II carved mahogany card table, 34in (87cm).
$10,000-13,500

A George II carved mahogany card table, on cabriole front legs headed with acanthus ornament and terminating in claw-and-ball feet, 34in (87cm).
$6,000-9,000

A pair of George III mahogany demi-lune card or tea tables, with fold-over tops and inlaid ruling, on square tapering supports, 36in (91cm).
$4,000-5,500

An early George III mahogany card table, on blind fret carved square chamfered legs headed by fretwork brackets, 36in (91cm).
$2,250-3,500

A George III mahogany serpentine card table, with later egg-and-dart carved edge, 36in (91cm).
$2,000-3,000

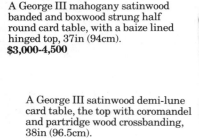

A George III mahogany satinwood banded and boxwood strung half round card table, with a baize lined hinged top, 37in (94cm).
$3,000-4,500

A George III satinwood demi-lune card table, the top with coromandel and partridge wood crossbanding, 38in (96.5cm).
$7,000-10,000

A George III mahogany, inlaid and crossbanded D-shaped card table, with fold-over top, square tapered legs and spade feet, 36in (91cm).
$2,000-3,000

A pair of late Regency rosewood folding card tables, with bead and reel carving to border, 36in (91cm).
$4,000-5,500

A Regency rosewood card table, the crossbanded top inlaid in cut brass, with brass paw caps and casters, 36in (91cm).
$4,000-5,500

A pair of William IV rosewood card tables, with baize lined D-end tops, on foliate knopped columns and quatrefoil platform bases, on reeded bun feet.
$5,000-7,500

A Regency mahogany fold-over card table, the top banded with rosewood, the frieze inlaid with a marquetry panel, with brass lion paw casters, 36in (91cm).
$2,000-3,000

A William IV rosewood swivel fold-over D-end card table, with green baize lining, on original brass casters, 36in (91cm).
$1,000-1,500

A pair of William IV rosewood card tables, with square section columns, veneers distressed, 36½in (92cm).
$1,500-2,500

A pair of William IV rosewood card tables, 36½in (92cm).
$10,500-15,000

A mahogany card table with carved pedestal and platform base with scroll feet, 19thC.
$1,000-1,500

A pair of Adam style D-shaped tables, comprising a side table and fold-over card table, 19thC, 36in (91cm).
$10,000-13,500

A rosewood folding card table, on carved pedestal with petal base and 4 paw feet, 19thC.
$1,200-1,750

A satinwood, rosewood and harewood crossbanded and inlaid half-round card table, with brass cappings and casters, early 19thC, 44in (112cm).
$9,000-12,500

An early Victorian burr walnut fold-over swivel card table with green baize lining, on original brass casters, 39in (99cm).
$1,300-2,000

A Chippendale carved mahogany card table, Pennsylvania, c1770, 33in (84cm).
$12,000-15,000

A Chippendale carved and inlaid mahogany card table, Pennsylvania, brackets restored, c1770, 34in (86.5cm).
$9,000-12,000

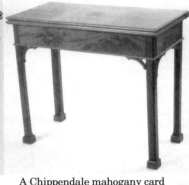

A Chippendale mahogany card table, New York or Philadelphia, brackets restored, small patch to left rear corner of top, c1770, 34in (86.5cm).
$4,000-5,000

A Federal inlaid mahogany card table, Eastern Massachusetts, small pieces of inlay missing, c1800, 36in (91.5cm).
$10,000-12,000

A Federal inlaid mahogany card table, Baltimore, some damage, c1800, 33in (84cm) diam.
$5,000-6,000

A Federal inlaid mahogany card table, Massachusetts, c1800, 36in (91.5cm).
$13,000-15,000

A Federal inlaid mahogany card table, Massachusetts or Rhode Island, c1800, 35½in (89cm).
$5,000-6,000

A late Federal mahogany card table, New York, warp and crack to top, restoration to banding, c1810, 36in (91.5cm).
$2,500-3,500

A Federal mahogany card table, Massachusetts, repair to leg, c1810, 35½in (90cm).
$2,000-2,500

A Federal inlaid card table, North Shore Massachusetts, top re-set, c1810, 35½in (90cm).
$4,000-5,000

A classical carved mahogany card table, New York, c1815, 37in (94cm).
$6,000-8,000

A classical carved mahogany card table, attributed to Anthony Quervelle, Philadelphia, c1825, 36in (91.5cm).
$1,500-2,000

A Victorian burr walnut fold-over card table, the shaped top decorated with satinwood foliate inlay, with ceramic casters, 39in (99cm).
$3,000-4,500

A Victorian burr walnut card table, the hinged demi-lune top above a plain frieze, on a turned and fluted column, with an overlapping leaf carved collar, 36½in (92cm).
$1,500-2,500

A Victorian burr walnut serpentine fronted card table, with a hinged swivel top and plain frieze, on a carved bulbous column with 4 splay legs, 26in (66cm).
$2,500-3,500

A Victorian rosewood card table, with a serpentine sided fold-over top, 36in (91cm).
$1,500-2,500

An Edwardian envelope top card table.
$1,300-2,000

A burr walnut card table, the figured top with outset corners, above a plain frieze, on cabriole legs with pad feet, 30in (76cm).
$2,000-3,000

A Louis XV style ebonised and boulle card table, applied throughout with gilt brass mouldings and inlaid in red tortoiseshell and cut brass, 36½in (92cm).
$1,500-2,500

Tables – Centre

A Regency mahogany centre table, with baluster shaft and arched moulded quadripartite base, 42in (106cm).
$1,500-2,500

A George IV rosewood centre table, with baluster shaft, on scrolled tripartite base, 51in (129cm).
$5,000-7,500

A George I walnut centre table, 35in (89cm).
$6,000-9,000

A pair of Regency ebonised centre tables, the brass edged tops inlaid premier partie and contre partie in cut brass and white metal with strapwork and scrolling foliage, 35in (88cm).
$6,000-9,000

Tables – Console

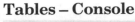

A Victorian burr walnut centre table, with serpentine edge, on carved cabriole legs with turned stretcher.
$2,000-3,000

A giltwood console table, the marble top above a beaded, gadrooned and key patterned banded frieze, on carved eagle support, on a rocky plinth base, part 18thC, 38in (96.5cm).
$6,000-9,000

A pair of William IV mahogany and bronze corner console tables, with moulded mottled green scagliola tops, 28in (71cm).
$6,000-9,000

A giltwood demi-lune console table, with neo-classical ornament, late 18thC, with later decorated top, 18in (48cm).
$1,200-1,750

A Swedish parcel gilt and blue painted console table, with white marble top, on simulated grey marble plinth base, 31in (78cm).
$8,000-11,000

A Regency parcel gilt and ebonised console table, with mottled black marble top and divided mirrored back, with plinth base and bun feet, 39in (99cm).
$6,000-8,000

A Regency parcel gilt and rosewood console table, with white marble top and frieze carved with egg-and-dart, on scrolling foliate supports and paw feet, with mirrored back, 48in (124cm).
$4,500-7,000

A carved silvered wood baroque console table, with a serpentine pink marble top, on 4 bold carved cabriole legs, with S-scroll stretchers, 55in (140cm).
$5,000-7,500

A Continental gilt gesso console table, the serpentine shaped marble top on rococo style base, 19thC, 54in (137cm).
$600-900

A Venetian giltwood console table, with moulded serpentine breccia marble top, restorations, mid-18thC, 43½in (111cm).
$8,000-11,000

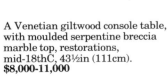

A French giltwood and gesso console table, 19thC, 52in (132cm).
$2,500-3,500

Tables – Dining

A Georgian mahogany snap-top dining table, bordered with a broad satinwood band, 62in (158cm).
13,000-17,500

A George II mahogany drop-leaf dining table, with elliptical leaves, on cabriole legs, carved with scallop shells and husks and claw-and-ball feet, 49in (125cm).
$3,000-4,500

A Chippendale mahogany drop-leaf dining table, mid-18thC, 63in (160cm) long extended.
$4,000-5,500

A George III style mahogany twin pedestal dining table, the top on plain turned columns and moulded outswept legs with brass casters, including one leaf, 91in (231cm) long.
$5,000-7,500

A George III mahogany two-pillar dining table, with thumb moulded edge, 66in (168cm) long including single extra leaf.
4,000-5,500

A Regency style mahogany twin-pillar dining table, on reeded quadruple supports, with brass claw feet and casters, 77in (195.5cm) extended, including one extra leaf.
$4,000-5,500

A Regency mahogany dining table, with Cumberland action, on turned supports and splayed legs with paw feet, 103½in (263cm).
$30,000-40,000

A mahogany triple pillar extending dining table, on quadruple supports with casters, early 19thC, 98in (248cm).
$9,000-12,500

Regency mahogany patent extending dining table, with -shaped folding top, dividing to reveal a telescopic action, inset with brass plaque engraved 'Titter & Co./Inventors and Manufacturers No.32/Pottergate St. Norwich', including 3 extra leaves, 111in (283cm) extended.
13,000-17,500

A George IV mahogany extending dining table, with turned and reeded legs, brass toes and casters, with 3 extra leaves, one leaf not original, 124in (314cm).
$7,500-10,500

A George IV dining table.
$7,000-10,000

George IV mahogany extending dining table, on 8 ring turned supports with brass casters, with extra leaves, 92in (233cm) extended.
3,000-4,500

A mahogany dining table, on waisted, faceted ribbed support, with finialled cruciform platform base, on casters, early 19thC, 53in (134.5cm).
$3,000-4,500

A George IV mahogany extending dining table, with twin flap top, on spiral twist legs, brass caps and casters, including 2 extra leaves, 80in (203cm) extended.
$2,000-3,000

A three-part mahogany D-end dining table, the centre section with drop leaves, on 12 reeded turned tapering legs, early 19thC, 89in (226cm) extended.
$5,000-7,500

A Victorian mahogany dining table, on 5 reeded turned tapering legs, including 4 extra leaves, 142in (360cm) extended.
$4,000-5,500

A George IV mahogany twin pedestal D-end dining table, on turned columns and hipped splayed legs, terminating in brass cappings and casters, including one extra leaf, 74in (189cm) extended.
$10,000-13,500

Tables – Display

A Victorian walnut pedestal dining table, with quarter veneered tilt-top, 54in (137cm).
$2,000-3,000

A Victorian walnut floral marquetry tilt-top dining table with carved pedestal and tripod base.
$7,000-10,000

A rosewood display table, inlaid with satinwood, 29in (73cm) high.
$1,500-2,500

A Regency mahogany vitrine table, with moulded top and sides filled with glass panels, the front with a door, inlaid with ebonised lines, on square tapering legs, 20½in (52cm).
$7,000-10,000

A Louis XV style rosewood and brass mounted vitrine table, on cabriole supports and cast brass sabots joined by a mirrored undertier, 36in (91cm).
$2,000-3,000

Tables – Dressing

A George III satinwood kneehole dressing table, with crossbanded top, on tapering legs with brass casters. 40in (101.5cm).
$6,000-8,000

A George III mahogany dressing table, with folding top enclosing a divided and lidded interior, previously with a mirror, 22in (56cm).
$2,000-3,000

A rosewood bijouterie table, with ormolu mounts, on cabriole legs, late 19thC, 24in (60cm).
$1,000-1,500

An inlaid mahogany kneehole dressing table, with reeded lift-up top enclosing fitted interior, with boxwood stringing and brass knob handles, on turned stump supports, 19thC, 49in (124.5cm).
$1,000-1,500

A George III mahogany and inlaid gentleman's enclosed dressing table, stamped Gillows, Lancaster, inlaid with boxwood and ebony lines, 31in (79cm).
$6,000-8,000

A Victorian burr-walnut Duchesse dressing table, with concave platform base, 54in (137cm).
$1,300-2,000

A Federal grain painted and stencilled dressing table, New England, with rosewood graining and gilt bronze stencilling, drawer branded S.R., c1830, 33in (84cm).
$2,500-3,500

A Danish satinwood and rosewood dressing table, the crossbanded top enclosing a fitted interior, including a mirror, with square tapering legs, late 18thC, 27½in (70cm).
$5,000-7,500

A Federal mahogany dressing table, New England, backboard replaced, c1825, 33in (84cm).
$2,000-3,000

Tables – Dropleaf

A Queen Anne maple drop-leaf table, New England, old crack to one leaf, c1750, 41½in (105cm).
$7,000-9,000

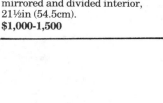

An Empire mahogany dressing table, with hinged lid enclosing a mirrored and divided interior, 21½in (54.5cm).
$1,000-1,500

A Chippendale mahogany drop-leaf table, Massachusetts, repair to one leg, c1770, 48in (122cm) long.
$2,500-3,500

A George II mahogany drop-leaf dining table, on plain cabriole legs, with pointed pad feet, 46in (116.5cm).
$1,000-1,500

Tables – Games

A Regency style rosewood and satinwood banded sofa games table, fitted with a dummy and a frieze drawer, on standard and dual splayed end supports, terminating in brass capping and casters, 45in (115cm) extended.
$5,000-7,500

A Regency mahogany games table, with baize lined twin flap top, on ring turned tapering legs, 35in (89cm) open.
$1,200-1,750

A Regency mahogany games table the top with a sliding centre section inlaid to the reverse with a chessboard and enclosing a backgammon board, 35in (89cm).
$2,250-3,500

A giltwood and composition games table, with square pietra dura top inlaid with chess squares, mid-19thC, 21in (53cm).
$2,000-3,000

A Victorian rosewood games table, the top inlaid with chessboard, flanked by cribbage scorers, 20in (51cm).
$800-1,200

A Victorian rosewood games tabl on a barley twist column, and hipped cabriole legs with scrolled feet, 20in (51cm).
$700-900

A Regency black and white penwork games table, with concave sided platform base and bun feet, 16in (40.5cm).
$4,000-5,500

A Victorian burr walnut and marquetry games/work table, the shaped folding swivel top inlaid and banded in amboyna, fitted with one drawer and a sliding bag, on end supports with splayed feet, 26½in (67cm).
$1,000-1,500

An Anglo-Indian ebony, ivory and penwork games table, inlaid with a chess board, the triangular base inlaid with ivory, on reeded bun feet, adapted, 21in (53cm).
$4,000-5,500

Tables – Gateleg

A gateleg table, on chamfered legs, joined by curvilinear stretchers, 36½in (92cm).
$1,000-1,500

A George II mahogany gateleg table, on slightly splayed turned legs with pad feet, 57in (145cm) diam.
$4,000-5,500

Tables – Pembroke

A Georgian mahogany Pembroke table, with a drawer at each end, on ring turned tapering legs with brass cappings and casters, 42in (106.5cm).
$1,200-1,750

A George III mahogany Pembroke table, stamped Gillows of Lancaster, the top banded with amaranth and boxwood, 23in (58cm) open.
$5,000-7,500

A George III crossbanded Pembroke table, on 4 tapering legs and casters, with end drawer.
$800-1,200

A George III mahogany Pembroke table, with crossbanded serpentine twin flap top and one bowed frieze drawer, on square tapering legs, 38in (96.5cm) open.
$5,000-7,500

A George III mahogany and marquetry Pembroke table, crossbanded in rosewood, on square tapered legs, terminating in brass cappings and casters, 35in (90cm).
$6,000-9,000

A George III mahogany Pembroke table, the satinwood crossbanded top with ebony and boxwood stringing, on square tapered legs, brass cappings and leather casters, bearing a label George Simson No. 19, Smithside, St. Paul's Church Yard, 37½in (96cm).
$3,000-4,500

A Regency mahogany Pembroke table, the top above an ebony lined frieze drawer, on a turned baluster shaft and moulded splayed quadripartite support, ending in cast brass paw feet, 48in (122cm) open.
$1,500-2,500

PEMBROKE TABLES

★ became popular in the mid to late 18thC, possibly designed and ordered by Henry Herbert, the Earl of Pembroke (1693-1751)
★ on early examples the legs were square which are by far the most desirable
★ later tables had turned legs
★ the turned and reeded legs are much less popular
★ those with oval or serpentine tops more desirable
★ flaps should have three hinges
★ rounded flaps and marquetry again increase desirability
★ satinwood was greatly favoured, particularly with much crossbanding and inlay
★ many 18thC Pembroke tables have chamfering on the insides of the legs
★ the Edwardians made many fine Pembroke tables which have been known to appear wrongly catalogued at auction
★ Edwardian tables now in great demand

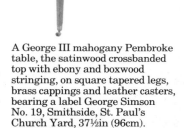

A Sheraton style Pembroke table with rosewood banded D-shaped flap top, on square tapering supports, 32in (81cm).
$3,000-4,500

A Regency mahogany Pembroke table, inlaid with ebonised lines, the quadruple down-curving legs with brass paw feet, 33in (84cm).
$4,000-5,500

A William IV Pembroke table, with brass terminals.
$1,500-2,500

A Federal mahogany Pembroke table, New York, small repair to one corner of top, c1810, 43in (109cm).
$5,000-6,000

A Federal inlaid mahogany Pembroke table, New York, some restoration to inlay, c1820, 34in (86cm).
$9,000-12,000

A Federal inlaid mahogany Pembroke table, Mid-Atlantic States, c1800, 49in (124.5cm).
$5,000-6,000

A Federal mahogany Pembroke table, New York, c1810, 36in (91.5cm).
$5,000-6,000

A late Federal figured maple and cherrywood Pembroke table, signed by A. J. Baycock, Brookfield, Madison County, New York, c1820, 42½in (107cm) open.
$6,000-7,000

A Federal inlaid mahogany Pembroke table, Mid-Atlantic States, c1800, 49in (124.5cm).
$6,000-8,000

A Federal inlaid mahogany Pembroke table, New York, restoration to inlay, c1800, 30in (76cm).
$3,000-4,000

Tables – Serving

A George III mahogany serving table, on stop fluted square tapered legs, headed by carved patera and terminating with spade feet, 66in (168cm).
$3,000-4,500

A Regency plum pudding mahogany serving table, 96in (243cm).
$6,000-9,000

A late Regency mahogany serving side table, with rope carved borders and tapering legs, on paw feet with foliate paterae headings, adaptations, 75in (190cm).
$3,000-4,500

Tables – Sofa

A Regency rosewood sofa table, with crossbanded top, 58in (147cm).
$2,250-3,500

A Georgian mahogany sofa table, crossbanded in coromandel, 34in (86cm).
$3,000-4,500

A rosewood sofa table, the top crossbanded in satinwood with canted angles, on splayed legs terminating in brass paw cappings and casters, 19thC, 59in (150cm).
$10,000-13,500

A mahogany sofa table, with hinged top, on square column, stepped concave supports terminating in brass cappings and casters, early 19thC, 37½in (96cm).
$7,000-10,000

A Charles X mahogany sofa table, on solid trestle ends, joined by a shaped stretcher and splayed feet, 61in (154cm) open.
$3,000-4,500

Tables – Supper

A mahogany supper table, with pad feet profusely carved with foliage, basically 18thC, 27½in (68.5cm).
$2,250-3,500

A Sheraton period mahogany sofa table, with 2 alternate boxwood line banded drawers and dummy drawers, with brass knob handles, 60in (152cm) open.
$6,000-9,000

Tables – Tavern

A Queen Anne maple tavern table, New England, 31in (79cm).
$5,000-6,000

A Georgian mahogany supper table, with richly inlaid D-shape top, with end drawer, 37in (94cm).
$2,250-3,500

Tables – Tea

A Queen Anne tea table, New England, c1750, 37½in (95cm).
$9,000-12,000

A Chippendale carved walnut dish top birdcage tea table, probably Lancaster, Pennsylvania, repairs to top and one foot, c1780, 32in (81cm) diam.
$3,000-3,500

A Chippendale walnut tea table, Pennsylvania, c1770, 34in (86.5cm) diam.
$4,500-5,500

A Victorian oval tip-up table with ebonised and satinwood banding, and a chased brass mounted border, on ebonised and gilt base, 50½in (128cm).
$1,500-2,500

Tables – Toilet

A French marquetry enclosed toilet table, on fluted square tapering supports, 32in (80cm).
$800-1,200

Tables – Tray

A George III mahogany butler's tray, with pierced three-quarter gallery, on later stand, with chamfered square legs and moulded stretchers, 33in (84cm).
$6,000-9,000

Tables – Tripod

A yew wood table, on bobbin turned shaft, with hexagonal platform and splayed triple supports with baluster feet, late 17th/early 18thC, 16in (41cm).
$1,500-2,500

A George III mahogany tray, with inverted corners and pierced gallery, on a later mahogany stand with square channelled chamfered legs, joined by an H-shaped stretcher, 22½in (57cm).
$2,000-3,000

A George III mahogany tripod table, with moulded tip-up top, the arched legs carved with husks, on claw-and-ball feet, 29in (73.5cm).
$7,000-10,000

A yew wood and elm tripod table, c1760, 26in (66cm) high.
$2,000-3,000

A George III mahogany tripod table, c1760, adapted from a polescreen, 18in (45.5cm).
$5,000-7,500

A mid-Georgian mahogany tripod table, the tilt top with scalloped edge, on columnar shaft, 34in (86.5cm).
$3,000-4,500

An ebony tripod table, the top with a partly fluted pedestal, on a baluster support carved with foliage on a pounced ground, 18th/19thC, 24in (60.5cm).
$3,000-4,500

Tables – Work

A Federal cherrywood mahogany work table, Pennsylvania or Kentucky, damage to top of 2 feet, c1820, 28½in (72cm).
$4,000-5,000

A late Federal mahogany worktable, New York, minor repair to legs, c1810, 20in (51cm).
$3,000-4,000

A late Federal inlaid mahogany work table, New York, c1825, 21½in (54.5cm).
$3,000-4,000

A Regency rosewood pedestal workstand, of sarcophagus form, with enclosed fitted upholstered interior, 17½in (44cm).
$1,500-2,500

A late George III thuya and rosewood crossbanded work table.
$13,000-17,500

A Federal inlaid mahogany sewing table, Massachusetts, split to top, minor repairs to one leg, c1810, 20in (51cm).
$3,500-4,500

A Regency rosewood work table, with easel top and frieze drawer, above a leather lined slide, formerly fitted with a work basket, 24½in (62cm).
$6,000-9,000

A Regency rosewood work table, the top with gadrooned border, enclosing a baize lined interior, 17in (43cm).
$2,250-3,500

A Regency coromandel work table.
$4,000-5,500

A William IV mahogany work table, 33½in (85cm).
$1,000-1,500

A Regency ladies rosewood writing/work table, with boxwood stringing, the corners and centre with harewood and satinwood shell inlays.
$2,250-3,500

Teapoys

A burr ash teapoy with fitted interior, on a lobed pedestal with platform base and bun feet, 19thC.
$1,200-1,750

Washstands

A George III black japanned corner washstand, variously gilt and decorated in colours, c1800, 51in (129cm) high.
$2,000-3,000

A mid-Georgian mahogany washstand, fitted with 2 drawers, the cabriole tripod base with dished centre, 31in (79cm) high.
$1,200-1,750

Whatnots

A mahogany four-tier whatnot, with frieze drawer, with casters.
$2,000-3,000

A Federal tiger maple washstand, New England, c1800, 16in (40.5cm).
$1,500-2,000

An inlaid mahogany washstand, stamped Edwards & Roberts, with satinwood crossbanding and boxwood and ebony stringing, 18½in (47cm).
$1,300-2,000

A Victorian mahogany three-tier whatnot, 36in (91cm) high.
$400-550

A Victorian figured walnut whatnot, on scroll feet, 29in (74cm).
$800-1,200

A walnut three-tier whatnot, c1880, 24½in (62cm).
$4,000-5,500

Wine Coolers

A Georgian mahogany cellaret, on carved bun feet.
$4,000-5,500

A George III mahogany and brass bound wine cooler on stand.
$4,500-7,000

A George III mahogany and brass bound wine cooler on stand, with a hinged top and lions' masks handles to the sides, on square tapered legs with brass cappings and casters.
$4,000-5,500

A George III mahogany brass bound cellaret, the rising top inlaid with chequer bands, 15in (38cm).
$2,250-3,500

A Regency mahogany wine cooler, the framed panel sides each inset with flame veneer mahogany, on carved paw feet and casters, 15½in (38cm).
$1,200-1,750

A late Georgian mahogany decanter box, with lift-up top, fitted interior, above 2 short drawers with brass drop ring handles, on bracket feet, 21½in (54.5cm).
$2,000-3,000

A pair of Georgian mahogany wine coolers, the bodies strung with boxwood and lead lined, the domed lids with later finials, on spreading feet and square plinth bases, 27in (69cm) high.
$4,500-7,000

A Regency mahogany wine cooler, with lead lined interior, the shaped body with spreading plinth base, formerly with a lid, 39in (99cm).
$6,000-8,000

A George III mahogany wine cooler, 25in (63.5cm).
$6,000-8,000

WINE COOLERS

★ cisterns for cooling wines were noted back in the 15thC and as objects of furniture became popular after about 1730. The cellaret is basically a cooler with a lid and fitted with a lock

★ there are two main types: those made to stand on a pedestal or sideboard and those with legs or separate stands to stand on the floor

★ octagonal, hexagonal, round or oval, the commonest form is of coopered construction with a number of brass bands

★ a cooler made to stand on a pedestal will often have the lowest brass band as near to the base as possible; a cooler made to fit into a stand will have the band slightly up the body to allow a snug fit

★ it is important that all mounts are original and condition should be good, but the absence of the old lead lining is not serious. An octagonal cooler or cellaret on stand may command a slightly higher price than a hexagonal model, but both are much in demand

★ after 1800, the sarcophagus shape became popular and later Regency models were made with highly figured mahogany veneers and large carved paw feet

★ there were not many new designs after the 1850s

Miscellaneous

An inlaid tiger maple document box, New England, late 18th/early 19thC, 10½in (27cm).
$1,000-1,500

A George IV mahogany bootjack, with reeded supports and shaped base, 32½in (82.5cm) high.
$900-1,300

A Federal cherrywood yarn winder, New England, c1810, 36in (91.5cm) high.
$500-1,000

A cherrywood document box, New England, replacements, late 18th/early 19thC, 13½in (34cm).
$350-450

A green leather covered and close nailed folding library ladder, 91in (231cm) high, closed.
$1,500-2,500

A George III mahogany hunting table, on folding X-shape square section stand, joined by stretchers, 35in (90cm).
$1,500-2,500

A George IV mahogany jardinière, the brass carrying handle and liner in a pierced urn shaped body and ribbed socle, the concave sided tripartite base with paw feet, 21in (53cm) high.
$2,000-3,000

A miniature stencilled sewing box, the top with gold stencilled fruit basket and inscribed Mrs. Susan Mathews, feet now lacking, 19thC, 14in (35.5cm).
$300-500

A set of Regency rosewood quartetto tables, with cockbeaded mouldings, the larger 22in (56cm).
$5,000-7,500

A mahogany waste paper basket, with waved toprail and pierced Gothic sides, 14in (35.5cm).
6,000-8,000

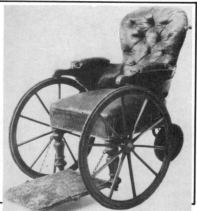

A Victorian bath chair, the mahogany frame button upholstered in black cloth, with a brass trade plate inscribed F.H. Miller, Maker, Newark Street, Bath, the wooden spoke wheels with a rubber rim, the seat on front turned mahogany legs to a carpet covered folding footboard, a fitment for a hood missing.
$1,200-1,750

A mid-Victorian child's see-saw, with chair at either end, flanking an open aperture and split cane shelf, 68in (172.5cm).
$5,000-7,500

A Dutch green painted and parcel gilt sleigh of rococo design, upholstered in red velvet, distressed, 52in (132cm) long.
$4,000-5,500

A George III Coadestone chimneypiece, with the arms of Beaumont and Wentworth, signed Coade 1796 London, distressed, 102in (259cm).
$1,300-2,000

A George III stripped pine mantel, 73in (185cm).
$1,000-1,500

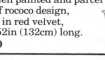

A pine fireplace, a 1920 copy of a Georgian style, 65in (165cm).
$800-1,200

A George III marble chimneypiece, with breakfront moulded overhanging cornice, above a frieze of Siena marble, 75in (190.5cm).
$4,000-5,500

A stripped pine fire surround, with tiled grate and iron doors.
$600-900

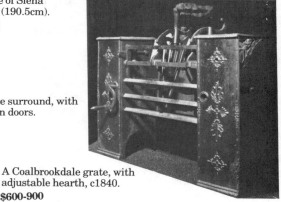

A Coalbrookdale grate, with adjustable hearth, c1840.
$600-900

A Victorian cast iron and brass grate.
$1,200-1,750

A Victorian cast iron interior with floral tiles.
$6,000-8,000

A Victorian cast iron and brass grate.
$1,000-1,500

A carved rosewood surround, inlaid with ivory and mother-of-pearl, 19thC, 78in (198cm) wide.
$4,000-5,500

A Victorian oak surround and shelf 84in (213cm) wide.
$1,300-2,000

A cast iron and tiled grate.
$7,000-10,000

An ornately carved oak chimneypiece, 19thC.
$2,250-3,500

A George III brass fender, 56in (142cm).
$6,000-8,000

A bronzed and ormolu adjustable fender, on plinth base edged with foliage, 48in (122cm) closed.
$1,300-2,000

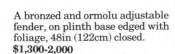

A George III brass serpentine fender, on claw feet, 54in (137cm).
$4,500-7,000

A giltmetal fender, stamped 1232 VI, 63in (160cm).
$1,200-1,750

A George III brass serpentine fender, 45½in (115cm).
$4,000-5,500

A pair of heavy brass andirons, with steel ball finials, 23in (58.5cm) high.
$700-900

A pair of brass and enamelled andirons, each moulded in relief in the form of the Royal coat of arms, supported by 2 naked men, with circular boss feet decorated with foliage and flowerheads, 26in (66cm) high.
$5,000-7,500

A George III cast iron blackened steel basket grate, one finial lacking, 28½in (72cm).
$2,000-3,000

A cast iron fireback, late 18thC.
$600-900

A Regency black painted cast iron basket grate, in the manner of George Bullock, with claw feet and plinth base, with an associated shovel, 31in (79cm).
$6,000-9,000

A Louis XVI style cast iron and brass fire basket, 22in (56cm).
$1,200-1,750

Miscellaneous

A circular window, 36in (91.5cm) diam.
$100-200

A 'marbled' corner basin, with decorative cast iron bracket.
$400-550

A cast iron lamp-post.
$200-350

A pair of cast iron gable finials, 42in (107cm).
$200-350

A Turtle stove, c1920, 30in (76cm).
$100-200

A set of 18 oak mullioned and leaded glass windows of various sizes.
$6,000-9,000

A pair of brass handles from an Edwardian chest.
$60-100

A brass lion's head door knocker, c1880.
$100-200

A brass bell pull.
$200-350

A black porcelain bell push, with gilt decoration.
$60-100

A black porcelain and brass bell pull.
$60-100

A brass bell push, 3½in (9cm).
$75-150

A rare Coadestone clock face, indented 'Coade London 1794', 38in (96.5cm) high.
$7,000-10,000

Coade is an artificial stone; Mrs. Eleanor Coade set up her factory at Lambeth in 1769. This item was recently found adapted as a garden fountain.

A black porcelain and brass servants bell pull.
$75-150

A brass bell push, 5½in (14cm).
$100-150

Late Victorian transfer printed floral patterned door knobs.
From **$45 per pair**

A porcelain bell push, with red and blue flowers.
$60-100

A hand painted porcelain door plate, 11½in (28cm).
$30-50

A cast iron door knocker in the form of a goats head, c1870.
$60-100

A pair of Georgian brass door stops, with moulded bases with weighted iron insets, inscribed with a sun mark and W.T.&S, 14in (35cm).
$1,000-1,500

A set of 6 brass coat hooks.
$100-200

A brass towel rail, 11½in (29cm).
$45-75

A pair of stone troughs, early 19thC, 24in (61cm) wide.
$250-350

A composition stone and bronze sundial, in the style of Coade, with bronze dial, inscribed Austin, Seeley & Co., New Road, London, the support carved with the three Muses, the plinth with stylised key pattern, mid-19thC, 50½in (128cm) high.
$6,000-9,000

A terracotta griffin, c1880.
$800-1,200

Victorian decorative railings.
$20-40 per foot *ARC*

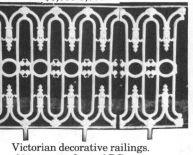

A pair of garden urns, early 19thC, 40in (101.5cm) high.
$2,500-3,500

An Italian garden vase, 19thC, 28in (71cm).
$800-1,200

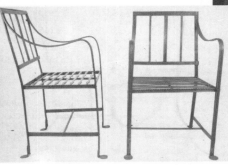

Two Regency wrought iron garden chairs with penny feet, c1820.
$3,000-4,500

Decorative railings.
$45-75 per foot

A pair of cast iron benches, by John McLean, New York, with grape and vine leaf open back above a reticulated seat with grape and vine skirt on leaf formed feet joined by a cross stretcher, late 19thC, 38in (96.5cm).
$2,000-3,000

A cast iron garden fountain, c1880, 60in (152cm) high.
$3,000-4,500

A white painted iron stickstand, modelled as a boy holding a serpent, 19thC, 34in (86cm).
$600-900

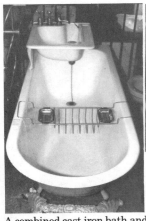

A roll top bath, 76in (193cm).
$700-900

A brass and copper soap rack.
$75-150

A carved oak bracket, from a church.
$800-1,200

A combined cast iron bath and basin, 66in (167.5cm).
$1,000-1,500

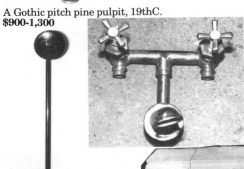

A pair of mahogany newel posts 60in (152cm).
$450-600

A Continental carved oak bar, c1900, 96 by 60in (243.5 by 182.5cm).
$10,000-13,500

A Gothic pitch pine pulpit, 19thC.
$900-1,300

A prison door, 19thC, 72 by 30in (182.5 by 76cm).
$300-400

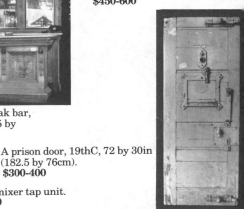

A brass mixer tap unit.
$300-400

A sandstone window, complete with leaded casements, 19thC, 60 by 108in (182.5 by 274cm).
$1,300-2,000

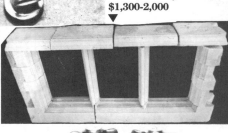

Telephone kiosks.
$600-900 each

A copper and brass shower unit, 35in (89cm).
$450-700

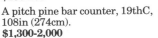

A pair of brass taps, E. Finch & Co. Ltd., Lambeth.
$150-200

A pitch pine bar counter, 19thC, 108in (274cm).
$1,300-2,000

A pitch pine pulpit, c1880
$7,000-10,000

CLOCKS

Longcase

An oak longcase clock, by Thomas Clare, Warrington, with 12in (30.5cm) brass dial, with engraved and spandrelled dial centre, subsidiary seconds and date aperture, 8-day 4-pillar rack striking movement with anchor escapement, 18thC, 82in (208cm).
$2,000-3,000

An oak and mahogany crossbanded longcase clock, by David Collier, Gatley, the brass dial with subsidiary seconds and date crescent with rolling moon in the arch, 8-day rack striking 4-pillar movement with anchor escapement, c1800, 86½in (219cm).
$2,000-3,000

A George III mahogany longcase clock, the brass dial with raised chapter ring and foliate spandrels, signed John Brand, London, with subsidiary seconds, date aperture and strike/silent ring in the arch, the 8-day movement striking on a bell, 100in (254cm).
$6,000-8,000

A walnut longcase clock, the arched brass dial with engraved wheatsheaf border and silvered chapter ring, with subsidiary seconds and date aperture and signed on a cartouche Hen. Batterson, London, with strike/silent in the arch, the movement with internal rack striking and anchor escapement, 18thC, with later gilt mounts to the hood 90in (229cm).
$3,000-4,000

A walnut longcase clock, 8-day movement, brass dial, silvered chapter ring, subsidiary dial for seconds, calendar aperture, the figured walnut case by John Blake of Fulham.
$9,000-12,500

A Regency mahogany longcase clock, the 12in (30.5cm) silvered dial with subsidiaries for seconds and for date, signed Grant, London, the 5-pillared movement with anchor escapement, 84in (214cm).
$8,000-11,000

A George III musical longcase clock, by Corban Cranefield, Sherringham, 3-train movement.
$7,000-10,000

A Dutch floral marquetry longcase clock, 18thC.
$8,000-11,000

Longcase/Tallcase Clocks

In the United States longcase clocks are commonly referred to as "tallcase". Both terms are equally correct and are becoming interchangeable

---

A Chippendale walnut longcase clock, the dial signed C. Warner, Pennsylvania, 91in (231cm) high. **$4,000-5,000**

A Federal painted longcase clock, possibly Berks County, Pennsylvania, the white painted dial with calendar dial, the case with maroon ground and gold details, paint restored, early 19thC, 96in (244cm). **$3,000-5,000**

A Chippendale inlaid walnut longcase clock, Pennsylvania, the brass dial engraved with a landscape, 88in (224cm). **$5,000-6,000**

A Chippendale carved mahogany longcase clock, dial signed by Thomas Claget, Newport, Rhode Island, the arched glazed door opening to an engraved brass dial with sweep seconds and calendar day dials, restorations to case, c1780, 88in (224cm) high. **$8,000-10,000**

A Chippendale cherrywood longcase clock, dial signed by Aaron Miller, Elizabethtown, New Jersey, minor repairs to hood, c1750, 80½in (204cm) high. **$10,000-12,000**

A Chippendale carved mahogany longcase clock, American, with white painted dial, sweep seconds and calendar day dials, unsigned, restorations to case, late 18thC, 95½in (242cm) high. **$6,000-7,000**

A walnut and seaweed marquetry longcase clock, with 12in (30.5cm) brass dial, signed Claudius du Chesne, Londini, with subsidiary seconds and date aperture, the 5-pillared movement with anchor escapement, early 18thC, 88in (224cm).
$9,000-12,500

A mahogany longcase clock, by W. B. Cornforth, Macclesfield, with 14in (35.5cm) convex enamelled dial, with rolling moon in the arch, subsidiary seconds and date crescent, 8-day rack striking movement with anchor escapement, c1820, 95in (241cm).
$1,000-1,500

An oak longcase clock, the dial with applied chapter ring and spandrels, signed Creighton B-Mena No. 120, ringed date aperture and winding holes, phases of the moon in the arch with lunar calendar and time of high tide scale, 91in (231cm).
$800-1,200

A marquetry and oak longcase clock, the 11in (28cm) dial with raised chapter ring, with inner quarter-hour ring, half-hour divisions and engraved Roman numerals with chased and faceted hands, signed A.M. Cressener, London, the movement with 4 ringing pillars and inside countwheel striking on a bell, 83in (210.5cm).
$4,000-5,500

A longcase clock by John Deacon, London, with early white dial, strike/silent and centre sweep hand for the calendar, subsidiary dial for seconds, 8-day movement, c1760, the case in the pagoda design, with inlaid brass columns, all brasswork original.
$15,000-21,000

A George III 8-day longcase clock, by John Darke, Barnstaple, with 12in (30.5cm) brass dial, signed silvered chapter ring, seconds dial, calendar aperture, phase of the moon in the arch and 'High Water at Barnstaple Key', the 4-pillar movement with anchor escapement striking on a bell, with pendulum and weights, in mahogany case, 89in (226cm).
$2,250-3,500

A country oak longcase clock with mahogany crossbanding, the 11in (28cm) dial engraved Wm. Edmunds, Madeley, the 30-hour movement striking on a bell, extensively restored, c1760, 77in (195.5cm).
$450-600

A Dutch oak longcase clock, the silvered chapter ring signed De Wancker TotLoo, with inscription, the gilt spandrels with vases amid scrolling foliage, the door with glazed apertures, slightly distressed, 18thC, 98in (249cm).
$1,300-2,000

A George III mahogany longcase clock, inscribed Daniel & Thomas Grignon, 3-train movement.
$6,000-8,000

A mahogany longcase clock, the brass dial signed Jas. Heron, New Town, subsidiary dial for seconds, date aperture, the 8-day movement striking on a bell, lacking bell, 87in (221cm).
$1,500-2,600

A Georgian mahogany longcase clock, with 12in (30.5cm) brass dial, silvered chapter ring, with subsidiary seconds and date aperture, signed on a cartouche William Haughton, London, with strike/silent in the arch, chiming the quarters on 8 bells, 97in (246cm).
$1,300-2,000

A mahogany longcase clock, the painted dial signed Geo. Hutchinson, Dullaghy, with subsidiary ring for seconds and date sector, rolling moon in arch with lunar calendar, the 8-day movement striking on a bell, 86in (218.5cm).
$1,300-2,000

An oak and mahogany banded longcase clock, the arched brass dial with pierced foliate spandrels and silvered chapter ring by Jonathon Ivison, fitted with an 8-day movement, 86in (218.5cm).
$1,000-1,500

Longcase Clocks

Longcase clocks are generally ordered alphabetically by the makers name

A George III mahogany longcase clock, the brass dial with silvered chapter ring, subsidiary seconds dial, date aperture and strike/silent in the arch, with brass cased weights and pendulum, 8-day strike, maker James Ivory, London, c1765, 97in (246cm).
$6,000-8,000

A mahogany longcase clock, the brass dial with engraved border and brass chapter ring, signed Philip Lloyd, Bristol, the engraved centre with subsidiary seconds and date aperture, with moon phase in the arch calibrated around and inscribed High Water at Bristol Key, the twin train movement with anchor escapement, 18thC, 88in (224cm).
$6,000-8,000

A mahogany 8-bell chiming longcase clock, the gilt brass dial with raised silvered chapter ring, subsidiary seconds and date aperture, strike/silent ring in the arch and signed on a silvered sector Willm and Jno. Kipling, London, the 8-day 3-train movement with 5 ringed pillars chiming the quarters on 8 bells with 12 hammers and a separate bell for the hours, 88in (224cm).
$7,000-10,000

HINTS TO DATING LONGCASE CLOCKS

Dials

8in square	to c1669	Carolean
10in square	from c1665-1800	
11in square	from 1690-1800	
12in square	from c1700	from Queen Anne
14in square	from c1740	from early Georgian
Broken-arch dial	from c1715	from early Georgian
Round dial	from c1760	from early Georgian
Silvered dial	from c1760	from early Georgian
Painted dial	from c1770	from early Georgian
Hour hand only	to 1820	
Minute hand introduced	c1663	
Second hand	from 1675	post-Restoration
Matching hands	from c1775	George III or later

Case finish

Ebony veneer	up to c1725	Carolean to early Georgian
Walnut veneer	from c1670 to c1770	Carolean to mid-Georgian
Lacquer	from c1700 to c1790	Queen Anne to mid-Georgian
Mahogany	from 1730	from early Georgian
Softwood	from c1690	from mid-Georgian
Mahogany inlay	from c1750	from mid-Georgian
Marquetry	from c1680 to c1760	from Carolean to mid-Georgian
Oak	always	

An oak and mahogany chiming longcase clock, signed Hugh Lough, Penrith, with Roman numerals, half-hour divisions and Arabic 5-minute numerals, sweep centre calendar, the massive 8-day movement playing a tune every 3 hours on 8 bells with 8 hammers and changing automatically every 24 hours, late 18thC, 93in (236cm).
$800-1,200

A mahogany longcase clock, the brass dial with silvered chapter ring, inscribed Maple & Co. Ltd., London, seconds dial, chime/silent ring in the arch, gilt metal cherub head and dolphin spandrels, the 3-train chiming 8-day movement with brass coated weights, 95in (241cm).
$1,300-2,000

A Georgian 8-day longcase clock with brass dial, signed Polglase, Helstone, with seconds dial, calendar aperture and pierced gilt spandrels, the 4-pillar movement with anchor escapement striking on a bell, with pendulum, weights, bell and keys, 2 hands missing, 85in (216cm).
$1,000-1,500

A green and gilt lacquered longcase clock, the brass dial with raised silvered chapter ring, recessed seconds disc and date aperture, gilt foliate spandrels, and strike/silent ring in the arch, signed Thos. Palmer, London, the 8-day movement with strike on bell, 93in (236cm).
$24,000-32,500

A Georgian walnut and inlaid longcase clock, signed Jon Sales, Dublin, with subsidiary seconds, date aperture and harboured winding holes, with an age of the moon dial in the added arch, the twin train movement with inside countwheel and anchor escapement, 102in (258cm).
$5,000-7,500

A walnut and panel marquetry longcase clock, with 11in (28cm) brass dial, with silvered chapter ring signed Thos Stubbs, London, with subsidiary seconds and date aperture, the movement with ringed pillars, internal rack striking and anchor escapement, early 18thC, 82½in (210cm).
$24,000-32,500

A walnut longcase clock, with 12in (30.5cm) brass dial with brass chapter ring, signed G. A. Smith, Barthomley, with subsidiary seconds and date aperture, the 6-ring pillared movement with inside countwheel strike and anchor escapement, the case with alterations, 18thC, 84in (213cm).
$3,000-4,500

A burr walnut longcase clock, the 12in (30.5cm) dial with raised chapter ring and spandrels, Roman numerals, Arabic numerals for the 5 minute divisions, subsidiary ring for seconds, date aperture, the chapter ring signed Sadler, London, the 8-day movement with rack strike, lacking bell, 18thC, 87in (221cm).
$6,000-9,000

A Scottish mahogany longcase clock, by D. Robinson, Airdrie, with painted dial, 8-day movement with seconds and date, 19thC, 84in (213cm).
$2,000-3,000

A Georgian mahogany longcase clock, the hood with swan neck pediment and spirally turned columns, the arched painted dial with subsidiary seconds and date, signed Geo. Ritchie, Arbroath, the twin train movement with anchor esapement, 82in (208cm).
$1,500-2,500

An Edwardian electric combination longcase clock, with 6in (15cm) brass dial, silvered chapter ring, the movement with alternative electric motor and 8-day chain fusee going train, striking the hours and the quarter hours on 9 gongs, in mahogany and inlaid case with concealed spirit level, strike/silent lever and glazed trunk door, with pendulum brass cased weight and 4 keys, 72in (182cm).
$5,000-7,500

A Regency mahogany longcase clock, now fitted with a 30-hour posted movement with 11in brass dial and silvered chapter ring, signed Jno. Mercer, Hythe, 78in (198cm).
$1,500-2,500

A Victorian mahogany and satinwood crossbanded longcase clock, the brass dial and silver chapter ring with Roman numerals, seconds dial and date aperture, with a silvered boss to the arch engraved William Patterson of Hamiltoun, fitted with an 8-day movement, 81in (206cm).
$1,500-2,500

A Victorian mahogany longcase clock, the silvered dial signed W. Ransone, London, with Roman numerals and blued steel hands, the weight-driven timepiece movement with 4 ringed pillars and anchor escapement, 69in (175cm).
$4,000-5,500

A German walnut cased pedestal clock, the pedestal fitted with a polyphon metal disc player, stamped 'Schutz -Marke', 19thC, 102in (258cm).
$10,000-13,500

A green lacquered longcase clock with caddy top, the brass dial with raised silvered chapter ring signed Sam Townson, London, half and quarter-hour marks and half-quarter divisions, silvered seconds ring, date aperture, and blued steel hands, hour hand broken, the 8-day movement with ringed pillars and outside countwheel striking on a bell, early 18thC, 94in (238cm).
$7,000-10,000

An oak 8-day longcase clock, with 10in (25.5cm) engraved brass dial, applied brass chapter ring and the 4 season spandrels with date indicator, maker William Webb, Wellington, with key, mid-17thC, 78in (198cm).
$1,500-2,500

A carved oak longcase clock, signed on a silvered plaque in the arch Edw. Whitehead, Wetherby, with subsidiary seconds disc and engraved silvered centre, the 8-day movement striking on a bell, 86in (218.5cm).
$1,300-2,000

A Georgian mahogany longcase clock, the 13in (33cm) brass dial with silvered chapter ring, subsidiary seconds and date aperture, the arch with moon phase signed Williams, Preston, the twin train movement with anchor escapement, 90in (230cm).
$6,000-9,000

A George III black and gilt japanned longcase clock, by John Wimble, Ashford, the 8-day 5-pillar movement with square brass dial, 90in (229cm).
$3,000-4,500

A walnut longcase clock, the silvered chapter ring signed E. Williamson, London, with subsidiary seconds, date aperture, harboured winding holes, the 5-ring pillared movement with inside countwheel strike and anchor escapement, late 17thC, with restoration, 81in (206cm).
$6,000-9,000

A walnut longcase clock, the 11in (28cm) brass dial with replaced winged cherub spandrels, and brass chapter ring, signed Jno Wise, London, with subsidiary seconds, date aperture and harboured winding holes, the movement with outside countwheel and later wheelwork, 18thC, with restorations and alterations, 82½in (210cm).
$3,000-4,500

A mahogany longcase clock with 8-day movement, the painted dial depicting Rent Day, c1800.
$1,200-1,750

A Lancashire mahogany longcase clock, with 15in (38cm) painted dial and rolling moon in the arch and centre date sweep, the dial centre with painted scene of the Death of Nelson, 8-day 4-pillar rack striking movement with anchor escapement, early 19thC, 94in (238cm).
$3,000-4,500

A mahogany longcase clock with boxwood inlay and stringing, the 12in (30.5cm) brass dial with early added arch, half and quarter-hour divisions and blued steel hands, the arch with silvered plaque flanked by dolphin spandrels, the 8-day movement with 5 ringed pillars, internal countwheel striking on a bell, 96½in (245cm).
$6,000-8,000

A mahogany longcase clock, the 7in (18cm) breakarch brass dial with raised chapter ring, Roman numerals, matted centre and applied spandrels, inscribed Tempus Fugit, the 8-day spring wound 3-train movement chiming quarter hours on 5 rods, 59½in (150cm).
$4,000-5,500

Regulators

A floor standing Vienna regulator, finished in walnut and ebony, with 8-day movement, maintaining power and deadbeat escapement, c1850, 95in (241cm).
$13,000-17,500

A walnut and ebony wall-hanging Vienna regulator, with 8-day movement, centre seconds sweep, Harrison's gridiron pendulum maintaining power.
$8,000-11,000

A small mahogany regulator, with white dial, signed Hepting, Stirling, 8-day 4-pillar movement with deadbeat escapement and Harrison's maintaining power, 19thC, 75in (190.5cm).
$1,500-2,500

A mahogany regulator longcase clock, the painted dial inscribed 'Thos Moreland, Chester', c1840, 89in (226cm).
$4,000-5,500

A Victorian walnut cased Vienna regulator wall clock, with 10-day deadbeat escapement and sweep second hand.
$1,500-2,500

Bracket Clocks

A single fusee bracket clock in ebony, by John Berry of London, 8-day movement, c1690, 14in (35.5cm).
$9,000-12,500

A verge bracket clock by Charles Gabrier of London, with applied gilt spandrels, c1740, 34in (86cm).
$16,500-23,000

An ebony and gilt brass mounted bracket clock, the brass dial with silvered chapter ring, signed Claudius du Chesne, London, with date aperture and harboured winding holes, and with strike/silent, early 18thC, with alterations, 17½in (45cm) high.
$8,000-11,000

A mahogany bracket clock with alarm, by Perigal, Coventry Street, London, c1775, 9½in (24cm).
$6,000-9,000

An ebonised bracket clock, with brass dial, strike/silent, by Thomas Gardner, London, the verge movement with 6 bell quarter repeating movement and engraved backplate, requires repairing, early 18thC, 18½in (47cm).
$3,000-4,500

An ebony bracket clock, the square brass dial with silvered chapter ring signed John Miller, London, now converted to anchor escapement, and originally with pull quarter repeat, now removed, the engraved backplate signed Johannes Miller, Londini fecit, early 18thC, on later bun feet, 16in (40cm) high.
$6,000-9,000

A tortoiseshell and cut brass inlaid bracket clock, the chased brass dial with enamel numerals, signed on a panel below Lepeltier a Paris, 19thC, 26½in (67cm).
$2,000-3,000

A French bracket clock, mercury gilded with painted panels, 8-day movement, hourly and half-hourly striking, c1840, 17in (43cm).
$3,000-4,500

An ebonised bracket clock, with inverted bell top, cast brass carrying handle, inscribed Richard Rayment, Bury St. Edmunds, with date aperture, mask and rococo spandrels, the movement converted to anchor escapement and with a backplate inscribed by the maker, feet replaced, 18thC, 19½in (49cm).
$2,000-3,000

HINTS TO DATING BRACKET CLOCKS		
Dials		
Square dial	to c1770	pre-George III
Broken arch dial	from c1720	George I or later
Round/painted/silvered	from c1760	George III or later
Case finish		
Ebony veneer	from c1660 to c1850	Carolean to mid-Victorian
Walnut	from c1670 to c1870	Carolean to Victorian
Marquetry	from c1680 to c1740	Carolean to early Georgian
Rosewood	from c1790	from mid-Georgian
Lacquered	from c1700 to c1760	Queen Anne to early Georgian
Mahogany	from c1730	from early Georgian

An ebony bracket clock, signed Thomas Science, London with mock pendulum and date apertures, and with strike/silent in the arch, the 5-pillared movement with fully engraved backplate and verge escapement, 18thC, 16in (41cm).
$5,000-7,500

A George III bracket clock in ebonised case, inscribed Thomas Wagstaffe, 3-train striking fusee movement.
$4,000-5,500

A George III mahogany bracket clock, with carrying handle to each side, with enamel dial, signed Biddell, London, with brass hands and with enamel subsidiaries above for regulation and for strike/silent, the twin fusee movement with anchor escapement, 21in (53cm).
$3,000-4,500

A French bracket clock, the case ebonised with tortoiseshell and brass inlays, the case with velveted brass dial and silvered chapter, with a gilt bronze figure of Father Time, signed beneath Gribelin, Paris, early 19thC, now with later spring driven movement, 21in (53cm).
$450-600

A Regency mahogany bracket clock with brass inlay, silver dial with strike, on 4 brass feet, by In. Lamb, London, 19½in (49cm).
$2,500-3,500

A Regency ebonised bracket clock, with white painted dial with Roman numerals and subsidiary date ring, signed Handley and Moore, London, with strike/silent ring in the arch, the 8-day repeating fusee movement striking on a bell, with engraved borders to the backplates, the pendulum with lock, 16in (40.5cm).
$2,500-3,500

A Regency Gothic mahogany bracket clock, the painted dial signed Manners & Sons, Stamford, with glazed cast brass bezel, the twin fusee movement with anchor escapement and strike on bell, the backplate with securing brackets to the case, 21½in (54.5cm).
$2,500-3,500

A Regency mahogany quarter chiming bracket clock, on gilt brass ball feet, the white painted dial with Roman numerals, signed Hanson, Windsor, with strike/silent ring in the arch, the 8-day 3-train movement similarly signed, one foot detached, 17½in (45cm).
$3,000-4,500

A bracket clock with 8-day movement, chimes on 8 bells and Westminster chimes, brass and ormolu dial in ebonised case with ormolu decoration, 19thC, 29½in (75cm).
$2,000-3,000

A French bracket clock, 8-day movement, hourly and half-hourly striking, in mahogany case, c1860, 13in (33cm).
$600-900

An oak cased ting-tang, fully restored and cleaned, c1890, 15½in (39cm).
$600-900

A Victorian walnut bracket clock, with silvered dial engraved with scroll decoration and with subsidiaries for regulation and strike/silent above, the twin fusee movement with anchor escapement, 26in (66cm).
$1,000-1,500

An English double fusee bracket clock, 8-day movement, hourly strike on the bell, in mahogany with fish-scale brass fretwork, by T. Farr, Bristol, c1830, 16in (41cm).
$3,000-4,500

An English double fusee bracket clock in oak, with ormolu mounts, with 8-day movement, quarter striking on 2 gongs, ting-tang, c1860, 17in (43cm).
$2,250-3,500

A mahogany 8-day bracket clock, with silvered dial with rise and fall regulator, quarter chiming on 2 gongs, with key, 19thC, 12in (31.5cm).
$450-700

A Victorian pollard oak Gothic cased 3-train bracket clock, chiming on 8 bells, by Thomas Myers, Sheffield.
$1,300-2,000

A small French bracket clock, hourly and half-hourly striking on a gong, with porcelain and enamel dial, c1860, 12in (30.5cm).
$1,300-2,000

A black marble bracket clock with applied gilt, 8-day movement and half-hourly striking, c1880, 11in (28cm).
$300-400

A Victorian pollard oak Gothic Revival bracket clock, with silvered brass dial with strike/silent in the arch, signed Muller, Twickenham, with substantial spring driven twin fusee mechanism, striking on a single gong, 42in (106.5cm) including bracket.
$1,500-2,500

Carriage Clocks

A silver and tortoiseshell cased carriage clock, maker William Comyns, London 1909, 4½in (11.5cm) in original fitted case.
$2,500-3,500

A gilt bronze English carriage clock, striking on a gong and signed on the backplate James McCabe, London, 3463, the signed silvered dial with subsidiary seconds, and with push repeat fitted through the top glass, 19thC, 10½in (26cm).
$10,000-13,500

An English carriage timepiece, in gilt brass case, with mother-of-pearl register plate, engraved silvered dial, the 8-day movement with lever beneath the balance wheel, the door inscribed Howell James & Co., Regent Street, London, 19thC, 6½in (16.5cm).
$4,000-5,500

A miniature oval carriage timepiece, with engraved mask, white enamel dial, Roman numerals, the 8-day movement with lever escapement, 3in (7.5cm).
$1,200-1,750

An English carriage timepiece, in gilt case, with Roman numerals and gilt halberd hands, the 8-day fusee movement signed on the backplate Bell and Sons, 131 Mount Street, Berkeley Square No. 14477, with platform escapement.
$2,000-3,000

A gilt repeating carriage clock, with ivory chapter ring, signed J.W. Benson, Ludgate Hill, London, the 8-day movement with silvered lever platform escapement striking on a gong, with the maker's stamp Drocourt, with original red leather numbered case, 6½in (16.5cm).
$2,000-3,000

A striking carriage clock, the case with bevelled glass window to the top, silvered mask with ivorine chapter ring, the 8-day repeating movement striking on a gong and with large silvered pointed lever platform escapement, 6in (15cm).
$900-1,300

An alarm carriage timepiece, in gilt case with gilt mask to the white enamel dial, with subsidiary alarm dial, the 8-day timepiece movement with gilt lever platform escapement and bimetallic balance, the alarm ringing on a bell in the base, with red leather travelling case, 3in (8cm).
$450-700

An English petit sonnerie carriage clock with white enamel dial, inscribed Lund & Blockley (to the Queen), No. 4095, with repeat button and silent/strike lever on the base, 6in (15cm).
$4,000-5,500

> **Clocks**
> All clock measurements refer to height unless otherwise stated

A French brass carriage clock, the lever movement striking on a gong, with push repeat and with the Margaine trademark on the backplate, with enamel dial, in an 'anglaise' case,19thC, 7in (18.5cm).
$1,000-1,500

A French brass carriage clock, the lever movement striking on gong with push repeat, the enamel chapter ring within an engraved gilt mask, in an 'anglaise' case, 19thC, 8in (20cm).
$1,200-1,750

A French gilt brass miniature carriage timepiece, the lever movement with enamel dial in an engraved case, 19thC, 4in (9.5cm), with a leather travelling case.
$2,000-3,000

A French gilt brass carriage clock, the lever movement striking on a gong and bearing the Drocourt trademark, with enamel dial, 19thC, 7in (18cm).
$2,000-3,000

A French gilt brass carriage clock, the lever movement striking on a gong with push repeat and enamel dial, in a bamboo style case, 19thC, 7½in (19cm).
$1,200-1,750

A French miniature brass carriage timepiece, the lever movement bearing the Margaine trademark and numbered 15556, with enamel dial, 19thC, 3½in (9.5cm).
$900-1,300

A French brass carriage clock, the lever movement striking on a gong, 19thC, 7in (18cm).
$1,000-1,500

A French brass carriage clock, the lever movement striking on a gong, with alarm and push repeat and bearing the Drocourt trademark, numbered 44663, with enamel dial, in a numbered case, 19thC, 6½in (16.5cm), together with a travelling case.
$1,000-1,500

A French gilt brass carriage clock, the lever movement striking on a bell, with enamel dial, 19thC, 6in (15cm).
$600-900

A French gilt brass grande sonnerie carriage clock, the lever movement striking on 2 gongs with push repeat numbered 3017, with enamel dial, 19thC, 8in (20cm).
$3,000-4,000

Mantel Clocks

A walnut mantel clock, the case with glazed top, side and back panels, the silvered dial with engraved spandrels, signed Chas. Frodsham, Clockmaker to the Queen, No. 2057, signed on the backplate, late 19thC, 12in (30.5cm).
$1,500-2,500

A Regency burr walnut mantel clock, surmounted by a bronze gadrooned top with brass side frets and stringing to the front, the silvered dial signed C. Lupton, Cornhill, London, the 8-day fusee movement striking on a gong, the pendulum with fine regulation and lock, 11in (28cm).
$4,000-5,500

A Regency mahogany and brass inlaid mantel timepiece, the painted dial signed Thwaites & Reed, London, the fusee movement with arched plates and anchor escapement, 16½in (42cm).
$1,500-2,500

A gilt porcelain-panelled mantel clock, with Brocot escapement, 15in (38cm).
$2,500-3,500

A Regency burr walnut, brass and ebony inlaid mantel timepiece, the silvered dial signed Grimalde & Johnson, Strand, London, the fusee movement with signed backplate and anchor escapement, damaged, 12in (31cm).
$5,000-7,500

A Regency white marble and gilt bronze mantel timepiece, the gilt dial with engine turned centre, signed Viner, London, the fusee movement with anchor escapement, 8in (20cm).
$1,000-1,500

A Regency rosewood and brass inlaid mantel timepiece, the silvered dial signed Carpenter, London, the fusee movement with shaped plates and anchor escapement, 9½in (24cm).
$4,000-5,500

A Regency mahogany and brass inlaid mantel timepiece, the enamel dial signed Scott, Horlr. to H.R.H. The Duke of Kent, 674, the fusee movement with anchor escapement and signed shaped plates, 10in (26cm).
$1,000-1,500

A mahogany and brass inlaid mantel clock, the painted dial signed Condliff, Liverpool, the twin fusee movement striking on a bell with anchor escapement, 19thC, 14in (35cm).
$1,500-2,500

An ornate cast brass mantel clock, decorated with birds and mask heads, 8-day striking movement, and claw feet.
5,000-7,500

A brass Eureka mantel timepiece, the movement with substantial compensated balance, numbered 7219, the signed enamel dial with subsidiary seconds, inscribed S. Fisher Ltd., 188 Strand, under a damaged glass shade, 13in (33cm).
$1,000-1,500

A French bronze and yellow marble mantel clock, the engine turned silvered dial signed Duval a Paris, the 8-day movement with silk suspension, outside countwheel and striking on a bell, early 19thC, 24in (61cm).
$1,300-2,000

A French ormolu and bronze mantel clock, the gilt dial with enamel numerals, the movement with silk suspension and countwheel strike, 19thC, 22in (56cm).
$1,300-2,000

French ormolu and porcelain mantel clock, 19thC, 15in (38cm).
,000-1,500

French ormolu and porcelain mounted mantel clock, the case with enamel dial, signed Chas. Frodsham, Paris, 19thC, 14in (35cm).
2,500-3,500

A French ormolu and enamel mantel clock, with polychrome champlevé decoration and circular gilt dial, 19thC, 12½in (32cm).
$1,200-1,750

A Federal carved cherrywood shelf clock, by David Wood, Newburyport, Massachusetts, the white painted dial with floral spandrels, seat board restored, minor repairs to applied moulding, c1800, 35in (89cm) high.
$9,000-12,000

A French white marble and bronze mantel clock, the case with decorated enamel dial raised on a column with a naked putto, 19thC, 15½in (39cm).
$1,200-1,750

A French gilt mantel clock, with 8-day striking movement, embossed with cherubs, 19thC.
$1,000-1,500

A French 8-day striking clock movement set in the stern of a ship mounted on black marble base with glass dome, the pendulum moving a sailor and the ship's wheel, late 19thC, 13½in (34cm).
$1,500-2,500

A Charles X ormolu and porcelain clock, with silvered face and floral and foliate bezel, the movement signed Le Roy Paris 1102, 16in (41cm) high.
$1,500-2,500

A French mahogany 4-pillar clock in Empire style, with flame mahogany veneers, the movement with gilt cast bezel and white enamel dial, the 8-day movement with 9-rod pendulum, anchor escapement and outside countwheel striking on a bell, 23in (58cm).
$1,000-1,500

A French mantel clock, with annular chapter ring and 8-day movement, in gilt brass case, late 19th/early 20thC, 22½in (57cm).
$900-1,300

A Louis XVI ormolu and biscuit mantel clock, the glazed enamel dial signed A Paris, 13½in (34cm) wide.
$2,250-3,500

A French red tortoiseshell and boulle mantel clock, the embossed gilt dial with blue Roman numerals on white porcelain cartouches with trefoil hands, the 8-day movement striking on a bell, 14in (36cm).
$1,000-1,500

A French bronze and gilt bronze mantel clock, with enamelled annular chapter ring with blue Roman numerals and regulator square above XII, and with 8-day movement by Japy Freres, 22in (56cm), with pendulum.
$3,000-4,500

A French ormolu mantel clock, the dial in green patinated frame surmounted by dying stag and hounds, by Leroy & Fils, Paris, 10in (25.5cm).
$6,000-8,000

An oak mantel clock, edged in boxwood, by W. H. of Germany, 8-day duration, striking on ting-tang chimes, c1880, 13in (33cm).
$400-550

A French bronze white marble and ormolu mantel clock, in the form of a globe, on a gilt base, the dial of applied gilt Roman numerals with hands in the form of a snake, the 8-day movement striking on a bell, with lever platform escapement, 14½in (37cm).
$2,500-3,500

An ormolu mounted white and red marble mantel clock, with glazed enamel dial signed Drouot à Paris, 15in (38cm) wide.
$4,500-7,000

A French tortoiseshell and brass inlaid mantel clock, with 8-day striking movement and gilt metal mounts to case.
$450-700

Lantern Clocks

An early Smith's lantern timepiece, c1920, 10½in (26cm).
$250-350

A late Stuart brass lantern clock of standard form, with anchor escapement and countwheel strike on bell above, with dolphin pierced frets above the dial, signed Nicholas Coxiter Londini fecit, within the florally engraved centre, 16in (41cm).
$1,300-2,000

A French brass lantern clock, the circular chased dial with enamel numerals, and pierced cresting, the movement with verge escapement and bob pendulum, originally designed for alarm, 16in (41cm).
$1,300-2,000

A brass lantern clock, with silvered chapter ring, half and quarter-hour divisions, engraved central field with single steel hand, signed Ninyan Burliegh, Durham, the weight driven movement with anchor escapement striking on a bell, early 18thC, with modern oak bracket, 15½in (39cm).
$2,500-3,500

A Georgian brass lantern clock, made for the Turkish market, the posted frame surrounded by a bell, with brass dial and chapter ring, signed on a cartouche in the arch Jno. Parks, London, the movement with verge bob pendulum escapement, 14½in (37cm).
$1,000-1,500

Skeleton Clocks

Wall Clocks

A Victorian skeleton clock, with passing strike, silvered chapter ring, the 8-day movement with chain fusee and deadbeat escapement, on wooden base with 4 bun feet, with a dome, 12in (30cm).
$800-1,200

A Swiss wooden wall clock, with arched side doors, the plates, wheels and pinions all of wood, with verge balance wheel escapement and outside countwheel strike, sounding on a bell mounted on top, 18thC, 11½in (29cm).
$9,000-12,500

A brass skeleton timepiece, the pierced spired plates with pierced silvered chapter ring, the fusee movement with lever, platform escapement, on a mahogany base under a glass dome, 19thC, 13in (33cm).
$1,200-1,750

A George III brass wall clock, the brass dial with date aperture, signed Edwd. Pashler, London, and with strike/silent lever at the IX, the twin fusee movement with anchor escapement, 18½in (47cm).
$3,000-4,500

A walnut Amsterdammertje, signee Etienne Hubert Amsterdam on the silvered chapter ring, the movement with anchor escapement and rack double strike, the wall case of standard form with figure finials, basically 18thC, 61in (155cm).
$1,000-1,500

An English inlaid mahogany dial clock, with brass bezel and convex 10in (25.5cm) circular dial, with twin fusee mechanism, striking on a bell with anchor escapement, early 19thC.
$9,000-12,500

A mahogany wall timepiece, the brass dial signed Mattw. & Thos. Dutton, London, the fusee movement with anchor escapement, 19thC, 26½in (67cm).
$4,000-5,500

A German carved wood wall clock, the brass movement striking the hours on a gong, and discharging an organ playing on 9 brass pipes, followed by a 4 air musical box, 19thC, 83in (211cm).
$1,000-1,500

Make the most of Miller's

When a large specialist well-publicised collection comes on the market, it tends to increase prices. Immediately after this, prices can fall slightly due to the main buyers having large stocks and the market being 'flooded'. This is usually temporary and does not affect very high quality items.

Miscellaneous

A Continental spelter mystery timepiece, the movement forming the upper part of the pendulum, which is supported in front of a cast figure of a kangaroo, 12½in (31.5cm).
$800-1,200

A carved oak cuckoo clock, the wooden dial with applied bone Roman numerals and bone hands, the skeletonised fusee movement striking on a gong, and operating 2 bellows and the cuckoo, 29in (74cm), with carved bracket.
$2,500-3,500

An ormolu and bronze clock, with glazed enamel dial, indistinctly signed … Armentieres, the case surmounted by an eagle supported by a classical semi-nude figure upon a fruiting platform, 32½in (83cm).
$3,000-4,500

A French clock, 18½in (47cm).
$6,000-8,000
Provenance: Original for Burghley House, Stanford, property of Lady Isabella Cecil.

A South German giltmetal tabernacle clock or Turmuhr, basically early 17thC, associated and with restorations, 19in (48cm).
$13,000-17,500

A Black Forest organ clock, the 4-key movement with 36 wood pipes, 8-air barrel and painted dial below a scene of classical figures in a landscape, in crossbanded and figured mahogany case with ebony and box stringing, unrestored, 97in (246cm).
$5,000-7,500

A silver gilt travelling watch, in engine turned case, with watch revealed by depressing the 2 sides, the matt silvered dial with Arabic numerals and moon hands, the movement jewelled to the centre with 17 jewels and signed Tavannes Watch Company.
$450-600

A German baroque brass and silvered Telleruhr, the circular plated movement with cylindrical pillars, resting barrel for the striking with pierced gates and numbered outside countwheel, chain fusee for the going with up-and-down ring engraved on the backplate signed Casper Sackerer, with loose ring suspension, basically early 18thC, with restorations, 17in (44cm) over pendant.
$2,500-3,500

An ormolu mounted Sèvres pattern
vase clock, the turquoise ground
oviform vase inset with central
glazed enamel dial, 23½in (59cm).
$1,300-2,000

An ormolu cartel clock, the glazed
dial with Roman numerals, signed
T. Martin, Paris, 27in (68.5cm) wide.
$1,300-2,000

A Louis XV cartel clock, with glazed
enamel dial signed Joannes Biesta
Paris, 32in (81cm).
$4,000-5,500

A Louis XV ormolu cartel clock, the
glazed enamel dial signed Leroy a
Paris, the movement with anchor
escapement and rack strike planted
on the backplate, the cartouche
shaped case cast with upspringing
foliage, 20in (51cm).
$2,500-3,500

A tôle piente Scwartzwald
clockmaker figure, naturalistically
painted, with a timepiece carried to
his front and a dummy one,
containing the key on his back, on
wood base simulating maple, 15in
(38cm).
$4,000-5,500

A Freise Stoelklok of standard form,
with cast lead frets to the canopy
and above the dial with moonphase
the movement with spiral angle
posts, 18thC, 31½in (80cm).
$5,000-7,500

A Swiss silver and enamel
miniature travelling timepiece, the
case surmounted by a handle and
decorated with purple guilloche
enamel, fitted with a watch
movement, 3.4cm, in a fitted
travelling case in the form of a
miniature briefcase.
$800-1,200

A brass mounted mahogany sedan
clock, with glazed dial and moulded
frame, early 19thC, 7in (18cm) diam.
$300-500

A Georgian gilt metal timepiece, the
verge movement with engraved
tapered plate signed Thomas
Greenstreet, fecit, the signed
24-hour dial with movable centre
disc engraved with 24 cities around
the world, and held aloft by
Father Time, 7½in (19cm).
$1,000-1,500

Watches

A quarter repeating jacquemart watch, in gold drum case with dark blue enamel surround to dial, applied with gold mounts, striking on 2 gongs.
$4,500-7,000

A French gold and enamel verge watch, the movement with pierced bridge cock, signed L'Epine a Paris, with later enamel dial, 3.9cm.
$1,500-2,500

A coaching watch, the cylindrical brass case contained within a brass bound mahogany box with recessed carrying handle, signed on the brass back 96 hours, Wregg, London No. 1649, Express No. 1., with unusual verge escapement, early 19thC, 12 by 9cm.
$5,000-7,500

A Swiss gold and enamel cylinder watch, the gilt bar movement signed H. Capt. Geneve, with enamel dial, the signed gold cuvette numbered 19119, 3.7cm.
$2,500-3,500

A French silver quarter repeating verge watch, the movement with pierced Egyptian pillars and bridge cock, signed Jacques Gloria à Rouen, early 18thC, with later gilt dial, 6cm.
$4,500-7,000

A gold Prest's keyless cylinder watch, by Jno. R. Arnold, Patent No. 134, London, the gilt movement signed on the bridge to the going barrel and on the top plate, casemaker TH, London 1825, 4.5cm.
$4,000-5,500

A German gold hunter cased keyless lever watch, the movement with compensated balance and overcoil spring, jewelled to the centre and signed Adolph Lange, Dresden 8667, the enamel dial, cracked, in numbered case, monogrammed to the front, 5.3cm.
$4,000-5,500

A Swiss gold minute repeating keyless lever dress watch by Cartier, the steel bar movement with compensated balance, signed Cartier, Paris 29, the signed silvered dial with subsidiary seconds, the case numbered 3088, with an inscription on the back to H. R. Coombs, Esq., 1917, 4.8cm.
$9,000-12,500

A Swiss gold and enamel cylinder watch, the movement signed Badollet a Geneve, with machined gold dial, the reverse decorated with a spray of lilies against a blue ground, 3.5cm.
$800-1,200

A Swiss gold and enamel cylinder watch, the gold cuvette inscribed Malignon a Geneve, No. 1805, 3.8cm.
$1,000-1,500

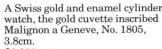

A gold and enamel form watch, the verge movement with pierced bridge cock, signed Fs Mayer a la Ville de Karlsbaad a Vienne, the case in the form of a viola, damaged, 19thC.
$3,000-4,500

A Swiss 8-day nickel cased keyless lever Goliath watch, the enamel dial signed Hy Moser & Cie, with subsidiary seconds, in a leather case, 10.3cm.
$800-1,200

A Swiss gold and enamel form watch, the keyless cylinder movement with enamel dial, contained in a jockey's racing cap decorated with black, blue and white designs, 2.7cm wide.
$4,000-5,500

A Swiss gold minute repeating keyless lever watch, signed Touchon & Co., Switzerland, with signed gilt dial, the case with repeat slide in the band, 4.4cm.
$2,250-3,500

A Swiss 18ct gold hunter cased minute repeating keyless lever chronograph, the movement with visible stopwork, compensated balance and extra jewelling to the repeat train, 5.8cm.
$5,000-7,500

A Swiss gold miniature hunter cased pendant watch, the keyless cylinder movement with enamel dial, the case set with a diamond in a heart shaped setting, 2.6cm.
$600-900

Wristwatches

A lady's brilliant and baguette cut diamond bracelet watch, on a fan and scroll design tapering flexible link bracelet.
$6,000-8,000

A Swiss gold keyless lever dress watch, the movement jewelled to the centre, signed European Watch and Clock Co. Ltd, the silvered dial signed Cartier, 4.5cm, in a signed presentation case.
$4,500-7,000

A lady's Continental wristwatch, with rose diamond bezel and winding button, with pearl 3 row bracelet and diamond and pearl clasp.
$4,500-7,000

A lady's diamond and platinum wristwatch, with white enamel dial with white gold abstract chapters and hands, signed by Jaeger-LeCoultre.
$30,000-40,000

A lady's wristwatch with diamond bezel, the dial signed Kutchinsky on an 18ct gold integral bracelet.
$2,000-3,000

A lady's diamond, sapphire and yellow gold wristwatch, with 18ct gold stylised half moon band, enhanced by a calibré cut sapphire arc, mounted in platinum and yellow gold, c1940, signed Vacheron & Constantin.
$8,000-11,000

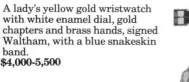

A lady's yellow gold wristwatch, signed by Concord, with quartz movement.
$800-1,200

A lady's yellow gold wristwatch with white enamel dial, gold chapters and brass hands, signed Waltham, with a blue snakeskin band.
$4,000-5,500

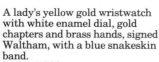

A gentleman's wristwatch by Vacheron & Constantin, Geneve, the matt white dial with applied gold numerals, the silvered movement signed, with certificate of origin and guarantee.
$2,250-3,500

An early chronograph wristwatch by Longines, with signed white enamel dial, blued steel moon hands, 24-hour ring in red Arabic numerals, red telemetric and black tachymetric scales, the central chronograph operated by a press button through the crown, movement numbered 5016649.
$5,000-7,500

A gentleman's wristwatch, signed on the matt silvered dial Rolex Oyster Elegante, Precision, with alternating baton and Arabic numerals, screwed down winder and screwed back.
1,300-2,000

An 18ct gold Omega wristwatch, with gilt dial signed Constellation Automatic Chronometer Officially Certified, day, date, bar numerals, with integral flexible brick link bracelet, 3.7cm.
$1,000-1,500

A gentleman's steel automatic wristwatch, signed on the black dial Rolex Oyster Perpetual Datejust, applied gold batons and white date aperture, screw down crown and integral steel bracelet with Rolex clasp.
$300-500

An early Rolex Oyster, in water resistant plated case, signed on the white enamel dial, the case numbered 7966, 3cm long.
$600-900

A 9ct red gold cased wristwatch, with applied gold numerals, and subsidiary seconds ring, signed Rolex, with screwed back to case, the signed movement jewelled to the 3rd with 15 jewels. ▶
$800-1,200

A gentleman's yellow gold wristwatch, with grey enamel dial and gold hands, signed by Piaget, in a black leather fitted case.
$5,000-7,500

◀

A German pilot's wristwatch of World War II, in grey metal case, with black dial and luminous minutes and hours, sweep centre seconds, hand lacking, the gilt three-quarter plate movement signed A Lange & Sohne, number 216339, 5.5cm.
$800-1,200

A gold wristwatch, with club foot lever escapement, the signed metal dial with Arabic numerals and batons formed from inset mother-of-pearl, with subsidiary seconds, c1935, 2.3cm.
$450-700

Barometers
Stick

A mahogany stick barometer, with domed cistern and broken pediment, the register signed Rizzi Fecit, with thermometer and pressure scales, early 19thC, 37in (94cm).
$900-1,300

A gentleman's wristwatch in gold bubble back case, signed Rolex Oyster Perpetual, Chronometre, the back numbered 46258 3131, with leather strap and gilt Rolex buckle, and a link mesh strap and clasp.
$5,000-7,500

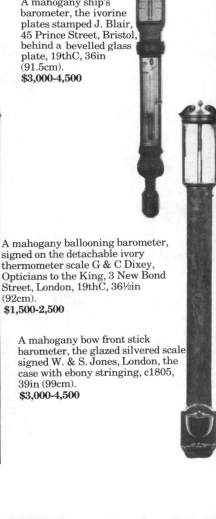

A stick barometer with painted dial, the mahogany case inlaid with Sheraton shells and boxwood stringing, c1820, 37½in (95cm).
$1,500-2,500

A walnut floral marquetry stick barometer, with silvered scales, the case with oak carcase, 49½in (126cm).
$3,000-4,500

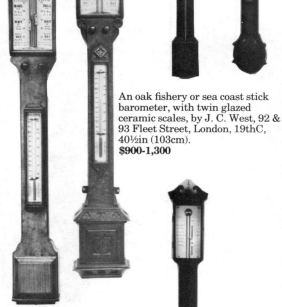

A carved oak stick barometer, c1840, 46in (116.5cm).
$1,000-1,500

A mahogany ship's barometer, the ivorine plates stamped J. Blair, 45 Prince Street, Bristol, behind a bevelled glass plate, 19thC, 36in (91.5cm).
$3,000-4,500

An oak fishery or sea coast stick barometer, with twin glazed ceramic scales, by J. C. West, 92 & 93 Fleet Street, London, 19thC, 40½in (103cm).
$900-1,300

A mahogany ballooning barometer, signed on the detachable ivory thermometer scale G & C Dixey, Opticians to the King, 3 New Bond Street, London, 19thC, 36½in (92cm).
$1,500-2,500

A walnut veneer fishery or sea coast stick barometer, with twin glazed ceramic scales, by R & J Beck, 31 Cornhill, London, 19thC, 39in (99cm).
$800-1,200

A mahogany bow front stick barometer, the glazed silvered scale signed W. & S. Jones, London, the case with ebony stringing, c1805, 39in (99cm).
$3,000-4,500

A stick barometer, by Gilbert & Wright of London, with swan arch pediment, edged in ebony stringing, silvered dial, c1800, 41in (104cm).
$2,250-3,500

Wheel

A lacquered brass aneroid barometer, signed J. Goldschmid, Zurich, fitted with a thermometer, 3in (7.5cm).
$800-1,200

A George III inlaid mahogany barometer, by Lione & Somalvico, with humidity gauge, thermometer, small convex mirror and barometer dial, some veneer chips, small cracks, late 18thC, 44in (111cm) high.
$1,500-2,000

A mercury banjo barometer, by J. Stopan of Aberdeen, with inlaid Sheraton shells, edged in ebony and boxwood stringing, c1820, 38in (96.5cm).
$900-1,300

An inlaid mahogany banjo barometer, with silvered dials, by I. Somalvico, Hatton Garden.
$1,000-1,500

A Federal inlaid mahogany barometer, dial signed A. Barnascone, Boston, Massachusetts, minor veneer and inlay chips, c1810, 38½in (97cm) high.
$5,000-6,000

Chronometers

An 8-day marine chronometer, the movement with separate subplate, with Arnold type spring detent escapement, Arnold stud, helical spring and later compensated balance and signed on the mainplate Jno R. Arnold, London, Invt. et fecit 294, the 3½in (9cm) silvered dial signed Arnold, London 294, in a brass case, possibly the original bowl, now fitted with carrying handle, on ball feet, early 19thC.
$3,000-4,500

The Chronometer Ledgers at Greenwich show that this piece was issued to the Beagle in 1837 and transferred to Erebus where it was presumed lost in the Arctic with the Franklin Expedition, see V. Mercer, John Arnold & Son, p237.

An 8-day chronometer, by Charles Frodsham, with spring detent escapement, c1930.
$5,000-7,500

A silver pocket chronometer, signed John Carter, Cornhill, London, No. 1573, the signed and numbered enamel dial with subsidiary seconds, the numbered case marked London 1842, 5.3cm.
$1,300-2,000

A 2-day marine chronometer, the movement with Earnshaw type spring detent escapement, the silvered dial signed Chadwick, Liverpool, No. 392, in a brass bowl hung in gimbals, with a safety key in a brass bound mahogany box, set with a signed and numbered ivory plaque, 19thC.
$2,250-3,500

Scientific Instruments
Globes

A miniature terrestrial globe, inscribed within a cartouche 'A/New/Terrestrial/Globe/by/ Nath.Hill/1754', with fishskin case, depicting the major constellations, 3in (7cm) diam.
$3,000-4,500

A Georgian 18in (46cm) terrestrial globe, by W. & A.K. Johnston, on mahogany tripod stand with scroll feet and casters, later map.
$5,000-7,500

A pair of 12in (30cm) J. & W. Cary globes, with coloured and varnished paper gores, set in divided brass meridian circles, titled 'Cary's New Terrestrial Globe . . . Made and Sold by J. & W. Cary, Strand, Septr 2nd 1816, with additions and corrections to 1818' and 'Cary's New Celestial Globe . . . precisely defined by Mr. Gilpin of the Royal Society . . . Jan.1, 1818', paper dial compass box, lacking one needle, 25in (63cm) high.
$18,000-25,000

A 14in (36cm) Betts's Portable Terrestrial Globe, by George Philip & Son Ltd, the collapsible colour printed linen globe on umbrella pattern frame, with suspension ring, in original wooden box, late 19thC, 30½in (77cm) wide.
$300-500

A French terrestrial globe, signed J. Forest, on turned ebonised base, slightly distressed, 23in (58.5cm) high.
$1,000-1,500

Surveying

A brass graphometer, signed I L M Ad 1702, the scales divided 0°-180°/180°-0°, with 2 fixed sights, compass box missing, early 18thC, 14in (35cm) wide.
$1,300-2,000

A Newton's 15in (38cm) terrestrial globe, the sphere applied with hand coloured gores and inscribed 'Newton's New and Improved Terrestrial Globe. Accurately delineated from the discoveries of the most esteemed navigators and travellers to the present time, published 1 July 1815, manufactured by J. & W. Newton, No. 66 Chancery Lane, London, slight damage, 29½in (75cm) high.
$1,300-2,000

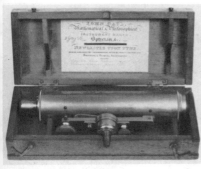

A surveyor's lacquered brass sighting level, signed John Cail Newcastle upon Tyne, with etched glass sights and maker's trade label, in mahogany case, 19thC, 9in (23cm) wide.
$400-550

A brass theodolite, signed on the plate Troughton & Simms, London, 19thC, 9½in (24cm) high.
$800-1,200

A brass folding arm protractor, signed Elliott Bros. London, with 2 verniers, fine adjustment tangent screw and clamp, late 19thC, 8in (20cm) wide, in mahogany case.
$300-500

A brass pantograph, by Watkins & Hill, London, in fitted wooden box with trade label, the box 26in (66cm) long.
$800-1,200

A lacquered brass theodolite, by Troughton & Simms, some damage, mid-19thC, 11½in (29cm) wide, in the original mahogany case.
$1,000-1,500

A lacquered brass 15in (38cm) 'Y' level, with 1in (2.5cm) diam lens and dust cap, pins replaced, 18thC, in oak case.
$300-500

Telescopes

A rare Jesse Ramsden brass 2in (5cm) refracting library telescope mounted on tripod base, signed to the tube, with brass lens cap and accessories, c1800, in fitted mahogany case, 25½in (65cm) long overall.
$800-1,200

A brass 5in (13cm) astronomical telescope, with 52in (133cm) long white painted body tube, some damage, in mahogany case, applied with trade label of Dollond & Co, 1 Ludgate Hill, London, E.C., 19thC.
$800-1,200

A brass single-draw 1¼in (3cm) pocket telescope and stand, the draw-tube signed Dollond, London, with threaded dust cap, early 19thC, 7in (17cm) long extended, in pasteboard case.
$1,000-1,500

A brass 3in (7.5cm) refracting
telescope, by Lewis & Brereton,
18 Preesons Row, Liverpool, with
rack and pinion focusing, 19thC.
$800-1,200

Microscopes

A lacquered brass botanical
microscope, signed on the pillar
Cary London, with accessories in a
plush lined mahogany case, the lid
with mounting ferrule, early 19thC,
5½in (14cm) wide.
$600-900

A lacquered brass Watson
polarising compound binocular
microscope, the 'Y'-shaped base
signed T.W. Watson, 4 Pall Mall,
London, 320, 19thC, in mahogany
case, 17in (43cm) high, with an
18-drawer oak slide cabinet, with
some slides, 11½in (29cm).
$1,000-1,500

A telescope by Horne and
Thornthwaite.
$800-1,200

A lacquered brass 3in (7.5cm)
refracting telescope, signed Watson
& Son, 313 High Holborn, London,
with rack and pinion focusing and
dust cap, in a Broadhurst &
Clarkson case with 2 eye pieces,
45in (115cm) long.
$1,000-1,500

A rare lacquered brass solar
microscope compendium, signed
J. Cuff London on the rotating plate
one bead glass missing, 2 of 3 brass
sliders numbered 1 x 2/3 x 4, and
other items, 18thC, the case 9in
(23cm) wide.
$4,000-5,500

A lacquered brass botanical
microscope, unsigned, with rack and
pinion focusing, 3 objectives,
bull's-eye condenser and swivel
mirror, in a plush lined case, the lid
with mounting ferrule, early 19thC,
5½in (14cm) wide.
$300-500

Make the most of Miller's

*When a large specialist
well-publicised collection
comes on the market, it
tends to increase prices.
Immediately after this,
prices can fall slightly due
to the main buyers having
large stocks and the
market being 'flooded'.
This is usually temporary
and does not affect very
high quality items.*

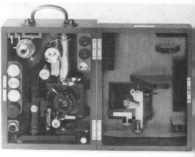

A black enamelled and lacquered
brass compound monocular
microscope, by E. Leitz Wetzlar,
No. 29852, 12in (30.5cm) wide.
$1,000-1,500

Medical Instruments

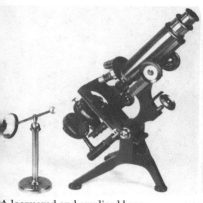

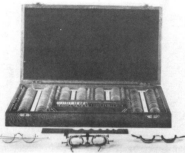

A lacquered and oxydised brass compound monocular microscope, by W. Watson & Sons Ltd, 313 High Holborn, London, with a comprehensive collection of accessories including 2 Abbe condensers, a wheel condenser, bull's-eye, polariser and other items in mahogany case, 13in (33cm) high.
$800-1,200

A brass Culpeper microscope by Lynch, Dublin, in original case, with a collection of eye pieces and slides.
$700-900

An optician's trial case in oak, containing lenses, coloured shades, 2 mirrors, 3 trial frames and an orthops rule, by Raphael Ltd London, the case 20½in (52cm) wide.
$300-500

A bone saw and 3 dental elevators, 19thC.
$200-350

An amputation saw by Weiss, signed Weiss's Improved Saw, 3 Strand, London, on the blade back, with anti-clog teeth and ebony handle, 19thC, 15½in (39cm) long.
$200-350

A pair of blued-steel framed 'D' folding sided spectacles, with blue tinted lenses, 19thC.
$150-250

A set of 6 folding trial spectacles, unsigned, numbered 2, 3, 4 and 5, with fractions ½ and ¾, the horn frame with centre brass interleaf and horn guards, 4¾in (12cm) long.
$300-500

A sectional model of the eye, the vitreous body decorated in colours and with glass lenses, mounted on an ebonised stand, late 19thC, 7in (17cm) high.
$800-1,200

A wax model of the human head showing the nerves, arteries, veins and muscles, each numbered with identification sheet, mounted in an ebonised and glazed case, by Lehrmittelwerke, Berlin, 10in (25cm) high.
$300-500

An anatomical plaster model of a human foot, 19thC.
$1,000-1,500

A cupping set by Weiss, 62 Strand, London, with 2 glass cups in plush lined fitted case, 19thC, 5½in (14cm) long.
$450-700

A sheet brass letter balance, signed
Parnell, London, and inscribed
Hall's Patent, the shaped plate and
pointer engraved, contained in the
original plush lined and fitted
leather case, 5in (13cm) wide.
$400-550

A Tate pump signed J.J. Griffin &
Sons, Garrick St. London, 19thC,
23in (59cm) wide, together with
4 bell jars.
$700-900

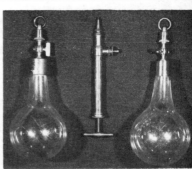

A lacquered brass hand vacuum
pump, unsigned, with 2 glass bulbs,
the brass bases with taps and end
caps, 19thC, 12in (30.5cm) high.
$450-700

A mahogany microscope slide
cabinet, with 21 drawers containing
a collection of entomological,
zoological and botanical slides by
various makers, including
F. Enoch, W.F. Stanley, E. Wheeler
and others, the cabinet with brass
carrying handle, late 19thC, 12in
(30.5cm) high.
$1,500-2,500

A demonstration diffraction prism,
mounted in brass frame, signed
W. & S. Jones, 30 Holborn, London,
early 19thC, 9½in (24cm) high.
$900-1,300

Cameras

A German silver perpetual
calendar, mounted on an ornately
decorated chased scrollwork panel,
18thC, 8½ by 2½in (21 by 6cm),
adapted as a notebook holder.
$1,500-2,500

A rare underwater housing for a
Leica camera, by Akustische und
Kinogerate GmbH, Vienna.
$1,500-2,500

A Wimshurst pattern plate machine
by Philip Harris Ltd, Birmingham,
with 2 contra-rotating plates,
2 Leyden jars, collector brushes and
combs, on a mahogany base, 22in
(55cm) wide, and a pair of brass and
ebonite discharge forks.
$1,000-1,400

A 5 by 2½in (13 by 6cm) Heag IX
Universal camera, with a pair of
C. P. Goerz Dagor III f6.8 90mm
lenses Nos. 253505 and 253496, and
Ernemann magazine back.
$300-500

A 1½ by 1½in (4 by 4cm) grey Baby
Rolleiflex camera No. 2056087, with
a Schneider Xenar f3.5 60mm lens
No. 7199161, by Franke and
Heidecke, in case.
$300-500

A 7 by 5in (18 by 13cm) No. 5
Folding Kodak camera, early
satchel type, with lens set into an
early sector shutter and an E.K. Co.
roll film pack stamped '7506'.
$700-900

A falling plate Svenska Express camera No. 2067 in black leather, stamped in gilt on reverse 'Hasselblad Svenska Express'.
$800-1,200

The camera was probably made by the German company Murer and bought in by Hasselblad's photographic department to sell under their own name.

A 28 by 28mm 'The Presto' camera by E. B. Koopman, with 4 glass plates in situ, and instruction book 'Presto Pocket Camera Primer'.
$800-1,200

A 2½ by 3½in (6 by 9cm) Rittreck IIa s.l.r. camera No. 2747 with a Musashino Koki Luminant f3.5 10.5cm lens No. 12001, extension tubes, a Luminant f4.5 21cm. lens No. 12108 and Rittreck roll film back and instruction book.
$600-900

A Leica I camera, No. 5640, with a Leitz Elmar f3.5 50mm lens, a Leitz rangefinder and cassette, all in Leitz leather case.
$1,300-2,000

The "TICKA"
Watch Pocket Camera.

HOUGHTONS L^{TD}

A rare and unusual hallmarked silver Ticka camera with lens cap and engraved with 'A' monogram and crown motif, by Houghtons Ltd.
$1,300-2,000

The silver Ticka is hallmarked for London 1906. The monogram refers to Princess Alexandra who was one of the more talented Royal photographers.
Houghtons Ltd advertised the fact that Princess Alexandra was a Ticka user although the Royal Archives have no record of this. The camera belonged to Francis Henry Smith who was a Royal Marine and served on the Royal Yacht. He apparently left the Marines c1909 to become the Queen's Wardrobe man and later became a King's Messenger for George IV.

A Boowu copying gauge in maker's original box, and a Ozwto cable release in maker's box, by Leitz.
$100-200

A Leica I camera No. 3001, with a Leitz Elmar f3.5 50mm lens, c1926.
$1,000-1,500

A rare 'mountain' Elmar 10.5cm f6.3 lens No. 136450, with reversible lens hood and caps, by Leitz.
$1,000-1,500

Made in 1932 during the first year of production.

A Leica 1 (Model C) camera No. 52102, non-standardised with a matched Leitz Elmar f3.5 50mm lens and a matched Leitz Elmar f3.5 35mm lens, both engraved on barrel '102'.
$4,000-5,500

The Leica with interchangeable lens facility was introduced in 1930 from when this camera dates. Lenses had to be individually matched to a body. The total number of non-standardised Leicas with interchangeable lens mounts is 2995.

A Xenon 5cm f1.5 lens No. 289110 with 2 rings, by Leitz.
$300-400

A good working cut-away demonstration Leica M5 camera, by Leitz.
$2,500-3,500

A Leica Ic camera, converted to a If No. 459934 with a Leitz Elmar 5cm f3.5 lens No. 805737, a 5cm brilliant viewfinder, in leather case and chrome FOKOS rangefinder in maker's box.
$1,000-1,500

An un-named tropical quarter plate detective camera with a built-in changing bag and seller's plaque 'Smith, Photo Chemist, Gosport'.
$600-900

A rare 'The Rover Patent' detective camera, by J. Lancaster & Son, with wooden casing and leather case, a Lancaster Patent See Saw shutter and internal brass plate holders.
$450-700

The Rover camera was based on W. J. Lancaster's patent of 1 October 1890 and used an unusual form of falling plate design. The unexposed plates were stacked horizontally in the top of the camera and a release knob on the side of the camera allowed each to fall into the focal plane. Once exposed they moved backwards. The Rover was also a variant on the disguised/hidden camera.

A half plate brass and mahogany camera, with a brass bound lens and focusing cloth, camera with seller's plaque 'McGhie & Co, 75 St Vincent St, Glasgow', all in canvas case.
$300-500

A rare No. 1 concealed vest camera No. 8364 with glass plate inside camera and 2 other circular glass plates.
$800-1,200

Viewers

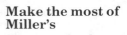

A Votra stereo transparency viewer.
$1,000-1,500

Five various direct vision viewfinders, including 13.5cm, 9cm, 5cm and others, 2 AUFSU waist-level finders, by Leitz.
$600-900

Make the most of Miller's

Every care has been taken to ensure the accuracy of descriptions and estimated valuations. Price ranges in this book reflect what one should expect to pay for a similar example. When selling one can obviously expect a figure below. This will fluctuate according to a dealer's stock, saleability at a particular time, etc. It is always advisable to approach a reputable specialist dealer or an auction house which has specialist sales.

ART NOUVEAU
Ceramics

An enamelled plaque, attributed to Harold Stabler, in soft cloisonné enamelled colours, within a silver coloured metal frame, 3in (8cm) diam.
$300-500

A pottery vase by Tiffany Studios, in mottled yellow, rust and brown glaze with crystalline-like elements, inscribed monogram, drilled, 6½in (16.5cm) high.
$600-700

An early Rozenburg pottery wall plate, the design attributed to Th. A. C. Colenbrander, probably painted by W. F. Abspoel, painted W.G. mark for W. Von Gudenberg, den Haag, date letter for 1888 and artist's device, 15in (38cm).
$1,000-1,500

An Austrian porcelain coffee set, painted in mauve, green and yellow with delicate flowers and further embellished with gilding, factory marks for Carl Knoll of Karlsbad, Austria.
$3,000-4,500

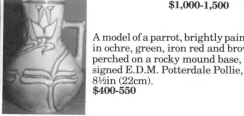

A Minton Art Studio jug in turquoise and honey colours, restoration, c1875, 8in (20cm).
$100-200

A model of a parrot, brightly painted in ochre, green, iron red and brown, perched on a rocky mound base, signed E.D.M. Potterdale Pollie, 8½in (22cm).
$400-550

A William de Morgan red lustre tile panel, made from 2 large tiles, and painted in shades of red and pink lustres, framed.
$1,500-2,500

An Ault pottery vase, the base with raised Ault mark, impressed C. W. Dresser, signature and No. 246, 7in (18cm).
$1,000-1,500

A Rookwood pottery 'Indian' flask and stopper, decorated by Harriet Elizabeth Wilcox, on a treacle coloured ground, impressed factory mark with date code for 1898, and artist's initials, 7½in (18cm).
$2,250-3,500

An Eltonware vase, decorated with gold and platinum crackle glaze, base with signature, 21½in (54cm).
$1,500-2,500

An Ault pottery twin-handled vase, designed by Christopher Dresser, decorated in red, white and apple green, relief factory mark, numbered 246 and facsimile designer's signature, 7in (18cm).
$1,300-2,000

An Ault pottery freeform vase, designed by Christopher Dresser, impressed facsimile designer's signature, 12½in (32cm).
$600-900

A Brannam pottery vase, decorated in sgrafitto technique by James Dewdney, in red, blue and yellow glaze, giving the appearance of green and brown colouring, signed and dated 1898, 19½in (50.5cm).
$600-900

A small Dalpayrat high fired porcelain vase, glazed in mixed shades of sang-de-boeuf, mauve, eau-de-nil and pale blue with the white body showing through in places, signed Dalpayrat and numbered 12, 2in (5cm).
$300-500

A pair of Mettlach Villeroy and Boch vases, each incised and painted in ochre, red and green on a blue ground, rim chip to one, incised marks and 2416, 16in (40.5cm).
$800-1,200

A Linthorpe pottery vase, possibly designed by Christopher Dresser, decorated in brown slip against a rich turquoise ground, impressed Linthorpe, numbered 2201 and signed F.B. for Fred Brown, 20in (51cm).
$600-900

A vase by Jessie Marion King, cracked, J.M.K. marks, 6in (15cm).
$300-500

A Royal Bonn jardinière, with painted decoration, c1900, 18in (46cm).
$300-500

A pair of Rozenburg vases, painted in vivid colours, crown and stork marks, Rozenburg, Den Haag and numbered 332, 15½in (39.5cm).
$1,000-1,500

A Pilkington's Royal Lancastrian lustre vase, by Forsyth, decorated with dragons, maker's marks, c1900.
$800-1,200

A large Pilkington Royal Lancastrian vase, painted by Richard Joyce, in golden lustre and red against a powder blue ground, impressed rosette mark and artist's monogram, 12in (30.5cm).
$1,000-1,500

A pair of Rozenburg pottery vases, on a green ground, painted marks with a date mark for 1898, 9½in (24cm).
$900-1,300

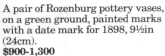

Clocks

A French Empire style clock, c1880, 14in (35.5cm).
$900-1,300

A Liberty & Co., English pewter timepiece, designed by Archibald Knox, with copper coloured numerals and red enamelled berry forms against shaded blue and green enamelling, stamped on base English Pewter 0609, Made in England and Rd. 468016, 8in (20.5cm).
$4,000-5,500

An Arts and Crafts brass clock with chased Celtic motifs on face, pendulum and weights, with simple Black Forest movement, reminiscent of Knox designs for Liberty's Tudric pewter, c1900, 15in (38cm).
$2,250-3,500

A Secessionist inlaid walnut longcase clock, inlaid in ebony and ivory, the movement by Gustav Becker, 77½in (197cm).
$1,500-2,500

366

A mantel clock in pottery case, printed in blue with pansies and convolvulus on a gold ground, indistinctly marked, late 19thC, 19½in (50cm).
$800-1,200

A Liberty & Co., pewter and enamel clock, marked Tudric and impressed no, c1900.
$2,000-3,000

A calendar clock in carved oak case.
$750-1,000

Figures

A Royal Dux figure, signed F. Otto, 24in (61cm).
$700-900

An oak electric mantel timepiece, the case applied with pierced brass, on ball-and-paw feet, the enamel dial signed The Brush Co. Ltd., Loughborough, 19in (48cm).
$800-1,200

A Royal Dux centrepiece, comprising 2 semi-nude nymphs with 2 leaves, on column decorated with water lilies, red triangular mark, 14in (35.5cm).
$800-1,200

A pair of white glazed figures modelled as Bruce and Wallace, some damage, 19in (48.5cm).
$600-900

A Goldscheider porcelain figure, 12in (30.5cm).
$800-1,200

A French porcelain figure, based on a design by the illustrator Umberto Brunelleschi, in grey and pink with gilt, marked on reverse Brunelleschi and Radiguet Ceramiste, Oissels France, 13½in (34.5cm).
$1,200-1,750

A gilded plaster figure, by William Banbury, on shaped ebonised wooden base, inscribed in ink on base William Banbury, plus indiscernable script, 12½in (31cm).
$200-350

A bronze figure of a naked girl, cast from a model by Küchler, inscribed Küchler and founder's mark of K and Vrais Bronce, Deposé, 14½in (37cm), with separate wooden base.
$2,000-3,000

A Zsolnay lustre glazed classical figure, modelled as the nude Venus, covered overall in golden green lustre shading to tones of reddish gold in places, signed in lustre Zsolnay Pecs in circle, and made in Hungary, 18in (45.5cm).
$2,500-3,500

An abstract bronze figure of a woman, cast from a model by Willi Soukop, R.A., signed on the underside Soukop, 11in (28cm).
$1,000-1,500

A gilt bronze group, cast from a model by Perrot, on marble base, inscribed Perrot, 10in (25.5cm).
$1,000-1,500

Furniture

An unusual Austrian bronze group, on marble base, inscribed Drah and marked Bronce M.N.F. Wien, 18½in (47cm).
$2,500-3,500

An amusing bronze figure of a poacher, wearing mediaeval costume and plumed hat, holding a knife between his teeth, wrestling with his 'prize' gripped between his legs, raised on marble base, unsigned but stamped 126/105, 9in (23cm).
$300-400

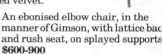

An Arts and Crafts walnut armchair.
$800-1,200

An Arts and Crafts armchair, c1910.
$300-500

A pair of mahogany armchairs, designed by Josef Hoffman, upholstered in buff textured velvet.
$4,000-5,500

An ebonised elbow chair, in the manner of Gimson, with lattice back and rush seat, on splayed supports.
$600-900

A bamboo drawing room suite, comprising a settee, 4 chairs, and an occasional table, each bearing a label Maison de Bamboos Perret et Vibert, 33 Rue du 4 Septembre, Paris.
$3,000-4,000

A nest of 2 tables, inset with tiles, largest 18in (46cm), and a shaped coffee table, 40½in (103cm), label Lazlo Hoenig, 54 South Audley St., Grosvenor Sq. London W1.
$300-500

An Arts and Crafts occasional table with inlaid plank legs, probably made by Wylie & Lockhead, c1900, 23in (58cm) square.
$1,500-2,500

An Arts and Crafts sideboard, 48in (122cm).
$900-1,300

An occasional table by Gallé, 17½in (44.5cm) square.
$1,300-2,000

A Gothic style oak side table, in the manner of Pugin, 42½in (107cm).
$1,000-1,500

An Arts and Crafts oak sideboard, by Stanley Davis of Windermere, marked under top with maker's monogram SDW 1927, and J.E.O. monogram, 54in (137cm).
$1,500-2,500

A mahogany escritoire with marquetry panel, by Shapland & Petter of Barnstaple, c1905.
$3,000-4,000

An Austrian mahogany kneehole desk, attributed to Otto Wagner, the top inset with green leather, with brass gallery, on flared brass feet, 47½in (121cm), and a matching mahogany chair, drop-in seat, with revolving action, on similar brass supports.
$4,000-5,500

An Aesthetic Movement walnut hanging cabinet, with hand painted panel, c1875.
$700-900

An Aesthetic Movement corner cupboard, the bow fronted doors enclosing 3 shelves and painted in colours, one door unfinished, on three-legged base with a single drawer and undertier, 27in (69cm).
$600-900

A mahogany and marquetry buffet, attributed to Louis Majorelle, with bronze mounts and marble tops, the gallery with a narrow shelf at the top, 56in (143cm).
$2,000-3,000

An Amsterdam School sideboard, rosewood bordered in coromandel, 65in (165cm).
$700-900

An Arts and Crafts pollard oak bedroom suite of 8 pieces, in the manner of C. F. A. Voysey.
$4,000-5,500

A Dutch Arts and Crafts tea buffet, designed by Jac. van den Bosch for 'het Binnenhuis', with metal tag 't Binnenhuis Raadhuisstraat, Amsterdam', and with branded monogram J. v.d. Bosch and the numbers 848, 61½in (156cm) high.
$2,500-3,500

An Arts and Crafts oak dresser, with brass hinges, 50in (127cm).
$2,250-3,500

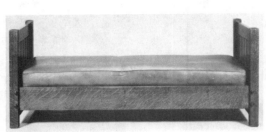

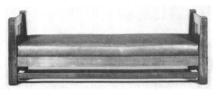

An oak 'knock-down' daybed, by
Gustav Stickley, branded with
firm's logo, 36in (91.5cm) wide.
$4,000-5,000

An oak double bed, by L. & J. G.
Stickley, c1910, 58in (147cm) wide.
$5,000-6,000

An oak daybed, by L. & J. G.
Stickley, model No. 292, c1912, 30in
(76cm) wide.
$5,000-6,000

An oak double door bookcase, by
Gustav Stickley, each door with
glass panes, branded with the firm's
logo, model No. 715, c1913, 35in
(89cm).
$5,000-6,000

An oak double door bookcase, by
Gustav Stickley, with red decal and
the Cobb-Eastman retailer's paper
label, model No. 715, c1904, 36in
(91.5cm).
$5,000-6,000

An oak 'Safecraft' secretaire, by
Gustav Stickley, the glazed
bookcase set on cabinet with 2 doors
with strap hinges, opening to a safe,
a red decal and paper label on base,
c1909, 35in (89cm).
$2,500-3,500

An oak and leather magazine
cabinet, by Gustav Stickley, the
open shelves with tacked leather
edging, red decal, model No. 546,
c1903, 44in (111.5cm) high.
$5,500-6,500

An oak china cabinet, designed by
Harvey Ellis, produced by Gustav
Stickley, model No. 803, with red
decal, c1903, 36in (91.5cm).
$6,000-8,000

A set of 4 oak spindle side chairs, by Gustav Stickley, with original rush seats, model No. 378, c1907, 40in (101.5cm) high.
$7,000-9,000

An oak salesman's sample chair, with drawer under seat converting to a table, c1910, 5½in (14cm), with original carrying case.
$400-500

An oak high back spindle side chair, by Gustav Stickley, with drop-in seat, branded with firm's logo, model No. 384, c1905, 46in (116.5cm) high.
$10,000-12,000

An oak spindle side chair, by Gustav Stickley, with original leather drop-in seat, black decal, model No. 384, c1905, 46in (116.5cm) high.
$11,000-13,000

An oak bow-arm Morris chair, by Gustav Stickley, with adjustable back, model No. 336, c1903.
$10,000-12,000

An oak spindle rocking chair, by Gustav Stickley, with remnants of a red decal, model No. 359, c1907.
$350-450

An oak ladderback rocking chair, by Gustav Stickley, with red decal under the arm, model No. 2632, c1902.
$1,000-1,200

A wicker armchair, attributed to Gustav Stickley, c1913, 37in (94cm) high.
$700-800

A wicker armchair, by Gustav Stickley, model No. 88, c1913, 39½in (100cm) high.
$1,000-1,200

A willow armchair, by Gustav Stickley, model No. 64, c1912, 33in (84cm) high.
$3,000-4,000

An oak banded chest of drawers, by Gustav Stickley, with branded signature, model No. 906, c1912, 41in (104cm).
$7,000-8,000

An oak table mirror, by Gustav Stickley, with branded signature, c1912, 26in (66cm).
$500-800

An oak buffet and serving table, by Roycroft, with metal tag 'Made by the Roycrofts and presented to Mr & Mrs E. W. Fellows as a wedding gift by his mother Martha C. Fellows, October 17, 1906', 42in (106.5cm).
$5,000-6,000

A leather topped desk, by Gustav Stickley, model No. 709, c1904, 47½in (119cm).
$2,000-3,000

An oak and leather desk, by Gustav Stickley, model No. 710, c1903, 48in (122cm).
$1,500-2,000

An oak settle, by Gustav Stickley, model No. 171, c1903, 78in (198cm).
$14,000-16,000

An oak settle, by L. & J. G. Stickley, model No. 275, c1910, 84in (213cm).
$10,000-12,000

An oak sewing table, by Gustav Stickley, the top with drop leaf top over 2 drawers, with red decal in drawer and brown paper label, model No. 630, c1909, 18½in (47cm).
$3,000-4,000

An oak and leather library table, by Gustav Stickley, with red decal, model No. 609, c1905, 36in (92cm) diam.
$4,000-5,000

An oak and copper cellaret, by Gustav Stickley, with black decal in drawer, model No. 86, c1907, 24in (61cm).
$7,000-9,000

An oak library table, by Gustav Stickley, model No. 619, paper label in drawer, c1910, 66in (167.5cm).
$4,000-5,000

An oak gateleg table, by L. & J. G. Stickley, with decal, model No. 553, c1912, 42in (106.5cm) diam.
$4,000-6,000

An oak waste basket, by Gustav Stickley, with vertical slats attached to 2 interior metal rings, model No. 94, c1910, 14in (35.5cm) high.
$3,000-4,000

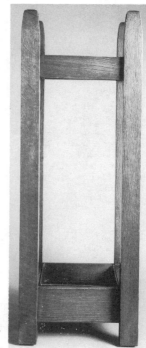

An oak child's wardrobe, by Gustav Stickley, model No. 920, c1907, 33in (84cm).
$3,000-4,000

A leather topped library table, by Gustav Stickley, model No. 633, c1903, 48in (122cm) diam.
$4,000-5,000

An oak umbrella stand, by Gustav Stickley, branded with firm's mark and paper label, c1912, 33in (84cm), high.
$1,200-1,500

An oak hall stand, with mirror and embossed copper panels, 36in (91.5cm).
$800-1,200

An Arts and Crafts plant stand, with copper strapwork, 36½in (92cm) high.
$300-500

A Limoges enamelled framed mirror, the bevelled glass flanked by panels enamelled in colours, 12½in (31cm).
$5,000-7,500

Glass

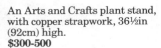

A Daum etched glass vase, the thick transparent brown ground deeply etched with wide zig-zag lines, inscribed, Daum Nancy, France, 9in (23cm).
$3,000-4,500

A Daum etched glass vase, in blue glass cut with thin vertical bands and small circles staggered throughout, inscribed Daum, Nancy France, 11in (28cm).
$1,200-1,750

A Daum overlaid and etched glass vase, on white ground overlaid in deep brown etched to depict full autumnal leaves, etched Daum Nancy, 14in (35.5cm).
$1,300-2,000

A Daum etched and enamelled glass vase, etched Daum Nancy, 21½in (54cm).
$5,000-7,500

A Daum two-layer cameo glass landscape vase, enamelled signature, 4½in (12cm).
$1,500-2,500

A Daum overlay glass vase, in shades of yellow, orange and brown, 5in (13cm).
$1,500-2,500

A Daum clear glass vase encasing blue, yellow and white, and overlaid in deep blue and grey/green, etched and carved with Rudbeckia and a martelé ground, repairs, engraved Daum Nancy, 16in (41cm).
$6,000-8,000

A Daum mottled amber tinted glass vase, relief decorated in deep pink morning glory flowers, inscribed Daum, Nancy, 327, 7in (18cm).
$1,500-2,500

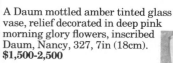

A large Daum glass vase, of transparent pale turquoise tone, signed on footrim Daum Nancy France, 12in (30.5cm).
$700-900

A Daum glass vase, with enamel decoration, 4½in (11.5cm).
$400-550

A Gallé glass vase, overlaid in pink and green, etched signature in the Chinese manner Gallé, 6in (15cm).
$2,000-3,000

A Gallé enamelled glass vase, enhanced with gilding, Cristallerie de Emile Gallé Nancy France in cameo, 13in (33cm).
$2,500-3,500

A Gallé 4 layer cameo glass vase, signed in cameo, 14½in (37cm).
$5,000-7,500

A Gallé glass vase, the white ground overlaid in light brown, with cameo signature Gallé, 9½in (24cm).
$2,500-3,500

A Gallé glass vase, the cream coloured ground overlaid in red, with cameo signature Gallé, 5in (13cm).
$1,500-2,500

A Gallé glass vase, the blue and white ground overlaid in olive green and brown, with cameo signature Gallé, 4in (10cm).
$2,000-3,000

A Gallé vase, the frosted and cream coloured ground overlaid with purple, with cameo signature Gallé, 5½in (14cm).
$3,000-4,000

A Gallé 4 layer cameo glass vase, decorated with chrysanthemum, signed in cameo, 6in (15cm).
$3,000-4,000

A Gallé 4 layer cameo glass vase, decorated with flowering clematis, signed in cameo, 6½in (17cm).
$5,000-7,500

A Gallé glass vase, the pinkish white ground overlaid in deep brown, with cameo signature Gallé, 5½in (14cm).
$2,000-3,000

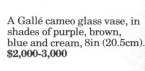

A Gallé cameo glass vase, in shades of purple, brown, blue and cream, 8in (20.5cm).
$2,000-3,000

A Gallé 2 layer cameo glass solifleur vase, decorated with wild flowers, signed in cameo, 7in (17cm).
$1,000-1,500

A Gallé 4 layer cameo glass vase, decorated with flowers and leaves, signed in cameo, 9½in (24cm).
$5,000-7,500

A Gallé 4 layer glass vase, decorated with clematis flowers, signed in cameo, 9in (23cm).
$1,500-2,500

A Gallé acid etched and enamelled vase, in green, amber, red and yellow, carved signature, 10½in (27cm).
$3,000-4,000

A Gallé cameo glass vase, base signed Gallé Depose, 16in (40.5cm).
$9,000-12,500

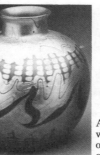

A glass vase by Loetz, with all-over silvery iridescence, inscribed Loetz Austria, 6in (15cm).
$6,000-8,000

A glass vase by Loetz, in pale green with blue green iridescence, raised on a small foot depicting a wave, c1900, 7½in (19cm).
$1,300-2,000

A French cameo glass vase, signed Le Vere Francais, c1900, 12in (30.5cm).
$800-1,200

A Loetz glass vase, with random splashes of golden iridescence shading through pale turquoise and violet, and applied with a silver coloured metal collar, 13in (33cm).
$800-1,200

An overlaid and carved glass vase, inscribed D. Christian Meisenthal, 3½in (9cm).
$2,000-3,000

A double overlay and carved glass vase, by Eugène Michel, in green and white and finely carved to depict water lilies in blossom, the interior with iridescence, 5in (13cm).
$5,000-7,500

A glass vase, overlaid in green and aubergine, with finely etched leaves, vines and blossoms depicting passion flowers, inscribed D. Christian Meisenthal Loth, 7in (18cm).
$2,000-3,000

A blue iridescent Favrile glass vase, inscribed X182, L.C. Tiffany-Favrile, 9in (23cm).
$2,000-3,000

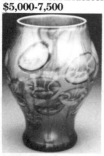

A Favrile glass paperweight vase, with many stylised morning glory blossoms amidst streamers encased in the clear glass, the interior with iridescence, crack to foot, engraved U4113 Louis C. Tiffany, c1904, 7½in (19cm).
$1,000-1,500

An iridescent Favrile glass comport, inscribed L. C. Tiffany Inc. Favrile W41N, 3in (7.5cm).
$2,000-3,000

An iridescent Favrile glass comport, in all-over blue and purple iridescence on a short stem and circular foot, inscribed 1531 2104 L L.C.T. Tiffany Favrile, 6½in (16.5cm).
$2,000-3,000

An iridescent gold Favrile glass flower bowl, with central detachable flower frog, both incised L.C. Tiffany Favrile 5344K, 14½in (36cm) diam.
$2,500-3,500

A Favrile glass centrepiece, the ribbed body with all-over blue iridescence, inscribed L.C. Tiffany Favrile 8412K, 10in (26.5cm).
$2,000-3,000

A pâté-de-verre dish, the translucent and red streaked ground carved with stylised blossoms, leaves and sinuous stem, moulded Decorchemont, 3in (7.5cm) high.
$800-1,200

A Daum cameo glass vase, etched and enamelled with a design of violets, the rim gilded, with enamelled signature, 5in (13cm) diam.
$1,500-2,500

A Daum cameo glass box and cover, the greyish body overlaid with acid etched green glass, heightened with gilding, applied with a silver coloured metal collar, signed in gold on base Daum Nancy, 5in (12.5cm) diam.
$2,500-3,500

A pair of pink cameo glass jars with silver screw top lids, 2in (5cm) high.
$250-350

A pâté-de-verre bust of a satyr, the bust modelled in amethyst glass, inscribed Despret and 1099, 6½in (16.5cm).
$1,000-1,400

A pâté-de-verre Buddha, the jade green figure sitting in typically cross-legged fashion, moulded A, Walter Nancy, 3in (8cm).
$700-900

Jewellery

A W.M.F. claret jug, the emerald green glass jug with plated mounts incorporating female masks and flowerheads, 16in (40.5cm).
$1,000-1,500

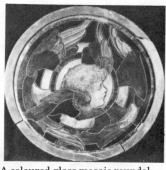

A coloured glass mosaic roundel, attributed to Powells and designed in the manner of Burne-Jones, 18in (45.5cm) diam.
$400-550

A glass and gold necklace, the green and violet woven cord necklace set with 9 moulded iridescent glass scarabs in 18ct gold, stamped Tiffany & Co, and 18ct, 16in (40.5cm) long.
$30,000-40,000

A Gip carved and pierced horn pendant, with bead link necklace, set with a silver backed moonstone, signed, 4½in (11cm).
$300-500

A cameo set, c1900, bracelet 6½in (16.5cm) long.
$10,000-13,500

A pâté-de-verre pendant, by G. Argy-Rousseau, with translucent ground, moulded with a bouquet of red and purple flowers on a fuchsia coloured cord, moulded A-R-G, 3in (7.5cm) diam.
$2,000-3,000

Lamps

A 'spiders web' leaded glass lamp shade, impressed Tiffany Studios New York 337, 15in (38cm) diam.
$6,000-8,000

A brass and glass oil lamp, c1910, 40in (101.5cm).
$300-400

A Favrile glass and bronze bell desk lamp, inscribed L.C.T. Favrile, the bronze base with green patina, impressed Tiffany Studios, New York 419, 11in (28cm).
$6,000-8,000

A bronze table lamp base, impressed Tiffany Studios, New York 531, 26½in (67cm) high.
$2,250-3,500

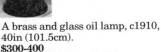

A leaded glass and gilt bronze table lamp, with white streaked amber and yellow panels, impressed Tiffany Studios, New York 1933, the gilt bronze base impressed Tiffany Studios New York 543, 21in (53cm) high.
$7,000-10,000

A leaded glass, bronze and Favrile glass table lamp, with tag impressed Tiffany Studios, New York, some damage, 26in (66cm) high.
$13,000-17,500

A stained and leaded glass table lamp, with a brass column cast with stylised foliage, on a leaf shaped base, the shade with a stylised floral border, 23in (58.5cm) high.
$1,500-2,500

A four-light lily Favrile glass and bronze table lamp, inscribed L.C.T. and impressed Tiffany Studios 313, 19in (48cm) high.
$5,000-6,000

A bronze figural lamp base, cast from a model by R. Sudre, modelled as a naked girl, with lamp fitment, signed R Sudre lere Epreuve and stamped Raymond Sudre, numbered 1910, 20½in (52cm) high.
$1,000-1,500

A bronze table lamp of a nude female figure, holding an adjustable lamp, on a circular base, not signed, 18in (46cm).
$4,500-7,000

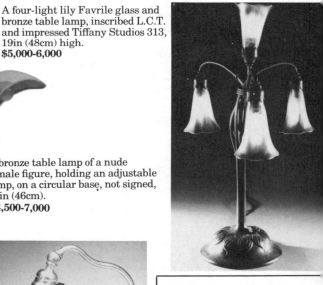

A Doré bronze and Favrile glass desk lamp, inscribed and impressed Tiffany Studios, New York, 416, shade cracked, 7in (18cm) diam of shade.
$2,500-3,500

Make the most of Miller's

Unless otherwise stated, any description which refers to 'a set' or 'a pair' includes a valuation for the entire set or the pair, even though the illustration may show only a single item.

Metal

A set of Georg Jensen Cypress pattern cutlery, comprising 61 pieces, designed by Tias Eckhoff, stamped in oval Georg Jensen sterling Denmark, 92oz gross.
$3,000-4,500

A German pewter bowl by Osiris, 5½in (14cm) high.
$300-400

An Arts and Crafts plated copper épergne, attributed to the Guild of Handicraft Ltd., and a design by Charles Robert Ashbee, 10½in (27.5cm).
$1,500-2,500

An Arts and Crafts stemmed bowl, attributed to John Paul Cooper, inscribed 'In memory of a Labour of Love, Ascension Day 1914', 6in (15cm).
$2,250-3,500

A WMF pewter dish with figure, 9in (23cm) high.
$1,200-1,750

A Jean Després plated bowl, with overall hammer textured finish, signed J. Després on base and JD poinçon on rim, 4in (10cm) high.
$2,000-3,000

A Liberty & Co. English pewter and Clutha glass stemmed bowl, the mount marked English Pewter and 0276, 6½in (16.5cm) high.
$1,000-1,500

A David Anderson bowl, the silver coloured metal stamped David Anderson, 830S and numbered 5485, 16½in (42cm) wide.
$900-1,300

A large comport, by Tiffany & Co., New York, the interior gilt, with script monogram, marked, c1880, 13½in (34cm) diam, 76oz 10dwt.
$10,000-12,000

WMF silvered pewter covered two-handled punch bowl and ladle, stamped, 21½in (54cm) high.
1,300-2,000

A set of Georg Jensen Scroll pattern cutlery, designed by Johan Rohde, comprising 79 pieces, stamped in oval Georg Jensen and Sterling Denmark, 136oz gross.
$3,000-4,500

Georg Jensen 57 piece continental pattern table service, stamped marks, London, import marks for 1934, 68oz not including eel.
,000-4,500

An Omar Ramsden silver soup ladle, stamped 'OR' with London hallmarks for 1924, 10½in (27cm), 6oz.
$1,500-2,500

A set of 6 Georg Jensen silver coffee spoons, stamped maker's mark, G.S. and London import mark for 1925, cased.
$200-350

A mixed metal and enamel vase, by Tiffany & Company, New York, marked on base, c1880, 11in (28cm) high.
$8,000-10,000

A flask, by Tiffany & Co., New York, the back with initials FTR and seaweed, marked on base, c1885, 8in (20.5cm) high, 11oz.
$2,000-3,000

A pair of salts, by Dominick & Haff, Newark, New Jersey, with small script monograms, marked, 1883, 3in (7.5cm) diam, 4oz 10dwt.
$300-400

A gold Favrile glass Jack-in-the-pulpit vase, by Tiffany Studios, inscribed LCT 6636A, and with partial paper label, 17in (43cm) high.
$7,000-9,000

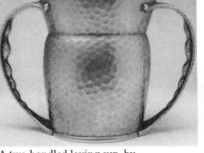

A centrepiece bowl, by Tiffany & Company, New York, marked on base, c1880, 7½in (19cm) diam, 17oz.
$7,000-8,000

A two-handled loving cup, by Tiffany & Co., New York, marked, c1885, 8in (20.5cm) high, 40oz.
$4,000-5,000

A mixed metal mug, by Tiffany & Company, New York, the base engraved with a presentation inscription 'Clyde Gordon Benedict' and dated 1882, the interior with traces of gilding, marked on base, 4in (10cm) high, 6oz gross.
$5,000-6,000

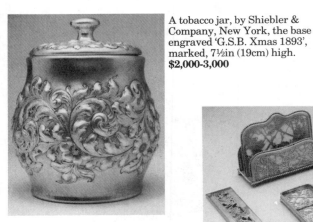

A tobacco jar, by Shiebler & Company, New York, the base engraved 'G.S.B. Xmas 1893', marked, 7½in (19cm) high.
$2,000-3,000

An eight-piece gilt bronze and onyx desk set, in the Grapevine pattern, by Tiffany Studios, each piece stamped.
$2,500-3,000

A sugar bowl and cream pitcher, by Whiting Manufacturing Company, with gilt interiors, marked, 2½in (6.5cm) high, 7oz 10dwt.
$500-600

A large pewter ale jug and cover, showing the influence of the designs of C. F. A. Voysey, unmarked, but probably Liberty & Co, 14½in (36.5cm) high.
$400-550

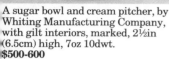

An Orfèvrerie Gallia plated tea and coffee set, stamped with factory marks, numbered 4643 and 4644, tray 20½in (52.5cm) wide.
$2,250-3,500

A Liberty's pewter tea service, designed by Archibald Knox, Solkets trade mark, English Pewter No. 0231.
$400-550

A Mappin & Webb silver coffee set, comprising: a coffee pot, 7in (18cm), hot milk jug and sugar bowl, maker's marks for Sheffield 1938.
$1,300-2,000

A pair of Georg Jensen candlesticks, designed by Johan Rohde, marked with Danish maker's marks, numbered 612 and with designer's monogram, 3in (7cm) high.
$1,000-1,500

A Modernist teaset, the silver coloured metal stamped 800 and 210ff in shaped punch, teapot 5in (13cm) high.
$1,500-2,500

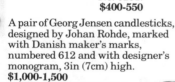

A pair of Kayserzinn five-light candelabra, designed by Hugo Leven, one sconce missing, marked in ovals on bases Kayserzinn 4486, 19in (48.5cm).
$4,000-5,500

A pair of Liberty's Tudric pewter candlesticks, each with detachable driptray, No. 01769, 8in (20.5cm).
$300-500

A pair of pewter candlesticks, by Just Anderson, c1920, 9in (23cm).
$700-900

A silver goblet, Chester 1905, 8in (20.5cm).
$400-550

A Gothic style cup and cover, with Manchester Reform Club monogram, with gilt interior, inscribed 'Omar Ramsden Me Fecit', London 1923, 15in (38cm), on oak socle with silver plaques and strapwork decoration.
$5,000-7,500

A Gothic style goblet, with Manchester Reform Club monogram, inscribed 'Omar Ramsden Me Fecit', London 1923, 7in (18cm), on silver mounted oak socle.
$900-1,300

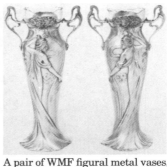

A Liberty & Co. Tudric Pewter flower vase, possibly designed by Archibald Knox, stamped marks, Tudric 0441, 4in (10cm).
$1,000-1,500

A bronze vase, signed J. Ofner, 13in (33cm).
$400-550

A pair of WMF figural metal vases, with glass liners, stamped marks on base, 14½in (36.5cm).
$2,250-3,500

A silver vase, maker's marks G & Co. Ld, and Birmingham marks for 1963, 10½in (26cm)
$300-500

A silver backed brush set, embossed with kingfishers and water lilies, Chester 1909, cased by Oldfields, Liverpool.
$600-900

A Hagenauer plated hand mirror, with linear decoration on one side, stamped on reverse with WHW in circle, 9½in (23.5cm).
$450-700

A hammered copper framed mirror, 21 by 15in (53 by 38cm).
$300-500

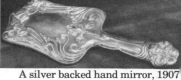

A silver backed hand mirror, 1907
$100-200

An Arts and Crafts mirror, with moth enamelled in relief, 19 by 15in (48 by 38cm).
$400-550

A silver and enamelled picture frame, marked H & A Birmingham 1904, 6½in (16.5cm).
$1,200-1,750

A brass flower, the petals remove to make individual ashtrays, c1900, 9½in (24cm).
$150-200

A pair of Liberty & Co., silver and enamelled picture frames, marked L & Co., Birmingham 1913, 5½in (13cm) diam, in original Liberty box.
$4,000-5,500

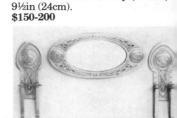

A pewter garniture by Margery Gilmore, comprising an oval mirror and a pair of double candle sconces each piece embossed with a Celtic interlaced design, each stamped M.G., the mirror 30in (76cm) wide.
$1,200-1,750

A bronze desk set, by Tiffany Studios, with firm's marks.
$1,000-1,500

A Glasgow style pewter and enamel cigar box, the hinged cover inset with an enamel plaque, 9in (23cm) wide.
$400-550

A Continental brass and wood tobacco jar.
$200-350

An Arts and Crafts copper and brass casket, 5½in (14cm) wide.
$100-150

Moorcroft

A Moorcroft Tudric candlestick, with pewter top, c1920, 4in (10cm).
$400-550

A Moorcroft tazza, with pewter base, 9in (23cm) diam.
$450-700

A Moorcroft bowl, c1920, 10in (25.5cm) diam.
$300-500

A Walter Moorcroft ginger jar and cover, with a turquoise and blue mottled ground, painted initials impressed facsimile signature, factory mark and potter to the Queen, c1945, 11in (28cm) high.
$450-700

A pair of Macintyre Florianware vases and covers, decorated by William Moorcroft with anemone-like flowers in blue and green on an ivory ground, one with slight hair crack, 8½in (22cm).
$1,000-1,500

A Moorcroft vase, 10½in (26cm) high.
$450-700

A Moorcroft pottery vase, painted with green trees on a yellow blue ground, green painted signature and printed Made for Liberty & Co., mark to base, 9in (23cm).
$1,300-2,000

A Moorcroft Florianware vase, signed, c1895, 10in (25.5cm) high.
$600-900

A Moorcroft vase, c1912, 10in (25.5cm) high.
$600-900

A Moorcroft Florianware vase, signed, 12in (30.5cm) high.
$1,000-1,500

A pair of Moorcroft Macintyre vases, signed, c1898, 10in (25.5cm) high.
$1,000-1,500

An early Moorcroft vase, with the Pomegranate pattern, c1912, 10½in (26cm) high.
$600-900

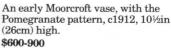

A Moorcroft Macintyre vase, painted with 18thC pattern, enriched with gilding, printed Macintyre marks, signed in green W. Moorcroft, 16in (40.5cm) high.
$1,000-1,500

A Moorcroft vase, painted on a tan brown ground, decorated in corn yellow, blue and green, with impressed facsimile signature W. Moorcroft Potter to H.M. The Queen, Made in England, also painted signature, c1935, 20in (51cm).
$1,000-1,500

Three Moorcroft Macintyre Florianware vases.
$5,000-7,500

A Moorcroft pottery vase, painted on a mottled blue green ground, blue signature on base and impressed Royal marks, 7in (18cm).
$800-1,200

A Moorcroft Burslem vase, with a flambé fish design on blue/lilac ground, c1910, 12½in (31cm).
$1,000-1,500

A Moorcroft vase, painted with a ▶ rich ruby glaze with impressed mark, Made in Burslem, signed W. Moorcroft, and with original paper label, slight chip to base, 16in (42cm).
$1,000-1,500

A Moorcroft Macintyre peacock pattern candlestick, c1900, 13½in (33cm).
$300-500

A large Moorcroft vase with wisteria design, green signature, c1914, 10in (25cm).
$800-1,200

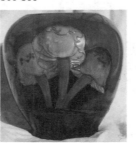

A Moorcroft vase with loop handles, with poppy design, c1925, 12in (30.5cm).
$1,300-2,000

A Moorcroft vase with a fish design on a pale flambé ground, c1930, 12in (31.5cm).
$1,300-2,000

A Moorcroft vase with the toadstool design, under a rare brown lustre glaze, 8in (20cm).
$1,300-2,000

A jardinière with the Claremont toadstool design, with a green signature, c1905, 7in (18cm).
$1,300-2,000

A vase with the Claremont toadstool design, on a mottled green ground, c1915, 9in (23.5cm).
$1,300-2,000

Posters

Louis Wain: 'A Day at the Seaside', pen and ink, signed in pencil, image area 7 by 5½in (18 by 14.5cm), framed and glazed.
$600-900

Nan M. Moffat: 'Gypsy Rondo', oil on canvas, signed in pencil on back of frame, dated 1922 and GSA Glasgow School of Art, image area 36½in square, framed.
$600-900

Louis Wain: 3 pencil drawings framed together and depicting a cat, a dog and another cat, entitled 'Sister Mary James Top Note', each picture signed, 30½ by 10½in (77 by 26.5cm), framed and glazed.
$600-900

Jules Chéret: 'Macassar de Naquet', a chromolithographic poster, signed en block, 53 by 38in (134.5 by 96cm), framed and glazed.
$600-900

Privat Livemont: 'Paintress', a chromolithographic panel signed en block and Brux. 1901, 19½ by 12½in (50 by 31.5cm), framed and glazed.
$300-500

E. McKnight Kauffer: 'You Can Be Sure Of Shell – Actors Prefer Shell', a chromolithographic poster for Shell petrol, signed en block, damaged, date '33, 30 by 45in (76 by 114cm).
$300-500

Privat Livemont: 'Sculptress', a chromolithographic panel signed en block, and Brux. 1901, image area 19½ by 12½in (50 by 31.5cm), framed and glazed.
$300-500

'Beatrice', a porcelain panel, painted by George Buttle, in natural colours, mounted in a silver plated frame, made by the Duchess of Sutherland's Cripples' Guild, and embellished in relief with theatrical figures and foliage and inscribed 'I was born to speak all mirth and no matter', signed on porcelain G. A. Buttle 1915, stamped on frame with crown and DSCG, 17½ by 13½in (45 by 34.5cm).
$4,000-5,500

George Buttle was a porcelain painter who worked for Wedgwood, Bishop & Stonier, Moore Brothers and Royal Doulton. The Doulton archives reveal him as a gifted figure painter in both the romantic and classical styles, whose other works also included miniatures, ceramic cameos and portrait heads of children. A large vase by Buttle was shown at the Brussels Exhibition in 1910. He left Doulton in 1911 to return to Bishop & Stonier as Art Director.

Walter Crane: engraved and printed by Duncan C. Dallas, Dallas Type Press, No. 5, Furnival St. London, J. M. Dent & Co., Aldine House 1893, a limited edition of 650, numbered 62, signed by the designer and the printer, in original box.
$800-1,200

Miscellaneous

A Belgian two-piece buckle, by Paul Dubois, unsigned, 4½in (11.5cm).
$300-500

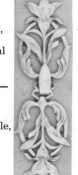

A Belgian two-piece foliate buckle, in white colour metal with an openwork design of leaves, engraved Paul Dubois, 8½in (21.5cm) wide.
$1,000-1,500

Doulton

A Perry & Co., chamber candlestick, designed by Christopher Dresser, painted overall in red, adapted, probably contemporary, maker's mark Dr. Dresser's design, and registration mark for 30th October, 1883, 7½in (19cm) high.
$450-700

A Perry & Co., chamber candlestick, designed by Christopher Dresser, and retailed through Liberty & Co., maker's mark, stamped Dr. Dresser's design, painted Liberty & Co., London and registration mark for 30th October, 1883.
$800-1,200

Two Doulton Lambeth brown salt glaze stoneware figures by George Tinworth, impressed marks and artist's monogram G.T., 5in (12.5cm).
$1,500-2,500

A Doulton 'Reynard the Fox' coffee service, pattern No. H4927.
$1,000-1,500

A pair of Doulton stoneware ewers, decorated by Hannah Barlow and Florence Roberts, impressed and incised marks, 11½in (29.5cm).
$800-1,200

A Doulton stoneware oil lamp, base with brass mounts, probably decorated by Florence Roberts, in shades of blue and green on a textured ground, complete with a frosted glass shade, impressed marks dated 1884, 18in (46cm).
$800-1,200

A Doulton Lambeth Isobath inkwell, stoneware glazed in shades of blue and brown, c1877, 6in (15cm).
$800-1,200

A pair of Doulton Lambeth vases, impressed marks Frank A Butler and 1883, 16in (41cm).
$800-1,200

A pair of Doulton faience vases, decorated on a two-tone brown ground, dated 1885, 9½in (24cm).
$300-500

A pair of Doulton faience Slaters Patent vases, late 19thC, 14½in (37cm).
$600-900

Royal Doulton

'Sarah Gamp', a Royal Doulton character teapot and cover, circle mark, lion and crown, date code for 1939, introduced 1939, withdrawn 1960, 7in (18cm) high.
$800-1,200

'Old Charley', a Royal Doulton character teapot and cover, circle mark, lion and crown, date code for 1939, introduced 1939, withdrawn 1960, 6in (17.5cm) high.
$800-1,200

'Mephistopheles', small, D5758, designer H. Fenton, introduced 1937, withdrawn 1948.
$600-900

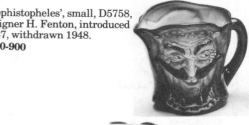

'Granny', a Royal Doulton character jug, toothless version, D5521.
$1,000-1,500

'The White haired clown', large, no number, should be D6322, designer H. Fenton, introduced 1951, withdrawn 1955.
$600-900

'The Clown', white hair, D6322, designed by H. Fenton, introduced in 1951, and withdrawn in 1955, 6in (15cm).
$600-900

'Mephistopheles', a large Royal Doulton two-sided character jug, withdrawn 1948.
$1,500-2,500

'Old King Cole', a Royal Doulton character jug, with yellow crown and grey/white hair, 6in (15cm).
$4,500-7,000

'One of the Forty', designer H. Tittensor, ivory decoration, no number, should be HN494, second version, model 298, introduced 1921, withdrawn 1938, 7in (18cm).
$800-1,200

'Ginger haired Clown', a Royal Doulton character jug, 6½in (16cm).
$800-1,200

'One of the Forty', designer H. Tittensor, ivory decoration, no number, should be HN492, 12th version, model 327, introduced 1921, withdrawn 1938, 7in (18cm).
$800-1,200

'Quality Street', HN1211, introduced 1926, withdrawn 1938, 7in (18cm).
$800-1,200

'One of the Forty', designer H. Tittensor, HN677, first version, introduced 1924, withdrawn 1938, 8½in (21.5cm).
$800-1,200

'Butterfly', designer L. Harradine, HN719, introduced 1925, withdrawn 1938, 6½in (16cm).
$1,000-1,500

'Kathleen', a Royal Doulton porcelain figure, designed by L. Harradine, HN1252, printed and painted marks, 8in (20cm).
$600-900

'Columbine', designer L. Harradine, HN1439, first version, introduced 1930, withdrawn 1938, 6in (15cm).
$700-900

'Sweet and Twenty', a Royal Doulton porcelain figure, designed by L. Harradine, HN1360, printed marks, 6in (15cm).
$400-550

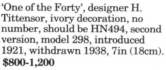

387

'Delight', a Royal Doulton figure, designed by L. Harradine, HN1772, printed and painted marks, 7½in (19cm), and 4 other pieces.
$200-350

'The Orange Lady', a Royal Doulton figure, green printed marks to base and HN1953, 8½in (21.5cm).
$200-350

'Young Miss Nightingale, a Royal Doulton porcelain figure, designed by M. Davies, HN2010, printed marks, 9½in (24cm).
$700-900

'Calumet', a Royal Doulton figure, green printed marks to base and HN2068, 6½in (16.5cm).
$400-550

'Easter Day', a Royal Doulton figure, HN2039, withdrawn 1969.
$300-400

'The Gaffer', a Royal Doulton figure, green printed marks to base and HN2053, 7½in (19cm).
$300-500

'Promenade', designer Margaret Davies, HN2076, introduced 1951, withdrawn 1953, 8in (20cm).
$1,500-2,500

'Midinette', a Royal Doulton figure, designed by L. Harradine, HN2090, printed marks, 7in (18cm).
$300-500

'The Wardrobe Mistress', a Royal Doulton figure, HN2145, withdrawn 1967.
$400-550

'Uriah Heep', a Royal Doulton figure, green printed marks to base and HN2101, 7½in (19cm).
$200-350

'Queen Elizabeth The Queen Mother', a Royal Doulton figure, produced to celebrate her 80th birthday, HN2282, No. 1422 of a limited edition, complete with stand, certificate and original box.
$600-900

A rare pilot figure, girl with pink skirt and pail under right arm, 7in (18cm).
$3,000-4,500

'Pierrette', designer L. Harradine, HN643, first version, introduced 1924, withdrawn 1938, 7in (18cm).
$900-1,300

'Fortune Teller', a Royal Doulton figure, HN2159, withdrawn 1967.
$400-550

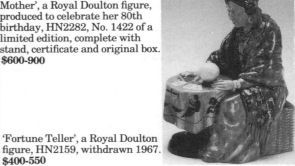

A pair of Royal Doulton stoneware vases, with panels of blue brown on green ground.
$200-350

A pair of Royal Doulton stoneware vases, by Hannah B. Barlow & Florrie Jones, heightened in brown on a buff ground, the base with green and blue lappets, incised H.B.B. & F.J. monograms, 5½in (14cm).
$400-550

A rare pilot figure, lady in blue and pink ball gown, foot and left hand defective, hair cracks, 9in (23cm).
$2,000-3,000

A pair of Royal Doulton vases, initialled WB, c1925, 13in (33cm).
$300-500

A pair of Royal Doulton vases, decorated in the Art Nouveau manner, in green and yellow on a gold decorated ivory ground, c1900, 10½in (27cm).
$300-500

A pair of Royal Doulton stoneware vases, incised monograms for Eliza Simmance & Bessie Newberry, 20thC.
$700-900

A Royal Doulton vase, covered in a thick multi-coloured crackled glaze, bearing the marks for Charles John Noke and Harry Nixon, 5½in (13.5cm).
$600-900

A Royal Doulton plate depicting Porchester, signed A. Holdcroft, c1925, 10in (25.5cm).
$250-350

A Royal Doulton 'Master of Foxhounds' presentation jug, No. 248 of a limited edition of 500, with original certificate of verification, 13in (33cm).
$700-900

A Royal Doulton stoneware Dewar's whisky jug, with green collar, c1895, 6½in (16.5cm).
$250-350

A pair of Royal Doulton blue ground stoneware vases.
$300-500

A Royal Doulton stoneware jardinière and stand, painted with deep blue and mottled green, stand chipped, late 19thC, 37½in (95cm).
$800-1,200

A Royal Doulton buff stoneware jardinière, by Hannah Barlow, with olive green glazed neck, incised with sheep in panoramic landscape, 9in (23cm) diam.
$600-900

A set of 5 Royal Doulton plates, signed A. Piper, with gilded rims, the centres painted with flowers and fruit, 9½in (24cm).
$900-1,300

ART DECO
Lalique Glass

A Lalique glass cockerel, script Lalique France marks, 8in (20.5cm).
$600-900

A glass cockerel's head, moulded Lalique France marks, chip to comb, 7in (18cm), on stepped Lalique glass base, script Lalique France marks.
$800-1,200

A clear and frosted glass car mascot of pale amethyst hue, Faucon R. Lalique, No. 1124, 6½in (16.5cm).
$2,000-3,000

A Lalique frosted glass car mascot, 'Coq Nain', with satin finish, moulded R. Lalique France, on circular base, 8in (20.5cm).
$1,200-1,750

A satin and polished car mascot, 'Victoire', modelled as an open mouthed maiden with stylised windswept hair streaming behind her, relief moulded mark R. Lalique, 10½in (26cm) long.
$14,000-19,000

A topaz frosted and polished car mascot, 'Coq Nain', moulded R. Lalique, No. 1135, 8in (20.5cm).
$6,000-9,000

A Lalique glass car mascot, 'Grand Libellule', modelled as a large dragonfly, moulded and signed on tail Lalique and R. Lalique France, 8in (21cm), with original electrical mount with green cell inside.
◄ $4,500-7,000

A frosted and polished car mascot, 'Petite Libellule', set in metal mount, moulded mark Lalique, 6½in (16.5cm) long.
$5,000-7,500

◄ A clear and polished car mascot, 'Cinq Chevaux', relief moulded mark R. Lalique and wheel cut France, in bronze mount and ebonised wood stand.
$5,000-7,500

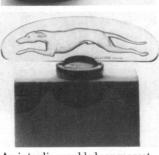

An intaglio moulded car mascot, 'Levrier', intaglio moulded mark R. Lalique France, 7½in (19.5cm) long.
$1,500-2,500

A clear and satin glass car mascot 'Faucon', moulded R. Lalique, etched No. 1124, 6in (15.5cm).
$2,000-3,000

A frosted car mascot, 'Vitesse', moulded as a naked female figure, slight chip, moulded R. Lalique, 7½in (18.5cm).
$8,000-11,000

A Lalique opalescent glass statuette, 'Naiade', moulded faintly R. Lalique and signed on underside of base Lalique, 5in (12.5cm).
$10,000-13,500

A Lalique frosted glass statuette, 'Source de la Fontaine', on wooden base, incorporating lamp fitment, 21in (53cm) high.
$4,000-5,500

An opalescent and frosted glass figure of a nude female dancer, 'Thais', her right hand slightly reduced, etched script mark R. Lalique, France, 8½in (21.5cm).
$5,000-7,500

A clear and frosted car mascot, 'Victoire – the Spirit of the Wind', R. Lalique, on Breves Galleries chrome light mount, 10in (25.5cm) long.
$13,000-17,500

A frosted glass figurine of a naked young woman, 'Grande Nue, Longs Cheveux', etched script mark R. Lalique, France, No. 836, 16in (40.5cm).
$15,000-21,000

An opalescent statuette, 'Sirene', moulded as a water nymph tending her hair, small chip, moulded R. Lalique, etched script mark R. Lalique, France, No. 831, 4in (10cm).
$3,000-4,500

l. A Lalique 'Alicante' vase, blue tinted with moulded budgerigar heads and wheat ears, etched signature R. Lalique, France, with removable fittings for use as a table lamp, 10in (25.5cm).
$2,000-3,000

r. A Lalique 'Laurier' vase, in blued opalescent glass, incised mark and No. 947, 7in (18cm).
$900-1,300

A Lalique frosted glass vase, moulded all over with a thistle design and stained in light blue, signed R. Lalique, France, No. 979, 8½in (21.5cm). **$1,200-1,750**

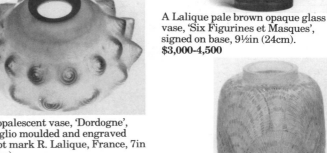

A Lalique pale brown opaque glass vase, 'Six Figurines et Masques', signed on base, 9½in (24cm).
$3,000-4,500

A large Lalique frosted glass vase, 'Penthièvre', signed on base R. Lalique France No 1011, 10½in (25.5cm).
$5,000-7,500

An opalescent vase, 'Dordogne', intaglio moulded and engraved script mark R. Lalique, France, 7in (18cm).
$2,000-3,000

A blue stained opalescent vase, 'Coquilles', etched script mark R. Lalique, France, 7½in (18.5cm).
$1,500-2,500

A clear, frosted and blue stained vase, 'Bordures Epines', with everted rim moulded with trailing thorned branches, wheel cut mark R. Lalique, 8in (20cm).
$1,200-1,750

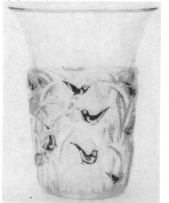

A clear, frosted and blue enamelled vase, 'Bornes', wheel cut mark R. Lalique, France, 9in (23cm).
$7,500-10,500

A Lalique opalescent glass vase, with frosted surface, etched R. Lalique on base, 7in (18cm).
$1,200-1,750

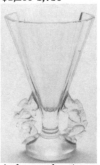

A clear and satin vase, 'Roitelets', stencilled R. Lalique, France, 11½in (29cm).
$2,000-3,000

A Lalique glass vase of trumpet shape, the sides moulded with ears of barley, with pale brown staining, marked on base R. Lalique, France, 6½in (16.5cm).
$1,000-1,500

A Lalique opalescent glass vase, 'Chardons', heightened with blue staining, marked R. Lalique France on base, 7½in (18.5cm).
$1,500-2,500

A smoked glass vase, 'Béliers', moulded at the rim with a pair of stylised rams, wheel cut R. Lalique, 7½in (19cm).
$3,000-4,500

A satin opalescent vase, 'Ronsard', the 2 handles moulded as semi-circular garlands of flowers, each enclosing a seated nude female figure, fracture to one arm, stencilled R. Lalique, engraved France, 8½in (21cm).
$3,000-4,500

A blue stained frosted vase, the ground detailed with vertical ribbing, stencilled R. Lalique, France, 6½in (16cm).
$1,000-1,500

A clear and frosted vase, 'Yvelines', the handles moulded with deer amidst foliage, the leaves spreading onto the body of the vase, etched R. Lalique, France, 8in (20cm).
$1,500-2,500

A frosted, clear and green stained vase, 'Camees', relief moulded mark R. Lalique, 10in (25.5cm).
$7,000-10,000

A Lalique glass vase, heightened with blue staining, signed on base R. Lalique, 9in (23cm).
$2,000-3,000

A George III
mahogany regulator,
the 10in silvered
dial signed Holmes,
London, later move-
ment, 72in (182cm).
$12,000-20,000

A walnut longcase
clock, 10in brass
dial signed Bird,
London, restored,
late 17thC, 81in
(204cm).
$26,000-40,000

A Federal longcase
clock, dial signed
David Wood, Newbury-
Port, Mass., c1790
damage, 90in (229cm).
$40,000-60,000

A walnut longcase
8-day clock, by
Jacob Lovelace,
Exeter, c1730,
101in (257cm).
$11,000-16,000

A walnut and floral
marquetry longcase
clock, 12in brass
dial signed Jona
Spencer, London,
early 18thC, 84in.
$14,000-20,000

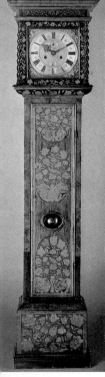

A floral marquetry
longcase clock, 11in
dial signed Thos.
Bradford Londoni
fecit, restorations,
1690, 78in (198cm).
$16,000-25,000

A mahogany longcase
regulator, the dial
signed Ollivant &
Son Manchester,
mid-19thC, 75in
(190cm).
$30,000-45,000

A walnut and panel
marquetry longcase
clock, with later
pierced fret, 11in
brass dial signed
J. Windmills London,
early 18thC, 86in.
$20,000-30,000

A mahogany longcase
sidereal regulator
with break circuit
work, signed
Wm.Bond & Sons,
Boston,
c1858, 64½in (164cm).
$34,000-38,000

A walnut and
marquetry
longcase clock,
dial signed
Wm. Sharpe,
Londini Fecit,
late 17thC,
85in (216cm).
$16,000-25,000

393

A Regency longcase regulator, with 12in engraved, silvered dial signed A. Samuel & Son, City London, No. 8388, 78½in (199cm). **$24,000-35,000**

A Black Forest Biedermeier organ automaton clock, mid-19thC, 106in (270cm). **$18,000-28,000**

A Federal maple and églomisé clock by Aaron Willard, Boston, Mass., c1815, No. 508, 35½in (90.5cm) high. **$14,000-23,000**

A Queen Anne twin-train month-going mean and sidereal longcase movement, by Daniel Quare and Stephen Horseman, London, No. 148, now in Regency pale mahogany case, 82½in (210cm) high. **$56,000-80,000**

l. A Queen Anne clock by Jacob Godshalk, Philadelphia, restored, 96in. **$14,000-23,000**

r. A Chippendale clock by David Rittenhouse, Philadelphia, c1770, 80in. **$12,000-20,000**

A giltmetal mounted Sèvres pattern vase clock and pedestal, late 19thC, vase 24½in (62cm) high. **$6,000-10,000** pedestal 45in. **$4,000-7,500**

A mahogany 8-day longcase clock, the dial signed by Wm. Fletcher of Gainsboro', c1800, 91in (231cm). **$10,000-15,000**

A walnut and marquetry long case clock, the dial signed by James Wightman, London, 17thC, 78½in (199cm). **$32,000-45,000**

A burr walnut longcase clock, by Thomas Tompion. **$90,000-125,000**

A French ormolu-mounted porcelain clock set, comprising clock with striking movement, 18in (46cm) high, the candelabra with 4 foliate candle nozzles, 17in (43cm). **$8,000-13,000**

A Louis XVI ormolu and terracotta mantel clock, the enamel dial with Roman numerals and days of the week, signed Sotiau A Paris, the case with figures of Minerva and attendants, 18in (46cm) wide. **$6,000-10,000**

An ebony veneered bracket clock by Clarke & Dunster, London, with Dutch strike and alarm, 8-day movement, repaired, early 18thC, 17in (43cm) high. **$10,000-15,000**

A Louis XVI ormolu-mounted Sèvres vase 'solaire' clock, cover restored, 18½in (47cm). **$20,000-30,000**

An Empire ormolu-mounted marble mantel clock, the enamel dial signed 'a Paris', the movement with outside countwheel strike, 21in (53cm) high. **$10,000-15,000**

An Empire bronze, ormolu and marble mantel clock, after a design by Thomas Hope, 21½in (55cm) high. **$12,000-18,000**

A Louis XVI ormolu and alabaster rotunda clock, signed Festeau a Paris, 16½in (42cm) high, with later glass dome. **$8,000-10,000**

A George III mahogany bracket clock, the 2-train movement with verge escapement, strike/silent regulation in the arch, a recessed plaque with maker's name William Garrett, London c1785, 20in (51cm). **$11,000-18,000**

South Bar Antiques

A Louis XV ormolu mantel clock, the dial and movement signed Etienne Le Noir a Paris, 13½in (34cm) high. **$9,000-11,000**

l. A Vienna regulator in walnut veneered case, by Lehrner in Pesten. **$10,000-18,000**
c. A late Biedermeier period Vienna regulator, by Mösslinger in Wien. **$6,000-10,000**
r. A lantern style Vienna regulator in fine mahogany case. **$24,000-45,000**

A grande sonnerie striking Vienna regulator, by S. Glink, Pesten, Budapest, with burr elm case. **$8,000-15,000**

A mantel clock, signed A. Duchesne, Lejeune à Paris, 18thC, 39in (99cm). **$5,000-8,000**

A French Directoire skeleton clock, by Laurent A Paris, c1790. **$40,000-60,000**

A Victorian bracket clock, the movement chiming on 8 bells with a gong, 30in (76cm) high. **$2,000-4,000**

An Empire mantel clock, with circular enamel dial in an urn-shaped case, 18in (46cm) high. **$8,000-12,000**

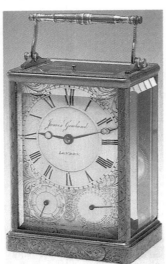

An 8-day carriage clock, signed in the centre James Gowland, London, the movement with lever escapement, in gilt brass case, 7in (18cm) high, with key and morocco travelling case. **$7,000-12,000**

A Federal gilt and eglomisé girandole clock, by Lemuel Curtis, Concord, Massachusetts, c1816, base glass replaced, 46in (117cm) high. **$16,000-25,000**

gold, enamel and jewelled singing bird cage, with clock watch, musical movement and double singing bird mechanism, by Freres Rochat and . Remond, with signature 'Fait par tüber', c1815, 8½in (21.5cm) high. 600,000+

A Regency mahogany wall regulator, the moulded case with oval mirror-glazed door, 65in (165cm) high. **$8,000-15,000**

An Empire ormolu cartel clock and matching barometer, the clock with dial signed Revel a Paris, each supported by winged classical female figures holding laurel sprays, 37½in (95cm) high. **$120,000-175,000**

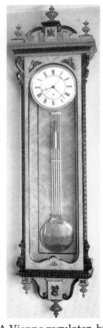

pair of gold watches formed from a aroque repousse watchcase, attributed Johann Andreas Thelot, movements y Goldney St. James St, London os. 5398 and 5497, Thelot's work 700, English movements c1820, .7cm diam. **$38,000-53,000**

A Vienna regulator, by Camerer, Cuss & Co., established 1788 in London, with a seconds beating 5-rod gridiron pendulum, 11in (28cm) diam. enamelled dial, clock with finials, 77in (196cm) high. **$10,000-15,000**

A gold double cased watch, by Breguet, No. 3876, the movement of Lepine calibre with ruby cylinder escapement, 4.1cm diam, with original gold chain and tipsy key. **$20,000-35,000**

gold double glazed half-uarter repeating Robin nontre perpetuelle', signed lugnier Horloger de S.M. 'Empereur et Roi No. 1009, ith Breguet hands, push endant and compensated alance, mid-19thC, 5.6cm iam. **$34,000-48,000**

A George III giltwood cartel clock, with associated silvered dial signed William Linderby, London, the case surmounted by an eagle, 34in (86.5cm) high. **$10,000-15,000**

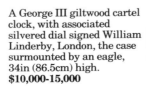

A black enamelled and lacquered brass theodolite, the telescope with rack and pinion focusing, signed T. Cooke & Sons York, England, No. 2250, 16in (41cm) high. **$4,000-7,500**

A gold perpetual calendar bracelet watch, signed Patek Philippe & Co, Geneve, No. 967639, 3.4cm diam. **$63,000-75,000**

A lacquered brass compound monocular microscope, unsigned, with various accessories, in a fitted mahogany case, late 18thC, 9in (23cm) long. **$5,000-10,000**

A lacquered brass compound binocular microscope, signed Powell & Lealand, 170 Euston Road, London, dated 1884, original mahogany case 19in (49cm). **$10,000-18,000**

A lacquered brass doctor's compound monocular microscope, signed Ross, London 4089, 19thC, in fitted case, 11in (26cm) wide. **$2,500-4,000**

A George II mahogany stick barometer, with silvered face, signed F. Watkins, London, 40½in (102cm) high. **$52,000-70,000**

A brass surveying sextant, signed Ramsden, London index arm with vernier, magnifier, tangent screw and clamp, late 18thC, 4in (10cm) radius, in original fitted mahogany case. **$6,000-10,000**

A brass theodolite, by Benjamin Cole the telescope with single draw tube focusing with level, dust cap and slide mid-18thC, 16in (40cm). **$4,000-7,50**

A 2-day marine chronometer, signed Barraud, 41 Cornhill, London, No. 2388, 19thC, 10cm diam of dial. **$12,000-18,000**

A lacquered brass solar microscope, the draw tube stamped B. Martin, London, 18thC, the mahogany wall plate 5½in (14cm). **$4,000-7,500**

A tulip leaded glass and bronze table lamp, impressed Tiffany Studios New York 1548 and 28620, 29½in (75cm) high. **$44,000-62,500**

An overlaid and etched glass table lamp, the shade etched Daum Nancy France, the base with similar design on a circular foot, 13in (32cm) high. **$18,000-55,000**

A cameo landscape table lamp, the shade carved with Daum Nancy with the Cross of Lorraine, the base carved with DN monogram, 25in (63cm) high. **$18,000-25,000**

A pair of terrestrial and celestial globes, 'Ger et Leon Vath Amsterdam 1750', 19in high. **$20,000-30,000**

A pair of William IV terrestrial and celestial globes, by W. Harris, London 1836, distressed, 40in (101cm). **$36,000-45,000**

A lacquered brass universal equinoctial ring dial, signed Dollond London, early 19thC, 9½in (24cm), in original plush lined fishskin covered case. **$8,000-15,000**

A lacquered brass azimuth sighting instrument, signed Narrien, London, c1820, 9½in (24cm). **$4,000-7,500**

A fruitwood nocturnal dial, 17thC, index arm 7½in (19cm) long, main plate 4in (10cm) diam. **$4,000-10,000**

A planetary motion compendium, unsigned, with 9 brass framed movements, early 19thC, 14in (35cm) wide, in fitted case. **$4,000-7,500**

A copper and mica table lamp, the base of trumpet form, stamped Dirk Van Erp, c1915, 22in (56cm) high.
$24,000-35,000

A cameo glass table lamp, the conical shade acid-etched with pendant branches of honeysuckle, signed in cameo Gallé on shade and base, 8½in (21cm) high.
$20,000-35,000

An earthenware and glass table lamp, the shade of mirrored black glaze over green flambé inset with leaded glass, by Fulper, the base and shade printed with firm's logo and number 21, 15½in (39cm) high. **$18,000-30,000**

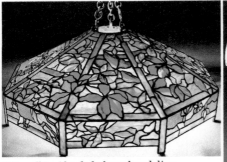

A 'woodbine' leaded glass chandelier, impressed Tiffany Studios New York 2-609, 27in (68cm) diam. **$24,000-35,000**

A 'trumpet vine' double overlay and etched glass table lamp, with cameo signature Gallé, 26½in (67cm) high.
$60,000-90,000

A 'hanging head dragonfly' leaded glass and bronze table lamp, both shade and base impressed Tiffany Studios New York, 1507 and 7984, 32½in (82cm) high. **$60,000-90,000**

An 'Oriental poppy' glass and bronze floor lamp, shade and base impressed Tiffany Studios New York 2404 and 378, 76in. **$85,000-115,000**

A 'woodbine' leaded glass and bronze table lamp, the shade stamped Tiffany Studios New York, 16in (40cm) diam, the base similarly stamped, 21in (53cm) high.
$60,000-85,000

A copper and mica tabe lamp, stamped Dirk Van Erp, c1910, 25½in (65cm) high.
$80,000-110,000

A double overlay and etched glass charger, with cameo signature Gallé, 15½in (39cm) diam. **$9,000-14,000**

l. A Gallé carved acid-etched triple overlay landscape vase, carved signature Gallé, 20in (50cm). **$16,000-25,000**

r. A blue cala-lily triple overlay mould-blown glass vase, cameo signature Gallé, 14in (35cm). **$50,000-70,000**

A mould blown vase, carved and acid-etched with rhodo-dendron, carved 'Gallé', 10in high. **$28,000-40,000**

A Gallé double overlay vase, repaired, 9in (23cm) high. **$3,000-5,000**

A bronze mounted Gallé vase, engraved signature Gallé ft. 1891-93, bronze foot signed with EG monogram, 11½in (28.5cm) high. **$44,000-67,500**

An acid-etched and enamelled vase, engraved Cristallerie d'Emile Gallé Nancy, 28in. **$8,000-12,000**

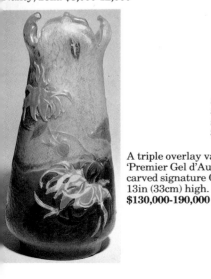

A triple overlay carved and acid-etched vase, carved signature Gallé, 9in (23cm). **$24,000-35,000**

An overlaid and etched glass vase, with 2 glass handles modelled as snails, etched Daum, Nancy, 8in (20cm). **$11,000-18,000**

A triple overlay vase, 'Premier Gel d'Automne', carved signature Gallé, 13in (33cm) high. **$130,000-190,000**

A pâte-de-verre vase, moulded signature G. Argy Rousseau and France, 3½in (9cm). **$18,000-28,000**

403

A black vase, 'Martins Pecheurs', moulded with songbirds in flowering branches, with impressed signature R. Lalique, 9½in (23.5cm) high. **$12,000-15,000**

A Carlo Bugatti ebonised and rosewood cabinet, with brass, pewter and ivory inlay, 35½in (90cm). **$18,000-25,000**

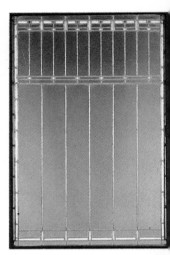

A leaded glass window, designed b Frank Lloyd Wright, c1900, 41½ by 27in (105 by 68cm). **$7,000-12,000**

An important oak dining table and 8 chairs, designed by Frank Lloyd Wright, c1903, table top 54½in (138cm) wide, chairs 46in (117cm) high. **$700,000+**

A Daum pâte-de-verre figure by Almaric Walter, moulded monogram AW and carved Daum Nancy with Cross of Lorraine, 6½in (17cm). **$16,000-25,000**

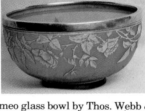

A cameo glass bowl by Thos. Webb & Sons, silver rim, H.M. London 1901, 8in (20cm) diam. **$3,500-5,000**

An oak side chair, by Charles Rohlfs, Buffalo, 1901, 47in (119cm) high. **$32,000-45,000**

An oak side chair, designed by Frank Lloyd Wright, c1902, 40in (101cm) high. **$28,000-40,000**

An Almaric Walter pâte-de-verre paperweight, designed by H. Bergé, moulded signature A. Walter Nancy H. Berge, 3in (8cm) high. **$20,000-30,000**

A Favrile glass vase, by Tiffany Studios, c1896, inscribed L.C. Tiffany E136, 20in (50cm) high. **$8,000-12,000**

An Arts and Crafts mahogany secretaire, the panelled drop desk flap enclosing central cupboard with mother-of-pearl inlay, possibly German, 48in (122cm). **$1,500-3,000**

A walnut and marquetry revolving bookcase, the top inlaid with various fruitwoods with swallows and Gothic pinnacle, on later revolving base, inlaid Gallé signature, 20in (51cm) wide. **$14,000-20,000**

A three-fold wood framed and leather covered screen, decorated across the top with a tooled and gilded frieze of seagulls, with sailing boats below, the lower frieze depicting fish, crabs and shells, 70in high. **$2,000-4,000**

An Austrian mahogany kneehole desk, attributed to Otto Wagner, with ivory, satinwood stringing and bronze plaques, 48in, and a chair. **$5,000-10,000**

Two jade table screens, carved in relief with birds in landscapes, Immortals gathered in groves and flowering peony, cracks to wood, 19thC, 7in high. **$36,000-50,000**

An oak bookcase, model No. 700, designed by Harvey Ellis, executed by Gustav Stickley, c1903, 36in (91.5cm) wide. **$12,000-20,000**

A Carlo Bugatti ebonised and rosewood ladies writing desk, with pewter and ivory inlay, signed Ricardo Telligrini 1897, 30in (76cm). **$9,000-15,000**

A repoussé tankard by Tiffany & Co, New York, for the world's Columbian Exposition, Chicago, 1893, the lid with stylised monogram, touchmark on base, 10in (25cm) high, 52oz 10dwt. **$32,000-45,000**

A Martelé vase, by Gorham Manufacturing Co, Providence, c1910, 15in, 61.5oz. **$8,000-12,000**

An Art Nouveau silver vase by Gilbert Marks, London 1902, 13½in (34cm) high, 30oz. **$6,000-10,000**

An early Ming gilt bronze figure of Vajrasattva, cast Yongle 6-character mark, 7in (18cm) high. **$28,000-40,000**

A three-piece demi-tasse service, by Tiffany & Co, New York, 1878-1891, coffee pot 8in (20cm) high, 23oz 10dwt. **$18,000-30,000**

A silver and enamel lidded tankard by Liberty & Co, attributed to a design by Archibald Knox, c1900. **$8,000-12,000**

A pair of pale celadon jade Mughal style tripod basins, 19thC, 7½in (18.5cm) wide, on pierced wood stands. **$10,000-15,000**

A rare Yixing stoneware wrist-rest, modelled as a section of bamboo, impressed with potter's seal mark of Chen Mingyuan, slight chip, late 17th/early 18thC, 8in (21cm), fitted box. **$26,000-35,000**

An inlaid waiter, decorated with an applied frog inlaid with gold alloy and copper, slight damage to sun, by Tiffany & Co, New York, 1878-1891, 9½in (24cm), 10oz. **$22,000-35,000**

A 142-piece mixed metal flatware service, with cast applied decoration of silver, gold and copper, in the Japanese taste, by Tiffany & Co, New York, c1880, marked 'ETC', 201oz 10dwt. **$110,000-150,000**

A Martele centrepiece bowl with scenes of the seasons, Gorham Man.Co. Providence 1906, English import marks of Birmingham 1908, 27in (68cm) long, 178oz 10dwt. **$42,000-60,000**

A 'Navajo' vase, by Tiffany & Co. New York, 1900, for the Exposition Universelle, Paris 1900, and the Pan-American Exposition, Buffalo 1901, Exposition touchmarks, damage, 8½in (22cm) high, 89oz. **$50,000-75,000**

A vase shaped ewer, by Tiffany & Co, New York, c1895, with applied sea motifs surrounded by seaweed, marked on base, monogram erased, 14in (36cm), 86oz 10dwt. **$20,000-40,000**

A 242-piece parcel gilt Persian pattern service, each engraved with a crest, by Tiffany & Company, New York, 1878-91, 332oz 10dwt. **$20,000-40,000**

A silvered bronze mantel clock, the drum body with Arabic chapters, on marble base, stamped E. Brandt, France, 12in (30.5cm) high. **$4,000-8,000**

A vase with the body formed of 5 rows of owls' heads and talons, by Tiffany & Co, New York, for Chicago Exposition 1893 touch, 10½in, 26oz. **$50,000-70,000**

An Imperial inlaid ink cake box and cover, with mother-of-pearl inlay, the black ink cakes moulded with floral sprays and inscriptions, minor chips, Qianlong, 12in (31cm) wide. **$16,000-25,000**

A pair of Liberty Cymric silver candlesticks, attributed to Archibald Knox, stamped maker's mark L & Co Cymric and Birmingham hallmarks for 1902, 8½in (22cm) high, 22oz 1dwt. **$8,000-12,000**

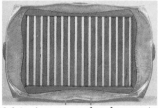

An 'Edelzinn' pewter and mahogany tray, designed by Joseph Maria Olbrich, c1904, unmarked, 22½in (57cm) long. **$6,000-10,000**

A silver gilt carved ivory tusk flagon set with stones, by Tiffany & Co. New York, 1910, marked, 23in, 466oz gross. **$40,000-60,000**

A green patinated bronze group, 'The Crowning of the Virgin', by T. B. Huxley Jones, 47in (120cm). **$3,500-6,000**

A bronze figure, 'Needless Alarms', cast from a model by Frederic Lord Leighton, unsigned, 18½in (47cm) high. **$5,500-8,000**

An early bronze statuette, 'Salomé', from a model by Carl Milles, signed, foundry mark for E. Colin & Cie, Paris, 12in (30cm). **$40,000-60,000**

A Guild of Handicrafts silver and enamel brooch by C. R. Ashbee, stamped, London 1907, 7.8cm. **$24,000-35,000**

An enamelled cigarette box, signed on the base Jean Goulden, numbered, dated LXVI28, 6½in long. **$3,500-5,000**

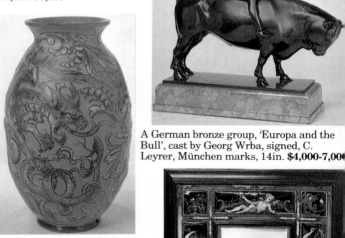

A German bronze group, 'Europa and the Bull', cast by Georg Wrba, signed, C. Leyrer, München marks, 14in. **$4,000-7,000**

A Martin Bros. stoneware vase, signed Martin Bros, London & Southall, 1891, 16in (40cm) high. **$6,000-10,000**

A Limoges enamelled framed mirror, 14 by 12in (36 by 31cm). **$5,000-8,000**

A Sibyl Dunlop necklace, pendant 7cm long, original case. **$6,000-9,000**

A Minton porcelain vase designed by
Dr. Christopher Dresser, painted in
colours, heightened in gilt, with
bands of stylised Gothic foliage,
damaged, 20in (20.5cm) high.
$10,000-15,000

A Rozenburg eggshell porcelain teaset, decorated
by H. G. A. Huyvenaar, with polychrome decoration
of daisies and birds on a cream ground, cracks,
painted marks Rozenburg Den Haag, painter's
monogram H, datemark for 1900, teapot 7in
(18cm) high. **$8,000-15,000**

A brass bust of a young woman,
the head with brass strip
forming long flowing hair and
features, stamped marks 1021
Franz Hagenauer Wien wHw Made
in Austria RD, 17in (43cm)
high. **$10,000-15,000**

A bronze table mirror, the
openwork base of overlapping
fern leaves, impressed
Tiffany Studios New York and
engraved E.C.T. June 8th
1909, 21in (54cm) high.
$20,000-35,000

A William de Morgan four-tile panel, with two
snakes amongst flowering foliage, each
impressed with W de Morgan Merton Abbey,
16½in (42cm) square. **$13,000-18,000**

A Salvatore Meli ceramic and glass
centre table, the stoneware base in the
form of a head of a mythical hound,
the ceramic inscribed Meli.58 Roma,
47in (120cm) wide. **$16,000-20,000**

A William de Morgan jar and
cover, painted in the Isnik
manner, underglazed blue
inscription W. De. Morgan
Fulham, 14½in (36.5cm) high.
$13,000-20,000

A Danny Lane float glass stack chair,
formed by irregular cut and polished
glass panels held by metal screws.
$8,000-12,000

A pair of birch laminated side chairs
by Gerald Summers. **$8,000-15,000**

The Bourne and Hollingsworth clock, with musical chimes on six bells by Gillett and Johnson, Croydon, England, the bells cast with the signature of Gillett and Johnson, Croydon, 1927. **$44,000-55,000**

A bronze and ivory figure, 'Eastern Dancer', on a green marble base, inscribed in the bronze Schmidt-Cassel, 15½in (38.5cm) high. **$30,000-50,000**

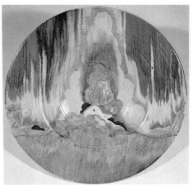

A Wilkinson Bizarre pottery charger, by Clarice Cliff, painted with cottages and trees, 18in (46cm). **$3,000-5,000**

A Macassar ebony veneered stationery cabinet, by Ernest Gimson, 25in (63cm) high. **$20,000-30,000**

A pair of Georg Jensen 5-branch candelabra, designed by Harald Nielsen, with fluted cylindrical branches, stamped marks, 18in (46cm) high. **$35,000-50,000**

A bronze and ivory figure, 'Bat Dancer', cold painted in red, turquoise and silver, on stepped marble base inscribed F. Preiss, 9½in (23.5cm) high. **$8,000-12,000**

A silvered bronze group, 'Diana', on black slate base, the bronze inscribed Lorenzl, 18in (46cm) high. **$10,000-15,000**

A Morris & Co. 'Hammersmith' hand-tufted woollen and mohair carpet, 122 by 169in (310 by 429cm). **$35,000-45,000**

Above. A silvered bronze electroplated dressing table mirror, the swivel glass on scroll supports, stamped E. Brandt, 21in (53cm). **$8,000-12,000**

Right. A bronze and ivory figure, 'Kamorna', by Demetre Chiparus, signed, 20in (51cm) high. **$50,000-75,000**

DISCOVER THE WORLD OF

ART DECO ORIGINALS

A wide selection of 20's/30's ceramics by Clarice Cliff, Susie Cooper, Charlotte Rhead Shelley, and others. Furniture, Lamps, Etc.

MUIR HEWITT
HALIFAX ANTIQUES CENTRE
(NOT THE PIECE HALL!)
Queens Road Mills
Queens Road/Gibbet Street
Halifax, West Yorkshire HX1 4LR
Tel: Halifax (0422) 366657
Evenings: Bradford (0274) 882051

Open 5 Days   Tuesday-Saturday 10am-5pm

A Clarice Cliff Bizarre pottery charger, painted in pastel shades with 2 gazelles in exotic tropical landscape, printed blue marks Hand Painted Bizarre by Clarice Cliff Wilkinson Ltd, England, 17½in (44.5cm). **$4,000-8,000**

A bronze and ivory figure, 'Con Brio', cast and carved from a model by Ferdinand Preiss, cold painted in pink and gold, on green onyx tray, inscribed F. Preiss, 11½in (29cm) high. **$14,000-20,000**

A painted bronze and ivory figure, 'The Butterfly Dancer', cast and carved from a model by Demetre Chiparus, signed, 17in (43cm). **$40,000-60,000**

A parcel gilt bronze and ivory statue, 'Valkyrie Rider', cast and carved by Louis Chalon, signed in the bronze, 21½in (54.5cm). **$11,000-15,000**

Left. A carved ivory figure on marble plinth, bow and arrow missing, some damage, signed F. Preiss, 7in (18cm) high. **$800-1,200**

Right. A carved ivory figure of a girl with feeding bowl and bird, on marble plinth, signed F. Preiss, 7in (18cm) high.   **1,200-1,500**

A bronze and ivory figure of a girl with clock, cast after a model by Ferdinand Preiss, base inscribed F. Preiss, 21½in (54.5cm) high. **$18,000-30,000**

A Linthorpe pottery vase, designed by Christopher Dresser, impressed Linthorpe with facsimile signature and HT monogram for Tooth, numbered '449', damage, 16½in (42cm) high. **$8,000-12,000**

A cold painted bronze and ivory figure, 'Girl on a Wall', cast and carved from a model by Ferdinand Preiss, the girl on a green onyx 'wall', signed on the reverse F. Preiss, 9½in (23.5cm) high. **$14,000-20,000**

A bronze and ivory figure, 'The Diver', cast after a model by Ferdinand Preiss, restored, signed F. Preiss, 12in (30cm). **$10,000-15,000**

An Art Deco 9ct gold brooch in the form of a bow, with a pair of earrings. **$300-500**

412

A frosted amber glass vase, 'Serpent', by René Lalique, moulded as a cobra, moulded R. Lalique, 10in (26cm) high. $16,000-25,000

A Monart ginger jar, with bluish green whorls, c1929, 10in (25cm). $1,000-1,500

A scent bottle, 'Bouchon Cassis', moulded R. Lalique, France No. 494, bruised, 4½in (11.5cm). $8,000-12,000

An etched glass table lamp, shade and base etched Daum, Nancy, France, 17in (43cm) high, shade 15in (38cm) diam. $20,000-30,000

A Monart bowl in mottled orange with silver flecks, c1930, 13in (33cm). $500-800

A Monart vase, in pale green, orange and brown with gold aventurine, c1930, 9in (23cm) high. $500-800

A Ray Flavell glass sculpture, 'A Thought About Art Deco', the smoky grey glass plate sandblasted with curved bands supporting a cased amethyst bowl with fluting, engraved Ray Flavell, 13in (32.5cm) high. $2,500-4,000

A James II posset pot, the front engraved, maker's mark TC conjoined, London 1686, 6½in long, 7oz. $80,000-120,000

A George I Irish coffee pot, engraved with a coat-of-arms in a baroque cartouche, by John Hamilton, Dublin, 1715, 9½in (24cm) high, 29oz gross. $10,000-12,000

A George I bullet teapot, the hinged cover with later mother-of-pearl finial, marked on base and cover, by John Eckfourd, London, 1727, later ivory scroll handle, 7in (18cm) long, 9oz 10dwt. $5,000-10,000

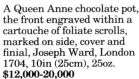

A Queen Anne chocolate pot, the front engraved within a cartouche of foliate scrolls, marked on side, cover and finial, Joseph Ward, London 1704, 10in (25cm), 25oz. $12,000-20,000

413

Two Victorian 10-light candelabra, by Barnard Bros. 1846 and C. F. Hancock, 1895, the nozzles unmarked, 32in (82cm), 458oz. **$30,000-42,000**

A Victorian 7-light candelabrum, by John S. Hunt 1846, No. 2792, 30in (76cm) high, 269oz. **$20,000-25,000**

A pair of Queen Anne tapering baluster candlesticks, engraved with armorials, by William Turell, 1713, 7½in (19.5cm), with later nozzles, 30oz. **$30,000-42,000**

A pair of Charles II candlesticks, bases engraved with initials S over IE, London 1683, maker's mark TA, pellet below, in circular punch, probably for Thomas Allen, 6in, 17oz. **$28,000-35,000**

A George III coffee pot, stand and lamp, engraved with crest, marked, by Paul Storr, London 1804, stand by Burwash and Sibley, 1806, 13in (32cm), 46oz 10dwt. **$6,000-10,000**

An early George III cast figure taper stick, modelled as a British sailor in traditional uniform, shown also in reverse, by William Cafe, 1761, 6in (15.5cm), 5.5oz. **$8,000-12,000**

A George I Irish chocolate pot, engraved with a later coat-of-arms and motto, by Thomas Williamson, Dublin, 1715, 11in (28cm) high, 32oz gross. **$12,000-18,000**

A George II chamber candlestick, engraved with a crest, by Paul de Lamerie, London 1746, 6in (16cm), 9oz 10dwt, the base with scratch weight 11*4. **$16,000-25,000**

A teapot, marked HM, New York, c1720 engraved on base IM, mark struck near rim on either side of handle, 6in (15cm) high, 16oz 10dwt gross. **$50,000-65,000**

A pair of George III 3-light candelabra, engraved with a crest, by Richard Cooke, 1800 and 1804, 17in (43cm) high, 128oz. **$24,000-35,000**

Four George II table candlesticks, cast and chased with flowers, foliage and scrolls, engraved with a crest, by Samuel Courtauld, 1757, 11in (28cm), 86oz. **$16,000-25,000**

A George III basket, with engraved coat-of-arms within a rococo cartouche, William Kidney, 1745, 15in (38cm) wide, 83oz. **$18,000-30,000**

A set of 6 Charles II shell shaped dishes, by Samuel Hood, 1675, one with maker's mark and leopard's head crowned only, 5in (12.5cm) wide, 10oz 7dwt. **$75,000-100,000**

A George I Irish monteith, with lion's mask and drop ring handles, with shaped detachable rim, by David King, 1715, 11in (28cm) high, 63oz. **$50,000-75,000**

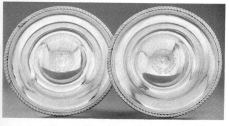

A pair of George I basins, with gadrooned borders, the domed centres engraved with a coat-of-arms in scalework, foliate scroll and laurel surround, by David Willaume, 1726, 15in (38cm) diam, 112oz. **$35,000-50,000**

A pair of wine coolers, the plain bodies half-fluted and engraved with a frieze of leaves and flowers, lion mask drop ring side handles, detachable rims and tinned liners, c1775, 9in (23cm). **$6,000-10,000**

A pair of George II sauceboats, engraved with a crest and coronet, by George Wickes, London, 1731, 9in (23cm) wide, the bases numbered and with scratch weights, 34oz. **$88,000-120,000**

A George II Irish engraved punch bowl, by Robert Calderwood, Dublin 1732, 8in (20cm) diam, 23oz. **$18,000-25,000**

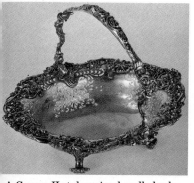

A George II style swing handled cake basket, on mask and scroll feet, by Charles Stuart Harris & Sons, 1912, 16in (40cm) long, 101.5oz. **$13,000-20,000**

A George II basket, by Benjamin Godfrey, 1741, engraved with later coat-of-arms, coronet and motto, 12in (30cm) long, 51oz. **$18,000-25,000**

A George III basin and Victorian ewer, the basin engraved, 1764, with maker's mark of John Jacob over-striking another, the ewer by Robert Garrard, 1841, 50oz. **$12,000-18,000**

A pair of George III baskets and covers, by William Pitts, 1803, with frosted glass liners, 12½in (31.5cm) long, 95oz. **$24,000-35,000**

A George II sauceboat stand from the Anson service, by Paul de Lamerie, London, 1739, 11in (28cm) long, 22oz.
$85,000-115,000

A set of 3 Charles II casters, engraved with initials AP, the smaller casters 1682, the larger 1683, maker's mark WB, a mullet below, 6 and 7in (15 and 18cm) high, 22oz.
$115,000-125,000

A William IV inkstand, with central taperstick and 2 mounted glass bottles, by Joseph & John Angell, 1830, 14in (36cm) wide, 42oz.
$8,000-15,000

A pair of George III vegetable dishes, covers and handles, by John Edwards, 1798, 12in (30.5cm), 85oz, and
A pair of George III sauce tureens and covers, by Robert Sharp, 1798, 10in, 47oz. **$10,000-18,000 each pair**

An Elizabeth I Communion cup and a cover paten, London 1571, maker's mark HW, the paten by John Jons, Exeter, c1576, 8in (21cm), 9oz 10dwt.
$8,000-15,000

Two pairs of nut crackers, inscribed, probably English, c1716, 4½in (11cm) long, 8oz.
$12,000-18,000

A soup tureen and stand, marked with initials of Carl Frederick Bredenberg, St. Petersburg, 1801, 20½in (52cm) high, 8,775 grammes
$16,000-25,000

A pair of George IV entrée dishes, covers and handles, by Philip Rundell, 1822, 12½in (31cm) wide, 148oz.
$12,000-18,000

A French centrepiece, the rim inscribed, by Christofle, Paris, 25in (63.5cm) high, 8,947 grammes. **$17,000-25,000**

A pair of donkey salts, by Mortimer and Hunt, fully marked, London 1840, each numbered 368, 4½in (11cm) high.
$18,000-25,000

A pair of George I toilet jars and covers apparently unmarked, but probably by Isaac Liger, c1728, 5in (12.5cm) high, 17oz, the bases with scratch weights 8 14 and 8 12.
$34,000-45,000

A frosted vase, 'Baies', heightened in black enamel, moulded mark R. Lalique, 10½in (26.5cm).
$6,000-9,000

A blue stained, clear and frosted vase, 'Paimpol', moulded in high relief with 6 panels of graduating conical projections alternating with spiny ribbed panels, stencilled Lalique and La Marquise De Sevigne, Paris, 10in (25cm).
$3,000-4,500

A grey stained opalescent vase, 'Oléron', moulded with a shoal of leaping fish, etched script mark R. Lalique, France, No. 1008.
$1,000-1,500

An opalescent and clear vase, moulded in relief beneath the rim with poppy flowerheads, stencilled mark R. Lalique, France, 5½in (14cm).
$2,500-3,500

A Lalique opaque glass vase, 'Ceylan', with blue stained decoration, below a narrow slightly everted rim, base chipped, etched R. Lalique, 9½in (24cm).
$3,000-4,500

A rare, blue stained clear and frosted vase, 'Chamois', moulded with panels of chamois antelope with curving stylised horns, stencilled R. Lalique, France, 5½in (14cm).
$1,200-1,750

A frosted and opalescent vase, 'Pinson', moulded with sparrows amongst berried branches, all above a narrow foot, stencilled mark R. Lalique, 7in (18cm).
$2,500-3,500

A blue stained opalescent vase, 'Tournai', moulded with vertical panels of leafy branches, stencilled R. Lalique, France, 5in (13cm).
$1,200-1,750

An amber vase, 'Ormeax', moulded with a carpet of beech leaves, engraved script mark R. Lalique, France, No. 984, 6½in (16.5cm).
$2,000-3,000

A frosted, clear and amethyst stained vase, 'Charmille', moulded with overlapping beech leaves, intaglio moulded R. Lalique, 14in (33.5cm).
$6,000-9,000

A red-amber vase, 'Aras', moulded on the body with crested parakeets amongst berried branches, intaglio moulded R. Lalique, 9in (23cm).
$9,000-12,500

An electric-blue frosted and polished vase, 'Perruches', moulded with pairs of billing parakeets upon blooming prunus boughs, traces of white stain, etched script mark R. Lalique, with France, No. 876, 10in (25.5cm).
$10,000-13,500

A frosted amber vase, 'Archers', moulded in relief with a design of nude male archers below swooping eagles, minor chip to rim, intaglio moulded mark R. Lalique, with France etched in script, 11in (28cm).
$7,000-10,000

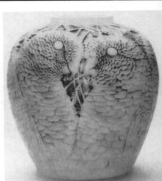

A cased opalescent frosted and black stained vase, 'Alicante', moulded with pairs of large parakeet heads in profile against a ground of millet seed, etched script mark R. Lalique, France, 10½in (26.5cm).
$8,000-11,000

A frosted, clear and blue stained vase, 'Aigrettes', moulded beneath the rim with egrets in flight, chips to footrim, wheel cut mark, R. Lalique, France, 10in (25cm).
$2,250-3,500

A large frosted opalescent vase, 'Sauterelles', moulded with grasshoppers perched on curving blades of grass, etched script mark R. Lalique, France, No. 888, 10½in (27cm).
$6,000-9,000

A rare early, bluish-grey stained frosted vase, 'Ceylan', moulded with facing pairs of budgerigars perched on budding branches, minute chips to rim, unsigned, 13½in (34.5cm).
$7,000-10,000

A Lalique frosted glass bowl, heightened with blue staining, marked on base R. Lalique, France, 9½in (24cm) diam.
$1,000-1,500

A frosted, clear and sepia stained surtout, 'Faisan', moulded with 4 panels each with an oriental pheasant and serpentine garland interspersed by slender panels with candle sconce surmounts, the base with stepped form, engraved script mark Lalique, France, 5in (14cm).
$1,500-2,500

A peppermint green and opalescent bowl, 'Muguet', the sides moulded with lily of the valley, stencilled mark R. Lalique, France, 9in (23cm) diam.
$6,000-9,000

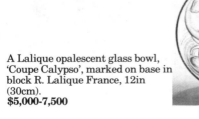

A Lalique opalescent glass bowl, 'Coupe Calypso', marked on base in block R. Lalique France, 12in (30cm).
$5,000-7,500

A Lalique bowl, inscribed
R. Lalique, France, 9½in (24cm)
diam.
$600-900

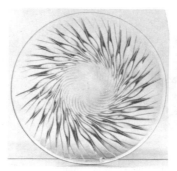

A Lalique opalescent glass shallow
dish, etched mark, 14in (35.5cm).
$1,000-1,500

A grey stained clear glass cendrier,
'Archers', the everted rim moulded
with panels of kneeling archers,
moulded R. Lalique, 4½in (11.5cm)
diam.
$450-700

A Cristal Lalique glass
paperweight, 'Perche', moulded as a
fish resting on its dorsal fins,
moulded on edge R. Lalique, and
signed on base Lalique France, 4in
(10cm) high.
$1,200-1,750

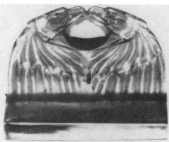

A sepia stained, clear and frosted
presse-papiers, 'Deux Aigles',
moulded as 2 eagle heads, jointly
gripping a sphere in their beaks,
moulded in intaglio R. Lalique, 3in
(8cm) high.
$700-900

A Lalique glass carafe and stopper,
moulded in high relief, heightened
with silver grey staining, the
stopper moulded with a shell like
spiral, moulded Lalique, with
extended L and engraved France,
14½in (36cm).
$3,000-4,000

A set of 6 Lalique glasses,
heightened with silver grey
staining, signed in script R. Lalique
France, 4in (10cm), in original
Lalique fitted case for '24 Place
Vendôme, Paris'.
$4,000-5,500

A Lalique blue stained scent bottle
and stopper, catalogued
'Amphitrite', inscribed R. Lalique,
France, 4in (10cm).
$2,000-3,000

A frosted and clear glass scent
bottle, 'Claire Fontaine', the stopper
moulded as a spray of lily of the
valley, etched Lalique, France, with
Made in France and Cristal Lalique
stickers, c1950, 4½in (12cm).
$200-350

A rare amethyst and clear glass
scent bottle, 'Flacon Muguet', the
stopper formed as a spray of lily of
the valley in frosted and polished
glass, unmarked, 4in (10cm).
$6,000-8,000

A Lalique blue stained glass
inkwell, moulded with 4 mermaids,
moulded Lalique signature, 6in
(15cm) diam.
$1,200-1,750

A Lalique clock, with Swiss 8-day
movement set in a milky blue panel
with naked female figures, in an
onyx and malachite frame, marked
Lalique in capitals, 5in (12.5cm)
high.
$3,000-4,500

A frosted powder box and cover, 'Amour Assis', moulded mark, 5½in (14.5cm).
$1,500-2,500

A clear and frosted box, 'Roger', with a design of opalescent cabochons and exotic birds, moulded mark Lalique, 5½in (13.5cm) diam.
$1,200-1,750

An opalescent and clear glass box and cover, 'Georgette', relief moulded mark, R. Lalique, and engraved in script at rim France, No. 51, 8½in (21cm) diam.
$1,500-2,500

An opalescent box and cover, 'Deux Sirênes', moulded R. Lalique, 10½in (26cm) diam.
$4,000-5,500

An opalescent box and cover, 'Libellules', moulded mark R. Lalique, 7in (17cm).
$1,200-1,750

An amber glass box, 'Grande Cyprins', with silk lined card base, the cover moulded with entwined oriental carp, moulded mark R. Lalique, 10½in (26cm) diam.
$4,000-5,500

Ceramics

A large Goldscheider wall mask of a lady holding beads, various makers' marks, Austria, c1930.
$700-900

A Swedish pottery Modernist bust, modelled as a girl with green curly hair, orange lips and an orange necklace, covered in a speckled green glaze, impressed 'b' within a crowned shield, 12in (30.5cm).
$1,200-1,750

A toast rack by Shorter, with purple anemones on a green base, c1930, 6in (15cm) long.
$45-75

A Carltonware dish with clematis on a green ground, c1930, 7in (18cm).
$75-150

A Carltonware sugar sifter with flower and leaves in relief, c1930, 5in (13cm).
$100-150

A Carltonware beaker with a design of anemones on a yellow ground, c1930, 4in (10cm).
$60-100

A Carltonware dish designed as pear fruit, flowers and leaves, c1935, 4½in (11.5cm).
$60-100

A Carltonware china coffee service of 15 pieces with gilt interiors and highlights, all painted and gilded in bright colours with exotic birds and stylised clouds.
$400-550

A Carltonware lustre jug with gilt loop handle, the body painted and gilded with stylised floral and fan decoration, 5in (13cm).
$250-350

A Carltonware oviform vase, the dark and pale blue ground with purple, lavender and green zig-zag motif outlined with gilt decoration, printed marks Carltonware, Made in England, Handcraft 8490, 10½in (27cm).
$400-550

A cream jug in Carltonware with anemones in relief on a yellow ground, c1930, 3in (7.5cm).
$75-150

Clarice Cliff

A Clarice Cliff Bizarre shallow dish, with slightly everted rim, boldly painted with brightly coloured flowers, 16½in (42cm).
$600-900

An Epiag porcelain part dinner service, painted in pale puce, yellow and red with stylised fuchsia and silver gilt rims, comprising: large tureen, cover and stand, a sauce boat with fixed stand, 6 dinner plates, 6 soup plates, a large fish plate, a circular serving dish, a square serving dish, a double salt with handle, 6 side plates, a tea and coffee pot, a milk jug, a sugar basin and cover, 12 cups and saucers, printed marks Epiag, Czechoslovakia, tureen 8in (19.5cm) high.
$800-1,200

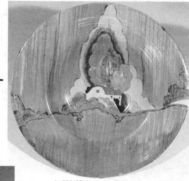

A Wilkinson Bizarre pottery charger by Clarice Cliff with dished centre, 18in (46cm).
$900-1,300

A Clarice Cliff breakfast set.
$200-350

A Clarice Cliff Bizarre dish, brightly painted with streaky glazes and pansies, 13in (33cm).
$600-900

A Clarice Cliff Fantasque coffee set, painted in orange, black and green, against a cream ground, printed factory marks and facsimile signature.
$1,300-2,000

A Clarice Cliff breakfast set, with
the Secrets pattern.
$600-900

A Clarice Cliff Bizarre tea service,
painted with concentric light and
dark brown rings on a cream
ground, and a crocus preserve jar
and cover, some damage.
$1,300-2,000

A Clarice Cliff vase,
8in (20cm) high.
$300-500

A Clarice Cliff Bizarre Latona vase,
boldly painted in blue with stylised
pink, purple, blue and green flowers
in panels, 12in (30cm).
$1,500-2,500

A Clarice Cliff Fantasque coffee
service, 'Summer House', painted in
red, yellow, green, black and blue,
comprising: a coffee pot and cover, a
milk jug, a sugar bowl and 6 cups
and saucers, minor chips, stamped
marks Fantasque Bizarre by Clarice
Cliff, Newport Pottery, England,
coffee pot 8in (20cm) high.
$3,000-4,000

A Clarice Cliff Bizarre pottery coffee
service, each piece boldly painted in
colour.
$700-900

A Clarice Cliff Fantasque vase,
boldly painted in colours, 7½in
(19.5cm).
$450-700

A Clarice Cliff Fantasque jug,
boldly painted in bright enamel
colours, 11½in (29cm).
$800-1,200

A pair of Clarice Cliff bookends,
6½in (16cm).
$250-350

A Clarice Cliff Bizarre jug, painted
in bright enamel colours, 11in
(28.5cm).
$450-700

A Clarice Cliff Delicia patterned jug.
$800-1,200

A Clarice Cliff wall pocket in the
form of 2 budgerigars, painted in
green, blue and yellow, 9in (23cm).
$150-200

A Clarice Cliff Bizarre biscuit
barrel, boldly painted in yellow and
green against a blue and orange
ground, with wicker handle, 6½in
(16cm).
$300-500

Ceramic Figures

A stylish pottery group, modelled as 2 girls of ample proportions, covered in a crackled cream glaze, indistinct monogram, possibly French, 17in (43cm).
$400-550

A china figure, unmarked, c1930, 12½in (31cm).
$300-500

A Goldscheider porcelain figure of a lady with a fan, signed on base, Austria, c1930, 17in (43cm) high.
$800-1,200

A Goldscheider ceramic figure, 14½in (37cm).
$450-700

A Goebels figure, German, 6in (15cm).
$400-550

Metal Figures

A Lenci figure with a box at the back with a frog on the lid, Italian, 10in (25cm).
$600-900

A Royal Dux figure, c1935, 12in (30.5cm).
$600-900

A figure of a girl with a hoop, cast and iron, signed Bertrand, c1920.
$600-900

A gilded spelter figure, Con Brio, of a young maiden with arms outstretched.
$400-550

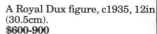

Bronze and Ivory Figures

A table lighter decorated with a silver plated spelter figure of a woman golfer, marked on base Fashioned by Ronson 16270 G.M. Silox, 11in (28cm) wide.
$200-350

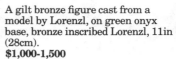

A bronze and ivory figure, 'Hoop Girl', by Chiparus, c1930.
$10,000-13,500

A gilt bronze figure cast from a model by Lorenzl, on green onyx base, bronze inscribed Lorenzl, 11in (28cm).
$1,000-1,500

A bronze and ivory figure of Harlequin by Lorenzl.
$1,500-2,500

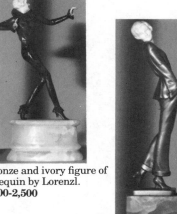

A gilt bronze figure cast from a model by Lorenzl, on green onyx base, bronze inscribed Lorenzl, 10in (26cm).
$1,000-1,500

A cold painted bronze and ivory figure by Lorenzl, enamelled in colours, on an onyx base, hairlines to base and one thumb lacking, signed Crejo, 10in (25cm).
$800-1,200

A bronze and ivory figure by Lorenzl, c1930.
$1,500-2,500

A cold painted bronze figure cast from a model by Nan Greb, inscribed Nan Greb, 11in (28cm).
$1,500-2,500

A bronze figure cast from a model by Le Faguays, signed on base, 25in (64cm) high.
$3,000-4,500

A cold painted bronze figure, 'Sword Dancer', cast from a model by Nan Greb, inscribed Nan Greb, 21in (54cm).
$3,000-4,000

A bronze and ivory figure, 'Gamine', cast and carved after a model by Ferdinand Preiss, cold painted in green, on a green marble base, hairlines to head, arms and legs, inscribed F. Preiss, 13½in (34cm).
$10,000-13,500

A bronze and ivory figure of a child by Preiss, c1930.
$1,500-2,500

A bronze figure of a dancer by Preiss, c1930.
$1,500-2,500

A bronze figure of a motorcyclist, unsigned but attributed to Bruno Zack, the marble base applied with metal tag stamped 'B. Zack Sculp. Argentor Vienna', 8in (20cm).
$4,000-5,500

A bronze and ivory figure in the manner of F. Preiss, on black marble plinth, 11in (28cm).
$10,000-13,500

A bronze and polychrome marble figure, 'Reading', cast and carved from a model by Schumacher, signed in the bronze Henry, 10in (26cm).
$2,000-3,000

A bronze and ivory figure, 'Dancing Girl', cast and carved from a model by Lorenzl, signed in the bronze Lorenzl, 9in (23cm).
$1,500-2,500

A bronze and ivory figure, 'Grecian with torch', cast and carved from a model by Ferdinand Preiss, on stepped pink striated base, signed in the bronze F. Preiss, 10in (25cm).
$6,000-9,000

A bronze figure, 'Spanish Flamenco Dancer', cast from a model by Sonher, inscribed Sonher, 13½in (34.5cm).
$2,000-3,000

A gilt bronze and ivory figure, 'Mystery', cast and carved from a model by V. Seifert, signed in the bronze V. Seifert, 11½in (29cm).
$7,000-10,000

A bronze figure, 'The Fencer', cast from a model by H. Müller, signed in the bronze H. Müller, 17½in (44.5cm).
$600-900

A bronze figure, 'Athlete', cast from a model by H. Henjes, signed in the bronze H. Henjes fec.10, 14in (35.5cm).
$800-1,200

A bronze and ivory figure, 'Feeding the birds', cast and carved from a model by L. Barthelemy, signed in the bronze L. Barthelemy, 12in (30.5cm).
$5,000-7,500

A spelter and ivorine group, 'Pierrot and Columbine', cast from a model by D. Chiparus, on striated marble plinth, 30in (76cm) wide.
$5,000-7,500

A bronze figure, 'Flower Girl', cast from a model by Tuch, a flower in her right hand, signed in the bronze Tuch, 17in (43.5cm).
$1,500-2,500

An Amsterdam School sideboard, designed by Richard Reens, in rosewood and coromandel, c1928, 119in (302cm).
$2,000-3,000

A sideboard enclosing satinwood interior shelves, and edged with satinwood.
$600-900

A nest of tables, 19in (48cm).
$800-1,200

A walnut and mahogany centre table, designed by W. F. Crittall and made by E. W. Beckwith, 44in (112cm) square.
$4,000-5,500

A mahogany dining table, designed by W. F. Crittall and made by E. W. Beckwith, 67in (170cm).
$6,000-8,000

A chrome base table with black glass top, 16in (40.5cm) diam.
$150-200

A copper base table, incorporating an electric light, with glass top, 30in (76cm) diam.
$400-550

A chromium frame and mirror glass two-tier tea trolley.
$150-200

A coffee table and set of 4 occasional tables, 34in (86cm) wide.
$700-900

A Rawley Gallery mirror, with original label on the back, c1930, 29in (74cm) high.
$200-350

A green lacquer piano, with chrome trim, 57in (144.5cm), and stool.
$700-900

Glass

A pair of glass book ends, c1930, damaged, 5in (12.5cm) high.
$45-75

A blue English bowl, c1930, 7in (18cm).
$200-350

A Moser Unica bowl, with blue centre and rim decorated with red and milky white dotted striations, engraved marks Chris Lebeau, Jan.1926, Moser-Fecit-Tchecoslovaquie, 10½in (27.5cm).
$900-1,300

A glass cocktail shaker, enamelled with 3 red and green spiders, insects and webs, with silver mounts, Birmingham 1936, 8in (20.5cm).
$1,000-1,500

Seven glass goblets and 8 finger bowls, signed Verdar.
$1,300-2,000

A decanter and glasses, in clear glass faceted with square panels and alternately flashed with amber, one chipped.
$400-550

A glass decanter set, decorated with panels of black enamel, frosted and engraved linear decoration.
$900-1,300

An Etling opalescent glass figure, moulded Etling France 50, 8in (20.5cm).
$1,500-2,500

A Venini patchwork vase, the clear glass internally decorated in red, green and blue, acid stamped Venini Murano Italia, 4½in (11cm) high.
$2,250-3,500

A Sabino opalescent glass lamp, signed on the glass Sabino France, 13½in (35cm) high, set in a chromed base incorporating lamp fitments.
$1,300-2,000

A Sabino opalescent glass figure, 'Suzanne Au Bain', unsigned, 9in (23cm), with wooden mount incorporating fitments for use as a lamp.
$3,000-4,500

A vase with black sunburst design, c1930, 5in (12.5cm) high.
$100-150

A heavy Orrefors green glass vase, by Edward Hald, inscribed on the base and dated 1938, 10½in (26.5cm).
$800-1,200

A Monart bowl, decorated with yellow whorls, and multi-coloured rim, c1930, 9in (23cm).
$400-550

l. A Monart powder box and lid, in orange and blue with gold aventurine clear knob, c1930, 5in (12.5cm) diam.
$700-900
r. A Vasart vase, in white and pale green with gold aventurine, c1930, 4in (10cm).
Acid etched signature **$30-50**
Without signature **$20-40**

A Monart vase in pale green, brown and gold aventurine, c1930, 3½in (9cm).
$150-250

A Monart vase, in lilac turquoise, paper label with the code VA.260, c1929, 9in (23cm).
$800-1,200

Metal

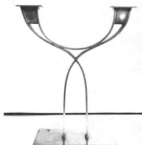

A pair of American bronze book ends, by Chase, 6in (15cm) high.
$400-550

A chrome and enamel cigarette box, 9½in (24cm) wide.
$150-250

A pewter candlestick, c1955, 8½in (22cm).
$150-250

A set of 6 Liberty & Co. silver and enamel handled cake forks, Birmingham 1931.
$400-550

A pair of George V table candlesticks, with carved oak barley-twist stems, hammered silver square bases and circular nozzles, A. E. Jones, Chester 1922, 9in (23cm), loaded.
$900-1,300

A pair of chrome Art Deco style uplighters, 75in (190.5cm).
$300-500

A French electroplated tea and coffee service, with rosewood handles and finials, stamped marks GM, tray 21in (52cm) wide.
$2,000-3,000

A four piece Art Deco style Walker & Hall teaset, Sheffield 1944, 50oz approx.
$900-1,300

A four piece tea service, by Edward Barnard and Sons Ltd., London 1934, 54oz gross.
$2,250-3,500

A Hukin & Heath electroplated toast rack, designed by Christopher Dresser, stamped maker's mark, 5in (13cm) high.
$3,000-4,500

A silver tea and coffee service by Mappin & Webb, with ivory handles, 1937 and 1939.
$5,000-7,500

Miscellaneous

A ceramic advertising cockerel for Eno's Fruit Salts.
$100-150

A plaster owl, c1910, 19in (48cm) high.
$450-700

A French enamel stove, c1930, 36in (91.5cm) high.
$100-200

An inkstand, with chrome trim, 14in (35.5cm) wide.
$100-200

A cigarette box, applied overall with square plaques of bleached petrified wood and a broad central band of red stained odonolite edged with brass, the interior lined with wood, 8½in (21cm) wide.
$1,000-1,400

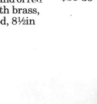

A marble box with clock in lid, damaged, 5½in (14cm) wide.
$30-50

A marble garniture, c1930.
$900-1,300

A Goebel figure table lamp, 9in (23cm) high.
$100-150

A chrome clock, 9in (23cm) wide.
$30-50

A Brazilian gourd electric floor lamp, with mushroom shaped shade and tapering conical illuminated column, 64in (162.5cm) high.
$1,000-1,400

A lamp, 16½in (42cm) high.
$600-900

A spelter figure lamp, c1930, 22in (56cm).
$450-700

A lamp by John Dowson, 20in (51cm) high.
$4,000-5,500

Post War Design

A paperweight by Paul Ysart, decorated in bright blue, yellow, green, red, purple and white, with PY cane, 3in (7.5cm) diam.
$600-900

A pottery wall mask, signed H. R. Rhodes, dated 1943.
$200-350

Brass candlesticks, c1955, 5in (12.5cm) high.
$100-200

A Wedgwood Windsor grey Travel pattern dinner service, designed by Eric Ravilious, each piece decorated in black and light blue with trains, liners, sailing boats, balloons, aeroplanes and buses, printed factory marks and designer's name.
$5,000-7,500

SILVER

Baskets

A George III bread basket, engraved with a coat-of-arms within shield shaped cartouche, by William Plummer, 1782, 15in (38cm) long, 42oz.
$10,500-15,000

A George III cake basket, with beaded borders and reeded swing handle, by Thomas Chawner, London 1783, 16in (41cm), 29.25oz.
$400-550

A George III cake basket, engraved with a coat-of-arms within a shield shaped cartouche, by Robert Hennell, 1787, 14in (35.5cm), 25oz.
$4,000-5,500

A George III sugar basket, with a band of bright cut engraving and a crest, by John Robins, London 1796, 7in (18cm), 8.33oz.
$1,000-1,400

A George III sugar basket, the sides with pierced fret band, with a contemporary initialled cartouche, fitted with a blue glass liner, maker's mark Thomas Daniel and W.H. London 1789, 6.5oz.
$1,000-1,400

A George III bread basket on spreading foot, by Henry Nutting or Hannah Northcote, 1801, 14in (35.5cm) long, 26oz.
$2,250-3,500

A George III crested sugar basket, with reeded swing handle on oval foot, by Peter and Anne Bateman, London 1791, 5½in (14cm), 5oz.
$1,200-1,750

A George III cake basket, with reeded swing handle, on raised foot, Dublin 1806.
$900-1,300

A George IV fluted swing-handled cake basket, with applied rococo floral and foliate rim, the handle with similar decoration, Thomas Bradbury & Co., Sheffield 1826, 10in (25.5cm), 22oz.
$1,000-1,500

An early Victorian sugar basket, maker's mark EE over JW, London 1846, 220 grammes.
$700-900

A Russian swing handled trompe l'oeil basket, applied with a red and blue enamelled Cyrillic monogram in one corner, by Ivan Chlebnikov, Moscow, c1885, 11½in (29.5cm) diam, 30.5oz.
$4,000-5,500

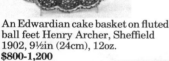

A pair of late Victorian dessert baskets, James Dixon & Sons, Sheffield 1896, 9½in (24cm), 21oz.
$1,300-2,000

A Victorian dessert basket, maker William Comyns, London 1893, 10in (25.5cm), 9½oz.
$450-700

A dessert basket, on pierced and carved panel feet, James Deakin & Sons, Sheffield 1901, 9½in (24cm), 9.75oz.
$450-700

An Edwardian cake basket on fluted ball feet Henry Archer, Sheffield 1902, 9½in (24cm), 12oz.
$800-1,200

A dessert basket, the pierced trellis sides with portrait medallions and floral swags, cast rococo borders and side handles, on scroll feet, B. Muller, Chester import mark 1904, 12in (30.5cm), 20oz.
$1,000-1,500

A dessert basket, maker's mark J.R., Sheffield 1913, 7½in (19cm), 7.5oz.
$400-550

A silver basket, Sheffield 1913.
$300-500

A pierced and engraved fruit dish, Robert Hennell, London 1788.
$3,000-4,500

Beakers

A julep cup, by Joseph Werne, Sr., Louisville, Kentucky, engraved WMB, marked on base, c1845, 4in (10cm), 3oz.
$1,000-1,500

A pair of beakers, by John McMullin, Philadelphia, engraved with script initial R, each marked with full name touch and eagle pseudo hallmark, c1820, 4in (10cm), 11oz.
$3,000-4,000

A pair of George III silver mounted horn beakers, Thomas & James Phipps II, London 1818, 6in (15cm).
$400-550

A beaker, by Eli C. Garner, Lexington, Kentucky, engraved 'Mattie Carrell', marked on base, c1838, 3½in (9cm), 4oz.
$500-1,000

A julep cup, by J. Coning, Mobile, Alabama, engraved MM, marked on base, c1845, 4in (10cm), 4oz.
$1,500-2,000

A julep cup, by Marquand and Company, New York, with inscription 'Catherine Davis, May 14th, 1829', marked on base, 3½in (9cm), 3oz.
$650-750

A julep cup, by Jaccard & Company, St. Louis, Missouri, c1845, 4in (10cm), 3oz.
$400-600

A German beaker and cover, on 3 ball feet, with silver gilt rim, the base with inscription dated 15th June, 1711, by Philipp Stenglin, Augsburg, 1708-1710, 5in (12.5cm), 199grammes.
$6,000-9,000

A julep cup, marked 'Gaither', possibly John Gaither of Alexandria, Virginia, engraved 'VHR' and 'Remember me', marked on base, early 19thC, 3in (7.5cm), 3oz.
$800-1,000

Bottles – Scent

A Victorian overlay blue glass scent bottle, applied with gilt mounts and stopper, enamelled in champlevé technique, with blue beading and scrolling foliage, and set with a carnelian finial, 4in (10cm).
$300-500

A Victorian ruby glass scent bottle, the body with canted corners, the base fitted with a vinaigrette, plain silver gilt mounts, S. Mordan & Co., London 1876, 3½in (9.5cm).
$600-900

A Victorian silver gilt and blue glass scent bottle, the centre with a hinged vinaigrette, the stoppers engraved with scrolling foliage, S. Mordan & Co., 5in (13cm).
$400-550

A Continental scent bottle in the form of a mandolin, with embossed decoration, import marks for London 1891, 5½in (14cm), 2.1oz.
$450-700

Bowls

A Queen Anne two-handled porringer, decorated with ropework girdle and band of fluting, engraved with armorial, Edward Wimans, 1704, 5in (12.5cm) diam, 10oz. **$2,000-3,000**

A George II Irish bowl, with a moulded rim, on a raised spread circular base, engraved with a contemporary cartouche and armorials, by David King, Dublin 1732, 6½in (17cm) diam, 14oz. **$7,000-10,000**

A George II fluted bowl, engraved with a crest, by Benjamin Godfrey, 1739, 7in (18cm) diam, 12oz 7dwt. **$6,000-9,000**

A pair of bowls, with stylised arms of James I, and the date '1610' and inscribed around the rim, one with 'Wine was made from the beginnings to make men glad and not for drunkennes (sic.). Wine measurably drunke and in time bringethe gladnesse and chearfulnesse of the mind', the other 'looke not thou upon the wine when it is red and when it sheweth his color in the cup or goeth downe pleasantly in the end thereof it will bite like a serpente and hurt like a cockatrice', 6in (15cm) diam, 31.5oz. **$5,000-7,500**

A George III sugar bowl and cover, on spreading foot, later chased with rococo flowers and foliage, the cover with flower finial and engraved with a crest, probably John King, London 1769, 5in (12.5cm). **$900-1,300**

A George III covered sugar bowl, with a detachable domed cover surmounted by a cast poupée finial, decorated all over with lobed fluting, reeded borders, by Rebecca Emes and Edward Barnard, 1814, 4½in (12cm) high, 12oz. **$1,300-2,000**

A silver compote, with 2 applied and chased polar bears on the inverted rim, by Gorham 1872, impressed with firm's marks and Sterling 125 E 4, 11in (28cm), 24.5oz. **$10,000-13,500**

A Victorian parcel gilt bowl and spoon, with beaded edging and frieze of classical and mythological figures on a matted ground, Martin Hall and Co., Sheffield 1870, 5.9oz, in fitted case. **$800-1,200**

An Edwardian reproduction of a Charles II porringer, embossed with leaping lions and unicorns, with beaded caryatid handles, by Charles Stuart Harris, 1902, 20.5oz. **$900-1,300**

A pair of Victorian rose bowls, decorated in Queen Anne Monteith style, on spreading bases and on wood plinth stands, Charles Stuart Harris, London 1891, 5in (12cm) high, 21.4oz. **$1,000-1,500**

A set of 12 Martele soup bowls on stands, by Gorham Manufacturing Company, Providence, each marked, c1908, stands 5in (12.5cm) diam, 84oz.
$10,000-15,000

An Edwardian rose bowl on stand, Goldsmiths & Silversmiths, London, 1903.
$600-900

A covered bowl, by Taylor and Laurie, Philadelphia, monogrammed, 10in (25cm) high, 40oz.
$1,600-2,000

A centrepiece bowl, by Gorham Manufacturing Company, Providence, the interior with traces of gilding and with script monogram, marked on base, c1885, 10in (25.5cm) diam, 17oz 10dwt.
$700-1,000

A George V silver sugar bowl, with decorative edge, on 6 feet, maker's mark O.R. for Omar Ramsden, London 1935, 5in (12cm) diam, 6oz 2dwt.
$800-1,200

An Edwardian hammered sugar bowl, A. E. Jones, Birmingham 1908, 4in (10cm) diam, 4.5oz.
$300-500

A medallion comport, by W. K. Vanderslice & Co., San Francisco, California, marked on base, c1865, 13½in (34cm) high, 53oz.
$4,500-5,500

A monteith bowl, by Samuel Kirk & Son, Baltimore, with engraved monogram in bottom of bowl, marked, c1885, 7½in (19cm) high, 29oz 10dwt.
$1,200-1,500

A Russian sugar bowl, with swing handle and gilt rim, Moscow 1894, 4½in (11cm), 8.5oz.
$600-900

A Martele bowl, by Gorham Manufacturing Company, Providence, light erasure to bowl, marked on base, c1905, 11in (28cm) diam, 29oz 10dwt.
$2,500-3,000

A two-handled bowl, on spreading foot with egg and dart border, engraved 'The Argentine Grand National Cup', by Elkington & Co., Birmingham, 1908, 13½in (34cm) diam, 100oz.
$4,000-5,500

A porringer, by William Moulton
IV, Newburyport, Massachusetts,
engraved with initials BN in script,
marked on back of handle, c1800,
5in (12.5cm) diam, 6oz.
$1,800-2,200

A porringer, marked 'Davis',
possibly Isaac Davis of Boston,
engraved in script W & CDW,
marked on back of handle, early
19thC, 5½in (14cm) diam, 8oz.
$1,600-2,000

A porringer, by John Burt, Boston,
engraved I*F on handle, wear and
repair to base, marked on back of
handle, c1740, 8in (20.5cm) long,
5oz.
$1,500-2,000

A footed bowl, by Shepherd & Boyd,
Albany, with engraved script
monogram HDH, marked on foot,
1815, 6½in (16.5cm) diam, 11oz
10dwt.
$1,000-1,500

A figural comport, by Gorham
Manufacturing Company,
Providence marked, c1868, 13in
(33cm) high, 41oz 10dwt.
$2,000-2,500

A Continental bowl, on 4 shell and
scroll feet, with 2 dolphins' masks
and ring handles, import marks,
1902, 13in (33cm) long, 47oz.
$4,000-5,500

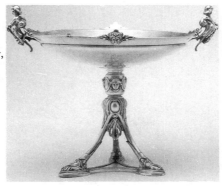

A comport, by Gorham
Manufacturing Company,
Providence, marked,
c1860, 10½in (28.5cm)
diam, 37oz 10dwt.
$2,500-3,500

A Dutch brandy bowl, the flat
handles cast and pierced with
recumbent cherubs and foliage, by
Volkaert Symonsz, Swaert,
Haarlem, 1661, 10in (25.5cm) wide,
210grammes.
$4,000-5,500

SILVER

Some dates of importance in
study of silver:–
★ 1660 restoration of
Charles II – beginning of
great era of domestic
English silver
★ c1670 influence of
acanthus leafage and
fluted baroque
★ 1685 The Revocation of
the Edict of Nantes –
brought Huguenot
silversmiths to England
★ 1697 introduction of
Britannia standard.
Lasted until 1702
★ 1740s early signs of rococo
★ 1750s revival of
chinoiserie
★ 1760s influence of
neo-classicism
★ 1800-20 tendency to add
decoration to plainer style
★ 1820s revival of rococo
style
★ by 1830s machines much
in use
★ 1880s Arts and Crafts
movement – influence of
Art Nouveau

Boxes

An English silver gilt needle case, the hinged cover engraved with a cherub mask, maker's mark William South, London, c1690.
$1,300-2,000

A tortoiseshell and silver tobacco box, the top inlaid with a silver crest of a rampant leopard, 18thC.
$1,000-1,500

A George III silver wrigglework snuff box, by W. Edwards, London 1806.
$200-350

A George III bag-shaped vinaigrette, by Joseph Taylor, Birmingham 1817.
$200-350

A George III articulated fish vinaigrette, by Samuel Pemberton, Birmingham 1817, 3in (7.25cm) long.
$700-900

A William IV engine turned snuff box, the lid chased with a castle landscape, Taylor & Perry, Birmingham 1835, 3in (7.5cm).
$400-550

A chased baluster shaped paint box and lid, London 1690, 3½in (9cm) high, 3.5oz.
$1,200-1,750

A box with mother-of-pearl base, the cover carved with huntsmen, dogs, scrolls and shells, engraved with monogram, unmarked, base damaged, early 19thC, 3in (7.5cm).
$150-250

A George III crested box, the domed cover with a gadrooned border and a shield shaped armorial, by Thomas Halford, London 1809, 3in (7.5cm).
$400-550

A George III shaped vinaigrette, with central laurel wreath, ray engraving and bright cut bands of flowers, by Joseph Willmore, Birmingham 1819, 1½in (3.5cm).
$600-900

A silver gilt filigree box formed as a heart, with detachable cover and plain base, probably English, 17thC, 2½in (6cm) wide.
$700-900

A Continental niello box, decorated with 2 figures, flowers, leaves and birds, 19thC, 3in (7.5cm).
$300-500

A George III bag-shaped snuff box, inscribed inside 'From an Individual Whose good fortune is to have a sincere Friend', by Robert Butterfield, London 1814, 2½in (6cm).
$600-900

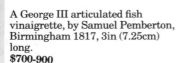

A George IV table snuff box, the hinged cover decorated in a Fragonard style rococo scene, with gilt interior, the engine turned base engraved with a monogram, John Shaw, Birmingham 1828, 3in (7.5cm), 4.5oz.
$1,000-1,500

A George V vesta box, the hinged lid enamelled depicting the cover of *Punch* magazine, maker's mark H.J. Birmingham 1931, 4.5cm.
$1,200-1,750

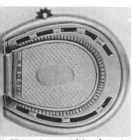

A Victorian combined vesta case and tinder box, engine turned around a vacant oval cartouche, maker's mark HJ, Birmingham 1880.
$400-550

A Victorian table snuff box, flat chased with scrolling leaves, George Unite, Birmingham 1884, 3½in (9cm), 4oz.
$400-550

A Victorian bell-shaped vesta case, with enamel panel of a floating buoy on a calm sea, Birmingham 1893, 4cm, 0.8oz.
$300-500

A late Victorian novelty vesta case, modelled as a Brazil nut, and inscribed 'One of the K-Nuts', by Henry Charles Freeman, 1896.
$300-500

A cedar lined cigar box, with central cutter, tools and spirit light, London 1899.
$1,200-1,750

An Edwardian vesta case, enamelled on cover with 2 huntsmen and their pack, small chips to enamel, by George Randle, Birmingham 1901.
$600-900

A box with pierced and embossed lid, by William Comyns, London 1903, 6in (15cm), 4oz.
$400-550

A book shaped box, Birmingham 1922, 3cm.
$100-150

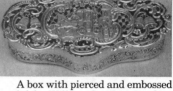

A silver gilt and enamel cigarette case, the cover enamelled in black and white with an oval panel of putti with garlands of flowers in a landscape, with borders of leaf scrolls, .800 standard.
$600-900

A mother-of-pearl and silver mounted box, the cover carved with a female bust beneath a canopy, trees, and animals, 7cm.
$300-500

A silver snuff box, import marks, 4in (10cm), 6oz.
$400-550

Candelabra

A pair of late Victorian four-light candelabra and 4 candlesticks, in neo-classical style, by Joseph & Horace Savory, 1884, one candelabrum stem 1866, candlesticks 11in (28cm), loaded and branches part loaded.
$15,000-21,000

A Russian cigarette case with hinged vesta compartment, and another compartment for a wick, probably Dmitri Nikolaiev, Moscow. c1890.
$300-500

A pair of German cast rococo style seven-light candelabra, by J. D. Schleissner & Sons, Hanau, with Dutch import marks, c1895, 21½in (54cm), 234.5oz.
$4,500-7,000

A Victorian five-light candelabrum, engraved with a monogram, Robert Garrard, 1841, 30½in (77.5cm) high, 254oz.
$9,000-12,500

A pair of George V five-light candelabra, Sheffield 1915, loaded, 22½in (56.5cm).
$5,000-7,500

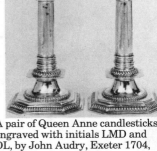

A pair of George I style two-light candelabra, Garrard & Co., London 1970.
$700-900

Candlesticks

A pair of Queen Anne cast candlesticks, Henry Lyon 1701, 5½in (14cm), 18oz.
$17,000-23,000

A William III cast taperstick, engraved with a crest, by Andrew Raven, 1701, 4in (10.5cm), 4.75oz.
$5,000-7,500

A pair of Queen Anne candlesticks, engraved with initials LMD and DL, by John Audry, Exeter 1704, 8in (20.5cm), 16oz 15dwt.
$8,000-11,000

A George II Scottish cast taperstick, by William Aytoun, Edinburgh 1739, 4½in (11.5cm), 4.25oz.
$1,500-2,500

A set of 4 George II table candlesticks, engraved with a coat-of-arms, by William Cafe 1757, 10in (25cm), 57oz.
$24,000-32,500

A pair of Russian cast candlesticks, maker's mark apparently AFH or AIH in script, untraced, Assay Master Nikifor Moshshalkin, St. Petersburg, 1795, 8½in (21.5cm), 27oz.
$3,000-4,000

l. A George II silver taperstick, with detachable nozzle, knopped baluster column and shaped square base, by John Priest, London 1749, 5in (12.5cm), 5oz 3dwt.
$8,000-11,000

r. A George III silver taperstick, with gadrooned detachable nozzle, knopped column, spreading foot and square gadrooned base, by William Cafe, London 1763, 4½in (11.5cm), 5oz 15dwt.
$800-1,200

A set of 6 George III table candlesticks, with detachable nozzles, by J & T Settle, Sheffield 1817 and 1818, also struck with the maker's mark of Samuel Hennell, 12in (30.5cm).
$9,000-12,500

A pair of late George II silver classical column candlesticks, odd sconces, one damaged, maker W.A., 1759, weighted, 14in (35.5cm).
$4,000-5,500

A pair of George II candlesticks, by John Robinson II, 1756 and 1766, 11½in (29cm).
$3,000-4,500

A set of 4 George III cast candlesticks, by William Cafe, 1762, 10in (25cm), 84oz.
$7,000-10,000

A pair of George III cast candlesticks, with contemporary nozzles, engraved with a crest, by Ebenezer Coker, 1762, 42oz.
$6,000-9,000

A pair of George III table candlesticks, engraved with a crest, by Jonathan Alleine, 1777, 10½in (26cm), 56oz.
$9,000-12,500

A pair of George III candlesticks, with detachable sconces, engraved with crests, maker's mark I.P. & Co. (John Parsons & Co.), overstruck T.P.A.H., Sheffield 1783, 11in (28cm).
$1,300-2,000

A pair of George III table candlesticks, one fractured at knop, makers George Ashforth & Co., Sheffield 1792, loaded, 11½in (29cm).
$2,250-3,500

A set of 4 George IV cast candlesticks, with knopped columns, chased with birds and flowers and engraved initial H., one nozzle missing, by Hyam Hyams, London 1834, 6in (15cm), 52oz.
$5,000-7,500

A pair of George IV silver gilt candlesticks, with detachable nozzles, maker's mark perhaps of James Ellis & Co., Sheffield 1822, 12in (31cm).
$5,000-7,500

A pair of figural chamber candlesticks, by Moore for Tiffany, monogrammed, c1865, 3½in (8.5cm), 21oz.
$2,000-2,500

A pair of Portuguese candlesticks, maker's mark initials LARA in a monogram, Oporto, 1853, 10½in (27cm), loaded.
$1,300-2,000

A set of 4 William IV candlesticks, engraved with crest, with detachable sconces, one sconce missing, maker's mark I & I.W. & Co. (Waterhouse, Hodson & Co.), Sheffield 1883, 11in (28cm).
$3,000-4,500

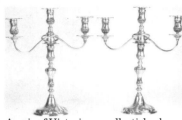

A pair of Victorian candlesticks, by
Robert Garrard, 1844, with a pair of
plated three-light branches to form
candelabra, 12in (31cm),
candlesticks 55oz.
$4,000-5,500

A set of 4 late Victorian candlesticks,
in the neo-classical manner, by
Hawksworth, Eyre & Co. Ltd.,
Sheffield 1894, 11½in (29cm),
loaded.
$3,000-4,500

A Victorian heart shaped silver
mounted tortoiseshell chamber
candlestick, with fluted nozzle,
gadrooned and pierced border, by
William Comyns, London 1894, 5in
(12.5cm).
$450-700

A pair of Victorian table
candlesticks, makers James Deakin
& Sons, Sheffield 1898, loaded.
$1,500-2,500

A pair of Edwardian candlesticks,
T.A.S., Sheffield 1907, 7in (18cm).
$900-1,300

A pair of Corinthian column table
candlesticks, Birmingham 1919,
8½in (21.5cm).
$800-1,200

A pair of late Victorian candlesticks,
with detachable nozzles, by Charles
Stuart Harris, London 1898, 11½in
(29cm), weighted.
$1,500-2,500

A pair of candlesticks, Birmingham
1920, 6½in (16.5cm).
$150-200

A set of 4 French candlesticks, with
fluted panelled bodies and floral
repousse decoration, on domed
bases, all drilled for electricity, 59oz.
$3,000-4,500

Casters

A pair of George II casters, the
pierced covers each with baluster
finials, engraved with cyphers, by
Thomas Bamford, 1728, 5in (13cm),
8oz.
$4,000-5,500

A set of 3 George I casters, engraved
with a coat-of-arms in baroque
cartouche, by Edward Vincent,
1716, largest 7½in (19cm), 27oz.
$1,500-2,500

A pair of Dutch silver gilt casters, by
Albert de Thomese, The Hague,
1733, chased later with scalework
and scrolls and engraved with a
coronet and cypher, 8in (20cm), 22oz.
$2,250-3,500

A pair of George II baluster casters, engraved with armorials, Jabez Daniell and James Mince, London 1759, 5½in (14cm), 6.3oz.
$6,000-8,000

A pair of George II sugar casters, engraved with armorials, by S. Wood, 1754, 6½in (17cm), 10.5oz.
$2,000-3,000

A George II Scottish caster, engraved with a crest and motto, by Charles Dickson, Edinburgh, 1744, the cover apparently unmarked, 5in (12.5cm), 5oz.
$900-1,300

Centrepieces

A George III épergne, with central oval basket pierced and chased, engraved with a crest, by Thomas Pitts 1766, the 4 branches unmarked, 98oz.
$18,000-25,000

A Victorian Imperial presentation centrepiece, engraved with initials and crown of Alexander II of Russia and with the inscription 'Ex Dono Imperatoris Russiae Alexandri II 1880', by Stephen Smith and William Nicholson 1856, on oval ebonised wood base, 11½in (29cm), 78oz.
$4,500-7,000

A neo-classical centrepiece, by Gorham, 13½in (34cm) high, 61oz.
$2,000-2,500

Coffee & Chocolate Pots

A George I coffee pot, the hinged domed cover with baluster finial, with wood scroll handle at right angles to the spout, by George Wickes, 1724, 9in (23cm), 22oz 0dwt gross.
$8,000-11,000

A Louis XV chocolate pot, with hinged flap to the moulded lip, the slightly raised cover with pivoting baluster finial and scroll thumbpiece, with baluster wood handle, by Jean Gouel, 1734, 10in (25cm), 840grammes without handle.
$5,000-7,500

A George II coffee pot, with domed hinged cover with turned finial, later foliate and scroll engraved decoration, London assay, marks rubbed, probably Richard Gosling, entered 1739, 10in (25cm), 28oz gross.
$2,000-3,000

A George II coffee pot, engraved with crest, armorial and motto, William Shaw II and William Preist, 1758, 11in (27.5cm), 31oz.
$3,000-4,500

A George II coffee pot, with leaf capped scroll spout and hinged domed cover, chased with foliage and scrolls, by Daniel Piers, 1754, 9in (23cm), 22oz gross.
$3,000-4,500

A George III coffee pot with engraved armorials, the domed lid with wrythen finial, wood handle, maker's mark rubbed, 1764, 25.5oz gross.
$3,000-4,500

A George III coffee pot, with polished wood double scroll handle and domed hinged cover with flower finial, Daniel Smith and Robert Sharp, London 1762, 11½in (29cm), 33.5oz gross.
$3,000-4,500

A George II coffee pot, with double scroll handle, Thomas Cooke and Richard Gurney, London 1752, 9in (23cm), 20.8oz gross.
$3,000-4,500

A George III chinoiserie coffee pot, T. Whipham and C. Wright, 1767, 12½in (31.5cm), 34oz.
$9,000-12,500

A coffee pot, by Simeon Soumaine, New York, repair to cover, marked, c1740, 11in (28cm) high, 32oz gross.
$10,000-12,000

A George III pedestal coffee pot, with scroll handle, reeded borders and engraved with a band of wrigglework, with shaped finial, by Henry Chawner, initialled, London 1795, 10½in (26cm), 22oz.
$2,000-3,000

A George III cylindrical coffee biggin, stand and detachable lamp, the biggin with applied reeded bands, detachable domed cover and ball finial, by John Wakelin and Robert Garrard, 1798, 11in (28cm), 28oz.
$2,000-3,000

A William IV coffee pot on scroll feet, with simulated bark and oak leaf spout, hinged domed cover and later Victorian acorn and oak leaf finial, engraved with coats-of-arms, by Paul Storr, 1836, finial by J. S. Hunt, 9in (23cm), 32oz.
$5,000-7,500

An early Victorian coffee pot with rustic handle, on 4 fish mask supports, Joseph Wilson, London 1838, 36oz.
$1,000-1,500

A Chinese export coffee pot, with dragon handle, dragon head finial, the body chased with elaborate battle scenes, on dragon mask and claw feet, the plain spout engraved with flowers and leafage, by Hung Chong of Canton and Shanghai, c1880, 8½in (22cm), 23.5oz.
$1,500-2,500

A Victorian coffee pot, probably William Cooper, London 1843, 10½in (27cm), 28.75oz.
$2,250-3,500

Cups

A Victorian coffee pot, E., E.J. & W. Barnard, London 1875, 11in (28cm), 27.8oz.
$900-1,300

A George I Irish two-handled cup, with harp shaped handles and moulded rim, engraved with a coat-of-arms within scrolling foliage cartouche, by Anthony Stanley, Dublin 1715, 9½in (24cm), 62oz.
$6,000-9,000

A Charles II plain cup, engraved with a coat-of-arms within plume mantling, the base with the name Henry Moore, MP, by Robert Williamson, York 1669, 3½in (9cm), 3oz 13dwt.
$6,000-9,000

A Provincial ascribed communion cup, mark only for William Bayrheed (Barehead) of Durham, c1610, 8in (20cm), 10oz.
$4,000-5,500

A George I two-handled cup and cover, on circular foot with moulded girdle, leaf capped scroll handles and baluster finial engraved with crest and armorial, by Abraham Buteux, 1727, 13in (33cm), 98oz.
$9,000-12,500

A George III two-handled cup and cover, with entwined serpent handles and fluted cover with beaded bud finial, by Andrew Fogelberg and Stephen Gilbert, 1789, 18in (46cm), 104oz.
$8,000-11,000

A pair of George III goblets, inscribed and dated, Samuel and Edward Davenport, London 1796, 6in (15cm), 13.6oz.
$2,250-3,500

A pair of George III goblets, Charles Aldridge, London 1791, 7in (18cm), 14.8oz.
$2,250-3,500

A pair of George III wine goblets, by Story & Elliott, 1810, 6in (15cm), 26oz.
$3,000-4,500

A Victorian boar's head stirrup cup, by William Edwards, 1872, 4½in (11cm), 7.25oz.
$7,000-10,000

A Continental silver betrothal cup, in the form of Queen Elizabeth I wearing long robes, import marks for London 1881, possibly Dutch, 8in (20cm).
$700-900

A George III silver gilt fox mask stirrup cup, by Thomas Pitts, 1771, 5½in (14cm) long, 5oz 13dwt.
$6,000-9,000

A Victorian fox's mask stirrup cup, engraved with the inscription 'Capt. Montague Legge To his Brother Officers 2nd. Batt. 1st Royals, in remembrance of 14 happy years spent with them, 1864', by John S. Hunt, 1850, 5in (12.5cm) long, 12oz 16dwt.
$4,000-5,500

A covered spouted cup, by Samuel Soumain, Annapolis and Philadelphia, marked, c1750, 3½in (9cm) high, 4oz.
$12,000-15,000

A handled cup, by Nicholas Roosevelt, New York, the base engraved with contemporary initials AS, patch to side, marked on base, c1750, 2½in (6cm), 1oz 10dwt.
$1,000-1,500

An Australian cup and cover, with horse finial, inscribed 'Mount Shank Cup presented by Capt. Gardiner to the Mount Gambier Turf Club, won by Mr. G. Riddoch's 'Mystery', January Meeting, 1875', by J. M. Wendt, Adelaide, South Australia, c1875, 13½in (34.5cm), 24.5oz.
$3,000-4,500

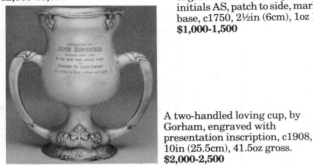

A two-handled loving cup, by Gorham, engraved with presentation inscription, c1908, 10in (25.5cm), 41.5oz gross.
$2,000-2,500

A pair of goblets, by Bailey & Company, Philadelphia, with script initial 'G', with gilt interior, marked on base, c1860, 6in (15cm), 16oz.
$2,000-2,500

A pair of goblets, by Gorham Manufacturing Company, Providence, retailed by Starr & Marcus, New York, engraved with an inscription and a monogram, marked, c1865, 10in (25.5cm) high, 27oz 10dwt.
$2,000-2,500

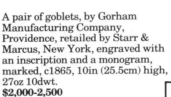

A George IV silver gilt travelling wine cup, by John Riley, 1824, 4½in (11cm), 6oz.
$1,000-1,400

An Australian trophy cup, embossed with fruiting vines and standing on a simulated tree trunk support terminating in a trumpet foot, inscribed, by J. M. Wendt, Adelaide, South Australia, c1880, 9½in (24cm), 6.75oz.
$1,500-2,500

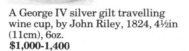

A Victorian commemorative goblet, engraved with a view of the St. Pancras Baths and Wash Houses, and inscribed 'St. Pancras – Presented to Mr. James Hoppey Commissioner for Public Baths and Wash Houses for St. Pancras to commemorate the laying of the first stone of the Baths and Wash Houses, Tottenham Court Road, May 8th, 1877', by D. & C. Hands, 1876, 6in (15.5cm), 5.75oz.
$1,300-2,000

Cutlery

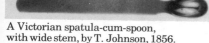

A Victorian spatula-cum-spoon, with wide stem, by T. Johnson, 1856.
$300-500

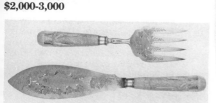

A pair of Victorian fish carvers, pierced and engraved with an underwater scene, by George Adams, 1856, the knife 14½in (37cm), in a fitted velvet lined leather case.
$2,000-3,000

A pair of Victorian fish carvers, the unusual handles of ivory and finely carved in the neo-Gothic style with a full figure of a draped woman within an alcove, by George Adams, 1868, in a fitted and lined case.
$1,300-2,000

A pair of Victorian cast sugar nips, decorated with leafage, flowers and waterlilies, the pivot modelled as a butterfly, by Joseph Willmore, Birmingham, 1840, 2.25oz.
$400-550

A pair of Victorian cast sugar nips, the handles modelled as swans, the finger loops as serpents entwined round the birds' necks, the grips cast and chased in the form of lily pads, Francis Higgins, London 1853.
$800-1,200

A pair of Victorian cast sugar nips, the handles modelled as a toper with cup and jug and a woman in rustic dress, by Francis Higgins, 1854, 2oz.
$450-700

A pair of Victorian novelty sugar nips, modelled as an outstretched monkey, by Albert William Barker, 1886, 2.5oz.
$600-900

A Victorian 6 piece fruit set, comprising a sifter spoon, ladle, and 4 serving spoons, makers Lias & Lias, London 1870, 11oz, the case labelled Carrington, Regent St.
$450-700

A Victorian fish slice and fork, the handles cast as Bacchante, the slice with pierced and chased blade depicting a nymph astride a sea monster, indistinct maker's mark, London 1864, slice 14in (35.5cm), 16oz.
$1,500-2,500

A pair of George III Irish sugar nips, with scroll decorated arms and floral engraved pivot, maker's mark rubbed, Dublin c1770.
$300-500

A matching set of 12 George IV teaspoons, and a pair of similar sugar nips, by Edward Farrell, c1826, 14oz, in fitted lined case.
$1,200-1,750

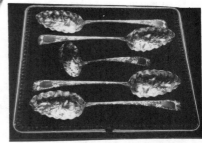

A set of 5 Regency silver gilt dessert spoons, the fluted bowls embossed and engraved, London marks for 1827, maker's marks JTH.JHM, 7oz 5dwt, in original case.
$450-600

A travelling canteen, by Benjamin Pyne, 1722, unmarked, 12oz 11dwt gross, without knife blade, in fitted shagreen case.
$3,000-4,500

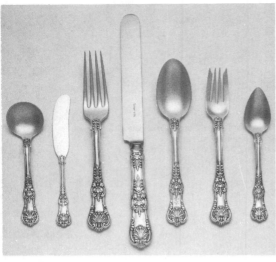

An English Kings pattern flatware service, comprising 94 pieces, by Tiffany & Co., New York, marked, c1885, 134oz 10dwt excluding dinner knives.
$7,500-8,500

A pair of fish servers and a set of 12 fish knives, by Tiffany & Co., New York, marked, c1880, slice 12in (30.5cm), 30oz 10dwt gross.
$1,600-2,000

An assembled medallion flatware service, by Gorham Manufacturing Company, Providence, comprising 140 pieces, each marked, late 19thC, 182oz 10dwt excluding ivory.
$6,000-8,000

A soup ladle, by Paul Revere Jr., Boston, with engraved script initials CVB, marked with full name touch on back of handle, c1780, 13in (33cm), 4oz 10dwt.
$8,000-9,000

A punch ladle, by Gorham, the bowl formed as a turtle shell with gilt interior, c1880, 11in (28cm), 7oz.
$2,500-3,500

A pair of servers, by Alvin Manufacturing Company, Providence, in Raphael pattern, each marked, c1905, 9in (23cm), 8oz.
$1,000-1,500

A stuffing spoon, by Samuel Kirk, Baltimore, King's pattern, with fluted shell bowl, engraved T, marked SK and 11oz on the back of handle, c1835, 3oz 10dwt.
$500-1,000

A Martele soup ladle, by Gorham Manufacturing Company, Providence, marked on handle, c1902, 14in (35.5cm), 8oz.
$2,000-3,000

A soup ladle, by Tunis D. Dubois, New York, with script initials JEL, marked, c1796, 14in (35.5cm), 5oz.
$2,000-2,500

Dishes

A covered butter dish, probably New York, with wood liner, unmarked, c1860, 7½in (19cm), 19.5oz.
$1,000-1,500

A set of 3 George III meat dishes, 2 with initials on undersides, William Bennett, London 1807, 13in (33cm), 67oz.
$3,000-4,500

An entree dish, with divider and detachable handle, Birmingham 1924, 54oz.
$1,000-1,500

A paua shell bon-bon dish, supported by silver and silver gilt cherub figure, London 1984, 6in (15cm).
$200-350

Inkstands

A George III meat dish, engraved with armorials and a similar cover with leaf scroll handle, London 1818, the dish by Paul Storr, 16½in (40.5cm), the cover by Philip Rundell, 14in (35.5cm), 115oz.
$9,000-12,500

A set of 3 Victorian dishes, engraved with armorials, by Robert Garrard, London 1874, and inscribed Garrards, Panton Street, London, 10in (25cm), 64oz.
$1,300-2,000

A German parcel gilt sideboard dish, with detachable pierced floral handles, by Erhard (I) or Isaak Warnberger, Augsburg, c1680, 27in (68cm) wide, 48.5oz.
$9,000-12,500

A George III inkstand, with claw-and-ball feet, fitted with 2 pierced, beaded and bright cut mounts, each containing a cut glass inkwell, the central reeded wafer box with a detachable reeded and beaded taper stick with vase shaped socket, William Plummer, London 1774, 7in (18cm) wide, 9.75oz.
$1,500-2,500

A Victorian breakfast turnover dish and 2 liners, the revolving cover monogrammed and reeded, on 4 tapering paw feet, London 1890, 14½in (35.5cm) wide, 106.9oz.
$3,000-4,500

A suite of one large and 2 smaller dishes on stands, with triform winged mask and paw supports, hung with fruiting floral festoons, the bowls with beaded rims and applied medallions, by Mappin & Webb, London 1919, the larger 11in (28cm) diam, 71oz.
$2,250-3,500

A pair of fluted hot water dishes, 7½in (19cm).
$600-900

A bonbonnière, the sides chased with leaves and husk swags, the domed pull-off cover similarly chased, and with bud finial, Birmingham 1936, 8in (20.5cm) high, 11oz.
$450-700

A George III inkstand, modelled as a cube with 2 pull-out drawers, the lower one with integral pounce compartment, the hinged cover opening to reveal a glass inkwell, by Phipps & Robinson, 1787, 13.75oz.
$5,000-7,500

447

A George III Provincial inkstand, with 2 silver mounted cut glass inkwells, each with hinged covers, the covers each engraved with a monogram, by R. Cattle and J. Barber, York 1807, 11in (28cm) wide, 32oz.
$3,000-4,500

A late Victorian inkstand, the 2 cut glass wells with flat hinged covers with gadroon and shell borders, London 1891, 8½in (21.5cm) wide, 11.5oz.
$450-700

A skull and crossbones inkwell, on slate base, H.M. Edinburgh, 1859, 4½in (11.5cm) high.
$2,500-3,500

An Edwardian inkstand, with 2 cut glass inkwells with hinged covers, Henry Lambert, London 1903, 11in (28cm), 23.75oz.
$1,500-2,500

A George IV inkstand, probably Joseph Angell, the inkstand with indistinct maker's mark, London 1828 and 1829, stand 10in (25cm), 30oz.
$3,000-4,500

Jugs

A Queen Anne hot water jug, with scrolled thumbpiece, slightly domed cover, scrolled handle and flanged foot, London 1707, 23oz.
$2,500-3,500

A George I sparrow beak cream jug, on a sloping collet foot, with scroll handle, by William Paradise, 1724, 3in (8cm), 2.5oz.
$1,000-1,500

A George II cream jug, monogrammed, with double scroll handle, Benjamin Sanders, London 1737, 3½in (9cm), 4.3oz.
$1,000-1,500

A George II bombé cream jug, the scroll handle with caryatid female head, by John Pollock, 4½in (11cm), 5oz.
$900-1,300

A George II cream jug, in rocaille manner, the handle with an entwined snake, its head forming the thumbpiece, gilt interior, by Peter Werritzer, 1756, 4½in (12cm), 5oz.
$3,000-4,500

A George III helmet shaped milk jug, by BM, probably Benjamin Mordecai or Benjamin Mountigue, London 1790, 6in (15cm), 3.75oz.
$300-500

A George III hot water jug, the domed cover with acorn finial, engraved with armorial within foliate swags, by Daniel Smith & Robert Sharp, 1773, 12in (30cm), 32.5oz.
$3,000-4,500

A George III milk jug, by R. & S. Hennell, 1802, 6in (15cm) long, 5.75oz.
$300-500

A George III cream jug, monogrammed, Samuel and Edward Davenport, London 1808, 5in (12.5cm), 3.9oz.
$300-500

A French Empire silver gilt ewer, by Martin-Guillaume, Biennais.
$60,000-87,500

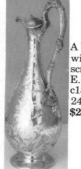

A Victorian claret jug, with hatched scroll work, by E. & J. Barnard, c1857, 14½in (37cm), 24.25oz.
$2,000-3,000

A Victorian jug and domed cover, with ivory pineapple knob, the handle with linen fold decoration, by George Fox, London 1875, 11in (28cm), 23oz gross.
$1,500-2,500

A water pitcher, marked by N.W. Silverware Manufacturing Company, Chicago, monogram removed, dented, marked, c1865, 10in (25cm) high, 19oz 10dwt.
$700-900

A medallion cream pitcher and sugar bowl, by Gorham Manufacturing Company, Providence, retailed by Tiffany & Company, c1865, later monogram LWT, marked, 6½in (16.5cm) high, 24oz.
$700-900

A silver gilt pitcher, by James Thomson, New York, marked on base, dated 1837, gilding later, 11½in (29cm) high, 30oz.
$1,000-1,200

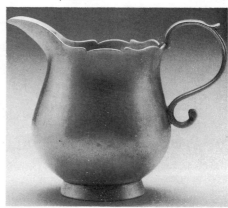

A cream jug, possibly by John Waite, South Kingston, Rhode Island, engraved with script monogram TEM, marked JW on base, c1770, 2½in (7cm) high, 2oz.
$800-1,000

A ewer, marked K & P and J Kitts, by John Kitts, Louisville, Kentucky, engraved South Western Agricultural and Mechanical Association, marked on base, c1850, 12in (30.5cm) high, 17oz.
$3,000-3,500

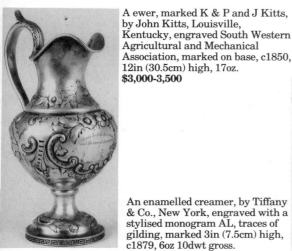

An enamelled creamer, by Tiffany & Co., New York, engraved with a stylised monogram AL, traces of gilding, marked 3in (7.5cm) high, c1879, 6oz 10dwt gross.
$1,500-2,000

Mugs and Tankards

A William and Mary tankard, with hollow handle, engraved with a later crest, by R. Timbrell, 1690, 6½in (17cm), 22oz.
$6,000-9,000

A George I Britannia Standard tankard, maker I.S, hallmarked London 1719, 6in (15cm), 21oz.
$3,000-4,500

A George II tankard, by John Langlands, Newcastle 1759, 5in (12.5cm), 11oz.
$900-1,300

A George III tankard, small repairs, by William Caldecott, London 1759, 7½in (19cm), 25oz.
$3,000-4,500

A George II tankard, inscribed and engraved with armorials, by William Soame, 1758, 10½in (26cm), 44.5oz.
$8,000-11,000

A tankard, by Otto Paul de Parisien, New York, the cover engraved with script initials, spout removed, marked twice on base, c1780, 7½in (19cm) high, 42oz.
$4,500-5,500

A George III tankard, by Solomon Hougham, 1792, 7½in (19cm), 27oz.
$3,000-4,500

A tankard, by Daniel Fueter, New York, marked on base, inside cover and on handle, c1790, 8in (20.5cm) high, 35oz 10dwt.
$5,500-6,500

A pair of George III christening mugs, each with gadroon base and applied shell and anthemion band, cast leaf handles and raised on pedestal feet, by Emes and Barnard, London 1813, 4½in (11cm), 13oz.
$1,500-2,500

A Victorian embossed presentation tankard, with rose pattern panels, London 1861, 4½in (11cm), 6.5oz.
$2,500-3,500

A Victorian christening mug, Chester 1898.
$200-350

A German parcel gilt tankard, the matted sides imitating shagreen, with C-scroll handle and double scroll thumbpiece, maker's mark QR (untraced), apparently Frankfurt-on-Main, c1680, 5½in (13.5cm), 16.75oz.
$8,000-11,000

An Edwardian waisted shaving mug, with a bracket handle, engraved with initials A.M.B., Birmingham 1904, 4in (10cm).
$400-550

A Scandinavian peg tankard, on fruit and foliage ball feet, the scroll handle with fruit and foliage thumbpiece, the hinged cover with Chiron and Achilles within guilloche border, maker's mark indistinct, probably 19thC, 8in (20.5cm), 1,295 grammes.
$5,000-7,500

A Norwegian peg tankard, the handle with eagle thumbpiece, the cover set with coins, by Anders Nielsen Borg, Trondheim, probably 1723, 6½in (16cm), 15.5oz.
$10,500-15,000

Salts

Six George III salt cellars, each with reeded rim, 4 engraved with a crest, by Robert and Thomas Makepeace, 1794, 3½in (8cm) diam, 26oz.
$3,000-4,500

A Norwegian peg tankard, the stepped domed cover inset with a gilt coin of Christian VI dated 1732, the barrel hinge surmounted by a cast crowned lion supporting a ball, with beaded scroll handle, one foot damaged, by Peter Gabriel Aamunosen, Peter Michael Blyth (Warden), Bergen 1815, a 19thC reproduction of an 18thC style, 6½in (16cm), 12oz.
$2,250-3,500

A set of 4 George III two-handled boat-shaped salts, on pedestal bases, with gilt interiors, engraved with a crest, by William Fountain, 1778, 6in (15cm) wide, 17.5oz.
$1,500-2,500

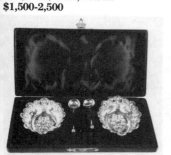

A set of 6 early Victorian salts, with blue glass liners, Charles Fox, London 1840, 24oz.
$2,250-3,500

A pair of Victorian embossed salts and spoons, Birmingham 1900.
$200-350

A set of 4 George III salts, by Thos. Robins, London 1819, 3in (7cm) diam, 18oz.
$900-1,300

A set of 4 Victorian salts, with white glass liners, apparently J. C. Eddington, 1849, 12oz.
$600-900

Salvers

A George II Scottish salver, with 3 hoof feet, scroll and foliage border, the ground chased with a similar band, by Robert Lowe, Edinburgh 1751, 9in (23cm), 16oz 7dwt.
$900-1,300

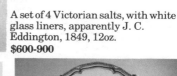

A pair of early George III salvers, by Richard Rugg, 1767, 7in (18cm), 23.5oz.
$2,250-3,500

A salver, by Tiffany & Company, New York, with stylised monogram A de L within foliage, marked, c1875, 10in (25.5cm) square, 22oz 10dwt.
$2,000-3,000

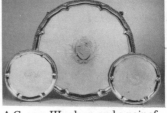

A George III salver, and a pair of matching smaller salvers, all engraved with the same coat-of-arms, by John Carter, 1772, the larger 14in (35.5cm), 65oz.
$7,000-10,000

A George III salver, with raised beaded border, on 4 claw-and-ball feet, maker possibly John Crouch, London 1772, 14½in (36.5cm), 44oz.
$1,300-2,000

A George III card tray, with shell and beaded border, on 3 claw-and-ball feet, engraved monogram to centre, by Robert Jones and John Schofield, London 1775, 6in (15cm), 7oz.
$600-900

A George III salver, with contemporary engraving of a coat-of-arms, maker's mark I.S. (John Schofield), London 1779, 12in (30.5cm), 28oz 2dwt.
$1,500-2,500

A George III salver, engraved with a coat-of-arms in a flower and scroll cartouche, by John Hutson, 1788, 18in (46cm), 68oz.
$8,000-11,000

A Victorian salver, on 4 cast scroll feet, by the Barnards, 1873, 16½in (41cm), 57oz.
$3,000-4,500

A silver salver, London 1876, 25oz.
$900-1,300

A salver with applied vine border, on 3 leaf chased and scroll pierced bracket feet, James Dixon & Sons, Sheffield 1900, 12½in (31.5cm), 31oz.
$1,000-1,500

A late Victorian dish, engraved Gilbert Marks 1900, 15in (38cm), 30oz.
$3,000-4,000

An Edwardian beaded salver, on openwork legs, the border pierced with Gothic arches and cast with rams' masks and drapery swags, with a plain ground, William Comyns, London 1910, 11½in (29cm), 33.5oz.
$800-1,200

Sauceboats

A pair of George III cast sauceboats, with applied laurel leaf festooning and flowerhead tassies, on pedestal bases and with laurel frieze and gadroon borders, engraved with a crest, by John Parker and Edward Wakelin, 1769, 10in (25cm) wide, 47.5oz.
$14,000-19,000

A George III mustard pot, with hinged cover, acorn finial and reeded scroll handle, engraved with a crest with blue glass liner, by John Wakelin and William Taylor, 1786, 7oz.
$1,500-2,500

A George III mustard pot, engraved with reeded bands, with blue glass liner, by Robert and David Hennell, 1779, 4oz.
$1,000-1,500

A pair of Victorian sauceboats, with leaf capped scroll handles and quatrefoil and scroll borders, by Robert Garrard, 1853, 8in (20.5cm), 43oz.
$7,000-10,000

Services

A five-piece breakfast tea and coffee service, by Crosby and Morse, Boston, with applied gold cypher initials, dents, handle of coffee pot broken, c1870, coffee pot 6½in (16.5cm), 36.5oz.
$1,500-2,000

A teapot and covered sugar bowl, by John McMullin, Philadelphia, the teapot with carved wood handle, each marked, c1810, 8in (20cm) high, 36oz 10dwt gross.
$1,000-1,500

A five-piece tea and coffee service, American, late 19th/early 20thC, coffee pot 14½in (37cm) high, 164oz.
$6,000-7,000

A three-piece tea service, by Nicholas Bogert, Newburgh, New York, with die-rolled decoration by Moritz Furst, each marked by maker on base, each die-rolled band bearing several die-cutters marks, c1835, teapot 10in (25.5cm) high, 62oz gross.
$3,000-3,500

A four-piece tea service, by William Thompson, New York, c1820, teapot 9½in (24cm) high, 71.5oz.
$2,000-3,000

A six-piece coffee and tea service, by
A. J. Crawford, New York, marked,
c1920, kettle 11in (28cm) high,
141oz gross.
$3,000-4,000

An assembled four-piece tea and
coffee service, the teapot and coffee
pot by Ebenezer Moulton, Boston,
engraved SH, marked, the covered
sugar urn and cream jug unmarked,
repairs to jug, c1810, coffee pot 11in
(28cm), 66oz 10dwt gross.
$2,500-3,000

A six-piece tea and coffee service, by
Gorham Manufacturing Company,
Providence, marked, c1865, coffee
pot 12in (30.5cm) high, 110oz 10dwt
gross.
$3,500-4,500

A six-piece tea and coffee service, by
Gorham Manufacturing Company,
Providence, in Marlborough
pattern, kettle 13½in (34cm) high,
marked, 1927, with matching tray
by Durgin for Gorham, 1928, 262oz
10dwt gross.
$6,000-7,000

A six-piece tea and coffee service, by
Robert & William Wilson,
Philadelphia, c1826, coffee pot
12½in (32cm) high, 149.5oz.
$4,500-5,500

A three-piece tea service, by
N. Taylor & Co., New York, the
teapot with a wood handle, c1810,
55oz gross.
$4,000-5,000

A Victorian tea and coffee service,
monogrammed and engraved, the
teapot and coffee pot with dove
knops, maker's mark R.P., London
1853-4, 71.6oz.
$3,000-4,500

A Victorian tea service, the sugar bowl and milk jug gilt lined, George Angell, London 1878, teapot 5in (12.5cm) high, 18oz.
$800-1,200

A tea service, engraved in the Aesthetic taste with bamboo and birds in water landscapes, crested, teapot inscribed, Elkington & Co., Birmingham 1884, 61.75oz.
$2,000-3,000

A Victorian tea and coffee service, comprising a teapot, coffee pot, hot water jug, sugar basin and cream jug, on scroll feet, on a two-handled tray with similar engraved decoration and moulded scroll border and handles, all engraved with a crest and motto, by Elkington & Co., Birmingham 1897 and 1898, the tray 25in (63.5cm) long, 234oz.
$1,000-1,500

A Victorian teaset, Messrs. Barnard and J. E. W. & J. Barnard, London 1889, 1891 and 1898, 47oz gross.
$1,000-1,400

A Victorian tea service, London 1893, 28.7oz gross.
$1,000-1,500

A five-piece tea and coffee service and a Victorian tray, 1897, 70oz.
$2,500-3,500

A Victorian fluted and floral engraved tea service, Atkin Bros, Sheffield 1895, 58.5oz.
$900-1,300

A silver teaset, maker's mark R.S. (perhaps R. Stewart), Glasgow 1901, 58.5oz.
$2,000-3,000

An Edwardian tea and coffee service, the milk jug and sugar basin gilt lined, Elkington, Birmingham 1904, coffee pot 10in (25.5cm), 69oz gross.
$2,500-3,500 ▶

An Edwardian tea and coffee service, with embossed scrolling leaf decoration, Birmingham 1902, teapot 12in (30.5cm) wide, 68oz 19dwt.
$2,000-3,000

A silver gilt coffee service, London 1911, and a pair of silver gilt sugar tongs, Sheffield 1909, 20oz.
$1,000-1,400

An Italian gilt tea and coffee service and matching tray, with ivory scroll handles, domed covers and vase shaped finials, each engraved with a monogram and coronet, unmarked, coffee jug 12in (31.5cm), 4,938 grammes.
$5,000-7,500 ▶

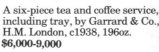

A six-piece tea and coffee service, including tray, by Garrard & Co., H.M. London, c1938, 196oz.
$6,000-9,000

An American coffee service, by Gale & Willis, New York, 19thC, .925 standard, 49.5oz.
$1,300-2,000

Tea Caddies

A George III tea caddy with central hinge, two covers and plain divider, engraved with wrigglework borders and a coat-of-arms and monogram, by Henry Chawner, 1788, 7in (18cm) high, 15oz 10dwt.
$5,000-7,500

A George I tea caddy, engraved with rocaille decoration, by Paul Crespin, 1724, 5in (13cm), 12.25oz.
$5,000-7,500

A George III tea caddy, the underbase engraved with initials HA, by Henry Chawner, 1790, 4in (10cm) high, 14oz.
$7,000-10,000

A Victorian tea caddy and cover, London 1890, also bearing a Russian control mark, 5in (12cm)
$600-900

A George IV tea caddy, cast and chased in the revived rocaille manner, with detachable raised cover surmounted by a cast floral bouquet, possibly by John Welshman, 1882, 6½in (16.5cm) high, 18oz.
$3,000-4,500

A mid-18thC style tea caddy, with sliding top and lift-off cover with baluster finial, chased with rococo flowers and foliage, with 4 vacant scroll cartouches, Chester 1911, 4½in (11cm).
$600-900

Tea Kettles

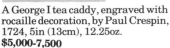

A Danish tea kettle on stand, with burner, by A. Dragstead, Copenhagen 1895, 66.25oz.
$1,200-1,750

A Victorian style part fluted compressed tea kettle, with a burner, probably George Fox, London 1912, 11½in (28cm), 45oz.
$1,200-1,750

Teapots

A George III tea kettle, stand and lamp, the kettle with curved spout, detachable cover with beaded rim and ivory finial, and partly wicker covered scroll swing handle, engraved with Sackville and West crests, motto and coronet, by Charles Wright 1780, the stand and lamp 1782, 15in (38cm) high, 56oz.
$3,000-4,500

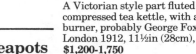

A George III teapot, engraved in the rocaille manner, with gilt interior, by Augustin Le Sage, 1763, 4in (10.5cm), 10oz.
$1,500-2,500

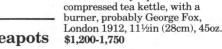

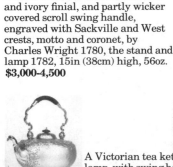

A Victorian tea kettle, stand and lamp, with swing handle and curved spout, the stand on 3 scroll and shell feet, and with pierced and cast apron, with circular lamp, by Harris Bros, 1896, 63oz.
$1,500-2,500

A George III teapot, with polished wood scroll handle and flat detachable cover with wood finial, engraved with an armorial, william Vincent, London 1777, 4½in (11.5cm), 13.25oz.
$1,300-2,000

A George III teapot and stand, with ivory pineapple finial, by William Stephenson, 1790, 19.5oz.
$4,000-5,500

A George III teapot, the domed cover with an ebony finial, scroll wood handle, spout repaired, Hester Bateman, London 1780, 13.75oz gross.
$1,000-1,500

A George III Irish teapot with domed cover, and ebonised handle, by Peter Wills, Cork c1790, 20.5oz gross.
$2,000-3,000

A Victorian teapot, by Edward, John & William Barnard, London 1844, 22.25oz.
$800-1,200

A George III teapot, with engraved silver knob, wood handle, by Samuel Hennell and John Terrey, London 1815, 22oz gross.
$900-1,300

A George III teapot and stand, the cover surmounted by a green ivory bud finial, contemporary engraved monogram either side, reeded wood handle, by Peter, Ann and William Bateman, 1799, the stand reeded and with similar frieze decoration, on 4 feet, overall height 7½in (19.5cm) high, 20oz.
$2,500-3,500

A teapot, by Gorham Manufacturing Company, Providence, one side engraved RB, marked, c1865, 8in (20.5cm) high, 32oz gross.
$1,000-1,200

Trays

A medallion teapot, by Gorham Manufacturing Company, Providence, the domed lid with pinecone finial, marked, c1865, 8in (20.5cm) high, 21oz gross.
$650-850

A Victorian two-handled tea tray, maker's mark J.H., probably of John Hall, London 1893, 15in (38cm) long, 119oz.
$3,000-4,500

A George III plain round waiter, by Elizabeth Jones, c1790, 7in (18cm), 5oz.
$700-900

A bread tray, by Samuel Kirk & Son, Baltimore, with script monogram MMS, marked, c1850, 14½in (37cm) wide, 23oz.
$900-1,200

A waiter, by Peter Quintard, New York City or South Norwalk, Connecticut, with engraved foliate script monogram WC, marked PQ on base, c1740, 6in (15cm) square, 8oz.
$30,000-35,000

Tureens

A George III soup tureen, with
conforming pedestal foot, with
engraved crest, lacking cover, by
William Pitts, London 1787, 14in
(35.5cm) wide, 31oz.
$1,200-1,750

A set of 4 George III sauce tureens
and covers, each on cast spreading
foot with reeded loop handles,
domed covers, engraved with
coat-of-arms and crest, by Robert
Sharp, 1788, 6in (15cm) high, 125oz.
$16,000-22,500

A George IV entree dish and cover,
the fluted domed cover with
detachable lion's mask and
acanthus foliage ring handle, by
Paul Storr, 1822, 12in (30.5cm)
long, 73oz.
$6,000-9,000

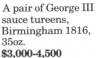

A pair of George III
sauce tureens,
Birmingham 1816,
35oz.
$3,000-4,500

A set of 4 George III entree dishes,
covers and handles, engraved with
coat-of-arms, crest and coronet, by
Robert Sharp, 1788, 10½in (26cm)
long, 155oz.
$16,500-23,000

Wine Antiques

A classical revival covered soup
tureen, by Tiffany, c1860, 15½in
(39cm) wide, 72.5oz.
$4,000-5,000

A Victorian articulated wine
wagon, decorated with vines,
maker's mark R & S, Roberts &
Slater, Sheffield 1859.
$4,000-5,500

A pair of William IV coasters, by
Henry Wilkinson & Co., Sheffield
1835, 7in (18cm) diam.
$2,250-3,500

A William IV claret jug, on shaped
foot cast and chased with dolphins,
foliage and shell ornament, with
vine tendril handle, the hinged
cover with crest finial, maker's
mark IW overstriking another,
perhaps that of Charles Fox, the foot
with retailer's mark of J. Walker,
Aberdeen, 1837, 17in (43cm), 65oz.
$4,500-7,000

A set of 4 William IV wine labels,
with suspensory chains, maker's
mark WR, London 1826.
$800-1,200

A wine bottle holder, by Lebolt &
Company, Chicago, the front with a
shield engraved with initial M,
marked, c1920, 9in (23cm), 12oz.
$900-1,200

A pair of George IV cast wine labels, pierced 'Bucellas' and 'Madeira', by Edward Farrell, 1824 and 1825.
$2,000-3,000

A pair of George III wine coasters, with turned wood bases, the sides with a monogram within oval cartouches, maker's mark indistinct, 1789, 5in (12.5cm) diam.
$4,000-5,500

A Dutch corkscrew, with fluted kidney shaped handle and fluted baluster stem, probably Cornelis Hilberts, Amsterdam, 1749.
$800-1,200

A William IV Farrow & Thompson type corkscrew, engraved with boar's head crest and monogram, lacking helical worm, by Reily & Storer, 1830.
$3,000-4,500

A set of 3 William IV cast silver wine labels for fortified wines, by Chas. Reily and Geo. Storer, London 1830.
$1,000-1,500

A claret jug, by The Goldsmiths & Silversmiths Co. Ltd., 1910, 14in (35.5cm), 42oz gross.
$2,250-3,500

A George III Provincial wine label, with cut-out title 'Claret', by Hampston, Prince & Cattles, H.P.C. incused, York, c1800.
$600-900

A Queen Anne style wine cistern, the handles formed as a winged female caryatid, engraved with a coat-of-arms, maker's mark RR, Britannia Standard, 1936, 24in (61cm) wide, 239oz.
$28,000-37,500

A pair of George III cast wine labels, incised 'White' and 'Claret', probably by Thomas Hemming, c1770.
$1,500-2,500

A claret jug, with hinged domed cover and openwork scroll finial, by The Goldsmiths and Silversmiths Co. Ltd., 1902, 14in (35.5cm), 42oz gross.
$3,000-4,500

A set of 3 George III wine labels, with raised titles 'Port', 'Claret' and 'Sherry', by Paul Storr, 1815.
$4,000-5,500

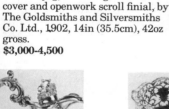

A pair of Victorian wine coasters, on a turned wood base, Charles Fox, London 1839, 5in (12.5cm) diam.
$4,000-5,500

A Victorian claret jug, with scroll handle and grape finial, by Henry Wilkinson, Sheffield 1838, 13½in (34cm), 24oz gross.
$2,500-3,500

A pair of George III wine coasters, with pierced sides, the silver bases with contemporary coats-of-arms, maker's mark W.B.R.S., William Burwash & Richard Sibley, London 1810, 6in (15cm) diam.
$7,000-10,000

A George III Irish dish ring, embossed with a classical urn, with blue glass liner, by Joseph Jackson, Dublin, c1775, 7in (17.5cm), 10oz.
$2,000-3,000

A silver sovereign and half-sovereign case, Birmingham 1905, 1.25oz.
$100-200

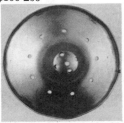

A George IV nipple shield, by T. & I. Phipps, 1821.
$100-200

A silver handled dusting brush, Goldsmiths & Silversmiths Co., London 1895.
$75-150

A Queen Anne baby's teether, the handle embossed in the baroque style, c1705, 5in (13cm) long.
$1,000-1,400

A George II Irish lemon strainer, applied with 2 openwork handles, one engraved with a crest, the reverse with initials, maker's mark only, struck twice, by George Cartwright, Dublin, c1735, 10in (25.5cm), 6oz 8dwt.
$2,000-3,000

A Georgian toothbrush set, comprising a toothbrush, 4½in (12cm) long, a two-part covered paste box, an unmarked tongue scraper, by James Barber II (?), 1793, in a fitted red shagreen case.
$450-600

An altar cross, the knop set with 8 amethysts, the cross with fleur-de-lys and Tudor rose terminals, and applied twice with the lamb and flag, the base engraved 'To the Glory of God and In Memory of Ellen Bertha Tufnell 1867-1930', by Omar Ramsden, 1932, 31in (79cm) high, 110oz gross.
$6,000-9,000

A Swiss travelling clock, with silver case, with translucent grey/blue guilloche and white enamelling, the white enamelled face inscribed Goldsmiths & Silversmiths Co. Ltd., 112 Regent Street, London, with London import marks for 1913, 2½in (6.5cm) high, in leather and gilt tooled case.
$13,000-17,500

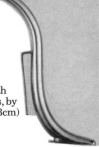

A Victorian feeding syphon, with hinged pierced strainer and clips, by William Saunders, 1875, 5in (13cm) long.
$300-400

Judaica

Victorian silver miniature Tephilin protective outer cases, 1in (2.5cm) high.
$1,000-1,400

A seven-light German brass Sabbath lamp, suspended from an ornate cast hook and chain, the oil tray with 7 spouts joined to the drip tray below by a short tapering column, the lower part of the drip tray with a serrated edge, some damage, c1790, 5½in (14cm) high.
$8,000-11,000

An English 18ct gold seal, of Judaica interest, inscribed 'Peace in Israel'.
$3,000-4,500

An olive wood Palestinian watch holder, signed Bezalel.
$200-350

A Ridgway blue and white Seder plate, for use on Passover, with scenes from Amsterdam Haggedah, 12in (30.5cm).
$200-350

A Swedish charity box, with lockable moulded hinged lid with a hinged cover over the slot for the money, mounted on the cover a cast bird of prey, marked on the base 'Nicolassen', slight damage, c1870, 4in (10cm) high.
$450-700

An Austrian siddur prayer book with silver mounts, printed on paper with Hebrew and German text on the same page in 2 columns, approx. 500 pages, the edges gilt, the cover in purple velvet with silver mounts, some damage, Vienna, c1864, 7½in (19cm).
$300-500

An Austrian alabaster and bronze bust of a Rabbi, the traditional Sephardic robes with long flowing sleeves finely formed in mottled white and beige alabaster, supported on an alabaster base, slight damage, late 19thC, 20in (51cm).
$5,000-7,500

A Syrian damascened brass table top, now used as a wall hanging plate, the surface of the plate profusely decorated with finely engraved silver and copper, some damage, c1870, 24½in (62cm).
$8,000-11,000

A Palestinian silver Bezalel Esther holder and scroll, the silver body finely chased and engraved with repousse work scenes taken from the Book of Esther, the Esther handwritten on 3 cemented pieces of parchment in 23 columns, retained by a silver keep with swivel catch, c1935, 9in (23cm).
$2,000-3,000

A Polish silver parcel gilt Esther holder and Esther scroll, the Esther handwritten on 4 sewn pieces of parchment in 19 columns, later metal keep with swivel catch inscribed 'Bezalel' in Hebrew, c1860, 9in (23cm).
$1,000-1,400

An Indian silver Esther scroll case with wooden handle, old repairs, c1850, 16in (40.5cm).
$800-1,200

The inclusion of hands in the design indicates that the original owner was probably a Cohen.

A Dutch silver table bell, maker's mark RH, Amsterdam 1792, 10oz.
$2,000-3,000

A Dutch Hanukah lamp, with fixed cast interior with 8 oval oil reservoirs, pierced back with cartouche, bearing the cast Hebrew inscription 'Hanukah', c1810, 11in (28cm).
$1,300-2,000

An American silver Art Deco 8-branch Hanukah lamp, with moulded square base with chased band, plain square section stem surmounted by a pierced Star of David finial, marked '925' on the star, c1930, 11in (28cm), 15oz.
$450-600

A late Victorian silver and silver gilt English Hanukah lamp, the removable silver gilt servant light is fitted centrally above the crown, a row of 8 silver gilt baluster candle holders, each with a removable silver gilt sconce individually mounted on the serpentine silver base, marked on the base, backplate and sconces, some restoration, hallmarked London 1897, 10½in (26.5cm), 32oz.
$6,000-9,000

An English silver plated steeple spice box, with 4 bells, plain tapering spire and flag finial, c1870, 9½in (24cm).
$600-900

This is a very unusual design for an English spice container.

A Palestinian silver steeple spice box, with hinged arched door, the small spire surmounted by a pierced ball and long wire stem for the flag, small filigree finial, marked on the base Silver Israel, minor damage, c1950, 8in (20.5cm), 2.3oz.
$400-550

An Austro-Hungarian filigree spice box, marked on the spice compartment and the top, c1885, 6in (15cm), 1.9oz.
$1,000-1,400

An English silver steeple spice box, marked on base, bells, terminals and flag, hallmarked London 1913, some damage, 11in (28cm), 7.5oz.
$1,500-2,500

A Russian silver steeple spice box, marked on the base, bells, door and flag, hallmarked 1892, some damage, 9in (23cm), 4.5oz.
$1,300-2,000

A German silver haudala and spice box holder, with pull-out drawer, c1860.
$4,000-5,500

A Polish Safed silver Kiddush beaker, engraved with 3 scenes from the Holy Land, titled in Hebrew 'Cave of Macpala – The Tower of David – Western Wall', marked 12 within a rectangle on the base, c1870, 3in (7.5cm), 2.4oz.
$2,500-3,500

An Austrian silver filigree spice box, mid-19thC.
$700-900

A Russian silver steeple spice box, slight damage, marked on the base and flag, hallmarked 1879, 9in (23cm), 5oz.
$1,200-1,750

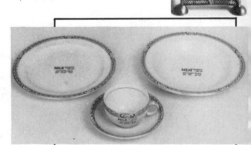

An Austrian silver filigree spice box in the form of a locomotive, c1870.
$3,000-4,500

A combined spice box and Kiddush, Vienna, c1860.
$3,000-4,500

A china tea service made for use by Jewish passengers aboard a Cunard liner. The service comprises a soup dish, cup and saucer, each decorated with a black band of Greek key decoration with foliage and grapes at intervals and gilt lining, the dish inscribed 'Meat' in English and Hebrew, the plate and cup 'Milk' in a similar manner, marked 'The Cunard Steamship Company Limited', 'Ridgway Potteries Limited', the soup dish made by Booths and Colcloughs, c1910.
$800-1,200

The inclusion of the English text was probably for the benefit of the catering staff to avoid incorrect use.

A German silver goblet, slight damage, maker's mark on the underside of the base, c1870, 4in (10cm), 2.5oz.
$250-350

A German silver goblet, with gilt interior, c1880, 4½in (11.5cm), 2.8oz.
$300-400

An Italian filigree spice box, 17thC.
$1,500-2,500

A late Victorian English silver filigree spice box.
$1,200-1,750

A French silver Kiddush cup, signs of gilding, maker's mark on the base, c1870, 3in (7.5cm), 2.3oz.
$300-500

A German Augsburg Kiddush cup, c1720, 4in (10cm).
$6,000-9,000

A German silver Kiddush cup, profusely chased with floral motifs, and small vacant cartouche, slight damage, c1840, 2½in (6.5cm), 1.7oz.
$250-350

A Turkish silver Kiddush cup, with gilt interior, c1850, 3½in (9cm), 3oz.
$200-350

Silver Plate

Candlesticks

A set of 4 George III Sheffield candlesticks, on square tapering beaded columns and square stepped beaded bases, engraved with a crest and motto 'Fear God in Life', of James, 14th Baron Somerville.
$2,500-3,500

A pair of Victorian dressing table candlesticks, the stems designed as bound palms on stepped square bases with tongue and acanthus edging, Sheffield 1866, 5½in (14cm), loaded.
$900-1,300

A pair of Edward VII Corinthian column dressing table candlesticks, the stepped square bases and detachable nozzles with gadrooned edging, Sheffield 1907, 6½in (16.5cm), loaded.
$1,000-1,500

A Sheffield plate oil lamp and shade, on 3 winged paw feet and supporting a glass reservoir, later converted for electricity, 26in (66cm).
$600-900

An electroplated Corinthian column oil lamp, with glass reservoir and shade, later converted for electricity, 23½in (60cm).
$600-900

A pair of silver plated candlesticks, with tulip-shaped hurricane shades with lift-out nozzles, on faceted shafts and moulded octagonal bases, 15½in (39cm).
$5,000-7,500

A set of 4 Sheffield plate candlesticks, 9in (23cm).
$700-900

OLD SHEFFIELD PLATE

★ old Sheffield plate made from c1740-1840 when it was replaced by electroplating
★ a problem arises with electroplating being called Sheffield plate and hence the original plate should be notated 'old' Sheffield plate, although frequently this title is omitted
★ aid to dating Old Sheffield plate by edge identification; until 1785 edges merely turned over or with simple punched-in beading
★ by 1789 beading, reeding or gadrooning
★ 1800 shells, dolphins, oak leaves
★ 1815 vine leaves and flowers, altogether much more elaborate
★ check for a seam on hollow ware as electroplate completely covers the piece

463

A set of 4 Sheffield plate candlesticks, each stamped Danl. Holy/Wilkinson & Co., 12in (30.5cm).
$1,200-1,750

Services

A three-piece teaset, the handles with scroll mountings, gadroon borders, c1815.
$600-900

A Victorian electroplated tea and coffee service, with beaded edging, decorated with cartouches and foliate bands.
$1,000-1,500

Tureens

A five-piece electroplated tea and coffee service, on spreading circular bases, with beaded edging, Elkington & Co., 1859.
$1,500-2,500

A four-piece electroplated tea and coffee service, with bright cut foliage, tied festoons and fronds, on spreading bases.
$600-900

A pair of Sheffield soup tureens, engraved with coat-of-arms and crest, c1820, 14in (35.5cm) high.
$6,000-8,000

The arms are those of Porter with Bothell.

An old Sheffield plate gadrooned sauce tureen and cover, on leaf capped paw feet, finely engraved with 2 armorials, the part fluted detachable cover engraved with 2 crests, 9in (23cm).
$750-1,000

A pair of French silver on copper raised sauce tureens, by Odiot of Paris, early 19thC, 7in (18cm).
$750-1,000

A pair of plated entree dishes, with vine decorated borders, 10in (25.5cm).
$200-350

A pair of entree dishes, covers and liners, with chased borders, engraved with armorials, with griffon head handles, by Elkington & Co., 19thC, 14in (35.5cm).
$900-1,300

An electroplated soup tureen and cover, 16in (40.5cm), and a matching dish.
$1,200-1,750

A pair of Victorian plated entree dishes, the domed covers with Egyptian Sphinx finials, the supports to the stands in the form of winged Egyptian female terms, with spirit burners, 11in (28cm).
$1,200-1,750

Miscellaneous

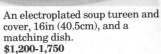

A two-handled cake stand, Sheffield 1923, 15½in (39cm) wide, with a pair of sweetmeat dishes, Sheffield 1922, 6½in (16.5cm) diam.
$2,000-3,000

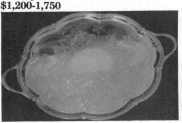

A Victorian tray with beaded handle and border, finely engraved centre, London 1874.
$6,000-8,000

A plated cigarette lighter, modelled as a ruler.
$150-200

A Sheffield plated pint tankard with lid, early 19thC, 7in (18cm).
$100-200

A plated breakfast dish, with strainer and lid, 14in (35.5cm) wide.
$250-350

A George III Sheffield plate cruet, the 4 sauce bottles with stoppers, and a set of 4 Regency bottle labels, c1785.
$700-900

A George III Sheffield tea caddy, bright cut engraved with swags of flowers, cartouche and ribbon tie, 5in (12.5cm).
$450-700

A silver plated kettle on stand, with spirit burner, c1890.
$700-900

A Victorian electroplated tea kettle on stand, with 3 scroll supports and burner, 14in (35.5cm) high.
$400-550

A George III bullet-shaped teapot, with baluster finial, floral border engraving, cast spout, wood handle, by Francis Crump, London 1769.
$600-900

An old Sheffield plate tea urn, on 4 ball feet, with lions' mask and ring handles, the domed cover with ball finial and with gadrooned borders, c1820, 16in (40.5cm) high.
$1,200-1,750

A glass claret jug, in the manner of Christopher Dresser, with angular plated mounts, flared star cut base, Hukin & Heath, 9in (23cm).
$600-900

An Edwardian novelty desk clip and pen brush in the form of a muzzled bear, on oak base, Birmingham 1908.
$600-900

A silver plated and crystal decanter set, one decanter cracked, impressed 12459, E & Co., with crown in shield Elkington & Co., 18½in (47cm) wide.
$1,500-2,500

A Sheffield plate inkstand with pen rests, fitted with a chamberstick and snuffer, pounce pot and inkwell, all with acanthus cast rims, on paw feet, early 19thC, 9½in (24.5cm) wide.
$700-900

A plated and engraved inkstand, with a pair of cut glass inkwells.
$200-350

A plated ink stand, with presentation inscription and vine pattern edging, supporting 2 glass wells with central reservoir and taperstick with snuffer, 13in (33cm).
$900-1,300

An Eastern silver coloured metal Scribes box, the engraved quill box with attached inkwell, engraved with stylised script and geometric patterns, with various marks.
$3,000-4,500

A silver lustre wig holder, by Bailey & Batkin, sole patentees, c1820, 9in (23cm).
$1,000-1,400

A Victorian silver plate surtout d'table, liner marked Prevost & Co., 16in (41cm) high.
$40,000-52,000

A silver plated model of General Gordon by Adrian Jones.
$3,000-4,500

A set of 5 Georgian Sheffield plated and crested livery buttons, c1820.
$75-150

A pair of George III coasters, with wrigglework band decoration, turned mahogany bases, Robert Hennell, London 1792.
$1,500-2,600

'The Milton Shield', an Elkington electrotype by L. Morel-Ladeuil, 1867, 33in (84cm) high.
$2,250-3,500

Gold

Miscellaneous

A gold cigarette case, the reeded panels bordered by scroll and foliate bands, with cabochon cut synthetic sapphire thumbpiece, 127 grammes.
$1,200-1,750

A 9ct gold reeded cigarette box, with plain thumbpiece, Cartier, London 1954, 2½ by 3in (6.5 by 7.5cm), 3.25oz.
$1,000-1,400

An English gold cigar box, the interior of the cover engraved with inscription dated 1933, wood lined, by Asprey, London, 1928, 18ct, 48oz 10dwt gross.
$16,500-23,000

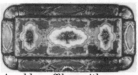

A gold snuff box with engraved scroll and foliate decoration, the cover set with 3 plaques with multi-coloured flower arrangements on white ground, probably Vienna, early 19thC, 94 grammes.
$2,000-3,000

Metal

Brass

A gold engine turned vinaigrette, with hinged lid, the thumbpiece inset with turquoise, the oval cartouche monogrammed, unmarked, c1830, 3 by 2.2cm.
$1,000-1,400

A brass and iron bed, 19thC, 55in (140cm).
$1,300-2,000

A brass cot, 19thC, 38in (96.5cm).
$1,000-1,400

A pair of engraved brass candlesticks, Continental, 18thC, 7in (17.5cm) high.
$1,800-2,000

A pair of George II brass candlesticks, one repaired, mid-18thC, 6½in (16.5cm) high, with brass scissor form candlesnuffer and stand.
$2,000-2,500

A pair of engraved brass candlesticks, Continental, 18thC, 7in (18cm) high.
$2,000-2,500

A pair of Federal bell metal andirons, American, c1800, 17in (43cm) high.
$1,000-1,500

A pair of late Federal brass andirons, American, early 19thC, 24in (61cm) high.
$3,000-3,500

A pair of brass and iron andirons, American, late 18thC, 22½in (57cm) high.
$2,500-3,500

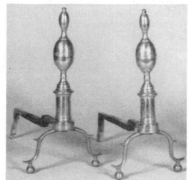

A pair of Federal brass andirons and matching fire tools, New York, c1820, andirons 20in (51cm) high.
$2,000-2,500

A pair of Federal brass andirons, New York, c1810, 18in (45.5cm) high.
$1,000-1,200

A late Federal brass and wire fireplace fender, American, on an iron base, late 19thC, 53in (134.5cm) wide.
$2,500-3,000

A pair of Federal brass andirons, American, c1815, 14in (35.5cm).
$1,200-1,500

A four-piece brass dressing table set, probably Austrian, Jugendstil, unmarked, candlestick 7in (18cm) high.
$300-500

A set of 4 Charles II style brass candlesticks, 10in (25.5cm).
$1,500-2,500

A brassed metal bust of Wellington, in military dress, on wood base, 6½in (16cm).
$100-200

A Spanish brass candlestick, c1700.
$150-250

A brassed metal wall piece profile portrait bust of Wellington, 6½in (17cm).
$100-200

A set of 4 Charles II style brass candlesticks, 16½in (42cm).
$3,000-4,000

A pair of brass candlesticks, mid-18thC, 8in (20.5cm).
$600-900

A pair of brass candlesticks, late 18thC.
$400-550

A pair of candlesticks with shell-shaped bases, 18thC.
$800-1,200

A pair of brass candlesticks, 19thC.
$100-150

A pair of brass candlesticks, c1830.
$900-1,300

A Regency brass desk lamp, with adjustable twin branches, shaped nozzles and drip pans, the base with twin rest for snuffers, lacking shades, 19in (48cm).
$1,500-2,500

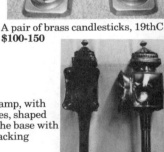

A pair of brass and copper carriage lamps, mid-19thC.
$2,000-3,000

A pair of Victorian ornamental brass candlesticks, with glass lustre decoration.
$900-1,300

A brass kettle on stand, the design attributed to Jan Eisenloeffel, the swing handle with wooden grip, 27½in (69cm).
$1,500-2,500

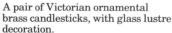

A brass kettle and stand, 19thC.
$150-250

A set of 3 George III brass fire-irons, with shaped ring handles and baluster shafts, comprising a poker, a pair of tongs and a shovel, 24in (61cm).
$3,000-4,000

A brass coal scuttle, 19thC.
$200-350

A set of 3 brass and polished steel fire-irons, with foliate bosses and fluted handles, 29½in (75cm) long.
$3,000-4,000

A steel balance with brass pans, by Charles De Grave, with some weights and label of values, in a fitted walnut case, 19thC, 6in (15cm) wide.
$450-700

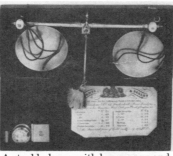

A steel balance with brass pans and weights, with trade label for Richard Vandome, in plush lined leather covered case, 19thC, 7in (18cm) wide.
$400-550

A pair of Dutch brass buckets, decorated with repousse fruiting foliage, and a brass 'cat and fiddle' brush.
$800-1,200

A Victorian brass postal balance, the beam signed Ortner & Houle, St. James's St. London, the 2 pans with painted porcelain plaques, 8in (20cm), and a set of 5 weights.
$2,000-3,000

A set of brass letter scales with 4 brass weights, on oak stand, 13in (33cm) wide.
$100-200

A brass stamp box, by W. Avery & Son, Redditch, No. 614, stamped with a registration mark, the sides arranged so as to fold, 2½in (6.5cm).
$450-600

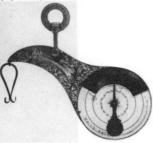

A sheet brass letter balance, signed Parnell London and inscribed Hall's Patent, in the original plush lined and fitted leather case, 5in (12.5cm) wide.
$300-500

A model brass and wooden cannon, c1830, 5in (12cm) long.
$100-200

A patinated brass telescope, the case mounted with a section of an ivory tusk, painted with Napoleon on horseback with the Imperial Eagle, stamped Ramsden, London, 8in (20cm) long when closed.
$1,500-2,500

A brass door stop, modelled as a saddled horse, 13in (33cm) wide.
$450-700

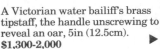

An English brass plate, the underside inscribed with ownership IT, and with traces of silvering, 18thC, 10½in (26.5cm) diam.
$3,000-4,500

A Regency brass inlaid rosewood inkstand, with 2 bottles.
$450-700

A Victorian water bailiff's brass tipstaff, the handle unscrewing to reveal an oar, 5in (12.5cm).
$1,300-2,000 ▶

A brass watering can, 19thC.
$150-250

A pair of martingale horse straps, 19thC.
$200-350

A pair of bronze busts of Sheakespear (sic) and Pope, or engraved gilt socles, on bronze pedestal columns, 19thC, 12in (30cm) high.
$3,000-4,000

A Louis XVI style gilded brass chandelier with vase turned column, late 19thC, 44in (111.5cm).
$1,500-2,500

Bronze

A bronze bust of Napoleon as First Consul, mounted on veined marble half column, 19thC, 14½in (36cm) high.
$800-1,200

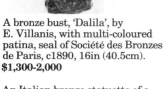

A bronze head, modelled as the head of a young faun with short wavy hair, on turned wooden socle, unmarked 10½in (26cm) high.
$800-1,200

A gilt bronze bust of Mary Queen of Scots, by Mathurin Moreau, on stepped socle, 19thC, 17in (43cm) high, with separate red marble plinth.
$1,500-2,500

A bronze bust, 'Dalila', by E. Villanis, with multi-coloured patina, seal of Société des Bronzes de Paris, c1890, 16in (40.5cm).
$1,300-2,000

An Italian bronze statuette of a bishop, 17thC, 10½in (26.5cm) high.
$3,000-4,000 ▶

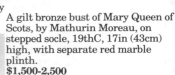

A bronzed spelter portrait bust desk ornament of Adolf Hitler, by Schmidt-Hoffer, Berlin.
$4,000-5,500

An Italian bronze of a lifesize blacksmith's apprentice, cast from a model by Commendatore Professore Rivalta, inscribed Fonderia Carradori, Pistoia, 19thC, 47in (120cm) high, on a carved wood pedestal.
$13,000-17,500

A German bronze group of Hercules and the Hydra, derived from a model by Giambologna, early 17thC, 17in (43cm) high.
$13,000-17,500

A gilt bronze figure of Hercules, in 17thC Venetian style, regilded, on plinth, 6½in (17cm) high.
$600-900

An English bronze figure of the young Prince of Wales, cast from a model by Thomas Fowke, standing on a bronze plinth inscribed T. Fowke Sc, London 1864, and bearing the silver label inscribed 'Honble. Artillery Company, Prince of Wales Prize, won by Corpl Hunt 1864', 33in (84cm) high.
$15,000-21,000

A French bronze group of the voyage of the Nations, cast from a model by Edouard Drouot, 19thC, 19½in (49cm) high.
$3,000-4,000

Drouot was born in France in 1859, he studied in Paris under the Moreaux family, and is best known as a genre painter, winning a medal at the salon of 1892 and receiving an honourable mention at the exposition of 1900.

A French bronze statuette of Bacchus, cast from a model by Louis Garnier, late 17th/early 18thC, 14½in (36cm) high.
$8,000-11,000

A pair of Continental bronze figures, after Giambologna, of Mercury and Iris standing on a puff of wind, 19thC, 30in (76cm) high.
$9,000-12,500

A 'new sculpture' bronze figure of The Catapult Boy, cast from a model by Sir William Reid Dick, signed Reid Dick, on a Siena marble base, string of catapult missing, 12½in (31cm) high.
$2,250-3,500

A pair of bronze figures of Mercury and Hebe, 19thC, tallest 32in (81.5cm) high.
$800-1,200

A bronze figure of Perseus, with the head of Medusa, the base incised in Greek and signed F. W. Pomeroy Sc, 1898, 20in (51cm) high, on antico verde pedestal.
$24,000-32,500

A pair of Italian bronze putti, late 19thC/early 20thC, 15½in (39cm).
$1,000-1,500

A bronze figure of a woman, signed Oscar Gladenbeck, c1900, 12in (30.5cm).
$300-400

A pair of gilt bronze figures, of Mercury after Giambologna, and another of Fortune, both on marble and gilt bronze plinths, 34in (86cm).
$2,250-3,500

A French bronze statuette of a seated classical man, cast from a model by Charles René de St. Marceaux, signed St. Marceaux, and with Susse Frères, Paris, inscription, seated on a marble plinth, broken top right and overpainted gold, late 19th/early 20thC, 23½in (60cm).
$600-900

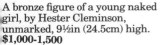

A bronze figure of a young naked girl, by Hester Cleminson, unmarked, 9½in (24.5cm) high.
$1,000-1,500

A bronze statue of a young hunter carrying a bow, his hound at his side, by Marcel Debut, signed, 30in (76cm) high.
$7,000-10,000

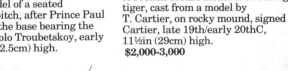

A bronze statuette of a French circus performer, holding a hoop and playing with a poodle, signed G. de Chemellier, 17in (43cm) high.
$300-500

A French bronze figure of a retriever, inscribed E. Delabrierre, 19thC, 10in (25.5cm) high.
$600-900

A pair of French bronze figures of Rousseau and Voltaire, 19thC, tallest 13in (33cm) high.
$1,500-2,500

A bronze statue of a nude male, inscribed 'Honor Patria', and signed E Picault, 32in (81cm).
$1,000-1,500

A French bronze figure of a racehorse, signed on the base I. Bonheur, 19thC, 11½in (29cm).
$2,250-3,500

An English bronze figure of a groom and a rearing horse, cast from a model by Joseph Edgar Boehm, the base incised, 19thC, 23½in (59cm) high.
$6,000-9,000

A bronze painted chicken and 3 chicks, late 19thC.
$150-200

A bronze figure of a deer hound, possibly Austrian and later gilded, late 19thC, 11in (28cm) high.
$800-1,200

A bronze model of a seated bloodhound bitch, after Prince Paul Toubetskoy, the base bearing the signature Paolo Troubetskoy, early 20thC, 9in (22.5cm) high.
$2,000-3,000

A French bronze model of a roaring tiger, cast from a model by T. Cartier, on rocky mound, signed Cartier, late 19th/early 20thC, 11½in (29cm) high.
$2,000-3,000

An Austrian cold painted bronze figure of a bulldog, 4in (10cm) high.
$1,000-1,500

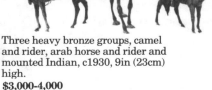

Three heavy bronze groups, camel and rider, arab horse and rider and mounted Indian, c1930, 9in (23cm) high.
$3,000-4,000

A reproduction bronze figure, 13in (33cm) high.
$300-500

An Austrian cold painted bronze figure of a magpie.
$1,000-1,500

A bronze equestrian study of a stallion, 58in (147cm) high.
$2,000-3,000

A bronze statuette, after a 19thC original, the base signed Kauba, on a green 'marble' plinth, 11in (28cm) high.
$600-900

A pair of bronze equestrian figures, signed J. Willis, 12in (30.5cm) wide on oak stands.
$6,000-8,000

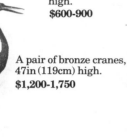

A pair of bronze cranes, 47in (119cm) high.
$1,200-1,750

A pair of bronze statues of Abyssinian cats, 31in (78.5cm) high.
$1,200-1,750

A bronze equestrian group Vainqueuer du Derby, signed P.J. Mêne, cast by F. Barbèdienne, 16in (40.5cm) high.
$2,000-3,000

A pair of Regency bronze candlesticks, 10½in (27cm) high.
$2,000-3,000

A pair of Regency bronze candelabra, on tapered columns, cast with laurel at the bases, on flared swagged feet and plinths, 28in (71cm) high.
$5,000-7,500

A pair of Continental bronze candlesticks, early 18thC, 9in (23cm) high.
$450-700

A pair of Italian bronze baluster shaped vases, with scrolling handles, 17thC, 7in (17cm) high.
$300-500

A pair of late Victorian French bronze candelabra, 32in (81cm) high.
$4,000-5,500

Rare because a man and a woman are depicted, whereas usually it is just men.

A bronze twelve-light chandelier in 2 tiers, 18thC, 27½in (70cm) high.
$4,000-5,500

A pair of French gilt bronze and champlevé vases of Japanesque form, on bronze and gilded bases with elephant's head supports, late 19thC, 14in (35cm) high.
$3,000-4,500

A pair of bronze inkwells, cast as male and female Nubian heads, studded with semi-precious stones, with ceramic eyes, and wearing parcel gilt burnouses, on black marble bases, his 'hair' replaced by a wig, 6in (15cm) high.
$3,000-4,500

An Empire gilt bronze encrier, on mahogany plinth with gadrooned half-round dishes to either side, and applied dolphin ornament, on ball feet, 10in (25cm) wide.
$2,250-3,500

A bronze and ormolu inkwell, with pierced Gothic arcaded frieze, the pierced scrolling shaft flanked by bosses on yellow marble square base, mid-19thC, 6in (15cm) wide.
$800-1,200

A James II bronze mortar by Edward Neale of Binford, the waist cast with his initials EN flanking an armorial, with the date 1688 and 2 mermaid reliefs, 5in (13cm) high.
$1,000-1,500

A Stuart bronze mortar, cast on each side with a roundel of the Royal Arms incorporating the initials CR, 17thC, 5in (13cm), and a pestle.
$200-350

Two Guernsey measures, both marked on the covers by Ns.L.C., Guernsey, between stamped roseheads, with ownership ELG and IRD, 18thC, 11in (28cm) high.
$900-1,300

A Guernsey measure, the cover stamped with the Carter arms touch and possibly workmaster's initials CM together with ownership ISM, mid-18thC, 11½in (28.5cm) high.
$450-700

A Dutch model of a cannon, with a bronze moulded band, dated 1631 and of the period, on a two-wheeled iron mounted wood carriage, barrel 15in (38cm) long.
$3,000-4,500

A large bronze cauldron, with iron swing handle, on tripod with masks, 16thC, 18in (46cm) high.
$3,000-4,500

A Flemish bronze plaque, depicting the Supper at Emmaus, stamped indistinctly to the base, late 16thC, 8½in (22cm) high.
$1,000-1,500

A bronze reduction of the Vendôme column, on white marble base, mid-19thC, 12in (30.5cm) high.
$5,000-7,500

Copper

An ebony and oval panelled jelly mould, 6in (15cm).
$100-200

A Victorian copper jelly mould, orb and sceptre mark, 5½in (14cm).
$200-350

A copper jelly mould, with swirl top, 5½in (14cm).
$200-350

A copper ale muller, 19thC.
$100-200

A copper kettle, 8in (20.5cm) diam.
$100-200

A copper kettle, c1800, 12in (30cm) high.
$300-500

A brass and wood trivet, c1880, 8in (20cm) high.
$100-200

A copper kettle, 19thC.
$100-200

A copper tea kettle, designed by Dr. C. Dresser, with brass and ebony handle, on 3 brass stump feet, with wrought iron stand and copper burner, 31½in (80cm) high.
$800-1,200

A large copper jug, 10½in (26cm) high.
$150-200

A copper kettle, mid-19thC.
$100-200

A copper helmet shaped coal scuttle.
$150-250

A copper charger, by John Pearson, signed and dated 1895, 24½in (62cm) diam.
$400-550

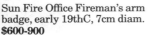

A copper coaching horn, c1870, 52in (132cm).
$200-350

Firemarks

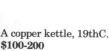

Royal Exchange Assurance, lead, raised Royal Exchange Building, policy No. 1072, G.
$3,000-4,500

Sun Fire Office Fireman's arm badge, early 19thC, 7cm diam.
$600-900

A pair of copper clad bronze wall appliqués, in the form of patinated cherubs supporting foliate branches, 25½in (65cm) high.
$3,000-4,500

> **FIREMARKS**
>
> **Glossary**
> M Mint
> E Excellent
> G Good
> F Fair
> P Poor
>
> Condition is stated as a matter of opinion, and takes into account the type of material and rarity of the mark. Policy numbers are impressed unless otherwise stated

The General Insurance Company of Ireland, lead, policy No. 2113, F to G.
$1,000-1,400

Sun Fire Officer, copper, original paint.
$75-150

Worcester firemark, lead, original paint.
$450-700

Dublin Insurance, lead, policy No. 1908, bowknot separated and rejoined, G.
$1,200-1,750

New Bristol Fire Office, lead, policy No. 4423, overpainted, numbers faint, G to E.
$1,200-1,750

Worcester Fire Office, lead, overpainted, G to E.
$600-900

Iron

A tin candlebox, c1790, 12in (30cm) long.
$75-150

Norwich Union Fire Insurance, lead, two holes to centre, G to E.
$1,000-1,400

A tin hogscraper candlestick, c1830, 8in (20cm).
$60-100

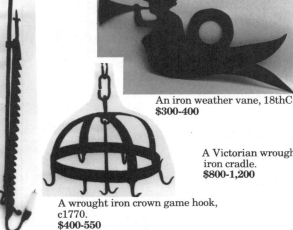

An iron weather vane, 18thC.
$300-400

A Victorian wrought iron cradle.
$800-1,200

A wrought iron adjustable candle holder, 18thC.
$400-550

A wrought iron crown game hook, c1770.
$400-550

A polychrome and gilt iron heraldic shield, Netherlandish, depicting the quartered Arms of the Royal House of the Netherlands, painted in green, red and cream with gilt highlights, inscribed Pletterij Den Haag, surface colour worn, 19thC, 47in (119cm) high.
$1,000-1,400

An iron painted pub sign of a bull, English, c1860.
$1,200-1,750

A mid-Victorian black painted cast iron stick stand, the back pierced with scrolling foliage and centred by a mask with semi-circular drip pan and foliate feet, 29in (74cm) high.
$700-900

A Nuremburg Armada chest, overlaid with strapwork, the interior with an elaborate locking mechanism with 13 locks turned by one key, also 2 padlocks with keys, with 2 heavy loop type carrying handles, 43in (109cm) wide.
$2,000-3,000

A Spanish iron strongbox, the hinged top and sides with strapwork, the sides with carrying handles, with key, 17thC, 20½in (52cm) wide.
$1,500-2,500

A Nuremburg iron casket, with an etched decoration of figures in panels divided by bands with foliage, on ball feet, 17thC, 7in (17.5cm) wide.
$1,500-2,500

A pair of cast iron whippets, American, each sitting on an oval base, 20thC, 17½in (44cm) high.
$3,500-4,000

A painted cast iron weathervane, American, modelled as a rooster, with sheet iron tail, 19thC, yellow paint of later date, 35in (89cm) high.
$3,000-3,500

A large sheet iron horse weathervane, shaped and pierced silhouette of a standing horse with supporting iron rod braces mounted on base with directional arrow, 8½in (21cm) long.
$600-800

A wrought iron double arm candlestand, the shaft with adjustable double candle-arm, on arched legs with disc feet, 46in (116.5cm) high.
$500-600

Ormolu

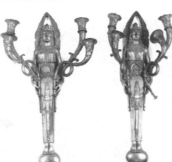

A pair of Regency ormolu wall sconces, 20½in (52cm) high.
$10,000-13,500

A set of 4 Louis XV style ormolu wall lights, drilled for electricity, 34½in (87cm) high.
$6,000-9,000

A Directoire ormolu lampe bouillotte, with adjustable green tôle shade, drilled, 26in (66cm) high.
$2,000-3,000

A pair of ormolu and white marble chenets, each modelled with a putto warming his hands by a tripod brazier while kneeling on a plinth hung with drapery swags, on a white marble base, 11½in (29cm) wide.
$1,200-1,750

A pair of Charles X ormolu vases, 14in (35.5cm) high.
$3,000-4,500

An ormolu and simulated bronze centrepiece, with fluted oval cut glass bowl, on a foliate circlet supported by 4 scantily clad classical maidens, probably Scandinavian, early 19thC, 11in (28cm) high.
$3,000-4,500

An ormolu door knocker, the classical mask with vine leaves and grapes, mid-19thC, 7½in (19cm) high.
$800-1,200

An ormolu reduction of The Warwick Vase, on moulded square onyx plinth, 17in (43cm) diam.
$2,250-3,500

A Regency ormolu pen tray, in the form of a classical bath with lion masks and claw feet, on green marble base, 7in (18cm).
$1,300-2,000

Pewter

A pair of pewter hexafoil wine ewers and flat covers, variously incised, late 17th/early 18thC, 6½in (17cm) high.
$1,200-1,750

A pewter tankard of gallon capacity, inscribed Wm. Dennis, White Swan, Ware, 19thC, 11½in (29cm) high, and an accompanying note.
$700-900

A French charger, the plain broad border with touchmarks dated 1667, 19in (48.5cm) diam.
$1,500-2,500

An important Royal portrait flat lidded pewter tankard, with ram's horn thumbpiece, serrated lip to lid, by William Eddon (Cotterell 1503), c1690, 6in (15cm).
$14,000-19,000

A set of 6 pewter plates, c1780, 9in (23cm).
$450-700

A pair of Portuguese 17thC style pewter candlesticks, the knopped stems raised on compressed domed shaped bases, 4in (10cm) high.
$300-500

A pewter plate, by Frederick Bassett, New York or Hartford, with Laughlin touches 463, 464 and 466, c1780, 9in (23cm).
$600-800

n English 17thC style pewter andlestick, the reeded knopped em raised on an octagonal base, ½in (21.5cm) high.
450-700

pewter plate, by Edward anforth, Hartford, minor pitting n front, Laughlin touches 387 and 88, c1790, 8in (20.5cm).
450-550

A pewter plate, by Samuel and Thomas Melville, Newport, Rhode Island, some scratches, small dents, Laughlin touches 326 and 327, c1795, 8½in (21.5cm).
$300-400

pewter plate, by Thomas D. bardman, Hartford, with Laughlin uch 424, c1860, 12in (30.5cm).
600-600

A pewter teapot, attributed to Cornelius Bradford, New York or Philadelphia, mark worn, some repairs, marked inside with rose and crown touch, c1775, 6½in (16.5cm) high.
$3,000-3,500

A pewter plate, by Nathaniel Austin, Charlestown, Massachusetts, scratches, repairs to edge, with Laughlin touches 299-a and 300, c1785, 12in (30.5cm).
$350-450

Miscellaneous

A pewter plate, by Robert Palethorp, Jr., Philadelphia, narked with Laughlin touches 560 and 561, c1820, 8in (20.5cm).
350-450

A spelter bust of Marie Stuart, c1880.
$100-200

vory & Shell

A Britannia metal coffee pot, by Keale, Parkin & Marshall, Sheffield.
$1,200-1,750

A South German iron box with gilt copper ajouré mounts, in the style of Michel Mann, internal lock mechanism in need of repair, 17thC, 5cm high.
$2,250-3,500

A Flemish carved ivory bust of a girl in a headscarf, inscribed Alph. van Beurden, on the left shoulder, on flared granite socle, late 19thC, 16½in (42cm) high.
$7,000-10,000

A Dieppe carved ivory bust of Louis XIV, 19thC, 2½in (6.5cm) high, on turned ebonised socle.
$1,200-1,750

An early French carved ivory figure of a young female in classical dress, 13in (33cm) high.
$4,000-5,500

A Preiss carved ivory figure of a young naked girl with skipping rope, 4in (10cm), on onyx plinth.
$1,000-1,500

A carved ivory portrait head of Wellington, on socle and column base, 5½in (14cm).
$450-600

A French carved ivory group of the Madonna and Child, after a 14thC original, 19thC, 11in (28cm) high, in a fitted tooled leather case.
$4,500-7,000

A Dieppe carved ivory group of a peasant couple, with resigned expressions, in typical costume, early 19thC, 4½in (11cm), on stained socle.
$1,200-1,750

A German wood and ivory figure of a saint, on square sectioned base, 2 fingers missing, 19thC, 8½in (21cm) high.
$800-1,200

A pair of carved ivory figures of Joseph and Mary, traces of gilding to the integral plinth base, 18thC, 9½in (24cm) high.
$4,500-7,000

A carved ivory figure of a male saint, holding a small figure of Christ standing on the bible, 5½in (14cm) high.
$800-1,200

An ivory statuette of a monastic saint with wings, on a shaped ornamental stand, wings separate, traces of gilding, padded modern Chinese box and shaped stand, 18thC, 8in (20.5cm) high.
$900-1,300

A miniature ivory automaton, on square section pedestal, traces of polychrome, one foot missing, his back hollowed, 18thC, 3½in (9cm) high.
$450-600

An ivory statuette of Saint Clare, holding a metal crucifix with bone or ivory Corpus Christi, with traces of gilding, 18thC, 7½in (18cm) high.
$700-900

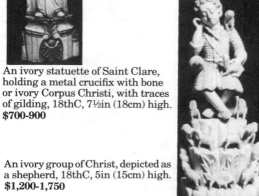

A carved ivory figure of the kneeling Virgin, with traces of polychrome, 18thC, 7in (17.5cm) high.
$3,000-4,500

An ivory group of Christ, depicted as a shepherd, 18thC, 5in (15cm) high.
$1,200-1,750

A Flemish ivory group of putti with a goat, in the style of Van Opstal, on an ebony and ivory pedestal, minor breaks and repairs, 18thC, 6½in (17cm) high.
$5,000-7,500

A carved ivory portrait relief, reputedly of Sir Richard Lovelace, in the manner of Van der Hagen, some repairs to border, 18thC, 3½in (8.5cm).
$700-900

A part set of 11 of 12 carved ivory portrait reliefs of Caesars, mounted in 2 ripple moulded ebonised frames, 18thC.
$4,000-5,500

An Indo-Colonial ivory pipe case, with hinged lid extensively applied with relief carved foliage and maskheads, terminating in a cone, 18thC, 21½in (55cm) long.
$7,000-10,000

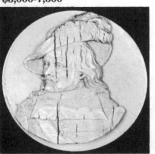

A Flemish carved ivory portrait relief, of a 17thC cavalier, on an ivory mount, 3in (7.5cm) high.
$400-550

A relief carved bone snuff box lid, depicting a couple in a wood, within a trailing vine surround, late 17thC, mounted on a later ivory box, 3½in (8.5cm).
$400-550

An ivory casket, on claw supports, probably French, mid-19thC, 15in (38cm) wide.
$9,000-12,500

A French ivory needle case, carved with shells and other rocaille in shallow relief, 18thC, 4½in (11.5cm).
$800-1,200

A carved ivory oliphant, probably Dieppe, c1860, 37in (94cm).
$4,000-5,500

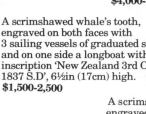

A pair of curved ivory elephant tusks, on stepped ebonised bases, 72in (182.5cm) high.
$4,000-5,500

An ivory horn, the upper part carved with a figural finial, the rest covered with leather, dark creamy patina, 21½in (54cm) high, on stand.
$1,300-2,000

A Flemish ebony, tortoiseshell and ivory mirror, with easel support, late 17th/early 18thC, 27½in (70cm) high.
$4,000-5,500

A scrimshawed whale's tooth, engraved on both faces with 3 sailing vessels of graduated size, and on one side a longboat with the inscription 'New Zealand 3rd Oct. 1837 S.D', 6½in (17cm) high.
$1,500-2,500

A scrimshaw whale's tooth, engraved on one side with the Battle of the Constitution and the Guerriere, engraved on the reverse with a woman amidst foliage, with foliate border, 6in (15cm) long.
$1,200-1,750

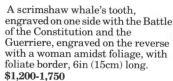

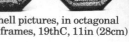

An ivory anatomical female figure, in the style of Stephen Zwick, South German, raised on 4 ivory ball feet, internal organs and one torso pin missing, late 17thC, 9½in (24cm) long.
$2,000-3,000

A Continental ivory ewer, 19thC, 10in (25.5cm) high.
$5,000-7,500

A carved ivory handle, in the form of a cherub, carrying a basket of fruit on his head, supporting a cartouche shaped embossed hand mirror, probably later, 18thC, 13in (33cm) high.
$800-1,200

An Indo-Colonial ivory cane handle, in the form of a dragon's head, 5in (13cm) high.
$600-900

A German lathe-turned ivory cup, some damage, 18thC, 11in (28cm) high.
$8,000-11,000

A pair of sailor's shell valentines, one arranged as a cross, the other with the motto 'Be True', in glazed octagonal frames, late 19thC, 21in (53cm) wide.
$800-1,200

Three shell pictures, in octagonal wooden frames, 19thC, 11in (28cm) wide.
$800-1,200

Tortoiseshell

A German tortoiseshell mounted crucifix, with silvered metal appliques, and bulbous Baroque style hexagonal foot, 17thC, 12in (30.5cm) high.
$800-1,200

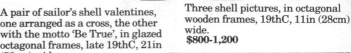

A tortoiseshell box and cover, inset with an ivory panel, carved with 2 reclining lovers, 3in (7.5cm).
$400-550

A Regency tortoiseshell clad sarcophagus tea caddy, 7½in (19cm) wide.
$8,000-11,000

Marble

A Milanese marble group of The Virgin and Child, by Agostino Busti called Il Bambaia, some damage, early 16thC, 9in (23cm) high.
$8,000-11,000

A white marble study of a partially nude female, on grey veined marble plinth, 19thC, 33in (84cm) high.
$2,500-3,500

A white marble figure of a barefoot peasant girl, on a grey marble plinth, some damage, 19thC, 22in (56cm) high.
$300-500

A marble figure of a nude maiden, seated on a pedestal, signed Pugi, 27in (69cm) high.
$3,000-4,500

A white marble sculpture, probably Diana, in her role as the great mother of Nature goddess, partially clad and holding her breasts, with 2 suckling dogs at her feet, 46in (116.5cm) high.
$8,000-11,000

A Victorian carved marble figure of a young girl feeding corn to a dove on her shoulder, 30½in (77cm) high.
$3,000-4,500

An Italian marble figure of Apollo Belvedere, some restoration, 19thC, 50in (127cm) high.
$14,000-19,000

An American marble group of 2 children asleep on a mattress, by William Rinehart, on an integral plinth signed W.H. Rinehart Sculpt., lower marble plinth, velvet covered wooden pedestal, 19thC, 35½in (90cm) wide.
$80,000-112,000

An English marble bust of General George Guy Carlton L'Estrange, inscribed on the reverse 'Lt. General George Carlton L'Estrange' and 'W. Theed 1853', 27½in (70cm) high, on marbleised pedestal.
$3,000-4,500

An English marble bust of an elderly gentleman, by Sir Francis Chantrey, wearing a toga, signed Chantry, Sculptor 1816, 24½in (62cm) high.
$8,000-11,000

A Victorian white marble bust of Sir John Knight by John Durham, 29in (74cm) high.
$1,200-1,750

A carved marble hound, 14in (35.5cm) high.
$300-500

A white marble bust of a young woman in 19thC dress and Neopolitan bonnet, on socle, 31in (79cm) high.
$2,250-3,500

A marble bust of 'Freddie', the sculptor's son, at the age of 6, signed on the reverse F. W. Pomeroy Sc. 1917, on antico verde socle, 20½in (52cm) high, with veined yellow marble pedestal.
$4,000-5,500

An Indian white marble low table, on baluster legs, Jaipur, 28in (71cm) wide.
$1,000-1,500

An Italian Sienna marble miniature sarcophagus, the lid with scrolling ends and inscribed Cornelio. C.N.F. Scipio, with an inscription on black marble base, 8in (20cm) wide.
$3.000-4.000

An Indian white marble bench, the solid seat on baluster legs, Jaipur, 48in (122cm) wide.
$3,000-4,000

A pair of Louis XVI style ormolu mounted rouge marble urns, fitted for electricity, early 20thC, 20in (51cm) high.
$3,000-4,000

◄ A blue marble vase of Louis XVI design, the ovoid body with twin ormolu satyr mask heads, on spreading foot and square plinth, 15½in (40cm) high.
$2,000-3,000

A gilt metal mounted red marble urn, in the style of Thomas Hope, fitted for electricity, 16½in (42cm) high excluding shade. ▶
$800-1,200

A pair of rouge marble Corinthian columns, with ormolu mounts, on square stepped bases, late 19thC, 52in (132cm) high.
$6,000-9,000

A pair of black and brown mottled marble pedestals, with turned capitals and socles, on square bases, 42½in (108cm) high.
$1,500-2,500

Terracotta/Stone

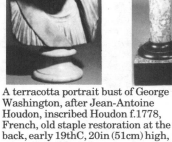

A German/Dutch terracotta bust of the young Bacchus, attributed to Guillaume de Groff, cracked and repaired, on terracotta socle, 17thC, 13½in (34cm) high.
$3,000-4,000

A terracotta portrait bust of George Washington, after Jean-Antoine Houdon, inscribed Houdon f.1778, French, old staple restoration at the back, early 19thC, 20in (51cm) high, on grey marble socle.
$2,000-3,000

A French terracotta bust of a child, by Gustave Deloye, signed on the rim Gustave Deloye 79, minor abrasions, on marble stand, late 19thC, 12½in (32cm) high.
$1,000-1,500

A terracotta portrait bust of Mlle. Vigee Lebrun, after Augustin Pajou, French, 19thC, 25in (63cm) high.
$3,000-4,000

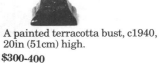

A Victorian terracotta bust of Marie Antoinette, 32in (81cm) high.
$1,500-2,500

A painted terracotta bust, c1940, 20in (51cm) high.
$300-400

A terracotta ridge tile, straddled by the figure of a winged dragon in the Gothic style, 19thC, 24in (61cm).
$150-250

A French moulded terracotta group, entitled Enfance de Silène, in the manner of Clodion, 19thC, 15in (38cm) high.
$800-1,200

A French terracotta group of a satyr and 2 putti, in the manner of Clodion, minor chips and damage to fingers, on octagonal plinth, 19thC, 18½in (47cm) high.
$300-500

A terracotta group, sculptured in the manner of George Tinworth, some damage, 18in (46cm).
$200-350

An Italian terracotta relief of The Madonna and Child, after Desiderio da Settignano's 'Sabauda Madonna', 16thC, in a carved walnut frame with sliding glass, 22in (56cm) high.
$3,000-4,000

An Italian terracotta relief of the raising of Lazurus, some damage, late 17thC, 19in (48cm) high, with a moulded wood frame and backing with old collection of gallery and customs labels.
$4,000-5,500

A Limestone otter, English, c1500.
$2,500-3,500

A stone lion, 18thC.
$2,500-3,500

Two hardstone planters, the green planter issuing 6 pink and white quartz peonies, the other of 8 flowers and green quartz leaves, 10in (25.5cm) high.
$1.500-2,500

A dark green and white flecked hardstone baluster vase and domed cover, 15in (38cm) high, on elaborate hardwood stand.
$5,000-7,500

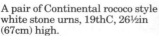

A pair of Continental rococo style white stone urns, 19thC, 26½in (67cm) high.
$6,000-9,000

A set of 4 Italian neo-classical style alabaster urns, fitted for electricity, 18in (46cm) high.
$4,000-5,500

An English Gothic sandstone water stoup, carved with a pair of Green Man faces and twisted foliage behind, with round receptacle in top, 14th/16thC, 11in (28cm) high.
$800-1,200

Woodcarvings

A Raeren brown glazed stoneware baluster tankard, with an inscription dated 1600, with contemporary hinged pewter cover, minor chips, 10in (25cm) high.
$2,000-3,000

An oak Renaissance carved panel, 16thC.
$300-500

A pair of walnut carvings, 17thC, 29½in (75cm) high.
$2,000-3,000

An oak panel of a dragon, 17thC.
$1,500-2,500

An oak panel, 16thC.
$300-500

A pair of oak carvings, 17thC, 16½in (42cm) high.
$300-500

A carved oak panel depicting Adam and Eve, Flemish, 17thC, 17in (43cm) high.
$1,000-1,500

A carved wooden cresting with cupids and flowers, probably Italian, 18thC, 86in (218cm) wide.
$450-700

A French polychromed carving with original decoration, c1710, 27in (68.5cm) high.
$600-900

A Continental carved wooden tankard, with hinged cover and lion finial, on 4 crouching lion supports, 8in (20cm).
$2,000-3,000

A carved lime group, early 19thC, 10in (25cm).
$300-500

A pair of Régence giltwood wall brackets, early 18thC, 9in (23cm) high.
$10,000-13,500

A pair of English carved oak dogs, 19thC, 9in (23cm).
$150-250

A European carved wood figure of a stag with a tree and glass flower epergne, 11½in (29cm) high.
$150-250

A carved lion's head, 19thC.
$300-500

◀ An Edwardian carved wood bear umbrella stand, 35in (89cm).
$800-1,200

A Swiss carved wood stick stand, 19thC, 35½in (90cm) high.
$2,000-3,000

A Black Forest carved wood smoker's stand, with musical movement playing 2 airs, the whole supported by a standing bear, 35in (89cm) high.
$1,000-1,500

▶

A carved wood polychromed shop sign, in the form of a gentleman in period costume, 18thC, 34in (86cm) high.
$9,000-12,500

A carved wood recumbent figure of a dog, with large ears and a bushy tail, 34in (86cm) wide.
$6,000-9,000

A carved wood midshipman, 48in (122cm) high.
$1,000-1,500

A pair of carved oak female figures, Flemish, c1580, 18in (46cm).
$1,500-2,500

A dummy board, in the form of Justice, balance missing, early 19thC, 71in (180cm).
$2,000-3,000

A Flemish wood figure of St. John, carved in relief, repairs to left thumb and forefinger, 17thC, 13½in (34cm) high.
$9,000-12,500

A walnut carving of a horse-drover and horse, pulling a section of a tree, from the workshop at Brienz, Switzerland, carved by A. L. B. Huggler, c1900, 34in (86cm) wide.
$2,000-3,000

A German pinewood skull, 17thC, 7½in (19cm) high.
$3,000-4,500

Antiquities

Marble

Metalware

A Roman marble commemorative tablet, the inscription reading 'Q. Pacuvius Stipius Giulio Isochruso Cognato Suo Locumdonavitob Meritis, 5in (13cm) square.
$600-900

A Roman marble relief of Eros, the face carved with up-turned reticulated pupils and framed by locks of wavy hair, surrounded by stylised wings, scrolls and foliage, 2nd-3rd Century AD, 8 by 12in (20 by 30cm).
$800-1,200

A Roman bronze figure of the child, Harpokrates, seated naked on an amphora, c2nd Century AD, 4.7cm long.
$100-200

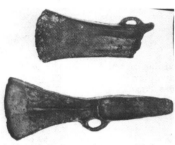

A British bronze palstave, with loop for securing to the haft, 6½in (17cm) long, and a British bronze socket celt with loop, 4½in (12cm) long, both early 1st Millennium.
$700-900

An Amlash bronze dagger, with leaf shaped blade and openwork conical hilt, c2000 BC, 11in (28cm).
$600-900

A pair of Roman bronze model feet, socketed, the sandals with dotted ornament, c2nd Century AD, 3in (8cm) long.
$300-500

A Syro-Palestinian bronze axe head, with concave ridges around the circular socket, c2000 BC, 6in (15.5cm) long.
$400-550

A Romano British bronze fibula, with linear decoration and onion shaped terminals, 3rd-4th Century AD, 2½in (6.5cm) long, and a Roman bronze weight in the form of a stylised winged figure, with a loop for suspension, 2½in (6.5cm) high.
$75-150

A Roman bronze bust of Athena, her hair swept back underneath a plumed helmet, wearing a draped tunic with incised scales, 2nd Century AD, 3½in (8.5cm) high.
$400-550

Pottery

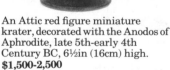

A Greek geometric pottery pyxis and cover, the rim and cover pierced for attachment, late 8th Century BC, 4½in (11.5cm) diam of rim.
$800-1,200

A Greek geometric pottery bowl, decorated with concentric banding, zig-zags and a rosette on the base, late 5th Century BC, 8cm diam of rim.
$300-500

An Attic red figure miniature krater, decorated with the Anodos of Aphrodite, late 5th-early 4th Century BC, 6½in (16cm) high.
$1,500-2,500

A collection of Roman red glaze bowls, with various potter's stamps, Lecoux Potteries, central Gaul, late 2nd Century AD.
$400-550

The 5 vessels were recovered from Puddingpan Rock, Herne Bay, Kent.

Miscellaneous

A Boeotian geometric terracotta figure of a horse, with high braided mane, decorated with stripes, rider missing, mid-6th Century BC, 5in (12.5cm) high.
$600-900

A Greek terracotta figure of a cockerel, with painted comb and tail feathers, Boeotia or Rhodes, 1st half 5th Century BC, 8.2cm high.
$600-900

A Boeotian geometric terracotta figure of a horse and rider, tail and rider's head missing, mid-6th Century BC, 4½in (12cm) high.
$300-500

A Khmer stone carving of Buddha, seated in dhyanasana on a stepped snake base, rising to a snake head canopy behind him, some damage, 13th Century, 11½in (29cm) high.
$400-550

An Egyptian Anthropoid wood mask, with traces of red pigment around the large bulbous eyes, Ptolemaic Period, 7in (18cm) high.
$300-400

A Boeotian terracotta 'Pappades' figure, decorated with stripes and wavy lines, mid-6th Century AD, 7½in (17.5cm) high.
$700-900

A wood ushabti, the front incised with a line of hieroglyphs, New Kingdom, 7½in (19cm) high.
$800-1,200

An Egyptian wood ushabti, painted in yellow, the details applied in black and red with a column of hieroglyphs at the front, New Kingdom, 6½in (16cm) high.
$600-900

An Egyptian turquoise glaze ushabti carrying a pick, hoe and basket, the back pillar impressed with hieroglyphs, 26th Dynasty, 7½in (19cm) high.
$1,000-1,500

A turquoise glaze ushabti, with details in dark blue, 21st-22nd Dynasty, 4½in (12cm) high.
$400-550

An Egyptian turquoise glaze ushabti, the inscription at the front and the pick and hoe painted in black, late Dynastic Period, 4½in (11.5cm) high.
$400-550

An Egyptian pale green mottled glaze ushabti, the front impressed with a column of hieroglyphs, 6in (15.5cm), and a pottery ushabti with traces of pale blue glaze with impressed hieroglyphs, 5in (12.5cm) high, both late Dynastic Period.
$600-900

An Egyptian blue glaze ushabti, the details and 6 lines of hieroglyphs in dark blue glaze, 21st Dynasty, 6½in (16.5cm).
$1,200-1,750

An Egyptian mummified hawk, complete with wrappings, late Dynastic Period, 8¼in (22cm) long.
$600-900

An Egyptian green glaze ushabti, the back clearly impressed with a column of hieroglyphs, late Dynastic Period, 4½in (11cm) high.
$3,000-4,500

An Egyptian cartonnage mask with inlaid eyes and gilded face, with scarab, glass paste eyes with blue surrounds and brows, the back of the wig painted with the mummified figure of a deity, Ptolemaic Period, 3rd-1st Century BC, 21in (53cm) high.
$10,000-13,500

Rugs & Carpets

GLOSSARY

Abrash	Variations of density in a colour seen in a carpet by irregular horizontal washes, can greatly add to the value
Aniline	Chemical dye, a derivative of coal-tar, first produced in the 1860s, most common in the red-blue-purple range, colours tend to fade (orange-pink, for instance can fade to walnut-brown)
Boteh	Widespread pattern of Persian origin (original meaning 'cluster of leaves'), used in Europe in the Paisley pattern
Ch'ang	Chinese endless knot, the inextricable knot of destiny
Chrome dye	A fast synthetic dye now used in all the major rug weaving areas, colours do not fade
Gol Henai Pattern	Floral pattern associated with Persian rugs, mainly found on Hamadan rugs
Hejira (or Hijra)	The beginning of the Muhammedan calendar, 16 July, AD 622
Herati Pattern	Also called the mahi or fish pattern. This common pattern originated in East Persia
Jufti	'False' knot, either Turkish or Persian, whereby the knots are tied to four, not two, warp threads
Kelim	Also spelled kilim, gilim, gelim. Principally from Anatolia
Madder	Deep red-brown dye
Palas	Caucasian name for kelim
Palmette	A flowerhead of heart-shape with many radiating lobes or petals
Sileh	A corruption of a now lost Caucasian place name. A form of Soumak, sileh pieces tend to be woven with rows of large S-motifs
Soumak	Sumak, Summak, Sumacq, Sumakh, thought to be a corruption of Shemaka, town in south east Caucasus
Spandrels	Architectural term for the space between the curve of an arch and the enclosing mouldings
Swastika	A hooked cross. Chinese symbol for 10,000 (wan) and happiness
Tiraz	Official weaving factory usually set up under Royal patronage

A Louis Philippe Aubusson rug, the floral sprays on a chocolate ground, 73 by 78in (185 by 198cm).
$5,000-7,500

A Bergama rug, with plum red field, 77 by 64in (196 by 162cm).
$1,300-2,000

A Bessarabian octagonal kelim of Western influence, with 2 flowerhead medallions, 84 by 57in (212 by 146cm).
$2,000-3,000

An Aubusson tapestry carpet, the plum field with ivory floral medallion, 19thC, 159 by 118in (404 by 300cm).
$6,000-9,000

A Beshir prayer rug, the ivory field around a brick red prayer panel, slight wear, repaired, 77 by 40in (196 by 102cm).
$4,000-5,500

A Bidjov rug, the indigo field covered with stylised birds, animals and human figures in panels of ivory, mauve, tan and light green, 77 by 52in (196 by 132cm).
$3,000-4,500

A Caucasian carpet, with 3 columns of palmettes, flowerheads, vine and lilies in a tomato red field, slight damage, repairs, late 18thC, 196 by 87in (497 by 222cm).
$10,500-15,000

A Chodor carpet, the brown field with 4 columns of Tauk Nuska guls divided by secondary guls, very slight wear, 108 by 70in (274 by 178cm).
$1,500-2,500

A Hamadan rug.
$600-900

A Ghiordes prayer rug, with plain ivory field, the stepped 'mihrab' with ivory and blue floral stripes, in an ivory and brown floral striped border between pale beige floral stripes, a short kilim strip at each end, slight overall wear, 83 by 58in (210 by 147cm).
$4,000-5,500

A Hereke rug, the ivory field with eau-de-nil tracery vine around a turquoise flowerhead lozenge and escutcheon panel within a similar broad red and pale turquoise floral border, signed, 71 by 48in (180 by 122cm).
$3,000-4,500

A silk Heriz prayer rug, the dark caramel field with scrolling vine and palmettes flanked by columns supporting a salmon pink 'mihrab', in an ivory palmette and vine border between light blue flowering vine strips, areas of slight wear, replaced selvedges, 72 by 53in (183 by 135cm).
$8,000-11,000

A Hereke carpet, the ivory field with scrolling vine in a multiple burgundy and ivory palmette, signature cartouche at one end, 172 by 117in (439 by 296cm).
$5,000-7,500

A large Hereke carpet, the shaded lilac field with an Ardebil design, in cream, lilac, burgundy and ivory, with signature cartouche, 195 by 162in (495 by 412cm).
$5,000-7,500

A Heriz carpet, the indigo field with terracotta, powder blue, rose and mustard palmette pendant medallion, 210 by 141in (535 by 360cm).
$8,000-11,000

An Isfahan rug, with ivory field, 84 by 57in (213 by 144.5cm).
$2,000-3,000

An Isfahan Serafian rug, the ivory field with a central red and ice blue medallion, signature cartouche at one end, 94 by 57in (238 by 145cm).
$14,000-19,000

A Hereke rug, the burgundy field with an Isfahan vase carpet design, a signature cartouche at one end, repaired, 101 by 84in (256 by 213cm).
$5,000-7,500

An Isfahan Tree of Life rug, the ivory field with trees, birds and animals, within a madder cartouche border and 4 guard stripes, 82 by 55in (208 by 139cm).
$2,000-3,000

An Isfahan rug, the crimson field with an ivory cartouche pendant medallion and all over floral and foliate stems, within mustard spandrels and a main indigo floral border, 84 by 56in (213 by 142cm).
$2,000-3,000

A pictorial hooked rug, depicting a ship at sea in green, blue and red with a black border, 19thC, 24 by 35in (61 by 89cm).
$100-150

A floral hooked rug, American, with oval medallion of flowerheads in green, blue, yellow and brown and surrounded by a geometric border in similar tones, late 19th/early 20thC, 104 by 69in (264 by 175cm).
$600-700

A Chinese carpet, the plain blue field with light blue angular spandrels, 136 by 107in (344 by 272cm).
$8,000-11,000

A Chodor rug, the fox brown field with stylised floral lozenges in ivory, burgundy, ice blue and sea green, some wear, repaired, 105 by 61in (266 by 155cm).
$800-1,200

A pictorial hooked runner, American, in 2 parts, depicting parrots with button eyes, urns and flowers in red, orange, blue, purple, green and brown, late 19thC, 54 by 16in (137 by 40.5cm).
$500-1,000

A Caucasian kilim, the field with serrated and stepped medallions in various colours, some damage, repairs, 117 by 68in (297 by 172cm).
$1,200-1,750

A Chinese carpet, the ivory ground woven with a peacock, a crane and 2 swimming ducks, with dark blue outer border, 116 by 84in (290 by 215cm).
$7,000-10,000

A Caucasian kilim, the field divided into broad ivory bands divided by multi-coloured smaller bands of stepped lozenges, 122 by 51in (309 by 130cm).
$1,500-2,600

A Caucasian kilim, the blue field with diagonal rows of ivory, red, yellow and brown lozenges, some damage, 116 by 61in (294 by 155cm).
$600-900

A Chichi rug, the indigo field with rows of hooked lozenges divided by rows of octagonal flowerheads, 77 by 49in (196 by 124cm).
$8,000-11,000

A Davarghin kilim, in dark brown and brick red, 127 by 58in (322 by 147cm).
$1,500-2,500

A Daghestan prayer rug, the ivory field with stylised plants and flowerheads, slight wear, 55 by 43in (140 by 109cm).
$3,000-4,500

A Dhurrie, the ivory field with rows of concentric blue, red and pale blue medallions, alternating with rows of stylised fleur-de-lys, in a shaded lilac border with red key pattern, 116 by 74in (294 by 188cm).
$1,200-1,750

A Derbend corridor rug, on blue ground.
$700-900

A Derbend runner, the rust field with 5 indigo medallions, octagons and scattered motifs enclosed by an ivory rosette meander border, dated 1890, 196 by 52in (500 by 132cm).
$3,000-4,500

A Dhurrie, the shaded pale blue field with central rust brown floral medallion and similar in each corner, areas of repair, one end stained, 192 by 165in (488 by 419cm).
$1,500-2,500

A Dhurrie, the light blue field with a stylised angular lattice enclosing large flowering plants, in a shaded buff border of hooked vine, repaired and stained, 157 by 113in (398 by 286cm).
$1,200-1,750

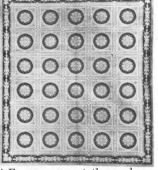

A Dhurrie, the pale green field with staggered rows of large pale blue flowerhead medallions surrounded by tendrils, in a broad purple flowering vine border, repaired and stained, 162 by 144in (412 by 366cm).
$1,500-2,500

A European carpet, the mushroom brown field with a square floral trellis, enclosing indigo flowerhead roundels with scrolling spandrels in an indigo spray border with outer plain stripe, 142 by 121in (360 by 307cm).
$5,000-7,500

A Fereghan rug, the indigo herati field with rose herati meander border, 70 by 58in (178 by 147cm).
$1,000-1,500

A needlework carpet, woven in bright colours with a central spray of summer flowers and oval band of foliage, the wide borders with scrolling foliage and fruit on an ivory ground, signed A. Galliard, 1804, repaired, mid-19thC, 109 by 82 in (276 by 208cm).
$10,500-15,000

A Karabagh kelim, the black ground with 2 bouquets in a floral spray frame, 164 by 74in (416 by 188cm).
$5,000-7,500

A Karabagh kelim, the black field with 3 bouquets surrounded by sprays with birds and stylised human figures, in an open spray border, repaired, 145 by 62in (368 by 157cm).
$2,000-3,000

A pair of Kashan rugs of prayer influence, the indigo field with powder blue floral spandrels, enclosed by red floral and indigo palmette panelled borders, 83 by 54in (210 by 138cm).
$6,000-9,000

A Karagashli rug, the indigo field with stylised flowerheads, flower vases and animals around 3 red floral medallions, a short kelim strip at each end, very slight overall wear, 54 by 38in (137 by 95.6cm).
$5,000-7,500

A pair of Kashan rugs, each indigo field with a floral design, madder medallion and spandrels, with twin guard stripes, 82 by 53in (208 by 135cm).
$4,000-5,500

A Kashgai rug, the indigo field with all over designs of stylised birds and flowers, with multi-coloured border, 109 by 60in (277 by 151cm).
$2,250-3,500

A Kashan rug, with central medallion, on a deep pink field, within a deep blue floral border, 72 by 48in (182 by 122cm).
$800-1,200

A Kashan rug with a Tree of Life, flowers and birds on a pale green field, one main camel ground border and several narrow borders, damaged, 81 by 52in (205 by 132cm).
$3,000-4,500

A Kazak rug, 82 by 57in (208 by 145cm).
$10,000-13,500

A Kashgai rug, the hooked rust red field with repeated rows of multi-coloured floral botehs, within an ivory serrated leaf and palmette meander border, 50 by 38in (126 by 98cm).
$1,500-2,500

A Kazak prayer rug, the red 'mihrab' with green lozenges, blue arch enclosed by an ivory leaf and calyx border, 48 by 40in (122 by 102cm).
$1,000-1,500

A Kazak rug, the red field with 2 columns of light blue and indigo medallions, in an ivory border, a short kelim strip at each end, 81 by 50in (206 by 127cm).
$2,250-3,500

A Khorrassan prayer rug, the ivory field with flowering tree with palmettes, 2 inscription cartouches between red and blue stripes dated AH 1316 (AD 1898), 90 by 65in (228 by 165cm).
$4,000-5,500

A pair of Kirman rugs, with ivory fields, central medallions and three line borders, 74 by 45in (188 by 114cm).
$800-1,200

A Kirman mille fleurs prayer rug, the shaded yellow field with floral sprays issuing from a baluster vase within a light blue floral frame, 109 by 82in (276 by 208cm).
$4,000-5,500

A Kirman carpet, the ivory field with all over floral and foliate 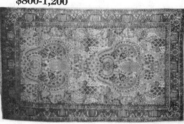 designs in pale blue, rose and ivory, with blue floral border, 110 by 73in (280 by 186cm).
$3,000-4,500

A Kirman rug, with an inscription cartouche at one end stating 'To the order of (?) Mukhya Kirmani', 84 by 53in (213 by 135cm).
$7,000-10,000

A Konya carpet, the shaded burgundy field with blue and deep aubergine octagons, with a broad blue border of stylised flowerheads and vine, areas of slight repair and wear, 149 by 67in (379 by 170cm).
$8,000-11,000

A Konagkend rug, the indigo field with stylised ivory floral lattice in a broad indigo stylised 'kufic' border between baton, zig-zag and skittle pattern stripes, slight overall wear, repaired, 61 by 49in (155 by 125cm).
$1,300-2,000

A Kuba rug, the dark brown field with stylised flowerheads, palmettes and animals around 3 ivory and red medallions, in an ivory stepped border, slight damage to one end, 77 by 50in (196 by 127cm).
$4,000-5,500

A Kuba Leshgi rug, the brick red field scattered with stylised flowerheads and blue and ivory octagons around 3 Leshgi medallions, a short kelim strip at each end, very slight overall wear, 55 by 47in (140 by 119cm).
$3,000-4,500

A Kuba Shirvan rug, the royal blue field scattered with ivory stellar octagons, stylised plants and animals around a string of ivory and royal blue palmette lozenges in a border of red, blue, apricot and green hooked lozenges, braided ends, 66 by 44in (168 by 112cm).
$4,000-5,500

An Afshar rug, with short kilim strip at each end, slight damage, 133 by 65in (337 by 165cm).
$3,000-4,500

An Abadeh rug, the ivory field with traditional vases of flowers, 78 by 56in (198 by 143cm).
$900-1,300

An Afshar rug, with double diamond panels on blue ground, 74 by 52in (188 by 132cm).
$1,500-2,500

An Agra carpet, the ivory field with wine floral spandrels, with turquoise guard stripes, 139 by 116in (353 by 295cm).
$5,000-7,500

An Afshar rug.
$150-250

A pair of Aubusson 'entre fenêtres', the ivory fields with neo-classical flower stands, some damage, 19thC, 117in (298cm).
$6,000-8,000

An Aubusson tapestry carpet, in deep rose and ivory within aubergine spandrels, 19thC, 116 by 98in (290 by 249cm).
$10,500-15,000

A Bergama rug, the rust field enclosed by an ivory quartered flowerhead border, 73 by 56½in (185 by 144cm).
$1,200-1,750

An Aubusson carpet, the central floral spray on a celadon ground, reduced, mid-19thC, 80½ by 76½in (204 by 194cm).
$7,500-10,500

A Chinese carpet, the golden-beige field with open floral roundel and sprays, plain outer stripe, 140 by 108in (355 by 275cm).
$9,000-12,500

An Empire Aubusson carpet, with central flowerhead and a circlet of summer flowers on a khaki ground, 184 by 197in (467 by 500cm).
$8,000-11,000

A Caucasian kilim, the field divided into alternate indigo and brick red bands of stepped and hooked lozenges, slight wear, repaired, 113 by 63in (286 by 160cm).
$2,000-3,000

A Kuba rug, the fox brown field with 3 ivory, red and blue Leshgi medallions, slight wear overall, 68 by 39in (173 by 99cm).
$2,500-3,500

A Melas prayer rug, the headed brown 'mihrab' with ivory spandrels enclosed by a saffron stella border and meander floral guard stripe, 56 by 47in (142 by 119cm).
$800-1,200

A Moghan rug, the ivory field with 2 columns of hooked stepped cruciform medallions, damaged, 92 by 43in (234 by 109cm).
$3,000-4,500

A Persian Qum, with ivory field and 3 inner and 5 outer guard stripes, signed, 163 by 122in (414 by 309cm).
$14,000-19,000

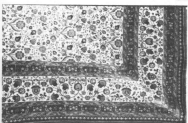

A Qashqai kelim, the brick red field with light blue, apricot and brown serrated lozenges, with an ivory border of concentric lozenges, and an outer reciprocal lozenge stripe, 86 by 57in (218 by 145cm).
$1,000-1,500

A Kuba rug, the fox brown field with blue, ivory, red and yellow Leshgi medallions, areas of slight wear, small repairs, 104 by 41in (261 by 104cm).
$1,500-2,500

A Moghan rug, the field divided into 2 columns of alternate red and royal blue panels containing octagons, a short kelim strip at each end, 67 by 48in (170 by 122cm).
$8,000-11,000

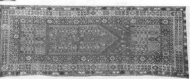

A Moroccan prayer carpet, the brick red field with columns of stylised plants and flower vases, the stepped and hooked green 'mihrab' with similar motifs, with an ivory stylised flowerhead and roundel border, very slight overall wear, Rabat, 216 by 78in (548 by 192cm).
$4,000-5,500

A Perepedil rug, the blue field with ram's horn and key design, some wear and damage, 70 by 53in (177 by 134cm).
$2,000-3,000

A Mahal rug, the brick red field with a column of flowerheads and flowering vine, between blue and ivory floral stripes, slight wear, 92 by 57in (234 by 145cm).
$1,500-2,500

A Malayir Kelleh, the brick red field with 'herati' pattern, around a string of cusped floral medallions, one end slightly damaged, 159 by 69in (403 by 175cm).
$2,000-3,000

A Ninghsia rug, the yellow field with a rice grain pattern around a cusped beige, pink and blue floral medallion, areas of corrosion and slight wear, 81 by 55in (206 by 140cm).
$4,000-5,500

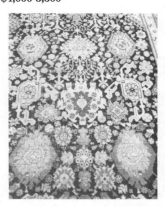

A North West Persian corridor carpet, with indigo field and brick red border between ivory strips, a few areas of slight wear, 238 by 76in (604 by 193cm).
$2,000-3,000

A Qashqai kelim, the brick red field with diagonal rows of multi-coloured hooked lozenges, embroidered skirts at each end, 118 by 62in (299 by 157cm).
$2,000-3,000

A Qashqai rug, the indigo field with 'herati' pattern, in a brick red flowering vine border between light blue and ivory flowering vine stripes, associated tassels, 77 by 55in (195 by 140cm).
$9,000-12,500

A Perepedil rug, the indigo field with 'wurma' motifs, stylised peacocks, enclosed by an indigo 'kufic' border, repaired, 61 by 42in (156 by 106cm).
$4,000-5,500

A Romanian carpet, the burgundy field with a Mughal design, very slight wear, 187 by 141in (474 by 358cm).
$2,000-3,000

A Rya rug, with chocolate brown field, a horse's head encircled by leafy sprays, in a plain red border inscribed 'MB 1885', 51 by 41in (129 by 104cm).
$1,200-1,750

A Sarouk rug, the indigo field with 'herati' pattern around a yellow hooked medallion, 78 by 52in (198 by 132cm).
$10,000-13,500

A Senneh rug, the indigo field with 'herati' pattern around ivory and indigo concentric 'boteh' with deer and lions, a kelim strip at each end, 78 by 55in (198 by 142cm).
$8,000-11,000

A Senneh rug, the stepped ivory 'herati' field with an indigo and red medallion, enclosed by a red 'herati' border, 72 by 51in (183 by 130cm).
$1,500-2,500

A Shirvan prayer rug, with a broad ivory border of multi-coloured hooked motifs between stripes, 64 by 37in (163 by 94cm).
$4,000-5,500

A Shirvan rug, the indigo field scattered with stylised flowerheads, birds and human figures, in a brick red stylised glass and serrated leaf border, 59 by 42in (150 by 107cm).
$3,000-4,500

A Shirvan prayer rug, the saffron 'mihrab' with a trellis design, and an ivory serrated leaf and calyx border, 53 by 37in (135 by 93cm).
$2,500-3,500

A Shirvan prayer rug, the pistachio green field with a lattice of multi-coloured serrated 'boteh', with stylised flowerhead and skittle pattern stripes, slight overall wear and repair, 57 by 43in (145 by 109cm).
$2,000-3,000

A Shirvan rug, the indigo field with stepped and serrated medallions, enclosed by a main stylised bird's head border, 64 by 52in (162 by 132cm).
$2,250-3,500

Textiles

Costume

An apron of ivory silk, embroidered in gold and silver thread, and blue, red and green silk, with gold netted insertions, English, c1730, framed and glazed.
$1,200-1,750

A pair of Chinese deep horseshoe cuffs of midnight blue silk, embroidered in coloured silks and gold thread, altered, 19thC.
$450-700

A Chinese midnight blue silk robe, embroidered in coloured silks, the sleeves with ivory silk sleeve bands, lined, 19thC.
$700-900

A coat of green linen ribbed silk, embroidered in pink and green with sprays of rosebuds, buttoned full length, with embroidered buttons, European, mid-18thC.
$1,000-1,500

A Chinese robe, of blue kossu silk woven in coloured silks and gilt thread, lined in dark sky blue silk damask, 19thC.
$2,000-3,000

A Chinese child's robe, of scarlet silk damask, embroidered in coloured silks, with blue silk lining.
$450-700

A Chinese vest, of midnight blue silk embroidered in coloured silks and metal thread in Pekin knot and satin stitch, lined, 19thC.
$1,000-1,500

A Turkish coat, woven with rows of florets in red, green and yellow silks on an ivory ground and trimmed with blue braid, lined, early 19thC.
$100-150

A grey velvet mantle, stencilled in silver and gold with a band of trailing flowers, leaves and cone motifs, with salmon pink lining, and bearing the maker's label as a silk roundel Mariano Fortuny Venise, c1920.
$3,000-4,500

A Chinese dragon robe, of chestnut brown silk embroidered in coloured silks and gilt thread, lined in blue silk damask, 19thC.
$600-900

A Chinese grey silk coat, embroidered in Pekin knot and satin stitch with coloured silks, with embroidered ivory silk sleeve bands, lined, 19thC.
$700-900

An evening dress, of royal blue loosely woven linen and silk mix gauze, with a deep bias cut frill at the hem and a matching stole edged with a frill, lined in blue silk, by Balenciaga, 10 Avenue George V, Paris, c1965.
$1,000-1,500

A dress, embroidered with bands of large and small black sequins and bugle beads, with simulated harness belt of clear beads, studded with strass, c1920.
$600-900

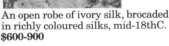

A black crêpe dress, the skirt with grey and cream crêpe insertions and ivory silk embroidery, c1920.
$400-550

An open robe of ivory silk, brocaded in richly coloured silks, mid-18thC.
$600-900

A red cotton gown, the trained skirt with flounced hem and trimmed with applied black and white cord, and a matching looped overskirt, c1870.
$700-900

A dusty pink velvet dress with full back bodice and bow trim, with maker's label Chanel, No. 47225, c1920.
$2,500-3,500

A burnt orange silk coat, with gold thread brocade, with deep cuffs and collar, c1920.
$200-350

A young girl's dress of dark green velvet and striped yellow silk, decorated with mother-of-pearl buttons, c1876.
$400-550

A cream crêpe dress, with bias cut skirt and pleated attached scarf, with underdress, the maker's label Molyneux, 48 Grosvenor Street, London, c1930.
$600-900

A white net dress, with bauble trim, the bodice and upper skirt with cotton cutwork and filet lace overlay, c1910.
$800-1,200

A black chiffon and silk dress, with tie to waistline and streamer hemline, bearing maker's label Molyneux, 5 Rue Royale, No. 35767, c1920.
$1,000-1,500

An ivory silk dress, with ivory chiffon and lace tiered overlay, c1910.
$1,000-1,500

An open robe and petticoat of ivory lustring, with padded decoration down the front, English, c1760.
$6,000-8,000

An unbleached linen child's frock and pantaloons, trimmed with white braid and buttons, c1810.
$600-900

A pink wool suit, with a matching blouse printed with an abstract design, in brown, orange, yellow and turquoise and woven with gilt thread, by Chanel, c1960.
$400-550

A boy's dress, of tartan silk trimmed with a band of sea green velvet and gilt metal buttons chased with a swirling design, lacking one button, c1868.
$600-900

A pair of saxe blue gentleman's silk stockings, embroidered with elaborate clocks in pink, yellow and white, c1740.
$1,000-1,500

A pair of glacé black kid slippers, the fronts embroidered with bouquets of flowers, trimmed with pale blue silk, c1840.
$1,000-1,500

The Court dress of King Otto of the Hellenes, comprising 'fermeli' and sleeved 'fermeloto ghileki' of blue facecloth, lavishly embroidered with silver braid and silvered metal ball buttons, and with standing collars of scarlet cloth with silver oak leaves and other lace in the Bavarian fashion, and one and a half pairs of leggings, and the court 'terliki' of Queen Amelia of black facecloth embroidered in gold braid and sequins, and a small 'ghileki' of silver lace with insertions of scarlet facecloth and gold lace and silver thread, pseudo buttons decorated with coral, c1835.
$18,500-26,000

A grey-blue wool frock coat, the collar, borders, cuffs and buttons embroidered in silver thread and sequins with garlands of flowers, lined with scarlet satin, lining torn, c1870.
$1,000-1,500

A pair of ivory silk stockings, initialled 'AB', numbered 36, the instep decorated with an inset of Brussels needlepoint lace, mid-19thC.
$1,000-1,500

A pair of slippers, of black silk and wool shawl material, woven with a Paisley design, c1840.
$800-1,200

A stomacher of undyed linen, embroidered mainly in green and red silks, c1700.
$1,000-1,500

A pair of shoes of mustard coloured ribbed silk, the toecaps trimmed with ruched ribbons, sequins and gold braid, the shoe also edged with gold lace, inscribed Miss Alsorne, English, worn, c1770, 3in (7.5cm) heels.
$3,000-4,000

A pair of glacé black kid slippers, embroidered in coloured silks on the front and heel, lined and trimmed with pink silk, c1840.
$1,200-1,750

An Edwardian lady's parasol, contained in a brass bound bamboo tube.
$150-250

A wide brimmed Sombrero, of white buckskin with floral decoration in violet silks and sequins on the band, by La Abeja, Talabarteria, Av.5 de Mayo 10 Mex, D.F., c1930.
$100-200

A North American plains Indian leather drawstring purse, with blue and white bead decoration, and an amulet shaped as an alligator worked in blue and white beads on leather, padded.
$200-350

The Lord Chancellor's bourse, of Lord Eldon, worked in high relief with royal arms in crimson silk, pink and blue silk metal threads, velvet and pearls, early 19thC, 16in (40.5cm) square, in carved wooden case.
$4,000-5,500

John Scot, first Earl of Eldon, 1751-1838, was Chancellor to George III and George IV and, having struggled to return to power under William IV, died in the reign of Queen Victoria. In 1800 a fresh bourse, possibly this one, would have been embroidered with the New Royal Arms, adopted upon the Act of Union. Lord Loughborough would have surrendered the Great Seal in it. At the King's death in 1820 all seals were defaced and became the property of their holders. Presumably this bourse with obsolete device became a perquisite of Eldon at the same time.

501

Embroidery

An embroidered panel for a stool, worked in coloured wools with a naturalistic spray of roses against a black background, c1875, 25 by 38in (63 by 96cm).
$1,000-1,500

An embroidered picture, worked in coloured wools, mostly browns and greens, with a lion and a tiger, c1860, 11 by 17in (28 by 43cm), framed and glazed.
$400-550

Lace

A fragment of Mezzo Punto bobbin and needle lace, possibly English, c1690.
$150-200

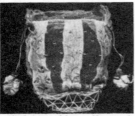

A lady's workbag of knitted and bobbin lace made straw, fastened with bauble trim, the whole worked in pink, brown and cream, mid-18thC.
$1,000-1,500

A bridal veil of tamboured net, designed with flower sprays and sprigs, late 19thC, 79in (200cm) square.
$400-550

A Canton embroidered cover, of peach pink silk satin worked in pastel silks, lined in sky blue silk, late 19th/early 20thC, 92in (233.5cm) square.
$200-350

Four panels from an embroidered screen, worked in coloured silks with various scenes, damaged, mid-18thC, each 16in (40.5cm) wide.
$1,000-1,500

A deep alb flounce of Flemish bobbin lace, designed with floral motifs, swags, canopies and scrolls, c1760, 104 by 15½in (266 by 39cm).
$200-350

A handkerchief of ivory silk, with scalloped edge trimmed with Valenciennes lace, the border embroidered with houses amidst sprays of leaves and flowers, one corner with initial 'L' surmounted by a coronet, late 19thC.
$400-550
Possibly bears the initial of Queen Victoria's daughter Louise 1848-1939, who married the Marquess of Lorne, Duke of Argyll.

A large embroidered picture of Nelson's tomb, worked mostly in red, white and blue wools, c1855, 21½ by 29in (54 by 74cm), framed and glazed.
$2,250-3,500

An embroidered screen, worked in pale coloured silks with 3 panels of the seasons, Spring, Summer and Autumn, damaged, 58 by 18in (147 by 46cm).
$400-550

A pair of joined lappets of Brussels needle lace, c1750.
$600-900

A flounce of ivory silk blonde lace, joined early 19thC, 157 by 21½in (400 by 55cm).
$300-400

A cotton voile Christening gown, embroidered and trimmed with lace.
$150-200

Quilts

An Amish pieced cotton quilt, probably Ohio or Indiana, with sawtooth diamond in a square pattern in dark green on a light green ground with lavender highlights, late 19th/early 20thC, 77 by 80in (195.5 by 203cm).
$600-800

An Amish pieced wool crib quilt, probably Pennsylvania, with alternating stripes of maroon and blue, with a maroon border, framed, holes, fading, border not original, late 19th/early 20thC, 35 by 27in (89 by 68cm).
$400-600

Samplers

A map sampler of England and Wales, with place names in black silk and the boundaries in coloured silk, 1809, 21 by 19in (53 by 48cm), framed and glazed.
$400-550

A Queen Anne strip sampler, by Mary Smith, in the Year of Our Lord 1702, worked in coloured silks with the alphabet and numbers, 18½ by 7in (47 by 18cm), unframed.
$800-1,200

A sampler with verse, figures of angels, dated 1828, 17 by 16in (43 by 40.5cm), in a maple frame.
$400-550

A needlework sampler, by Sarah Withington, 1840, the linen ground embroidered mainly in red and green wools, 20½in (52cm) square, in glazed maple frame.
$450-700

A needlework sampler, by Sarah Redfern, 1869, the canvas ground worked in colours, with a poem dedicated to the memory of the King, 41 by 30½in (104 by 77cm), framed and glazed.
$1,000-1,500

A sampler, by Mary Eades, aged 12 years, embroidered in silks using cross stitch, long stitch and chenille work, c1810, 15 by 12in (38 by 30.5cm), in a maple frame.
$1,300-2,000

The sampler commemorates the arrival of King William III at the Battle of Boyne in 1690, where he was guided across the river by David McKinley after whom the Orange Lodge of Enniskillen is named.

A sampler, with alphabet, verse and figures of plants and birds, dated 1824, 17 by 13in (43 by 33cm).
$700-900

A needlework sampler, by Nancy
Vredenburghs, Mount Tabor
Academy, East Chester, New York,
August 29th, 1838, 23 by 18in (58 by
46cm).
$1,200-1,500

A matched pair of embroidered and
drawn threadwork show towels,
probably Pennsylvania, by Mary
Myers 1842, and Catherine Myers
1841, one ink stain, 55in (139.5cm)
long.
$400-600

A silk-on-silk needlework picture,
American, signed on the mat 'MW,
The little Slumberer, 1801', mat
replaced, 24 by 29in (61 by 73cm).
$6,000-6,500

Three drawn threadwork show
towels, probably Pennsylvania,
some staining, 19thC, 57in (145cm).
$150-250

A papercut picture, American,
depicting 2 eagles with flags above
flower filled urns with yellow,
orange and green decoration, 19thC,
6 by 7½in (15 by 19cm).
$1,200-1,500

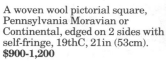

A woven wool pictorial square,
Pennsylvania Moravian or
Continental, edged on 2 sides with
self-fringe, 19thC, 21in (53cm).
$900-1,200

A sampler, by Mary Smith, aged 15 years, c1800, 16 by 12½in (40.5 by 32cm).
$600-900

A needlework sampler, by Mary Ann Cash, 1801, the linen ground worked in coloured silks, 14½ by 12in (37 by 30cm), framed and glazed.
$400-550

A needlework sampler, by Elizabeth Matilda Whitcomb, aged 11, worked at Miss Nicholl's Seminary, March 2, Orchard Street, Kidderminster, 1846, embroidered in coloured silks on a wool ground, 17 by 12½in (43 by 32cm), framed and glazed.
$700-900

An Armenian needlework sampler, by Souepile Kedeasian, the linen ground embroidered in red and pink threads, mid-19thC, 17½in by 23in (45 by 58cm).
$200-350

Tapestries

A Coptic fragment of tapestry woven in red and black wool and undyed linen, 5th/7thC, framed and glazed.
$300-500

Reputed to have originated from a tomb at Thebes.

A Peruvian fragment of tapestry, woven in coloured wools, 8th/10thC, mounted, framed and glazed.
$450-700

A verdure tapestry, woven in shades of blue, green, brown and red, 17thC, 83 by 78in (210 by 198cm).
$10,500-15,000

A Brussels tapestry panel, depicting possibly the Israelites receiving water in the desert, enclosed by a blue acanthus leaf border with fleur-de-lys feathers in panels to the corners above, 17thC, 93 by 55in (237 by 139cm).
3,000-4,000

A tapestry picture, woven in shades of cream, green, blue and red, mid-18thC, 16½ by 12in (42 by 30.5cm), framed.
$1,500-2,500

A gros and petit point arched firescreen panel, worked in coloured wools, mid-18thC, 34 by 26in (87.5 by 67cm), in a walnut veneered glazed frame.
$1,000-1,500

A small altar frontal, worked in coloured wools, with Joseph and Christ, flanked by roses in blue and white vases, mounted in ormolu with swags of pink roses against a beaded ground, North European, late 17thC, 26 by 42in (66 by 106cm).
$2,250-3,500

Miscellaneous

A patchwork coverlet, the centre worked in plain and printed cottons, surrounded by mainly pink and blue striped and floral cotton, the reverse worked with alternating panels of patchwork and quilted cotton, 19thC, 110 by 102in (280 by 260cm).
$400-550

A collection of manufacturer's samples of textiles for children's bedroom curtains, early 20thC, each 11½ by 5in (29 by 12.5cm).
$300-500

A beadwork pin cushion, in the shape of a book, the 'binding' worked in coloured beads, against a green ground, the 'spine' with the intitials MH, the inside lined with pink silk, 5 by 3in (12.5 by 7.5cm).
$200-350

An Oriental panel, the fuchsia ground worked in coloured silk threads, with heavy silk thread fringing, lined, with 2 pairs of fringed silk tassels, 102 by 95in (260 by 240cm).
$10,500-15,000

A quilt, depicting a blazing star in pastel shades of crepe, bound in white, some of the patches quilted, American, c1930, 80in (203cm) square.
$400-550

Two pairs of Chinese yellow silk satin curtains, painted in colours, each with later blue border, slightly worn, 72in (182.5cm) high, lined and interlined.
$200-350

A patchwork coverlet, in brightly printed cottons with a dark border, variously quilted, 105in (266cm) square.
$800-1,200

A border of French brocade, the ivory silk ground woven in coloured silks, early 19thC, lined.
$450-700

A damask banquet cloth, depicting the glorification of the Virgin Mary, 17thC, 103 by 81in (262 by 206cm).
$5,000-7,500

A set of 3 Aubusson entre-fenêtres, in deep rose pink and beige, woven in many colours, 19thC, 70in (177.5cm) high, fringed.
$7,000-10,000

A pair of silkwork panels, some staining, 18thC, 12 by 7½in (30.5 by 19cm).
$1,000-1,500

A Victorian embroidered pelmet, with deep scallops worked in brightly coloured wools, highlighted in silk, c1880, 19 by 62in (48 by 157cm).
$400-550

Fans

An unmounted printed fan leaf, 'St. Batholomew's Fair in 1721', the aquatint engraving tinted, with text, published by J. F. Setchel, the margins overpainted in white, c1780, 22in (56cm) wide, framed and glazed.
$4,000-5,500

A fan, the leaf painted with the family of Darius, the mother-of-pearl sticks carved and pierced, silvered and gilt and backed with mother-of-pearl, guardstick damaged, mid-18thC, 11in (28cm), in glazed fan case.
$1,500-2,500

A fan, the leaf an etching in brown of heraldic devices, inscribed 'Pubd. as the Act directs Feb 11 1792, by F. Martin & Co., Enter'd at Stationer's Hall and Sold by Sarah Ashton Fan Maker No. 28 Little Britain', with ivory sticks, 10in (25cm) long.
$700-900

A fan with ivory sticks, the initial guard carved with the head of a lady, c1890, 14in (35cm) long, in original box inscribed J. Duveileroy, London 167 Regent Street W.
$800-1,200

A French fan, with carved, pierced, painted and gilt ivory sticks decorated with mother-of-pearl, c1760, 11in (28cm) long.
$2,500-3,500

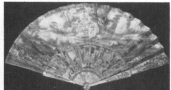

A fan with carved, pierced, silvered and gilt mother-of-pearl sticks, probably German, c1760, 12in (30cm) long.
$1,000-1,500

A Canton carved ivory, painted and embellished paper fan, in gouache, fabric and bright coloured ivory, with silver swivel and silk tassels, 19thC, 20in (51cm) wide, in original gilt and black lacquered fitted box.
$1,000-1,500

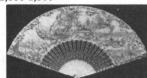

A French fan, the carved, pierced and painted ivory sticks decorated with red and green florets, with gilt highlights, c1750, 10½in (26cm) long, and a shaped case.
$1,300-2,000

A fan, with carved, pierced, silvered and gilt mother-of-pearl sticks, signed Donzel, c1870, 14in (35cm) long, in a shaped, glazed case with gilt gesso frame.
$3,000-4,500

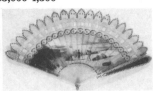

A gilded horn brisé fan with piqué work, c1810, 6½in (16cm) long.
$450-700

A gauze leaf fan, painted and decorated with sequins, the mother-of-pearl sticks pierced, gilt and hinged for folding, c1890, and another distressed fan.
$100-150

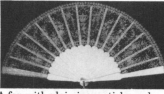

A fan with plain ivory sticks and 18ct gold loop at pivot, c1890, 10½in (27cm) long, in a box.
$1,000-1,500

A Chinese fan, with carved and pierced shaped sticks of tortoiseshell, mother-of-pearl, stained and unstained ivory and metal filigree with enamel decoration, c1840, 11in (28cm) long, in a black and gilt lacquer box.
$1,000-1,500

A fan, the leaf painted with the Judgement of Paris, the ivory sticks carved, early 18thC, 10½in (27cm).
$600-900

A fan with plain ivory sticks, the leaf with a hand coloured etching of The Visitation, inscribed M. Gamble 1743, 10in (25.5cm) long.
$300-500

The Casino fan, the leaf a hand coloured etching, with the rules of the game, published by I. Cook & J. P. Crowder, Wood Street, London, April 1st. 1793, with wooden sticks, leaf damaged, 10in (25.5cm).
$450-700

A French fan, the ivory sticks carved and pierced, c1760, 11in (28cm) long.
$1,000-1,500

A fan, the silk leaf painted, the reserves embroidered with spangles and sequins, the mother-of-pearl sticks carved, pierced and gilt, French, damaged, c1760, 11in (28cm), in contemporary fan box.
$400-550

A French fan with gilded ivory sticks, c1770, 11in (28cm) long.
$600-900

A fan, the leaf painted in French with an illustrated encyclopaedia, the ivory sticks pierced, damaged, c1790, 10in (25.5cm).
$1,000-1,500

A fan, the leaf painted and signed Michaels, the verso with monogram I.L., with smoked mother-of-pearl sticks, French, repaired, c1895, 14in (35.5cm), in box monogrammed I.L. by A. Howeiler, Paris.
$1,500-2,500

A French fan with carved, pierced, silvered and gilt mother-of-pearl sticks, c1770, 11in (28cm) long, in a shaped, framed and glazed case.
$600-900

A fan, the leaf painted with pink, red and yellow roses and honeysuckle, signed Mathilde 1889, with tortoiseshell sticks, one guardstick piqué in gold with the initial C.B. or L., with coronet above, 13in (33cm), in box by Vanier Chardin, 82 Boulevard Haussman.
$1,500-2,500

A parasol fan, the mount of strawberry pink silk embroidered in ivory and deeper pink silks, edged with a silk fringe and boned with 5 whalebones, which together with the patent mechanism allow the fan to form a half parasol, the ivory handle carved and pierced, and the metal band inscribed De Givry, rue Romarin 20, Lyon, c1865, 14in (35.5cm) folded.
$4,000-5,500

A Chinese cabriolet fan, with black, pink, silver and gilt lacquer sticks, c1830, 11½in (28.5cm) long, in original box covered in painted silk with label printed in Spanish.
$1,500-2,500

A Chinese telescopic fan, with black and gilt lacquer sticks, the leaf painted and hand coloured both sides, c1840, 11in (26cm) long extended, in original box.
$700-900

An unmounted fan leaf, painted on chicken skin with a Roman marriage after the antique, Italian, c1800, 21in (53cm) wide, in box inscribed from 21 St. James's Place, 23.1.30.
$1,200-1,750

A Chinese silver gilt filigree fan, with mainly blue and green enamel decoration, c1830, 7½in (19.5cm) long.
$1,200-1,750

A Canton ivory brisé fan, carved with birds and flowers, coronet monogrammed C.P.W., c1810, 8in (20cm).
$600-900

Possibly for Charlotte, Princess of Wales.

A Chinese fan of carved and pierced ivory, designed with a central shield, monogrammed DB, c1760, 10in (25.5cm) long.
$900-1,300

Dolls

Wax

A poured wax child doll with fixed blue eyes, the long blonde hair inset in groups into head, the stuffed body with wax limbs, wearing underclothes, striped sailor dress and bronze shoes, with Lucy Peck oval stamp on the body, 21in (53cm).
$600-900

A poured wax child doll, with swivel head and shoulder plate, fixed blue eyes, pierced ears and blonde mohair wig, the stuffed waisted body dressed in white, body melted, 19in (48cm) high.
$450-700

A poured wax child doll, the blonde hair inset in slashes, the stuffed body with wax limbs, dressed in sailor dress with red braid and cap band embroidered 'HMS PET', with Lucy Peck oval stamp on body, 20in (51cm) high.
$600-900

A poured wax child doll, with blonde hair inset in slashes, blue eyes, stuffed body and wax limbs, dressed in striped pink silk, with Lucy Peck oval stamp on the body, replaced and damaged foot, 21in (53cm) high.
$450-700

A poured wax child doll, with fixed blue eyes, wearing original purple silk frock with pleated hem and lace decoration, underclothes and petticoat embroidered in purple wool, English underdome, 16in (40.5cm) high.
$1,000-1,500

Wooden

A Grödenthal wooden doll, painted in grey, yellow, brown and red, in contemporary tucked cotton dress with pantalettes and petticoat, c1830, 7½in (19cm).
$800-1,200

A Grödenthal wooden doll, in white printed coat and dress, c1820, 15in (38cm).
$1,300-2,000

A bisque character baby doll, with blue painted eyes, jointed at shoulder and hip, marked 390214, on the leg 10P 6, 6½in (16.5cm).
$800-1,200

A turned and carved wooden doll, with inset eyes, stitched brows and lashes and bright pink cheeks, the white painted body joined at the hip and shoulder, crack encircling face, c1810, 11½in (29cm).
$1,000-1,500

A bisque headed character baby doll, in original clothes, Bahr & Proschild, 14in (35.5cm).
$400-550

Bisque

A bisque shoulder head doll with swivel neck, with fixed grey/green paperweight eyes, pierced ears, by François Gaultier, minor damage, incised 8 top back of the crown, 25in (64cm).
$9,000-12,500

A Kaiser baby glass-eyed doll, with open/closed mouth, 14½in (37cm).
$2,250-3,500

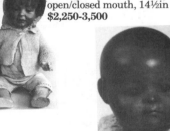

An all bisque Kaiser baby, with painted features and hair, the bent limbed body wearing baby gown, marked 5, 7½in (19cm).
$800-1,200

A brown bisque headed baby doll, with brown sleeping eyes, dressed in white, marked R 127A, 14½in (36.5cm).
$600-900

A bisque headed child doll, with blue sleeping eyes, pierced ears and blonde mohair wig, the jointed composition body in pink smocked dress, white underwear, black shoes and straw hat with feather, marked 192 by Kestner, 12in (30.5cm).
$900-1,300

A bisque headed child doll, with blue lashed sleeping eyes, brown mohair wig and pierced ears, the jointed composition body in blue spotted dress, marked ABG 1362.8, 35in (89cm).
$1,200-1,750

An all bisque boy doll, with blue intaglio eyes, open/closed mouth with 2 teeth, moulded and painted shoes and socks, dressed in a navy wool military costume, marked 150/10, possibly by Hertel, Schwab & Co., 8½in (21.5cm).
$300-500

Bru

A French fashion doll, with glass eyes, pierced ears, with a gusset jointed kid leather body, by Ferdinand Gaultier, 19thC, 13in (33cm).
$3,000-4,500

A French bisque headed closed mouth doll, with applied pierced ears and paperweight eyes, dressed in original clothes, Paris bébé, Tête Deposee 16, 35in (89cm).
$10,000-13,500

A Bru Jeune bisque headed doll, with fair mohair wig over cork pate, fixed blue paperweight eyes, open/closed mouth, pierced ears and bisque shoulder plate with moulded breasts, the white kid leather body with kid covered wood upper arms and painted wood lower legs, damage to arms, incised BRU JNE 6, and the shoulder plate incised BRU JNE, 18in (46cm), together with a pair of brown leather shoes, incised BRU JNE PARIS, and 4 items of clothing.
$13,000-17,500

A Bru Jeune R bisque head walking doll, with wig over cork pate, weighted blue eyes, pierced ears, open mouth with upper teeth, and dressed wood and composition body with squeaker, straight limbed legs and jointed arms, marked BRU JNE R 9, 21in (54cm).
$3,000-4,500

Gebruder Heubach

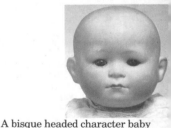

A black bisque headed baby doll with closed mouth, brown sleeping eyes and pierced ears, the composition baby body dressed in original felt petalled skirt, marked Heubach Koppelsdorf 399 2/0, 15in (38cm).
$450-700

A bisque headed character baby doll, with blue sleeping eyes, closed mouth and painted and moulded hair, the stuffed body dressed in white baby gown, marked Heubach Koppelsdorf 339, 3/0, 14½in (37cm).
$600-900

A bisque headed character baby doll, with blue intaglio eyes and blonde mohair wig, the bent limbed composition baby's body dressed in white cotton broderie anglais baby gown and carrying cape and bonnet, marked 6970 4 Germany, with the Gebruder Heubach sunburst, 11½in (29cm).
$450-700

A bisque headed child doll, with blue lashed sleeping eyes, hair wig and jointed composition body, in contemporary dark blue girl guide uniform with compass and whistle, marked AWW9, 5 Heubach Koppelsdorf by Adolf Wislizerus, 24in (61cm).
$400-550

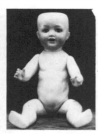

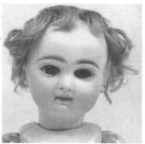

A bisque figure of a seated fat baby, marked 95 and the Heubach square mark, stamped in green 68, 5in (12.5cm).
$150-200

A German bisque headed doll, Heubach Koppelsdorf, No. 3422, early 20thC, 16in (40.5cm).
$450-700

Jumeau

A bisque headed bébé, with blue sleeping eyes, the jointed composition body dressed in blue watered silk with white underclothes, and brown leather shoes, stamped in red Tête Jumeau: Bébé Jumeau diplôme d'honneur sticker on body, 24in (61cm).
$2,000-3,000

A bisque headed bébé, with closed mouth, fixed brown eyes, pierced ears, blonde wig and fixed wrist, jointed wood and composition body, stamped in red DEPOSE TETE JUMEAU Bte. S.G.D.G. 6, and on the body in blue with the Medaille d'Or mark, 14½in (37cm).
$3,000-4,500

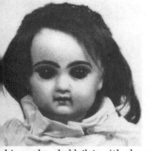

A bisque headed bébé, with closed mouth, fixed brown eyes, pierced ears, long chestnut wig and jointed composition body wearing petticoat tucked frock with lace insertions and bébé Jumeau bronze shoes, stamped in red DEPOSÉ TETE JUMEAU bte S.G.D.G. 2 impressed, stamped on body Jumeau Medaille D'Or Paris, 11in (28cm).
$3,000-4,500

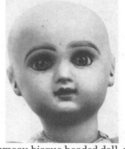

A Jumeau bisque headed doll, with cork pate, fixed blue paperweight eyes, pierced ears, closed mouth and jointed composition body, dressed in lace trimmed green silk, dress distressed, stamped in red Depose Tête Jumeau Bte S.G.D.G.3, the body stamped in blue Jumeau Medaille d'Or Paris, 12in (30cm).
$3,000-4,500

A bisque headed bébé, with fixed blue eyes, brown wig and jointed composition body, dressed in contemporary red and white spotted dress, white underwear and brown leather boots, crack to neck, the head stamped Tête Jumeau in red and body with Bébé Jumeau Diplôme d'Honneur sticker, 25½in (63.5cm).
$2,000-3,000

A Jumeau bisque headed doll, with brown wig, fixed brown eyes, pierced ears, jointed composition body dressed in lace trimmed silk, small chip to left eye, paint damage to hands, 25in (63.5cm).
$2,250-3,500

A Jumeau bisque headed doll, with wig, fixed blue paperweight eyes, the jointed composition body dressed in whitework, some repainting to body, marked 1907 12, 26in (66cm).
$2,250-3,500

An Emile Jumeau bisque headed doll, with original clothes, and a trunk of accessories, 12½in (31.5cm).
$8,000-11,000

A Jumeau bisque headed doll, in original clothing with accessories, marked Depose Tête Jumeau Bte SGDG 14, 30½in (76cm).
$10,000-13,500

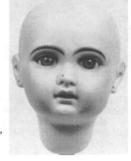

A Jumeau bisque headed doll, with sleeping blue eyes, jointed composition body, dressed in whitework, socks and leather shoes, one hand missing, incised 1907 10.
$3,000-4,500

511

J. D. Kestner

A Kestner all-bisque dolls house doll, in original felt outfit, with closed mouth and glass eyes, 3½in (9cm).
$300-500

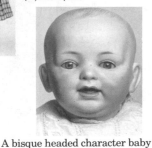

A J. D. Kestner bisque headed googly eyed doll, with dark mohair wig, brown eyes, and straight limbed composition body dressed in red gingham, marked B 6 J.D.K. 221, 10in (25cm).
$3,000-4,500

A bisque headed character baby doll, with blue sleeping eyes, open/closed mouth and composition body, in lace edged embroidered frock, marked J.D.K.12, 14½in (37cm).
$1,200-1,750

A Kestner bisque headed character doll, with blue sleeping eyes, blond wig and jointed body, dressed in white with velvet caped coat, marked J13 143, 20in (51cm).
$1,200-1,750

A bisque headed character baby doll, with blue sleeping eyes, open/closed mouth, dressed in cream silk and lace, marked JDK.Y, 10½in (27cm).
$600-900

A J. D. Kestner bisque headed googly eyed doll, with weighted blue eyes, and dressed jointed composition body, body repainted, marked A 5 JDK 221, 12in (30cm).
$6,000-8,000

A bisque headed character baby, with brown lashed sleeping eyes and composition body, marked 25 J.D.K.44, 18½in (47cm).
$800-1,200

A bisque headed character baby doll, with moulded and painted curl on forehead and above ears, double chin and jointed toddler body, marked JDK 8 and stamped in red on the body Germany, 13½in (34cm).
$1,200-1,750

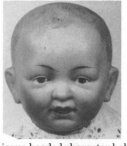

A bisque headed character baby, with brown painted eyes, open/closed mouth and bent limbed baby body, dressed in whitework gown, marked 7, probably Kestner, 11½in (29cm).
$300-400

A bisque headed character doll, with brown fixed eyes, the bent limbed body dressed in blue silk suit and white shoes, marked J.D.K. 257, 16in (40.5cm).
$900-1,300

A bisque headed character doll, with painted eyes, open/closed mouth, the bent limbed composition body in knitted outfit, marked J.D.K. 11, 15in (38cm).
$700-900

A Kestner bisque headed child doll, with fixed brown eyes, blonde wig, fixed wrist jointed composition body dressed in fawn, marked 192 3, 12in (30.5cm) high, with a Scotts string and wood dolls swing, with trade label, 25in (63.5cm).
$800-1,200

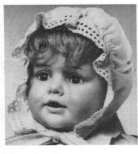

A bisque headed character baby doll, with brown flirting, sleeping eyes, quivering tongue, dimpled cheeks, short blonde wig and composition baby body, wearing nightgown, marked K14 247 J.D.K. 14, 17in (43cm).
$1,500-2,500

A Lenci painted felt child doll, with blonde wool wig, original hunting pink and black jodhpurs, boots and hat, c1930, 16½in (41cm).
$800-1,200

A Lenci cloth child doll, with painted face and blonde mohair wig, dressed in original blue and white check felt dress and white apron, c1920, 9in (23cm).
$600-900

Armand Marseille

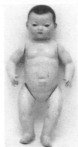

An Armand Marseille 'Just Me' bisque headed doll, with weighted blue eyes, and 5-piece composition body, dressed in lace trimmed cotton, socks and white leather shoes, one hand missing, marked A 310/11/OM, 7in (18cm).
$1,200-1,750

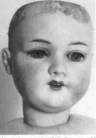

An Armand Marseille bisque headed doll, with open/closed eyes and jointed composition limbs, 390, lacking hair, some damage, 27in (69cm).
$300-500

An Armand Marseille Oriental doll, with biscuit Chinese character head, brown glass eyes, slightly yellow coloured composition body, marked A.M. Germany, 353/8k, c1920, 24½in (62cm).
$3,000-4,000

CHARACTER DOLLS

★ in 1909 Kammer & Reinhardt introduced a large number of character dolls

★ these were modelled from life, showing all the nuances of childish temperament

★ a model was made and then a mould taken, which was used about fifty times

★ Simon and Halbig cast and painted the heads for many other manufacturers, including Kammer & Reinhardt, such heads are marked K & R, Simon & Halbig, or K & R, S & H and the model number

★ early K & R character dolls are of exceptional quality

★ the French had remained supreme in the manufacture of dolls, in the 19thC, with Jumeau one of the main exponents

★ however, from the 1890s the Germans had perfected equal skills

★ after K & R introduced their characters many other makers followed: Heubach, Armand Marseille, Bruno Schmidt, Kestner, and S.F.B.J. (the Societe Francaise de Fabrication de Bebes et Jouets)

★ obviously these dolls were expensive and so they were hardly produced in large quantities

★ K & R Model 117 is usually considered to be one of the most desirable, in fact any 'pouty' doll is highly collectable

★ the most common is model 126

★ there are more Heubach characters than any other

★ as one gets nearer to the First World War quality tends to decrease and character dolls produced after the war are in many cases, poor quality

An Armand Marseille bisque headed doll, with open mouth and sleeping eyes, marked A 15M, 34in (86cm).
$1,300-2,000

An Armand Marseille bisque headed Oriental doll, with sleeping eyes, and dressed composition toddler body, marked 353/4K, 14in (36cm).
$1,500-2,500

An Armand Marseille bisque headed dream baby, marked AM 351 7/K, 18in (46cm).
$200-350

A bisque headed child doll, with jointed wood and composition body, dressed in brown velvet, with white underwear and shoes, marked 390 A.M., 37in (94cm).
$2,000-3,000

An S.F.B.J. bisque headed character doll, with fixed blue glass eyes, open/closed mouth and dressed straight limbed composition body, marked S.F.B.J. 226 8, 18in (46cm).
$1,200-1,750

An S.F.B.J. bisque headed character doll, with sleeping brown eyes, open/closed mouth and composition toddler body, hairline crack to forehead, marked 236 12, 24in (61cm).
$900-1,300

Simon & Halbig/ Kammer & Reinhardt

A bisque headed character doll, with painted features and blonde mohair wig, the jointed composition body in whitework dress, white underwear and leather shoes, wig damaged, marked K*R 114 49, 18in (46cm).
$4,000-5,500

Schoenau & Hoffmeister

A Schoenau & Hoffmeister 'Princess Elizabeth' bisque headed doll, with blue sleeping eyes, upper moulded teeth, fair hair wig, on composition toddler body, in cream silk embroidered dress, impressed Porzellanfabrik Burggrb, made in Germany, 23in (58cm).
$1,000-1,500

A bisque headed character boy doll, with jointed toddler composition body dressed in red knitted suit, marked S.F.B.J. 236 Paris, 13in (33cm).
$1,000-1,500

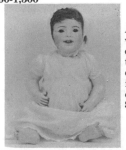

An S.F.B.J. bisque headed doll, with weighted black glass eyes, no pupils, open/closed mouth, and composition toddler body, in white cotton embroidered dress and bonnet, impressed SFBJ 236 Paris 12, c1910, 24in (61cm).
$1,300-2,000

A Kammer & Reinhardt/Simon & Halbig bisque headed character doll, with brown glass eyes, ball jointed composition body, in cream net and lace dress with undergarments and cotton shoes, impressed K*R, Simon & Halbig 117 55, 22in (56cm).
$6,000-9,000

A bisque headed character boy doll, with brown sleeping eyes, golden brown mohair wig, the jointed composition toddler body in cream suit with brown leather shoes, marked K*R Simon & Halbig 115/a 48, 19½in (49cm).
$4,000-5,500

S.F.B.J.

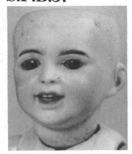

A bisque headed character baby doll, with open/closed mouth, sleeping dark eyes and baby body, marked SFBJ 236 Paris 4, 12½in (32cm).
$800-1,200

A bisque character headed doll, with open/closed mouth, dark sleeping eyes, composition baby body and silk dress with spare embroidered frock, marked S.F.B.J. 236 Paris 11, 22½in (57cm).
$800-1,200

A Simon & Halbig bisque headed doll, with sleeping eyes, 2 moulded upper teeth, fair hair wig, voice box and composition body, in white cotton gown and bonnet, impressed Simon & Halbig Oo Germany 60, 23½in (60cm).
$700-900

A bisque headed character doll, with grey painted eyes, closed mouth and jointed composition body, marked K*R 114 60, 21in (53cm).
$4,000-5,500

A Simon & Halbig bisque headed doll, with sleeping eyes, pierced ears and composition ball jointed body, clothed, marked S & H Halbig 1079, Germany 14, 30in (76cm).
$1,300-2,000

Jules Steiner

A Kammer & Reinhardt bisque headed character doll, with painted blue eyes, the jointed composition body dressed in whitework, marked K*R 114 46, 18in (46cm).
$4,000-5,500

A bisque headed bébé, with brown eyes, pierced ears, skin wig and composition jointed body, wearing a wool sailor's outfit, with extra clothing, marked Ste.C l and written in red Steiner A.S.G.D.G. Paris Bourgoin Jne, 15in (38cm).
$4,000-5,500

Automata

An automaton of a young girl, by Simon & Halbig, when the musical mechanism is wound her head, eyes and arms move from side-to-side and the chest shows a positive breathing action, dressed in a sequinned net blouse with matching headdress and blue/grey woven silk costume, trimmed with braid, head marked 1300, 28in (71cm), including musical box base.
$2,250-3,500

A Simon & Halbig bisque headed automaton doll, four movement with music, 21in (53cm).
$3,000-4,500

An American clockwork doll, c1862, 10in (25.5cm).
$800-1,200

A mechanical kid bodied doll, crying 'Mama' and 'Papa', in original clothes, 19thC, 19in (48cm).
$6,000-9,000

An automaton, modelled as a Scottish terrier, on small wheels, by Descamps, 11in (28cm).
$400-550

A Bing jumping monkey clockwork automaton, with rust fur covering and felt paws, marked with 2 metal tags, 6in (15cm).
$300-500

A Bing 'cat skier' clockwork automaton, with grey fur body, white shirt and red breeches, leather boots, on metals 'skis' with wheels and holding a wooden stick, the key mechanism concealed in body, marked with metal tag in ear, 8in (20cm).
$900-1,300

An automaton, of a cow which moos when the head is turned from side-to-side, patented, c1890, 10in (25.5cm) high.
$600-900

A tiger automaton, covered in animal skin, pounces, c1880, 14in (35.5cm) long.
$1,300-2,000

A musical automaton of a lady at her dressing table, by Ferdinand Gaultier, 19thC.
$8,000-11,000

Dolls Houses

An eight-piece matching suite, late 19thC.
$450-700

An Edwardian dolls house, the front elevation with a portico flanked by bay windows, 33in (84cm) wide.
$2,250-3,500

A mahogany dolls house, with glazed windows, sliding front wall revealing plain interior, c1900, 37in (94cm) wide.
$2,250-3,500

A dolls mahogany bed, with turned ends and Chinese embroidered mattress and pillow, 19½in (49cm) long.
$300-500

Teddy Bears

A golden plush covered teddy bear, in the form of a child's muff, with black boot button eyes, embroidered snout and silk neck cord, 15in (38cm).
$400-550

A Steiff gold plush teddy bear, slightly worn, pads renewed, with metal Steiff disc in left ear, c1907, 25in (63cm).
$4,000-5,500

A golden plush covered teddy bear, with boot button eyes, pointed muzzle, hump and elongated limbs, with growler, Steiff button in ear, 24in (61cm).
$5,000-7,500

A silver grey plush covered teddy bear, with boot button eyes, pointed muzzle, hump and elongated limbs, growler inoperative, Steiff button in ear, 28in (71cm).
$5,000-7,500

A teddy bear, 23in (58cm).
$400-550

A Steiff teddy bear, with button in ear.
$1,500-2,500

A pair of twin teddies with button eyes, well loved, c1930, 12in (30.5cm).
$300-500

A golden plush covered teddy bear, with boot button eyes, cut muzzle, hump and elongated limbs, replaced pads, Steiff button in left ear, 19in (48cm).
$1,000-1,500

A golden plush covered teddy bear, with boot button eyes, growler, possibly by Steiff, c1930, 12½in (32cm).
$700-900

A golden plush covered teddy bear, with pronounced hump, growler inoperative, with Steiff button in ear, 29in (74cm).
$6,000-8,000

A cinnamon plush covered teddy bear with glass eyes, large hump and elongated limbs, 12in (30.5cm).
$200-350

A honey plush covered teddy bear, the cut muzzle with central seam, wide set eyes, with elongated pads and small hump, growler inoperative, probably Steiff, c1908, 17in (43cm).
$1,500-2,500

Miscellaneous

A pair of advertising dolls with composition shoulder heads, modelled as the 'Bisto Kids', designed by Will Owen, the cloth bodies in original clothes, c1948, 11in (28cm).
400-550

A painted felt character doll, in original red and white romper suit, with Lenci metal button, probably from the 111 series, c1922, 13in (33cm).
$400-550

A collection of dolls clothes, including whitework gowns, shoes and bibs.
$5,000-7,500

A composition headed parasol doll, with fixed blue eyes, blonde wig and pink silk lace bonnet, the skirt forming the parasol covering, the matching cape covering her composition arms, her wooden legs forming the handle, 21in (53cm).
$600-900

A doll's trunk, containing a quantity of clothes, shoes and sandals, including a blue silk velvet and satin dress with watered silk front, 17in (43cm).
$600-900

A set of painted composition headed Punch & Judy glove puppets, in original clothes, with wooden hands and legs.
$450-700

Two dolls hats.
$150-250

Toys
Lead Soldiers

Britains set No. 2077, King's Troop,
Royal Horse Artillery, at the walk,
in review order, slightly retouched,
1 plume broken.
$400-550

Britains set No. 9419, Royal Horse
Artillery Gun and Team, repainted
in original box, lid with torn sides.
$400-550

Heyde set No. 919, Knights in
Armour, 1 lance and 6 plumes
broken, 50mm scale, c1880, in
original box.
$200-350

Britains set No. 37, Band of the
Coldstream Guards, 1 missing.
$300-500

Britains rare set No. 2171, Royal
Air Force Colour Party, slightly
chipped, in original Regiments of all
Nations box.
$4,000-5,500

Britains set No. 63, 10th Bengal
Lancers, at the canter, in
original box.
$1,500-2,500

Britains very rare
set No. 1450,
Royal Army
Medical Corps, slight
damage, c1940, in
original box.
$6,000-9,000

Britains display set No. 54, Types of
the British Army, including
Queen's Bays (2nd Dragoons), 9th
Lancers and 1st Life Guards, one
sword broken, 3 Life Guards
missing.
$600-900

Britains rare set No. 1287, Military
Band, some damage, in original box.
$1,000-1,400

Britains rare special set for
Hamleys, Royal Marines Colour
Party, rubbed, in original Types of
the British Army box.
$4,000-5,500

Britains set No. 460, Colour Party of
the Scots Guards, some damage, in
original Types of the World's
Armies box.
$800-1,200

Tinplate

Money Banks

A cast iron money box of a golliwog,
6in (15.5cm).
$200-350

A Bing printed and painted tinplate
English houseboat, No. 13662/1,
c1904, some damage, 14in (35.5cm)
long.
$3,000-4,500

A Bing three-funnel liner, with
clockwork mechanism, repainted in
red and cream, black lining and tan
decks, 2 reproduction flags, mast
missing, c1925, 15in (38cm) long.
$800-1,200

A Bing three-funnel Dreadnought No. 155/115, with clockwork mechanism, finished in battleship grey, lacks masts and flags, worn, c1912, 16in (40.5cm) long.
$700-900

A Bing battleship, with removable deck to reveal clockwork mechanism, finished in dark grey below waterline, grey above, with black painted portholes, tan decks, 2 flags, some retouching, steering wheel broken, c1915, 16in (40.5cm) long.
$800-1,200

A Carette painted tinplate three-funnel liner, 'Manxman', in original paintwork with white repainted ensign, some chipping, lacks flag on mast, c1910, 11in (28cm).
$700-900

A Metalcraft, No. 820 'Spirit of St. Louis', with instructions, U.S.A., c1928, in original box, worn.
$400-550

An Ernest Plank riverboat, the painted tinplate steamer with live steam spirit fired mechanism, finished in red below waterline, black above, with white side panels, slight damage, c1920, 16in (40.5cm) long.
$450-700

A Lehmann rare printed and painted early monoplane, 'Ikarus', No. 653, the clockwork mechanism firing a two-bladed propeller, with yellow paper wings, all finished in red and yellow, c1920, 10½in (27cm) long.
$3,000-4,500

An Arnold printed and painted tinplate motorbike and rider, 'Mac 700', with clockwork mechanism causing the rider to hop on-and-off, in original paintwork, W. German, c1955, 7½in (19cm).
$600-900

A Gunda-Werke lithograph tinplate motorcycle and sidecar, with clockwork mechanism, c1920, 6½in (16.5cm).
$1,500-2,500

A Lesney Massey Harris 745D tractor.
$300-500

A Dinky Spratts van, No. 514, boxed.
$400-550

An Arcade Toys cast iron 2-piece motorcycle 'COP', in blue, 4in (10cm), with farm tractor in red, 3½in (8cm).
$400-550

A Tekno Mercedes Tuborg Pilsner delivery lorry, boxed.
$100-200

Two Spot-On Ford Zodiacs No. 100, with original boxes.
$200-350

A Dinky J. Lyons & Co., van No. 514, boxed.
$450-700

A Spot-On London Transport bus.
$600-900

Five Corgi Toys Gift Sets No. 5.
British Racing cars, including
Vanwalls, Lotus Mk.XI's and
B.R.M.'s, c1960, in original boxes.
$600-900

A C.I.J. P2 Alfa Romeo painted
tinplate 2-seater Grand Prix racing
car, with clockwork mechanism
powering rear axle, finished in
green, French, some damage, c1926,
21in (53cm) long.
$1,000-1,400

Walt Disney's Donald Duck Duet,
by Marx, boxed.
$450-600

A painted and lithographed tinplate
vis-a-vis, c1910, 5in (12.5cm).
$700-900

A Karl Bub atom rocket ship, boxed.
$200-350

Tootsietoy No. 5210 trucks,
including a Mack Express
semi-trailer 1925, a Mack trailer
truck, a Greyhound bus, a fire
engine, a wrecker truck and
4 pick-up trucks, one vehicle
damaged, c1938, in original box.
$400-550

A Bub lithographed limousine, with
clockwork mechanism, battery
operated headlamps and rear 'stop'
plate, finished in blue and light
green, with yellow and blue lining,
some damage, c1928, 14½in (37cm)
long.
$400-550

A Lehmann early printed and
painted tinplate motorcyclist, Echo,
EPL 725, with clockwork
mechanism, c1910, 9in (23cm).
$4,000-5,500

A Lehmann printed and painted
tinplate rickshaw with running
coolie, Masuyama, EPL 773, with
clockwork mechanism, in original
paintwork, some damage, c1925,
7in (18cm) long.
$450-700

An Ingap 4-door limousine, with
clockwork mechanism, in blue over
red, with yellow and black lining,
some chipping, right rear wheel
damaged, c1930, 11in (28cm) long.
$800-1,200

An Ichiko printed and painted
tinplate Cadillac, with defective
friction drive mechansim, finished
in red with chrome trimming,
c1967, 28in (71cm) long.
$800-1,200

A Doll & Co., printed and painted
carousel, with a hand cranked
clockwork mechanism, in red and
pink, lacking flag, c1914, 11½in
(29cm).
$600-900

An S. Gunthermann clockwork
painted and printed tinplate
billiards player, the mechanism
causing 3 balls to be potted and
returned to the player, c1900, 8in
(20cm) long, in original box.
$2,000-3,000

A German tinplate clockwork army motorcycle and sidecar, with machine gunner, key missing, c1930.
$1,500-2,500

A German plated tinplate clockwork pool player at table, 11½in (29cm) long.
$800-1,200

A Lehmann clockwork zig-zag, No. 640, in good condition, boxed.
$1,300-2,000

Miscellaneous

A German clockwork boxing match, post war, boxed, no lid.
$150-200

A quantity of Elastin 70mm scale cowboys and indians, 8 by Lineol, some slight damage, c1938.
$450-700

A group of painted bronze miniature figures of animals, mainly characters from Beatrix Potter's books.
$1,200-1,750

A set of Erzegebirge painted carved wood and flock covered composition animals, in original wood box, German, some slight damage, c1860.
$600-900

A toy tin circus, the 14-part ring with 16 various artists and horses, c1830.
$6,000-9,000

An Erzegebirge painted wood Noah's Ark, with opening side panel to reveal 74 carved wood animals and birds and 5 members of the Noah family, in original paintwork, inscribed 'Harry Burney, Keeper of Wild Beasts, Birds, Fishes and Insects', German, some slight damage to animals, c1870, 15½in (38cm) long.
$1,200-1,750

An Erzegebirge straw-work Noah's Ark, with opening side panel to reveal 236 animals, birds and insects, Mr & Mrs Noah and 5 members of the family, German, some slight damage, c1870, the ark 19in (48cm) long.
$2,500-3,500

Britains and other makers farm items.
$200-350

Britains Famous Football Teams, Chelsea, in original box.
$600-900

Britains Home Farm items, some damage, all in original boxes.
$600-900

A Noah's Ark, complete with animals, 19thC.
$1,000-1,500

Two wooden rod puppets, with painted faces.
$150-250

An acrobat toy, comprising 4 papier mâché acrobats standing and sliding down on 2 ropes stretched in a stand, in original wood box with sliding top.
$1,500-2,500

A wood box with 3 drawers containing Meccano, with 2 instruction booklets, not complete and slightly worn.
$300-500

A pull-along nodding duck, with green velvet head and painted feathers, factory stamp on base, c1880, 6in (15cm) long.
$300-400

A clockwork fur-covered giraffe with clown rider, 12½in (31cm) high.
$100-150

A Steiff grey cloth covered elephant on wheels, with boot button eyes and red blanket, late 19thC, 8in (20cm) high.
$300-500

A lavender plush covered monkey, the head removing to reveal a scent bottle with stopper, jointed at shoulders and hips, with felt ears and feet, probably by Schuco, c1920, 3½in (7.5cm) high.
$300-500

A cream plush goose, with felt beak possibly German, 14in (35.5cm) long.
$100-200

A complete boxed set of Snow White and the 7 Dwarfs, in original clothes, the dwarfs 9½in (24cm) high, in boxes labelled Chad Valley Hygienic Textile Toys, with the name of each toy beneath.
$6,000-9,000

A terracotta headed creche figure, with painted hands and feet, in original cream shirt and tweed breeches, Neapolitan, early 19thC, 16½in (42cm) high.
$700-900

A terracotta headed creche figure, modelled as a Turk, with painted wooden hands and feet, in original blue and gold embroidered jacket and gold Turkish trousers, Neapolitan, early 19thC, 19in (48cm) high.
$700-900

A Chad Valley felt headed character doll, modelled as Snow White, 16½in (41.5cm) high, and 7 dwarfs.
$2,000-3,000

A wood and brass toy sleigh, upholstered in blue velvet, with brass runners, late 19thC, 13in (33cm) long.
$1,300-2,000

A Victorian child's tricycle, with leather seat, wooden handlebars and horse's head, on metal wheels.
$8,000-11,000

A Victorian dolls perambulator.
$400-550

A Victorian child's sledge, painted red, on shaped metal runners.
$800-1,200

A three-wheeled perambulator, with metal rimmed wooden wheels and porcelain handle, the bodywork black with blue and yellow lines, 50in (127cm) long.
$800-1,200

A Victorian wooden rocking horse, with leather saddle, repainted, 86in (218.5cm) long.
$1,000-1,500

Models

A Lehmann printed and painted tinplate monorail car, Vineta, EPL No. 656, slightly worn, c1920, 10in (25.5cm) long.
$800-1,200

A Bing tinplate clockwork tram car.
$400-550

A Bing gauge 0 clockwork model of an early tramcar, in original claret and cream paintwork, with original lining, slightly chipped, c1906, 7in (18cm) long.
$800-1,200

A Benefink & Co., model of a horse drawn cart.
$800-1,200

A scale model Romany caravan, in the style of Dunton, with fully fitted interior, 72in (182.5cm) high.
$1,500-2,600

An early fret-work Type B London bus, British, some very slight damage, c1920, 20½in (51cm) long.
$600-900

A model Guinness brewery wagon, drawn by a pair of horses.
$700-900

A silver presentation model Chinese coal minehead, with plaque inscribed 'presented to E.J. Nathan, Esq., O.B.E., Joint Chief Manager of the Kailan Mining administration by the members of the senior staff as a token of their esteem and gratitude Autumn 1945', the roof opening to form a cigar box, 21 by 37in (53 by 94cm).
$1,500-2,500

A detailed 2in (5cm) scale static display model of a Merryweather twin cylinder horse drawn fire appliance 'Birmingham Fire Brigade', 17 by 26in (43 by 66cm).
$5,000-7,500

A model of the Cotswold Coffee Roasting and Grinding Mill, by R. J. Sare, c1925, 10 by 13in (25.5 by 33cm).
$400-550

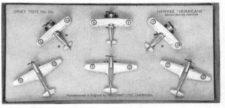

Dinky 60p Gloster Gladiator Bi-planes, with 62s Hawker Hurricane fighters, in 62s set of 6 box.
$1,000-1,500

Aircraft identification models from the 1939-45 war.
$300-500

A fully rigged bone and horn model of an 86-gun man-of-war, 23 by 30½in (58 by 77cm).
$3,000-4,500

A ¼ scale flying model of the Stampe SV4C bi-plane, serial letters G-AYWT, with external details, finished in green with gilded decoration and white letters 'Jaguar', wingspan 83in (210.5cm).
$1,200-1,750

A fully planked and framed wood pinned rigged model of the ketch Nonsuch of 1650, built by T. E. J. Manning, 29 by 30in (73 by 76cm).
$700-900

A model of H.M.S. Bounty, with planked wooden hull, the masts fully rigged with linen sails, 20thC, 26in (66cm) high, in glazed display case.
$400-550

A bone and baleen model of H.M.S. Star, with 46 guns, the stern named and carved in relief, 19thC, 23½in (63cm) long, on wooden stand with glazed case.
$7,000-10,000

A model of the sailing yacht Shamrock III, with gaff rig and paper sails, early 20thC, 75in (190.5cm).
$7,000-10,000

A wooden model of H.M.S. Victory, 19½in (50cm) long, in glazed mahogany case.
$8,000-11,000

A Swedish model of the sailing boat, Wardo, c1895, 33½in (85cm) long.
$200-350

A Bing 3RE 4–4–2 LNWR tank locomotive No. 44, wheels and motor replaced, pre World War I.
$700-900

A Basset Lowke gauge 0 3-rail electric model of the GWR 2–6–0 Mogul locomotive and tender No. 4331, in original paintwork, slightly chipped.
$900-1,300

A Bing for Basset Lowke 3RE 4–4–0 George The Fifth and tender No. 2663, pre World War I.
$300-400

A Bing gauge 1 3-rail electric model of the G.C.R. 4–6–0 locomotive and 6-wheeled tender No. 423, Sir Sam Fay, in original paintwork, converted from clockwork, very slightly chipped, 2 lanterns missing, c1914.
$2,000-3,000

A Bing tinplate clockwork King Edward VII 0 Gauge locomotive, No. 1902 in black livery, with red and gold lines, marked G.B.N. Dep.
$150-250

A Hornby gauge 0 3-rail electric 20V model of the SR 4–4–2 No. E36 locomotive and tender No. 1759, in green livery, with smoke deflector plates, repainted, lacks bulb.
$300-400

A Hornby gauge 0 3-rail electric 20V model of the LMS No. E220 Special Compound locomotive and tender No. 1185, in original paintwork, with boxes, worn.
$450-600

A Hornby gauge 0 clockwork model of the LNER No. 2 4–4–4 tank locomotive, in original paintwork and box.
$250-350

Two Hornby gauge 0 No. 2 LMS saloon coaches and a No. 2 Pullman coach, all in original paintwork, slightly worn, all lacking connectors, with boxes.
$300-400

A finely engineered 3½in (9cm) gauge model of the 2–8–2 locomotive and tender, Kratos, built by H. G. Horn, 10 by 55in (25.5 by 139.5cm).
$3,000-4,000

A 2in (5cm) scale model of the Burrel Gold Medal double crank compound, 2 speed, 3 shaft tractor, Reg. No. AD 7782 'Pouss-Nouk-Nouk', built by G. S. Lane, 20 by 29in (50 by 73.5cm).
$6,000-9,000

A well engineered 5in (12.5cm) gauge model of the B.R. 0–4–0 side tank locomotive built to the designs of Ajax, 14 by 28in (35.5 by 71cm).
$2,000-3,000

Games

Chess Sets

A Jaques Staunton ivory chess set, stained red and natural, both kings stamped Jaques London under the base, some variation in red staining, late 19thC, king 3in (7.5cm), in original leather casket, gilt stamped The 'Staunton' Chessmen, with green label to the base.
$2,500-3,500

A Jaques Staunton 'Club' weighted set, in boxwood and ebony, 20thC, king 4in (10cm), in mahogany box with green label, and a mahogany framed holly and coromandel veneered board with Jaques & Son label, 22in (56cm).
$2,500-3,500

An early Jaques Staunton ivory set, stained red and natural, white king stamped Jaques London under base, king 3in (7.5cm), contained in a carton pierre casket, with red label bearing registration No.
$1,500-2,500

An Anglo-Indian stained green and plain ivory chess set, one replacement piece, with a Cantonese ivory and tortoiseshell chess board, c1800, 18in (46cm).
$3,000-4,500

A Chinese carved ivory chess set, in blonde and magenta, elaborately carved upon canted bases, 19thC, red king 5in (13cm).
$1,500-2,500

A British Chess Company 'Staunton Chessman' ivory set, stained red and natural, king 4½in (11cm), in original rosewood box with label, torn, 11in (28cm) wide.
$2,000-3,000

The British Chess Company of Stroud, Glos., were in production c1900, and the smaller 'Royal' set in boxwood and ebony was produced in large numbers.

A Lund ivory playing set, the white king stamped Willm. Lund, Maker, 24 Fleet Street, red queen lacking knop, one red pawn base only, early 19thC, king 3in (8cm).
$1,000-1,500

A Vizagapatam horn and ivory set, the knopped stems and spreading bases with egg-and-tongue carving, black king lacking finial, 19thC, king 4in (10cm).
$800-1,200

An Indian 'Muslim' ivory set, the 2 sides stained with brown and red rings, the pawns, king and queen of domed form, king 2in (5.5cm).
$2,000-3,000

A bone 'pulpit' set, dark stained and natural, one black pawn missing, upper section of black king lacking, some restoration required, probably 19thC, king 5in (13cm).
$5,000-7,500

A Lund pattern ivory set, the pieces stained red and natural, 19thC, king 3½in (9cm), in mahogany box.
$800-1,200

A Wedgwood jasper part chess set, to the design of John Flaxman, each pawn to a different design, some damage, king 3½in (8.5cm).
$3,000-4,000

Two letters and a photograph from Josiah Wedgwood & Sons, dated 1923, indicate that this is an early example of its type.

Musical Instruments

A violin by Sebastian Kloz in Mittenwald, bearing the label AN 1780, length of back 14in (35.5cm), with a bow, in case.
$6,000-9,000

A violin by Benjamin Banks, bearing the label Benj. Banks, Catherine Street, Salisbury, 1773, length of back, 14in (35.5cm).
$8,000-11,000

A violin by Charles J. B. Collin-Mezin, bearing the maker's label Rue de Faub Poissonniere No. 29, dated 1899, and signed on the inner lower back, length of back 14in (35.5cm), in case.
$3,000-4,000

A violin by William H. Luff, bearing the maker's label in London, dated 1976, length of back 14in (35.5cm).
$7,000-10,000

A violin by Joan Carol Kloz, bearing the maker's label In Mittenwald An 1741, length of back 14in (35.5cm), with a silver mounted bow by G. Winterling, in a shaped leather case.
$2,500-3,500

A violin by Giuseppe Pedrazzini, bearing the maker's label in Cremonese fece in Milano L'Anno 1937, with maker's signature and brand, a second label of Boosey & Hawkes, sale agents London above, length of back 14in (35.5cm), with a bow, in case with cover.
$14,000-19,000

A violin by George Pyne, bearing the maker's label G. Pyne, Maker, London, dated 1887, with maker's script brand above, length of back 14in (35.5cm), in case.
$5,000-7,500

A violin by Antonio Bagatella, bearing the maker's label Antonius Bagatella delectans fecit Pata VII anno 1749, length of back 14in (35.5cm), with nickel mounted bow in a velvet lined shaped case.
$24,000-32,500

A violin by Paul François Blanchard, after Guarneri, bearing the maker's label Fait par Paul Blanchard a Lyon en 1896, No. 385, length of back 14in (35.5cm), in case.
$8,000-11,000

A violin by Albert Laurent in Brussels, bearing the maker's label dated 1913, length of back 14in (35.5cm), with 2 silver mounted bows, one with nickel adjuster, and leather case with cover.
$7,000-10,000

A violin by Johannes Barnardus Cuypers fecit L'Hage, bearing a manuscript label dated 1810, length of back 14in (35.5cm), in case.
$10,000-13,500

An English viola, probably by John Wilkinson, unlabelled, the one-piece back of plain wood, the scroll of faint figure, the table of medium grain, the varnish of a deep golden colour, length of back 16½in (42cm).
$3,000-4,500

An English viola by Charles Craske, labelled George Craske... Sold by / William E. Hill & Sons, London, the varnish of a red brown colour over a golden ground, length of back 16in (40.5cm), in case.
$4,500-7,000

A French viola, labelled Mansuy à Paris, the varnish of a red brown colour, c1890, length of back 16in (40.5cm), in case.
$1,500-2,500

A French viola, labelled Jean-Baptiste Vuillaume à Paris/3 rue Demours-Ternes/1870, length of back 16in (41.5cm), in case.
$35,000-46,000

An Italian viola, labelled Ferdinandus Gagliano Filius/ Nicolai fecit Neap 1775, the front and back double-purfled and decorated with fleur-de-lys design, the varnish of a dark golden colour, length of back 14in (35.5cm), in case.
$24,000-32,500

An Italian viola, attributed to Stefano Scarampella in Mantua, c1870, length of back 16in (41.5cm), in case.
$10,000-13,500

An English violoncello by Henry Jay, unlabelled, length of back 29in (73.5cm).
$10,000-13,500

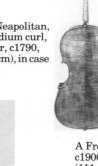

A violoncello, probably Neapolitan, the two-piece back of medium curl, the ribs and scroll similar, c1790, length of back 29in (73.5cm), in case with bow.
$15,000-21,000

A French double bass, unlabelled, c1900, length of back 44in (111.5cm).
$4,500-7,000

An English double bass, labelled Thomas Kennedy / London 1831, the table of medium grain, length of back 44½in (112cm).
$30,000-40,000

A single manual harpsichord, by Jacob & Abraham Kirkman, the nameboard inscribed Jacobus et Abraham Kirckman Londini Fecerunt 1774, in a crossbanded mahogany case with brass strap hinges, with walnut interior, 37½in (95cm) wide, on modern trestle stand.
$30,000-40,000

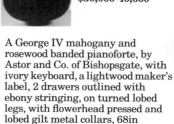

A George IV mahogany and rosewood banded pianoforte, by Astor and Co. of Bishopsgate, with ivory keyboard, a lightwood maker's label, 2 drawers outlined with ebony stringing, on turned lobed legs, with flowerhead pressed and lobed gilt metal collars, 68in (172.5cm) wide.
$3,000-4,000

Musical Boxes

A cylinder musical box by George Bondon, with 3 mandarins striking 6 bells, 8 airs, c1880, 19 by 10in (48 by 25.5cm), with original tune sheet.
$6,000-9,000

A polyphon 15⅝in (39.5cm) periphery-drive disc musical box, the case with quartered veneer and inlaid lid, lid interior restored, with winding handle and 12 discs.
$7,000-10,000

A 12 air musical box, in inlaid rosewood case.
$3,000-4,500

A Swiss musical box, by Nicole Freres, Geneva, No. 45006, with six 13in (33cm) cylinders, each playing 6 tunes, contained in a rosewood and marquetry cabinet mounted on a writing table, with tulipwood and walnut crossbanding, a drawer fitted with a writing slide, and pen and ink compartments, on hexagonal legs, late 19thC, 38½in (96.5cm) wide.
$2,000-3,000

An 18-key chamber barrel organ, by Longhurst (?), London, in mahogany case with simulated pipes to the Gothic front, on square reeded legs with barrel compartment, pipes dismantled and in poor condition, 71in (180cm) high.
$2,000-3,000

A 2-air manivel, c1880, 3in (7.5cm) diam.
$100-200

A Lépee mandolin pinned cylinder musical box, playing 4 airs, contained in rosewood case, with brass and pewter inlay, c1870, 24in (61cm) wide.
$6,000-9,000

Phonographs

A Pandora phonograph model, manufactured by Excelsior, plays 2 minute cylinders, complete with play back head and recording head, German, c1905.
$600-900

An Edison Diamond Disc phonograph, Chippendale Laboratory Model (C19) No. SM106640, with gilt fittings, mahogany case and Edison record pan, 51½in (130cm) high, with 19 discs.
$1,000-1,500

An Edison Amberola 1A phonograph, No. SM950, in mahogany case, with maroon enamelled 2-minute and 4-minute traversing mandrel mechanism, Diamond A and Model M combination reproducers, grille fret removed, 49in (124.5cm) high.
$1,500-2,500

A coin-in-slot phonograph, Type BS, in oak case with curved glass front and transfer, now with adapted Zonophone horn.
$1,500-2,500

Gramophones

An oak cased horn gramophone, with soundbox and brown embossed fluted tinplate horn.
$300-500

Miscellaneous

An oak Berliner 7in (18cm) record cabinet with folding lid, carved plinth moulding and spaces for 32 records, containing 7 American issue Berliners by Cal. Stewart and others.
$1,000-1,500

The Emor 'globe', by Emor Radio Ltd., made for the domestic market, the stem and globe chromium plated, tuned by rotating globe, other controls in stem, 1947, 54in (137cm).
$450-700

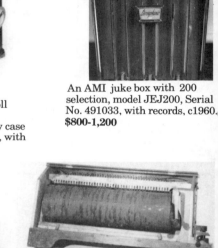

An Edison Bell discophone, with trumpet speaker.
$450-600

An Amourette organette in the form of a chalet, with 2 mirrored compartments with dancing dolls, one doll missing, the 16-note mechanism mounted behind, with 17 discs, various case parts loose or missing, 14in (35.5cm) wide.
$1,000-1,500

A Melodia table top paper-roll organette, by the American Mercantile Co., in mahogany case with gilt transfer decoration, with 9 rolls, 12½in (32cm) wide.
$450-600

An AMI juke box with 200 selection, model JEJ200, Serial No. 491033, with records, c1960.
$800-1,200

A musical picture clock, with 2-train French movement, striking on wire gong and 3-air snuff box musical movement, in giltwood frame, 29½ by 34½in (75 by 87cm).
$3,000-4,500

A miniature barrel organ, with 7 tunes, signed Josef Celis.
$5,000-7,500

A 44-key dumb organist, pinned for 6 listed hymn tunes, in plain mahogany case with crank, 31in (79cm) wide.
$1,500-2,500

A French singing bird, c1860, 11in (28cm) high.
$2,000-3,000

A wireless and horn speaker with eliminator for running off mains electricity, c1920.
$1,500-2,500

'His Master's Voice' model dog, 15in (38cm) high.
$2,000-3,000

Boxes

A satinwood and a rosewood tea caddy, 19thC.
$300-400

A Dutch parquetry tea caddy, 18thC.
$150-250

A mahogany and curled paper tea caddy, stained and inset with urns, flowers and lambrequin ornament, the top with chequer stringing, late 18thC, 6in (15cm).
$800-1,200

A George III mahogany tea caddy, decorated with marquetry panels and boxwood stringing, 6½in (16.5cm).
$800-1,200

A mahogany tea caddy, 18thC, 8½in (21cm).
$1,500-2,500

A Georgian fruitwood tea caddy, in the form of an apple, 4½in (11cm).
$1,000-1,500

A tortoiseshell 2 compartment caddy, inlaid with mother-of-pearl floral decoration, late Georgian.
$1,500-2,500

A Georgian mahogany Sheraton pattern knife box, with boxwood inlay, 9in (23cm) wide.
$10,000-13,500

An Adam ivory caddy, with tortoiseshell angles and shell pique decoration, 5in (15cm).
$1,500-2,500

A Sheraton style satinwood tea caddy, with marquetry decoration on harewood to lid, 6½in (16.5cm).
$1,300-2,000

A William and Mary walnut crossbanded marquetry lace box, 19½in (50cm).
$1,500-2,500

A William and Mary style oyster veneered lace box, the lid with boxwood stringing, 21in (53cm).
$1,500-2,500

A pair of George III mahogany knife boxes, with ebony line borders, one with fitted interior, the other with interior fittings removed.
$2,000-3,000

A Regency tortoiseshell veneered tea caddy, with ribbed front, enclosing a pair of lidded compartments, with turned ivory knop and ball feet, c1820, 5½in (14cm) wide.
$1,500-2,500

A North Italian oak fall-front casket, inlaid in foliate carved marine ivory, with fitted interior, 17thC, 9in (23cm) wide.
$600-900

A Dutch marquetry set of 6 gilded spirit flasks, stoppers and matching wine glass.
$1,500-2,500

A Continental agate box, the cover overlaid with gold mounts, 19thC, 3in (7cm).
$8,000-11,000

A George III mahogany serpentine front knife box, the kingwood crossbanded front enclosing an interior now fitted for stationery, with a crested silver escutcheon, 15in (38cm) high.
$600-900

A brass bound rosewood box, containing a set of 2 gilded ruby glass tea caddies, a spirit flask and stopper, a sugar bowl and cover, the box 10in (25.5cm) wide.
$1,500-2,500

A box, the top with gilt floral spray within a cartouche, the base with painted floral sprays on a lilac ground, 2in (5cm) wide.
$1,500-2,500

An oak bible box, with fitted interior, 18thC, 24½in (62cm).
$100-150

A matching pair of boxes, painted with floral sprays in panels, with blue and pink grounds, 2cm.
$450-600

A giltmetal mounted mother-of-pearl casket, the domed lid applied with straps and carrying handle, 19thC, 10in (25.5cm).
$250-350

A Georgian Stilton box.
$30,000-40,000

A patch box, the lid printed with black on white named view of Salisbury Cathedral, turquoise base, 1½in (4cm) wide.
$300-500

An oak box, 18thC, 9in (23cm).
$100-200

A mahogany collectors box, with brass stringing and vacant name plate, with turned brass handles, c1850, 7½in (19cm) wide.
$300-500

A box, painted with doves, with green base, 2in (5cm) wide.
$250-350

A Batavian silver mounted burr walnut casket, with foliate angle mounts and coat-of-arms, with escutcheon and carrying handles, mid-18thC, 13in (33cm) high.
$1,500-2,500

An Oriental floral and foliate carved ivory box, with finely decorated gilt hinged cover, 3in (7.5cm) wide.
$800-1,200

An Italian gilt metal box, one side with micro-mosaic allegorical panel, the other with ROTIA in raised letters, 19thC.
$9,000-12,500

A French black lacquered and buhl perfume box, the interior covered with silk, with 3 bottles and matching stoppers decorated in gold leaf.
$450-700

Electrical

A brass electric fire, c1900, 34 by 23in (86 by 58cm).
$100-200

A William and Mary lace box, veneered in walnut with oyster top and front, 21 by 16½in (53 by 42cm).
$2,000-3,000

A mahogany Tunbridgeware box, 19thC, 9in (23cm).
$100-200

Enamel

A George III South Staffordshire enamel tea caddy, painted with designs after J. Pillement and C. Fenn, damage, c1765, 6in (15cm) high.
$2,000-3,000

A Limoges enamel plaque of a Turkish bath, signed R-Blanchet, Limoges, 9½ by 8in (24 by 20cm).
$30,000-40,000

A Staffordshire enamel box, damaged, 18thC, 5½in (14cm) diam.
$450-600

An inlaid wall salt box, mid-19thC.
$450-600

Typewriters

A red Mignon No. 2 typewriter, with English type and spare German keyplate, serial No. 1907, in a bentwood case, lacks folding paper table, case recovered, handle detached.
$2,500-3,500

A Merrit typewriter, with rubber type, in wooden case, some damage.
$450-600

A pair of mahogany cased wall telephones, of Prof. D. E. Hughes/Crossley loose carbon electrode microphone type, with bells beneath and 2 similar ebonite earpieces, late 19thC, 9½in (24cm) high.
$300-500

Transport

A single Victoria, finished and upholstered in green, 95in (241cm) long.
$3,000-4,000

A 1901 International charette side entrance tonneau, Engine No. 42.
$22,000-30,000

A 1919 A.B.C. Scootamota, designed by Granville Bradshaw, Engine No. IB239.
$1,500-2,500

A 1924 Buick Regent 1½ ton van, converted from a hearse, Engine No. 1216436.
$14,000-19,000

A 1927 Austin Seven (Chummy) 2-door tourer, Engine No. M12427.
$10,000-13,500

A 1950 B.S.A. A10 Golden Flash 650cc solo motorcycle, plunger model, Engine No. ZA10-2043, with maker's handbook and tool kit.
$2,000-3,000

A 1942 Harley Davidson 1,200cc side valve motorcycle combination.
$10,000-13,500

An Ordinary bicycle, Humber Meteor, with iron frame, wood handles and solid rubber tyres, renewed, c1878, 40in (101.5cm) diam.
$800-1,200

An Edwardian baby's pram, with black paintwork and upholstery.
$300-400

l. A brass Lucas Kings Own No. F144 oil sidelight, 8½in (21.5cm) high.
$200-350

r. A black painted and nickel plated Lucas Kings Own No. F141 oil sidelight, 8½in (20.5cm) high.
$100-150

A collection of 6 motoring and cycling colour posters, advertising the Triumph Fifteen, Bean Cars, Wolseley and Morris.
$2,000-3,000

A gradient meter, by Tapley & Co., Southampton, with a silvered rise-and-fall dial, nickel plated brass case and dashboard brackets.
$100-200

Three Riley Alpine instruction books.
$100-200

A catalogue for Bugatti Competition and Racing Models, for the year 1932, missing card, containing a print of the Type 51 Grand Prix Standard 2-seater.
$300-400

A North British Railway copper lamp with bull's-eye lens, mounted with brass plate inscribed Hawick Up Home, internals missing, 24in (61cm) high.
$300-400

A pair of brass Bleriot oil sidelights, 14in (35.5cm) high.
$800-1,200

A Watford dashboard clock, with silvered dial, heavy brass case with bevelled glass, 8-day movement and button activated hand setting, c1910, 3½in (9cm) diam.
$150-250

A Bentley winged 'B', stamped J. Fray Ltd., c1920, on early original Bentley radiator cap, 8in (20cm) wide.
$800-1,200

Aero Club, a Brooklands badge, numbered 188, good enamel, post 1930.
$900-1,300

A pair of Lucas new 'Alto-de-Luxe grill fronted horns, with restored chrome cases, 5in (12.5cm) diam.
$400-550

An Austin winged steering wheel mascot, mounted on radiator cap, inscribed Austin Motor Co., stamped Rd 286069, c1910, 4 by 5in (10 by 12.5cm).
$2,000-3,000

An R.A.C. associated member's badge, in nickelled brass with enamel crest and disc for 1914, 6in (15cm) high.
$5,000-7,500

The cast brass nameplate from Lifeboat No. 12, S.S. Titanic, 12½in (32cm).
$9,000-12,500

A chrome plated mascot, victory, a female standing on one leg with arms outstretched, holding a ribbon.
$300-400

An MG radiator, restored, c1950, 24in (61cm) high.
$300-400

A brass R.A.C. full member's badge, stamped No. DF384, c1910, chipped, 5in (12.5cm) high.
$150-250

A Jaguar mascot, the shaped base stamped Gordon Crosby, c1930, 8in (20cm) long, on original SS 100 Jaguar radiator cap.
$450-600

A glass car mascot of a butterfly girl, the base inscribed Red-Ashay-Reg. 611338, 1935, 9½in (24cm) high.
$900-1,300

Leather & Luggage

A travelling dressing set, with silver mounts, 1901, Birmingham, in an alligator skin case.
$900-1,300

A tan leather cocktail hamper, made for Brooks Brothers, New York, 15in (38cm) wide.
$700-900

A Hermes python bag, with box, c1950.
$4,000-5,500

A Louis Vuitton trunk, fitted with 2 trays, covered with a brown chequer board design, labelled Louis Vuitton, 454 Strand, Paris, 1 Rue Scribe, No. 35832, c1890, 30in (76cm) wide.
$1,300-2,000

A British officer's valise, formerly the property of Col. H. Harford, 1852-1937, Adj. of the 99 Foot, the Duke of Edinburgh's Regiment.
$1,500-2,500

This valise was actually used by the Colonel during the Zulu Wars.

A crocodile cased clock, c1920.
$300-500

A wicker travelling 'en route' set, by Drew & Sons, Piccadilly, 12in (30.5cm) wide.
$450-700

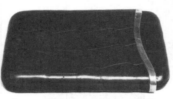

A crocodile cigar holder, c1930.
$400-550

A hunting decanter set in leather box, with brass decoration, early 19thC.
$1,300-2,000

A crocodile suitcase, the interior fitted with folding tray/dressing case, canvas cover.
$800-1,200

A crocodile and silver wallet.
$400-550

An Asprey crocodile travelling case, with integral folding toilet case, containing extensive silver gilt fittings, including lidded bottles, brushes, and a mirror, marked London 1914, the reverse of the lid stamped Asprey, London, with initialled waterproof canvas cover.
$3,000-4,500

An Edwardian lady's crocodile carry-all.
$400-550

A snakeskin suitcase, c1940.
$1,000-1,500

A Louis Vuitton crocodile lady's necessaire, fittings in crystal and tortoiseshell, c1920.
$10,000-13,500

An Australian crocodile case, c1940.
$1,200-1,750

A crocodile attaché case, c1920.
$1,000-1,500

Two pieces of vellum luggage, and one other.
$100-200

An Edwardian Gladstone bag.
$800-1,200

A school satchel, 13in (33cm).
$30-50

An American crocodile hat box, c1940.
$1,500-2,500

An Asprey fitted travelling case, the fittings in silver and crystal, c1920.
$10,500-15,000

A Victorian coaching trunk.
$450-700

A leather folding stool.
$30-50

A Louis Vuitton hide gentleman's suitcase, with crystal and silver fittings.
$8,000-11,000

A pair of ladies crocodile sling-back shoes, c1950.
$300-500

A Victorian crocodile jewellery box, c1890.
$1,500-2,500

A Drew & Sons fitted crocodile case, with tortoiseshell fittings, c1930.
$10,000-13,500

A pair of gentleman's crocodile shoes, c1940.
$250-350

A pair of field boots, with wooden trees, c1914.
$300-400

A crocodile suit/dressing case, opening into 3 sections, one lined with ivory watered silk, the other with compartments and 5 glass bottles with silver and tortoiseshell tops, monogrammed L.S., the suitcase lid similarly initialled, lacking some fittings, 18in (46cm) long, in foul weather case.
$400-550

Two crocodile wallets, with gold corners, c1950.
$450-700

A lady's leather carrying toilet case, the fittings with silver mounts, and an ebony brush set.
$200-350

A Louis Vuitton shoe carrier, c1950.
$1,500-2,500

A Louis Vuitton suitcase, c1950.
$1,000-1,500

Make the most of Miller's

Miller's is completely different each year. Each edition contains completely NEW photographs. This is not an updated publication. We never repeat the same photograph.

A shagreen cigarette box, c1920.
$300-500

A shagreen clutch bag, c1920.
$800-1,200

A crocodile leather case, lined with suede, with key, 16in (40.5cm) long.
$6,000-9,000

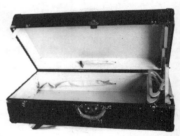

A Louis Vuitton travelling case, c1950.
$2,000-3,000

A Hermes crocodile bag, with jewellery box under, c1950.
$8,000-11,000

Sport
Fishing

A Hardy brass Perfect, with ivory handle and Bickerdyke nickel silver lineguard, c1891, 3½in (9cm).
$3,000-4,500

A nickel plated brass Hardy crankwind trout fly reel, with offset pillars and horn handle, c1890, 2¼in (6cm).
$1,000-1,500

l. A Hardy St. John fly reel, c1925, 4in (10cm).
$75-150

r. A Hardy L.R.H. lightweight trout fly reel, c1935, 3in (7.5cm).
$75-150

A Hardy salmon Perfect with duplicated Mk II check, c1925, 3¾in (9.5cm).
$400-550

An electroplated fishing prize cup, dated 1844, 10½in (27cm) high.
$75-150

A Hardy Bougle trout dry fly reel with offset pillars, c1915, 3in (7.5cm).
$1,300-2,000

A brass collar fitting wynch by Hayward of Birmingham, with turned bone handle, drum locking mechanism and horsehair line, c1860, 3½in (9cm) overall.
$400-550

A geared crankwind gut twister, c1880, 4 by 5½in (10 by 14cm).
$200-350

Top. A wooden pike lure, by DAM of Berlin, c1950, 5in (12.5cm).
$15-30

Bottom. An Edward Vom Hofe of New York spoon bait, the SAMS, nickel silver, patented 1908, 4½in (11.5cm).
$15-30

A leather rod butt holder for big game fishing.
$15-30

A keep net.
$30-50

A Hardy case showing examples of different sizes of spinning lines, 2 missing, c1930.
$15-30

l. A Hardy Sunbeam trout fly reel, c1938, 3¼in (8cm).
$75-150

r. A Hardy Sunbeam trout fly reel, c1930, 3in (7.5cm).
$75-150

A drum alloy Hardy trout dry fly Perfect, c1901, 2½in (6.5cm).
$800-1,200

A Hardy Zane Grey game fishing reel, in Monel metal with leather thumb brake guard, c1930, 4¼in (11cm).
$1,000-1,500

A Greasaline gun, a device for permanently greasing a fly line, to be fixed to the rod butt with line running through 2 holes, c1935.
$15-30

Three early style fly-tying vices and holders, c1900.
$20-40

Golfing

A Mills, Niblick N.K. model aluminium alloy golf club, by the Standard Golf Co., the hickory shaft stamped Mitchell, Manchester.
$400-550

An M.S.D. 2 model aluminium alloy golf club, by the Standard Golf Co., the hickory shaft stamped Finnighans, Manchester.
$75-150

A Copeland jug, decorated with a golfing scene, on a green ground with biscuit ground borders, 6in (15cm) high.
$300-500

A bronze metal statue of a golfer, 10½in (26.5cm) high.
$300-500

A silver ashtray, by James Dixon & Sons, Sheffield, 1928, mounted with a figure of a devil smoking a pipe, standing next to a silver golf bag containing 5 clubs, 8in (20cm) diam, 20 grammes gross.
$800-1,200

Miscellaneous

An iron saddle rack.
$20-40

A Riley billiard marker, 25in (63.5cm) long.
$60-100

A Sussex stove ball bat, 11in (28cm).
$20-40

A cast iron painted bridle rack.
$75-150

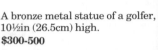

A Victorian mahogany quarter-size snooker/dining table, with 3 leaves to top, with cues, set of balls and scoreboard, 89 by 48in (226 by 122cm).
$1,000-1,400

A pair of leather boxing gloves, pre-war.
$75-150

A riding tack rack.
$60-100

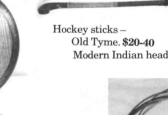

Hockey sticks –
Old Tyme. **$20-40**
Modern Indian head. **$20-40**

A discus, 8in (20.5cm) diam.
$20-40

A Continental silver chalice-shaped trophy, Montreux Lawn Tennis Club, 24th April 1905, 9½in (24cm).
$800-1,200

Edwardian hoops.
$20-40

An Edwardian leather skipping rope.
$20-40

A football.
$30-50

A bronzed metal figure of a tennis player, 11½in (29cm) high.
$600-900

A B.A.N. Co. automatic 'penny arcade' football machine, c1915.
$2,250-3,500

A 15ct. gold Football League Championship medal, for the season 1911-12, the medal having been presented to Mr. R. B. Middleton, the secretary of Blackburn Rovers Football Club.
$450-700

A pottery jug, inscribed on the front 'Sheffield Wednesday, English Cup Winners, April 18th, 1896', the reverse giving details of each match won during the competition, 4½in (11.5cm) high.
$1,000-1,500

A programme for the F.A. Cup Final of 1923, the first occasion that the game was staged at Wembley Stadium.
$400-550

A silver footballing vesta case, Birmingham 1907, the front of the case embossed with 3 footballers in action.
$400-550

A modern plaster portrait bust of Sayers, overcoloured in bronze, on inscribed plinth, 12in (30.5cm).
$200-350

A china figure of a boxer, 10½in (27cm).
$300-500

A creamware mug, with an image of Johnson and Perrins at Banbur on the side, some wear, 4½in (12cm) high.
$400-550

A mid-Victorian wine goblet, finely engraved with an image of 2 unidentified boxers in combat in the ring, 6½in (17cm) high.
$600-900

A white jug with red markings, 5½in (14cm).
$400-550

Crafts

A stoneware vase, by Lucie Rie, impressed LR seal, 10½in (27cm) high.
$1,500-2,500

A stoneware bottle vase, by Lucie Rie, covered with a mottled turquoise, bluish-green and pale lavender spiral with matt bronze and fluxed rim, impressed LR seal, c1975, 11in (28cm) high.
$3,000-4,500

A stoneware shallow bowl, by Lucie Rie, covered in a thick white pitted glaze with iron brown flecks, the centre with unglazed band, impressed LR seal, c1955, 13in (33cm).
$3,000-4,500

A stoneware vase, by Hans Coper, the manganese brown body covered in a buff slip with burnished areas to body and foot revealing brown body, the foot with ochre blistering, slight rim restoration, impressed HC seal, c1970, 16in (41cm).
$15,000-21,000

A stoneware beaker, by Lucie Rie and Hans Coper, the exterior covered in a pitted matt manganese glaze, the interior in a shiny white glaze, impressed LR and HC seals, c1958, 4in (10cm) high.
$600-900

A pair of stoneware plates, by Michael Cardew, covered in a light mushroom coloured glaze with olive brown, and blue brushwork, impressed MC and Wenford Bridge seals, c1978, 10in (26cm) high.
$400-550

A stoneware black bottle form, by Hans Coper, covered in a matt manganese glaze, impressed HC seal, c1970, 6in (15cm).
$10,000-13,500

A stoneware teapot, by Michael Cardew, with strap handle and grip, covered in a mushroom coloured glaze with iron brown and blue brushwork, impressed MC and Wenford Bridge Pottery seals, c1970, 9½in (23.5cm) high.
$1,300-2,000

A stoneware sculpture of a cat, by Rosemary Wren, covered in a matt white, pale green and iron brown glaze, impressed Wren seal, 9½in (24.5cm) wide.
$200-350

A stoneware asymmetrical vase, by Ewen Henderson, the hand built form laminated with pale lavender and brown clays covered in pitted and textured turquoise, white, amber and buff glazes, 22in (56cm) high.
$2,250-3,500

A stoneware baluster shaped vase by Janet Leach, covered in a mottled iron brown and mirrored black glaze over which run a pale lavender glaze stopping short of the foot, impressed JL and St. Ives seals, c1960, 12½in (31cm) high.
$400-550

An early slip decorated raku bowl, by Bernard Leach, covered in a translucent pitted and flecked pale beige glaze with cobalt blue band to outer rim, trailed with amber slip grape clusters, kiln damage, impressed BL and St. Ives seals, c1928, 9½in (24cm) wide.
$1,000-1,500

A stoneware jar, by John Leach, decorated in wax resist, with speckled greenish white dolomite glaze, impressed JL seal and Muchelney, 12in (30.5cm).
$450-700

A thickly potted stoneware vase, by William Staite Murray, covered in a finely crackled semi-translucent mushroom coloured glaze with iron brown and grey brushwork of stylised foliage, impressed M seal, 8in (20.5cm) high.
$1,000-1,500

A large slab-built porcelain vase, by Ljerka Njers, textured and decorated with muslin lace and leaves glazed in shades of green, amber, blue and white, with stylised flowers and foliage, painted monogram LN, 11½in (29cm) high.
$450-700

A stoneware pebble, by Eileen Lowenstein, covered in a run pale olive green glaze decorated with finely crackled translucent lime green flowerhead, impressed EL, 8in (20cm) high.
$200-350

A stoneware flared bowl, by Estella Camparias, covered on the interior with a streaked lavender, purple, and turquoise glaze, the exterior with a run turquoise glaze, impressed E seal, 10in (25.5cm) diam.
$400-550

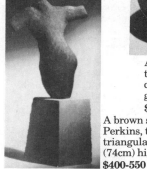

A grey earthenware bowl, by Birch, the interior covered in a finely crackled translucent pale blue glaze, 10½in (26.5cm) wide.
$200-350

A brown stoneware torso, by Roger Perkins, the sculpted figure on triangular section stone base, 29½in (74cm) high.
$400-550

A porcelain bowl, by Henry Hammond, painted with bands of fishes, covered in a finely crackled translucent celadon glaze, impressed seal, 2½in (6cm) high.
$400-550

A stoneware plate, by Seth Cardew, decorated in iron brown and blue brushwork against a pale mushroom ground, impressed SC and Wenford Bridge seals, 14in (35.5cm) diam.
$300-500

An early St. Ives slip decorated eathenware jug, with strap handle, covered in a lustrous pale brown glaze and decorated with mustard yellow, slip flaking, impressed St. Ives and obscured square seals, 9in (23cm).
$100-200

A stoneware pouring vessel by Walter Keeler, covered in a mottled blue grey salt glaze, 5½in (13.5cm) high.
$400-550

A pair of Studio pottery vases, slight damage to one, c1900, 9in (23cm) high.
$100-150

A stoneware vase, by John Ward, covered in a matt white glaze over a speckled pale greenish brown glaze, slight restoration, impressed J W seal, 7½in (19cm) high.
$200-350

A stoneware sculpture, by Gordon Baldwin, covered in a white slip with pink tinges, impressed GB seal and painted title 'For Nic Barbow Box for a friend GB 74', 14in (35.5cm) high.
$450-700

Tribal Art

A Baga head for an altar, Elek etc. with glossy dark patina, old damage, 17½in (44cm).
$800-1,200

A Tiv wood table, the figures with scarification on their heart-shaped faces, dark glossy patina, replacement circular top, 27in (68cm) high.
$800-1,200

An Awka (Ibo) stool on curved supports, with dark glossy patina, 13½in (34cm) high.
$1,000-1,500

A Trobriand Islands wood washboard, with a seated figure at the top, 29in (73cm) high.
$1,000-1,500

A Pokot wood headrest, on 3 legs flaring from central support, 6½in (16cm) high.
$200-350

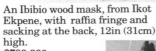

A Hawaiian wood spear, ihe laumake, of kauila wood, minor chips, 102in (260cm) long.
$4,000-5,500

An Ibibio wood mask, from Ikot Ekpene, with raffia fringe and sacking at the back, 12in (31cm) high.
$700-900

A New Guinea wood pigment dish, with dark glossy patina with extensive remains of lime and pale mud, middle Sepik, 16in (40cm).
$14,000-19,000

A Jivaro shrunken head, with curling black hair and finely woven fibre suspension cord from the top of the head.
$9,000-12,500

A Mbete wood dance crest, minor damage, 23½in (60cm) high.
$3,000-4,500

A female Ibeji, from Oro, near Ila-Orangun, 10½in (27cm) high.
$2,000-3,000

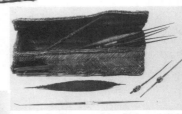

An Inca workbasket containing spinning instruments, 12in (30.5cm) wide.
$800-1,200

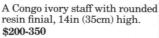

A Maori bone comb, 5in (12.5cm) high.
$300-500

A Congo ivory staff with rounded resin finial, 14in (35cm) high.
$200-350

An Australian aborigine wood club, 21in (53cm) long, with another aborigine club from New South Wales and a Fiji ula with incised grip.
$800-1,200

An unusual mask for the Malanggan cult, painted in red, black and white, 37in (94cm) high.
$6,000-9,000

A French bronze group of Roger and Angelica borne by the Hippogriff, cast from a model by Antoine-Louis Barye, by the master founder H, Henri at Hector Brahme foundry, stamped H, signed Barye, Roger Ballu, L'oeuvre de Barye, Paris, 1890, 20 by 27½in (51 by 70cm). **$150,000-200,000**

A bronze figure of Mephistopheles, the massive granite base engraved on one side in gold Antocolski, after Markus Antokolski, 19thC, 34in (86cm) high. **$10,000-18,000**

An Austrian bronze model of an owl pouncing on 3 mice, by Caspar Gras, 17thC, 6in (15cm) high, on turned wood socle. **$22,000-35,000**

A French bronze group of an Arab falconer, cast from a model by Pierre Jules Mène, signed, inscribed Susse Frères Editeurs, Fauconnier a Cheval de P.J. Mene, 19thC, 31 by 30in (78 by 76cm). **$20,000-30,000**

An Italian gilt bronze figure of Hercules supporting a celestial globe, late 16th/early 17thC, 15in (38cm) high. **$210,000-275,000**

An English bronze statuette of Peter Pan, after Sir George Frampton, inscribed on the base, early 20thC, 19in (48cm) high. **$8,000-12,000**

A Venetian gilt bronze statuette of Neptune, in the style of Girolamo Campagna, on a marble pedestal with pietre dura inlaid coat-of-arms of a bishop, with a tower overgrown with ivy, 16thC, 16½in high. **$14,000-20,000**

A pair of French gilt and bronze urns, with classical figures in market scenes inscribed EN THI AT OPAI and EK THEAT OPAE, above friezes of sphinx and Athenian decoration, 19thC, 4½in (11cm) high. **$24,000-35,000**

A bronze group of Aeneas carrying his father Anchises followed by Ascanius, after François Girardon and Pierre Lepautre, French, 18thC, 22in (56cm) high. **$10,000-15,000**

A Charles X ormolu casket, with English porcelain plaque, carrying handles, 9½in (24cm) wide. **$9,000-14,000**

A pair of ormolu and filigree candle-sticks, possibly Italian, c1800, 10in (25cm) high. **$4,000-8,000**

A pair of Louis XVI ormolu-mounted alabaster pot pourri vases, with bearded satyr's mask handles, 13½in (34.5cm) high. **$12,000-18,000**

A pair of ormolu and bronze 3-branch wall lights in the Regency style, 19in (48cm) high. **$8,000-12,000**

A French ormolu caryatid herm, a bearded male figure, on a tapering support, early 18thC, 52in (132cm) high. **$84,000-110,000**

A pair of Louis XVI bronze and ormolu chenets, with recumbent lions on lambrequin and fluted shaped pedestals, 23in (58.5cm) wide. **$50,000-75,000**

A Peter the Great parcel gilt Imperial presentation kovsh, the silver centre with the Russian double-headed eagle, exterior with Cyrillic engraving, unmarked, c1697, 13½in (34cm) long. **$32,000-45,000**

A pair of ormolu mounted Chinese red and blue porcelain 8-light candelabra, 19thC, 35in (89cm) high. **$8,000-12,000**

A pair of George III bronze, ormolu and white marble cassolettes, 10in (25cm) high. **$16,000-20,000**

A pair of Louis XV ormolu and bronze 3-light candelabra, the central shaft entwined by a snake, the white marble plinths on square bases, 19½in (49.5cm) high. **$6,000-10,000**

A pair of Empire patinated bronze and ormolu 6-light candelabra, 31½in (80cm) high. **$30,000-45,000**

A pair of ormolu and bronze urn-shaped vases, fitted for electricity as lamps, with pleated silk shades, 34½in (88cm). **$18,000-30,000**

547

A pair of Empire ormolu-mounted bronze ewers, c1815, 22½in (57cm) high. **$20,000-30,000**

An Empire painted and gilded 8-light chandelier, with stepped circular spreading central support surmounted by a classical maiden, re-decorated, 36in (91.5cm) high. **$10,000-15,000** C

An Empire patinated bronze and ormolu 6-light candelabrum, with scrolling foliate candle branches ending in rosettes, 42in (107cm) high. **$18,000-30,000**

A Charles X ormolu and bronze encrier, surmounted by a bust of Minerva, on a Siena marble base, 14in (35.5cm) wide. **$10,000-15,000**

A pair of Empire ormolu and patinated bronze chenets, formed as recumbent sphinxes, on shaped plinth bases, 15½in (39cm) long. **$36,000-50,000**

An Empire ormolu and bronze fender, 36in (91cm) wide. **$8,000-12,000**

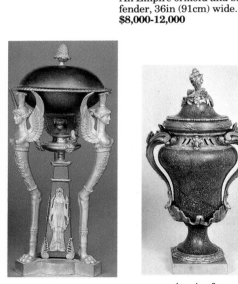

A pair of ormolu wall lights, of Louis XV style, fitted for electricity, 13½in (34cm) high. **$5,000-8,000**

A pair of Empire patinated steel and ormolu Athéniennes, 17in (43cm) high. **$12,000-18,000**

A pair of ormolu mounted porphyry urns, stamped Ch. Bussierre, 22½in (57cm) high. **$38,000-50,000**

A pair of Louis XVI style ormolu mounted rock crystal covered urns, 19thC, 17in (43cm) high. **$24,000-45,000**

A Louis XV ormolu mounted Japanese lacquer and Meissen porcelain encrier, group modelled by J. J. Kändler, damage and repair, blue crossed swords mark, c1749, 17½in (44cm) wide. **$30,000-45,000**

A Flemish ivory statue of St. Sebastian, damage, 17thC, 17in high. **$115,000-150,000**

A pair of Dieppe ivory mirrors, the frames with foliage, lions masks and figures of Pan, initialled FAR, late 19thC, 33in high. **$14,000-20,000**

A German ivory cadaver, in the manner of Stephen Zick, slight damage, 17thC, 10in (25cm) long. **$4,000-8,000**

A pair of ormolu mounted Sèvres bleu nouveau pot pourri vases, 16in (41cm) high. **$52,000-70,000**

An English carved marble portrait bust, reputedly Admiral Byng, damage, 18thC, 17in high. **$6,000-10,000**

A white marble bust of Napoleon I, signed by R. Trentanove, Italian, damaged, early 19thC, 21in (54cm) high. **$3,000-5,000**

An English walrus ivory games piece, damaged, mid-12thC, 7cm diam. **$50,000-55,000**

A pair of ormolu-mounted granite urns, 17½in (44cm) high. **$10,000-15,000**

A pair of Florentine marble figures of Love Found and Love Abandoned, by Pasquale Romanelli, Firenze 1876/77, minor chips, 63 and 61in. **$95,000-130,000**

549

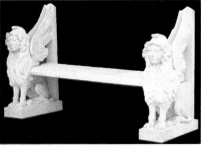

A white marble garden bench, the seat supported by winged sphinxes, 19thC, 70in (178cm) wide.
$18,000-30,000

An Italian white marble statue of a nude figure by Alfredo Pina, signed in the marble, early 20thC, 32in (81cm) high.
$20,000-35,000

A matched pair of George III blue-john vases, on stepped square plinths, partly of white marble and slate, 9in (23cm) high. **$12,000-20,000**

Three North German oak statues of Apostles, St. James of Compostela in pilgrim's hat, and 2 others, late 15thC, 2 hands damaged.
$18,000-30,000

A pair of mottled pink marble urns, with everted lips and tapering bodies, with shaped socles and square bases, 19thC, 30in (76cm) high.
$8,000-12,000

An English marble figure of Susannah, by Jospeh Gott, 19thC, 48in (120cm), on original pedestal.
$110,000-130,000

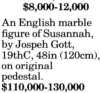

An English marble figure of Ino teaching Bacchus to dance, by Joseph Gott, 57in (145cm) high, on veined marble pedestal.
$450,000-550,000

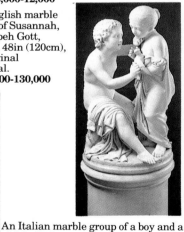

An Italian marble group of a boy and a girl, by V. Lusardi, repaired, c1875, 35½in (90cm). **$12,000-20,000**

A wood sculpture of St. Catherine, with traces of polychrome, late 15thC, 45in (114cm) high.
$40,000-90,000

A terracotta group of a Bacchant and 3 Bacchantes, by Claude-Michel, Clodion, French, c1800, 25in (64cm) high, on later base. **$400,000-500,000**

An Italian marble figure of a child pulling a thorn from a spaniel's foot, by Giovanni Maria Benzoni, damage, c1846, 43in (110cm).
$20,000-30,000

An Etruscan bronze figure of a nude ephebe, with beaded decoration around his neck, on marble base, early 5th Century B.C., 4½in (12cm) high. **$84,000-120,000**

A green basalt head of an official wearing a striated wig, Saite Period, mid-7th Century B.C., 4½in (12cm) high. **$60,000-80,000**

An antique Chinese pillar rug, 127 by 67in (323 by 170cm). **$16,000-20,000**

An Attic red figure pelike, by the Painter of the Louvre Centauromachy, repaired, minor restoration, c440 B.C., 14in (35.5cm) high. **$20,000-30,000**

A Bidjar carpet, the ivory field surrounded by indigo arabesque vine, 153 by 84in (390 by 215cm). **$18,000-25,000**

An Aubusson tapestry rug, with shaped ivory field and rose surround, 19thC, 71 by 55in (180 by 140cm). **$12,000-20,000**

An Aubusson carpet, the cream ground with a central floral bouquet, surrounded by a gold and rust leaf-tipped border, damage and repairs, c1870, 216 by 127in (574 by 323cm). **$24,000-35,000**

A George III needlework carpet, designed by Robert Adam, with opening for a hearth, 177in (448cm) diam. **$60,000-80,000**

A Bessarabian carpet, repaired, c1890, 101 by 72in (256 by 183cm). **$6,000-10,000**

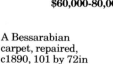

An Aubusson carpet, with an inscription Spe Vivitur, some wear, repaired and backed, mid-19thC, 276 by 232in (701 by 590cm). **$30,000-50,000**

An 'Imreli' carpet, the rust brown field with rows of 'spread eagle' guls, reduced, slight wear, early 19thC, 117 by 62in (297 by 157cm). **$24,000-40,000**

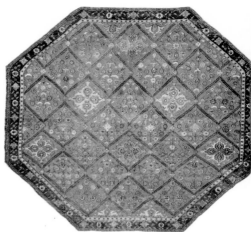

An East Persian octagonal carpet, the shaded burgundy field with a lattice enclosing various floral palmettes and sprays, some wear, repairs, backed, 139 by 127in (352 by 322cm). **$18,000-25,000**

A Kashan silk prayer rug, c1920, 56 by 41in (142 by 104cm). **$44,000-65,000**

This exceptionally fine rug contains approximately 1,200 knots per square inch and by repute was woven over a period of 8 years.

A Kuba prayer rug, the teal blue ground covered by a pattern of stylised floral and geometric devices, c1890, 59 by 50in (150 by 127cm). **$22,000-30,000**

A Melas rug, the rust ground covered by multi-coloured rosettes and leaves, damaged, late 19thC, 71 by 48in (180 by 122cm). **$6,000-10,000**

A Herez carpet, the terracotta field with allover angular designs, 148 by 109in (376 by 278cm). **$12,000-20,000**

A Savonnerie carpet, woven in bright colours with summer flowers in picture frame borders, restored, mid-19thC, 262 by 208in (666 by 528cm). **$130,000-180,000**

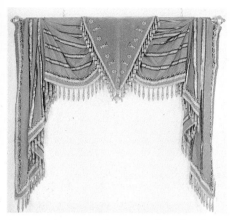

A set of 3 Regency pelmets, attributed to George Bullock, 58in (147cm) high. **$8,000-12,000**

A Buddhist priest's kesi robe, lined in silk, Kangxi, 42 by 108in (106.5 by 274cm). **$9,000-15,000**

A sampler, by Ann Tafsell aged 14 in 1830, 18in (46cm), in original frame. **$1,500-2,500**

A lady's informal flowered silk robe, full length, with front overlap closing to the right, 56in (142cm) long. **$4,000-8,000**

A needlework purse, English, late 16thC, 5in (12.5cm). **$18,000-25,000**

A sampler by Sarah Gaull, aged 14, dated April 27, 1827, 24½in (62cm) high. **$800-1,500**

A Scottish sampler, by Isobel Williamson, c1790. **$2,000-4,000**

A sampler by Mary White, dated August 17, 1835, 4½in (11cm). **$200-400**

A pair of embroidered gloves, English, c1600, slight wear. **$8,000-12,000**

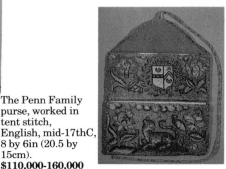

The Penn Family purse, worked in tent stitch, English, mid-17thC, 8 by 6in (20.5 by 15cm). **$110,000-160,000**

A needlework casket, the doors concealing 4 drawers and a secret drawer, the lid opening to reveal a mirror and writing compartment, English, mid-17thC, 10 by 12in (25 by 30cm), with key. **$16,000-25,000**

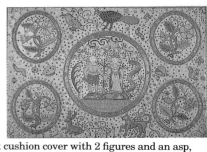

A silk cushion cover with 2 figures and an asp, and 4 roundels of flowers in coloured silks, worked with the initials DTM, early 17thC, 14 by 22in (36 by 56cm), framed, glazed. **$14,000-20,000**

A box covered in petit point, and 4 boxes, English, early 18thC, 5 by 8in (13 by 20cm), in glazed case. **$30,000-42,000**

A cushion of ivory silk embroidered with the story of Bathsheba, English mid-17thC, 20 by 22in (51 by 56cm), framed and glazed. **$36,000-45,000**

An Aubusson tapestry entre fenêtre, with neo-classical urn of flowers and sprays, 19thC, 140 by 65in (356 by 165cm). **$8,000-12,000**

A needlework casket, with mirrored compartment, secret drawers and 2 glass bottles, restored, English, mid-17thC, 11in (28cm) wide. **$36,000-50,000**

A needlework casket, containing a mirror, drawers including secret drawers, 2 bottles, English, mid-17thC, 15½in (39cm) wide. **$14,000-20,000**

A casket, the lid and sides of ivory satin decorated with scrolled paper work, and 3 other smaller boxes, English, 1687, main box 17in (43cm) wide. **$24,000-35,000**

A needlework panel for a cushion cover, worked with the Adoration of the Magi, within a blue border with flowers, fruit and insects, with a unicorn, leopard, lion and stag at each corner, English, c1600, 20 by 22in (51 by 56cm), framed and glazed. **$14,000-20,000**

A Brussels tapestry, The Death of Decius Mus, after a cartoon by Peter Paul Rubens, signed in the selvedge Raet with Brussels town mark, 133 by 188in (338 by 477cm). **$20,000-30,000**

A Brussels tapestry woven in silks and wools, with Anthony and Cleopatra and their attendants, with Brussels town mark, late 16thC, 135 by 155in (344 by 394cm). **$36,000-45,000**

A Brussels verdure tapestry, depicting swans on a river with a stone bridge and buildings in the background, repaired, 17thC, 136in (347cm). **$7,000-12,000**

An Italian tapestry woven in silks and wools with a Muse above a figure of Athena flanked by masks and figures, lacking bottom border, Florence or Ferrara, late 16thC, 136 by 160in. **$30,000-50,000**

A valance worked in tent stitch, with Tobias and the very large fish, and the marriage of Tobias and Sara at Ecbatana, c1600, 21 by 66in (53 by 168cm), framed and glazed. **$12,000-20,000**

A Brussels tapestry woven in silks and wools, lacking top and bottom border, signed V.Leyniers D.L, c1725, 126 by 158in (320 by 401cm). **$20,000-30,000**

A Brussels tapestry, woven in wools and silks with King Numitor and his attendants, with Romulus and Remus to the left, outside the city of Albalonga, late 16thC, 120 by 152in. **$36,000-50,000**

A Brussels tapestry woven in silks and wools with Bacchus seated in a chariot, lacking borders, 17thC, with later slip, 109 by 148in (277 by 376cm). **$36,000-50,000**

A Britains Royal Horse Artillery at the gallop in steel helmets, No. 1339, some damage and repairs, c1940. **$16,000-25,000**

A Britains The Sovereign's Escort, No. 2081, comprising 222 pieces, in good condition, 1953. **$8,000-12,000**

A Britains Royal Horse Artillery at the halt, No. 318, service dress, some damage and wear, 1933. **$14,000-20,000**

Left. A Steiff dark plush teddy bear, worn, Steiff button to l. ear, 26in (66cm). **$4,500-6,500**

Right. A Danel & Cie French bisque head Paris-Bebe, marked, 16in (40cm). **$5,000-8,000**

Britains Vertunni, Louis XV of France, his wife, mistress, mother, 2 Royal Guards and a gentleman, original paint. **$400-600**

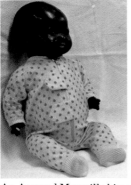

A Britains scale figure of the Colonel-in-Chief, the Welsh Guards, excellent, 1947, 70mm. **$3,000-5,000**

Above. A French bisque doll, in original dress, marked 14, 9½in (24cm). **$3,000-5,000**

Left. An Emile Jumeau bisque head doll, incised 6 EJ and stamped, damaged, 17in (43cm). **$2,000-3,000**

An Armand Marseille bisque head negro baby doll. **$200-400**

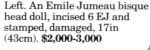

Left. A German tinplate sentry box and guard, 1890. **$600-1,000**

Right. A German tinplate sentry box with mounted sentry of the Royal Horse Guards, 1890. **$800-1,200**

A William and Mary wooden doll, English, with painted face, damage, clothing distressed, c1690, 12½in (32cm). **$50,000-75,000**

A double manual harpsicord, by Jacob Kirkman, 1761, 37in (94cm) wide. **$160,000-200,000**

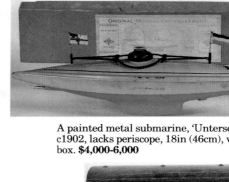

A painted metal submarine, 'Unterseeboot', by Bing, c1902, lacks periscope, 18in (46cm), with damaged box. **$4,000-6,000**

A Marklin PLM 2nd class bogie coach, in original livery, c1921, 12½in (32cm), in original wood box. **$2,500-4,000**

A Marklin gauge 1 live steam, spirit fired model of GWR 4–6–2 Pacific locomotive and tender No. 111, The Great Bear, c1909, 27in long. **$6,000-9,000**

A mounted figure by Roger Berdou, entitled 'Garde Impériale TARTES LITHUANIENS Trompette 1812', signed, 5.4cm. **$400-600**

A grand pianoforte, 7 octaves, No. 82771, by Erard, Paris, with amboyna case with ebonised lines, 55½in (140cm) wide. **$10,000-12,000**

A chitarrone, by David Tecchler, 1725, 71in (180cm) long. **$40,000-60,000**

A violoncello, by Carlo Antonio Testore, 1766, 29½in (75cm) long. **$70,000-95,000**

A columnar alto recorder, by Hans Rauch von Schratt, mid-16thC, 20in. **$90,000-120,000**

A Louis XVI style ormolu mounted purplewood and marquetry grand piano, the works by Erard, the case by P. Sormani, 75in (190.5cm) wide. **$20,000-30,000**

A 1956 Bentley S1 Continental 2-door drophead coupé, coachwork by Park Ward, Registration No. PLG 123, Chassis No. BC 77 BG, Engine No. BA 76128 UE 3764. **$120,000-160,000**

A Bing tinplate clockwork omnibus, the sides litho-graphed with Auto-Omnibus Gesellschaft, in near mint condition, c1911, 12in (30cm), with box base. **$18,000-25,000**

A 1931 Rolls Royce 20/25 doctor's coupé, coachwork by Windover, Registration No. GP5803, Chassis No. G0510, Engine No. D9E. **$80,000-110,000**

A gilt brass mounted kingwood coffre fort, with inlaid oyster veneered top, late 17thC, 25in (64cm) wide. **$5,000-8,000**

A 1962 Mercedes-Benz 300SL roadster, Chassis No. 1980421000298, Engine No. 19898010003022, left hand drive. **$130,000-175,000**

A Chinese export brass bound painted leather coffer, early 19thC, 47in (119cm) wide. **$7,000-10,000**

A leather travelling writing cabinet, with fitted interior, gilt tooled SG monogram, French, early 18thC, 10½in (26cm) high. **$1,500-4,000**

An Empire morocco leather despatch box, 27in (69cm) wide. **$10,000-15,000**

A French walnut and ebony casket, early 17thC, 18in (46cm) wide. **$18,000-25,000**

A leather travelling canteen, tooled with the cypher of Catherine II, the box late 18thC, 13in (33cm) high. **$24,000-40,000**

A Victorian mother-of-pearl inlaid and painted papier mâché tea caddy, impressed on base Clay, King Street, Covent Garden, 7½in. **$200-400**

A stoneware bottle vase, by Hans Coper, impressed HC seal, c1955, 19½in (49cm) high. **$18,000-30,000**

A Seguso 'valva' vase, designed by Flavio Poli, c1958, 6in (15cm) high. **$8,000-15,000**

An Archimede Seguso 'Compisizione Piume' carafe, c1960, 11½in (29cm) high **$10,000-18,000**

A stoneware bottle vase, by Elizabeth Fritsch, with painted design, 11in (28cm) high. **$12,000-18,000**

A Venini vase, acid stamped Venini Murano Italia, engraved Fulvio Bianconi 60, 11in (28cm) high. **$40,000-80,000**

A stoneware bottle, by Lucie Rie, impressed LR seal, 16½in (41.5cm) high. **$9,000-15,000**

A tall 'hour glass' vase, by Hans Coper, the matt manganese body covered in a buff slip heavily burnished on waist, and ochre blistering, impressed HC seal, 18in (45.5cm) high. **$38,000-50,000**

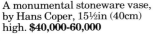

A monumental stoneware vase, by Hans Coper, 15½in (40cm) high. **$40,000-60,000**

A stoneware 'spade form', by Hans Coper, impressed HC seal, 7in (18cm) high. **$10,000-15,000**

A stoneware bowl, by Lucie Rie, covered in a thick pitted glaze run pooling to reveal turquoise glaze beneath with iron brown and cobalt blue flecks, impressed LR seal, 13in (33cm) diam. **$10,000-15,000**

A Paul Ysart pre-World War II paperweight, black glass with PY cane and Monart label, c1935, 3in (7.5cm). **$1,500-2,500**

A Vasart paperweight, with yellow ground and concentric millefiori rings and multi-coloured filigree spokes, c1955, 2½in (6cm). **$60-150**

A Paul Ysart paperweight, with PY cane, a rose with millefiori border, on a black ground, c1975, 3in (7.5cm). **$700-1,000**

A Paul Ysart paperweight, with red aventurine dragonfly on a blue ground, unsigned, c1960, 3in (7.5cm). **$500-700**

A Paul Ysart paperweight, a blue flower on a dark blue ground with millefiori border, unsigned, c1960, 3in (7.5cm). **$250-450**

A Paul Ysart paperweight, with PY cane, millefiori on a black ground, c1975, 3in (7.5cm). **$550-800**

A lady's lacquered wood chair, with kidney-shaped seat, some damage and restoration, Kangxi, 32½in (82.5cm) high. **$6,000-10,000**

A Huanghuali altar table, 17th/18thC, 57in (145cm). **$12,000-16,000**

A Ming Huanghuali and Huangyangmu Kang table, the underside with traces of lacquer, 21in (53cm) square.
$10,000-18,000

A scarlet and gold lacquer low table, with foliate ormolu frame, 44in (111cm).
$10,000-15,000

A pair of painted lacquer chairs, Mieguishi, Jiaqing.
$10,000-15,000

A pair of Huanghuali armchairs, minor repair, 17thC.
$12,000-20,000

A pair of Huanghuali armchairs, with caned seats, 17th/18thC, 47in (119cm) high. **$12,000-20,000**

A lithograph in colours, by Jules Chéret, 1893, 48½in high. **$2,000-4,000**

l. Anchor Line poster. **$700-1,000**
c. Lithograph in colours, Leopoldo Metlicovitz, 1904, 56in (142cm) high.
$4,000-6,000
r. The Royal Mail Line poster.
$300-500

A massive cloisonné enamel and gilt bronze tripod censer and cover, late Qing Dynasty, 33in diam. **$12,000-20,000**

A gilt splashed bronze sectional beaker vase, Qing Dynasty, 25in (63cm) high. **$10,000-15,000**

A tilemaker's incense burner and cover, restored, Wanli mark, 41in (104cm). **$5,000-8,000**

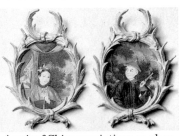

A pair of Chinese paintings on glass, 18thC, in later giltwood frames, 5½ by 3½in (14 by 8.5cm). **$12,000-16,000**

A Peking enamel and gilt copper box and cover, slight damage, Yongzheng/early Qianlong. **$2,000-4,000**

A cloisonné enamel panel, minor pitting, 18thC, 46in (117cm) high. **$8,000-15,000**

A pair of Chinese export reverse painted glass pictures, after a European print, with carved wooden frames, one cracked, c1795, 16in (41cm). **$8,000-12,000**

A pair of cloisonné and champlevé enamel vases, minor pitting, mid/late Qing Dynasty, 25in. **$10,000-15,000**

A pair of cloisonné enamel vases, minor damage, c1800, 27in (68cm). **$6,000-10,000**

A pair of cloisonné enamel vases, restored, some pitting, Qianlong 6-character seal marks and of the period, 10½in (26.5cm) high. **$8,000-15,000**

A pair of cloisonné enamel and gilt bronze censers and covers, late 18th/19thC, 15½in (39cm) wide. **$10,000-16,000**

A pair of cloisonné enamel horses, minor damage, late Qing Dynasty, 28in (71cm) wide. **$10,000-15,000**

A pale celadon and jade two-handled cup, Qianlong 4-character seal mark and of the period, 5½in (14cm) wide. **$10,000-15,000**

A celadon jade vase and cover, deeply carved with archaistic dragons, with lion mask ring handles, 18th/19thC, 16in (41cm). **$15,000-18,000**

A spinach jade two-handled bowl, small chips, 18thC, 10½in (26cm) wide, in fitted box. **$7,000-12,000**

A Korean inlaid black lacquer box and cover, inset in shell with a fruiting vine, fitted with bronze hinges, side handles and front lock, minor damage, 17th/18thC, 8½in (21.5cm) wide. **$20,000-30,000**

A wooden model of a reclining falcon, realistically modelled, on socle base, Dynasty XVIII, 5in (13cm) high. **$10,000-15,000**

A pair of Chinese painted carved wooden figures, with nodding heads and plaited hair, late 18th/early 19thC, the gentleman 46in (117cm) high, on later painted plinths 21in (53cm) high. **$24,000-35,000**

A jade group of 3 Immortals, 18thC, 6in (15cm) wide. **$15,000-20,000**

A jade fish bowl, 18thC, 5½in (14.5cm) diam, with wood stand. **$40,000-60,000**

A six-tiered lacquer box and cover, Ming Dynasty, 11in (28cm) high. **$20,000-30,000**

A four-tiered inlaid black lacquer box and cover, inset with shell, 16thC, 10½in (27cm). **$10,000-15,000**

A pale celadon jade double gourd shaped vase and domed cover, Qianlong, 12in (30cm) high. **$20,000-30,000**

A gilt lacquered figure of the Buddha, Ming Dynasty, 41in (104cm) high. **$16,000-25,000**

A stained and inlaid ivory netsuke, Temple Servant, signed Yasumasa, late 19thC, 4.9cm. **$5,000-8,000**

An ivory netsuke, Daruma Doll, signed Mitsuhiro and kao, 1810-75, small age cracks, 4cm high. **$5,000-8,000**

A stained and painted ivory netsuke, Fly on an Octopus Tentacle, signed Mitsuhiro and kao, 1810-75, 5.6cm long. **$16,000-20,000**

An ivory netsuke, Ox and Calf signed Mitsuharu, 18thC, 5.7cm long. **$14,000-20,000**

An ivory netsuke, Crane, signed Masatoshi, 20thC, 4.5cm long. **$14,000-20,000**

An ivory netsuke, Wild Duck, signed Ohara Mitsuhiro 1810-75, 4.8cm. **$14,000-20,000**

An ivory netsuke, Dog and Awabe Shell, signed Tomotada, 18thC, 3.5cm high. **$14,000-20,000**

An ivory netsuke, Songoku the Magical Monkey, Mitsuhiro, Ohara, 1810-75, 5cm. **$16,000-20,000**

An ivory netsuke, Ryujin, signed Masatoshi, 20thC, 9.2cm high. **$8,000-15,000**

A netsuke carved from stag antler, Owl, signed Masatoshi, 20thC, 4.5cm high. **$7,000-10,000**

An ivory netsuke, Karashishi and Young with a tama, signed Eijusai Masayoshi, 19thC, 4cm. **$18,000-25,000**

An ivory netsuke, Young Wrestler, signed Masanao, of Kyoto, age crack, 18thC, 4.9cm high. **$10,000-16,000**

An ivory netsuke, Seated Kirin, signed Yoshimasa, c1800, 10.5cm high. **$55,000-75,000**

An ivory netsuke, Tiger and Monkey, signed Kaigyokusai, with seal Masatsugu, 1813-92 3.9cm long. **$30,000-45,000**

An ivory netsuke, Omori Hiko-shichi and the Witch, signed Shoko, 20thC, 5cm. **$16,000-25,000**

A neo-classical ormolu and cut glass chandelier, fitted for electricity, early 19thC, 36in (91cm) high. **$16,000-25,000**

An early Victorian brass 18-light chandelier, restorations, 56in (142cm) high. **$10,000-15,000**

An ormolu and rock crystal 8-light chandelier, fitted for electricity, 34in (86cm) high. **$4,000-6,000**

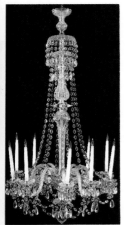

A cut glass 10-light chandelier, mid-19thC, 65in (165cm) high. **$10,000-16,000**

An Empire ormolu chandelier in the manner of Thomire, 28½in (72cm). **$17,000-25,000**

A pair of Regency ormolu and cut glass twin light candelabra, 16in (40.5cm) high. **$4,000-7,000**

A Russian ormolu and tôle 10-branch chandelier, lacking one wreath, early 19thC, 25in (63.5cm) wide. **$7,000-12,000**

A cut glass chandelier, 72in (182cm). **$55,000-75,000**

A pair of Louis XVI ormolu and bronze 3-light candelabra, 29in (74cm) high. **$14,000-20,000**

A pair of Louis XV ormolu candelabra, formed as river Gods, possibly Italian, 8½in (22cm) wide. **$20,000-30,000**

A pair of Regency bronzed and ormolu lamps, fitted for electricity, 31in (79cm). **$36,000-50,000**

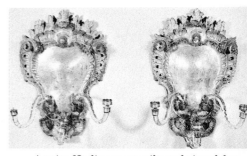

A pair of Italian rococo giltwood girandoles, with glass shades, restorations, one shell scroll lacking, mid-18thC, 37in (94cm). **$10,000-15,000**

A two-tiered brass chandelier, in the Flemish Gothic style, wired for electricity, with later fittings, 48½in (123cm) high. **$14,000-20,000**

A pair of Charles X ormolu and bronze oil lamps, 32in (81cm) high. **$10,000-15,000**

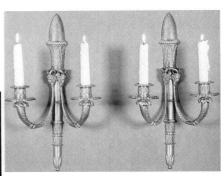

A set of 4 Empire ormolu wall lights, 19thC, 16in (40.5cm) high. **$7,000-12,000**

A pair of Empire style ormolu and rock crystal candelabra, 28in. **$26,000-40,000**

Walter Tyler, mahogany and brass bi-unial magic lantern. **$1,500-2,500**

A pair of silver mounted rhodonite candlesticks, by Fabergé, workmaster Anders Nevalainen, St. Petersburg, c1880, 5½in high. **$24,000-30,000**

A pair of ormolu and bronze candle-sticks, 30in, c1825. **$10,000-15,000**

A Russian ormolu cut glass chandelier, late 18thC, 17in (43cm). **$26,000-40,000**

A pair of Charles X ormolu and bronze three-light candelabra, 21in (53cm) high. **$4,000-8,000**

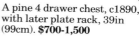

A pine pedestal desk, c1880, 48in (122cm) wide. **$1,200-2,000**

A pine 6 drawer chest, c1870, 24in (61cm) wide. **$700-1,000**

A pine 4 drawer chest, c1890, with later plate rack, 39in (99cm). **$700-1,500**

A pine kneehole desk, c1880, 51in (130cm). **$700-1,500**

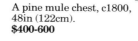

A pine cupboard, c1890, 39in (99cm). **$700-1,000**

A pine mule chest, c1800, 48in (122cm). **$400-600**

A pine display cabinet, c1890, 45in (114cm). **$600-1,000**

A pine washstand, c1840, 30in (76cm). **$250-350**

A pine 4 drawer chest, c1880, 39in (99cm). **$450-650**

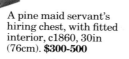

A pine maid servant's hiring chest, with fitted interior, c1860, 30in (76cm). **$300-500**

An oak hand stripped dressing chest, c1895, 38in (96.5cm). **$500-700**

A composite 'Maximilian' half-armour, some damage and repairs, partly German and partly Italian, 16thC. **$26,000-40,000**

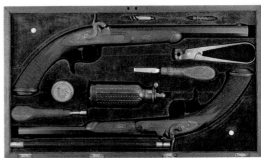

A cased pair of percussion duelling pistols, by Joseph Jakob, signed, mid-19thC, 16in (41cm), with velvet lined case and accessories. **$4,000-7,000**

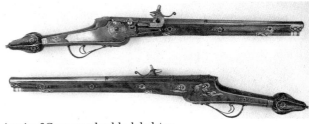

A pair of German wheel-lock holster pistols, by Hans Fleischer, dated 1610, maker's mark CT, Christopher Dressler, minor damage, restorations, 29½in (75cm). **$56,000-75,000**

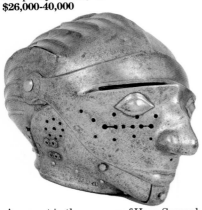

An armet in the manner of Hans Seusenhofer of Innsbruck, damaged, repaired, c1520, 9in (23cm). **$70,000-90,000**

An Austrian hunting trousse, comprising a cleaver and 5 extra pieces, possibly Viennese, mid-18thC, 21in (53cm). **$16,000-25,000**

A Russian flintlock gun by G. Permjakov, c1770, restored, 32in. **$18,000-25,000**

Above. A Colt Hartford-English dragoon percussion revolver, mid-19thC, 14½in (37cm). **$16,000-25,000**

A 12-gauge D.B. hammerless sidelock gun by J. Woodward, No. 7004, 14½in. **$24-40,000**

A pair of percussion pistols, by John Dickson & Son, Edinburgh, London proof marks, 1894, 12in. **$12-20,000**

Above. A 12-gauge D.B. hammerless self- opening sidelock ejector gun by J. Purdey **$18,000-30,000**
Right. A German 12-gauge D.B. hammerless sidelock ejector gun, **$10,000-18,000**

An etched close helmet in Wolfgang and Franz Grosschedel of Landshut style, repaired, c1560, 11in. **$28,000-40,000**

A Zuni pottery jar, decorated in brown and red on a white ground, 10½in (27cm) high.
$3,000-4,500

A Fiji wood paddle club, incised with circles, triangles and diamonds, 46½in (118cm) long, together with a Sudanese hide shield.
$200-350

A Senufo bird, porpianong, with square wings, painted with black and red dots on a white ground, 53in (135cm) high.
$2,250-3,500

A Bambara iron horseman, the right leg deficient, 8in (20cm) high.
$1,000-1,500

A Kongo female figure, one glass eye missing, one foot chipped, 3in (8cm) high.
$4,000-5,500

A Baule mask, with black patina, damaged, 15½in (39cm) high.
$2,250-3,500

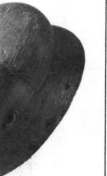

A Baule mask, with finely carved face, reddish-brown patina, 11in (28cm) high.
$18,000-25,000

A small square box and cover, 3in (8cm), with another box and 2 covers, damaged.
$300-500

l. A covered flask woven with multi-coloured bands with figures, 10½in (26cm).
$300-500

r. A covered flask, damaged, 5½in (14cm), and another flask woven with geometrical bands, 7in (18cm).
$100-200

A rare Lobi figure carved with 2 necks side by side, crusty patina, 26in (65cm) high.
$30,000-40,000

A Solomon Islands shell ornament, with 4 figures within bands of geometric motifs, 4½in (11cm) wide.
$1,200-1,750

A Yoruba beaded crown, orikogbofo, sewn all over with coloured beads, with central bird and 4 smaller birds about the rim, 14in (35cm) wide.
$1,000-1,500

Ephemera
Cigarette Cards

Wills, unissued series, The Life of H.M. King Edward VIII, a set of 50, minor edge staining.
$450-700

John Sinclair, World's Coinage, a set of 50.
$450-700

National Cigarette and Tobacco Company, National Types, sailor girls, a set of 25.
$300-500

American Tobacco Co., Beauties, 'Star Girls', black typeset back, a set of 24 plus one other.
$100-200

Postcards

A woven silk postcard, R.M.S. Titanic, unused.
$400-550

A photographic postcard of Colonel W. F. Cody mounted on his horse, inscribed by subject 'Buffalo Bill'.
$700-900

A Valentine mobile, addressed to 'Miss Josephine J. Morrison, 201 West 55 St., New York City, repaired, c1903, 21in (53.5cm) high.
$700-900

A head and shoulders portrait postcard of Montgomery Clift, inscribed.
$150-250

A collection of 180 Valentines and greetings cards, contained in 2 albums, c1900.
$700-900

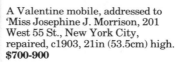

A collection of German Victorian and Edwardian Valentines.
$45-75

Three Victorian Valentines, c1870.
$150-250

Victorian Valentines, embossed, in pierced and gilded paper lace, now pasted on loose sheets.
$60-100

Miller's is a price Guide not a price List
The price ranges given reflect the average price a purchaser should pay for similar items. Condition, rarity of design or pattern, size, colour, pedigree, restoration and many other factors must be taken into account when assessing values.

Posters

John Hassall-Little Tich in Lord Tom Noddy at the Garrick Theatre, lithograph in colours, printed by David Allen & Sons, 30 by 20in (76 by 51cm), and 3 others.
$600-900

H.M. Queen Alexandra, a cabinet card portrait study, 1899, with another.
$450-700

G. C. R. England's Greatest Poet, Shortest and Quickest Route to Stratford on Avon, double royal, on linen.
$300-500

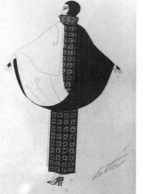

Erte, a watercolour and gouache costume drawing, signed, framed and glazed, 14 by 10½in (35.5 by 27cm).
$1,000-1,500

Austin Cooper, Take Your Car by L.N.E.R. and Save Road Fatigue.
$200-350

Nestle's Milk advert, 2 cats on wall.
$30-50

Sainsbury's Cocoa, Negro Boy advert, slight scruffing.
$20-40

Frank H. Mason, Havens and Harbours on the L.N.E.R., Lowestoft.
$100-200

E. Hamilton, Ellerman's City Line To and From India.
$300-500

John Hassall, Skegness Is So Bracing, by L.N.E.R.
$1,000-1,500

Tom Purvis, East Coast by L.N.E.R.
$4,000-5,500

Fred Taylor, Why Not Visit London For A Few Days, by L.N.E.R.
$1,300-2,000

E. McKnight Kauffer, Great Western To Devon's Moors, No. 12, dated 1932.
$1,300-2,000

Septimus E. Scott, To Edinburgh By Pullman, by L.N.E.R.
$1,000-1,500

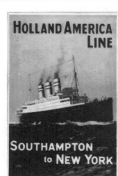

G. H. Davis, Holland America Line, Southampton to New York, and United States Lines, damage.
$700-900

Peek Frean & Co., a coloured lithograph, 40½ by 24½in (102 by 62cm), in wooden frame.
$450-700

A. R. Thomson, Take Me By The Flying Scotsman, by L.N.E.R.
$1,200-1,750

Weber, Winter Sports Expresses, by Southern Railway, double royal, 1934.
$200-350

Tom Purvis, Yorkshire Moors, L.N.E.R., quad. royal.
$800-1,200

T. D. Kerr, Golfing In Southern England And On The Continent Southern Railway, double royal, 1932.
$450-700

H. G. Gawthorn, Saltburn By The Sea, L.N.E.R., double royal.
$700-900

Adolphe Mouron Cassandre, The Continent via Harwich, double royal.
$1,500-2,500

Severin, The Devon Belle, by Southern Railway, 1947.
$450-700

A Bovril mirror, 8in (20.5cm) diam.
$45-75

An enamel sign, c1950, 22 by 16in (56 by 40.5cm).
$150-250

Thorne's Draught Beers, 19in (48cm) high.
$100-200

Suffragette banner, in cream cotton edged with purple satin, and press cuttings.
$300-500

An advertising poster, 1860, 23 by 18in (58 by 45.5cm).
$75-150

Norman Hartnell, a design for H.M. Queen Elizabeth II Coronation dress, signed, dated December 18, 1952.
$450-700

Photographs

Sir Winston Churchill, a half-length portrait study, mounted on card, 5 by 4½in (12.5 by 11cm), with a typescript note, A Souvenir of 10 Downing Street, 1940-45.
$1,000-1,400

Dorothy Wilding, a pair of portrait photographs of George VI and Queen Elizabeth, in silver Cartier frames, with silver gilt crowns, signed on mounts 'Elizabeth R' and 'George R 1947', in original fitted cases, 10½ by 14in (26 by 35cm).
$7,000-10,000

W. & D. Downey, an official portrait study of the future King Edward VIII's Christening group, inscribed by subjects on image, 'Victoria R. I. & little Edward Albert, July 6, 1894' 'Albert Edward' and 'George', 11½ by 7in (29 by 18cm).
$4,000-5,500

W. & D. Downey, a half-length portrait photograph of H.R.H. Edward, Prince of Wales, inscribed 'Edward Christmas 1910', 5½ by 4in (14 by 10cm), framed and glazed.
$150-250

A full length portrait photograph, H.M. Queen Elizabeth and H.R.H. Prince Philip, mounted on card, inscribed 'Elizabeth R' and 'Philip, 1957', 9½ by 7in (24 by 18cm), framed and glazed.
$900-1,300

A half length portrait photograph of the young Winston Churchill, by J. Russell & Sons, signed by subject, mounted on card, 6 by 4in (15 by 10cm).
$1,500-2,500

Walt Disney Productions, 'Peter Pan', watercolour, pen and ink, heightened in white, initialled, c1953.
$300-500

Disneyalia

Walt Disney Productions, 'Nana', from Peter Pan, initialled.
$200-350

Walt Disney Productions, 'Captain Hook' from Peter Pan, watercolour, pen and ink, heightened in white, initialled, c1953.
$300-500

Walt Disney Productions, 'Tinkerbell', from Peter Pan, c1953.
$200-350

A tin bucket, c1950.
$45-75

Snap cards, c1930.
$20-40

A battery operated plastic clock,
c1960, 12in (30.5cm) square.
$60-100

A wooden Mickey Mouse from a
fairground, c1930, 30 by 27in (76 by
68.5cm).
$3,000-4,500

Scripophily

Banque de Syrie et du Grand-Liban,
1 Livre, unadopted, slight staining
left side, 1925.
$450-700

Imperial Bank of Persia, 100
Tomans, outline seal, payable at
Yezd only, handwritten signatures,
18 Jun 1913.
$4,000-5,500

Banque de Syrie et du Liban,
Lebanon, 100 Livres, Specimen,
1945, uncirculated.
$900-1,300

Trinidad and Tobago, Royal Bank of
Canada, 5 Dollars, Jan 2, 1909.
$60-100

South Africa, Zuid Afrikaansche
Republiek, £1, arms at centre,
green, pin hole, 25.1.1872.
$30-50

Russian State Credit Note, 100
Roubles, portrait of Catherine II on
reverse, right corner torn, 1892.
$150-250

Film & Theatre

Stan Laurel and Oliver Hardy, a
half length publicity photograph,
and an autographed postcard.
$600-900

Charlie Chaplin, a head and
shoulders profile publicity
photograph, inscribed, 10 by 8in
(25.5 by 20.5cm), re-issue of a c1920
photograph, and a half length
photograph of Chaplin, c1920, 7 by
5in (18 by 12.5cm).
$300-500

Laurence Olivier and Vivien Leigh,
a signed head and shoulders portrait
of Vivien Leigh and a film still
signed by Laurence Olivier.
$200-350

Charlie Chaplin, a plaster
advertising figure, 12in (30.5cm).
$900-1,300

A bamboo cane with metal tip,
allegedly used by Charlie Chaplin
in City Lights, 1931, 36½in (92.5cm)
long, with a crooked walking stick
used by Harry Lauder.
$10,500-15,000

Charlie Chaplin, a china portrait
bust with manufacturer's printed
stamp on base, Flesh Pots,
Stoke-on-Trent, England, 1978,
12in (30.5cm) high.
$100-200

Charlie Chaplin, a glazed china salt cellar, c1925, 4in (10cm), and a cruet, c1920, 5½in (14cm) high.
$150-250

Charlie Chaplin, two pressed tin confectionery moulds, 8in (20cm), and 2 complementary cast figures, c1920.
$200-350

Charlie Chaplin, Motion Picture Employee Identification Card No. 42655, issued 6.11.42.
$8,000-11,000

Charlie Chaplin, a collection of 5 photographs, one by Witzel.
$100-200

Charlie Chaplin, a typescript letter, signed, dated April 11 1916, framed and glazed.
$400-550

Mary Pickford and Douglas Fairbanks, a full length seated portrait photograph by Abbe, signed, dated July 14th 1924, 14 by 10½in (35.5 by 26cm), framed and glazed.
$400-550

Douglas Fairbanks, Snr., a pair of imitation steins, and one other, in hand painted moulded plaster, 1954.
$150-200

I. Claudius, a theatrical copy of a Roman Soldier's brigandine, 1937.
$200-350

Two hundred and fifty postcards and publicity stills, mostly signed by subjects, contained in one album and loose.
$600-900

Bing Crosby, an imitation printed silk dressing gown, worn by Bing Crosby whilst making the film We're Not Dressing, 1934.
$450-700

Marilyn Monroe, a skin-tight 'shimmy' black satin dress, worn in the film Some Like It Hot, 1959.
$36,000-47,500

Star Wars, the original fibreglass mould used to make the robotic head of C.3.P.O., 1977.
$400-550

Louis Armstrong, signed programme, 1959.
$200-350

A programme for the opening of Going My Way, signed, creased.
$150-250

Katharine Hepburn, signed photograph, 8 by 10in (20.5 by 25.5cm).
$300-400

Bette Davis, signed, 8 by 10in (20.5 by 25.5cm).
$100-200

Rudolph Valentino as the Sheik, scuffed, 14 by 16in (35.5 by 41cm).
$1,000-1,400

Miscellaneous

A white Bakelite plaque, c1945, 30 by 12in (76 by 30.5cm).
$100-200

Four gold and silver watch chain fobs, one inscribed Lieut. H. G. Lowe, R.N.R. Titanic.
$4,000-5,500

A cast brass plate, inscribed Edinburgh Castle, 1948-1976, 8 by 14in (20 by 36cm), mounted on wood plaque.
$600-900

An iron ship rivet, inscribed R.M.S. Titanic 1912, 4.5cm diam.
$1,000-1,400

An autographed letter, 'On board R.M.S. Titanic', on official writing paper, signed by Thomas Mudd, April 11th, 1912.
$1,200-1,750

A bronze Carpathia medal, the reverse inscribed 'Presented to the Captain, Officers and crew of R.M.S. Carpathia, in recognition of gallant and heroic services from the survivors of the SS Titanic, April 15th, 1912', 1½in (4cm).
$1,500-2,600

A leather bound visitors book, used at Windsor Castle and St. James' Palace, 1909-1922.
$600-900

ORIENTAL
Bamboo

A bamboo stick stand, c1870, 34in (86cm) high.
$200-350

A saddler's carved wood painted sign, in the form of a caricature of the jockey Fred Archer, 51in (130cm).
$1,500-2,600

A bamboo carving of a jovial Immortal, possibly representing Liu Hai, 18th/19thC, 8in (20cm) high.
$450-700

A bamboo carving of a group of Buddhistic lions, damage, 18thC, 12½in (32cm) high.
$900-1,300

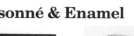

A bamboo magazine rack, c1870, 18½in (47cm) high.
$100-200

Cloisonné & Enamel

An enamelled earthenware figure of a nio, restored foot, 19thC, 21½in (54cm) high.
$1,200-1,750

A cloisonné enamel incense burner, in the form of a caparisoned elephant, 6in (15cm) high, and a blue ground cloisonné enamel jar and cover, some damage, Qianlong, 10½in (27cm) high.
$800-1,200

A polychrome cloisonné enamel tripod censer and domed cover, slight damage, c1800, 20½in (52cm) high.
$7,000-10,000

A cloisonné enamel figure of a quail, feet damaged and repaired, Qianlong/Jiaqing, 5in (12.5cm) high.
$600-900

Furniture

A pair of Hongmu spindleback armchairs, 18thC, 33in (84cm) high.
$5,000-7,500

A pair of Tielimu spindleback armchairs, 17th/18thC, 39in (99cm) high.
$3,000-4,500

A pair of Hongmu armchairs, the backs and sides carved with 'linghzi' clusters growing on contorted branches, some repair, 19thC, 39in (99cm) high.
$5,000-7,500

A pair of carved and gilt red lacquer armchairs, slight damage, 40in (101cm) high.
$800-1,200

A folding zig-zag chair, with North Italian penwork, 19thC.
$800-1,200

A Chinese export hardwood pedestal table, inlaid with marquetry and bone, late 19thC, 54in (137cm).
$1,500-2,600

A Hongmu deck armchair, 19thC.
$1,000-1,400

A Japanese hardwood shodana, decorated with shibayama panels depicting birds, flowers and parcel gilt, 53in (134.5cm).
$6,000-9,000

A Canton gilt and black lacquer sewing table, the hinged cover opening to reveal a fitted interior with pierced ivory accessories, including bobbins and pin boxes, slight wear, mid-19thC, 28in (71cm) high.
$3,000-4,500

A mother-of-pearl inlaid stepped low table, the superstructure fitted with a single drawer, with pierced apron below, some damage, late Ming, 40in (102cm) wide.
$4,000-5,500

A Manchurian Huali, Huamu and Changmu chow table, in two halves, inlaid in parquetry style with a central figured medallion, some damage, 19thC, 54½in (138cm) diam.
$3,000-4,500

A gilt and black lacquer miniature cabinet, chips, sealmark under lid, Meiji period, 14in (35.5cm) high.
$1,500-2,600

A Chinese black and gold lacquer coffer, the sides with brass carrying handles, basically mid-18thC, 54in (137cm) wide.
$7,000-10,000

An Islamic Syrian table, inlaid with silver, mother-of-pearl and ivory, with Mashrabiya panels and geometric top, 19thC, 28in (71cm) high.
$1,500-2,600

A Turkish table in ebony, sandalwood and mother-of-pearl, 19thC, 20in (51cm) high.
$900-1,300

A Victorian Damascan folding screen, with Mashrabiya turnings, 80in (203cm) high.
$1,000-1,400

Miller's is a price Guide not a price List

The price ranges given reflect the average price a purchaser should pay for similar items. Condition, rarity of design or pattern, size, colour, pedigree, restoration and many other factors must be taken into account when assessing values.

A pair of Japanese lacquer cabinets on stands, each with an arrangement of drawers, hinged compartment and doors, decorated with birds and poultry in landscapes, metal mounts, 19in (48.5cm) wide.
$1,500-2,600

A Chinese padouk altar table, 48in (122cm) wide.
$2,000-3,000

Glass

A Chinese rock crystal koro and cover, early 19thC.
$900-1,300

Horn

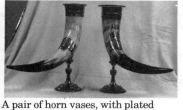

A pair of horn vases, with plated mounts and stands.
$600-900

Ivory

A Chinese carved ivory figure of a sage with red, blue and gilt decoration, on shaped base, 19thC, 9½in (24cm) high.
$700-900

A Japanese carved ivory tusk vase, finely detailed and shaded with elephant attacked by tigers, on carved hardwood stand, Meiji period, 28½in (72cm) high.
$2,000-3,000

An ivory okimono of a girl standing, dressed in a kimono, holding a bunch of millet in one hand, signed Hideyuki on a red tablet, 8½in (21.5cm) high.
$1,200-1,750

A rhinoceros horn libation cup, some damage, 18thC, 7in (17.5cm) wide, on fitted wood stand.
$5,000-7,500

Jade

A mother-of-pearl inlaid and jade set hardwood sceptre, of 3 variously sized celadon jade plaques, carved with Immortals, repaired, 22in (56cm) long.
$1,000-1,400

A rhinoceros horn libation cup, carved on one side at the foot with 4 figures on a small punt, 17thC, 6½in (16cm) wide, with wood stand carved as a lotus cluster.
$8,000-11,000

A celadon jade group of a buffalo and boy, 14in (35.5cm) wide.
$4,000-5,500

A Chinese pale grey speckled jade bowl and cover, carved in archaic style with Tao T'ieh masks on a key pattern ground, 6½in (16.5cm) wide.
$1,300-2,000

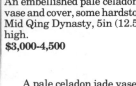

A pair of white jade bangles, 17th/18thC, 3in (7.5cm) diam.
$2,000-3,000

A creamy celadon jade standing Buddhist figure, carved from a thin section of stone, late Qing Dynasty, 8in (20cm) high, wood stand.
$2,250-3,500

An embellished pale celadon jade vase and cover, some hardstone loss, Mid Qing Dynasty, 5in (12.5cm) high.
$3,000-4,500

A pale celadon jade vase and cover, with animal mask loose ring handles, 7½in (19.5cm) high, wood stand.
$9,000-12,500

A Mughal celadon jade box and cover in the form of a leaf, the finial with a gilt and red glass inset agate top, interior chips, early 19thC, 4in (9.5cm) high.
$3,000-4,500

A green and russet jade carving of a phoenix, seated with its head on its back and holding a lotus spray in its beak, 19thC, 9in (23cm) wide.
$2,500-3,500

Lacquer

A black and gilt lacquered tea chest and hinged cover, cover repaired, 19thC, 13in (33cm) wide.
$2,500-3,500

Two Ming style gilt lacquer figures of seated dignitaries, each enthroned on red lacquered horseshoe-backed chairs, the top rails terminating in gold dragons' heads, their detachable heads with official hats, one figure holding a gold ingot in his right hand, also detachable, minor damage, 36in (91.5cm) high.
$10,000-13,500

A gilt and dry lacquer figure of a martial official, his crimson lined robes in dark red, some gilt, some flaking, Ming Dynasty, 39½in (101cm) high.
$8,000-11,000

A pair of Indian silver anklets, Kutch Valley dowry pieces.
$1,500-2,500

Metal

A Ming bronze arrow vase, some damage, possibly 16thC, 20½in (52.5cm) high.
$4,000-5,500

A gold and silver inlaid bronze wheel fitting, Warring States, 4½in (11cm) long.
$4,000-5,500

A bronze figure of Buddha on a tortoise base, in 3 sections, mandorla missing, late Ming, 18½in (47cm) high.
$3,000-4,500

A Sino-Tibetan gilt bronze figure of a monk, 17th/18thC, 6½in (16.5cm) high.
$1,000-1,400

A Japanese bronze ornamental incense burner, cast as a caparisoned trumpeting elephant, minor damage, incised 2-character mark on an applied plaque inscribed 'Shomin', late 19thC, 24½in (62cm) high.
$2,500-3,500

A bronze mount, probably a sword chape, Zhou Dynasty/Warring States, 3½in (8.5cm) long, fitted box.
$2,000-3,000

A bronze model of a trumpeting elephant, 32in (81cm) long.
$1,200-1,750

A bronze TLV mirror, cast with a central pierced boss within a square panel with small knops, Han Dynasty, 5½in (14cm) diam, fitted box.
$2,500-3,500

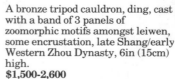

A group of gilt bronze ornaments, Tang Dynasty, 1 to 2in (2.5 to 5cm) wide.
$2,000-3,000

A bronze tripod cauldron, ding, cast with a band of 3 panels of zoomorphic motifs amongst leiwen, some encrustation, late Shang/early Western Zhou Dynasty, 6in (15cm) high.
$1,500-2,600

Netsuke

A gilt bronze figure of a recumbent unicorn, areas of gilt rubbed, 17thC, 10½in (27cm) long.
$4,000-5,500

A carved ivory netsuke, man with kiln, 4.5cm.
$100-200

A carved ivory netsuke, figures on raft.
$30-50

A carved ivory netsuke, rat, signed.
$200-350

A carved ivory netsuke, figure of a monkey, signed.
$150-250

A lacquered wood netsuke, of a seated karashishi on a pierced brocade ball, 18th/19thC, 1½in (4cm).
$300-400

Tsuba

A bronze alloy Tsuba, Japanese sword guard, adorned with crane standing under a pine tree.
$150-250

Wood

A rustic style two-handled censer, minor repairs, 9in (23cm) wide.
$900-1,300

A hardwood carving of Liu Hai, the jovial Immortal standing with his left leg resting on the back of his three-legged toad, base cracks, 19thC, 15in (38cm).
$600-900

Miscellaneous

A coral carving of 2 female Immortals, on the back of a phoenix, some repair, 6in (15cm) high, fixed wood stand.
$600-900

An Islamic tortoiseshell, mother-of-pearl and ivory box, 19thC, 16½in (42cm) wide.
$700-900

A pair of Chinese Lotus shoes, for bound feet, 19thC.
$150-250

Two Mandarin hat buttons, worn on the top of hats to represent rank by their colour, 19thC.
$60-100

A pair of bronze and gilt decorated Oriental figures, Thai dancers, late 19thC.
$900-1,300

A Japanese ebonised Aesthetic clock set, 18 to 10in (45.5 to 25.5cm) high.
$1,000-1,500

RUSSIAN

Icons and Works of Art

An icon of the Resurrection surrounded by feasts, with brass basma, 19thC, 12½ by 10½in (31 by 27cm).
$1,200-1,750

An icon, the Image of the Saviour 'not made with hands', tooled gilt background in blue, white, purple, red and green to resemble enamel, 10½ by 8½in (26.5 by 21.5cm), ebonised frame.
$600-900

Four panels from a portable iconastas, each painted in 3 rows, with the Prophets, Festivals and Saints, 19thC, each panel 33 by 4in (84 by 10cm).
$2,500-3,500

The Annunciation, painted in subdued colours with architectural background, 18thC in 16thC style, 12 by 10in (30.5 by 25.5cm).
$2,250-3,500

The Pokrov, 19thC, 18 by 15in (46 by 38cm).
$2,250-3,500

Tolga Mother of God, painted on gold ground in shades of brown in a traditional manner, c1800, 25½ by 19in (64.5 by 48cm).
$3,000-4,500

Saint John the Baptist, with silver chased and repoussé halo and engraved basma on the borders, c1700, 12½ by 10½in (31.5 by 26.5cm).
$2,250-3,500

Archangel Gabriel of the Deisis, painted in vivid colours on gold ground, Palekh School, c1800, 21 by 11in (53 by 28cm).
$4,000-5,500

Iverskaya Mother of God, realistically painted with silver gilt repoussé and chased oklad and applied shaded enamel haloes, marked with initials of Ivan Alexseev Alexeevich, Moscow, 1899-1908, 9 by 7in (23 by 18cm).
$2,000-3,000

Vladimirskaya Mother of God, realistically painted, with a silver gilt repoussé and engraved oklad, marked with unrecorded Cyrillic marks CG, 12 by 10½in (30.5 by 26.5cm).
$2,000-3,000

Mother of God of Vladimir, painted in sepia in the traditional manner, some restoration, 17thC, 11½ by 9in (29 by 23cm).
$2,000-3,000

The Resurrection and Descent into Hell, painted in the traditional manner, 19thC, 14 by 12½in (35.5 by 31.5cm).
$1,500-2,600

A wing of a Greek triptych with the Nativity painted on shaped panel, in vivid colours, restoration, c1600, 8½ by 5in (22 by 12.5cm).
$4,000-5,500

A Greek triptych, painted in vivid colours on gold ground, with silver repoussé haloes, probably Macedonian, c1700, 13 by 21in (33 by 54cm).
$5,000-7,500

Miscellaneous

A set of 12 shaded enamel teaspoons, white metal, marked with initials of Constantin Skvortsov, Moscow, c1910.
$3,000-4,500

An openwork enamel gold locket, opening to reveal 4 rotating photograph frames, with blue ground plaque with gold figure 'XXV', with initials FW, St. Petersburg, c1870, 1½in (3.5cm).
$1,200-1,750

A Russian parcel gilt sugar basket and cream jug, in raised coloured enamels, stamped 88, 11 MA, late 19thC.
$3,000-4,500

A parcel gilt silver kovsh, engraved in Cyrillic, the base with inscription 'given by Mamamie Countess of Pembroke to her daughter Countess of Clanwilliam' marked with unrecorded initials CC, Moscow, 1856, 7in (18cm), with matching sugar sifter, 337 grammes.
$3,000-4,000

A five-piece tea service, with knop finials, minor dents, white metal, marked A. Hempel and unknown maker's marks PJS, St. Petersburg, c1900, tray 22in (56cm) long, 4,950 grammes.
$4,000-5,500

An enamel military cigarette case, the cover with opaque white enamel order of Saint George suspended from an enamelled black and orange ribbon, with cabochon sapphire, marked with unrecorded Cyrillic initials AF, St. Petersburg, c1912, in a red leather case stamped 'Annerl, 3 December, 1898 Weihnachten 1915', 4in (10cm), 140 grammes gross.
$4,000-5,500

A silver cake basket, engraved with initials AMS and dated 23 August 1896, with swing handle, marked Klebnikov, St. Petersburg, 1880, 10in (25.5cm), 111.5 grammes.
$1,500-2,600

A porcelain Easter egg, the white ground with gold panels enclosing blue blossoms, 19thC, 3½in (9cm) high.
$1,500-2,500

A large silver mounted cut glass kovsh, applied with 4 cabochon semi-precious stones, some damage, marked Khlebnikov with Imperial Warrant, Moscow, c1890, 18in (45.5cm) long, 619 grammes gross.
$6,000-9,000

A porcelain kovsh, with gilt and green border, by Kornilov Factory, St. Petersburg, 19thC, 8½in (21cm) wide.
$1,000-1,400

A crystal vase, with white metal rim and base, by the 15th Artel, Moscow, c1910, 15in (38cm).
$2,000-3,000

A porcelain sauce boat and stand, from the service of the Grand Duke Alexander Alexandrovitch, with the Imperial cypher of the Grand Duke, within large gold ring, by the Imperial Porcelain Factory, period of Alexander II and Alexander III.
$1,000-1,400

A porcelain Easter egg, painted on blue ground, late 19thC, 4in (10cm) high.
$1,300-2,000

A Russian pastille burner, probably Gardner, some restoration, c1820.
$1,000-1,400

A porcelain figure of a young girl, by the Popov Factory, with underglaze blue impressed mark and impressed Cyrillic K, c1845, 5in (12.5cm) high.
$1,500-2,500

A bronze group of a father and son seated on a sleigh, both dressed in fur-trimmed overcoats and hats, mounted on a malachite base, 19thC, 7½in (19cm).
$2,000-3,000

A malachite and ormolu clock, with enamel chaptered cast ormolu dial, c1850, 4½in (11.5cm) wide.
$2,250-3,500

A quartz desk seal, designed as a seated brown bear holding a clear bottle, realistically carved, 19thC, 3½in (9cm) high.
$1,300-2,000

A carved oak chair, each arm rest formed as an axe, the front legs and back formed as a yoke duga with carved Russian adage, a pair of gloves resting on the back of the seat, the third foot formed as a branch, the back leg bifurcated, attributed to V. P. Shutov.
$2,250-3,500

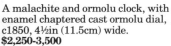

A papier mâché lacquer photograph album, with velvet spine and plain black lacquered back cover, enclosing 19 pages, with clasp, stamped Lukutine Factory, with gilt Imperial Eagle, mid-19thC, 9in (23cm) long.
$700-900

Lighting

A giltmetal hall lantern, with glazed panels and 3 candle branches, fitted for electricity, 32in (81cm) high.
$3,000-4,000

A mid-Victorian giltmetal and blue glass column oil lamp, with Corinthian capital and stepped square plinth, fitted for electricity, 38in (95.5cm) high.
$3,000-4,000

A pair of giltmetal sconces of 17thC design, the shaped embossed backplates with portrait busts and baldacchinos with single scrolling branches, 15in (38cm) high.
$800-1,200

A pair of French Barbedienne candlesticks, signed, late 19thC, 14in (35.5cm).
$1,500-2,500

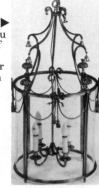

A pair of ormolu hall lanterns of Louis XVI design, fitted for electricity, 17in (43cm) diam.
$8,000-11,000

A Continental bronze gasolier, c1880, converted for electricity, 42in (122cm) high.
$4,000-5,500

A pair of Austrian bronzed and gilded 3-light wall lights, late 18thC, 14in (35.5cm) high.
$3,000-4,500

A pair of rock crystal and giltmetal pricket candlesticks, with hexagonal drip-pans and faceted multi-baluster stems on stepped hexagonal bases, 11in (28cm) high.
$4,000-5,500

An Edwardian cast brass chandelier, with cut glass pineapple shades, fitted for electricity, c1905, 36in (91.5cm) high.
$2,000-3,000

A giltmetal hall lantern, with Gothic pattern glazed body, 19thC, fitted for electricity, 37in (94cm) high.
$9,000-12,500

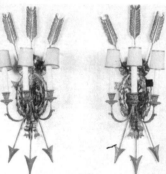

A pair of giltwood 3-branch wall lights, with ribbon tied arrow-and-wreath backplates and scrolling branches, fitted for electricity, 36in (91.5cm) high.
$2,250-3,500

A Dutch style chandelier, 19thC, 24in (61cm) diam.
$700-900

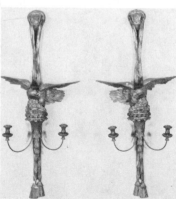

A pair of George III style giltwood wall lights, 47½in (120cm) high.
$3,000-4,500

Papier Mâché

A Victorian papier mâché and inlaid nursing chair.
$450-700

An early Victorian black lacquered papier mâché tray, decorated with gilt, slight damage, 32in (81cm) wide.
$1,000-1,400

Two Regency black lacquered papier mâché trays, decorated in colours and gilt, some damage, the larger 30in (76cm) wide.
$2,500-3,500

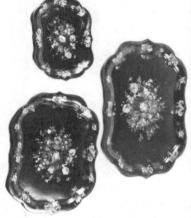

A graduated set of 3 Victorian papier mâché trays, with gilt foliate decoration.
$1,500-2,600

A papier mâché snap-top occasional table, with black lacquer and mother-of-pearl, 19thC, 26in (66cm) diam.
$700-900

An early Victorian papier mâché tray, painted in colours and gilt, registration tablet for 1846, 32in (81cm) wide.
$1,000-1,400

A papier mâché and mother-of-pearl inlaid inkstand and pair of glass inkwells, 19thC, 11in (28cm) wide.
$150-250

A papier mâché tray, with serpentine raised borders, decorated with gilt foliage and insects, old repair, early 19thC, 29½in (75cm).
$1,000-1,400

A Stockmann painted papier mâché snuff box, the lid painted with 'Loth avec les filles', after Raphael, the interior of the lid inscribed with title, the interior of base inscribed with '1475 St.St', early 19thC, 4in (10cm) diam, cased.
$900-1,300

A Victorian ebonised and gilt papier mâché table, 24½in (62cm).
$1,500-2,600

A Victorian papier mâché occasional table, inlaid with mother-of-pearl, with adjustable column.
$800-1,200

A pair of papier mâché pole screens, 19thC.
$1,300-2,000

Sewing

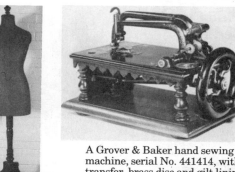

A Wheeler & Wilson-type S. Davis & Co., walnut 'Davenport' treadle sewing machine, serial No. 21535, some damage, c1870, 38in (96cm) high.
$3,000-4,000

A tailor's dummy, 59in (150cm) high.
$100-200

A Grover & Baker hand sewing machine, serial No. 441414, with transfer, brass disc and gilt lining, on mahogany base, c1873.
$2,250-3,500

A mahogany sewing box, the central handle flanked by 2 hinged lids, with sectioned interior, early 19thC, 7½in (19cm) square.
$100-200

A French satinwood workbox, decorated with painted panels, the fitted interior lined in blue silk, containing needlework tools, early 19thC, 14in (35cm) wide.
$3,000-4,000

Miniatures

A miniature of a gentleman, wearing a red uniform with dark blue and gold facings, c1810, 3in (7.5cm).
$600-900

A miniature of a gentleman, wearing a blue uniform, his powdered hair en queue, c1875, 4cm, later chased gold and silver frame.
$400-550

A miniature of an officer, in a red uniform with cream coloured collar, silver epaulettes and black sash, and black feathered beret, in bright cut gold frame, c1770, 4.5cm.
$400-550

A miniature portrait of the Duchess of Montagu, daughter of the Great Duke of Marlborough, documented, by Bernard Lens, signed monogram on ivory, c1720, 5 by 4½in (12.5 by 11cm).
$450-600

A miniature of a gentleman, in a dark blue coat and white cravat, his powdered hair tied back, gilded metal frame with plaited hair reverse, c1790, 6cm.
$400-550

Pine Furniture
Beds

A cane and pine carved bed head and foot, 66in (167.5cm) wide.
$1,000-1,400

A pine bed, c1860, 36in (91.5cm) wide.
$400-550

A George III style pine breakfront bookcase, 74in (188cm).
$5,000-7,500

Bookcases

A beech bed, c1870, 43in (109cm) wide.
$400-550

A William IV bookcase, with false drawers, 50in (127cm).
$1,000-1,400

A pine glazed bookcase, 49in (124.5cm).
$1,200-1,750

A pine bookcase, the glazed doors enclosing a green watered silk interior between entrelacs, on a plinth base, 57in (145cm).
$6,000-9,000

A Continental bookcase, c1860, 43in (109cm) wide.
$900-1,300

Chairs

A pine chair, c1840.
$150-200

A turned stick-back chair.
$100-150

A miniature elm rocking chair, c1900, 11in (28cm) high.
$200-350

An Irish chair, c1860.
$200-350

A scroll back Windsor chair.
$75-150

A child's chair, 26in (66cm) high.
$45-75

A lathe back chair.
$100-200

A wheel back chair.
$300-500

Chests

A pine, walnut and fruitwood chest, applied with split bobbin mouldings, on bun feet, 17thC, 31in (79cm).
$2,000-3,000

A bowfront chest of drawers, painted in blue, c1820, 41½in (105cm).
$600-900

A pine mule chest with 2 drawers, unused, c1830, 42in (107cm).
$800-1,200

A painted pine linen chest, c1830, 43in (109cm).
$1,500-2,600

An original painted pine chest of drawers, c1850, 41in (104cm).
$900-1,300

A painted pine chest of drawers, c1840, 42in (106.5cm).
$600-900

A chest of drawers, with scroll decoration, c1850, 36in (91.5cm).
$600-900

A miniature chest of drawers, c1870, 15½in (38cm).
$200-350

A pine combination chest of drawers, c1860, 40in (101.5cm).
$600-900

A pine dressing chest, c1850, 42in (106.5cm).
$700-900

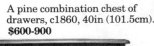

A chest of drawers, c1880, 33in (84cm).
$150-250

A Continental four drawer chest, c1860, 42in (106.5cm).
$450-600

A pine flight of drawers, with original brass handles, c1860, 37in (94cm).
$300-500

A chest of drawers.
$1,000-1,400

A Victorian mule chest.
$600-900

A pine nest of drawers, 19in (48cm) wide.
$600-900

A bowfront chest of drawers, unusually sound, 34in (86cm).
$800-1,200

A painted pine wedding chest, possibly Scandinavian, 30in (76cm).
$700-900

591

A specimen chest, 29in (74cm).
$1,000-1,400

A pine specimen chest, with fitted drawers, 23in (58cm).
$600-900

A dressing chest, with mirror front, the lifting lid revealing a secret drawer, 35in (89cm).
$800-1,200

A small pine chest of drawers, with new brass handles, 30in (76cm) high.
$400-550

A painted pine chest of drawers, 42in (106.5cm).
$1,000-1,400

A painted pine chest of drawers, 40in (101.5cm).
$450-700

Commodes

Cupboards

A pine commode, c1850, 25in (63.5cm).
$400-550

A pine corner cupboard, with painted dome, c1760, 50in (127cm).
$8,000-11,000

An Irish glazed cupboard, c1780, 56in (142cm).
$1,500-2,600

An Irish food cupboard, c1780, 57in (144cm).
$2,500-3,500

A French armoire, c1780.
$4,000-5,500

A Normandy buffet, c1780, 58in (147cm).
$4,500-7,000

A two-piece corner cupboard, c1780, 44in (112cm).
$1,300-2,000

An Irish panelled food cupboard, c1780, 50in (127cm).
$1,500-2,600

A food cupboard, c1850, 58in (147cm).
$1,300-2,000

An Irish food cupboard, with fitted interior, c1800, 51in (129.5cm).
$1,500-2,600

An Irish astragal glazed cabinet, c1800, 49in (124.5cm).
$1,500-2,600

A mid-European drapers cabinet, 71in (180cm).
$2,500-3,500

A pine huffer, c1840, 39in (99cm).
$450-700

A spice cupboard, c1860, 19in (48cm).
$200-350

A George III painted pine dome-shaped fitment, decorated with gilt, 35in (89cm).
$1,500-2,600

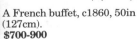

A two-door panelled cupboard, c1840, 75½in (191cm) high.
$1,000-1,400

A French buffet, c1860, 50in (127cm).
$700-900

A glazed corner cupboard, c1860,
35in (89cm).
$700-900

A butler's cupboard, c1870, 106in
(269cm).
$3,000-4,500

A bedside cabinet, c1910.
$200-350

A pine cupboard, 52in (132cm).
$1,300-2,000

A pine linen press, 50in (127cm).
$1,300-2,000

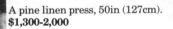

A hand painted pine cupboard,
c1900, 25½in (65cm).
$250-350
Two Scandinavian boxes, c1820.
$100-150
A bargeware watering can.
$75-150

A Normandy marriage armoire,
51in (129.5cm).
$7,500-10,500

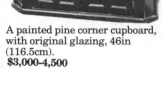

A painted pine corner cupboard,
with original glazing, 46in
(116.5cm).
$3,000-4,500

A corner cupboard, 43in (109cm).
$1,300-2,000

A pine cupboard, 20in (51cm).
$150-250

Desks

A pedestal desk,
61in (155cm).
$1,300-2,000

A carved pine desk,
with cabriole
legs, c1880,
72in (182.5cm).
$4,000-5,500

A Queen Anne bureau, with fitted
interior, 35in (89cm).
$1,500-2,600

A pine desk, with later leathered
slope, c1860, 53in (134.5cm).
$1,000-1,400

An Irish plate rail dresser, c1800,
61in (155cm).
$1,000-1,400

Dressers

A dresser base, c1700, 90in
(228.5cm).
$7,500-10,500

A dresser base, c1840,
73in (185cm).
$900-1,300

A Devonshire dresser, with glazed
top, 51in (129.5cm).
$1,500-2,600

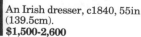

An early pine dresser, 48in (122cm).
$900-1,300

A pine dresser, c1840, 42in
(106.5cm).
$900-1,300

An Irish dresser, c1840, 55in
(139.5cm).
$1,500-2,600

Dressing Tables

A painted pine dressing table, 18thC, 42in (106.5cm).
$2,000-3,000

A dressing table, with mirror, 42in (106.5cm).
$450-700

Settles

An Irish high back settle, c1820, 74in (188cm).
$800-1,200

Mirrors

A pine frame, c1860, 30 by 26½in (76 by 67cm).
$150-250

A carved pine mirror, 68in (172.5cm) high.
$1,500-2,600

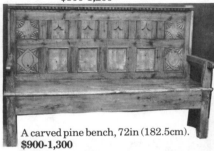

A carved pine bench, 72in (182.5cm).
$900-1,300

Sideboards

A pine sideboard, 72in (182.5cm).
$800-1,200

A Dutch carved pine bench in the baroque taste, on trestle end supports, with blue squab, 18thC, 74in (188cm).
$4,000-5,500

A Victorian sideboard, 72in (182.5cm).
$800-1,200

A pine sideboard, 47in (119cm).
$450-700

Two George III grained pine serving tables, one inscribed underneath 'This next to Servants Hall', the other '. . . East table', the larger 59in (149.5cm).
$16,500-23,000

Stools

A pine piano seat, c1900.
$300-500

Tables

Wardrobes

A pine console table, heavily carved, c1850, 46in (116.5cm).
$4,000-5,500

A large pine table, c1850, 120in (304.5cm).
$900-1,300

A painted pine armoire, with domed top, 48in (122cm).
$800-1,200

A painted pine table, c1830, 36in (91.5cm).
$700-900

A Regency painted pine side table, fitted with frieze drawer, 30in (76cm).
$2,500-3,500

A cricket table, c1850, 29in (73cm) diam.
$450-700

A side table, c1880, 60in (152cm).
$450-700

A combination pine wardrobe, c1870, 79in (200.5cm) high.
$1,500-2,600

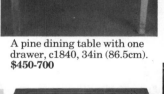

A bedside adjustable table, c1850, 32in (81cm) high.
$300-500

A pine dining table with one drawer, c1840, 34in (86.5cm).
$450-700

A Scottish pine two-door wardrobe, with carved decoration, 45in (114cm).
$900-1,300

A pine table with slotted shelf, c1850, 59in (149.5cm).
$600-900

A painted pine table, 31in (78.5cm).
$450-600

A double wardrobe, 96in (243.5cm).
$3,000-4,500

A French pine armoire, c1780, 50in (127cm).
$3,000-4,000

Miscellaneous

A pine stand, c1860, 55in (139.5cm).
$200-350

A pitch pine box, 44in (111.5cm).
$150-250

Washstands

A painted pine washstand, 19thC, 36in (91.5cm).
$300-500

A pine flax crusher, 37½in (94cm).
$150-250

Pine bookshelves, 48in (122cm) high.
$200-350

A pine washstand, with shelf and one drawer, c1830, 25in (63cm).
$300-400

A set of steps, 23in (58.5cm) high.
$60-100

A small pine box, 29in (74cm).
$60-100

A small pine box, 15in (38cm).
$100-150

A pair of pine sculpted greyhounds, 42in (106.5cm).
$900-1,300

A pine corn bin, 37in (94cm).
$150-250

A pine box, 36in (91.5cm).
$100-150

A small pine box, c1850, 20in (53cm).
$100-150

A pine lead lined double trough, 46in (116.5cm).
$600-900

From the Dairy Department of Reading University.

A pine hall stand, carved in the form of a bear, 85in (216cm) high.
$2,000-3,000

Pine shelves, with bobbin supports, c1850, 50in (127cm) high.
$250-350

A cattle trough, c1860, 120in (304cm).
$450-600

Pine hanging shelves, 38in (96.5cm).
$150-250

A pair of French carved fireplace surrounds, 19thC, 59 by 79in (150 by 200cm).
$10,500-15,000

A pine croquet box, 35½in (90cm).
$60-100

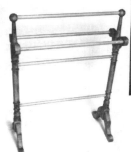

A pine towel rail, 25in (63.5cm).
$60-100

A pine reeded fire surround, 51 by 59in (130 by 150cm).
$450-600

Pine hanging shelves, 17½in (44.5cm) wide.
$150-250

A hatters block, 8in (20cm) high.
$60-100

A set of pine hat stands, 2 with original pads, 13 to 38in (33 to 96.5cm) high.
$30-50

Shipping Goods

A grandmother miniature oak longcase clock, 65in (165cm) high.
$450-700

A mahogany wall clock, damaged, 24in (61cm) high.
$100-150

A Victorian mahogany waisted clock.
$250-350

A bronze model of a pointer dog, on marble base.
$200-350

A pair of Satsuma vases, 13½in (34cm) high.
$150-250

A short handled copper warming pan, 32in (81cm).
$100-150

An oil lamp, in Continental glass, converted, 28in (71cm).
$100-150

A box commode, 19in (48cm) high.
$100-150

A mahogany toilet mirror.
$100-150

A mahogany toilet mirror, with drawers, 26in (66cm) high.
$200-350

A spinners oak chair, 37in (94cm).
$100-150

A set of 4 Queen Anne style mahogany chairs, 41in (104cm).
$200-350

A captain's chair in elm, 28in (71cm).
$150-250

An oak lowboy, a late Victorian copy, 30½in (78cm).
$600-900

An Arts and Crafts plant holder, 37in (94cm).
$75-150

A Victorian mahogany pot cupboard, 32in (81cm) high.
$150-250

A mahogany chest of drawers, with brass handles, 42in (106.5cm).
$450-600

A walnut desk conversion, with featherbanded top, free standing, 42in (106.5cm).
$400-550

A mahogany dressing table, converted to a desk, 48in (122cm).
$400-550

A Georgian mahogany bureau, 42in
(106.5cm).
$1,300-2,000

A Victorian walnut specimen chest,
15in (38cm).
$300-500

A mahogany chest of drawers, with
bracket feet, 40in (101.5cm) high.
$400-550

A mahogany linen press, with brass
handles, 42in (106.5cm).
$900-1,300

A mahogany nest of tables, 24in
(61cm) high.
$200-350

An Edwardian walnut games table,
24½in (62cm) high.
$150-250

A washstand, c1820, 41in (104cm).
$300-500

A Victorian mahogany bidet, used
as a coffee table, 23in (58cm).
$100-150

A pine bench, c1850, 54in (137cm).
$100-150

A pine and elm box,
39in (99cm).
$300-500

A pitch pine serving table, 29in
(73cm) high.
$200-350

A drop-leaf table, 65in (165cm)
extended.
$450-700

Kitchenalia

A milk bucket and measure, late 19thC.
$100-150

A lignum vitae coffee grinder, c1770.
$900-1,300

A Norwegian finely carved pudding box, with original polychrome decoration, dated 1839.
$1,500-2,600

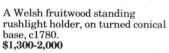

A Welsh fruitwood standing rushlight holder, on turned conical base, c1780.
$1,300-2,000

A Norwegian kasa, with original painted decoration, c1780.
$2,500-3,500

A Welsh walnut spoon, early 19thC.
$600-900

A pair of George III turned yew candlesticks.
$900-1,300

A pair of figure carved nutcrackers, English, c1650.
$800-1,200

A pair of turned oak egg cups, with silver plaques, inscribed NB 1798, 3in (7.5cm) high, and two copper measures, engraved with N below a crown and St. Cloud on the bases, 2in (5cm) diam.
$1,500-2,600

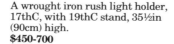

A wrought iron rush light holder, 17thC, with 19thC stand, 35½in (90cm) high.
$450-700

A creamware jelly mould, c1775, 6in (15cm) long.
$60-100

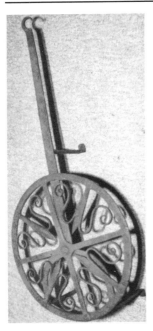

A wrought iron revolving grill, early 19thC.
$300-500

An oak candle box, 18thC, 17½ by 5in (44 by 13cm).
$150-250

A rhubarb forcer, 28in (71cm) high.
$100-150

A set of ceramic feet, for standing a dresser on stone floors.
$75-150

A tin bell-shaped chocolate mould, 5½in (14cm) high.
$45-75

A selection of Mauchline ware napkin rings, with transfer picture of Isle of Wight and Beachy Head.
$15-30

A Macintosh's tin, 16in (40.5cm) high.
$30-50

A copper saucepan, stamped H.E. Cars.
$60-100

A selection of tin scoops, 5½ to 12in (14 to 30.5cm).
$15-30

Three toffee hammers:
Sharps, 4in (10cm).
$15-30
Blue Bird, 4in (10cm).
$15-30
Bone handle, 5in (12.5cm).
$15-30

A Victorian egg basket, 6½in (16.5cm) high.
$60-100

A stone hot water bottle, now filled with sand for use as a door stop, 12in (30.5cm) long.
$30-50

A T. G. Green spot pattern jug, 4in (10cm) high.
$15-30

Enamel scoops:
Top. 4½in (11.5cm).
$15-30
Bottom. 3½in (9cm).
$15-30

A T. G. Green spot pattern plate, 7in (18cm).
$15-30

A clothes dryer, 32in (81cm) high.
$60-100

Two T. G. Green & Co. Cornish kitchenware oval cups and saucers.
$15-30

Easimix bowl, with platform for easy mixing.
$25-35

T. G. Green & Co. Cornish kitchenware,
Sultanas and Flour
5in (12.5cm),
Sugar 4in (10cm).
$20-40

Two wooden flour barrels:
l. 10in (25.5cm).
$75-150

r. 6½in (16.5cm).
$60-100

A bee collection box and comb, 18in (46cm).
$100-150

Three milk cans, tin with brass rim, 3 to 8in (7.5 to 20.5cm).
$45-75

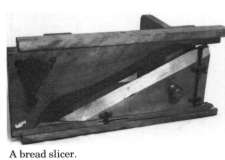

A bread slicer.
$100-150

A wall egg rack for one dozen eggs,
15in (38cm) high.
$60-100

China eggs.
$15-30 each

An Edwardian marmalade slicer.
$45-75

An egg rack.
$30-50

A Spong miniature knife sharpener
and cleaner.
$30-50

A wooden
draining spoon.
$15-30

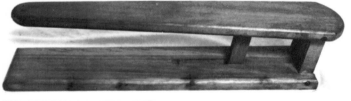

A pine sleeve board.
$20-40

A grater/slicer.
$45-75

A pine plate rack.
$100-150

A wooden rolling pin.
$20-40

A rub-a-tub, 16½in (42cm) diam.
$60-100

A wooden trough, 18 by 12in (46 by 30.5cm).
$30-50

Cleaver.
$20-40

Butter pat.
$15-30

A meat tenderiser.
$20-40

A pair of baby scales, 15in (38cm) high.
$75-150

An enamel candlestick.
$20-40

Sundry Trades

A wrought iron thatcher's needle, 19thC.
$60-100

A chemist's ball, 21in (53cm) high.
$1,200-1,750

A metal bound oak tub, 19thC, 14in (36cm).
$150-250

An oak costrel, with glass ends, 19thC, 10½in (26cm) high.
$150-250

A lacemaker's lamp with hollow baluster stem and plain moulded foot, c1880, 10½in (27cm).
$200-350

An oak silk thrower, 18thC, 25½in (64cm) long.
$150-250

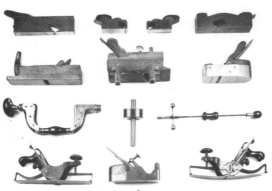

A selection of carpenter's tools.
$900-1,300

A collection of farm and country trade tools, gag 19in (48cm), thatcher's comb 10in (26cm), castrating iron 10in (26cm) and balance 9in (23cm).
$45-75

The Dining Room

A mahogany cigar box, 19thC, 8in (22cm).
$300-400

A multi-blade defence stick, with 6 spring-out blades operated from the handle, c1900.
$700-900

Games & Pastimes

A Victorian horse measuring stick, with boxwood rule and brass pull-out level, c1890.
$250-350

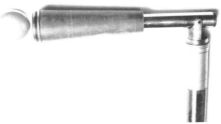

A telescopic bird spotter cane, Continental, with malacca shaft, c1890.
$400-550

A pair of twig armchairs and a table, chair 34in (86cm) high.
$1,200-1,750

Miscellaneous

A French walnut spinning wheel, 19thC, 28in (71cm) high.
$450-700

A naval rum barrel, with Royal coat-of-arms, late 19thC, 25in (63cm) high.
$300-500

A wooden framed wire bird cage.
$300-400

Jewellery

An old cut diamond and pearl three-stone ring, centre stone approx 1.65ct.
$4,000-5,500

A large sapphire cluster ring, 19thC.
$1,200-1,750

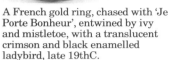

A French gold ring, chased with 'Je Porte Bonheur', entwined by ivy and mistletoe, with a translucent crimson and black enamelled ladybird, late 19thC.
$400-550

A Victorian gold, diamond and turquoise ring.
$600-900

A diamond cluster ring, the 2.85ct centre stone surrounded by 9 white diamonds, set in silver with gold band and under bezel.
$14,000-19,000

A hardstone cameo, with 19ct gold surround, set with 4 pearls.
$3,000-4,500

A deep carved coral brooch, in 18ct gold filigree surround, c1850, 1½in (4cm).
$1,200-1,750

A shell cameo, with 18ct gold surround set with turquoise stones, c1870.
$2,500-3,500

An Italian shell cameo brooch, set in Victorian gilded pinchbeck mount.
$600-900

A shell cameo, of a Grecian lady's head, with 9ct gold leaf effect surround, c1880.
$600-900

A diamond mounted bracelet, the leaf shaped links with rows of graduated brilliant and baguette cut stones.
$5,000-7,500

A Victorian sardonyx cameo brooch/pendant, c1865.
$5,000-7,500

An Edwardian Italian shell cameo, in low content Continental gold, possibly 7ct.
$200-350

A shell cameo of a cherub, with 18ct gold surround, c1870.
$1,300-2,000

A shell cameo with 9ct gold surround, c1880, 2½in (6cm) wide.
$1,000-1,400

A Georgian shell cameo of a gentleman's head, with 18ct gold surround, c1860, 3in (7.5cm).
$1,500-2,600

A pair of sardonyx cameo earrings, set in gold oval mounts with a beaded and ropetwist border, 19thC.
$1,000-1,400

A large cameo on stand, surrounded by mosaic floral pattern, c1880.
$1,500-2,600

A shell cameo brooch, with 15ct gold mount, c1875.
$1,300-2,000

A pair of Victorian deep green enamelled pendant earrings, mounted in 9ct gold, with matching pendant, a few seed pearls missing.
$700-900

A pair of sapphire and diamond pendant earrings, from The Duchess of Windsor's collection, with 2 Burmese blue sapphires 75.33ct.
$500,000+

A Victorian 9ct gold bangle, with 3 sapphires and 2 diamonds.
$800-1,200

A pair of Victorian tortoiseshell drop earrings, with carved monogram centres and mounted by family crest, c1875.
$1,200-1,750

A carved coral bracelet, c1870.
$1,200-1,750

A sapphire and diamond flexible bracelet, from The Duchess of Windsor's collection, by Van Cleef and Arpels of Paris, for 'The Marriage Contract 18.5.37'.
$1,300-2,000

A natural pearl and blue enamel snake bracelet, c1840.
$9,000-12,500

An 18ct gold bracelet, with 8 sapphires alternating with 7 diamonds.
$700-900

An Art Deco 18ct white gold bracelet, set with diamonds.
$10,500-15,000

A Victorian gold and half pearl star-shaped brooch/pendant with suspension ring, in case.
$600-900

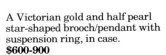

A white gold and platinum bracelet set with brilliant cut diamonds, c1935.
$10,000-13,500

A gold, ruby and diamond insect brooch, in the form of a bee.
$1,200-1,750

A gold, ruby and diamond brooch, mid-19thC.
$6,000-9,000

A gold and diamond ribbon bow brooch, late 19thC.
$2,500-3,500

A gold and diamond crescent brooch, late 19thC.
$2,000-3,000

A layered agate cameo brooch, mid-19thC.
$1,300-2,000

A gold, sapphire, diamond, ruby and seed pearl butterfly brooch, late 19thC.
$1,500-2,600

A diamond set scroll double dress clip, set in white gold.
$2,500-3,500

A sapphire and diamond frog brooch, with collet set sapphire eyes, set in silver and gold, 19thC.
$8,000-11,000

A 15ct gold and enamelled ceremonial coat-of-arms pendant, with motto 'Salus Populi', by Spencer of London.
$300-400

An old cut diamond crescent brooch, with 15 stones set in gold and silver, late 19thC.
$900-1,300

An amethyst brooch, bordered by small rose cut diamonds, calibre jet and seed pearls with open scroll platinum setting, one pearl missing.
$1,000-1,400

A pietra dura floral brooch, in gold scalloped mount, mid-19thC.
$100-200

A French agate cameo, with 18ct gold surround, blue enamel and diamonds set in 4 stars and 4 arrows, c1840.
$1,300-2,000

A Victorian reverse carved intaglio brooch, c1870, 1in (2.5cm) diam.
$1,500-2,600

A diamond set brooch, with flower shaped suspension, 53 variously sized stones set in gold.
$4,000-5,500

An Art Deco brooch, set with 5cts of diamonds mounted in platinum, c1925, 4cm.
$8,000-11,000

A Kutchinsky 18ct gold, diamond and ruby brooch.
$2,250-3,500

A diamond crescent brooch, 19thC.
$3,000-4,000

A diamond brooch/clasp, 19thC.
$4,000-5,500

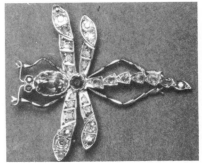

An amethyst pale sapphire, ruby and rose diamond dragonfly.
$800-1,200

A Victorian double moonstone and rose diamond heart brooch.
$1,300-2,000

A Victorian gold, pearl and sapphire bar brooch.
$600-900

A diamond geometric brooch.
$3,000-4,000

A sapphire and diamond bar brooch.
$3,000-4,000

A diamond and pearl pendant, 19thC.
$7,000-10,000

A late Victorian silver and gold brooch, set with sapphires, diamonds, natural pearls, garnets and rubies, with detachable pin to make into a pendant, 4.5cm.
$3,000-4,000

A brilliant and baguette cut diamond brooch, set in platinum and white gold, c1930.
$5,000-7,500

An 18ct gold, diamond and baroque pearl floral spray brooch.
$3,000-4,000

A mid-Victorian 15ct gold brooch, set with an emerald.
$700-900

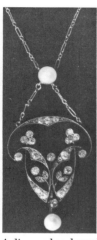

A diamond and pearl pendant.
$800-1,200

A 15ct gold floral and scroll design articulated pendant, set with pearls.
$450-700

A Victorian opal and diamond pendant.
$2,500-3,500

A Victorian gold, pearl and turquoise heart locket and chain, c1880, 3cm long.
$3,000-4,000

A ruby and diamond necklace, from the Duchess of Windsor's collection, a birthday present from the Duke of Windsor to the Duchess on the occasion of her 40th birthday, on 19th June 1936, re-made by Van Cleef and Arpels in 1939.
$3,000-4,000

A 15 row simulated pearl necklace, from the Duchess of Windsor's collection, the clasp of 2 tubular rings of gold set with diamonds and a row of cultured pearls, by Darde et Fils, c1960.
$60,000-87,500

A red coral bead necklace.
$200-350

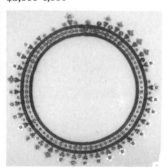

A Victorian 18ct gold, turquoise and pearl necklace.
$5,000-7,500

A cushion shaped blue 206.82ct sapphire, from the Duchess of Windsor's collection, surrounded by 11.31ct baguette and brilliant cut diamonds, by Cartier, Paris, 1951.
$400,000+

A tiara, formed as 3 flowerhead and leaf sprays pavé set with brilliant cut diamonds, centre stone .75ct, dividing to form 3 spray brooches, c1880, the fitted velvet lined case stamped E. White, 20 Cockspur St., Pall Mall.
$8,000-11,000

An Art Nouveau pendant, the carved ivory face set in silver and enamel with baroque natural pearls and cut tourmalines, c1890, 12cm overall.
$2,250-3,500

Arms & Armour
Armour

A composite half-armour, European, slightly damaged, mid-16thC.
$2,500-3,500

A composite Innsbruck half armour, some damage, c1555.
$10,500-15,000

A Japanese suit of armour.
$1,300-2,000

A half-scale model of a Gothic armour, in 15thC Southern German style, 16in (40.5cm).
$400-550

A close helmet made for Pisan Bridge Festival.
$3,000-4,000

A close helmet, a modern copy of a 16thC helmet, 13in (33cm) high.
$450-700

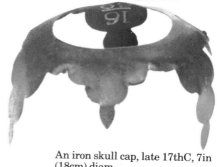

A Cuirassier helmet, probably Italian, old riveted and brazed internal patches, c1600, 11½in (29cm) high.
$2,000-3,000

A Cuirassier helmet, probably German, early 17thC, 13in (33cm).
$3,000-4,000

An iron skull cap, late 17thC, 7in (18cm) diam.
$400-550

A Dutch Zwolletown guard spontoon.
$800-1,200

A German mace, mid-16thC.
$6,000-8,000

A close helmet, mainly 17thC.
$1,500-2,600

A German peaked burgonet.
$2,000-3,000

Edged Weapons – Bayonets

A Nazi Wehrmacht dress bayonet, slight wear to hilt plating.
$10,500-15,000

A bayonet, British pattern 1859, minor damage to scabbard leather.
$400-550

Daggers

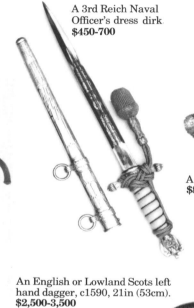

A 3rd Reich Naval Officer's dress dirk.
$450-700

A silver mounted Omani Jambiya.
$800-1,200

A scabbard for a Landsknecht's dagger, c1550.
$600-900

An English or Lowland Scots left hand dagger, c1590, 21in (53cm).
$2,500-3,500

Knives

A French combination knife and double barrelled pistol, signed Dumonthier (sic) Paris, c1850.
$1,300-2,000

Swords

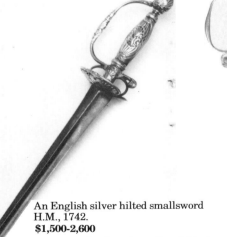

A swept hilt rapier, c1600.
$4,000-5,500

An English silver hilted smallsword H.M., 1742.
$1,500-2,600

An American silver hilted smallsword, c1730, blade 33in (84cm).
$1,200-1,750

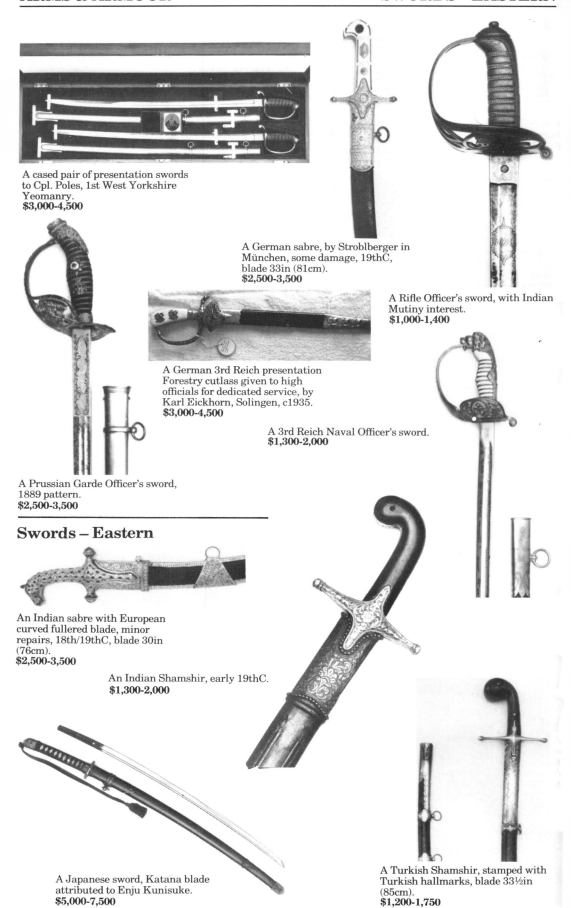

A cased pair of presentation swords
to Cpl. Poles, 1st West Yorkshire
Yeomanry.
$3,000-4,500

A German sabre, by Stroblberger in
München, some damage, 19thC,
blade 33in (81cm).
$2,500-3,500

A Rifle Officer's sword, with Indian
Mutiny interest.
$1,000-1,400

A German 3rd Reich presentation
Forestry cutlass given to high
officials for dedicated service, by
Karl Eickhorn, Solingen, c1935.
$3,000-4,500

A 3rd Reich Naval Officer's sword.
$1,300-2,000

A Prussian Garde Officer's sword,
1889 pattern.
$2,500-3,500

Swords – Eastern

An Indian sabre with European
curved fullered blade, minor
repairs, 18th/19thC, blade 30in
(76cm).
$2,500-3,500

An Indian Shamshir, early 19thC.
$1,300-2,000

A Japanese sword, Katana blade
attributed to Enju Kunisuke.
$5,000-7,500

A Turkish Shamshir, stamped with
Turkish hallmarks, blade 33½in
(85cm).
$1,200-1,750

Blunderbusses

A brass barrelled flintlock blunderbuss, fore-end restored, barrel 15½in (39.5cm).
$1,000-1,400

A brass barrelled flintlock blunderbuss, the engraved lock signed Waters & Gill, 12in (30cm).
$1,500-2,600

A brass barrelled flintlock blunderbuss, engraved London, signed Joyner, and stamped with an ordnance mark, 14in (36cm).
$1,500-2,600

Muskets & Sporting

A flintlock blunderbuss with bayonet, by REA.
$1,300-2,000

A flintlock blunderbuss by Wilson.
$1,300-2,000

A matchlock musket, the two-stage sighted barrel struck with maker's mark C.R. at the breech, North European, c1630, 41in (104cm).
$1,300-2,000

An Austrian rifled flintlock sporting carbine, c1770.
$1,000-1,400

An Elliott flintlock Cavalry carbine.
$2,000-3,000

An Italian matchlock musket, 16thC.
$2,000-3,000

A British Naval flintlock musketoon.
$4,000-5,500
A seven shot volley gun.
$4,000-5,500

Two Japanese matchlocks,
gun. **$1,000-1,400**
rifle. **$1,500-2,600**

A double barrelled 12-bore sidelock ejector shotgun, by George Gibbs, Serial No. C581, nitro proof, re-barrelled by makers in 1979, barrels 28in (71cm), in plush lined leather case with maker's trade label.
$2,500-3,500

Rifles

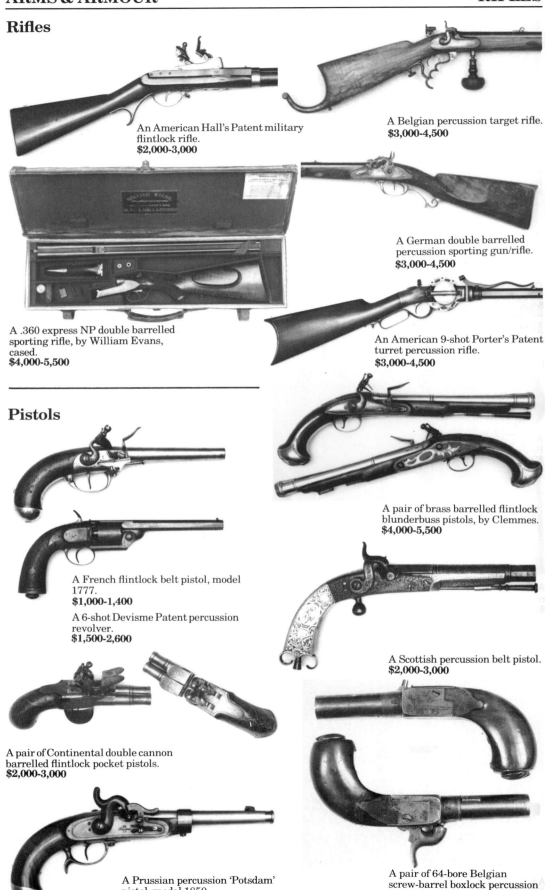

An American Hall's Patent military flintlock rifle.
$2,000-3,000

A Belgian percussion target rifle.
$3,000-4,500

A German double barrelled percussion sporting gun/rifle.
$3,000-4,500

A .360 express NP double barrelled sporting rifle, by William Evans, cased.
$4,000-5,500

An American 9-shot Porter's Patent turret percussion rifle.
$3,000-4,500

Pistols

A French flintlock belt pistol, model 1777.
$1,000-1,400

A 6-shot Devisme Patent percussion revolver.
$1,500-2,600

A pair of brass barrelled flintlock blunderbuss pistols, by Clemmes.
$4,000-5,500

A Scottish percussion belt pistol.
$2,000-3,000

A pair of Continental double cannon barrelled flintlock pocket pistols.
$2,000-3,000

A Prussian percussion 'Potsdam' pistol, model 1850.
$2,000-3,000

A pair of 64-bore Belgian screw-barrel boxlock percussion muff pistols, c1855, barrel 4cm.
$400-550

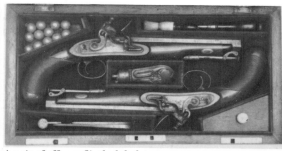

A pair of officers flintlock holster
pistols by Hamburger & Co., cased.
$2,500-3,500

A pair of brass barrelled flintlock
pistols by Wilson, cased.
$4,000-5,500

A 7.63 Mauser model 96 semi-auto
pistol with holster stock.
$4,000-5,500

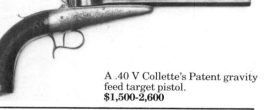

A .40 V Collette's Patent gravity
feed target pistol.
$1,500-2,600

Revolvers

A 5 shot 2nd model pepperbox by
Budding.
$2,000-3,000

An 8-shot Austrian pepperbox
revolver.
$2,000-3,000

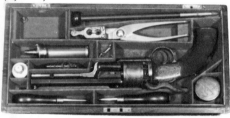

A 6-shot transitional percussion
revolver by T. K. Baker, cased.
$2,000-3,000

A 120 bore Beaumont-Adams 5-shot
double action percussion pocket
revolver, serial No. 461, retailed by
Deane & Son, 30 King William
Street, London Bridge, on an 1851
model frame, barrel 4in (10cm).
$1,500-2,600

Medals & Orders

A 5-shot double action percussion
revolver, by Daw, cased.
$1,500-2,600

A 6-shot Colt Hartford-English
Dragoon percussion revolver.
$6,000-9,000

Louisbourg silver medal, 1758.
$1,300-2,000

Militaria, Badges & Plates

Shoulder belt plate Royal Monmouth Regt.
$450-600

Imperial Austrian Pilots badge.
$700-900

Officer's plain brooch, Highland Lt. Infantry.
$800-1,200

Powder Flasks

A Sykes Patent revolver flask, the brass collar and top with 3 position charger, bag shaped copper body, minor damage, 6in (15cm).
$150-200

Third Reich Auxiliary Cruiser badge, with diamonds.
$9,000-12,500

A presentation signed photograph of Kaiser Wilhelm II.
$2,250-3,500

Miscellaneous

A Victorian set of surgeon's instruments, cased.
$900-1,300

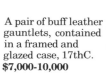

Prussian Order of the Black Eagle, Grand Cross.
$6,000-9,000

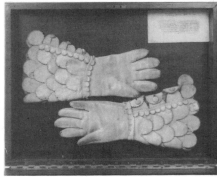

A pair of buff leather gauntlets, contained in a framed and glazed case, 17thC.
$7,000-10,000

Thirteen toy soldiers, Nazi period.
$900-1,300

DIRECTORY OF INTERNATIONAL AUCTIONEERS

This directory is by no means complete. Any auctioneer who holds frequent sales should contact us for inclusion in the 1990 Edition. Entries must be received by April 1989. There is, of course, no charge for this listing.

America

Acorn Farm Antiques,
15466 Oak Road, Carmel,
IN 46032
Tel: (317) 846-2383

ALA Moanastampt Cain (David H Martin),
1236 Ala Moana Boulevard,
Honolulu, HI 96814

Alabama Auction Room Inc,
2112 Fifth Avenue North,
Birmingham, AL 35203
Tel: (205) 252-4073

B Altman & Co,
34th & Fifth Avenue, New York,
NY 10016
Tel: (212) OR 9 7800 ext 550 & 322

Ames Art Galleries,
8729 Wilshire Boulevard, Beverly
Hills, CA 9021
Tel: (213) 655-5611/652-3820

Arnette's Auction Galleries Inc,
310 West Castle Street,
Murfreesboro, TN 37130
Tel: (615) 893-3725

Associated Appraisers Inc,
915 Industrial Bank Building,
Providence, RI 02906
Tel: (401) 331-9391

Atlanta's ABCD Auction Gallery
(Clark, Bate and Depew),
1 North Clarendon Avenue,
Antioch, IL 30002
Tel: (312) 294-8264

Bakers Auction,
14100 Paramount Boulevard,
Paramount, CA 90723
Tel: (213) 531-1524

Barridoff Galleries,
242 Middle Street, Portland,
ME 04 101
Tel: (207) 772-5011

C T Bevensee Auction Service,
PO Box 492, Botsford, CT 06404
Tel: (203) 426-6698

Frank H Boos,
1137 S Adams, Birmingham,
MI 48011
Tel: (313) 644-1633

Richard A Bourne Co Inc,
Corporation Street, PO Box 141/A,
Hyannis Port, MA 02647
Tel: (617) 775-0797

Bridges Antiques and Auctions,
Highway 46, PO Box 52A,
Sanford, FL 32771
Tel: (305) 323-2801/322-0095

George C Brilant & Co,
191 King Street, Charleston,
SC 29401

R W Bronstein Corp,
3666 Main Street, Buffalo,
NY 14226
Tel: (716) 835-7666/7408

Brookline Auction Gallery,
Proctor Hill Road, Route 130,
Brookline, NH 03033
Tel: (603) 673-4474/4153

Brzostek's Auction Service,
2052 Lamson Road, Phoenix,
NY 13135
Tel: (315) 678-2542

Buckingham Galleries Ltd,
4350 Dawson Street, San Diego,
CA 92115
Tel: (714) 283-7286

Bushell's Auction,
2006 2nd Avenue, Seattle,
WA 98121
Tel: (206) 622-5833

L Butterfield,
605 W Midland, Bay City,
MI 48706
Tel: (517) 684-3229

Butterfield,
808 N La, Cienega Boulevard, Los
Angeles, CA 90069

Butterfield & Butterfield,
1244 Sutter Street, San Francisco,
CA 94109
Tel: (415) 673-1362

California Book Auction Galleries,
358 Golden Gate Avenue, San
Francisco, CA 94102
Tel: (415) 775-0424

C B Charles Galleries Inc,
825 Woodward Avenue, Pontiac,
MI 48053
Tel: (313) 338-9023

Chatsworth Auction Rooms,
151 Mamaroneck Avenue,
Mamaroneck, NY 10543

Christie, Manson & Wood
International Inc,
502 Park Avenue, New York
Tel: (212) 826-2388 Telex: 620721

Christie's East,
219 East 67th Street, New York,
NY 10021
Tel: (212) 570-4141

Representative Offices:
California:
9350 Wilshire Boulevard, Beverly
Hills, CA 902 12
Tel: (213) 275-5534

Florida:
225 Fern Street, West Palm Beach,
FL 33401
Tel: (305) 833-6592

Mid-Atlantic:
638 Morris Avenue, Bryn Mawr,
PA 19010
Tel: (215) 525-5493

Washington:
1422 27th Street NW, Washington,
DC 20007
Tel: (202) 965-2066

Midwest:
46 East Elm Street, Chicago,
IL 60611
Tel: (312) 787-2765

Fred Clark Auctioneer Inc,
PO Box 124, Route 14, Scotland,
CT 06264
Tel: (203) 423-3939/0594

Cockrum Auctions,
2701 North Highway 94,
St Charles, MO 63301
Tel: (314) 723-9511

George Cole, Auctioneers and
Appraisers,
14 Green Street, Kingston,
NY 12401
Tel: (914) 338-2367

Coleman Auction Galleries,
525 East 72nd Street, New York,
NY 10021
Tel: (212) 879-1415

Conestoga Auction Company Inc,
PO Box 1, Manheim, PA 17545
Tel: (717) 898-7284

Cook's Auction Gallery,
Route 58, Halifax, MA 02338
Tel: (617) 293-3445/866-3243

Coquina Auction Barn
40 S Atlantic Avenue, Ormond
Beach, FL 32074

Danny's Antique Auction Service
(Pat Lusardi),
Route 46, Belvidere, NH 07823
Tel: (201) 757-7278

Douglas Galleries,
Route 5, South Deerfield,
MA 01373
Tel: (413) 665-2877

William Doyle,
175 East 87th Street, New York,
NY 10128
Tel: (212) 427-2730

DuMochelle Art Galleries,
409 East Jefferson, Detroit,
MI 48226
Tel: (313) 963-6255

John C Edelmann Galleries Inc,
123 East 77th Street, New York,
NY 10021
Tel: (212) 628-1700/1735

Robert C Eldred Co Inc,
Box 796, East Dennis, MA 02641
Tel: (617) 385-3116/3377

The Fine Arts Company of
Philadelphia Inc,
2317 Chestnut Street,
Philadelphia, PA 19103
Tel: (215) 564-3644

Fordem Galleries Inc,
3829 Lorain Avenue, Cleveland,
OH 44113
Tel: (216) 281-3563

George S Foster III,
Route 28, Epsom, NH 03234
Tel: (603) 736-9240

Fred's Auction House,
92 Pleasant Street, Leominster,
MA 01453
Tel: (617) 534-9004

S T Freeman & Co,
1808 Chestnut Street,
Philadelphia, PA 19103
Tel: (215) 563-9275

Col K R French and Co Inc,
166 Bedford Road, Armonk,
NY 10504
Tel: (914) 273-3674

Garth's Auctions Inc,
2690 Stratford Road, Delaware,
OH 43015
Tel: (614) 362-4771/369-5085

Gilbert Auctions,
River Road, Garrison, NY 10524
Tel: (914) 424-3657

Morten M Goldberg,
215 N Rampart Street, New
Orleans, LA 70112
Tel: (504) 522-8364

Gramercy Auction Galleries,
52 East 13th Street, New York,
NY 10003
Tel: (212) 477-5656

Grandma's House,
4712 Dudley, Wheatridge,
CO 80033
Tel: (303) 423-3640/534-2847

The William Haber Art Collection
Inc,
139-11 Queens Boulevard,
Jamaica, NY 11435
Tel: (212) 739-1000

Charlton Hall Galleries Inc,
930 Gervais Street, Columbia,
SC 29201
Tel: (803) 252-7927/779-5678

Hampton Auction Gallery,
201 Harwick Street, Belvidere,
NH 07823
Tel: (201) 475-2928

Hanzel,
1120 S Michigan Avenue, Chicago,
IL 60605
Tel: (312) 922-6234

Harbor Auction Gallery,
238 Bank Street, New London,
CT 06355
Tel: (203) 443-0868

Harmer's of San Francisco Inc,
49 Geary Street, San Francisco,
CA 94102
Tel: (415) 391-8244

Harris Auction Galleries,
873-875 North Howard Street,
Baltimore, MD 21201
Tel: (301) 728-7040

Hart,
2311 Westheimer, Houston,
TX 77098
Tel: (713) 524-2979/523-7389

Hauswedel & Nolte,
225 West Central Park, New York,
NY 10024
Tel: (212) 787-7245

G Ray Hawkins,
7224 Melrose Avenue, Los
Angeles, CA 90046
Tel: (213) 550-1504

Elwood Heller & Son Auctioneer,
151 Main Street, Lebanon,
NJ 08833
Tel: (201) 23 62 195

William F Hill Auction Sales,
Route 16, East Hardwick,
VT 05834
Tel: (802) 472-6308

Leslie Hindman,
215 West Ohio Street, Chicago,
IL 60610
Tel: (312) 670-0010

The House Clinic,
PO Box 13013A, Orlando, Fl 32859
Tel: (305) 859-1770/851-2979

Co Raymond W Huber,
211 North Monroe, Montpelier,
OH 43543

F B Hubley Et Co,
364 Broadway, Cambridge,
MA 02100
Tel: (617) 876-2030

Iroquois Auctions,
Box 66, Broad Street, Port Henry,
NY 12974
Tel: (518) 942-3355

It's About Time,
375 Park Avenue, Glencoe,
IL 60022
Tel: (312) 835-2012

Louis Joseph Auction Gallery
(Richard L Ryan),
575 Washington Street, Brookline,
MA 02146
Tel: (617) 277-0740

Julia's Auction Service,
Route 201, Skowhegan Road,
Fairfield, ME 04937
Tel: (207) 453-9725

Sibylle Kaldewey,
225 West Central Park, New York,
NY 10024
Tel: (212) 787-7245

Kelley's Auction Service,
PO Box 125, Woburn, MA 01801
Tel: (617) 272-9167

Kennedy Antique Auction
Galleries Inc,
1088 Huff Road, Atlanta,
GA 30318
Tel: (404) 351-4464

621

Kinzie Galleries Auction Service,
1002 3rd Avenue, Duncansville,
PA 16835
Tel: (814) 695-3479

La Salle,
2083 Union Street, San Francisco,
CA 94123
Tel: (415) 931-9200

L A Landry (Robert Landry),
94 Main Street, Essex, MA 01929
Tel: (603) 744-5811

Jo Anna Larson,
POB 0, Antioch, IL 60002
Tel: (312) 395-0963

Levins Auction Exchange,
414 Camp Street, New Orleans,
LA 70130

Lipton,
1108 Fort Street, Honolulu,
HI 96813
Tel: (808) 533-4320

F S Long & Sons,
3126 East 3rd Street, Dayton,
OH 45403

R L Loveless Associates Inc,
4223 Clover Street, Honeoye Falls,
NY 14472
Tel: (716) 624-1648/1556

Lubin Galleries,
30 West 26th Street, New York,
NY 10010
Tel: (212) 924-3777

Main Auction Galleries,
137 West 4th Street, Cincinnati,
OH 45202
Tel: (513) 621-1280

Maison Auction Co Inc,
128 East Street, Wallingford,
CT 06492
Tel: (203) 269-8007

Joel L Malter & Co Inc,
Suite 518, 16661 Ventura
Boulevard, Encino, CA 91316
Tel: (213) 784-7772/2181

Manhattan Galleries,
1415 Third Avenue, New York,
NY 10028
Tel: (212) 744-2844

Mapes,
1600 West Vestal Parkway,
Vestal, NY 13850
Tel: (607) 754-9193

David W Mapes Inc,
82 Front Street, Binghamton,
NY 13905
Tel: (607) 724-6741/862-9365

Marvin H Newman,
426 South Robertson Boulevard,
Los Angeles, CA 90048
Tel: (213) 273-4840/378-2095

Mechanical Music Center Inc,
25 Kings Highway North, Darien,
CT 06820
Tel: (203) 655-9510

Milwaukee Auction Galleries,
4747 West Bradley Road,
Milwaukee, WI 53223
Tel: (414) 355-5054

Wayne Mock Inc,
Box 37, Tamworth, NH 03886
Tel: (603) 323-8057

William F Moon & Co,
12 Lewis Road, RFD 1, North
Attleboro, MA 02760
Tel: (617) 761-8003

New England Rare Coin Auctions,
89 Devonshire Street, Boston,
MA 02109
Tel: (617) 227-8800

Kurt Niven,
1444 Oak Lawn, Suite 525, Dallas,
TX 75207
Tel: (214) 741-4252

Northgate Gallery,
5520 Highway 153, Chattanooga,
TN 37443
Tel: (615) 842-4177

O'Gallerie Inc,
537 SE Ash Street, Portland,
OR 97214
Tel: (503) 238-0202

Th J Owen & Sons,
1111 East Street NW, Washington,
DC 20004

Palmer Auction Service,
Lucas, KS 67648

Park City Auction Service,
925 Wood Street, Bridgeport,
CT 06604
Tel: (203) 333-5251

Pennypacker Auction Centre,
1540 New Holland Road,
Kenhorst, Reading, PA 19607
Tel: (215) 777-5890/6121

Peyton Place Antiques,
819 Lovett Boulevard, Houston,
TX 77006
Tel: (713) 523-4841

Phillips,
867 Madison Avenue, New York,
NY 10021
Tel: (212) 570-4830

525 East 72nd Street, New York,
NY10021
Tel: (212) 570-4852

Representative Office:
6 Faneuil Hall, Marketplace,
Boston, MA 02109
Tel: (617) 227-6145

Pollack,
2780 NE 183 Street, Miami,
FL 33160
Tel: (305) 931-4476

Quickie Auction House,
Route 3, Osseo, MN 55369
Tel: (612) 428-4378

R & S Estate Liquidations,
Box 205, Newton Center,
MA 02159
Tel: (617) 244-6616

C Gilbert Richards,
Garrison, NY 10524
Tel: (914) 424-3657

Bill Rinaldi Auctions,
Bedell Road, Poughkeepsie,
NY 12601
Tel: (914) 454-9613

Roan Inc,
Box 118, RD 3, Logan Station,
PA 17728
Tel: (717) 494-0170

Rockland Auction Services Inc,
72 Pomona Road, Suffern,
NY 10901
Tel: (914) 354-3914/2723

Rome Auction Gallery (Sandra A
Louis Caropreso),
Route 2, Highway 53, Rome,
GA 30161

Rose Galleries Inc,
1123 West County Road B,
Roseville, MN 55113
Tel: (612) 484-1415

Rosvall Auction Company,
1238 & 1248 South Broadway,
Denver, CO 80210
Tel: (303) 777-2032/722-4028

Sigmund Rothschild,
27 West 67th Street, New York,
NY 10023
Tel: (212) 873-5522

Vince Runowich Auctions,
2312 4th Street North, St
Petersburg, FL 33704
Tel: (813) 895-3548

Safran's Antique Galleries Ltd,
930 Gervais Street, Columbia,
SC 29201
Tel: (803) 252-7927

Sage Auction Gallery,
Route 9A, Chester, CT 06412
Tel: (203) 526-3036

San Antonio Auction Gallery,
5096 Bianco, San Antonio,
TX 78216
Tel: (512) 342-3800

Emory Sanders,
New London, NH 03257
Tel: (603) 526-6326

Sandwich Auction House,
15 Tupper Road, Sandwich,
MA 02563
Tel: (617) 888-1926/5675

San Francisco Auction Gallery,
1217 Sutter Street, San Francisco,
CA 94109
Tel: (415) 441-3800

Schafer Auction Gallery,
82 Bradley Road, Madison,
CT 06443
Tel: (203) 245-4173

Schmidt's Antiques,
5138 West Michigan Avenue,
Ypsilanti, MI 48 197
Tel: (313) 434-2660

K C Self,
53 Victory Lane, Los Angeles,
CA 95030
Tel: (213) 354-4238

B J Selkirk & Sons,
4166 Olive Street, St Louis,
MO 63108
Tel: (314) 533-1700

Shore Galleries Inc,
3318 West Devon, Lincolnwood,
IL 60659
Tel: (312) 676-2900

Shute's Auction Gallery,
70 Accord Park Drive, Norwell,
MA 02061
Tel: (617) 871-3414/238-0586

Ronald Siefert,
RFD, Buskirk, NY 12028
Tel: (518) 686-9375

Robert A Siegel Auction Galleries
Inc,
120 East 56th Street, New York,
NY 10022
Tel: (212) 753-6421/2/3

Robert W Skinner Inc,
Main Street, Bolton, MA 01740
Tel: (617) 779-5528

585 Boylston Street,
Boston, MA 02116
Tel: (617) 236-1700

C G Sloan & Co,
715 13th Street NW, Washington,
DC 20005
Tel: (202) 628-1468

Branch Office:
403 North Charles Street,
Baltimore, MD 21201
Tel: (301) 547-1177

Sotheby,
101 Newbury Street, Boston,
MA 02116
Tel: (617) 247-2851

Sotheby Park Bernet Inc,
980 Madison Avenue, New York,
NY 10021
Tel: (212) 472-3400

1334 York Avenue, New York,
NY 10021

171 East 84th Street, New York,
NY 10028

Mid-Atlantic:
1630 Locust Street, Philadelphia,
PA 19103
Tel: (215) 735-7886

Washington:
2903 M Street NW, Washington,
DC 20007
Tel: (202) 298-8400

Southeast:
155 Worth Avenue, Palm Beach,
FL 33480
Tel: (305) 658-3555

Midwest:
700 North Michigan Avenue,
Chicago, IL 60611
Tel: (312) 280-0185

Southwest:
Galleria Post Oak,
5015 Westheimer Road, Houston,
TX 77056
Tel: (713) 623-0010

Northwest:
210 Post Street, San Francisco,
CA 94108
Tel: (415) 986-4982

Pacific Area:
Suite 117, 850 West Hind Drive,
Honolulu, Hawaii 96821
Tel: (808) 373-9166

Stack's Rare Coin Auctions,
123 West 57th Street, New York,
NY 10019
Tel: (212) 583-2580

Stalker and Boos Inc,
280 North Woodward Avenue,
Birmingham, MI 48011
Tel: (313) 646-4560

Classic Auction Gallery
(formerly Sterling Auctions),
62 No. 2nd Avenue, Raritan,
NJ 08869
Tel: (201) 526-6024

Stremmel Auctions Inc,
2152 Prater Way, Sparks,
NV 89431
Tel: (702) 331-1035

Summit Auction Rooms,
47-49 Summit Avenue, Summit,
NJ 07901

Superior Stamp & Coin Co Inc,
9301 Wiltshire Boulevard,
Beverly Hills, CA 90210
Tel: (213) 272-0851/278-9740

Swann Galleries Inc,
104 East 26th Street, New York,
NY 10021
Tel: (212) 254-4710

Philip Swedler & Son,
850 Grand Avenue, New Haven,
CT 06511
Tel: (203) 624-2202/562-5065

Tait Auction Studio,
1209 Howard Avenue,
Burlingame, CA 94010
Tel: (415) 343-4793

Tepper Galleries,
110 East 25th Street, New York,
NY 10010
Tel: (212) 677-5300/1/2

Louis Trailman Auction Co,
1519 Spruce Street, Philadelphia,
PA 19102
Tel: (215) K1 5 4500

Trend Galleries Inc,
2784 Merrick Road, Bellmore,
NY 11710
Tel: (516) 221-5588

Trosby Auction Galleries,
81 Peachtree Park Drive, Atlanta,
GA 30326
Tel: (404) 351-4400

Valle-McLeod Gallery,
3303 Kirby Drive, Houston,
TX 77098
Tel: (713) 523-8309/8310

The Watnot Auction,
Box 78, Mellenville, NY 12544
Tel: (518) 672-7576

Adam A Wechsler & Son,
905-9 East Street NW,
Washington, DC 20004
Tel: (202) 628-1281

White Plains Auction Rooms,
572 North Broadway, White
Plains, NY 10603
Tel: (914) 428-2255

Henry Willis,
22 Main Street, Marshfield,
MA 02050
Tel: (617) 834 7774

The Wilson Galleries,
PO Box 102, Ford Defiance,
VA 24437
Tel: (703) 885-4292

Helen Winter Associates,
355 Farmington Avenue,
Plainville, CT 06062
Tel: (203) 747-0714/677-0848

Richard Withington Inc,
Hillsboro, NH 03244
Tel: (603) 464-3232

Wolf,
13015 Larchmere Boulevard,
Shaker Heights, OH 44120
Tel: (216) 231-3888

Richard Wolffers Inc,
127 Kearney Street, San
Francisco, CA 94 108
Tel: (415) 781-5127

Young,
56 Market Street, Portsmouth,
NH 03801
Tel: (603) 436-8773

Samuel Yudkin & Associates,
1125 King Street, Alexandria,
VA 22314
Tel: (703) 549-9330

Australia

ASA Stamps Co Pty Ltd,
138-140 Rundle Mall, National
Bank Building, Adelaide, South
Australia 5001
Tel: 223-2951

Associated Auctioneers Pty Ltd,
800-810 Parramatta Road,
Lewisham, New South Wales 2049
Tel: 560-5899

G J Brain Auctioneers Pty Ltd,
122 Harrington Street, Sydney,
New South Wales 2000
Tel: 271701

Bright Slater Pty Ltd,
Box 205 GPO, Lower Ground
Floor, Brisbane Club Building,
Isles Lane, Brisbane, Queensland
4000
Tel: 312415

Christie, Manson & Woods
(Australia) Ltd,
298 New South Head Road, Double
Bay, Sydney, New South Wales
2028
Tel: 326-1422

William S Ellenden Pty Ltd,
67-73 Wentworth Avenue,
Sydney, New South Wales 2000
Tel: 211-4035/211-4477

Bruce Granger Auctions,
10 Hopetoun Street, Huristone
Park, New South Wales 2193
Tel: 559-4767

Johnson Bros Auctioneers & Real
Estate Agents,
328 Main Road, Glenorchy,
Tasmania 7011
Tel: 725166 492909

James A Johnson & Co,
92 Boronia Road, Vermont,
Victoria 3133
Tel: 877-2754/874-3632

Jolly Barry Pty Ltd,
212 Glenmore Road, Paddington,
New South Wales 2021
Tel: 357-4494

James R Lawson Pty Ltd,
236 Castlereagh Street, Sydney,
New South Wales
Tel: 266408

Mason Greene & Associates,
91-101 Leveson Street, North
Melbourne, Victoria 3051
Tel: 329-9911

Mercantile Art Auctions,
317 Pacific Highway, North Sydey,
New South Wales 2060
Tel: 922-3610/922-3608

James R Newall Auctions Pty Ltd,
164 Military Road, Neutral Bay,
New South Wales 2089
Tel: 903023/902587 (Sydney ex)

P L Pickles & Co Pty Ltd
655 Pacific Highway, Killara, New
South Wales 2071
Tel: 498-8069/498-2775

Sotheby Parke Bernet Group Ltd,
115 Collins Street, Melbourne,
Victoria 3000
Tel: (03) 63 39 00

H E Wells & Sons,
326 Rokeby Road, Subiaco, West
Australia
Tel: 3819448/3819040

Young Family Estates Pty Ltd,
229 Camberwell Road, East
Hawthorn, Melbourne 2123
Tel: 821433

New Zealand

Devereaux & Culley Ltd,
200 Dominion Road, Mt Eden,
Auckland
Tel: 687429/687112

Alex Harris Ltd,
PO Box 510, 377 Princes Street,
Dunedin
Tel: 773955/740703

Roger Moat Ltd,
College Hill and Beaumont Street,
Auckland
Tel: 37 1588/37 1686/37 1595

New Zealand Stamp Auctions,
PO Box 3496, Queen and
Wyndham Streets, Auckland
Tel: 375490/375498

Alistair Robb Coin Auctions,
La Aitken Street, Box 3705,
Wellington
Tel: 727-141

Dunbar Sloane Ltd,
32 Waring Taylor Street,
Wellington
Tel: 721-367

Thornton Auctions Ltd,
89 Albert Street, Auckland 1
Tel: 30888 (3 lines)

Daniel J Visser,
109 and 90 Worchester Street,
Christchurch
Tel: 68853/67297

Austria

Christie's,
Ziehrerplatz 4/22, A-1030 Vienna
Tel: (0222) 73 26 44

Belgium

Christie, Manson & Woods
(Belgium) Ltd,
33 Boulevard de Waterloo, B-1000
Brussels
Tel: (02) 512-8765/512-8830

Sotheby Parke Bernet Belgium,
Rue de l'Abbaye 32, 1050 Brussels
Tel: 343 50 07

Canada

A-1 Auctioneer Evaluation
Services Ltd,
PO Box 926, Saint John,
NB E2L 4C3
Tel: (508) 762-0559

Appleton Auctioneers Ltd,
1238 Seymour Street, Vancouver,
BC V6B 3N9
Tel: (604) 685-1715

Ashton Auction Service,
PO Box 500, Ashton, Ontario,
KOA 180
Tel: (613) 257-1575

Canada Book Auctions,
35 Front Street East, Toronto,
Ontario M5E 1B3
Tel: (416) 368-4326

Christie's International Ltd,
Suite 2002, 1055 West Georgia
Street, Vancouver, BC V6E 3P3
Tel: (604) 685-2126

Miller & Johnson Auctioneers Ltd,
2882 Gottingen Street, Halifax,
Nova Scotia B3K 3E2
Tel: (902) 425-3366/425-3606

Phillips Ward-Price Ltd,
76 Davenport Road, Toronto,
Ontario M5R 1H3
Tel: (416) 923-9876

Sotheby Parke Bernet (Canada)
Inc,
156 Front Street, Toronto, Ontario
M5J 2L6
Tel: (416) 596-0300

Representative:
David Brown,
2321 Granville Street, Vancouver,
BC V6H 3G4
Tel: (604) 736-6363

Denmark

Kunsthallens,
Kunstauktioner A/S,
Købmagergade 11 DK 1150
Copenhagen
Tel: (01) 13 85 69

Nellemann & Thomsen,
Neilgade 45, DK-8000 Aarhus
Tel: (06) 12 06 66/12 00 02

France

Ader, Picard, Tajan,
12 rue Favart, 75002 Paris
Tel: 261.80.07

Artus,
15 rue de la Grange-Batelière,
75009 Paris
Tel: 523.12.03

Audap,
32 rue Drouot, 75009 Paris
Tel: 742.78.01

Bondu,
17 rue Drouot, 75009 Paris
Tel: 770.36.16

Boscher, Gossart,
3 rue d'Amboise, 75009 Paris
Tel: 260.87.87

Briest,
15 rue Drouot, 75009 Paris
Tel: 770.66.29

de Cagny,
4 rue Drouot, 75009 Paris
Tel: 246.00.07

Charbonneaux,
134 rue du Faubourg Saint-
Honoré, 75008 Paris
Tel: 359.66.57

Chayette,
10 rue Rossini, 75009 Paris
Tel: 770.38.89

Delaporte, Rieunier,
159 rue Montmartre, 75002 Paris
Tel: 508.41.83

Delorme,
3 rue Penthièvre, 75008 Paris
Tel: 265.57.63

Godeau,
32 rue Drouot, 75009 Paris
Tel: 770.67.68

Gros,
22 rue Drouot, 75009 Paris
Tel: 770.83.04

Langlade,
12 rue Descombes, 75017 Paris
Tel: 227.00.91

Loudmer, Poulain,
73 rue de Faubourg Saint-Honoré,
75008 Paris
Tel: 266.90.01

Maignan,
6 rue de la Michodière, 75002 Paris
Tel: 742.71.52

Maringe,
16 rue de Provence, 75009 Paris
Tel: 770.61.15

Marlio,
7 rue Ernest-Renan, 75015 Paris
Tel: 734.81.13

Paul Martin & Jacques Martin,
3 impasse des Chevau-Legers,
78000 Versailles
Tel: 950.58.08

Bonhams, Baron Foran,
Duc de Saint-Bar, 2 rue Bellanger,
92200 Neuilly sur Seine
Tel: (1) 637-1329

Christie's, Princess Jeanne-Marie
de Broglie,
17 rue de Lille, 75007 Paris
Tel: (331) 261-1247

Sotheby's, Rear Admiral J A
Templeton-Cotill, CB,
3 rue de Miromesnil, 75008 Paris
Tel: (1) 266-4060

Monaco

Sotheby Parke Bernet Group,
PO Box 45, Sporting d'Hiver, Place
du Casino, Monte Carlo
Tel: (93) 30 88 80

Hong Kong

Sotheby Parke Bernet (Hong
Kong) Ltd,
PO Box 83, 705 Lane Crawford
House, 64-70 Queen's Road
Central, Hong Kong
Tel: 22-5454

Italy

Christie's (International) SA,
Palazzo Massimo Lancellotti,
Piazza Navona 114, 00186 Rome
Tel: 6541217

Christie's (Italy) SR1,
9 Via Borgogna, 20144 Milan
Tel: 794712

Finarte SPA,
Piazzetta Bossi 4, 20121 Milan
Tel: 877041

Finarte SPA,
Via delle Quattro, Fontane 20,
Rome
Tel: 463564

Palazzo Internationale delle Aste ed
Esposizioni SPA,
Palazzo Corsini, Il Prato 56,
Florence
Tel: 293000

Sotheby Parke Bernet Italia,
26 Via Gino Capponi, 50121
Florence
Tel: 571410

Sotheby Parke Bernet Italia,
Via Montenapoleone 3, 20121
Milan
Tel: 783907

Sotheby Parke Bernet Italia,
Palazzo Taverna, Via di Monte
Giordano 36, 00186 Rome
Tel: 656 1670/6547400

The Netherlands

Christie, Manson & Woods Ltd,
Rokin 91, 1012 KL Amsterdam
Tel: (020) 23 15 05

Sotheby Mak Van Waay BV,
102 Rokin 1012, KZ Amsterdam
Tel: 24 62 15

Van Dieten Stamp Auctions BV,
2 Tournooiveld, 2511 CX The
Hague
Tel: 70-464312/70-648658

Singapore & Malaysia

Victor & Morris Pte Ltd,
39 Talok Ayer Street, Republic of
Singapore
Tel: 94844

South Africa

Ashbey's Galleries,
43-47 Church Street, Cape Town
8001
Tel: 22-7527

Claremart Auction Centre,
47 Main Road, Claremont, Cape
Town 7700
Tel: 66-8826/66-8804

Ford & Van Niekerk Pty Ltd
156 Main Road, PO Box 8,
Plumstead, Cape Town
Tel: 71-3384

Sotheby Parke Bernet South
Africa Pty Ltd,
Total House, Smit and Rissik
Streets, PO Box 310010,
Braamfontein 2017
Tel: 39-3726

Spain

Juan R Cayon,
41 Fuencarral, Madrid 14
Tel: 221 08 32/221 43 72/222 95 98

Christie's International Ltd,
Casado del Alisal 5, Madrid
Tel: (01) 228-9300

Sotheby Parke Bernet & Co,
Scursal de Espana, Calle del
Prado 18, Madrid 14
Tel: 232-6488/232-6572

Switzerland

Daniel Beney,
Avenue des Mousquines 2,
CH-1005 Lausanne
Tel: (021) 22 28 64

Blanc,
Arcade Hotel Beau-Rivage, Box
84, CH-1001 Lausanne
Tel: (021) 27 32 55/26 86 20

Christie's (International) SA,
8 Place de la Taconnerie, CH-1204
Geneva
Tel: (022) 28 25 44

Steinwiesplatz,
CH-8032 Zurich
Tel: (01) 69 05 05

Auktionshaus Doblaschofsky AG,
Monbijoustrasse 28/30, CH-3001
Berne
Tel: (031) 25 23 72/73/74

Galerie Fischer,
Haldenstrasse 19, CH-6006
Lucerne
Tel: (041) 22 57 72/73

Germann Auktionshaus,
Zeitweg 67, CH-8032 Zurich
Tel: (01) 32 83 58/32 01 12

Haus der Bücher AG,
Baumleingasse 18, CH-4051 Basel
Tel: (061) 23 30 88

Adolph Hess AG,
Haldenstrasse 5, CH-6006 Lucerne
Tel: (041) 22 43 92/22 45 35

Auktionshaus Peter Ineichen,
CF Meyerstrasse 14, CH-8002
Zurich
Tel: (01) 201-3017

Galerie Koller AG,
Ramistrasse 8, CH-8001 Zurich
Tel: (01) 47 50 40

Koller St Gallen,
St Gallen
Tel: (071) 23 42 40

Kornfeld & Co,
Laupenstrasse 49, CH-3008 Berne
Tel: (031) 25 46 73

Phillips Son & Neale SA,
6 Rue de la Cité, CH-1204 Geneva
Tel: (022) 28 68 28

Christian Rosset,
Salle des Ventes, 29 Rue du Rhone,
CH-1204 Geneva
Tel: (022) 28 96 33/34

Schweizerische Gesellschaft der
Freunde von Kunstauktionen,
11 Werdmühlestrasse, CH-8001
Zurich
Tel: (01) 211-4789

Sotheby Parke Bernet AG,
20 Bleicherweg, CH-8022 Zurich
Tel: (01) 202-0011

24 Rue de la Cité, CH-1024 Geneva
Tel: (022) 21 33 77

Dr Erich Steinfels, Auktionen,
Rämistrasse 6, CH-8001 Zurich
Tel: (01) 252-1233 (wine) &
(01) 34 1233 (fine art)

Frank Sternberg,
Bahnhofstrasse 84, CH-8001
Zurich
Tel: (01) 211-7980

Jürg Stucker Gallery Ltd,
Alter Aargauerstalden 30,
CH-3006 Berne
Tel: (031) 44 00 44

Uto Auktions AG,
Lavaterstrasse 11, CH-8027
Zurich
Tel: (01) 202-9444

West Germany

Galerie Gerda Bassenge,
Erdener Strasses 5a, D-1000 West
Berlin 33
Tel: (030) 892 19 32/891 29 09

Kunstauktionen Waltraud Boltz,
Bahnhof Strasse 25-27, D-8580
Bayreuth
Tel: (0921) 206 16

Brandes,
Wolfenbütteler Strasse 12, D-3300
Braunschweig 1
Tel: (0531) 737 32

Gernot Dorau,
Johann-Georg Strasse 2, D-1000
Berlin 31
Tel: (030) 892 61 98

F Dörling,
Neuer Wall 40-41, D-2000
Hamburg 36
Tel: (040) 36 46 70/36 52 82

Roland A Exner,
Kunsthandel-Auktionen,
Am Ihmeufer, D-3000
Hannover 91
Tel: (0511) 44 44 84

Hartung & Karl,
Karolinenplatz 5a, D-8000
Munich 2
Tel: (089) 28 40 34

Hauswedell & Nolte,
Pöseldorfer Weg 1, D-2000
Hamburg 13
Tel: (040) 44 83 66

Karl & Faber,
Amiraplatz 3 (Luitpoldblock),
D-8000 Munich 2
Tel: (089) 22 18 65/66

Graf Klenau Ohg Nachf,
Maximilian Strasse 32, D-8000
Munich 1
Tel: (089) 22 22 81/82

Numismatik Lanz München,
Promenadeplatz 9, D-8000
Munich 2
Tel: (089) 29 90 70

Kunsthaus Lempertz,
Neumarkt 3, D-5000 Cologne 1
Tel: (0221) 21 02 51/52

Stuttgarter Kunstauktionshaus,
Dr Fritz Nagel,
Mörikestrasse 17-19, D-7000
Stuttgart 1
Tel: (0711) 61 33 87/77

Neumeister Münchener
Kunstauktionshaus KG,
Barer Strasse 37, D-8000
Munich 40
Tel: (089) 28 30 11

Petzold KG- Photographica,
Maximilian Strasse 36, D-8900
Augsburg 11
Tel: (0821) 3 37 25

Reiss & Auvermann,
Zum Talblick 2, D-6246
Glashütten im Taunus 1
Tel: (06174) 69 47/48

Gus Schiele Auktions-Galerie,
Ottostrasse 7 (Neuer Kunstblock),
D-8000 Munich 2
Tel: (089) 59 41 92

Galerie,
Paulinen Strasse 47, D-7000
Stuttgart 1
Tel: (0711) 61 63 77

J A Stargardt,
Universitäts Strasse 27, D-3550
Marburg
Tel: (06421) 234 52

Auktionshaus Tietjen & Co,
Spitaler Strasse 30, D-2000
Hamburg 1
Tel: (040) 33 03 68/69

Aachener Auktionshaus, Crott &
Schmelzer,
Pont Strasse 21, Aachen
Tel: (0241) 369 00

Kunstauktionen Rainer
Baumann,
Obere Woerthstrasse 7-11,
Nuremburg
Tel: (0911) 20 48 47

August Bödiger oHG,
Oxford Strasse 4, Bonn
Tel: (0228) 63 69 40

Bolland & Marotz,
Feldören 19, Bremen
Tel: (0421) 32 18 11

Bongartz Gelgen Auktionen,
Münsterplatz 27, Aachen
Tel: (0241) 206 19

Christie's International Ltd,
Düsseldorf:
Alt Pempelfort 11a, D-4000
Düsseldorf
Tel: (0211) 35 05 77

Hamburg:
Wenzelstrasse 21, D-2000
Hamburg 60
Tel: (4940) 279-0866

Munich:
Maximilianstrasse 20, D-8000
Munich 22
Tel: (089) 22 95 39

Württenberg:
Schloss Langenburg, D-7183
Langenburg

Sotheby Parke Bernet GmbH,
Munich:
Odeonsplatz 16, D-8000 Munich 22
Tel: (089) 22 23 75/6

Kunstauktion Jürgen Fischer,
Alexander Strasse 11, Heilbronn
Tel: (07 131) 785 23

Galerie Göbig,
Ritterhaus Strasse 5 (am
Thermalbad ad Nauheim)
Tel: (Frankfurt) (611) 77 40 80

Knut Günther,
Auf der Kömerwiese 19-21,
Frankfurt
Tel: (611) 55 32 92/55 70 22

Antiquitaeten Lothar Heubel,
Odenthaler Strasse 371, Cologne
Tel: (0221) 60 18 25

Hildener Auktionshaus und
Kunstgalerie,
Klusenhof 12, Hilden
Tel: (02103) 602 00

INDEX